BEST OF THE BEST IN THE U.S.

Library of Congress Catalogue Card Number 84-62320

ISBN 0-931073-01-4 (paperback edition)

ISBN 0-931073-00-6 (hardcover edition)

EDITORIAL STAFF

Editor & Publisher:	Mike Michaelson
Managing Editor:	Jennifer Murduck
Staff Writer/Editor:	Michael Sweeney
Contributing Writers:	Sarah Aldridge, Christine Benton, Robert H. Bradford, Peter Garino, Jim Hargrove, Bill Martin, Keith Ray, Elizabeth Rhein, Michael Schwanz
Design & Production:	Sawyer Design Ltd.
Research:	Barbara Kaurin
Administrative Assistant:	Marie Dubauskas

BEST OF THE BEST IN THE U.S.

A NATIONAL BESTSELLER PUBLICATION

National BestSeller Corporation
1740 Ogden Ave.
Downers Grove, IL 60515

CONTENTS

CONTENTS

BEST OF THE BEST IN THE U.S.

Great America, Santa Clara, CA

The Forks, ME

Photo: Charles Hathaway

Little Rock, AR

Old Sturbridge Village, Sturbridge, MA

Galveston, TX

The Very Best To You

When this book was conceived, the idea was to create a unique source book for travelers in the United States—no matter whether they were traveling cross-country, taking a weekend trip into the country, or even riding a bus across town. Catering to a multiplicity of interests is not an easy task—trying to please the golfer as well as the fisherman, the canoeist as well as the museum-goer. Yet, as individuals, we *do* have varied interests; as family groups, the variety is infinite. Thus, tennis enthusiasts also may enjoy visiting historic landmarks, skiers may appreciate learning how pioneers worked at their crafts, travelers who enjoy being pampered at luxury resorts are not necessarily adverse to roughing it in the wilderness. And almost everyone loves a festival!

All things to all people? Perhaps not. But, with this volume, we have attempted to be many things to many people. And therein lies its uniqueness. In owning this one-of-a-kind travel guide, you now possess—in a single volume— guides encompassing hundreds of different interests in 21 separate chapters. You'll find within these covers the famous and the little known, the offbeat and the unusual, as well as the expected.

Do you know where in the United States you can dig for diamonds— and keep any you find? Or where you can go skiing in midsummer? Or how about a restaurant where you can eat breakfast while watching a cascading waterfall that is higher than Niagara, or a series of charming inns that you can canoe to? You'll find lots of unusual recreational ideas in the pages that follow, from watching dog-sled races to putting yourself behind the wheel of a Formula racing car and circling an Indy-style track at 125 mph.

This volume is designed as an *idea* book as well as a reference work with suggestions on where to go, what to do, and where to stay. Looking for a romantic rendezvous, an island escape, or a vacation afloat—all within the United States? Or a fast-paced weekend in the city, a unique restaurant, or a get-in-shape visit to a fully-equipped health spa? Or the country's most scenic drives, its best man-made and natural wonders, or top-rated museums? You'll find the very best within these pages. For high adventure, there are suggestions for hot-air balloo- ning, hang-gliding, white-water rafting, and much more, plus the top dude ranches and winter-sports spots. And fine resorts, prime fishing and hunting spots, and the best in golf and tennis facilities. If festivals are your thing—or amusement parks, ethnic-flavored villages, or vacations down on the farm — you'll find our critics' choices for these, too, in this versatile guide.

If you're looking for something really different for a vacation, perhaps a Mississippi trip aboard a luxury steamboat, an island where wild ponies roam, or a storytelling festival below the Mason-Dixon Line, you'll find this volume indispen- sible as a trip planner. But it's great for weekend outings, too, and even day trips — perhaps a visit to a German village in the midwest, an outing to a brand-new amusement park in the south, or an unusual way to experience the excitement of a major city. Our goal has been to help you decide where to go, where to stay (from cozy, comfortable and inexpensive inns to some of the world's finest resorts), and what to do when you get there—and along the way. With each chapter divided into six geographic regions, you're sure to find an interesting outing or a rejuvenating getaway within easy driving distance of wherever you happen to live.

The best? "Best" is necessarily a subjective term, but in presenting the 1000-plus suggested destinations within these pages we have sought superla- tives. The book has been prepared by veteran travel writers and by authors specializing in specific recreational subjects. In researching the book and seeking out "the best," we culled a huge body of literature, books and magazines, sought the recommendations of travel-industry professionals, used many personal visits and evaluations, and harnessed the research capabilities of our computer. We also have tempered our selections to achieve variety and regional balance. And, in all probability, we have missed some obvious choices.

In fact, some of our ideas have come, not from travel experts, but from expert travelers. Thus, we invite you the reader to contribute to future editions of this book (and we'll give credit for any we use!).

A final word. We have striven for accuracy in detailing addresses, phone numbers, directions, hours open, and other factual information. Also, wher- ever appropriate we have attempted to provide either actual costs or a range of prices that were applicable at press time. Inevitably, places close or move, hours open (and even seasons open) change, and inflation catches up with costs. We recommend that you always check these details before you depart.

Chapter 1

INN PLACES

Rustic, secluded, historic—America's inns provide much more than mere accommodations. You'll brush with history and enjoy personal, cossetted treatment when you choose this unique way in which to enjoy a vacation or a weekend getaway. Home cooking, antique furnishings, idyllic, restful settings, friendly hosts . . . inns offer all this and more.

Unlike many of the other subjects covered in this book, where the numbers are finite—national parks, for example—our treatment of inns is unique. Because there are so many inns of so many different types, we have attempted to provide in this section a representative sampling of the various types of hostelries, from large and elegant to small and homey. We also sought to strike a geographic balance—so that in all likelihood you'll find an inn near you, no matter where you live. With these criteria and goals in mind, this chapter should be regarded as a "sampler" of prime examples of *all types* of inns, large and small, rather than as an unqualified guide to the best regardless of type and location.

Thus, these inns range from historic 18th century roadhouses and secluded luxury resort-type inns to old hotels in small towns and mansions on large estates. Also included are many examples of that new breed of bed-and-breakfast inns that are popping up around the country like muffins in a pan.

NORTHWEST

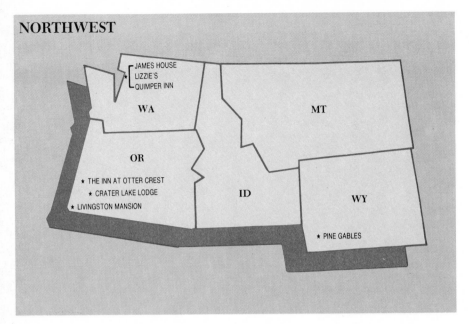

JAMES HOUSE
★ LIZZIE'S
QUIMPER INN

WA

MT

OR

★ THE INN AT OTTER CREST
★ CRATER LAKE LODGE
★ LIVINGSTON MANSION

ID

WY

★ PINE GABLES

THE INN AT OTTER CREST

Otter Rock, OR

Perched on a cliff high above the crashing Pacific surf, this "getaway" spot combines the intimacy of a secluded country inn with the amenities of a luxurious oceanfront resort. Two-story, cedar-sided lodges house 250 guest rooms, many with fireplaces, and fully-equipped kitchens, all with view decks, refrigerators and cable TV. The resort is loaded with amenities: Heated pool, tennis courts, saunas, basketball, volleyball, shuffleboard, badminton, putting green, jogging paths, recreation room and gift shop. But there are simpler pleasures: Strolling a secluded beach to watch a whale, exploring a tide pool to gather seashells and agates; wandering through 40 acres of forest; enjoying a duck skim across the surface of a silent pond tucked between the trees. The Flying Dutchman offers candlelight dinners, marvelous seascapes and local seafood specialties such as Dungeness crab and Yaquina Bay oysters. The Wardroom Lounge is the place for entertainment and dancing.

Rates: *Bedroom 1-4 persons or Studio 1-2 persons $55-$65; Loft suite 1-6 persons $85-$105; 1-bedroom suite $98-$118; 2-bedroom suite $130-$160. Substantial savings on package plans from $31 per person including meal for two and 2-for-1 cocktail. The Inn at Otter Crest, PO Box 50, Otter Rock, OR 97369,* **1-800-547-2181** *(in OR)* **1-800-452-2101.**

CRATER LAKE LODGE

Crater Lake, OR

Formed by eruptions eons ago, Crater Lake in Oregon's Cascade Mountains attracts 600,000 visitors annually to the state's only national park. If you plan to be among those who admire the lake's deep, azure blue waters and rugged shoreline with stands of Ponderosa pine, you may wish to arrange a stay at the park lodge. This beautiful brick building blends harmoniously with its surroundings and offers accommodations (many rooms with lake views) from mid-June to mid-September. Cottages are available May to October, depending upon snow conditions. (Snow has been recorded in parts of the park every month of the year.) The lodge has a spacious lobby and a rustic, red-toned dining room. The Watchman Restaurant and Lounge offers food, cocktails and spectacular views of the lake. Highlight your visit with a two-hour launch trip around the lake's 25-mile shoreline—or take a 10-passenger guided tour bus around its 35-mile rim. There's fishing for rainbow and brown trout and kokanee salmon (no license required).

Rates: *Hotel rooms $39-$59; suite $67; Ponderosa cottages $39-$51; Sleeping cottages $19-$32. Crater Lake Lodge, Crater Lake, OR 97604.* **503/594-2511.**

LIVINGSTON MANSION

Jacksonville, OR

This stately bed-and-breakfast inn sits on four acres amid towering oaks. Jacksonville was founded in 1851 following the discovery of gold in Rich Gulch. Today, it is a National Historic Landmark that offers a walk back in time. Rooms offer sweeping vistas of the Rogue Valley and Mt. McLoughlin. The Regal Suite has private entrance, fireplace, bay window and antique bed (adjoining room available). The Amour, once the maid's chamber, has a queen bed. The Vagabond can be arranged with twin beds or king (shower only). There's a swimming pool on the grounds and airport pick up. Lodging includes complimentary breakfast and wine and sherry in the evening on the porch or in front of the fire. Guests celebrating special occasions are treated to flowers, candles, and other extra touches. Nestled between the Coast Range and the Cascade Mountains, southern Oregon offers a variety of diversions, from white water rafting and downhill skiing to Shakespeare and fine dining.

Rates: *Regal Suite or Armour $75, Vagabond $65 ($10 less Nov. 1-Mar. 31). Livingston Mansion, 4132 Livingston Rd, Box 1476, Jacksonville, OR 97530,* **503/899-7107.**

QUIMPER INN

Port Townsend, WA

A flourishing seaport of the late 1800s, Port Townsend has retained much of its Victorian charm. This bed and breakfast inn built in 1880, offers six guest rooms, some with views of the bay and village, others with mountain outlooks. A two-room suite has a double brass bed and an antique tin tub. Room price includes a Continental breakfast with fresh-ground coffee and baskets of French breads. Use the inn as your base for exploring the Pacific Northwest's sandy beaches, walking tours of historic Port Townsend, bicycling country lanes or visiting nearby Seattle. For an unusual experience, take a four-hour sail aboard the schooner *Alcyone.*

Rates: *2 persons with breakfast $46-$64. Quimper Inn, 1306 Franklin, Pt Townsend, WA 98368,* **206/385-1086.**

The Inn At Otter Crest, Otter Rock, OR

Quimper Inn, Port Townsend, WA

JAMES HOUSE

Port Townsend, WA

This grand Victorian mansion, overlooking the bay, was built in 1891 and features Queene Anne style architecture, with gables, dormers, porches and five chimneys. It reflects the original owner's love of fine woods and commands a sweeping view of Port Townsend and the waterways. Each of the cheery, spacious rooms has a different character. All are furnished with antiques, some original to the house. They offer water and mountain views. The bridal suite, originally the master bedroom, has a fireplace, parquet floor, clawfoot tub bath, and a private balcony off a bay-windowed sitting room. Two-room garden suites have fireplace or parlor stove. A garden cottage has twin beds and private bath. The main floor has two parlors, dining room and fireplaces that invite relaxation and conversation. Breakfast is served in the kitchen around a big oak table next to a wood stove.

Rates: Single $35-$40, double $45-$50, bridal suite $75, garden suites $60-$75. Breakfast incl. James House, 1238 Washington St, Port Townsend, WA 98368, **206/385-1238.**

LIZZIE'S

Port Townsend, WA

In Port Townsend, Washington's "Victorian seaport," Lizzie's bed and breakfast inn offers guests a taste of elegant living as it existed at the turn of the century. Built in 1887 by a wealthy ship owner, the Italianate mansion has been carefully restored from its floors to its 12-foot ceilings and filled with antiques. Lizzie's offers six bed-sitting rooms, some with views of bay or mountains. Rooms have antique furnishings, brass, half-canopy or other antique beds and baskets of books; bathrooms feature leaded glass and wood-burning stoves. The parlor and drawing rooms have fireplaces and inviting leather sofas. Guests are invited to play the grand piano. Adding to the opulence are Belgian and Oriental carpets, Chinese tapestries and silk hangings from the Broadway production of "Flower Drum Song." Breakfast, included in the price of a room, features fresh fruit, brown farm eggs cooked in their shells, freshly-baked bread or scones, homemade jams, juice, and beverages. Guests gather to enjoy this repast around a 12-foot country kitchen table.

Rates: Double $42-$79. Lizzie's, 731 Pierce, Port Townsend, WA 98368, **206/385-4168** or **9826.**

PINE GABLES BED AND BREAKFAST INN

Evanston, WY

Next to the historical downtown business district of Evanston, this 100-year-old mansion offers antique-furnished guest rooms featuring high carved oak beds, brass bed with satin comforter, oak Morris chairs, oak washstands and dressers, marble-top dresser with matching washstand and wing back rocking chairs. There are comfortable parlor rooms, a front sun porch and an antique shop. For guests who enjoy an evening walk, your hosts will conduct a tour of town and relate the story of the coming of the Union Pacific Railroad in 1869. Nearby there are hiking, fishing and sightseeing in the Wasatch National Forest and the scenic Uinta Mountains with more than 500 basin lakes. Other tours take you over the original Union Pacific Railroad grade and to charcoal kilns built in 1868 and to Fort Bridger, a restored military post. Your hosts will supply information, road maps and a picnic lunch.

Rates: start at $28.50; additional persons $6. Mini-vacation package available. Pine Gables Bed & Breakfast Inn, 1049 Center St, Evanston, WY 82930, **307/789-2069.**

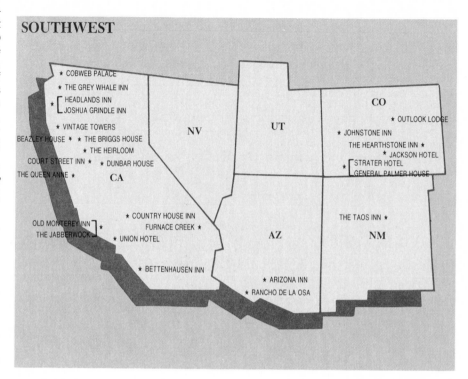

HEADLANDS INN

Mendocino, CA

Beginning life in 1868 as a barber shop, this inn has undergone additions and transformations, including stints as a saloon and hotel annex and, in 1893, a move (literally by horse power and logs used as rollers) to its present location. Today, the restored inn offers six guest accommodations, each distinctly individual. Third-floor rooms have window seats offering views of the Pacific coastline; a spacious second-floor room opens onto a private balcony; a cottage behind the inn has a Victorian tin ceiling (plus modern comforts). In the common room, guests may peruse local restaurant menus, select a book or choose a game. The front deck provides a sheltered spot to enjoy the spectacular ocean view. Three rooms and the cottage have wood-burning fireplaces; another has an old-fashioned parlor stove. Breakfast features coffee or tea, home-baked breads or muffins, freshly squeezed orange juice or fresh fruit—plus the morning paper every day except Sundays. The coastal village of Mendocino offers shopping and gallery browsing, an art center, and sandy beaches with tidepools to explore. Nearby are hiking in five state parks, golf, and canoeing on the Big River.

Rates: $57-70; cottage $62. Headlands Inn, PO Box 132, Mendocino, CA 95460, **707/937-4431.**

JOSHUA GRINDLE INN

Mendocino, CA

Named after its builder, a New England lumberman who was attracted to Northern California by virgin redwood forests, this lovely home dates back to 1879. Located on two acres in Mendocino, about 130 miles north of San Francisco, the inn offers a view of the village, the bay and the ocean. Antiques from the 17th and 18 century from the private collection of innkeepers Bill and Gwen Jacobson decorate each room. Some guest rooms feature antique brass beds, one has an antique four-poster. Rooms also feature fireplaces—two with hand-made 19th Century English tiles; two rooms are equipped with Franklin stoves. There is a comfortable parlor, a dining room with an early 19th Century pine table and many tasteful etchings and paintings throughout. All guest rooms have private bath. Breakfast is included with the price of a room—a hearty meal featuring homemade breads, eggs, fresh fruit and tea or coffee. A short walk from the inn is the local art center, galleries, shops, restaurants, the beach and a stretch of rugged Pacific coastline.

Rates: $57-$63 single or double occupancy incl. breakfast. Joshua Grindle Inn, 44800 Little Lake, PO Box 647, Mendocino, CA 95460, **707/937-4143.**

VINTAGE TOWERS

Cloverdale, CA

A quaint, wine-country town with tree-lined streets, old houses and stately churches, about 1½ hours north of San Francisco, is the setting for this bed-and-breakfast inn. Housed in a 20-room mansion built at the turn of the century by a wealthy merchant, the inn is set on shaded, landscaped grounds that feature a rose garden, venerable rose tree and a gazebo that is used for concerts. There are three tower suites—one round, one square and one octagonal. Each of the seven guest rooms is architecturally unusual and has been restored and decorated with period pieces. Breakfast is served in a formal dining room, in the gazebo, or on the veranda (fitted with a porch swing). The Calico Tower also has a private balcony where breakfast can be served. Within minutes of the inn are many wineries, including Italian Swiss Colony. Also nearby are secluded beaches on the Russian River, river rapids for tubing, and hiking trails. The inn provides bicycles as well as inner tubes for river running. It owns a 25-foot sailing sloop harbored at a nearby lake that may be reserved by guests.
Rates: *Double $35-$65. Vintage Towers, 302 N Main St, Cloverdale, CA 95425,* **707/894-4535.**

THE BRIGGS HOUSE

Sacramento, CA

Surrounded by stately trees, this restored Victorian home is just a few blocks from the State Capitol. European and American antiques are set in spacious rooms of rich wood paneling, inlaid hardwood floors, oriental rugs and delicate lace curtains. You'll find fresh flowers in your room and English china and silver for your morning dining. In the evening there is complimentary wine, fruit and nuts. Recline on the porch swing, sit by the fire, relax in the soothing spa or sauna in the shaded backyard or take a sunset bicycle tour of the Capitol. In the morning you are greeted with complimentary fresh-ground coffee, juice and a gourmet breakfast.
Rates: *Single or double, $45-$75 Sun.-Thu., $50-$90 Fri-Sat. (Higher rates quoted are for occupancy of a secluded carriage house.) The Briggs House, 2209 Capitol Ave, Sacramento, CA 95816,* **916/441-3214.**

THE HEIRLOOM

Ione, CA

Nestled among the foothills of the great Sierras, Ione is one of the small communities settled during the gold rush of 1848. This bed-and-breakfast inn, circa 1863, offers guest rooms decorated with antiques, handmade quilts, and other tasteful accessories. Some rooms have a fireplace and/or balcony. Breakfast varies from day-to-day and may be taken in bed, on your veranda, in the dining room, or in a garden lush with foliage. Included in the breakfasts are fresh fruit in season, juice, a cheese board, crepes, popovers, quiche and tea or dark-roasted coffee. Located southeast of Sacramento, this gold country offers plenty of diversions to satisfy the nature lover, history buff, antique enthusiast, wine connoisseur, little-theater goer, sportsman, artist and poet.
Rates: *$35 including breakfast. The Heirloom, PO Box 322, 214 Shakeley Lane, Ione, CA 95640,* **209/274-4468.**

COBWEB PALACE

Westport, CA

Back in the 1880s Westport was the largest seaport between San Francisco and Eureka, with 14 hotels and 17 saloons. Today, it is a tiny coastal village with one remaining hotel, housing a restaurant, bar and six-room guest house. The ocean is its front yard (just 200 yards from the door), the mountains its backyard. The village, with a small cove and secluded beach, is surrounded by miles of virtually untouched wilderness, ideal for hiking and exploring. Although the inn has a Victorian western ambience, it also may remind visitors of an English inn—or of New England, situated as it is along the rugged north Mendocino Coast in a community reminiscent of a coastal village in Maine. The menu offers a selection of seafood and meat entrees, with country-style vegetables and desserts. Room rates include Continental breakfast.
Rates: *$33-$58. Cobweb Palace, PO Box 132, Westport, CA 95488,* **707/964-5588.**

BEAZLEY HOUSE

Napa, CA

Napa's first bed and breakfast inn is just an hour from San Francisco, in the heart of the Napa Valley's wine country. Within minutes are ballooning, cycling, gliding, wine touring and hot mineral baths. You can walk to old Napa's restored shopping area with its fine restaurants and some of the most beautifully restored neighborhoods in California. The inn sits on half an acre of lawns and gardens. It features a stained glass entry, music room and spacious living room with a huge fireplace. The newly built carriage house is modeled after a 75-year-old original. All carriage house rooms have private baths, fireplaces and separate entrances. Two loft rooms each have a two-person spa. Complimentary breakfast includes home-baked muffins, fresh fruit, cheese, coffee, tea and juice. In the evening you'll find tea, coffee and sherry on the tea cart.
Rates: *Main house $65-$75, Carriage House $85-$95. Beazley House, 1910 First St, Napa, CA 94559,* **707/257-1649.**

DUNBAR HOUSE

Murphys, CA

An Italianate-style house, built in 1880, this bed-and-breakfast inn offers five warmly decorated guest rooms with such amenities as air conditioning, electric blankets and a parlor where, awaiting your pleasure, are books, games, and sherry served from a crystal decanter. On cold mornings you may enjoy Continental breakfast in the dining room where a fire crackles in a free-standing fireplace; on warm, sunny mornings, the porch and gardens beckon. Breakfast consists of fruit compote, homemade breads, a selection of cheeses and cereals, and milk, tea or coffee. A short walk away is Main Street, rich with historical buildings, shops and restaurants. Located in the heart of the southern Mother Lode region of California, the inn is a good headquarters for visiting Calaveras Big Trees State Park, Mercer Caverns, Mt. Reba/Bear Valley ski area and the charming Mother Lode towns.
Rates: *$50-$55 double including breakfast. Dunbar House, 271 Jones St, Murphys, CA 95247,* **209/728-2897.**

The Heirloom, Ione, CA

Vintage Towers, Cloverdale, CA

Union Hotel, Los Alamos, CA

BETTENHAUSEN INN

Seal Beach, CA

Housed in a refurbished 1924 lodge, this Orange County inn has 23 suites and rooms, each with private baths and most with kitchen-bars. It has pretty gardens with a quiet pool area, a cozy library with a fireplace, and lots of collectibles and antiques. An old-fashioned tea room is used to serve complimentary Continental breakfast featuring freshly squeezed orange juice, fruit in season, assorted pastries and breads, jam and honey, and coffee, tea or hot chocolate. Among the artifacts that adorn this inn are fences from Paris, old English phone booths, Victorian corbels, antique tile scenarios, Victorian ceilings, many brass chandeliers, and antique lace. The exterior presents a French Mediterranean seaside mood with blue canopies, burgundy street lights, flower boxes, and cream colored fences and gates. Located in a seaside village community, the inn is only 300 yards from the beach. Within a 30 minutes drive are such attractions as Disneyland (see Amusement & Theme Parks) Knotts Berry Farm (see Amusement & Theme Parks) and the Queen Mary (see Manmade & Natural Wonders).

Rates: *Double $70-$100. Bettenhausen Inn, 212 5th St, Seal Beach, CA 90740,* **1-800/854-3380,** *in CA* **1-800/432-7045,** *local* **213/493-2416.**

THE GREY WHALE INN

Fort Bragg, CA

Located in the coastal town of Fort Bragg, about 3½-4 hours' drive north of San Francisco, this weathered redwood inn was built in 1915 and originally served as a hospital. Today, with 13 guest rooms—many offering views of the ocean—it serves as a charming bed-and-breakfast inn. Two penthouse rooms have decks; some of the other rooms feature kitchens; another has an interior patio. In one of the oceanview suites, an old gimballed surgery lamp is a reminder of the building's past. You can view the picturesque town of Fort Bragg from the Sunrise Room, or watch the annual grey whale migration (Dec.-Mar.) from the Sunset Room. Complimentary breakfast includes home-baked coffee cakes, pastries or nut breads, fresh fruit and beverages and is served buffet-style. Books and magazines are available in guest rooms and in the lounge; nearby are the indoor city swimming pool and a health club. The famous Skunk Train is within walking distance; a few minutes drive will take you to stake parks with hiking trails through redwood forests and to unspoiled beaches. Fort Bragg and nearby Mendocino offer art galleries, unique shops and fine dining. Theater, opera, concert performances and special celebrations are scheduled throughout the year.

Rates: *Single $40-$50, double $45-$60 (incl. breakfast). The Grey Whale Inn, 615 N Main St, Fort Bragg, CA 95437,* **707/964-0640.**

COURT STREET INN

Jackson, CA

In the heart of California's Mother Lode country, this inn, a registered National Historic Landmark, circa 1870, offers antique-filled guest rooms and complimentary breakfast served in your room, in a large dining room, or in the garden patio. The inn's Victorian charm and elegance is enhanced by lace curtains and fresh flowers in every room. Accommodations comprise of five guest rooms in the main house (some with private baths), including a two-room suite (with private bath) featuring Queen Anne period furnishings and an adjoining sun room. Recently opened are additional accommodations in the adjacent India House, featuring a huge sitting room with a fireplace and an 1860 square grand piano, a private bathroom with a claw-foot tub and two bedrooms. (The India House normally is rented to one couple or to two couples traveling together.) A short walk away are the Amador County Museum, historic pioneer churches and cemeteries and downtown Jackson. Within a 10-mile radius are two rivers for rafting or gold panning; within a 20-mile radius are six lakes for boating, waterskiing and fishing. Nearby are the wineries of the Shenandoah Valley, offering tours and tasting; premier skiing is an hour's drive from the inn.

Rates: *Rooms $45-$60; Suite $60-$70; India house $95 one couple, $145 two couples. Court Street Inn, 215 Court St, Jackson, CA 95642,* **209/223-0416.**

FURNACE CREEK INN RANCH RESORT

Death Valley, CA

In a lush oasis fed by a mountain spring, shaded by swaying date palms, Furnace Creek offers a choice of accommodations either at the inn, a Spanish-style grande hotel, or at the ranch. Inn activities include tennis on lighted courts and swimming in an enormous spring-fed pool. A superb dining room menu and The Oasis Supper Club are widely acclaimed. The ranch has the genuine flavor of the Old West. Activities include swimming, golf, tennis, horseback riding, bicycling and hiking. The ranch has its own general store with a wide variety of gift items, including handcrafted jewelry. Sightseeing close to the ranch includes The Visitor Center of Death Valley National Monument and the Borax Museum. (This luxurious resort began life as a way station for 19th Century borax wagons.) The inn is on Modified American Plan (includes breakfast and dinner).

Rates: *Single $120-$139; double $140-$159; additional person in room, adult $37, child 5-12 $22. Open Oct-May. Furnace Creek Inn, Death Valley, CA 92328,* **619/786-2345.**

COUNTRY HOUSE INN

Templeton, CA

This 1886 home has only six rooms for rent—but enough warmth and ambience to make it well worth a visit. Wake up to the aroma of fresh coffee and cinnamon rolls. Enjoy breakfast and watch hummingbirds entertain at the dining room window. Walk in the rose-bordered gardens shaded by huge oak trees or play the player piano by the fireside. This Victorian home, a Designated Historic Site, offers rooms furnished with queen and king size beds and antiques. Two baths down the hall are a reminder of family living in days gone by. One room has a half bath, private entrance and double bed. The inn is filled with antiques and fresh flowers and provides complimentary breakfasts and tea-time refreshments. Six wineries with tasting rooms are within five miles, Hearst Castle is just a short drive, and the missions San Luis Obispo and San Miguel also are close by. Templeton, a railroad boom town of the 1880s (it had three hotels, 18 saloons and a population of nearly 5000), has an old west atmosphere, many antique shops and good eateries.

Rates: *$55 per couple including taxes. Country House Inn, 91 Main St, Templeton, CA 93465,* **805/434-1598.**

UNION HOTEL

Los Alamos, CA

"This is my home, hobby and occupation," says Dick Langdon, owner of this restored 1880 Wells Fargo stagecoach stop. That's why he only opens three days a week—Friday, Saturday, Sunday. Beyond that, he says, "it becomes work." Overnight guests receive welcoming wine and a complimentary breakfast of juice, fresh fruit, homemade cinnamon rolls and coffee. Then comes a local tour in a 1918 15-passenger White touring car, vehicles originally made to replace stagecoaches in Yellowstone National Park. Upstairs, there's a parlor for use by overnight guests only, complete with an 1880 Brunswick pool table, game table, reading area and extensive library. Each guest room is unique, with a variety of wallpapers, antique furniture, china wash bowls and pitchers, and handmade quilts. Downstairs is a dining room and saloon, both featuring an eclectic collection of antiques, from 100-year-old hand-carved oak sideboards to a lamp used in *Gone With the Wind.* Outside is a swimming area, barbecue and buffet, and a backdrop of mountain scenery. At the push of a button, a structure that is by day a Victorian gazebo converts at night to a whirlpool for 20 guests. The dining room features homemade soups, country-baked chicken, platters of beef and cornbread and honey butter.

Rates: *$65-$75, shared bath; $80-$90, private bath. Union Hotel, 362 Bell St, Los Alamos, CA 93440,* **805/344-2744.**

The Hearthstone Inn, Colorado Springs, CO

Bettenhausen Inn, Seal Beach, CA

Rancho de la Osa, Sasabe, AZ

Headlands Inn, Mendocino, CA

Beazley House, Napa, CA

The Queen Anne, San Francisco, CA

THE QUEENE ANNE

San Francisco, CA

This restored 19th Century landmark was originally completed in 1890 by one of the Comstock Lode Silver Kings as an elite private boarding school for young girls. Today, the midtown guest house blends European charm with modern luxury and convenience. The 49 large guest rooms are individually decorated with a potpourri of antiques, marble sinks, shelves of books, brick fireplaces and cozy reading nooks. Parlor suites are available and The Townhouse Suite offers a two-story, two-bedroom suite with private courtyard. Guest services include complimentary Continental breakfast with morning newspaper served in the guest's room (or in the parlor by the fire)—including fresh-squeezed orange juice or other beverage, flaky, fresh croissants, sweet butter, homemade fruit preserves and 100% Colombian dark French roast coffee. There's complimentary afternoon tea and sherry service in the parlor and free valet registered guest parking.

Rates: *Daily $80-$140, suites $185; Weekly $480-$840, suites $1,110. The Queene Anne, 1590 Sutter St, San Francisco, CA 94109,* **415/441-2828.**

OLD MONTEREY INN

Monterey, CA

This handsome, Tudor-style, half-timbered house sits on an oak-studded hillside in a quiet residential neighborhood—yet within the sounds of the waves and barking sea lions of close-by Monterey Bay. The Inn, built in 1929, sits on an acre of landscaped gardens which abound with fuchsias, begonias and rhododendrons. There are a formal rose garden, sheltering pines, oaks and redwoods, secluded sitting areas and inviting hammocks. Stained glass windows, warm natural woods, skylights and many wood-burning fireplaces enhance the charm of this intimate inn. With European goosedown comforters and pillows, period furniture and family antiques, each of the 10 guest rooms is individually styled. The day begins with a Continental breakfast of juice, fruit in season, freshly baked pastries and coffee or tea. You may join the other guests downstairs to enjoy the antique fireplace and view of the garden, or be pampered with breakfast in your room. In the evenings, a fire burns in the high-ceilinged living room where guests gather for wine, cheese and conversation. Complimentary wine is always available in the living room, as are a collection of menus from nearby restaurants. Old Fisherman's Wharf, historic Monterey and many fine shops and restaurants are a short walk from the inn. Nearby is Cannery Row and Carmel-by-the-Sea.

Rates: *$85-$120; garden cottage $150. Old Monterey Inn, 500 Martin St, Monterey, CA 93940,* **408/375-8284.**

THE JABBERWOCK

Monterey, CA

Once a convent, this charming country inn offers spectacular views of Monterey Bay and meandering strolls along Cannery Row (just four blocks away). It was built in 1911 and retains its original flavor, from garrett to gardens and waterfalls. Each of five quaint guest rooms are distinctively decorated and furnished with antique beds. For example, The Borogrove is a large, old-fashioned king size room with cozy fireplace and sitting area in addition to a private bath and dressing area with a view of the bay. Unique touches include goose down pillows and comforters, lace sheets and fresh flowers in every room. Enjoy a complimentary breakfast in the elegant dining room or in your room. Every evening, you're invited to enjoy complimentary hors d'oeuvres and aperitifs by the fireplace or in the estate gardens. Cookies and milk at bedtime complete the day. Nearby are Carmel and the famous 17-mile Drive in Pebble Beach. Fisherman's Wharf abounds with restaurants.

Rates: *Per room, $70-$105 plus tax. The Jabberwock, 598 Laine St, Monterey, CA 93940,* **408/372-4777.**

RANCHO DE LA OSA

Sasabe, AZ

In the high Sonoran desert, close to the Mexican border, this guest ranch provides a relaxed, homey atmosphere by accommodating no more than 35 guests at a time. Located at an altitude of 3,600 feet, 66 miles southwest of Tucson, La Osa has been in continuous operation as a guest ranch since the early 1900s, except during the Mexican Revolution when its owner turned the main building into a hospital and tended wounded revolutionaries. The ranch's adobe guest rooms (some are family-size suites) and main building are decorated in a Southwestern and Mexican motif. Each room has a fireplace or wood-burning stove which crackles with mesquite logs on cool winter evenings. Rates are full American plan and include all meals, horseback riding and instruction, swimming in a heated pool and movies in the Cantina (where cocktails are available—but not included). This picturesque desert, where hawks wheel overhead and wildlife and wild flowers abound, is a timeless place for quiet exploration. Side trips can be made to Kitt Peak Observatory, Nogales, Mexico for shopping, Mt. Lemon's ski slopes, the Papago Indian Reservation and other southern Arizona attractions.

Rates: *American plan; Double, per person, weekend rate, $92.50-$97.50; weekly rate (7 days/6 nights) $300-$390. Rancho de la Osa, PO Box 1, Sasabe, AZ 85633,* **602/823-4257.**

ARIZONA INN

Tucson, AZ

For more than 50 years, the Arizona Inn has been a Tucson landmark, known for elegance and service. Discriminating guests have included the Roosevelts and Rockefellers, as well as such luminaries as Spencer Tracy, Howard Hughes, Frank Sinatra and Burt Reynolds. Adobe-type cottages house 85 rooms, each one-of-a-kind, many with private patio, balcony or fireplace and walk-in closets. Fourteen acres of immaculate lawns and gardens include a heated swimming pool, clay tennis court, fountain and ramada. Golf and horseback riding can be arranged nearby. Make the inn your headquarters for exploring the surrounding mountains and desert, tiny pioneer towns and old Spanish missions. Guests enjoy the Library, with its fireplace, handcrafted furniture and antique card tables. The cocktail lounge, with Audubon prints, is another popular setting for conversation. A second bar is located poolside where food may be ordered. Outstanding cuisine is prepared by a championship chef.

Rates *vary with three basic tourist seasons. Average rates, not including 16% gratuity and 7% sales tax, are: May 1-Sept 30, single $44-$59, double $54-$78, Suites $90-up; Oct 1-Dec 31, single $55-$75, double $68-$85, suites $95-up; Jan 1-Apr 30, single $66-$96, double $75-$108, suites $115-up. Arizona Inn, 2200 E Elm St, Tucson, AZ 85719,* **602-325-1541.**

JOHNSTONE INN

Telluride, CO

When Butch Cassidy made his first illegal withdrawal at Telluride in 1889, the town already was more than 20 years old. Today, with a population of 1,100, it is a popular mountain resort, headquarters for skiing, fishing, rafting, canoeing, horseback riding, jeeping, and hiking. It also is noted for its festivals, a full calendar celebrating such interests as film, dance, jazz, wine, hang gliding and country music. This inn offers eight guest rooms, some with private baths, furnished with such antiques as a hand-carved oak bedroom set, a satin settee, needlepoint seats on walnut chairs. Guests relax in a lounge decorated with an antique crazy quilt, matching love seats, a comfortable sofa, and an oak piano. Continental breakfast is served in a dining area filled with antiques; after-ski refreshments are served in the parlor. There's a sunny wooden porch for relaxing outdoors. Originally a boarding house for miners, the inn was built in 1893. It is located within walking distance to ski lifts and adjacent to many historical buildings, restaurants and shops.

Rates: *Doubles $30-$48. Johnstone Inn, 403 W Colorado Ave, Box 546, Telluride, CO 81435,* **303/728-3316.**

OUTLOOK LODGE

Green Mountain Falls, CO

Enjoy the Rockies at this Victorian lodge in a small mountain village on the slope of Pike's Peak. Drink in the mountain view as you sip your coffee on a veranda featuring hand-carved Victorian balustrades . . . in the evening, roast marshmallows on a crackling pine-scented fire . . . start the day with a complimentary breakfast of fresh fruit, juice, and homemade rolls, muffins, scones, and croissants. The main lodge was the parsonage for the Little Church in the Wildwood and is nestled in pines and spruce above the church. The lodge, a Victorian structure with the original furnishings, was built in 1889 and is on the Historic Homes Tour. Victorian antiques also furnish a summer annex. The lodge is within walking distance of swimming pool, volleyball and tennis courts, stables, a fishing lake, shops, and restaurants. Hiking trails start at the door, and the many attractions of the Pike's Peak area (see Manmade and Natural Wonders) are only minutes away.
Rates: *Double, share bath, $25; Annex, half and full baths, $30-$35. Open Mem Day—Lab Day. Outlook Lodge, Box 5, Green Mountain Falls, CO 80819,* **303/684-2303.**

THE TAOS INN

Taos, NM

Taos, which sits on a 7,000-ft. mesa, has a unique Spanish/Indian flavor, and this inn blends in harmoniously. Located in the center of a town that's noted for its international art colony (it boasts 60 galleries), clear sunny skies and unpolluted mountain air, the inn, parts of which date back to the 1600s , is a Historic Landmark. It offers 42 rooms furnished southwestern style with handloomed Indian bedspreads, antique armoires, furniture custom-built by local artisans and fireplaces in the Pueblo Indian tradition. Its restaurant, Doc Martin's, offers regional specialties and an outdoor dining patio; the Adobe Bar is a popular meeting place for local artists, writers, musicians and craftsmen. Activities abound. The inn will pack you a picnic lunch, complete with wine, for horseback riding, rafting down the Rio Grande or hiking to a hot spring in the 53,000 acres of Carson National Forest. Nearby is first-class Alpine and Nordic skiing. Or explore the galleries, shops and restaurants of Taos—or simply enjoy the inn's pool and Jacuzzi.
Rates: *Single $45-$65; Double $55-$75. Special packages available. The Taos Inn, PO Drawer N, Taos, NM 87571,* **1-800-TAOS INN.**

JACKSON HOTEL

Poncha Springs, CO

An authentic taste of the Old West is offered by this rustic, wood-frame hotel built in 1878 and once host to such famous and infamous guests as Ulysses S. Grant, Rudyard Kipling and Frank and Jesse James. The lobby features such artifacts as the old cash register and an early guest book; the dining room has a diamond-dust mirror, sparkling chandeliers, a large, native rock fireplace and an antique rosewood square grand piano. There is a well-stocked bar and a coffee shop and saloon for lunch and light evening meals. Any time is right to enjoy coffee or cappuccino from a steaming espresso machine and home-baked pastries. The hotel sits at the junction of three mountain ranges and is central to many summer and winter activities including fishing, hiking, horseback riding, rock hounding, hunting, and four-wheel driving tours. Nearby are some of the world's most challenging white water rafting and kayaking. Many peaks in the area exceed 14,000 feet and the region offers excellent downhill as well as cross-country skiing.
Rates: *Double $22-$28. Jackson Hotel, PO Box 25, Poncha Springs, CO 81242,* **303/539-3122.**

STRATER HOTEL

Durango, CO

Built in 1887, the Strater Hotel long has been the hub of activity in Durango's Historic District. It also serves as headquarters for a broad assortment of cultural and recreational activities that range from skiing at the famed Purgatory Ski area, touring Mesa Verde National Park (see Nat'l Parks & Monuments), riding to Silverton on the scenic Durango & Silverton narrow-guage railroad, and enjoying turn-of-the-century threatre at the Diamond Circle Theatre located next to the hotel. The hotel houses what has been noted as the largest single collection of authentic American Victorian walnut antiques in the world. These pieces are distributed throughout public areas and in every guest room. Amenities include the Opera House and Columbian dining rooms which offer both casual and formal dining and are open during all three meal periods, and the Diamond Belle, an Old West saloon that features Victorian decor, bar maids in comely costumes and ragtime piano entertainment nightly. The hotel carries a Four Diamond AAA rating.
Rates: *Winter $40-$65, Summer $47-$85. Strater Hotel, PO Drawer E, Durango, CO 81301,* **303/247-4431.**

GENERAL PALMER HOUSE

Durango, CO

Nestled in a valley of red mesas and green forest, Durango sits at the foot of the Western Slope of the Rockies. To the north, the mountains rise quickly to 14,000 feet. Here are the ghost towns of the great Gold and Silver Rushes and the very-much-alive mining towns of Silverton, Ouray and Telluride. One of the region's most popular attractions are the narrow-guage steam locomotives that make daily trips to the mountains. Located next to the historic station of the famed Silverton train is the General Palmer House, a major victorian landmark since 1898 (completely restored in 1982). Its Victorian furnishings combine with modern conveniences to make it a fine headquarters for exploring nearby art galleries, shops, boutiques, restaurants and theatres. This Four-Diamond AAA rated hostelry is close to Purgatory, a major ski resort with seven chairlifts.
Rates: *Summer $45-$64; Winter $40-$58. General Palmer House, 567 Main Ave, Durango, CO 81301,* **303/247-4747.**

THE HEARTHSTONE INN

Colorado Springs, CO

In the shadow of soaring Pike's Peak, this 25-room Victorian mansion is completely furnished with turn-of-the-century antiques. Each room of this award-winning inn is individually decorated, with elaborate walnut, cherry and oak beds, marble-topped dressers and ornate sofas. There are handmade quilts, an abundance of plants and brass lighting fixtures that sparkle from another era. Some rooms have working fireplaces while some have private balconies where guests may have breakfast served. Hearty breakfasts include homemade specialty breads such as almond lime bread, blueberry muffins, pumpkin doughnuts, spicy orange bread and gingerbread; fresh fruits, such as strawberries and sour cream, baked apples and pears poached in cinnamon sauce; and an entree, such as eggs in cream sauce, cheese souffle, quiche lorraine and German pancakes. Tennis courts and public swimming are nearby and there's a jogging trail in the city park directly behind the inn. And, of course, the famous lineup of Colorado Springs attractions is at hand.
Rates: *$48-$75 per room. The Hearthstone Inn, 506 N Cascade Ave, Colorado Springs, CO 80903,* **303/473-4413.**

The Hearthstone Inn, Colorado Springs, CO

The Taos Inn, Taos, NM

Strater Hotel, Durango, CO

MIDWEST

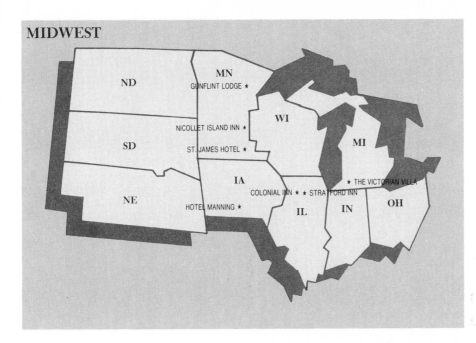

(Map showing states with labels: ND, MN, SD, NE, WI, MI, IA, IL, IN, OH. Inn locations marked: GUNFLINT LODGE ★, NICOLLET ISLAND INN ★, ST. JAMES HOTEL ★, HOTEL MANNING ★, COLONIAL INN ★, STRATFORD INN ★, ★ THE VICTORIAN VILLA)

NICOLLET ISLAND INN

Minneapolis, MN

This inn is something of an enigma. It is totally modern, opened in 1982, yet it is housed in a 90-year-old limestone building. It is reminiscent of a country inn, yet it is located in downtown Minneapolis. Certainly, the building has a colorful history. Built in 1893 on the bustling Mississippi riverfront as a manufacturing plant, it later was occupied by the Salvation Army for nearly 60 years. Today it houses a fine restaurant that already has received acclaim, a cozy pub and 24 guest rooms. Each of the rooms is individually decorated in the manner of a Victorian-era country inn, complete with armoires, wing chairs, writing desks, framed antique graphics, old-fashioned comforters and fresh flowers. Accommodations include a complimentary cordial upon arrival, a bedtime chocolate, Continental breakfast and the morning newspaper. For dining, you can choose seating near the antique oak fireplace or on the four-season, glassed-in porch overlooking the Mississippi.

Rates: *$70-$100; Double $82-$112. Special packages available. Nicollet Island Inn, 95 Merriam, Nicollet Island, Minneapolis, MN 55401,* **612/623-7741.**

ST. JAMES HOTEL

Red Wing, MN

This town, nestled between limestone bluffs carved by the Mississippi, houses a hotel reminiscent of the days when steamboat traffic plied the river. Built in 1875, the 60-room St. James reopened in 1979 after two years of restoration and expansion. Each guest room is furnished differently and distinctively with antiques and antique reproductions. Wallpaper, carpeting and hand-quilted bedspreads add to a homespun Victorian flavor. Nearly half of the guest rooms offer views of the Mississippi and soaring bluffs. A restaurant and bar, sculptured from rough limestone quarried from the bluffs, provides a pub-like atmosphere and serves lunches, dinners and cocktails. The more formal Victorian Room, furnished with antiques from around the country, offers dinners from an a la carte Continental menu. There's also a coffee shop overlooking the river (with alfresco dining in good weather) and twice-a-week barbecues during the summer months. Summer activities include hiking, boating, sailing, fishing and picnics along the river banks or atop the bluffs. In winter there is downhill and cross-country skiing nearby.

Rates: *$54.50 to $75 per room. St. James Hotel, 406 Main St, Red Wing, MN 55066,* **612/388-2846.**

Colonial Inn, Grand Detour, IL

Gunflint Lodge, Grand Marais, MN

GUNFLINT LODGE

Grand Marais, MN

In the northwoods country close to the Canadian border, this secluded, rustic lodge is ideal for restful family vacations and popular with fishermen. In fact, special fishing packages include meals, accommodations, boat, motor, gas and fish filleting and freezing. Guides are available, and you'll have the opportunity to sample a north-country tradition—a shore lunch in the heart of the wilderness. Accommodations are in modern lakeside cottages or suites in the main lodge—all with maid service. Three hearty meals a day are home-cooked. Dinner, for example, includes homemade soup, salads, breads, and a big platter of meat and vegetables followed by a dessert fresh from the kitchen. There's fishing for lake trout, northern pike, walleye and smallmouth bass. Plus waterskiing, hiking to nearby Bridal Falls, berry-picking, motor-boat cruising, and exploring by canoe the nearby lakes and the outer reaches of the Boundary Waters Wilderness. Open early May—mid Oct.

Rates: *Family plan packages (including lodging, all meals, boat and motor, two canoes, gas, unlimited waterskiing and wilderness activities program including an overnight canoe trip if desired FOR A FAMILY OF 3) range from $570 for 4 nights to $895 for a full week. Gunflint Lodge. Grand Marais, MN 55604,* **218/388-2294,** *outside MN* **800/328-3325.**

HOTEL MANNING

Keosauqua, IA

Edwin Manning started out in 1837 in this bustling river town with a log cabin trading post. When that burned down, he opened, in 1854, a general store and a bank in what later became the first floor of the Hotel Manning. The upper two stories were added in the late 1890s. Today, you can step back in time and rent a room restored with antique beds, commodes and dressers, patterned wallpaper and quilts. Hearty meals are served in three dining rooms and the rustic Sandbar Lounge in the cellar is a unique watering hole. Nearby are golf, tennis, canoeing, fishing, hiking and pool or lake swimming. Across the Des Moines River are Lacey-Keosauqua State Park (Iowa's largest) and Bentonsport, a "ghost town" with the Mason House Museum, Iowa's largest country store, pottery and glass works and artist studios.

Rates: *An overnight package for two includes champagne dinner, accommodations in a restored room and a full breakfast served in your room; Cost $65 for two. Hotel Manning, Keosauqua, IA 52565,* **319/293-3232.**

COLONIAL INN

Grand Detour, IL

If you'd like to spend the night, the weekend—or longer—in a 19th Century mansion surrounded by beautiful Victorian antiques, head for the sleepy village of Grand Detour, Illinois. This picturesque little community of 600—once a thriving town of 6,000 until it was by-passed by the railroad—was named by early French explorers because it is nestled in an oxbow bend of the Rock River. Later, the town gained fame as the site where John Deere invented his famous plow that opened up the west. The John Deere Historic Site features a replica of his blacksmith shop and the houses where he lived, now restored and authentically furnished. The Colonial Inn has 12 guest rooms, many with fireplaces (now purely decorative) and some with private baths. Guest rooms are decorated with antique or reproduction wallpaper, painted in authentic Victorian colors and include such furnishings as a six-foot Victorian carved headboard, a chest-of-drawers with teardrop poles and a hand-rubbed walnut bureau. Guests relax in a lounge decorated with rich red-and-gold flocked wallpaper and featuring a grand piano *and* an organ. Antique lovers can do some shopping as well as admiring—the inn's front parlor also serves as an antique shop.

Rates: *With bath $25, shared bath, $20. Colonial Inn, Rte 3, Dixon, IL 61021,* **815/652-4422.**

STRATFORD INN

Sycamore, IL

Modern luxury and antique ambience blend in this comfortable inn which has risen, Phoenix-like, within the shell of a totally refurbished commercial hotel built in the 1920s. Furnishings also combine period and modern. Rooms feature deep-pile carpeting, fluffy thick comforters, writing desks, easy chairs and armoires; doors are handsome solid oak with brass fixtures. Nor has expense been spared on the attractive new lobby, which features a "club" look, with oak wainscoting and imported wool carpet in a rich Hunter green. An oddity of this inn is that within its core remains the shell of a house built in 1882 by the town's first mayor. The new inn actually wraps around this old mansion, two of the rooms of which have been converted into luxury suites—one with a loft bedroom and rooftop garden, both with king-size whirlpools. The inn offers two additional suites in the main section and 34 rooms. The restaurant, Carls Fargo Coach Room, is locally popular, with an extensive menu ranging from burgers and sandwiches to baked French onion soup and steak and seafood dinners. In late October, Sycamore's annual Pumpkin Festival attracts 80,000 visitors.

Rates: *Master suites $75 single, $80 double; corner suites $54 single, $59 double; rooms $31-$47. Stratford Inn, 355 W State St, Sycamore, IL 60178,* **815/895-6789.**

THE VICTORIAN VILLA

Union City, MI

In keeping with its name, this 19th-century guesthouse offers no rooms. Instead, it accommodates guests in five overnight "guest chambers," each furnished and decorated in a popular style of the 1880s. Included in the price is an afternoon beverage and Continental breakfast with imported teas and coffee, fruit juice, home-baked Amish pastries, muffins and seasonal Michigan fruit—plus chocolates on your pillow at turn-down time. By reservation, the innkeepers will provide an afternoon Victorian "tea for two." Chilled champagne, wine, cheese plates and floral service are available on request. Located in a quaint river village in South Central Michigan, this guesthouse is quiet and relaxing—yet close to a variety of diversions. Within a 25-mile radius are 45 antique shops, six Victorian homes/museums, several 19th century historical walking tours, good restaurants and three summerstock theaters. Nearby are good fishing, regular country antique auctions and lots of summer festivals.

Rates: *Rooms, $40/couple; suite $60/couple. The Victorian Villa, 601 N Broadway, Union City, MI 49094,* **517/741-7383.**

St. James Hotel, Red Wing, MN

Nicollet Island Inn, Minneapolis, MN

St. James Hotel, Red Wing, MN

Hotel Manning, Keosauqua, IA

Colonial Inn, Grand Detour, IL

SOUTHCENTRAL

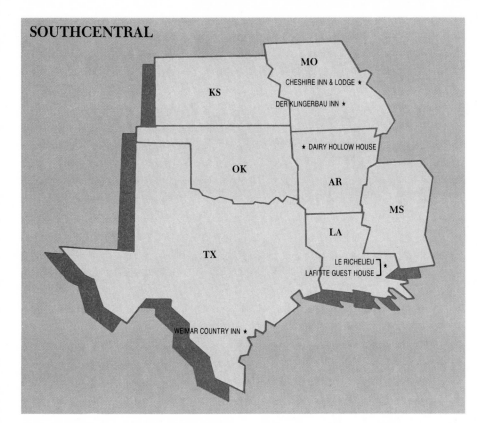

DER KLINGERBAU INN

Hermann, MO

In the "Rhine Country of Missouri," this elegant mansion is furnished to reflect its Victorian beginnings. Built in 1878 by the community's flour miller, the restored inn offers spacious, antique-furnished guest rooms, with a "stitchery museum" on the third floor—three bedrooms decorated with an extensive collection of Victorian needlework. Each morning a complimentary light breakfast is served by the fireside in the dining room. Hermann is an historic river town that contains more than 100 buildings and two districts on the National Register of Historic Places. There are two wineries offering tours and tastings, a museum, restaurants, antique shops, a craft center and a golf course. Owners of the inn also operate The Calico Cupboard, a restaurant overlooking the Missouri River. It is filled with "a collection of collections"—blue willow, spongeware, graters and choppers—and offers a varied German-American menu featuring such favorites as weiner schnitzel, bratwurst, German potato salad, fried chicken and country-baked ham ... plus homemade bread, strudel, jams, jellies and pickles.

Rates: *Special 2-night package includes all meals and tours of wineries and museums, $99.50 per person. der Klingerbau Inn, 108 E 2nd St, Hermann, MO 65041,* **314/486-2030.**

DAIRY HOLLOW HOUSE

Eureka Springs, AR

This tiny inn is a restored 1888 Ozarks farmhouse furnished with antiques and traditional folk arts, with fresh flowers in every room. There are only two guest rooms, each with a private bath and private entrance and each distinctive in character. The Rose Room has a double bed, handmade quilt, gentleman's bureau, antique hooked rug, hand-woven window shades, clawfoot tub, skylight and etched glass. The Iris Room features twin beds of ornate cast iron with handmade quilts and oak bureau. Breakfast (included) features coffee, tea, herb tea or cafe au lait (served in your room, if you wish, with morning paper by your door), fresh fruit in season or just-squeezed orange juice served in the sunny parlour, followed by a basket of fresh-baked wholewheat butterhorns and a loaf of sweet bread, or a generous helping of German baked pancakes—accompanied by homemade jams and butter. The inn also will prepare dinners for guests only: A 6-course French-accented meal billed as Haute Country Cuisine.

Rates: *Single $45-$55; Double $49-$59 plus 6% sales tax. Dairy Hollow House, Rte 2, Box 1, Eureka Springs, AR 72632,* **501/253-7444.**

WEIMAR COUNTRY INN

Weimar, TX

Here's a tale of a town that lost a hotel ... and regained it. This corner of town has been the site of a hotel since the 1870s. The present building, erected in 1909, is the third. The business closed in 1970. For a time the building was used as a nursing home. Later it was vacant and threatened with demolition. In 1981 a new group undertook its complete restoration. Nine guest rooms upstairs (most with private baths) and the dining facilities on the main floor have been restored and decorated in keeping with the building's original style—but with all modern conveniences. Also available is a three-room suite with two baths. The Texas-style dinner menu features a selection of reasonably-priced steaks; for lunch there are burgers, sandwiches, chili and mugs of cold beer. Complimentary Continental breakfast is included in the price of a room.

Rates: *$30-$65; Suite $125. Weimar Country Inn, 101 Jackson, Weimar, TX 78962,* **409/725-8888.**

CHESHIRE INN & LODGE

St. Louis, MO

Ride an English double-decker to the Municipal Opera or a sporting event. Splurge and explore St. Louis in a chauffeured Rolls Royce Silver Cloud. Quaff a half yard of beer and enjoy strolling minstrels. These are the touches designed to recreate an English hostelry—American style. Despite its pseudo-Englishness, this is a comfortable, fun place to stay. There's an English-style pub with nightly entertainment (and rare, old Scotch!) and another with a piano bar. There's dining in an award-winning restaurant, complimentary Welsh rarebit during the cocktail hour, an ice cream parlor and an antique shop. There's also a courtyard pool (food and drinks served poolside) and health-club facilities.

Rates: *Single $61-$67; Double or Twin Double $72-$79; Suites (including breakfast) $127. Taxes not included. Cheshire Inn & Lodge, 6300 Clayton at Skinker, St. Louis, MO 63117,* **1-800-325-R-E-S-V** *or (in Missouri)* **1-800-392-RESV.**

Le Richelieu, New Orleans, LA

Daily Hollow House, Eureka Springs, AR

Der Klingerbau Inn, Hermann, MO

LE RICHELIEU

New Orleans, LA

In a city known for its fine small hotels, here's one that has been multiply-acclaimed as one of the best: Movie stars, politicians and other celebrities stay there. Ex-Beatle Paul McCartney took the VIP suite (said by *Business Week* to be "the South's most luxurious suite") for two months. The hotel, located in the famous French Quarter, is the result of a meticulous restoration that combined a row mansion and a macaroni factory. It exudes elegance and good taste, offering 88 large, clean, newly and individually decorated rooms and suites, free self-parking and lock on premises, intimate lounge and terrace cafe, landscaped patio and pool, and a staff that knows the true meaning of "Southern hospitality." All of the sights and sounds of the Vieux Carre are within walking distance.
Rates: *Singles $55-$70; Doubles and twins $65-$80; Suites $85 up. Le Richelieu Motor Hotel, 1234 Chartres St, New Orleans. LA 70116,* **1-800-535-9653** *(in LA call collect* **504-529-2492).**

LAFITTE GUEST HOUSE

New Orleans, LA

Typical of New Orleans' French Quarter, this 1849 brick French manor has ivy-covered walls, wrought-iron balconies, and a charming little courtyard. Guest rooms feature 14-foot ceilings, crystal chandeliers, and black marble and carved-mahogany mantels; many have private balconies. Fine antiques and reproductions from around the world add grace to this inn. Furnishings include four-poster beds and antique armoires. The Victorian parlor, with plush, red velvet drapes, Oriental rugs and a period settee, offers reading material and a comfortable place to relax. The price of a room includes a Continental breakfast of freshly squeezed juice, French roast coffee, croissants or brioches, and butter, jelly and jam. You may enjoy this in the courtyard or, perhaps, on the balcony of your room. Located in the heart of *Vieux Carre,* the inn offers easy access to its antique shops, museums and world-famous restaurants. Whatever your pleasure in this exciting city—jazz, fine dining, a quiet stroll through rows of colorful Creole and Spanish cottages, or the non-stop lively pace of Bourbon Street—this delightful inn puts you in the center of the action.
Rates: *Double $68-$95. Lafitte Guest House, 1003 Bourbon St, New Orleans, LA 70116,* **504/581-2678.**

Weimar County Inn, Weimar, TX

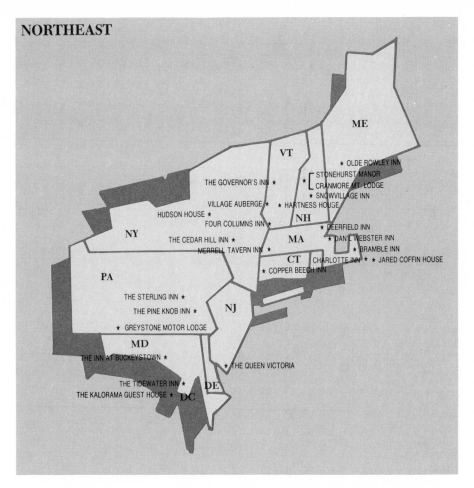

NORTHEAST

ME
VT
★ OLDE ROWLEY INN
STONEHURST MANOR
THE GOVERNOR'S INN ★ ★ CRANMORE MT. LODGE
★ SNOWVILLAGE INN
VILLAGE AUBERGE ★ ★ HARTNESS HOUSE
HUDSON HOUSE ★ NH
FOUR COLUMNS INN ★ ★ DEERFIELD INN
NY ★ DAN'L WEBSTER INN
THE CEDAR HILL INN ★ MA
MERRELL TAVERN INN ★ ★ BRAMBLE INN
CT
CHARLOTTE INN ★ ★ JARED COFFIN HOUSE
★ COPPER BEECH INN
PA
THE STERLING INN ★
THE PINE KNOB INN ★ NJ
★ GREYSTONE MOTOR LODGE
MD
THE INN AT BUCKEYSTOWN ★
★ THE QUEEN VICTORIA
THE TIDEWATER INN ★
THE KALORAMA GUEST HOUSE ★ DE
DC

THE PINE KNOB INN

Canadensis, PA

This 30-room, pre-Civil War inn provides comfortable accommodations and superb food in the heart of the Pocono Mountains. It offers guest rooms with antique furnishings, including mahogany four-poster and Victorian carved beds, and a parlor with a cheery fire, shelves of books and a grand piano, where you can enjoy good conversation and sip an aperitif or after-dinner drink. Hearty breakfasts include eggs, French toast and pancakes plump with blueberries. Dinner menus feature homemade soups and chowders, Quiche Maison (a creamy broccoli and cheddar quiche is a wonderful specialty) and such entrees as veal Marsala, duckling with orange sauce, Coquilles St. Jacques Mornay and juicy prime rib—plus homemade desserts such as praline pecan cheesecake. Breakfast and dinner are included in room prices. This year-around inn has a swimming pool and a trout creek and offers tennis, badminton, shuffleboard and other lawn games. Nearby are hiking trails that meander past rushing waterfalls and placid lakes, plus golf courses, horseback riding, professional summer theater, antique and craft shops and night clubs. Skiers are five minutes from Timber Hill and Buck Hill, 30 minutes from Camelback and Jack Frost ski areas. Snowmobiling and ice skating are only five minutes away. Nearby state parks offer some of the state's best cross-country skiing.
Rates: *Daily $42-$48, weekly $252-$288, per person incl. dinner and breakfast. The Pine Knob Inn, Rte 447, Canadensis, PA 18325,* **717/595-2532.**

THE STERLING INN

South Sterling, PA

High in the Pocono Mountains, this year-around resort offers accommodations in a charming lodge or in secluded cottages. Guest rooms are airy and comfortable; the main lounge has a huge fireplace of native stone; there is a spacious game room that includes a small library. Rates include three meals daily, with entrees such as roast leg of lamb, standing rib roast, fresh veal and fresh fish. The dining room is set with fresh flowers. Luncheons also are served lakeside. Summer activities include tennis, shuffleboard, putting, hiking and swimming in the lake; nearby are championship golf courses, good fishing and water skiing, horseback riding, night clubs, theaters and Summer playhouses. In winter, there's ice skating on the lake, cross-country skiing and sledding, with a variety of other winter sports nearby.
Rates: *Daily rates $44-$56.60 midweek, $49-$58 weekends, per person, double occupancy including three meals. The Sterling Inn, S. Sterling, PA 18460,* **717/676-3311.**

GREYSTONE MOTOR LODGE

Bird-In-Hand, PA

The term "motor lodge" is unquestionably a misnomer for this attractive Victorian mansion. It dates back to 1883, having been constructed from a farmhouse built in the mid-1800s. Each of the guest rooms are individually furnished, some with antiques, and some of them feature such items as stained glass windows, cut-crystal doors, original woodwork and antique bath fixtures. The lobby, with its Victorian decor, features leaded beveled glass doors and plaster-cast wall and ceiling sculptures. The carriage house was originally a barn built about the same time as the farm house. The inn, which sits on a two-acre lot with manicured lawns and tall shade trees, also offers multi-room suites for families and some suites with full kitchens. It is centrally located for exploring the Pennsylvania Dutch Country.

Rate: *$20-$47. Greystone Motor Lodge, 2658 Old Philadelphia Pike, Bird-In-Hand, PA 17505,* **717/393-4233.**

THE TIDEWATER INN

Easton, MD

Ringed with tree-lined streets studded with craft shops and boutiques, this inn along Maryland's storied Eastern Shore is a handsome structure of Federal design. It has 120 modern rooms and suites. Its restaurant, famous for food and service, includes many epicurean dishes, some of which must be ordered 24 hours in advance. Its Decoy Bar, reflective of the area's prime goose hunting, offers warm ambience and a distinctive decor. Within easy walking distance, in Easton's Historic District, are more than 100 residences and sites which date back to the beginning of the Federal period of architecture. The Third Haven Meeting House, built by Quakers in 1682, is believed to be America's oldest wooden house of worship in continuous use. Nearby Oxford, one of America's chief colonial deepwater ports, has its own quaint charm, while at St. Michaels is a maritime museum, an antique lighthouse and an aquarium of Chesapeake Bay underwater life. In season, you can see the nation's last working sailfleet as it goes out for a day's oyster dredging—or you can go charterboat fishing for striped bass and fighting blues.

Rates: *Single $34-$40, double $46-$56, suite $105-$155. The Tidewater Inn, Easton, MD 21601,* **301/822-1300.**

THE INN AT BUCKEYSTOWN

Buckeystown, MD

This 1890s restored Victorian mansion is in the heart of Buckeystown, a nationally registered historic village with pre-revolutionary roots and a strong Civil War influence. The village is on the Monocacy River and is surrounded by Civil War sites, monuments and markers. Shaded by chestnut and dogwood trees, the house has a wrap-around porch ideal for relaxing. The decor features ornate crystal chandeliers, working fireplaces and a golden oak-paneled staircase leading to guest rooms. Service is on

Victorian china, period silver and glassware. The price of a room includes breakfast and dinner, with complimentary wine at dinner and port wine served in the room. Dinner cuisine is eclectic, running the gamut from classical French and Pennsylvania Dutch through Basque and Southern-style.

Rates: *Weekends and holidays $105 per couple, per night; Mon.-Thu. $75. The Inn at Buckeystown, 3521 Buckeystown Pike, Buckeystown, MD 21717,* **301/874-5755.**

HUDSON HOUSE, A COUNTRY INN

Cold Spring, NY

On the banks of the Hudson River, you'll find hospitality at the second oldest inn in continuous operation in New York State. Built in 1832 to accommodate an increase in river passenger traffic brought on by the advent of the paddle steamer, this inn has been completely restored, filled with antiques and tenderly embellished with Colonial crafts. Fourteen antique-filled guest rooms with private baths occupy two original floors of this inn that recently was designated a Historic Landmark Building. In the Half Moon Bar you can enjoy drinks around a warming fire, in the peaceful garden, or on the porch, watching the sun set behind West Point across the river. The menu emphasizes American country cooking with homemade breads, pastries and cottage meat pies, fresh fruits and vegetables, meats butchered and cured right on the premises and a sumptuous Yankee Doodle Sunday brunch. Explore historic Cold Spring. The entire downtown section has been selected as an Historic Landmark District. George Washington is said to have watered his horse at the cold spring in town.

Rates: *Single $55; Double $65; Suite $100. Hudson House, A Country Inn, 2 Main St, Cold Spring, NY 10516,* **914/265-9355.**

THE CEDAR HILL INN

Ghent, NY

For getaways to a "comfortable home in the country," this secluded bed-and-breakfast inn in the heart of rural upstate New York fits the bill. It offers eight bedrooms with half baths, two living rooms with fireplaces for quiet conversation, a baby grand piano and shelves full of books, plus swimming pool, courts for tennis and croquet and 20 acres of lawn and rambling countryside. A night's lodging includes breakfast. Blueberry pancakes, banana French toast and homemade muffins and granola are frequent specialties. Dinner is available on weekends. Or you might coax the kitchen into preparing one of your personal favorites. Several restaurants are nearby. The setting is the richly textured mosaic of the Hudson Valley: mountains, fields, forests, lakes and streams. Hiking and cross-country ski trails start right from the inn door. Within an hour's drive are downhill skiing, fishing, the Appalachian Trail, Tanglewood Music Festival, regional theaters, fairgrounds, state parks, museums and historic homes. The area is studded with antique dealers.

Rates: *Double, 1 night, 2 persons (inc. full country breakfast), $72; Single, $57; Reduced rates for 3 nights or more. The Cedar Hill Inn, Ghent, NY 12075,* **518/392-3923.**

Stonehurst Manor, North Conway, NH

The Cedar Hill Inn, Ghent, NY

Village Auberge, Dorset, VT

Deerfield Inn, Deerfield, MA

Historic Merrell Tavern Inn, South Lee, MA

THE QUEEN VICTORIA

Cape May, NJ

Close to the beaches of Cape May and Cape May Point, this bed and breakfast inn offers romantic accommodations and hearty country breakfasts. Rooms are decorated with authentic Victorian furnishings in walnut, wicker, oak and pine. Colorful quilts, antique bedsteads and fresh flowers are featured in guest rooms. Breakfast includes fresh fruits, imported coffees and teas, farm-fresh eggs and cream and homemade hot breads. During the day the inn will provide bicycles that will enable you to enjoy the ocean breezes as you visit local historic landmarks, art galleries, craft shops and antique emporiums. In the evening, you can relax in the parlor by a crackling fire, perhaps with a book from the inn's extensive library. Christmas is a favorite season at this year-around inn. Each weekend in December is highlighted by special events . . . decorating the inn, carolling, Dickens readings by the fire.

Rates: *Shared bath $35-$55; Large room with private bath $70-$80. Discounts for longer stays. The Queen Victoria, 102 Ocean St, Cape May, NJ 08204,* **609/884-8702.**

THE KALORAMA GUEST HOUSE

District of Columbia

This Victorian townhouse in the fashionable DC embassy district functions as a European style bed-and-breakfast guest house. Its six guest rooms feature plush comforters, brass headboards, warm Oriental carpets, and relaxing wing chairs. Turn-of-the-century artwork and lots of greenery enhance the charming ambience. In keeping with tradition, you can enjoy a complimentary Continental breakfast in the dining room each morning and, each afternoon, repair to the upstairs parlour for sherry by the fireside. Just a block away are a melange of ethnic restaurants, night spots, and antique shops. Fashionable Connecticut Avenue stores are close by for shopping or browsing.

Rates: *Single $30-$35, double $35-$40. The Kalorama Guest House, 1854 Mintwood Place, NW, Washington, DC 20009,* **202/667-6369.**

THE GOVERNOR'S INN

Ludlow, VT

Ludlow is surrounded by five lakes, the Black River, Okemo Mountain (less than a mile) and all of Vermont! Located on the village green, this late 19th century Victorian home offers eight stylish guest rooms, each furnished with antiques. Six have private baths, the other two share a bath and may be used as a suite. Common rooms include a spacious foyer with fireplace and a whispering alcove, a living room with an ornate slate fireplace, dining and breakfast rooms and a den with full beverage service. Snuggle under a puff in a century-old brass four-poster and wake to hot oatmeal, apple pancakes and fresh coffee. Enjoy a six-course dinner by candlelight or order a picnic hamper packed with chilled soup, cheese, fruit, juice, a sandwich, nut bread, cream cheese and wine.

Rates: *Per person double occupancy (including full breakfast and dinner) $49-$55 plus 5% state tax and 15% service charge. The Governor's Inn, 86 Main St Ludlow, VT 05149,* **802/228-8830.**

HARTNESS HOUSE

Springfield, VT

There's a private forest for walking, 32 acres of woodland for cross-country skiing, a lighted clay tennis court, heated swimming pool and fine food and wine. You'll find it all at this turn-of-the-century house on a hillside in southeastern Vermont. It is the former home of Governor James Hartness, also an imaginative inventor and an astronomer. He designed one of the first tracking telescopes in America, which remains in working order on the front lawn. The inn also houses a museum displaying a collection of telescopes and priceless drawings and paintings. There are 42 rooms (each with private bath). In the old house, rooms are cozy with period wallpaper and furniture; additions contain comfortable modern interiors. Public areas are decorated with plants, original works of art, antique furniture and old and new country Vermont pieces. Nearby is superlative skiing—plus maple sugaring, covered bridges, antiqueing and striking scenery.

Rates: *Rooms $41-$44; Suites $53. Modified American Plan $36 per person. Weekend package $100 per couple. Hartness House, 30 Orchard St, Springfield, VT 05156,* **802/885-2115.**

VILLAGE AUBERGE

Dorset, VT

Set back from a picturesque country lane and backdropped by the foothills of the Green Mountains, this country inn is owned and operated by Alex and Hanneke Koks of the Netherlands. The Dutch affection for things that grow is apparent in the blooming flowers in the gardens and containers; under large maples guests will find wrought iron tables and chairs from which to enjoy this serene setting. There are four guest rooms in the white clapboard inn (a restored farmhouse) and two suites in adjacent converted cottages. Rooms are warmly furnished with four-poster beds, antique dressers and patterned wallpapers. The dining room, highlighted by a tin ceiling and broad bay window, has built-in china closets stocked with a fine collection from Holland, linen tablecloths, and settings of crystal, china and New England pewter lamps. An intimate bar is complete with a stained-glass window. Continental cuisine features such as rack of lamb, medallion of lamb en croute with wine and goat cheese, sweetbreads, veal kidneys, and breast of duck with a raspberry vinegar sauce. Homemade deserts include fruit tarts, French chocolate cakes, and mousses. Nearby is good skiing, tennis, golf, fishing, and hiking. The Dorset Playhouse is the oldest summer theater production in Vermont.

Rates: *$50-$85 EP. Village Auberge, Rte 30, Dorset, VT 05251,* **802/867-5715.**

The Governor's Inn, Ludlow, VT

Jared Coffin House, Nantucket, MA

Greystone Motor Lodge, Bird-in-Hand, PA

The Inn at Buckeystown, Buckeystown, MD

The Bramble Inn, Brewster, MA

The Dan'l Webster Inn, Sandwich, MA

The Queen Victoria, Cape May, NJ

FOUR COLUMNS INN

Newfane, VT

Perhaps the most picturesque town common in Vermont is to be found in the small village of Newfane, north of Brattleboro. Surrounding the wide, grassy common, the village is entirely comprised of white clapboard, green-shuttered buildings, a steepled church, and a country general store. One of these buildings, dating back to 1830, is the Four Columns Inn. The main house and barn were renovated and opened as an inn and restaurant in 1965. Twelve guest rooms all contain private baths and are furnished with brass and canopy beds, wing back chairs and colonial wallpapers and curtains. The original wide planked floors of the inn now hold an elegant array of country antiques and period reproductions. Accent in the kitchen is on nouvelle cuisine, including such dishes as saute of veal in caper and nasturtium sauce, and sliced double breast of duck in a rhubarb and relish sauce. The dining room has a huge brick fireplace. Continental breakfast is included in the price of a room. Nearby is good downhill and cross-country skiing, plus skating on the inn's pond. The inn has a swimming pool, trout stream and is central to good hiking and biking country.
Rates: *$50-$75 double occupancy. Four Columns Inn, Newfane, VT 05345,* **802/365-7713.**

SNOWVILLAGE INN

Snowville, NH

In a picturesque setting 100 feet high on Foss Mountain at the edge of the famed White Mountains and Lakes region, this year-around country inn once was a summer home, built in 1916. Fourteen guest rooms are decorated in Early American country style. A large fireplace in a living room stocked with books and game invites relaxation and conversation. There is a porch with a striking view where cheese and crackers are served for a "happy hour" get together, and a grand piano and guitar for guests to play. Extra touches include fresh flowers in rooms and on dining tables, a fresh fruit basket for guests, and complimentary tea and coffee always available. Lodging includes breakfast and dinner, the latter featuring such dishes as veal piccata, roast beef with Yorkshire pudding, and coq au vin. Breakfast includes eggs or pancakes, with eggs benedict and champagne served on Sunday. Soups and bread are made fresh daily; in season, fresh vegetables come from the garden. Nearby activities include canoeing, hiking and fishing. The inn has its own clay tennis court and cross-country ski trails start at the door. Excellent downhill skiing nearby.
Rates: *MAP (incl. breakfast and dinner), per person double occupancy, summer $47.50, Winter $49.50. Snowvillage Inn, Snowville, NH 03849* **603/447-2818.**

STONEHURST MANOR

North Conway, NH

In the heart of the White Mountains, this English-style country manor is filled with rich old oak, stained glass crafted in Europe, elegant appointments and plush carpeting. Relax in a fan-back wicker chair in one of four dining rooms as you work your way through an extensive dinner menu. It includes 14 appetizers, 10 veal specialties, a variety of fish and such favorites as Beef Wellington and rack of lamb. There's an espresso bar, a variety of coffee liquor drinks and an array of sinfully rich desserts. Guest rooms and suites are individually decorated, some have porches—one has a stained glass door connecting the porch. There's a large pool (with summer cocktail service), tennis courts, volleyball courts and shuffleboard. In winter, the mountains and ski trails of Mt. Washington Valley are within minutes of the manor's 33-acre, pine-forested grounds.
Rates: *Double $42; Two doubles $58-$82; Two doubles & balcony $92; Suites from $92. Special package plans available. Stonehurst Manor, Box 1900, N Conway, NH 03860,* **603/356-3113.**

CRANMORE MT. LODGE

North Conway, NH

This country inn, in the heart of the White Mountains, combines a rustic lifestyle with an array of resort facilities. The main building, in an old New England farmhouse, has a cozy sitting room with fireplace, a TV and game room and 13 guest rooms. There's a dining room offering home cooking, and an Alpine ski rental shop and waxing room. Additional accommodations in a modernized barn (the original beams have been left exposed) in rooms furnished with oak antiques. Acres of trails wind through pine woods and past a mountain stream; a trout pond offers fly fishing. There's an outdoor pool, all-weather tennis court, basketball court, hot spa and poolside barbecue. Mt. Washington Valley offers a host of activities—hiking, kayaking, canoeing, bicycling, golf, horseback riding, antiquing, art galleries, summer theater and many fine restaurants. Cross-country ski enthusiasts will find miles oftrails unwinding from the inn's back door. Downhill skiers are within minutes of Cranmore, Attitash, Wildcat and Black Mountain. The inn has its own lighted toboggan hill, skating pond and snowmobiling.
Rates: *Winter, double from $27.50 to $37.50 per person (including breakfast and dinner). Summer, $28 to $39 (including full country breakfasts). Group rates and packages that include ski equipment and snowmobile rides are available. Cranmore Mt Lodge, PO Box 1194, Conway, NH 03860,* **603/356-2044.**

OLDE ROWLEY INN

North Waterford, ME

Built in 1790, this restored inn once was a stagecoach stop servicing the line through the White Mountains. A "tightwinder" staircase ascends to five guest rooms. Softly lit by tin lanterns, the cozy rooms feature period furniture, reproduction wallpaper, exposed beam ceilings and pumpkin pine floors. In the "keeping room," guests relax by an open fireplace. Three intimate dining rooms offer home-cooked specialties. Room rates include a full country breakfast: fresh fruit, eggs, blueberry pancakes; in winter a hot dish of oatmeal with butter and cream by a morning fire. Dinner may include such dishes as Chicken Veronique and Steak Diane, and a bread basket containing, perhaps, Shaker herb loaf and blueberry buckle. Nearby are four seasons of sports and activities . . . clear mountain lakes for swimming, fishing and boating; excellent skiing and hiking; fine golf courses and biking.
Rates: *Single $30; Double $36; Additional person $18, Discounts for extended stay. Olde Rowley Inn, PO Box 87, Rte 35, N Waterford, ME 04267,* **207/583-4143.**

HISTORIC MERRELL TAVERN INN

South Lee, MA

In the heart of the Berkshires and less than a mile from Norman Rockwell's beloved Stockbridge, this former stagecoach inn dates back to 1800. Emphasis is on historical accuracy and authenticity. Most of the furnishings date from 1790 to 1820. Guest rooms have canopy or four poster beds, antique furnishings and fireplaces. Breakfast varies according to seasons—fresh fruit with cereal, homemade breads, omelettes. Garnishes are picked from the inn's garden and herb bed. Throughout the growing season the breakfast tables are decorated with fresh-cut flowers. Many guests enjoy curling up in front of the fireplace during evening hours with wine and cheese. The grounds have old stone fences and the Housatonic River borders the property. The looming mountains nearby are beautiful year-around, spectacular in fall.

Rates: *A new special package offers a room with a fireplace, check-in on Friday, full breakfast Saturday and brunch (with the New York Times) Sunday with late 5pm check-out (for a chance to linger by the fire before journeying on). Cost: $140 double occupancy. Historic Merrell Tavern Inn, Main St, Rte 102, South Lee, MA 01260,* **413/243-1794.**

DEERFIELD INN

Deerfield, MA

This charming inn, which has won national acclaim, is located along the village Street in Old Deerfield. Originally built in 1884, the completely restored and redecorated inn has 23 beautifully appointed guest rooms, all with private bath and individual heat and air conditioning controls. It also features two cocktail lounges, a bar, two dining rooms and a coffee shop. The Main Dining Room, with its two large oriental rugs, features Chippendale and Federal style chairs and glistening mahogany tables. The informal Flintlock Room on the lower level has an outdoor terrace and is open for breakfast daily. The luncheon menu includes broiled or fried scallops, shish-kebab, broiled fresh haddock and daily specials featuring a crepe du jour and fresh fish. The dinner menu is more specialized, featuring such dishes as New England baked stuffed shrimp, veal Orloff, tournedos au-poivre and boneless breast of chicken Kiev. Located in the Upper Connecticut River Valley of western Massachusetts, the inn is a few minutes stroll from Historic Deerfield with its 12 beautifully restored museum houses containing a distinguished collection of early American furniture, silver, textiles, ceramics and household objects.

Rates: *$65-$70 single or double occupancy. Deerfield Inn, The Street, Deerfield, MA 01342,* **413/774-5587.**

JARED COFFIN HOUSE

Nantucket, MA

Located 30 miles off the southern coast of mainland Massachusetts, the island of Nantucket is an historic outpost of the 18th and 19th century whaling fleet. In the center of town is the well-preserved Old Historic District, and among the sea captain's homes and tree-lined lanes is the Jared Coffin House. This three-story brick building, built in 1845, is one of several old 18th and 19th century homes that comprise the inn. In all, the inn has 58 guest rooms, all with private baths. Period antiques, many brought back from whaling voyages to the far corners of the world, furnish the rooms. The common rooms have working fireplaces, oil paintings and traditional woven fabrics. The dining room features classic American fare, including native game and seafood dishes. Food and potables are served in the Tap Room, which features live entertainment. An adjoining patio, furnished with umbrella tables, offers alfresco luncheons and refreshments. Just a short walk from the inn are the stores on Main Street or Steamboat Wharf.

Rates: *$35 single; $65-$110 double, EP. Reduced rates (including Continental breakfast) Jan-Mar, Jared Coffin House, 29 Broad St, Nantucket, MA 02554,* **617/228-2400.**

THE DAN'L WEBSTER INN

Sandwich, MA

This picture-postcard inn rests on the main street of Sandwich, Cape Cod's oldest town, dating back to 1639. Recreated after the original was destroyed by fire in 1971, the inn is named after its most famous guest (Daniel Webster kept a standing reservation there from 1815-1851), and offers 41 guest rooms and four suites with fireplaces. Furnishings include canopy beds, wing back chairs, and other period antiques and fine reproductions. Chef Richard Catania, a graduate of the Culinary Institute of America, prepares Continental fare as well as a variety of fresh, local seafood dishes. Selections include veal Oscar and scallops baked in a stuffing with artichoke bottoms, mushrooms, shrimp and almonds in lemon, wine and shallot butter. Breakfast is served in a sunny conservatory. The authentic reproduction of the old tap room, the detailed recreation of the fireplaces, and the furnishings in the restaurant and guest rooms give the traveler and vacationer a welcome change of pace. Guests can enjoy a happy refresher in the tavern, an evening relaxing by the hearth side, or an elegant dinner in the 18th century Webster Room, which displays glass artifacts on loan from the Sandwich Glass Museum.

Rates: *Winter $42-$67 MAP; Summer $60-$105 MAP, double occupancy. The Dan'l Webster Inn, 149 Main St, Sandwich, MA 02563,* **617/888-3622.**

THE BRAMBLE INN

Brewster, MA

Within walking distance of the ocean, this Civil War inn is in the heart of the Historic District of Cape Cod. The main inn, built in 1861, houses a restaurant and art gallery on the first floor with guest rooms above. A separate building of similar Greek Revival style architecture dates from 1849 and houses additional guest rooms. Open from Memorial Day through October, it offers a small, cozy, intimate spot to stay while visiting Cape Cod. Complimentary Continental breakfast is included in the room price. Dinners at the inn's restaurant feature quiche, crepes, fancy cheese plates, gourmet soups (including Cape Cod clam chowder), fine wines and imported beers. The inn is adjacent to tennis courts and close to golf, fishing, museums, a state park, summer theaters and many other resort and recreational activities.

Rates: *Private bath $56-$62; Shared bath $46-$52. The Bramble Inn, Rte 6A, PO Box 159, Brewster on Cape Cod, MA 02631,* **617/896-7644.**

THE CHARLOTTE INN

Edgartown, MA

"This inn, one of the nation's handsomest, is a museum of art that takes boarders. Paintings, etchings, and engravings are hung along the corridors and in the rooms and there is a gallery and a gallery shop on the main floor." So noted nationally syndicated columnist, Horace Sutton, in picking favorite lodging places that have provided "extra pleasure." And with good reason. Beautifully situated on the island of Martha's Vineyard, this inn is a former sea captain's home, topped by a widow walk and surrounded by manicured gardens. Built circa 1860, the main house and its accompanying buildings (one dating from 1790), offers 24 lovely rooms. Furnishings include early American four posters, ladder-back rockers and wing-back chairs. Some guest rooms have working fireplaces; all have private baths. Guests receive complimentary breakfast Monday-Saturday. On Sunday, brunch is offered at an additional charge. Lunch and dinner are served at Chez Pierre, the inn's distinguished French dining room, specializing in Continental fare, fresh local seafood and game dishes. Selections include such entrees as Chateaubriand, Nantucket quail, roast pheasant with orange chutney glaze, mango chutney and wild rice, lobster saute with cognac cream sauce with mussels, and veal rib with wild mushroom cream sauce. Edgartown, with quiet, leafy lanes and tall, white church spires poking above hourglass elms offers excellent shopping. Nearby are sailing, fishing, golfing, tennis, summer theater and fine beaches for swimming and sunbathing.

Rates: *Double room $34-$135; Suite with fireplace $78-$195; Full apartment with fireplace $78-$125; Carriage house rooms $65-$195. The Charlotte Inn, S Summer St, Edgartown, MA 02539,* **617/627-4751.**

The Pine Knob Inn, Canadensis, PA

Stonehurst Manor, North Conway, NH

Hartness House, Springfield, VT

COPPER BEECH INN

Ivoryton, CT

If you enjoy elegant, imaginative dining, here's a country inn that puts the emphasis on food. Shaded by a huge copper beech tree, this 1886 white mansion offers four dining rooms and five bedrooms for overnight guests. Dining rooms have comfortable Chippendale or Queen Anne chairs (white wicker on the dining porch) and are decorated with antiques, old prints, gleaming brass and elegant china and crystal. Specializing in Country French cuisine, the inn is a consistent award winner—four stars from Mobil, voted number one restaurant in the state three years in a row by *Connecticut* magazine. From 15 or more innovative appetizers to about the same number of homemade desserts, the menu is the comprehensive kind that makes selection a pleasant chore. Thick lobster bisque and hot country pâté are acclaimed, while recommended entrees include Chataubriand, salmon in puff pastry with sole mousse, trout meunière, sweetbreads with mustard butter and veal stuffed with bluepoint oysters. Reservations a **must** for accommodations and dining.

Rates: *$55-$85 double. Copper Beech Inn, Main St, Ivoryton, CT 06442,* **203/767-0330.**

Four Columns Inn, Newfane, VT

The Sterling Inn, South Sterling, PA

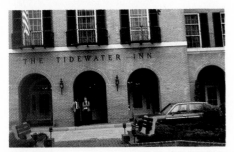

The Tidewater Inn, Easton, MD

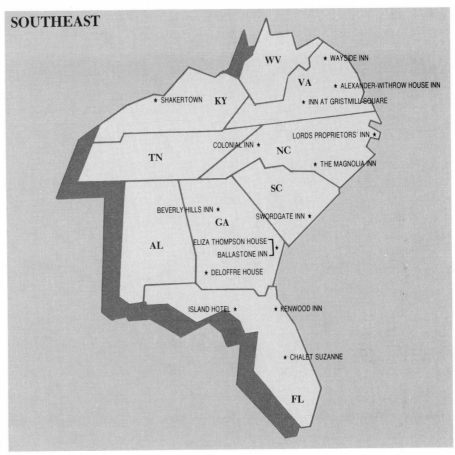

SOUTHEAST

WV
★ WAYSIDE INN
VA
★ ALEXANDER-WITHROW HOUSE INN
★ SHAKERTOWN   KY
★ INN AT GRISTMILL SQUARE
LORDS PROPRIETORS' INN ★
COLONIAL INN ★
TN   NC
SC
★ THE MAGNOLIA INN
BEVERLY HILLS INN ★
SWORDGATE INN ★
GA
AL
ELIZA THOMPSON HOUSE
BALLASTONE INN ★
★ DELOFFRE HOUSE
ISLAND HOTEL ★   ★ KENWOOD INN
★ CHALET SUZANNE
FL

SHAKERTOWN

Harrodsburg, KY

Probably, you've visited restored historic villages. Well, here's a chance to *stay* in one. Shakertown is the only historic site in the country that offers all overnight accommodations in original buildings—72 lodging rooms scattered among 14 different buildings. Rooms are furnished with reproduction Shaker pieces and hand-woven rugs and curtains. All are air-conditioned and have private baths. The Shaker Village of Pleasant Hill preserves 27 original 19th century buildings. On a self-guided tour you can sit in a cantilevered meeting house . . . learn about the medicinal uses of herbs in the Farm Deacon's Shop . . . watch broommakers, joiners, coopers, spinners, weavers and quilters . . . explore kitchen and herb gardens . . . hike across the fields or down to the Kentucky River . . . enjoy a ride on a paddlewheel riverboat. Dine amid the 19th century charm of the Trustees' Office Inn on Kentucky country fare—hearty breakfast buffets, lunches and dinners with a choice of meats, salads, relishes, vegetables passed at the table, fresh-baked breads, pies, cakes and tarts. Two craft shops offer a wide assortment of handmade items. Shaker Heritage Weekends highlight different interests—music, ballet, leatherworking, tinsmithing, hearth cooking, etc.

Rates: *Single $26-$50; Double $40-$67. Shakertown at Pleasant Hill, Inc, Rte 4, Harrodsburg, KY 40330,* **606/734-5411**

ISLAND HOTEL

Cedar Key, FL

This small island community off Florida's northwest Gulf coast (about 150 miles north of St. Petersburg) is the antithesis of the glittering Florida resort. A sleepy little fishing port, it seems almost untouched by time. Built around 1850, the Island Hotel is a two-story galleried building coated with "tabby," a mix of crushed shells and stones popular in Florida construction. During its checkered career, it has housed troops of the Union and Confederate armies and has served as a hideaway for gun runners. Today, the charming hotel is an ideal out-of-the-way place to relax from the pressures of modern day living. It offers 10 guest rooms and has a newly-renovated dining room with multiple French doors and a dining veranda. Food at the hotel, which features spicy chowders, hearts of palm salads, key lime pie and a bounty of fresh fish from local waters (including, in season, succulent stone-crab claws) has for years induced knowing visitors to make the trip to Cedar Key just to dine there. Two local museums, Cedar Key State Museum and Cedar Key Historical Museum, provide interesting background on this tiny town of 700 that once was one of the largest in the state. Annual events include a sidewalk art festival in late Apr and a seafood festival mid-Oct.

Rates: *$45 (private bath), $35 (semi-private bath—connecting), $30 (shared bath)—all rates for doubles. Island Hotel, Main St, Cedar Key, FL 32625,* **904/543-5111.**

The Deloffre House, Columbus, GA

Wayside Inn, Middletown, VA

The Kenwood Inn, St. Augustine, FL

The Lords Proprietors' Inn, Edenton, NC

CHALET SUZANNE

Lake Wales, FL

In the heart of Florida's citrus belt, this 30-room inn, owned and operated by the Hinshaw family since 1931, has become famous for its exquisite cuisine, its fascinatingly jumbled architecture and its eclectic collection of artifacts. There are spires, steeples, balconies, turrets, and a clock tower in pinks, greens, yellows and a variety of other hues. No two rooms in the inn are alike—nor are any two tables in the dining rooms. There are tiles from Persia, ironwork from Spain, copper from Egypt, wooden beds from Norway—objets d'art from around the globe. The food is reason enough for many to visit this unlikely inn. The restaurant received four stars from Mobil, was rated by *Life* as one of the 49 finest in the U.S. and nominated by Craig Claiborne as one of the 121 best in the world. The soups are so famous that they are shipped around the world and even travelled to the moon with the Apollo astronauts. At mealtime you can sample such offerings as the inn's famed romaine soup, baked grapefruit with a touch of cinnamon, hot home-made potato rolls, relishes made from tropical fruits, miniature versions of crepes Suzette, building a meal around such entrees as king crab thermidor, shrimp curry, lobster Newburg, or chicken Suzanne, tender and golden brown.
Rates: *$45-$80 double occupancy, additional person $6. Anyday Hideaway Special offers dinner, room and breakfast for two persons for $131. Chalet Suzanne, PO Drawer AC, Lake Wales, FL 33859,* **813/676-6011.**

THE KENWOOD INN

St. Augustine, FL

Located in the heart of our nation's oldest city—St. Augustine packs in 417 years of history—this inn was operating as a private boarding house as early as 1886. Now, lovingly restored (with central heat and air conditioning added) and furnished with Victorian antiques, it offers bed and breakfast to tourists. Guest rooms feature brass or high, walnut headboarded beds, walnut marble-topped dressers and tables, lots of wicker and plants and original paintings. Accommodations range from large rooms with fireplaces and kingsize beds to smaller, cozier quarters. Complimentary Continental breakfast includes tea, coffee, juice and home baked breads. Located two blocks from a park and half a block from a marina on the Intracoastal Waterway.
Rates: *$25-$45, single or double occupancy, plus tax. Extra person $5. The Kenwood Inn, 38 Marine St, St. Augustine, FL 32084,* **904/824-2116.**

WAYSIDE INN

Middletown, VA

Tucked away in the Shenandoah Valley, this inn first started offering bed and board to weary travelers in 1797. Twenty years later, when rugged roads were hacked out of the wilderness, it became a stagecoach stop. Today, the 21-room inn has been restored and refurbished with hundreds of antiques, capturing the flavor of the 18th century. Each room is a veritable museum; yet the inn also is functional and comfortable. Some guest rooms have canopied beds and working fireplaces. There are seven

uniquely decorated dining rooms, with costumed serving staff reinforcing the Colonial ambience. The Old Slave Kitchen is a popular eating place—especially on a cold winter's night when a fire crackles in the hearth. The room is decorated with high-backed chairs and bare tables—perhaps as it was when Stonewall Jackson rode through town as the Civil War swept by. The menu has a strong local flavor, with country-cured ham processed by local farmers, peanut soup, spoon bread and pan-fried chicken. Vegetables are valley-grown and apple juice has been a famous Shenandoah product for 200 years. Activities abound nearby, from fishing, golf, boating and skiing to antique hunting and visiting historic sites.
Rates: *$50-$100. Wayside Inn, 7783 Main St, Middletown, VA 22645,* **703/869-1797.**

THE INN AT GRISTMILL SQUARE

Warm Springs, VA

Originally the site of a mill built in 1771, this cluster of restored buildings includes the inn, a country store, a restaurant, an art gallery, and a Bath and Tennis Club with swimming pool and sauna. Every room or suite in the inn is decorated differently, some with antiques and old prints, others with a more contemporary motif. Guest accommodations may include such accessories as an antique clock, a spinning wheel or a fireplace mantel dating from the Revolutionary War. Many rooms have wood burning fireplaces. Included in the price of accommodations is a Continental breakfast—coffee, juice, muffins, jam and butter—served in the room. The acclaimed Waterwheel restaurant—fashioned from the original mill, with waterwheel still intact—features such specialties as boneless mountain trout stuffed with crabmeat, chicken cooked in a mushroom and tarragon cream sauce, barbecued baby spareribs, dry-cured country ham, rack of lamb, and several veal dishes. After dinner, guests may repair for potables at a tiny, cozy pub. This tiny village in the rolling farmland of the uplands of southwest Virginia is central to good riding, hiking, fishing, hunting, and skiing. Golf is minutes away at the famous Cascades and Lower Cascades courses—or "take the waters" at local springs.
Rates: *Double suites $55-$80. The Inn at Gristmill Square, PO Box 359, Warm Springs, VA 24484,* **703/839-2231.**

ALEXANDER-WITHROW HOUSE INN
THE McCAMPBELL INN

Lexington, VA

These two country inns are located in the center of historic Lexington across the street from each other and operated by the same management. The Alexander-Withrow House Inn was built in 1789 as a town house and served variously as a school, a bank and a store. Completely restored in 1972 and furnished according to the period, it offers six suites, each with a bedroom with double bed, living room with double hide-a-bed and a refreshment center. The McCampbell Inn was built in 1809 as a home, with additions in 1816 and 1857 by subsequent owners. Over the years the building has housed a jewelry store, doctor's office, the town's telegraph and post office, and a hotel. In 1982 the inn was completely restored and furnished according to the period. There are two suites and 14 rooms, each with a refreshment center. Refreshment centers include refrigerator, kitchen area, hotpot, mugs, glasses, coffee, juice and tea. There is a bakery adjacent. Besides exploring historic Lexington, visitors can drive out to Goshen Pass or Cyrus McCormick's farm, view the majestic mountains from the Blue Ridge Parkway and visit Natural Bridge. There's skiing at nearby Wintergreen and Snowshoe and summer stock at a playhouse on Main Street.

Rates: *$40-$55 single occupancy, $7 each additional person. Historic Country Inns, 11 N Main ST (in the McCampbell Inn), Lexington, VA,* **703/463-2044.**

ELIZA THOMPSON HOUSE
Savannah, GA

Located in the heart of the Historic District, this inn, originally completed in 1847, is a restored architectural landmark. Inside are gleaming heart pine floors, period furnishings and a parlor with a private bar where guests are invited to mix their own drinks—plus such modern amenities as direct-dial phones, color television, and private baths. Outside is a landscaped courtyard with splashing fountains and fragrant southern foliage. Complimentary Continental breakfast is a tradition at the inn with rich coffee and fresh baked butter croissants. Also served are corncakes made from Miss Eliza's recipe which was discovered during restoration. Legend has it that it's the same recipe the "ladies of property" made corncakes from to sell to Union soldiers during the winter of 1864 when the city was under General Sherman's blockade. A concierge is available to assist with dining suggestions, reservations, or tour and travel arrangements.

Rates: *$68-$88. Eliza Thompson House, 5 W Jones St, Savannah, GA 31401,* **912/236-3620.**

BALLASTONE INN
Savannah, GA

You'll enjoy being pampered at this 1835 inn from the moment you checkin at an antique English reception desk and receive a glass of port or sherry to enjoy in your room or in the parlor. Fresh fruit and flowers greet your arrival, shoes are polished overnight and velour robes await in the bathroom. Complimentary breakfast—served in your room or in a charming courtyard—includes fresh fruits and juice, Southern-style pastries and rich, dark coffee . . . accompanied by the morning paper. Afternoon tea and late afternoon cocktails are served each day for guests and their friends. In the courtyard, lemonade or mint julep in hand, you can relax under wisteria amid the pungent fragrance of magnolia, gardenia and jasmine. Treat yourself to Southern tea-time sweets or cocktail hors d'oeuvres. Each of 19 rooms displays its own unique Victorian character. Oriental, Egyptian, Greek Revival, English Heritage or Colonial American can be your choice for the night. Rooms feature poster and canopy beds, marble-topped tables and dressers, chavall mirrors, comfortable love seats and wing chairs.

Rates: *Single from $65; Double from $80; Double queen or single king from $100; Master rooms from $140. Ballastone Inn, 14 E Oglethorpe Ave, Savannah, GA 31401,* **912/236-1484.**

THE DELOFFRE HOUSE
Columbus, GA

Blending Victorian charm and Southern hospitality, this 1863 townhouse has been elegantly restored and modernized. Located on a brick-paved street, it is just a block from the historic Iron Works Trade and Convention Center and is within walking distance of the downtown business district and the Historic District's finer restaurants. Guest rooms have original fireplaces and are furnished with antiques. You'll find a complimentary bowl of fruit and a decanter of wine awaiting you, and enjoy a complimentary Continental breakfast in a handsomely-appointed candlelit dining room—with newspaper, antique china and homemade date-nut bread. All rooms have phone and television.

Rates: *Single $43-$45, double $50-$55. The DeLoffre House, 812 Broadway, Columbus, GA 31901,* **404/324-1144.**

BEVERLY HILLS INN
Atlanta, GA

This European-flavored city retreat, housed in a converted apartment house built in 1929 in the then-popular Hollywood-style architecture, offers city conveniences in a fine old residential neighborhood. Accommodations include five one-bedroom suites and 12 studio apartments, all with private baths and kitchenettes. Rooms are distinctively decorated with period furniture. The original natural wood floors have been retained, and the high-ceilinged rooms have balconies adorned with pretty baskets of flowers. The decor features Oriental print chintz, framed Art Deco posters and a collection of antiques. Room prices include Continental breakfast—fresh orange juice, coffee and croissants—served in the Garden Room or on the patio. For evening relaxation there's a cozy library with current periodicals, books, and an inviting baby grand. Located in the Buckhead neighborhood, this bed-and-breakfast inn is a 15-minute drive from downtown Atlanta and only five minutes from the 200-store Lenox Square/Phipps Plaza premier shopping area. Nearby are many historical houses and fine restaurants.

Rates: *Single $48-$53; Double $57-$62; Suites weekly $160-$260. Beverly Hills Inn, 65 Sheridan Dr NE, Atlanta, GA 30305,* **404/233-8520.**

COLONIAL INN
Brevard, NC

Located in the scenic mountains of western North Carolina—the "Land of Waterfalls"—this bed-and-breakfast inn recaptures the grace and charm of an old Southern home. In 1911, this white-columned mansion hosted a reunion of troops that served the Confederacy under Gen. Stonewall Jackson. Inside, you'll find original brass hardware, carved fireplaces and other furnishings that recall the turn of the century. Most of the 12 guest rooms are furnished with antiques. Guests receive a complete, country-style breakfast and complimentary afternoon tea or coffee. Enjoy the clear air and cool mountain breezes as you explore this scenic region or visit nearby Brevard Music Center.

Rates: *Single $24-$34; Double $28-$38, plus tax, $5 extra adults, $3 extra children. Colonial Inn, 410 E Main St, Brevard, NC 28712,* **704/884-2105.**

Shakertown, Harrodsburg, KY

Chalet Suzanne, Lake Wales, FL

Shakertown, Harrodsburg, KY

THE LORDS PROPRIETORS' INN

Edenton, NC

It's impractical to describe many of the antique furnishings in this bed-and-breakfast inn because they are liable to change at any given time. When they opened this restored mansion in 1982, the innkeepers invited antique dealers to provide the furnishings as a kind of living showroom. Thus, everything, from Chippendale chairs to quilts on the beds, is for sale. Edenton has been called "the prettiest town in the South." Nestled on a bay at the head of the Albemarle Sound, its beautiful 18th and 19th century homes look out over water that once bustled with commercial shipping but now see only pleasure boats. The inn itself, on more than an acre of land in the Historic District, consists of two restored and refurbished adjacent houses—one built in 1787 and remodeled in Victorian style 100 years later, the other built in 1901. It offers 12 spacious guest rooms, each with private bath and furnished with beds hand-made by local craftsmen in 18th and 19th century styles. There is a guest parlor, dining room and quiet porch with rockers. Included in the price of a room is a Continental breakfast with homemade breads, muffins and preserves and fruits of the season. During winter months, weekend packages include a gourmet dinner. A guided walking tour takes visitors to homes that were built in the 18th Century when the town was the seat of government for the Province of North Carolina. The inn also offers bicycles to guests.
Rates: *Single $41, double $50 incl. breakfast. The Lords Proprietors' Inn, 300 N Broad St, Edenton, NC 27932,* **919/482-3641.**

THE MAGNOLIA INN

Pinehurst, NC

Golfers and inn fanciers can combine both interests with a visit to the historic, 12-room inn, built in 1896 by the Tufts family, founders of Pinehurst. Golf? Pinehurst (See Golf & Tennis Places) is famous for it, with six courses built on ideal sandy soil on gently rolling terrain with a climate tempered by nearby mountains and Gulf Stream breezes. Here, in a golfing hub that may have hosted more championships than any other spot in the country, is the World Golf Hall of Fame, a fascinating storehouse of memorabilia for linkspersons. Guests of the inn are invited to play the famous courses of the Pinehurst Country Club. This modernized old southern inn, which always has been used as a guest house, offers air conditioned rooms with private baths, and includes breakfast in the price of lodging. The living room has a large fireplace and provides card tables for guests, and TV. Breakfast is served in a bright, cheerful dining room. An attractive, kidney-shaped swimming pool is available for summer use. Georgian-Colonial mansions dot the streets of this charming, year-around resort village. Within easy walking distance of the inn are numerous shops and restaurants. In addition to the Pinehurst links, there are 20 other golf courses in the area.
Rates: *$14.50 per day per person, including breakfast. The Magnolia Inn, Pinehurst, NC 28374,* **919/295-6900.**

THE SWORDGATE INN

Charleston, SC

Among the many charms of this historic 19th century guesthouse is the fact that it knows how to start off the day in grand style. It serves a "Charleston breakfast" under the morning sun at wrought-iron tables on the patio. It's an informal Southern treat, served buffet-style, with a spread that includes such delectables as baked ham, scrambled eggs, sausage, hash browns, omelettes, baked apples, homemade pastries and biscuits, fruit and juice—and, of course, grits; a mix of yellow and white grits simmered overnight and served with butter and a shaker of cinnamon. Five guest rooms feature four-posters and brass beds, lots of antiques and luxurious accessories, such as thick, thirsty towels. Guests receive complimentary fruit and sherry in their rooms. Located in the heart of Charleston's famed historic district, the inn is close to antique stores, boutiques and the city's celebrated open-air vegetable and flea market. Bicycles are available to guests free of charge.
Rates: *Single $50, double $68-80. The Swordgate Inn, 111 Tradd St, Charleston, SC 29401,* **803/723-8518.**

The Lords Proprietors' Inn, Edenton, NC

Chalet Suzanne, Lakewales, FL

Colonial Inn, Brevard, NC

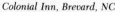

Chapter 2

REGAL RESORTS

Basin Harbor Club, Vergennes, VT

I f homes are castles, resorts are kingdoms! "All the comforts of home" is an understatement for these sanctuaries of self-indulgence—that is, unless your house has gold plated bath fixtures and a computerized dial-a-martini dispenser in the bedroom. Modern-day resorts luxuriously outdo themselves, cossetting guests with private Jacuzzis and swimming pools for every suite, bathrooms equipped with TV and telephone in reach of the tub, and balconies overlooking scenic backdrops of mountains, ocean, or desert.

These posh retreats are communities unto themselves and offer a melange of activities—supplying the demands of today's active vacationer. Guests can arrive via private airplanes, limousines, or even yachts, and choose from golfing on the rugged Pacific coast, to scuba diving off the tip of Florida. Choices in between include fishing, sailing, wind surfing, boating, skeet shooting, hiking, and gambling.

Plush resorts are for winter, too, with many offering superlative downhill and cross-country skiing, as well as more esoteric pursuits, such as snowshoeing and ice sculpting . . . or perhaps the romance of a moonlight sleigh ride. Many have suites equipped with wood-burning fireplaces and provide such comforts as handmade quilts and a bedtime snifter of cognac.

Whatever your preference, perfect days can begin either on the horse trails or foot paths that wind through the rugged, stirring beauty of the Acadia National Park wilderness, or in the shadow of the snow-capped White Mountains. And perfect days could perhaps end with a candlelit dinner for two beneath crystal chandeliers, a tension-easing massage, or hot toddies sipped in front of a crackling fire.

NORTHWEST

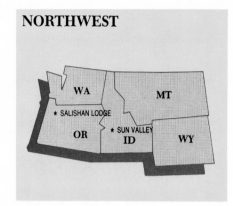

SOUTHWEST

and two of the original buildings remain. The former wine cellar is now the Plow and Angel Bar; what once was a fruit-packing house is now the dining room which features such specialties as sauteed veal tips and prawns in a mustard sauce. Top off the evening with a cordial or cocktail in front of the flagstone hearth in the Hacienda Lounge—guests prepare their own drinks and keep a running tab.

Rates: $99-$124 rooms; $179-$198 suites. San Ysidro Ranch, 900 San Ysidro Ln, Montecito, CA 93108, **805/969-5046.**

SALISHAN LODGE

Gleneden Beach, OR

Imagine watching seals drifting with the tide, seagulls diving for fish, and crabs scurrying along the beach. It's all available at Salishan Lodge, a rustic resort hugging the shore of Siletz Bay on the Oregon coast. Miles of white sand beaches and wooded hiking and jogging trails lure guests from their rooms. A resident naturalist conducts nature walks and birding trips. Modern two-story villas of native wood contain the rooms, 150 in all. Each room has a wood-burning fireplace, balcony overlooking the 18-hole golf course or the bay, and a covered walkway connecting it to the main lodge. The lodge houses an art gallery and several restaurants. Diners can choose from an elegant candlelit table for two or a fresh salmon barbecue on the patio.

Rates: $68+ per person, dbl occupancy. Salishan Lodge, Gleneden Beach, OR 97388, **503/764-3600.**

SUN VALLEY LODGE & INN

Sun Valley, ID

Since the mid-1930s when Averell Harriman, Chairman of the Board of Union Pacific Railroad, first sought the ideal ski center to attract people to his railroad, the Sun Valley area has grown to become a world-famous mecca for winter sports enthusiasts. Such luminaries as Ernest Hemingway and Gary Cooper graced the lodge in the 1940s. Today there are a total of 64 ski runs on Baldy and Dollar/Elkhorn, the longest around three miles of continuous challenges. Novices, however, should not be intimidated by the quality of the runs. A ski school provides expert instruction for children and adults. The area also has many summer attractions including four golf courses, three hydrotherapy pools, two Olympic-sized pools, and nearly 50 tennis courts. Nearby stables offer hay rides, fox hunts, dressage clinics, and sleigh rides. The lodge and surrounding buildings are chalets with steeply sloping roofs. The rooms are panelled with rustic siding and have mock fireplaces. A unique dining experience is offered at the Trail Creek Cabin where a horse-drawn sleigh transports guests to this secluded restaurant for a feast of hearty American fare.

Rates: $68+ 1 or 2 persons. Sun Valley Co, Sun Valley, ID 83353, **208/622-4111.**

SAN YSIDRO RANCH

Montecito, CA

In the foothills of the Santa Ynez Mountains are the storybook cottages of the San Ysidro Ranch. Each cottage has a rich history all its own—one served as a retreat for Winston Churchill, another as a honeymoon suite for Senator John F. Kennedy and his young bride Jackie, and a third as working office for Somerset Maugham. Once owned by the actor Ronald Coleman and used as a hideaway for personal friends, the resort has been refurbished and the cottages now blend modern amenities with old-fashioned comfort. The cozy cottages are furnished with antiques, overstuffed love seats, oriental rugs, and brass beds. Some have private Jacuzzis set into redwood decks that are bathed in the heady perfume of lilies, eucalyptus, and other native plants from the nearby garden. Hikers and horseback riders can explore the 550 acres on well-marked trails. Meanwhile, back at the ranch, swimmers can enjoy poolside barbeques and cocktails. Tennis players are forewarned that concentration may be hindered by the view—the three courts overlook the Pacific Ocean on one side and the mountains on the other. In the 1880s the ranch was the site of a Franciscan mission

HARRAH'S RENO

Reno, NV

Originally opened as a bingo parlor in 1937, Harrah's has evolved into a quality resort and world famous casino. The 24-story, 565-room highrise in downtown Reno, while best known for its gaming tables and dazzling cabaret, also offers a variety of activities to its guests. The rooms feature contemporary decor with plush furnishings and black-out curtains for total privacy day or night. When the sun is shining (which it does for the better part of the year) a swim in the outdoor pool is refreshing. Jane Fonda proteges can "do the burn" in the exercise room and then slip into the sauna or whirlpool for a welcome respite. Outdoor enthusiasts will revel at the sight of the Sierra Nevadas with their miles of hiking trails and challenging ski runs in winter. Day trips to a nearby ghost town or to the Ponderosa Ranch, immortalized by the Cartwrights on the TV show "Bonanza," can be arranged. Harrah's has its own collection of antique autos—more than 1000 of the gleaming gems. Patrons can get their fill of surf and turf at The Steak House or the Seafare.

Rates: $63-$90 dbl; suites from $165. Harrah's Reno, PO Box 10, Reno, NV 89504, **800/648-3773** *(CA, OR, UT, ID, AZ),* **702/329-4422** *(NV, HI, AK),* **800/648-5070** *(all others).*

Durango, Colorado

C Lazy U Ranch, Granby, CO

Photo: © Rod Walker

CAESARS PALACE

Las Vegas, NV

With its marble statues of Roman goddesses, cascading fountains, and palatial courtyards, Caesars Palace is more than a casino. No expense has been spared to treat guests to the ultimate in luxury and self-indulgence. The rooms and suites, 1600 in all, are large and plush. The new Villa Suites are tastefully done in art deco style. Each suite has its own computerized Jacuzzi, gold plated bath fixtures, marble floors, and personal captain to wait on guests hand and foot. After a long day of blackjack or playing the slot machines, guests can take out their aggressions on the tennis courts or relax in one of two pools. The Olympic-sized pool in the lush Garden of the Gods is made of 8000 pieces of hand-cut Carrara marble, probably best known in the statues of Michelangelo. The second pool caters to ardent sunbathers—three "lounging islands" are continuously washed by layers of cool, refreshing water. Guests can take in a movie at the Omnimax Theatre with its "sensaround" audio system or buy souvenirs at a variety of shops and boutiques. At night, Caesars Palace comes alive with big-name entertainers, boxing matches, and tennis tournaments at The Circus Maximus Showroom. Thirsty patrons can sink into silken cushions to enjoy an aperitif at Cleopatra's Barge—an entertainment lounge that floats on its own gently swaying "Nile." There are six restaurants to choose from, including the elegant Palace Court, housed in a mini-museum setting, which serves French haute cuisine, offering 100 specialties as well as a score of souffles. Diners are surrounded by lush tropical plants, fine art and antique furnishings in the atmosphere of a private palazzo. A stained glass dome overhead retracts to unveil the star-studded Nevada sky.
Rates: $95-$105 dbl; suites from $170. Caesars Palace, 3570 Las Vegas Blvd, S, Las Vegas, NV 89109, **702/731-7324.**

The Wigwam, Litchfield Park, AZ

HARRAH'S LAKE TAHOE

Stateline, NV

Although the word "casino" conjures up visions of smoke-filled rooms, tumbling dice, and the shuffling of card decks, Harrah's is also a luxurious resort—one of only three in the entire US to win both the five-star rating from Mobil Travel Guide and the five-diamond rating from AAA. The modern 18-story resort rising above the pines was built to blend with its surroundings. Luxurious rooms, decorated in the colors of the four seasons, each contain two bathrooms, complete with personalized his/her toiletries, phones, and TVs, a computerized drink dispenser, and a blackout curtain insuring total darkness when desired. Private balconies offer breathtaking views of the snow-capped Sierra Nevadas and shimmering Lake Tahoe. Suites on the 16th floor are attended by personal foot servants who not only handle reservations and plan private parties, but also do last minute tailoring. The Casino keeps its guests stacking the chips at more than 183 gaming tables, or pumping coins into the 2300 slot machines. After a day of playing the odds, guests can count on a refreshing dip in the dome-covered pool, a good soak in the Jacuzzi, or a total body massage in the health club. The Summit restaurant on the top floor combines romantic candlelit dinners with panoramic views of the city lights

twinkling below. After dinner diversion is provided by top-name entertainers at the Stateline Cabaret.
Rates: $95-$135 dbl; suites from $400. Harrah's Lake Tahoe, Stateline, NV 89449, **800/648-3773** *(CA, OR, UT, ID, AZ),* **702/329-4422** *(NV, HI, AK),* **800/648-5070** *(all others).*

ARIZONA BILTMORE

Phoenix, AZ

A quarter of a century of quality service, food, accommodations, and five-star ratings from Mobil Travel Guide, have elevated this elegant resort to a category all by itself. Built by a protege of Frank Lloyd Wright, the architecture itself is worth noting. Many of the rooms and suites have patios overlooking the famous Olympic-sized blue tile pool or the luxurious garden. The 39-acre garden is a feast for the senses—palm trees and flowering cacti are interspersed with fruit-bearing citrus trees. The Orangerie is noted for its seafood and fresh game selections. A climate-controlled glass wine room has a fine selection of domestic and imported labels. Those wishing to burn off a few calories have their choice of 17 lighted outdoor tennis courts, jogging trails, or two more pools. Overworked muscles can be soothed by a massage at the Health Club and/or trip to the steam room and sauna.
Rates: $155 dbl (lower June-Aug). Arizona Biltmore, 24th St & Missouri, Phoenix, AZ 85016, **602/955-6600.**

SHERATON TUCSON EL CONQUISTADOR

Tucson, AZ

At first glance you may believe you are seeing a mirage, but a closer look will reveal that you have arrived at southern Arizona's newest and most hospitable desert oasis. The picturesque Santa Catalina Mountains provide a breath-taking backdrop for this 440-room resort amid towering palms, sparkling fountains and cascading waterfalls. A 27-hole championship golf course, 16 lighted tennis courts, riding stables and, of course, swimming are just a few of the many amenities. Catering to hearty appetites generated by vigorous fun in the sun are diverse menus—ranging from continental cuisine to such gourmet delicacies as pheasant and quail. If you prefer meals indigenous to your environment, you may wish to dine at the Last Territory or the Sundance Cafe and savor the flavor of a rack of ribs or Mesquite-broiled steaks. The White Dove Restaurant provides more opulent surroundings. Numerous boutiques and craft shops populate the area making browsing one of the most popular activities. If you prefer something more adventurous—not to mention exotic—you may choose to accompany the resident naturalist in search of the elusive flourescent scorpion.
Rates: $115-$130 dbl; $145 suites. Sheraton Tucson El Conquistador, 10000 N Oracle Rd, Tucson, AZ 85704, **602/742-7000.**

MARRIOTT'S CAMELBACK INN

Scottsdale, AZ

This resort, situated at the base of Mummy Mountain and nearby Camelback, is blessed with more than 300 days of sunshine each year. The 413 rooms, renovated in 1983 at a cost of $3 million, are located in "casas"—contemporary adobe-like buildings patterned after the dwellings of the pueblos. Each suite has its own kitchen, fireplace, and pool. The grounds, 125 acres in all, bloom with flowering desert flora, while guests can soak up the sun on two PGA-approved golf courses, in two swimming pools with adjacent whirlpools, on 10 tennis courts, or on miles of hiking trails. For those wishing to cover more terrain, horseback rides, and bicycles are available for a fee.

Rates: From $160 sngl or dbl. Marriott's Camelback Inn Resort & Golf Club, PO Box 70, Scottsdale, AZ 85252, **602/948-1700.**

THE WIGWAM

Litchfield Park (Phoenix), AZ

The blazing sun and arid climate don't keep guests from enjoying themselves at this resort. Popular attractions include horseback trips into the desert where steaks (accompanied by panfried potatoes, sourdough bread, and apple pie) are grilled over hot coals, and golfing on three championship courses (two designed by Robert Trent Jones). The Wigwam, built in 1919 to house business executives visiting the nearby Goodyear cotton plantations, became so popular that it was opened to the public 20 years later. The rooms, 440 in all, are situated in 1- or 2-story stucco casas, modeled after the original building which has been preserved as part of the lobby. There are eight tennis courts (six lighted) and a complete health spa in the Goodyear Golf and Country Club. Equestrians will have a hard time choosing from the stable's diversity of activities—breakfast rides, hay rides, and stagecoach rides are offered in addition to trail rides. A 14,000-acre ranch nearby has miles of meandering desert bridle trails.

Rates: $100 per person; incl meals (golf, horseback, and tennis pkgs). The Wigwam, Litchfield Park, AZ 85340, **800/421-0000** *or, from CA (except LA):* **800/252-0211, 602/935-3811.**

C LAZY U RANCH

Granby, CO

If you've always wanted to have your own horse and ride the range in Big Sky country, your dreams can come true at this rustic ranch resort which overlooks the Continental Divide at 8300 feet above sea level. Guests are matched according to ability with one of the 145 horses on the range. The horse then is theirs for a week of trail riding, breakfast rides, and instruction in the ring. Children get to show off their abilities in a "shodeo"—a horse show on Saturday. The lodge, an A-frame constructed of pine logs and siding, houses six rooms. The other 32 rooms are located in cottages with wood-burning fireplaces. The C Lazy U Ranch is not for the horsey set only, it has an outdoor pool, two tennis courts, and a skeet range. Don't

forget your waders—the ranch supplies everything else for anglers who want to catch "the big one" in a nearby trout stream. After a vigorous game of racquetball in a glass court, those knotted muscles can be soothed in one of two saunas or the whirlpool. Family-style dinners in the lodge, or outdoor cookouts, allow guests to recap the day over hearty fare. In winter, the ranch becomes a ski lodge luring guests to miles of machine-groomed trails, while other diversions include tubing, snowshoeing, ice skating, and sleigh rides.

Rates: $85 - $115dbl, incl meals. C Lazy U Ranch, PO Box 378B, Granby, CO 80446, **303/887-3344.**

THE BROADMOOR

Colorado Springs, CO

With its pink, Mediterranean-style buildings, red-tile roofs, and location along the shore of a large lake, the Broadmoor is often called the "Riviera of the Rockies." The luxurious original hotel was opened in 1918, the 144-room Broadmoor South in 1961, and the 150-room Broadmoor West in 1976. The hotel maintains a European flavor in its restaurants—from steak and kidney pie in the Golden Bee, to haute cuisine in the lavishly decorated Penrose Room. Three 18-hole golf courses, the newest designed by Arnold Palmer, are nestled at the foot of Cheyenne Mountain. The Broadmoor World Arena building, often open to the public for skating, has hosted a number of world figure skating championships, ice hockey games, and other sporting events in recent years. Three heated swimming pools, including one on the Lake Terrace, provide year-round swimming, while snow machines and a double chair lift ensure quality skiing. There are 16 tennis courts, two of which are covered by a heated, illuminated bubble for winter play. Pikes Peak is nearby (see Man-Made and Natural Wonders).

Rates: $120-$160 sngl or dbl; suites from $200. The Broadmoor, PO Box 1439, Colorado Springs, CO 80901, **303/634-7711.**

TAMARRON RESORT

Durango, CO

As the coal-fired 1882 replica Silverton train winds its way across the narrow-gauge tracks from Silverton to Durango, passengers catch a glimpse of the rustic Tamarron Resort. Situated 7500 feet above sea level in the protected valley of the San Juan Mountains, this resort offers guests a smorgasbord of hands-on experiences. Fish for trout in clear-running streams, shoot the rapids in a raft or kayak, or horseback ride to a naturally-formed cave. Milder adventures include bus or jeep tours along old stagecoach trails to abandoned mining towns. A 45-minute helicopter ride provides an eagle's perspective of breeze-ruffled and jewel-like hidden lakes. The resort also offers golf, swimming, tennis, and platform tennis. Skiiers find plenty of challenges on the slopes of Purgatory or on well-groomed nordic trails. Guests stay in rustic rooms and suites in the inn. The rooms are decorated in warm earth tones and some have lofts overlooking the kitchenette and fireplace. After a day of activities in the crisp mountain air, appetites can be satisfied at Le Canyon, an elegant restaurant where diners are serenaded by harp music, or at the informal San Juan Club, popular with the apres ski crowd who gather near the roaring fireplace.

Rates: Suites from $54 (summer golf, tennis, & honeymoon pkgs). Tamarron Resort, PO Box 3131, Durango, CO 81301, **800/525-5420.**

KEYSTONE LODGE

Keystone, CO

As the colorful hot air balloon floats lazily above the aspens, guests are treated to a breathtaking view of the Colorado Rockies. But sky rides are but one of a host of activities that keep guests busy year-round at this resort situated on 512 acres in the Snake River Valley. Guests stay in rooms at the lodge or in condominiums. The rooms

The Wigwam, Litchfield Park, AZ

are large and comfortable with a lounging area and bedroom loft. The rustic condos, built from rough-hewn pine logs, have one to three bedrooms, full kitchens, and flagstone fireplaces. Mornings in Colorado are crisp and clear, perfect for tennis on one of the 14 courts at the John Gardiner Tennis Club. Earlybird golfers can get in a round of golf on the 18-hole course expertly sculptured out of the valley by Robert Trent Jones. The nearby Arapaho National Forest awaits backpackers, rock climbers, and horseback riders—all outfitted by the lodge. For anglers, there is good fishing—for brook, brown, and rainbow trout—in the clear-running streams. A late afternoon swim, sauna, or Jacuzzi will invigorate tired muscles. Food is served in three different settings—The Brasserie, a coffee house, offers freshly brewed coffees and pastries; the Garden Room serves continental cuisine in a tropical environment; and the Bighorn Steakhouse serves thick slabs of barbecued ribs and juicy sirloin steaks. The skiing season is nine months long here and guests often ski in short-sleeved shirts during June. A $15 million expansion has added a six-person gondola that whisks skiers to the pristine summit of North Peak. It's the resort's third ski mountain with 200 acres of challenging runs, new chair lifts, and ski village.

Rates: $66-$123 dbl; $75—$173 1 bedroom condo (tennis, golf, holiday pkgs). Keystone Resort, Box 38, Keystone, CO 80435, **303/468-4242.**

RANCHO ENCANTADO

Santa Fe, NM

Santa Fe, steeped in Indian lore and Spanish traditions and the home of a thriving artist's colony and superb opera company, also is the home of Rancho Encantado—the enchanted ranch. Guests' accommodations, ranging from terra-cotta colored casas to condominiums, feature a southwestern-style motif—Navajo rugs in geometric designs, wood-burning adobe fireplaces, red-tile floors, and beamed ceilings. Some have cozy sitting rooms with love seats and antique tables; others have sun porches overlooking desert gardens. The sunny, dry climate is perfect for hiking, tennis (two courts available), swimming, or soaking in the hot tub. A natural-wood portal provides shade from the intense sunshine. The ranch has a stable and offers breakfast rides and steak broils in the desert. The restaurant in the Main Lodge serves a diversity of cuisines, including American, Continental, and Mexican.

Rates: Cottages from $115; suites from $155. Rancho Encantado, Rte 4, Box 57C, Santa Fe, NM 87501, **505/982-3537.**

The Woodstock Inn & Resort, Woodstock, VT

MIDWEST

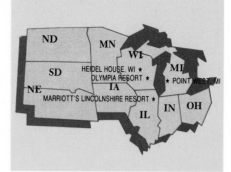

MARRIOTT'S LINCOLNSHIRE RESORT

Lincolnshire, IL

Situated in a beautifully wooded community 35 miles northwest of the urban noise and sprawl of downtown Chicago, this is one of the most complete resorts in northern Illinois. Within its self-contained world of recreation and rejuvenation is an 18-hole championship golf course, a private lake with sail- and paddleboats available in summer, an indoor climate-controlled tennis/racquetball complex, a fully-equipped health club, and the award-winning Marriott's Lincolnshire Theatre. The Lincolnshire is also aware of the special needs of business travelers, providing extensive meeting space, an audio-visual staff to handle business equipment, and on-site secretarial services. And when your day of golf or conferences is over, you can look forward to a relaxing session in the resort's sauna or spa, followed by a fine meal at the King's Wharf or Fairfield Inn restaurants. Or if you don't feel like leaving your room, you can order your dinner from room service and enjoy fine movies or premiere sporting events on the in-room cable television system. All this comfort and enjoyment, only 10 minutes from Woodfield (the world's largest shopping mall), 15 minutes from Six Flags Great America (see Theme & Amusement Parks), and 25 minutes from Chicago's O'Hare Airport (regularly scheduled hotel van service from airport available).

Marriott's Lincolnshire Resort, Lincolnshire, IL 60015, **312/634-0100.**

POINT WEST INN

Macatawa, MI

If a lakeside resort is what you're looking for, this one satisfies your requirements twice! Located on a scenic peninsula between Lake Michigan and Lake Macatawa, Point West Inn is a year-round resort combining the relaxed elegance of a country inn with the expertise and service of a big-city hotel. With all that water around, swimming, sailing and fishing are obvious choices for recreation, but Point West also features such nonaquatic activities as tennis, golf, and tours of area wineries. And Point West visitors are granted membership privileges to the nearby Holland Tennis Club, enabling them to use sauna, whirlpool, and exercise facilities there. Other highlights in neighboring Holland include a 200-year-old windmill and the annual Tulip Time Festival (see Fun At Festivals). Point West is also a favorite for business meetings and conferences, offering a number of spacious rooms and free use of audio-visual equipment for these events. For a special treat, start your day watching the sunrise over Lake Macatawa, and end it with a spectacular sunset on Lake Michigan.

Point West Inn, Macatawa, MI 49434, **616/335-5894.**

HEIDEL HOUSE RESORT

Green Lake, WI

This resort is on the shores of Wisconsin's Green Lake . . . and sometimes on the lake itself! No, it isn't sinking; the part of the resort that floats is Heidel House's large party boat, punningly named "Yachts of Fun." From late April through October, the boat glides over the lake, carrying resort guests on special dinner, party, or excursion cruises. But fear not if you're a confirmed landlubber—there's plenty to do here on dry land. Heidel House recently became the proud owner of Tuscumbia, the oldest golf course in Wisconsin, and has begun improving these historic links. And what would a Wisconsin vacation be without fishing? Green Lake is Wisconsin's deepest inland lake, and is known for its excellent muskie and lake trout fishing, and for bountiful catches of white bass (which the hotel dining room will prepare for your table). For vacationing couples, the resort's Pump House is a charming cottage featuring antique furnishings, an elegant brass bed, and the perfect ingredient for a memorable honeymoon or romantic getaway: seclusion. Dining choices range from snacking at the German-style Rathskeller to full meals at the main dining room. Of special note is the Fondue Chalet, featuring the cheese-dipping Swiss specialty and authentic Swiss decor, including a 200-year-old alpine horn. Unlike many other northern resorts, Heidel House keeps humming during winter months: Green Lake becomes an ice fishing paradise, and cross-country ski trails are laid out at Tuscumbia Golf Course.

Heidel House Resort, Illinois Ave, Box 9, Green Lake, WI 54941, **414/294-3344.**

OLYMPIA RESORT/SPA

Oconomowoc, WI

(See Health Spas.)

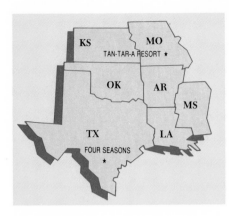

FOUR SEASONS

San Antonio, TX

With its red-tile roof, sun-drenched climate, tranquil court-yards, and splashing fountains, the Four Seasons Hotel captures the spirit of 19th century Spain. Each of the 250 rooms has its own private balcony overlooking the outdoor pool and terraced gardens. In the European manner, a full-time concierge helps arrange business meetings and guest travel and ensures that each room has fresh-cut flowers, turndown service at night with a chocolate mint on each pillow, and a complimentary morning newspaper at the doorstep. The hotel is within walking distance of the historic district, noted for its victorian mansions and as the site of the ill-fated Alamo, where Texas fought valiantly for its independence in the 1800s (See Historic Landmarks). Nearby is Riverfront, an area dotted with shops and out-door cafes along the meandering San Antonio River. The hotel offers tennis (two lighted courts), plus an exercise room and sauna. Restaurants include the casually elegant Anaqua, featuring brass chandeliers and sparkling crystal, and The Restoration Pub, a German home with fireplaces and pedimented porches built in the 1850s and renovated as a tavern serving imported beers and wines, and offer-ing a variety of games. Light lunches or snacks are served in a garden setting at the Palm Terrace or the Arbor. Three historic homes on the premises have been modernized and now host business meetings, banquets, and recep-tions. (See Ethnic & Historic Villages.)
Rates: $85-$110 sngl; $105-$130 dbl; suites $220-$440. Four Seasons Hotel, 555 S Alamo at Durango St, San Antonio, TX 78205, **512/229-1000.**

MARRIOTT'S TAN-TAR-A RESORT

Osage Beach, MO

In the language of the Blackfoot Indians, Tan-Tar-A meant "one who moves swiftly." That saying aptly applies to this resort, which has grown from 12 lakefront cottages in 1960, to its present size of more than 800 rooms, suites and villas spread over 420 acres on the shores of the Lake of the Ozarks. Along this shimmering lake you can partake in active water sports such as water-skiing and sailing, or you can just relax while sunbathing and fishing. For vaca-tioning linksmen, Tan-Tar-A offers a total of 27 holes of championship-quality golf, plus a full-time staff of PGA professionals to help golfers sharpen their skills. And for tennis buffs, there are six outdoor courts, and an indoor

sports center with all-weather tennis and racquetball courts. Other recreational activities include bowling, bil-liards, miniature golf, canoeing, and Broadway-style shows at the Mainstage Theatre. Tan-Tar-A is also known as "The Honeymoon Capital of the Midwest," and offers special cruises and free champagne to newlyweds. All of this, plus more than 15 convenient shops and 20 tempting restaurants and lounges on a wooded lakeshore make this a perennially popular resort.
Rates: $75-$108; suites from $120 (golf and honeymoon pkgs). Marriott's Tan-Tar-A Resort, State Rd KK, Osage Beach, MO 65065, **314/348-3131, 800/228-9290.**

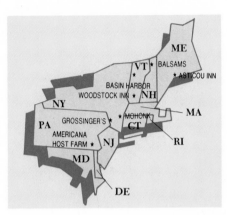

MOHONK MOUNTAIN HOUSE

New Paltz, NY

In distance, less than 100 miles north of New York City, in time, Mohonk Mountain House may well be a century removed. It's a perfect retreat from the onslaught of noise, the crush of people, and the hurried pace of the city. This imposing 300-room mansion *commands* peace and quiet—cars must be left at the end of two-mile drive from the gatehouse, motor boats are banned on the lake, and TVs are conspicuously absent in the rooms. In keeping with the 19th century atmosphere, the rooms are decorated in period furnishings; many have wood-burning fireplaces. Originally built by Quakers, the resort still frowns on the consumption of alcoholic beverages. However, private consumption in the rooms is permissible. The steep, rugged terrain of the 2000-acre estate is best traversed by hiking, mountain climbing, horseback riding, or by horse-drawn carriages. More than 100 outdoor gazebos provide convenient places to rest and observe the spectacular countryside. The clean mountain air can also be taken in on the 18-hole golf course, on six tennis courts, or on the lake—swimming, boating, and fishing are popular. In the winter, the sports change to ice skating on the frozen lake, cross-country skiing or snowshoeing on well-marked trails, and sleigh rides through the woods.
Rates: $85+ for room w/private bath. Mohonk Mt House, Mohonk Lake, New Paltz, NY 12561, **914/255-1000.**

Mohonk Mountain House, New Paltz, NY

GROSSINGER'S HOTEL & COUNTRY CLUB

Grossinger, NY

Until the 1950s, this venerable resort catered exclusively to Jewish clientele but now is multi-sectarian. The 600-room Tudor-style hotel is situated on more than 800 acres of rolling hills in the Catskill Mountains. Guests can commune with nature on the miles of jogging trails, in a boat on the mile-wide lake, or on a 27-hole championship golf course. Recreational facilities include Olympic-sized indoor and outdoor pools, 12 outdoor and four indoor tennis courts, and sauna. After a good snowfall, skiers can enjoy cross-country trails or downhill runs. The hotel maintains two kitchens to comply with the strict dietary customs of kosher Jews. Classic American fare is also served. Convention facilities accommodate more than 450 conferences each year.

Rates: $70-$90 dbl; suites from $270. Grossinger's Hotel & Country Club, Grossinger, NY 12734, **914/292-5000, 212/563-3704, 800/431-6300 (resrv).**

AMERICANA HOST FARM RESORT

Lancaster, PA

The former Host Corral, in the heart of the Pennsylvania Dutch country of Lancaster County, has built a championship reputation by catering to business executives. In addition to a regulation 18-hole golf course, a challenging 9-hole executive course allows the early-bird golfer to test every club in the bag and still attend a morning meeting. Each of the 510 rooms includes a hospitality bar, refrigerator, coffee maker, and color TV. The resort has superb conference accommodations as well as a diversity of recreational activities—everything from badminton and billiards to paddleboating, indoor and outdoor swimming, softball, and volleyball. The more adventuresome can rent a bike, tour cart, or horse-drawn cart or take a riding lesson—all for a modest fee. After a game of tennis (outdoor free, indoor $16/hour during prime time), one can relax and unwind with a sauna, whirlpool bath, or massage. Winter activities include skiing and outdoor ice skating.

Rates: $100 per person, dbl occupancy; incl 2 meals. Americana Host Farm Resort, 2300 Lincoln Hwy E (Rte 30), Lancaster, PA 17602, **717/299-5500.**

THE BALSAMS

Dixville Notch, NH

This grand resort hotel in northern New Hampshire virtually pioneered the American Plan (all meals included) concept in hotels and resorts. Over the years, the plan has been expanded so that a single rate covers virtually everything the resort has to offer, including an 18-hole Donald Ross-designed golf course, a challenging 9-hole executive course, tennis, water sports (including trout fishing), hiking in the 15,000-acre private estate, skiing (downhill and cross-country) and ice skating. Hot toddies in front of the crackling fireplace and live entertainment warm the cold winter evenings. Nestled between a man-made lake and the snow-capped peaks of the White Mountains, the Balsams could be mistaken for a castle in the Swiss Alps.

Rates: $78-$100 per person, dbl occupancy; incl 3 meals. The Balsams, Dixville Notch, NH 03576, **603/255-3400.**

Boca Raton Hotel & Club, Boca Raton, FL

ASTICOU INN

Northeast Harbor, ME

Nestled amid the rugged wilderness of Acadia National Park, the Asticou Inn has been a part of Maine's vacation heritage for more than 100 years. Overlooking Northeast Harbor on Mt. Desert Island, the inn is just a short sail away from Somes Sound, the only natural fjord in North America. The four-story rambling inn has many cozy rooms; guest houses with kitchen facilities are also available. The Northeast Harbor Golf Club welcomes Asticou guests and there are three other nearby courses. Grounds around the inn are beautifully landscaped and invite strolling—especially through the lovely formal gardens. Miles of mountain trails and carriage roads await the more adventuresome. Open late-Apr—late-Oct.
Rates: $112-$140 dbl, 2 meals incl. Asticou Inn, Northeast Harbor, ME 04662, **207/276-3344.**

BASIN HARBOR CLUB

Vergennes, VT

Along with crisp mountain air and dense woods, this resort offers guests a chance to photograph Champy, the Loch Ness Monster of Lake Champlain who reportedly has been seen, but never captured. The Basin Harbor Club, which celebrated its centennial in 1983, accommodates guests in several renovated houses. Secluded lakeview cottages with wildflower gardens are ideal for honeymooners or families. For those willing to test the water, the Club offers everything from sailing to water skiing. An Olympic-sized heated pool, five tennis courts, and a well-groomed golf course grace the property. A 3200-foot airstrip, popular with private airplane pilots, is situated nearby. Convention facilities are available for a unique business retreat.
Rates: $65-$100 sngl (tennis, golf and honeymoon pkgs). Basin Harbor, Vergennes, VT 05491, **802/475-2311.**

THE WOODSTOCK INN & RESORT

Woodstock, VT

Covered bridges, steeple bells cast by Paul Revere, and a quaint landmark village lure guests to this resort in historic Vermont. The Woodstock Inn, a three-story colonial style resort, opened in 1969 but the site has been occupied by village inns since 1793, when Richardson's Tavern first opened. The rooms, 120 in all, are decorated in an early American style with handmade Vermont furniture and colorful quilts. Contemporary attractions include the Woodstock Country Club with its 18-hole Robert Trent Jones golf course, 10 tennis courts and a 25' × 50' swimming pool. Nearby are hiking and horseback riding in the rolling hills, and fishing in the Ottauquechee River. Antique shopping is a popular diversion, as is photographing, or simply admiring the region's fabled, multi-hued fall foliage. The area also is well known to skiers as the home of the Suicide Six ski area. Facilities include a 30-acre snow-making machine, two double chair lifts, and 18 trails. Cross-country skiers are not neglected—47 miles of marked trails provide scenic views of the Green Mountains. Other winter activities include snowshoeing and moonlight sleigh rides.
Rates: From $76 sngl; $78 dbl. The Woodstock Inn & Resort, 14 The Green, Woodstock, VT 05091, **802/457-1100.**

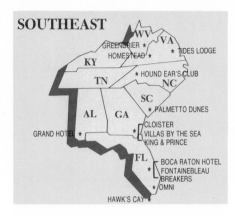

SOUTHEAST

HAWK'S CAY

Marathon, FL

You don't need a ferry boat to get to this island. It's accessible by auto along the scenic Overseas Highway (see Man-made & Natural Wonders). Hawk's Cay, formerly the Indies Inn, is a 60-acre West-Indies-style resort in the Florida Keys. It underwent extensive renovation in 1983 and now boasts a landscaped tennis garden, two oceanside Jacuzzis, a new dockside restaurant, and 20 new suites, all with private balconies. Once frequented by Harry Truman, Dwight Eisenhower, and Lyndon Johnson, this resort has maintained quality service and accommodations. Fishing is the name of the game here—three charter boats transport avid anglers to some of the best game fishing in the world. Just four miles from Hawk's Cay is the largest barrier reef in America, teeming with snapper, grouper, yellowtail, and mackerel. Deeper waters are home for dolphin, marlin, and tuna. The day's catch usually ends up as the fish of the day, broiled over mesquite in the Ship's Galley restaurant. A unique Starter's Program for adults offers basic instruction in scuba diving, sailing, fishing, and tennis. Students can then do their "homework" on a sailboat, in or under the water, or on five clay tennis courts shielded from the sun by tropical shade trees. Golf is available at the nearby Sombrero Golf Course.
Rates: $130-$180 dbl, incl breakfast. Hawk's Cay, Mile Marker 61, Marathon, FL 33050, **305/743-7000.**

BOCA RATON HOTEL & CLUB

Boca Raton, FL

One of the world's most famous resorts, remodeled and added to many times since its debut in 1926, now offers four unique vacation environments. The Spanish-style Cloister, the original building, is noted for its quiet elegance, antique furnishings, and tropical gardens covering 1000 acres. The Tower is a modern high-rise on the Intracoastal Waterway with a panoramic view of the Gold Coast. The Golf Villas, smaller and more private, is the ultimate for golf fanatics—greens are just steps from suites. The Boca Beach Club, the newest of the four, is touted for its beach and water sports—everything from volleyball to sailing, windsurfing, water skiing, and serious sunbathing. The four share facilities and, when combined, can boast of 22 tennis courts, three 18-hole golf courses, fitness and aerobic classes, a spa, and seven restaurants. Supervised programs for children.
Rates: From $235, dbl occupancy. The Boca Raton Hotel & Club, PO Box 225, Boca Raton, FL 33432, **305/395-3000.**

OMNI INTERNATIONAL

Miami, FL

Just minutes from downtown Miami, Miami Beach, and the airport, the soaring glass and marble walls of this city-within-a-city offer an attractive, climate-controlled environment for vacationers and business executives alike. The mega-structure includes 556 luxurious rooms, six movie theatres, scores of restaurants, two department stores, 165 shops and boutiques, an indoor amusement park, and rooftop tennis courts, swimming pool, and 5000-square-foot playground. A 24-hour child-care center and nursery school is available. The rooms are large and comfortable. The suites have their own private terrace overlooking Biscayne Bay where luxury liners dock. Other popular attractions include The Terrace Cafe overlooking the roof-top gardens and Biscayne Bay, the Scaramouche disco, and the Fish Market which specializes in broiled and steamed seafood.
Rates: $85-$130 per person, dbl occupancy; suites from $170. Omni Int'l Hotel, Biscayne Blvd at 16th St, Miami, FL 33132, **305/374-0000.**

Fountainebleau, Miami Beach, FL

The Greenbrier, White Sulphur Springs, WV

FONTAINEBLEAU HILTON

Miami Beach, FL

Like the phoenix, the mythical bird that rose from ashes, the Fontainebleau has risen from a state of neglect and disrepair, to re-establish itself as one of the most glamorous resorts in America. Since 1978, $30 million has been spent to renovate the hotel with a new tropical motif. The rooms have been redone in a Caribbean decor with over-stuffed chairs, plush carpeting, and ornamental fireplaces. The redesigned lobby provides a view of the ocean and a rock grotto. The grotto, with its own cascading waterfall, surrounds an enormous free-form swimming pool. Lush tropical trees around the perimeter provide shade. Other temptations include three outdoor whirlpools, two 18-hole golf courses, and a bi-level tennis complex with seven lighted courts. Water sports, pursued off the private 300-foot-wide beach, include windsurfing and sailing. Chartered fishing boats are available for anglers anxious to hook some of the famous Atlantic sport fish. Appetites can be satisfied at the Steak House which serves thick planks of meat and 22 imported beers.
Rates: From $115 dbl. Fontainebleau Hilton, 4441 Collins Ave, Miami Beach, FL 33140, **305/538-2000.**

THE BREAKERS

Palm Beach, FL

Architecture buffs, or those who like to treat themselves like royalty, will be attracted to the grand design of this Italian Renaissance-style resort. The lobby and ballrooms are adorned with Flemish tapestries, frescoes, marble, and gilt. The crystal chandeliers are not the only things that sparkle—social-register elite from Europe and America flock here to see and be seen. The rooms are large and luxurious and offer views of the ocean or the gardens. The Florentine Dining Room, offering seafood and prime beef entrees, specializes in nouvelle cuisine. The wine collection, awarded for its diversity and quality, contains over 400 vintages. For those who need a spot of fresh air, there is a private beach to explore. The more energetic will enjoy two 18-hole golf courses, 14 tennis courts, an indoor freshwater pool, or an outdoor saltwater pool. A supervised children's program tempts the little ones with trips to the zoo, amusement parks, and water shows.
Rates: $200 dbl in winter (lower off-season); golf & tennis pkgs. The Breakers, Palm Beach, FL 33480, **305/659-8440.**

THE CLOISTER

Sea Island, GA

Although Tara, the plantation home of Scarlett O'Hara in *Gone With the Wind*, was fictitious, this plantation-style resort revives the Tara spirit with its expanse of lawn, beautiful gardens, and 10,000 acres of swaying palms and moss-covered oaks. The Cloister is out to pamper its guests by offering them top-notch service and a variety of accommodation choices. Besides the main building, there are beachfront villas and cottages. Food is served on your own private patio, in the solarium, in the dining room, or even on the beach. The beach is five miles long and is considered one of the finest on the East Coast. Golfers are challenged by 36 holes divided into four distinct nines. Each nine is ornamented with ocean views and magnolias, and can be played in any combination or order. Tennis buffs can improve their game with play on the 18 clay courts or with lessons at a clinic taught by a staff of pros. Other outdoor activities include skeet shooting, miniature golf, wind surfing, sailing, biking, and swimming in two outdoor pools. The Cloister has its own riding stable and a canter along the beach at sunset is the perfect way to end the day.
Rates: $75+ per person dbl occupancy, incl 3 meals. The Cloister, Sea Island, GA 31561, **800/841-3223** *(resrv),* **800/342-6874** *(in GA),* **912/638-3611.**

VILLAS BY THE SEA

Jekyll Island, GA

Looking for a secluded one-, two-, or three-bedroom villa overlooking 1800 feet of beachfront on the Atlantic Ocean? This island resort off the coast of Georgia offers it all. Each villa has full kitchen facilities, but many guests prefer to dine in the resort's restaurant or at one of the 10 others found on the island. For swimmers, a year-round pool competes with the ocean surf. Attractions on Jekyll Island include three 18-hole golf courses, one 9-hole course, eight lighted outdoor tennis courts, and one indoor court. There are miles of nature trails for cyclists and hikers. Musicals are performed at an outdoor amphitheatre during summer. Nearby is Millionaires Village, once home of the world's richest—now a museum offering walking tours. (See Island Escapes.)
Rates: $60 sngl; $78 dbl; $98 3-bedroom. Villas By the Sea, 1175 N Beachview Dr, Jekyll Island, GA 31520, **912/635-2521.**

KING & PRINCE BEACH HOTEL

St. Simons Island, GA

History abounds on the island home of this Spanish colonial-style hotel and adjacent villas. The hotel is elegantly furnished with antiques, stained glass, and chandeliers. The villas, with kitchen facilities, have their own private view of the sunrise over the Atlantic. History buffs will enjoy trips to either nearby Fort Frederica, a British Fort built in 1736, to a lighthouse built in 1870, or to Christ Church, where Charles Wesley (the co-founder of the Methodist Church) preached in 1736. More vigorous activities can be pursued on five tennis courts, in an indoor pool, or aboard a rental sailboat. A major expansion including 55 suites, an indoor pool, shops, and convention facilities was slated for completion by late 1984.
Rates: $50-$90 dbl; $140-$170 villas. The King & Prince Hotel & Villas, PO Box 798, St Simons Island, GA 31522, **912/638-3631.**

THE GREENBRIER

White Sulphur Springs, WV

Wake up to sunrise over the Allegheny Mountains, don your jodphurs and riding boots and pick up your frisky mount at the riding circle for an early morning jaunt on this sprawling 6500-acre estate. The Greenbrier, built in 1778 and patronized by Robert E. Lee, is one of the most famous grand old resorts in America. The rooms, 700 in all with no two alike, are located in the main building or in guest houses. Horse-drawn carriages transport guests over the grounds and past the Spring House, a landmark for the "curative" waters of White Sulphur Springs. Outdoor enthusiasts will find a host of activities from golf (three 18-hole courses, one designed by Jack Nicklaus) to tennis, swimming, hiking, and fishing. For those who tend to overdo it, the spa offers massages, saunas, and mineral baths (see Health Spas). The Greenbrier has won many culinary awards and started its own cooking school in 1981. An artist's colony "on the hill" sells pottery and other hand-crafted items. A summer children's program offers a potpourri of supervised activities.
Rates: $100 per person, dbl occupancy. The Greenbrier, White Sulphur Springs, WV 24986, **800/624-6070.**

THE HOMESTEAD

Hot Springs, VA

If George Washington and Thomas Jefferson were still alive to stroll once again this 16,000-acre estate, they would certainly be satisfied with the traditional elegance maintained by this classic resort in the Allegheny Mountains. Afternoon tea in the Great Hall—an expanse of pillars, chandeliers, and log-burning fireplaces—is accompanied by a string orchestra. The 700 rooms are all comfortable and the "cottages" sport spiral staircases leading to bedrooms. A formal dress code is observed—men must wear jackets and ties after 7pm. Women usually come to dinner in designer gowns. Recreational facilities include three 18-hole golf courses, a trout stream, graded walks and paths for hiking or jogging, and four skeet and trap shooting fields. After a strenuous ride on a horse from the resort's own livery, a soak in the naturally-heated mineral water pool will feel like heaven. An indoor and outdoor pool and 19 tennis courts are also available. Winter sports enthusiasts can do figure eights on the Olympic-sized ice skating rink or perfect their stem turns on the downhill runs.
Rates: $205-$255 dbl. The Homestead, Hot Springs, VA 24445, **703/839-5500.**

THE TIDES LODGE

Irvington, VA

Start the day with breakfast on your private balcony overlooking the Rappahannock River in historic Tidewater, Virginia. The Tides Lodge, a small, intimate resort on a private 175-acre peninsula, prides itself on perfection and a courteous, personable staff. The rooms are situated in 2-story villas and have a homey, rustic decor. After breakfast, guests can take in a round of golf on a course designed by a Scotsman from St. Andrews. A refreshing dip in the freshwater or saltwater pool can be followed by building your own triple decker sandwich at the poolside sandwich bar. Afternoons can be active or leisurely spent snoozing in a swaying hammock. Tennis (a lighted court), sailing, and canoeing are popular. The Binnacle Restaurant serves romantic dinners near the blazing hearth. Regional delicacies, such as soft-shelled crabs and roasted oysters, are specialties. The perfect way to end the day is on a twilight yacht cruise around the peninsula.
Rates: From $52 per person; $71 for suites. The Tides Lodge, Irvington, VA 22480, **800/446-5600.**

The Cloister, Sea Island, GA

MARRIOTT'S GRAND HOTEL

Point Clear, AL

Watching the sunset over Mobile Bay while sipping a refreshing mint julep has become synonymous with this elegant grand resort. The rooms, 310 in all, have recently been renovated and historically preserved. Ceiling fans, plush sitting rooms, and gorgeous views of the bay, marina, or lagoon are now offered. The internationally known Lakewood Golf Club has a challenging 27-hole course and PGA instructors. The resort's 53-foot yacht, complete with crew, is available for deep-sea fishing, where the day's catch often becomes dinner for two, prepared to your specifications in the Birdcage Lounge. The grand scale of this southern resort includes a 750,000-gallon swimming pool, a 40-slip marina (providing anchorage for boats owned by guests), and Sunday afternoon polo matches. Trail riding offered by the hotel livery allows guests to slip away and experience solitude beneath the moss-draped oaks. Other diversions include 10 tennis courts and a sauna.
Rates: From $180, incl 2 meals. Marriott's Grand Hotel, Point Clear, AL 36564, **800/228-9290, 800/268-8181** *(from Canada).*

HOUND EARS CLUB

Blowing Rock, NC

Named for an unusual rock formation, this exclusive private club in the Blue Ridge Mountains also provides 25 rooms and suites for guests. Balconies offer panoramic views of the verdant mountains named for the blue haze that lingers over the treetops. Privately owned chalets and condominiums are available for longer stays. The 18-hole golf course—a challenge for any flatlander—traverses the undulating topography of the area. A swimming pool is built under the overhang of a natural rock grotto. Tennis clinics for refresher tips prepare players for matches on the four grass-textured tennis courts. Nearby state and national parks boast of well-groomed trails for hiking or horseback riding. The resort maintains two ski slopes and has a snow-making machine for when mother nature does not comply.
Rates: $90 per person, dbl occupancy, 2 meals incl. Hound Ear's Club, PO Box 188, Blowing Rock, NC 28605, **704/963-4321.**

PALMETTO DUNES

Hilton Head Island, SC

You don't have to go to Hollywood to see celebrities—it's a well-kept secret that many vacation on Hilton Head Island, attracted by warm ocean breezes, a lush, semi-tropical setting, and championship golf courses. Palmetto Dunes Resort, located on 1800 acres in the center of the island, accommodates guests in two hotels or in private villas. The Hyatt recently underwent a $1 million facelift on its 360 rooms and suites, as well as its nightclub, the Club Indigo. The Mariner, opened in 1983, offers rooms surrounding a central courtyard that contains an outdoor pool and lush groupings of tropical trees and flowers. Outdoor sports are almost a science here—two golf courses (one designed by Robert Trent Jones) are the site of many tournaments, including the Hilton Head Island Celebrity Golf Classic, a benefit for the Muscular Dystrophy Foundation. The Rod Laver Tennis Center with its 25 courts (six lighted) and staff of pros might seem intimidating to the novice. However, personal instruction, clinics, and exhibitions take the edge off. The more adventuresome can explore the eight-mile lagoon system in a canoe or paddleboat. You can also relax and leave the driving to the captain of the *Adventure*, a tour boat docked at Shelter Cove Harbour specializing in nature, dinner, or moonlight cruises. Fishermen will be pleased to know that the day's catch, often snapper, flounder, or bass, is broiled over mesquite and served for dinner at the Pisces Restaurant.
Rates: $80-$270 dbl. Palmetto Dunes Resort, Hilton Head Island, SC 29928, **803/785-1234, 800/228-9000.**

Chapter 3

MANMADE & NATURAL WONDERS

The crème de la crème of natural and man-made wonders highlighted in this chapter flicker like inviting flames to the curious moth. Almost 300 million times each year we pay homage to our national parks, drinking in their splendor, scene by scene, never tiring of their grandeur. The same is true of our great bridges, dams and other attractions.

These works of awe, created by man and nature alike, often inspire a kind of instant spirituality rarely found in the workaday world. We absorb from them mystical qualities that defy articulate description—the Grand Canyon is one; others, such as Watkins Glen State Park, help quench a perpetual thirst for the aesthetic marvels of our environment.

The works of man often are moving tributes to his determination as a builder. For example, the unheralded philosophy of the diminutive Golden Gate Bridge engineer Joseph Strauss, is as inspiring as is his creation. He devised elaborate safety precautions in constructing this gem; only one life was lost until a few months before completion, when 10 more perished. Yet, this monumental project, built at a cost of $27 million, shattered the once inflexible rule that one life must be paid for each $1 million in construction cost.

Wonders seem to beget wonders. Even the most isolated of those described here—and they span the continent—are close to other dramatic vistas or worthwhile events. You can sample Creole cooking and whoop it up with Cajuns at the Sugar Cane Festival along with a visit to Mississippi's bayou country . . . ski the slopes of Sun Valley after a morning at Craters of the Moon . . . or soak up the early life of an American legend with a visit to Abe Lincoln's Kentucky birthplace after spelunking Mammoth Caves.

NORTHWEST

GRAND COULEE DAM

WA
★ MOUNT ST. HELENS
MT

ID
OR
GRAND CANYON
OF YELLOWSTONE
★ BIGHORN ★ DEVIL'S
CANYON TOWER
CRATERS OF THE MOON ★
WY

MOUNT ST. HELENS & SPIRIT LAKE

Near Cougar, WA

This long-dormant volcano erupted on May 18, 1980, blasting 1500 feet off the top of the mountain, and sending millions of tons of ash, ice and rock high into the atmosphere. It created an eerie environment over a vast area. The view from the north, where most of the crater's rim was blown away, allows even ground-level spectators to see into the sometimes steamy crater. The view from Hopkin's Hill in the town of Morton is especially dramatic. Travel in the immediate area of the volcano is restricted, but there are numerous viewpoints along highways skirting the restricted area. The ash is sold commercially in several spots and the Mount St. Helens National Volcanic Mountain Visitor Information Center, located just north of the town of Toledo, has displays showing the geologic features of the mountain and explaining how it came to blow its top. Area hazards include blowing ash, wet ash on roads, heavy winter snows and, of course, the possibility of a repeat performance of the ultimate hazard of May, 1980. Evacuation routes are marked on major highways.

Mount St Helens Nat'l Volcanic Monument Visitor Center, Toledo, WA 98591, 206/864-6699.

GRAND COULEE DAM

Near Grand Coulee, WA

The mammoth dam, constructed during the height of the Great Depression, was the symbol of the future and hope for millions of people who had little else to believe in. Half a century later, it remains an incredible sight and a recreation area of unsurpassed beauty, especially for boaters. The Visitor Arrival Center offers splendid views of the facilities, free movies and printed information. A glass-enclosed incline elevator takes spectators to a 330-foot-high balcony where spectacular views of the spillway await, and upward another 135 feet to a point where you can walk into the world's largest hydroelectric generator station. Other area attractions include the 151-mile-long Lake Roosevelt (all within Coulee Dam Nat'l Recreation Area), Banks Lake and the Colville Indian Reservation. Campsites at Spring Canyon Campground.

Coulee Dam Nat'l Recreation Area, PO Box 37, Coulee Dam, WA 99116, 509/633-1360.

THE GRAND CANYON OF THE YELLOWSTONE

Yellowstone Nat'l Park, WY

Some 1500 feet below the rim, trumpeter swans, the largest waterfowl in Yellowstone, spread their snow-white wings—seven feet from tip to tip—searching for food along the rivers. They emit a distinctive "beep" as they glide gracefully in flight. But birds aren't the only attraction in this canyon, sliced from yellow rock by the Yellowstone River. Dramatic vistas heighten the wilderness; in one area, two waterfalls can be seen simultaneously. The Lower Falls sends the Yellowstone River tumbling more than 300 feet (almost twice the height of Niagara Falls) to the canyon floor. The Upper Falls arches gracefully along a verdant shoreline, set off by black glass canyons. Literally thousands of hot springs and mud pools dot the park, and there's a petrified forest as well. Old Faithful is there, steadily spouting tons of steam and water into the atmosphere about once every 70 minutes; nearby are Mammoth Hot Springs and Yellowstone Lake. Hayden Valley is one of the best places for observing wildlife. (See Nat'l Parks & Monuments.)

Yellowstone Nat'l Park, WY 82190, 307/344-7381.

The Grand Canyon of Yellowstone, Yellowstone Nat'l Park, WY

The House on the Rock, Spring Green, WI

Grand Coulee Dam, Near Grand Coulee, WA

Photo: U.S. Bureau of Reclamation

from coyotes to mule deer call the barren scape home. Apollo astronauts trained here to become accustomed to the pock-marked terrain they would find on the moon. The landscape is painted black by volcanic lava lying in huge fields—overlooked by cinder cones that sometimes soar as high as 800 feet. Several layers of lava cover the broad valley in central Idaho from the three outbursts of volcanic activity during the last geological age. The 83 square miles, preserved as a national monument since 1924, show traces of Indian inhabitation with mysterious crescent-shaped piles of rocks, stone artifacts and mounds made as trail markers. At the visitor center are geologic displays which also feature information on plants and wildlife; a seven-mile loop drive starts there. Permission to strike out on your own must be obtained at the visitor center. Caves, actually tubes through which lava flowed, are common at Craters of the Moon and throughout Idaho, but less than a day's drive away are the Crystal Ice Caves, unusual for the area because they are a fissure cave with stalactites and columns of ice instead of stone. They stay frozen, even in summer. Sawtooth Lake, near the Sawtooth Primitive Area, has excellent campsites, but you have to hike to them. Arco, near the craters, has a museum dedicated to the monument. In contrast to this stark terrain, the sybaritic comforts of Sun Valley are only 65 miles away.

Craters of the Moon Nat'l Monument, PO Box 29, Arco, ID 83213, **208/527-3257.**

Devils Tower Monument, Sundance, WY

DEVILS TOWER NAT'L MONUMENT

Near Sundance, WY

There's no mistaking the Devils Tower; once you've seen it you'll never forget it. Young Teddy Roosevelt was so smitten by it that he made the tower the country's first National Monument once he became President. The Devils Tower is forbidding—the kind of real estate no one readily would claim. But it is impressive, rising almost 1300 feet above the valley, making it the tallest rock formation of its kind in the US. Film buffs will recognize it as the site chosen by aliens to land their spacecraft in the movie, *Close Encounters of the Third Kind.* Tower Trail offers hikers close-up views of the changing face of the fluted formation as well as the opportunity to listen for the bugle of a bull elk or glimpse the ever-present yellow-bellied marmot. Darting prairie dogs are particularly abundant; they've built a "town" about half a mile from the monument's entrance. Deer, turkey,. cottontail rabbits and other small animals can be seen occasionally. The area is rich in Western lore—this used to be Sioux Indian country and General George A. Custer bivouacked here in 1874 looking for gold. And the town of Sundance is where Harry Longabaugh, alias the Sundance Kid, shot a deputy sheriff and then hot-footed it to Hole-In-The-Wall with Butch Cassidy.

Devils Tower Nat'l Monument, Devils Tower, WY 82714. Wyoming Travel Commission, **307/777-7777.**

BIGHORN CANYON NAT'L RECREATION AREA

Near Billings, MT

You need not be a descendant of General Custer to appreciate the importance in northern Wyoming of the name, Big Horn. The name stems from the sheep that have now all but vanished from the area, though free-roaming wild horses are seen often. Upstream from Yellowtail Dam, the Big Horn River slices through the Big Horn Mountains, exposing layers of rock spanning more than 500 million years. The national recreation area surrounding it offers opportunities for hunting, fishing, boating, water skiing, camping and hiking. A look-see at Bradford Brinton Memorial Ranch (open mid-May—Lab Day) is worth a side trip for Western art buffs; it's located near Big Horn, 12 mi S of Sheridan.

Bighorn Canyon Nat'l Recreation Area, Supt, PO Box 458, Ft Smith, MT 59035, **406/666-2412.**

CRATERS OF THE MOON

Arco, ID

There is life here, though at first glance you would never suspect it. Nevertheless, birds and animals ranging in size

SOUTHWEST

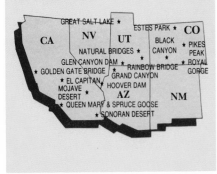

MOJAVE DESERT

San Bernardino County, CA

This county is larger than some states, and most of it is desert, but there are some unusual sights here; and, unexpectedly, snow-skiing on the fringes at Wrightwood and Big Bear. It's also the improbable site of a naval installation (yes, US Navy!) at China Lake. Dry desert lake beds, one of which is fittingly called El Mirage, are part of the varied package in this area. The Mojave is a 15,000-square-mile desert of barren valleys, spectacular rock-mountains, and glorious and grotesque vegetation such as the well-nigh useless, Joshua tree. But on the glorious side is the desert rose and several different forms of cacti. Favorite areas for sightseeing include the agricultural Antelope Valley and the Joshua Tree Nat'l Monument. The dappled desert mountains lent a hand in naming Calico Ghost Town near Barstow. Highlights include a tour of an abandoned silver mine and a museum displaying mining implements circa 1880. Near Victorville is a cliff that looks like the profile of an Indian and close by are ancient petroglyphs. Here, too, are some fine golf courses, as well as Roy Rogers' Apple Valley Inn, and the Stoddard Jess Turkey Ranch where you can see thousands of gobblers in and out of their hutments before and after—but not during—Thanksgiving. In Nevada, the Red Rock Canyon area is noted for spectacular views of the Spring Mountains, which form a backdrop for the cactus gardens that don't quite flourish on the canyon floor.

Office of Tourism, 1030 13th St, Ste 200, Sacramento, CA 95814, **916/322-1396.**

EL CAPITAN

Yosemite Nat'l Park, CA

Beginning in early April, rock climbers swarm to meet El Capitan's challenge and don't give up until the end of summer. It is one of the best known rock mountains in "the Incomparable Valley," as the 7-square-mile Yosemite Valley has been called. The mountain has a broad appeal, beckoning artists and photographers like a magnet ever since John Muir explored the territory a century ago. The mighty El Capitan is the product of alpine glaciers that rumbled through the canyon of the Merced River, scouring the weaker sections of granite and leaving behind the more solid hunks of rock, such as El Capitan and its equally well-known neighbor, the rock mountain called Half Dome. In the same area competing in superb grandeur for attention are Yosemite Falls and Bridalveil Falls. And 50 miles to the northeast a scenic highway crosses the crest of the Sierra at Tioga Pass, the highest automobile pass in California, and the view is magnificent. You can see the awesome contrast of peaks and meadows to the west, and high desert vistas to the east. (See Nat'l Parks & Monuments.)

Yosemite Nat'l Park, PO Box 577, Yosemite, CA 95389, **209/372-4461.**

THE QUEEN MARY & THE SPRUCE GOOSE

Long Beach, CA

Two seafaring vessels sit side by side in drydock in Long Beach harbor: The "Queen of the Seas," a title held for more than 30 years by Britain's *Queen Mary*, the largest passenger ocean liner afloat, and Howard Hughes' flying boat, commonly called the "Spruce Goose." The legendary ocean liner's staterooms form the nucleus of a hotel with all the luxury pertaining thereto. But if you can't spend the night, you can take a walking tour of the superannuated ship, browse shops, dine on gourmet dishes prepared in elegant restaurants, dance in an attractive art deco lounge, and enjoy great views of the harbor and the California coastline. Nearby, the world's largest free-standing aluminum dome houses the globe's largest airplane; two DC-10s would fit under each wing. It was the brainchild of industrialist Henry J. Kaiser for ferrying troops during World War II, but it was built by the eccentric Hughes. A stormy Congressional investigation into Hughes' war contracts focused on the issue of the mammoth plane's ability to fly. Hughes put the question to rest with a one-minute flight in 1947 and then hid it behind closed doors for three decades. The interior bespeaks TLC, looking as if it has just rolled off the assembly line. About 750 troops could be carried in the cargo hold. Interpretive talks by flight information officers flesh out the details. Nicely-presented audio-visual programs trace Hughes' career in aviation and as a movie magnate.

Wrather Port Properties, Ltd, PO Box 8, Long Beach, CA 90801, **213/435-3511.**

SONORAN DESERT

Southern AZ and CA

The statuesque Saguaro cactus, state symbol for Arizona, flexes its great arms throughout this vast desert. This region stretches from Phoenix, touching the Colorado River in California and nearly surrounding the Gulf of California (also called the Sea of Cortez) and Mexico's Baja Peninsula. Of America's four great deserts, the Sonoran Desert is the most diverse. It includes some of the continent's most arid land, as well as spectacular mountains (often thickly forested), extinct volcanoes, underground caves and an unusually varied spectrum of flora and fauna. The Roadrunner (beep, beep!) can divert your attention on remote roads, and nature's brilliant display of wildflowers blooming in early spring beside I-10 at Picacho Peak can take your breath away. Organ Pipe National Monument near the Ajo Mountains is a popular attraction; so is Old Tucson, originally built as a movie set (for which it is still used). A good introduction to the natural mysteries of this land can be found at the Arizona-Sonora Desert Museum (see Masterful Museums) near Tucson. It is a living museum with more than 300 plants and animals, the only combined botanical and zoological garden west of the Mississippi. Displays are in natural surroundings indoors, outdoors and underground over a 12-acre area.

Arizona-Sonora Desert Museum, Rte 9, Box 900, Tucson, AZ 85743, **602/883-1380.**

GOLDEN GATE BRIDGE

San Francisco, CA

Four more eyes would be of considerable help as you drink in the sights crossing the Golden Gate Bridge—there's that much to see: the sea below, the glorious sky above, the sparkling East Bay cities, and "the City," San Francisco. But the Mona Lisa of bridges is the main attraction in this gallery of visual arts, edging gracefully into its golden anniversary in 1987. More than a mile long, it is one of the longest of the world's single-span suspension bridges and the two great towers, rising 746 feet above the Pacific Ocean inlet, are the world's tallest. The bridge was built by Joseph Strauss, aided by the John A. Roebling's Sons Company, which was founded by the family who built the Brooklyn Bridge. The firm spanned the gap between the two towers by spinning 80,000 miles of wire between them. Inside the towers is a maze of strength-building square boxes so extensive that a 26-page manual was written to guide workmen traveling inside. When the bridge opened to traffic in 1937, celebrating San Franciscans staged a blow-out that made front-page news for a week; the party in '87 should be a humdinger. Golden Gate Park on the San Francisco side offers great viewing sites as well as scenic drives, golf, concerts all year long, and museums. Sausalito, the western terminus of the bridge, is for shoppers.

Office of Tourism, 1030 13th St, Ste 200, Sacramento, CA 95814, **916/322-1396.**

The Spruce Goose, Long Beach, CA

Photo: Mike Michaelson

Photo: © ASDM, Doris Ready

Photo: © ASDM

Photo: © ASDM

Photo: © ASDM

Photo: © ASDM, Al Morgan

Photo: © ASDM, Willis Peterson

Sonoran Desert, Southern AZ and CA

HOOVER DAM

AZ, NV Border

Here, quite literally, is the wellspring of abundance. As you travel the Southwest, through a land of bountiful crops and bustling industry, you can get an idea (by stopping at Hoover Dam) as to how the metamorphosis of vast arid western desert lands occurred. The magnificent structure tamed the raging Colorado River and now provides enormous electrical energy, resulting in managed waterflow, agricultural productivity and jobs for great portions of several states. The dam is sometimes called Boulder Dam, because the original Congressional legislation called it that. But in 1947 that body officially bestowed the name Hoover because Herbert Hoover had much to do with its construction—as an engineer in private life, as Secretary of Commerce, and as President. It could very well be called Mammoth Dam—it is 660 feet thick at the base, 45 feet thick at the top, 1,244 feet long at the crest, 726 feet high and weighs more than 6½ million tons. Like so many huge structures, it was the final resting spot for 110 of its makers. Behind the dam, the waters of the Colorado form Lake Mead, an almost illimitable source of outdoor recreation and unparalleled scenic beauty. One entire building is dedicated to exhibits, including a model of the river basin and a recorded lecture; elevators carry you down to the powerplant for a 35-minute guided tour. Las Vegas-style gambling is only four miles west of the dam at the Gold Strike Inn.

Office of Tourism, 3507 N Central Ave, Phoenix, AZ 85012, **602/255-3618.**

GLEN CANYON DAM

Near Page, AZ

An awesome view of wild water harnessed in concrete, houseboats and other watercraft plying a placid lake, and a rugged desert-mountain landscape embracing cacti, wildflowers and multi-hued sandstone formations greet visitors to the Glen Canyon Dam complex. Completed in 1966 at a cost of more than $272 million, the dam was created to control seasonal variations and flooding of the Colorado River, and to provide hydroelectric power to cities in large areas of the West. Behind the dam is Lake Powell which, when full, has a shadowed, fjord-like shoreline of nearly 2000 miles and is the prime attraction of the enormous Glen Canyon National Recreation Area. Guided tours of the 583-foot-high concrete dam are offered June 1—Sept 30 from the Carl Hayden Visitor Center; self-guided tours at other times. Exhibits include a digital counter that registers the dollars this powerplant is returning to the US Treasury by the sale of electricity. Boaters on Lake Powell can make a 50-mile-long trip to Rainbow Bridge National Monument (see Rainbow Bridge), site of the largest natural bridge on earth (290 feet high, 270 feet across).

Glen Canyon Nat'l Recreation Area, PO Box 1507, Page, AZ 86040, **602/645-2471.**

GRAND CANYON NAT'L PARK

Northern AZ

The Grand Canyon is one of those marvels for which the word "awesome" was created. Other words fail to describe the great pleasure of simply looking at the labyrinthine vista . . . but we'll try. Gouged into the earth by the Colorado River, the canyon is 277 miles long—you can travel its entire length by raft from Lee's Ferry. It's more than a mile deep at the North Rim, and in places it's 10 miles or more across as the crow flies. Earth's time zones, recording geological history dating back two billion years, are displayed on the canyon walls, between which live a small band of Havasupai Indians. The South Rim is the big attraction because it's open all year long (North Rim roads are open only mid-May—Oct). Campgrounds and cabins are located within the canyon. You can walk down steep trails to the river, pack in by mule, or enjoy the view from a hired helicopter or airplane. The hikes are for the hardy; the mules are safe and sure-footed, but require stamina from the passengers. The canyon is home to a unique squirrel with tassel-like ears, and other wildlife, but tiny burros, who grew too numerous and too troublesome, are no more. Best bets for a satisfying visit are one-day guided tours and overnight trips to Phantom Ranch in the bottom of the canyon (602/638-2401).

Supt, Grand Canyon Nat'l Park, PO Box 129, Grand Canyon, AZ 86023, **602/638-7888.**

GREAT SALT LAKE

Salt Lake City, UT

You can bob like an apple in a barrel in the buoyant waters of this lake, but be forewarned that swimming sometimes is uncomfortable and the land surrounding it often is inhospitable. Great Salt Lake is the largest brine lake in North America—72 miles long and 30 miles across, but with a maximum depth of only 27 feet. It is but a tiny reminder of the huge prehistoric Lake Bonneville that once held 500 times as much water. Today, the lake is far from one of America's prettiest natural wonders, but awesome nevertheless (and beauty, after all, is in the eye of the beholder). West of the lake is Bonneville Salt Flats, famed site of land speed trials and world records. The east side of Great Salt Lake provides homes for some of the largest waterfowl sanctuaries in the US. The area includes Farmington Bay and Antelope Islands (where herds of bison, not antelope, roam), and northward are Bear River and Locomotive Springs (on the north shore). Great Salt Lake Park includes part of Antelope Island. Stansbury Island, an 11-mile peninsula along the southern shoreline, has a large population of rabbits and mule deer. The golden spike driven to symbolize the link between east and west by rail is memorialized at a national historic site west of Brigham City.

Utah Div of Parks & Recreation, 1636 W North Temple, Salt Lake City, UT 84116, **801/533-6011.**

NATURAL BRIDGES NAT'L MONUMENT

Near Blanding, UT

There's less here than meets the eye; that is, there's no water flowing under these bridges. Nevertheless, there they are, three sandstone bridges making up the grandest collection of such features found anywhere on earth. The display is situated along an 8-mile paved road about 42 miles west of Blanding. A visitor center at the entrance houses geologic exhibits, offers historical information covering the 225-million-year-old formations, and presents slide shows about the area. The three natural bridges, Kachina, Sipapu, and Owachomo, are formed from Cedar Mesa sandstone, which is the principal subject of the geologic exhibits. Also of interest is one of the largest solar power installations in the US which, at peak power, provides 100 kilowatts of electricity for the visitor center and other facilities. The site is reached via UT 95 about 42 miles west of Blanding. Note that this area of southeastern Utah is the site of other spectacular scenery such as Capitol Reef, Canyonlands and Arches National Parks (See Nat'l Parks & Monuments). Zion and Bryce Canyons are in southwestern Utah (see Nat'l Parks & Monuments).

Canyonlands Nat'l Park, 446 S Main St, Moab, UT 84532, **801/259-7164.**

Great Salt Lake, Salt Lake City, UT

RAINBOW BRIDGE

Near Bridge Canyon Landing on Lake Powell, UT

The National Park Service prizes Rainbow Bridge, the largest natural bridge on earth, as one of the seven natural wonders of the world. It is isolated against a backdrop of steep cliffs high above Lake Powell. The Navajos call the colorful arch "Nonnoshoshi" or "the rainbow turned to stone." It is possible to reach this national monument on foot or by horseback from the Navajo Trading Post or from the now abandoned Rainbow Lodge. Most visitors, however, travel by boat on Lake Powell 50 miles from Wahweap marina to the landing in Bridge Canyon and then walk about a half mile up the canyon to the bridge. There are virtually no improvements within the monument area; nearest services are in Page, AZ. Rainbow Bridge is 290 feet high and 270 feet across.

Glen Canyon Nat'l Recreation Area, PO Box 1507, Page, AZ 86040, **602/645-2471.**

PIKES PEAK COUNTRY

Near Colorado Springs, CO

When Zebulon Pike discovered the mountain named in his honor in 1806, he remarked that the sides were so steep he doubted that anyone would ever climb to the top. Today, there's an annual marathon (for purists, it's only 13 miles, but consider that it's run over some of the steepest terrain imaginable), a famous annual auto race and daily visits by adventurous and curious sightseers. You can reach the 15-acre summit via a well-constructed highway, the world's highest railway, and even on horseback. The 14,110-foot summit, although not the highest in the Rockies, is noted for its spectacular views of the surrounding area, and the snowy fantasy of Christmas even in July. The adjacent area is rich in tourist attractions. Among them: Garden of the Gods, Colorado Car Museum, Mt. Manitou Incline (with the world's longest cable railway), US Air Force Academy, Cripple Creek, and more. Reservations suggested for the Pikes Peak Cog Railway to the summit; take it up, enjoy a scenic bus trip down.

Convention & Visitors Bureau, 801 S Tejon, Colorado Springs, CO 80909, **303/635-1723.**

The Grand Canyon National Park, Northern AZ

BLACK CANYON OF THE GUNNISON NAT'L MONUMENT

Near Montrose, CO

Verticality rules every aspect of life in this area because the Black Canyon of the Gunnison is among the deepest abysses in the world. Gaping—up, usually—is compelled by the rugged scenery. The 12 miles within the national monument combine depth, narrowness, and sheerness in a somber and dizzying display. Nearly half a mile deep in some places, the canyon's width at one point is 1100 feet at the top and as little as 40 feet at the river below. To the uninitiated, there is nothing quite like it. Scenic drives are aided by a dozen lookout points along the 8-mile rim, but the river can be reached only by steep, treacherous trails. The park is noted for camping, hiking, technical rock climbing (experts only), fishing, and cross-country skiing in the winter. Numerous tourist facilities nearby.

Black Canyon of the Gunnison Nat'l Monument, PO Box 1648, Montrose, CO 81401, 303/249-9661.

ROYAL GORGE

Canon City, CO

High and remote, this is one of the most dramatic canyons in the US. Located a few miles south of Pikes Peak, Royal Gorge affords a spectacular view in the state's heartland along the main east-west thoroughfare linking Pueblo and Gunnison. The area is virtually awash in superlatives: To traverse the canyon, highway builders constructed the world's highest suspension bridge—more than 1000 feet above the canyon floor—to span the gorge; next came the world's steepest incline railway, which carries passengers to the level of the Arkansas River, which gouged out the massive gorge. Newest major attraction is the Aerial Tram, a cable car system that glides across the canyon 1200 feet above the river. The tram allows leisurely sightseeing along both sides of the rim. Unlike some other popular spots in the area, the roads (US 50 via US 25) leading to Royal Gorge allow it to remain open year-round.

Chamber of Commerce, 816 Royal Gorge Blvd, PO Box 366, Canon City, CO 81212, 303/275-2331.

ESTES PARK

Near Boulder, CO

Really "high" living is the hallmark of Estes Park; it is high in the Rockies and is perhaps the most spectacular part of this extraordinary national park. Rocky Mountain National Park embraces one of the most easily accessible high mountain areas in North America with elevations to well over 14,000 feet. Situated along the eastern border of the 405-square-mile park, the resort town of Estes Park claims only a few thousand permanent residents—but literally millions of visitors each year. It's a cafeteria of outdoor culture, offering cross-country and downhill skiing, professional and amateur bike racing, beautiful tall aspens sighing in the breeze and an aerial tramway. For those who prefer to pursue indoor activities, the art galleries, await. The massive, elegant Stanley Hotel, dwarfed by the granite mountains surrounding it, has long been an Estes Park landmark. It was built by F.O. Stanley, creator of the once popular Stanley Steamer automobile. Advance reservations recommended.

Chamber of Commerce, PO Box 3050, Estes Park, CO 80517, 303/586-4431.

MIDWEST

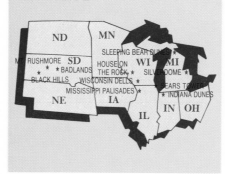

MOUNT RUSHMORE NAT'L MEMORIAL

Near Keystone, SD

Gutzon Borglum's famed shrine to four of democracy's finest leaders was actually the work of 360 individuals. They used dynamite, jackhammers and hand tools to carve the granite faces of George Washington, Thomas Jefferson, Abraham Lincoln and Theodore Roosevelt into a 16,000-foot mountain in the Black Hills. The sculpture is best viewed under morning light. From Mem Day—Lab Day an evening sculpture lighting program is presented in the amphitheater, which includes a talk by a ranger, a film, and the playing of the National Anthem. From May 25—Sept 3, special programs about the history and development of the monument are presented in the Sculptor's Studio, which can only be reached following a strenuous walk on rock stairways.

Supt, Mount Rushmore Nat'l Memorial, Keystone, SD 57751, 605/574-2523.

BLACK HILLS

Southwestern SD

Best known for Mt. Rushmore National Monument (see) and wild, rolling countryside, the Black Hills still hold some surprisingly well-kept secrets. One is Jewel Cave, 13 miles west of Custer, which contains more than 70 miles of passageways, making it the second longest cave in the US. Custer State Park, 5 miles east of Custer, and Wind Cave National Park (see Nat'l Parks & Monuments), 10 miles north of Hot Springs, together are home for the largest concentration of American bison in the world. Another gem in the area is the Black Hills Petrified Forest, where ancient petrified cypress trees still stand. Other spelunking delights include Bethlehem Cave and Black Hills Caverns. For youngsters and inquisitive adults there is Rapid City's Dinosaur Park, a playground of life-size replicas of prehistoric reptiles. Among the great many attractions around Mt. Rushmore is the Parade of Presidents Museum which houses life-sized wax figures of our past Chief Executives.

Black Hills, Badlands & Lakes, PO Box 910, 2436 S Junction Ave, Sturgis, SD 57785, 605/347-3646.

THE BADLANDS

Around Badlands Nat'l Park, SD

The parched area now known as the Badlands once was home to a wondrous array of prehistoric animals, including 40-foot marine reptiles, which flourished in the soggy environment. But that was 40 million years ago and times have changed. Today, erosion from limited water and sands driven by wind has created a topography of colorful canyons, peaks, ridges, cliffs and spires. But the denizens of the past have made this area one of the richest sources of prehistoric fossils in the US. Much of the most interesting scenery is within the National Park (see Nat'l Parks & Monuments), but there are attractions of note outside the park. They include the Badlands Petrified Gardens at Kadoka, featuring prehistoric and local history exhibits, and the Mammoth Site in Hot Springs, where you can see fossils of giant creatures that once roamed the area. The single-industry town of Wall—the industry being the famous Wall Drug Store—is just off Interstate 90 about 7 miles north of the National Park. Free ice water is the biggest attraction for the 10,000 thirsty tourists who stream through the doors during the season; a nickel cup of coffee ranks high, too. Among Wall Drug's numerous free attractions are an animated mechanical orchestra, an exhibit of Arikara Indian artifacts and a Western art gallery.

Black Hills, Badlands and Lakes, PO Box 910, 2436 S Junction Ave, Sturgis, SD 57785, 605/347-3646.

Sears Tower, Chicago, IL

WISCONSIN DELLS

Near Madison, WI

P.T. Barnum would have loved this place—he may even have visited it, because it has been a tourist attraction since an enterprising boater began excursions in the 1850s. Life under the Big Top, however, isn't the big draw here that; rather, it's a 25-mile stretch of the Wisconsin River eroded into fascinating formations. Modern cruise ships carry visitors through the Upper Dells and the Lower Dells mid-Apr—Oct (608/254-8336). The cruise through the Upper Dells is longer and more varied. The Wisconsin Dells—the word being a corruption of an Indian term meaning "narrow passage on the river"—has a sister community called Lake Delton and it is on their main streets where you will find most of the commercialization. The pizzazz include hot-air-balloon rallies and the Parsons Post Indian Pow Wow. Tommy Bartlett's Water Show (608/254-8336) is worth a look, as well as the Enchanted Forest and Prehistoric Land, Stand Rock Indian Ceremonial, Wilson Deer Park, Royal Wax Museum and several amusement parks. Other good bets extend for a 25-mile radius of the Dells; they include the excellent Circus World Museum (see Masterful Museums) in Baraboo and the Mid-Continent Railway Museum at North Freedom.

Visitor & Convention Bureau, PO Box 390, Wisconsin Dells, WI 53965, **800/362-8414, 800/356-6611** *(outside WI).*

The House on the Rock, Spring Green, WI

THE HOUSE ON THE ROCK

Spring Green, WI

One look at this place and you can readily understand the spellbinding magnetism that drew architect Alex Jordan to exploit the natural beauty of Deershelter Rock, a 60-foot tower of stone which he first saw it in 1944. Jordan, a veritable Renaissance Man—art collector and sculptor—built a natural structure into the patterns and contours of rock, originally for his private use. But he yielded to public pressure and opened it to the public in 1961. Since then, the architectural marvel has become the state's most popular privately-owned tourist attraction. The first-time visitor is startled at the sight of a house where trees grow through the roof, a bookcase stretches three stories high, and a two-story waterfall forms an entire wall. Each of the 15 rooms is unique, though alike in beauty and elegance. The "Streets of Yesterday" section features a nostalgic exhibit of charming shops and homes from the 1880s; it is a prelude to the "Music of Yesterday," housing huge music boxes that render tunes ranging from classics to contemporary. Numerous art works and antiques, many of them priceless, provide accents throughout the structure. They range from suits of armor to a collection of Bauer and Coble leaded glass lamps and shades, to ancient Chinese root carvings. The Organ Building, so named for the world's largest theatre organ console, from which 29 of the 52 grand pianos situated throughout the house are wired, is relatively new. You enter the building through a "devil's head" staring from behind moveable eyes and surmounted by horns. About an hour's drive west of Madison.

House on the Rock, Spring Green, WI 53588, **608/935-3639.**

INDIANA DUNES NAT'L LAKESHORE

Near Porter, IN

Visions of some Arabic oasis come to mind when you first encounter the Indiana Dunes, but the gigantic heap of shifting sands is no mirage. A calf-stretching climb to the 135-foot summit of Mt. Baldy is rewarded by a restful view of Lake Michigan. A frolicking slide down the slopes eases the memory of the ascent. This is an ideal spot for bird watchers; more than 200 species come here, some for stopovers in the north-south migrations, others because it offers a hospitable ecosystem. This ice-age remainder is home to numerous forms of life along the southern shore of the lake. Unusual vegetation dapples the dunes with diversity, from flowering dogwood to cacti and other varieties not usually found in this part of the country. Almost constant winds continuously change the topography of the 13,000-acre preserve, especially areas closest to shore; back-dunes are more stable, having been settled by soil and the plants growing in it. At the visitor center on Kemil Rd and US 12, slide shows and exhibits describe how the area developed; park rangers are available to conduct tours. Hiking trails are numerous; most famous is the Old Sauk Trail, once used by Indians. The dunes are flavored by festivals throughout the year: the Duneland Folk Festival (July), Autumn Harvest Festival (Sept), Traditional Christmas, and Maple Syrup Time (Mar). For anglers, some of the finest coho fishing in Lake Michigan is a short distance away at Michigan City, where charter boats are available.

Indiana Dunes Nat'l Lakeshore, 1100 N Mineral Springs Rd, Porter, IN 46304, **219/926-7561.**

SLEEPING BEAR DUNES

Eastern MI

This 34-mile-long cluster of sand dunes, thought to resemble a snoozing bruin by Indians who named it, isn't hibernating; it's actually moving inland more than two feet a year. In some places the dunes rise almost 500 feet above scenic Lake Michigan, ranking them among the highest in the world. They are alive with forests, inland lakes and small-to-large animals, including deer. Sheer bluffs are topped by a plateau stretching inland as much as 2½ miles, creating a huge sandpile where adults and children alike frolic in unrestrained glee. Dune buggies based in Glen Haven will take you for a heart-stopping tour or you can drive over a 6-mile road that slices through the sand and forest. Water sports, including fishing in the fall for tenacious coho salmon, may be found throughout the National Lakeshore area, but few accommodations exist within the Dunes because authorities want to keep the area unspoiled. As you might expect, it's crowded in summer. March is a good time to visit, when you can catch the maple syrup festival; the spring cherry blossom festival also is a treat. The entire area is awash in color during the fall season; see it from a tour based at Glen Arbor.

Sleeping Bear Dunes Nat'l Lakeshore, 400 Main St, Frankfort, MI 49635, **616/352-9611, 616/334-4017.**

SILVERDOME

Pontiac, MI

See Astrodome (Houston, TX).

SEARS TOWER

Chicago, IL

In a city that sprouts skyscrapers—indeed, Chicago was the birthplace of the modern cloud-huggers—it's no surprise to find the Sears Tower, the world's tallest inhabited building (1454 feet)—an uninhabited structure a thousand feet higher is located in Canada. Built in the Soaring Seventies, the Tower is headquarters for Sears Roebuck, and the building is somewhat of an architectural wonder—aside from its height, it is constructed of prefabricated welded steel frames that form a core for the 110 stories and it is called a "bundled tube" by architects. At the 1353-foot level is a fully enclosed Skydeck observatory offering a sweeping view of the Windy City seven days a week, 9am—midnight. Admission: $1.50; under 12 $1. Nearby are several attractions of note: the city's financial center on La Salle Street; the Loop, so-called because of the elevated train tracks that circle an eight-block-square area; and the major commodity and stock exchanges. Other features include: the State Street pedestrian mall; scenic Michigan Avenue, which parallels the Lake Michigan shoreline; and the city's most enduring symbol, the Water Tower—built in 1869 and one of the few buildings to survive the Great Fire. Several blocks north of the Sears Tower is Rush Street, center of Chicago's night life.

Sears Tower, 233 S Wacker Dr, Chicago, IL 60606, **312/875-9696.**

MISSISSIPPI PALISADES STATE PARK

Near Savanna, IL

The Indians had an eye for the land, and a word for everything. Here, the word was "Manitoumi," the Land of God, but modern Americans re-named it for the high rock cliffs that border the upper Mississippi in this region, forming the park's boundary. From the top are magnificent views of the Mississippi River Valley, while at the bottom the palisades themselves provide scenery that is relatively rare in the Midwest. On the banks of one of the tributaries is Galena, the "Town That Time Forgot." A charming relic of the past, it reached its zenith when lead mining was king in the 1850s. The Victorian architecture of the period is preserved throughout the town and in it are antiques, arts and crafts shops, and a museum devoted to Civil War artifacts. Home-town hero U.S. Grant's mansion is here. There are horseback trails at Chestnut Mountain Lodge, and the Lock and Dam 13 provide an interesting look at water traffic. Scenic drives line both the Illinois and Iowa shorelines. The 2500-acre state park includes 350 campsites and 11 miles of well-marked trails for hikers. Excellent boating facilities.

Chamber of Commerce, PO Box 315, Savanna, IL 61074, **815/273-2722.**

The House on the Rock, Spring Green, WI

Photo: Allen Ruid

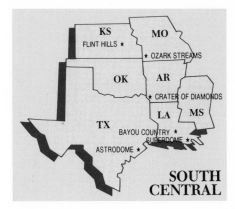

SOUTH CENTRAL

Crater of Diamonds, Near Murfreesboro, AR

FLINT HILLS

From Manhattan to Eureka, KS

This can be an exciting place to explore at round-up time in the fall. You can find herds of cows and cowboys driving them along the 40-mile-wide Kansas plateau undulating from the Nebraska border to the Oklahoma line. The flinty outcroppings for which the region is named are overlain by a sea of rippling grass. Historically, the hostile earth denied tillers of the soil, but at the turn of the century someone discovered that the protein-rich grass would fatten cattle in a hurry—by as much as 100 pounds in 30 days—and an industry was born. The tall grasses (left to themselves they'll reach eight feet) bar trees from growing on the escarpment, but small wildlife such as rabbits, skunks, beaver, gray foxes and weasels are everywhere; birdlife also is plentiful. Marine fossils can be found embedded in the 200-million-year-old limestone cliffs. Spectacular views in any season. From Eureka you can make a 150-mile drive over county and state roads, looping the heart of the hills. The countryside is basically flat, heightening the spectacle of four chalk spires towering 70 feet above the plains at Castle Rock. Water sports, picnicking and other recreation facilities at Cedar Bluff State Park.

Kansas State Park & Resources Authority, 503 Kansas Ave, Box 977, Topeka, KS 66601, **913/296-2281.**

ASTRODOME

Houston, TX

You don't have to be a professional athlete, or even a fan, to enjoy the domed spectacles of sport. They may foretell the future, as H.G. Wells predicted a hundred years ago, producing the technology to cover entire cities. But technology marches on and the Astrodome's linear descendant, the Superdome of New Orleans, may be the last of the old breed of rigid structure domes, because air-supported buildings are cheaper to build. The Superdome cost $121.6-million, while the Silverdome in Pontiac, MI, the largest air-supported, fabric dome stadium in the world, cost a mere $41.8-million. Nevertheless, the Superdome is a stupendous structure, rising 205 feet from the playing surface and seating more than 80,000 fans. But the grandaddy of these stadiums, the Houston Astrodome, still is larger in some respects and especially as a tourist attraction. The dome is 218 feet high (surpassing the Silverdome), spanning 642 feet. Its pioneering scoreboard, still one of the world's largest, is four stories high

and 474 feet across. When no afternoon events are scheduled, guided tours are conducted daily at 11am, 1 and 3pm. In summer months, when no night events are scheduled, an additional tour is given at 5pm. A multimedia presentation chock-full of Texas-size statistics is featured during all tours.

Astrodome, PO Box 288, Houston, TX 77001, **613/799-9500.**

CRATER OF DIAMONDS

Near Murfreesboro, AR

Some days a diamond, some days a stone . . . and sometimes you find both in one, a fabulous gem in the 40-acre diamond field open to the public since its discovery in 1906. More than 60,000 diamonds, some as much as 40 carats, have been found at the "crater," an eroded volcanic pipe. In 1983 diamond diggers, who paid the Arkansas State Parks system $3 for the privilege of looking, found 1500 of the precious stones; minor miners (under age 6) are admitted free. You can rent mining equipment and even have your find appraised free at the site. Genuine diamonds aren't the only lure; semi-precious gems and minerals such as amethyst, agate, jasper, quartz and others are yours for the taking. The "upside down" eruption that carried hot gases from the earth's core to the surface, brought with it the age-old diamond treasures. Orientation programs at the Visitor Center cover subjects ranging from history to geology; gift shop, interpretive and audio-visual displays as well as a short-order cafe are on the site. The diamond mine is part of a 900-acre pine-covered park lining the banks of the Little Missouri River.

Supt, Crater of Diamonds State Park, Rte 1, Box 364, Murfreesboro, AR 71958, **501/285-3113.**

MISSISSIPPI BAYOU COUNTRY

Lafayette, New Iberia & St. Martinville, LA

The heart of the bayou—*bayuk* in French—was settled by soft-spoken Acadians (Cajuns), whom the English routed from their Nova Scotia homeland more than 200 years ago. Their travail was chronicled in Longfellow's poem, Evangeline. The huge swamplands where they settled are alive with slow-moving waters, which is the definition of a bayou, and crowned with lush vegetation. Brilliant azaleas fire the countryside around Lafayette, home to gorgeous gardens and a lively Mardi Gras festival of its own. The peculiar patois of the Cajuns is characterized by a distinctly French flavor, evidenced by the Gallic names given quaint villages and towns that dot the land. A curtain of Spanish moss drapes the trees, lending a dream-like quality to the region, inhabited by alligators, profuse birdlife and fish. Paddlers can see a big chunk of the 1300-square-mile territory from chartered canoes, or capture the flavor of it in scenic drives, such as the mile-long Pine and Oak Alley near St. Martinville. Near New Iberia on Avery Island, a great salt dome rearing up from flat marshland, is Bird City, a refuge for one of the largest egret rookeries in the US. Spicy hot peppers, better known as the chief ingredient of Tabasco Sauce, are cultivated here. As a tasty alternative, you can join merrymakers at the Sugar Cane Festival in the Fall and sample the sugar formed from liquid pressed from cane. Beaux Bridges proclaims itself Crawfish Capital of the World and celebrates in even-numbered years. Natchez Trace Parkway in Mississippi, following an old Indian Trail, offers a scenic drive through the bayou.

Chamber of Commerce, 804 E St Mary Blvd, PO Box 51307, Lafayette, LA 70505, **318/233-2705.**

SUPERDOME

New Orleans, LA

See Astrodome (Houston, TX).

OZARK STREAMS

Southeastern MO

These gentle rolling hills are coursed by some of the finest waterways in America, and 140 miles of them are under the official care of the National Park Service as the Ozark National Scenic Riverways. The area encompasses 113 square miles characterized by bursts of color, courtesy of flowering dogwood and redbud trees, and brilliantly-blooming wild flowers, but is better known for the greatest concentration of springs in the world. They feed the Current River, which is abundant with fighting smallmouth bass and scrappy bluegill. The river is a potpourri of pleasures for all who enjoy the water: canoeists, anglers, campers and tourists. The Current's headwaters are near Montauk State Park, south of Salem. Pitched tents are a common sight on the frequent gravel bars. Springs-fed Jack's Fork and nearby Eleven Point rivers are also in the same region. Other highlights in the area include picturesque Alley Springs where there's a historic red mill that works (occasionally), a cable ferry that crosses the river at Powder Mill Ferry, and an awesome plunge of water which flows from a massive bluff at Big Spring. Whitetail deer, wild turkey and some 200 species of birds populate the region. In season, informative talks are given at Round, Big and Alley Springs, where there are marked nature trails.

Ozark Nat'l Scenic Waterways, PO Box 490, Van Buren, MO 63965, **816/323-4236.**

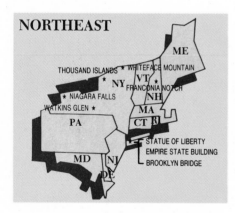

NORTHEAST

WATKINS GLEN STATE PARK

Watkins Glen, NY

Within this 700-acre park, nestled in scenic beauty near the southern edge of Seneca Lake, lies world-famous Watkins Glen Gorge, laced with walking trails throughout the stupendous sculptured chasm. The narrow, secluded valley itself drops about 700 feet in two miles. It features 18 waterfalls and many unusual rock formations. A 165-foot-high bridge spans the glen, and cliffs soar 200 feet up from the river below. Visitors can walk behind Rainbow Falls, where sunlight often produces a rainbow in the

Niagara Falls, Niagara Falls, NY

spray—or trek across Mile Point Bridge and then hoof it up Jacob's Ladder, a steep rock staircase leading back to the upper entrance. At the park entrance, a pavilion features a geological display and gift shop. Wines and fruit juices, as well as upstate New York cheeses, are sold at the Bandstand inside the Victorian Courtyard. Twice nightly the curtain rises on Timespell—a computerized sound and light extravaganza utilizing stereo, lasar beams and other high-tech equipment to illustrate the geological history of the glen. Advance reservations suggested (607/535-4960 or 535-2466). Scenic boat rides on Seneca Lake depart from Watkins Glen. Nearby Elmira contains the grave of Samuel Clemens (Mark Twain); the Mark Twain Study, constructed to resemble a Mississippi riverboat pilothouse, is on the campus of Elmira College.

Dept of Commerce, 99 Washington Ave, Albany, NY 12245, **518/474-5143.**

THOUSAND ISLANDS

St. Lawrence Seaway, NY

See Island Escapes.

EMPIRE STATE BUILDING

New York, NY

For several decades this was the world's tallest building at 1250 feet, then, much to the chagrin of New Yorkers, Chicago's Sears Tower (see) captured the honor at 1454 feet. Even the nearby World Trade Center (1353 feet) has surpassed the once superior height of the Empire State Building. But with buildings, just as it is with people, height isn't everything; the structure's history and long dominance continue to make it a worthwhile landmark for visitors. The remarkable structure, built in 1931 and containing 2-million square feet of office space, has survived not only the ravages of time, but also a devastating blow from an airliner. Millions have been inspired to visit after seeing the Hollywood-inspired climb up its exterior by a gigantic ape called King Kong. The view from the top is still remarkable and at night the building is illuminated with lights in an ever-changing spectacle of color. Observatories located on the 86th and 102nd floors; open daily 9:30am—midnight. Rates: $2.75; children $1.50.

Empire State Building, Fifth Ave & 34 St, NY, NY 10118, **212/736-2100.**

NIAGARA FALLS

Niagara Falls, NY

Niagara's thundering waters beckon four million visitors each year. The American Falls, and the even larger Canadian Horseshoe cataract, which cascades 173 feet through a gap half a mile wide, stand side by side in awesome splendor joining two of the world's largest lakes, Erie and Ontario. In a crashing display of monumental proportions, the tremor and tympany at the base of the falls is seen, felt and heard on misted wooden walkways dubbed the "Cave of the Winds" after the rock-filled cave behind the American Falls. Visitors routinely toured these walkways until dangerous slides commenced in 1920. Since 1885, raincoat-clad tourists have boarded a *Maid of the Mist* boat for an up-close view of the spectacle. Today, modern vessls run mid-May—late Oct (716/284-8897). Attractions dot both shores, including the Daredevil Hall of Fame at the Niagara Falls Museum on the Canadian border, which houses a collection of barrels and other stunter's devices used to ride the falls; on the U.S. side, films, displays and exhibits covering the 500-year geological history of the area can be found at the Schoell-kopf Geological Museum and at the Niagara Art Center. The New York State Power Authority maintains extensive exhibits about the Niagara hydroelectric project, and offers an exceptional vantage point for viewing the gorge (716/285-3211). At night, the falls are lighted in spectacular color shows; in winter, the frosted display of water is exceptionally stunning—and the walkways are uncrowded.

Convention and Visitors Bureau, Box 786, Falls St Station, Niagara Falls, NY 14303, **716/278-8010.**

BROOKLYN BRIDGE

New York, NY

Once considered to be the eighth wonder of the world, this utilitarian link between Manhattan and Brooklyn is celebrated as a major work of art. Designed to straddle New York's East River, the 5,989-foot-long span claimed the lives of more than two dozen of its builders. It is the only bridge in the world with an elevated promenade, and is crossed daily by walkers, joggers and cyclists. Its pre-eminence among the world's bridges is a tribute to the determination and iron will of architect John Roebling and his engineer son, Col. Washington A. Roebling, who built it after his father died while working on the site. Wire ropes radiating from the 276-foot-high twin stone towers at either end are crossed by vertical steel suspenders joining the cables to the beam of the roadway. The result is a photogenic fishnet effect. The bridge was the first major use of steel in New York. Ironically, instead of boosting the fortunes of Brooklyn as a city (as it was then) over its island neighbor, builders borrowed the concept of structural steel to mold metropolitan Manhattan's soaring skyline, and more people settled there as a result. Nearby on the Brooklyn side is Williamsburg, an old community of Hasidic Jews where bearded, black-clothed men and their severely dressed families live in daily observance of their faith.

Brooklyn Bridge, 206 St John Place, Brooklyn, NY **212/636-1920.**

WHITEFACE MOUNTAIN

Adirondack Mountains, NY

Getting away from it all is pretty easy in the Adirondack Mountains; there are few roads—only 1100 miles of highway and a scant 120 miles of railway—and nearly half of the 6-million-acre area is wilderness. The Adirondacks are among the oldest mountains on earth, and they were once higher than the Rockies are today. But Whiteface Mountain, located deep in the chain near Wilmington is high enough—almost a mile above sea level—and sufficiently rugged for the most avid skier. It is, in fact, the highest skiing mountain in the eastern US. Ascent of this mountain, whether by scenic toll road or modern chair lift, provides perhaps the best view of mountain scenery in the East. A macadam highway near NY 431 climbs to a parking area near the summit, which can be reached by foot or by an unusual elevator set into the cone of the mountain. The highway and elevator are in use late May—mid-Oct. Nearby are: Ausable Chasm, a steep gorge with perpendicular cliffs and soaring falls; the resort town of Lake Placid, where the 1980 Winter Olympic games were held; and Lake George, a small community that boasts an opera festival mid-July—Aug.

Chamber of Commerce, Box 277, Wilmington, NY 12997, **518/946-2255.**

STATUE OF LIBERTY

New York, NY

The nation's most enduring symbol, the Statue of Liberty, celebrates her 100th birthday in 1986. And the old girl will look as grand as the day she was born due to restoration efforts begun in 1984. Cosmetics are being applied to her upraised right arm, and to the 168-step spiral staircase leading to her crown. Major surgery includes replacement of her torch and some inner organs, and the addition of a glass elevator to whisk you from ground level to the top of the pedestal on which she stands. Take the ferry boat over from Battery Park in Manhattan. Unless you're a KGB agent, you'll get a lump in your throat as you approach the plot of soil (actually New Jersey soil) the 151-foot centenarian calls home. The French-born beauty (she was a gift from France) shelters the American Museum of Immigration, which features multi-media exhibits about the "huddled masses" who remember her as their first glimpse of their adopted country. Few superlatives describe the panoramic view from Liberty's crown, and there is a paucity of adjectives to match the exhausting climb to it (if you opt to try out your fitness). There are three rest stops; it gets awfully hot sometimes in summer. Before or after your tour, explore Battery Park. Among sights to see: Castle Clinton, an ancient fort now a National Monument; the Marine Memorial, dedicated to those who went down with their ships at sea; and various statues along a circular walk.

Statue of Liberty Nat'l Monument, Tour Coordinator, Liberty Island, Manhattan, NY 10004, **212/732-1286** *(recorded info),* **212/732-1236.**

FRANCONIA NOTCH STATE PARK

Near Franconia, NH

This is one of the crowning glories in a land renowned for its picture-postcard beauty. For nearly two centuries, millions have enjoyed the rugged scenery within this natural pass between the Kinsman and Franconia mountain ranges of New Hampshire. The Flume and the Great Stone Face stand out along the 8-mile route between towering peaks. The Flume is a narrow canyon never more than 20 feet wide with vertical granite walls rising nearly 100 feet above Flume Brook, which at one end of the canyon spills over the 45-foot Avalanche Falls. The Great Stone Face, also called Old Man of the Mountains, is an entirely natural structure that bears a striking resemblance to a craggy old mountaineer. Within the setting are the Basin Waterfall, high and clear Lonesome Lake, Cannon Mountain, the Cannon Mountain Aerial Tramway and Echo Lake. Good skiing in winter.

Franconia Notch State Park, New Hampshire Div of Parks & Recreation, PO Box 856, Concord, NH, 03301, **603/823-5563.**

Statue of Liberty, New York, NY

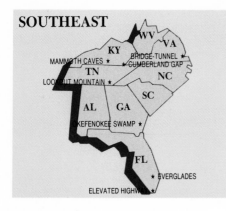

SOUTHEAST

FLORIDA KEYS ELEVATED HIGHWAY

Southern Tip of FL

A disastrous storm in the mid-1930s wiped out the rail line linking the Florida Keys from Miami to Key West. It was replaced by an overseas highway that opened up the Keys to the motoring public in 1938. Most of the 128-mile highway is over water. The Seven Mile Bridge (really about a quarter-mile shorter than its name suggests), one of 42 bridges along the route to Key West, is one of the longest in the world. The name "Keys," is a corruption of the Spanish word *cayo,* meaning "small island." At Islamorado is the Coral Underwater Sea Garden. The living reef formations there can be seen up-close and underwater by snorkelers, or from above in a glass-bottom boat. Fishing boats can be chartered almost anywhere in the Keys. Saltwater bounty includes toothsome stone crab, drum, bluefish, flounder, grouper, snapper and a host of other species. A serving of the unique stone crab is worth a journey of almost any length; for the sweet tooth, Key Lime pie, confected from home-grown limes (distinctively smaller and more tart than the supermarket varieties), ends any meal with delight. At Plantation Key you can see gold doubloons, pieces of eight and other scavanged treasures at McKee's Museum of Sunken Treasure. At Key West, America's southernmost city, the Conch Train (pronounced "conk") takes you for a 14-mile, 90-minute tour that includes Truman's erstwhile abode, one of Ernest Hemingway's favorite watering holes (Sloppy Joe's Bar) and the famous writer's home.

Florida Upper Keys Chamber of Commerce, PO Box 274-C, Key Largo 33037, **305/451-1414.**

THE EVERGLADES

Near Homestead, FL

(See Nat'l Parks & Monuments.)

MAMMOTH CAVES

Bowling Green, KY

(See Nat'l Parks & Monuments.)

Mammoth Caves, Bowling Green, KY

LOOKOUT MOUNTAIN

Chattanooga, TN

There's no escaping the Civil War influence on this part of the country. Memorials, civic and commercial, crop up everywhere, but the natural beauty of Lookout Mountain is the chief coin of the realm. The strategic battlefield, scene of both the Yankee blue and Confederate gray of occupation forces during the war, can be reached by chair lift, by the world's steepest incline railway, or by auto via TN 58. At the top you can see seven states from Lovers Leap. Tours of historic Cravens House, headquarters for both armies during hostilities, are conducted by National Park Service guides in period costumes; a museum exhibits life-sized dioramas of historic events and memorabilia. Not far from Cravens House is the entrance to Ruby Falls, a natural waterfall 1120 feet beneath the mountain in Lookout Mountain Caverns. The falls, reached by an elevator through 260 feet of solid rock, spills 145 feet. If you have the time, try the Alpine slide down the mountain; you can regulate the speed yourself. Chattanooga is a central spot for other explorations: The Great Smoky Mountains (see Nat'l Parks & Monuments), Nashville, and Oak Ridge Museum of Science and Industry, and Jack Daniel Historic Distillery are only a couple of hours away by auto.

Convention & Visitors Bureau, Civic Forum, 1001 Market St, Chattanooga, TN 37402, **615/756-2121.**

CUMBERLAND GAP NAT'L HISTORICAL PARK

KY, VA and TN

It's difficult to visualize the pioneers pushing through this rugged mountain country on foot, but it was the route used to cross the Appalachian Mountains during the great westward migration. Daniel Boone was the first white man to mark the trail that became known as the Wilderness Road, leading through the gap to Kentucky. This expansive wilderness area is most popular with hikers and campers. There are about 50 miles of hiking trails, some providing the only access to such park highlights as Sand Cave and White Rocks. A 160-acre campground is located on US 58 in Virginia. Nearby and noteworthy: Lincoln Memorial University in Harrowgate, TN (4 miles from park), which houses a collection of Lincolniana (books, paintings, sculptures); Mountain Drive Mine; and "Song of the Cumberland Gap," an outdoor musical drama about the life of Daniel Boone. Park officials also present numerous demonstrations and guided tours.

Cumberland Gap Nat'l Historical Park, PO Box 840, Middlesboro, KY 40965, **606/248-2817.**

CHESAPEAKE BAY BRIDGE-TUNNEL

Delmarva Peninsula & Norfolk, VA

This is another candidate for the eighth wonder of the world, and thoughtful builders placed a pier in the Atlantic waters where you can pause and ponder its place in that pantheon. However, most visitors prefer to fish; it's free, except for the bait, which you can buy nearby. You also might enjoy dining in the restaurant, also located on Sea Gull Island, one of four man-made islands that dot the

Okefenokee Swamp Park, Near Waycross, GA

Photo: Tourist Division, Department of Industry and Trade

crossing. From your perch on the pier or from high above the bay you will see ocean liners porting industrial goods from the four corners of the earth, gray navy warships and other sea-going vessels. They are above and beneath you when you cross the Chesapeake Bay between the Delmarva Peninsula and Norfolk, VA. The 20-mile bridge-tunnel is a complex series of bridges, tunnels and causeways, its design facilitating sea traffic streaming through the main channels. Most of the roadway is actually a series of causeways joining two separate tunnels, each about a mile long, dug under the main channels of the bay. The bridge-tunnel was built at a cost of $200-million and opened in 1964. On the Delmarva Peninsula, named for the states of Delaware, Maryland and Virginia, are numerous recreational facilities, especially appealing to boaters and anglers. Norfolk is home to a vast US naval base, where ship tours are available. Whether the fleet is in or out, there's seaside camping, swimming at well-maintained beaches, and thrilling rides at nearby amusement parks.

Chesapeake Bay Bridge & Tunnel District, Box 111, Cape Charles, VA 23310, **804/464-3511.**

OKEFENOKEE SWAMP PARK

Near Waycross, GA

Pogo and his cartoon friends seem to come to life here in this natural sanctuary for alligators, otters, wildcats, bears, deer, turtles, and several other species of mammals, reptiles and birds. The huge Okefenokee Swamp, a National Wildlife Refuge and a recent addition to the National Wilderness System, is a significant part of America's heritage. It is more than half a million acres of soggy land which the Indians once called "Trembling Earth." Okefenokee Swamp Park gives us a peek at this otherwise nearly impenetrable world. The park features interpretive exhibits, lectures, wildlife shows, boat tours, wilderness walkways, an observation tower, and Pioneer Island, site of a reconstructed swampland homestead. Open daily 9am—6:30pm spring and summer (to 5:30pm fall and winter). Nominal admission charge.

Okefenokee Swamp Park, Waycross, GA 31501, **912/283-0583.**

Chapter 4

FUN AT FESTIVALS

Bluegrass Music Festival—Louisville, KY

Just as it is with parades, it seems that everyone loves a festival. Certainly, there is an abundance of supply to meet the demand, with literally thousands of events, large and small, held around the country each year.

There are festivals to mark the changing seasons, such as the Cherry Blossom Festival in DC and the yuletide Dickens Evening on the Strand in Texas, and to celebrate such special occasions as Lent, Independence Day, and Halloween. There are festivals woven around such special interests as aviation, hot-air ballooning and water sports and winter sports—and around ethnic cultures, such as Michigan's Dutch-flavored Tulip Time and the St. Paul Festival of Nations that each year brings together more than 50 different cultures.

Good old Americana is represented by festivals celebrating folklore, rodeo and bluegrass music, and by such events as Hannibal's Tom Sawyer Days. Of course, music, from classical to jazz is the focus of many festivals, as are arts and crafts and a whole range of edibles.

Selecting the ''best'' in this category was a particularly challenging and necessarily subjective task, particularly with limitations of space. Unquestionably, there are enough fine events to fill an entire book, let alone a single chapter! For further selections we invite readers to request calendars of events supplied by most state tourism offices.

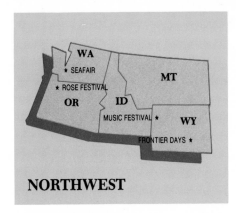

NORTHWEST

SEAFAIR

Seattle, WA

This fair started in the years following World War II and has gradually grown into a three-week festival with more than 50 major events, most with a nautical theme. The Chevron Milk Carton Boat Race requires entrants to build their own boats entirely out of milk cartons. Other sporting events include a hole-in-one contest, a triathlon, a sailboat race, and the nationally acclaimed hydroplane race. A Miss Seafair Scholarship Pageant awards $15,000 in scholarships and prizes to its chosen queen. Major festivities include Harborfair, the Des Moines Waterland Festival, and Underwater Seafair. During the celebration, 16 Puget sound communities host picnics, parades, dances, arts and crafts shows. Held late July-Aug.

Seafair, 901 Occidental S, Seattle, WA 98134, 206/623-7100.

ROSE FESTIVAL

Portland, OR

The venerable Portland Rose Society has been host to Rose Festival visitors for more than 75 years. Guests numbering in the hundreds of thousands come to experience more than 50 events. Three giant parades culminate with the Grand Floral Parade, second in size only to the Pasadena Tournament of Roses Parade (see). Marching bands, dance bands, and jazz groups perform at the Civic Stadium and numerous downtown locations. Early in the 17-day festival is the Golden Rose Ski Classic, with slalom competitions held at Mt. Hood's Timberline Lodge. Within the city limits is the giant Festival Fun Center which sprawls for many blocks bordering the Willamette River. During the festival, more than a score of naval ships line the McCall Waterfront Park. New in 1984 was the Portland 200 Indy-style car race held at Multnomah County Exposition Center. Held 1st part of June.

Portland Rose Festival Assn, 1 SW Columbia, Portland, OR 97258, 503/227-2681.

GRAND TETON MUSIC FESTIVAL

Teton Village, WY

The festival orchestra draws its members from many of the best orchestras in the US, as well as from a number of universities, and features several concert masters and gold medalists from international competitions. Orchestras represented include Baltimore, Hong Kong, Honolulu, Indianapolis, Metropolitan Opera, Milwaukee, New Orleans, New York Philharmonic, San Francisco, Seattle, and the St. Paul Chamber Orchestra. Performances are held in an acoustically splendid hall in the shadow of the towering, snow-capped Teton Mountains. Celebrity guests in recent years have included Itzhak Perlman, Yehudi Menuhin, and the 465-member Mormon Tabernacle Choir. Musicians-only seminars are offered in early June. Other attractions include chamber groups and guest soloists. Held late July-Aug.

The Grand Teton Music Festival, (summer) PO Box 310, Teton Village, WY 83025, 307/733-3050, (winter) 2373 Terwood Dr, Huntingdon Valley, PA 19006, 215/947-3928.

FRONTIER DAYS

Cheyenne, WY

As a roaring pioneer town, Cheyenne earned the dubious sobriquet, "Hell on Wheels." It's tamer now, but livens up the last week of July when the grandaddy of all frontier festivals (dating from 1897) lassos top-notch entertainment for young and old alike. Headlining the events are nine full days of Professional Rodeo Cowboys Association sanctioned rodeos, followed each evening by chuckwagon races. Southern Plains Indians perform ritual dances afternoons and early evenings at the Indian Village. Other highlights include a variety of parades in downtown Cheyenne, free square dancing at the City Center parking lot, free pancake breakfasts, a chili cook-off, and top-name country and western entertainers. The Cheyenne Frontier Days Old West Museum is open 8am-9pm throughout the festival.

Cheyenne Frontier Days, PO Box 2666, Cheyenne, WY 82003, 800/443-2723 (outside WY), 800/442-4191 (within WY).

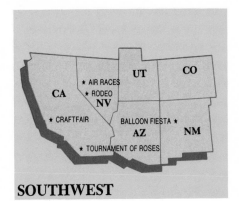

SOUTHWEST

AMERICAN CRAFT COUNCIL CRAFTFAIR

San Francisco, CA

This craftfair is held four times a year, in San Francisco, Dallas, Baltimore, and West Springfield (MA), and each site carefully selects many pieces of art for display— including very expensive works. Artists often prefer to make limited editions or one-of-a-kind items. Examples include: furniture made from exotic woods or those with unusual grain; woven metal vessels of bronze, brass, and copper; porcelain flutes; and painted steel models of hats, boots, and shoes. More than 120,000 people attend the craftfairs, and sales from recent events have totalled around $11 million. The West Springfield and San Francisco sites were added in 1984; and more may be selected soon. Schedules vary each year; call in advance. The ACC also provides info regarding reduced transportation and lodging.

American Craft Enterprises, Inc, PO Box 10, 256 Main St, New Paltz, NY 12561, 914/255-0039.

TOURNAMENT OF ROSES PARADE

Pasadena, CA

More than 125 million people watch this parade each year on TV, and 1 ½ million more spectators come to watch curbside. Regulations govern the making of the elaborate floats which cannot be covered with any manmade materials. Decorations range from dried and real flowers to seeds and vegetations, but 95% of the trimmings are fresh plants. Guests can view the building of floats in various locations in the area throughout the year. Builders start months in advance with the chassis and chicken wire, and finish by glueing on fresh foliage in the last three days. The parade itself features 23 award-winning bands, and more than 200 equestrians. For best views of the 60 floats, the tournament recommends Sierra Madre Blvd. between Washington and Sierra Madre Villa. Following the parade is the Rose Bowl football classic. Held 1st of Jan.

Pasadena Tournament of Roses Parade, 391 S Orangegrove Blvd, Pasadena, CA 91184, 818/449-7673.

NAT'L. CHAMPIONSHIP AIR RACES

Reno, NV

Since acres of sagebrush were removed from Nevada flatlands some 20 years ago, Reno's National Championship Air Races have become the largest and oldest such event in the US. Events in the four-day air spectacular include military fly-bys, wing walks, parachute team demonstrations, aerial acrobatic displays, demonstrations of ultra-lights, and, of course, a wide variety of races for all sorts of aircraft. In past years, such luminaries as the Navy's Blue Angels, the Air Force's Thunderbirds, and the Army's Golden Knights have made appearances, along with renowned racers, daredevils, and acrobats. The qualifying trials are free for a few days prior to the festival. Held mid-Sept.

Reno Air Racing Assn, PO Box 1429, Reno, NV 89505, 702/826-7500.

RENO RODEO

Reno, NV

Strap on your chaps and join about 45,000 other buck-a-roos at one of the biggest, richest professional rodeos in the world. The total purse is around $300,000 and more than 900 of the most skillful cowboys and cowgirls from around the nation compete in seven events including saddle bronc riding, bareback riding, bull riding, steer wrestling, calf roping, team roping, and barrel racing. A parade downtown and a fireworks display kick-off this week-long event. Come watch the fun at the steer-decorating contest where one team member holds a 400-700 lb. steer by a rope, as his partner tries to tie a ribbon on its tail. Other attractions include a Buckaroo Breakfast before the parade, exhibits, a carnival, a chili cook-off, and the Budweiser Clydesdales. Held mid-June at the Nevada State Fairgrounds.

Reno Rodeo Assn, 1350 N Wells, PO Box 20580, Reno, NV 89515, **702/329-3877.**

INT'L. BALLOON FIESTA

Albuquerque, NM

The self-styled "Hot Air Balloon Capital of the World" annually presents what is acclaimed to be the biggest event of its kind anywhere. The festival began in 1972 as a one-day, 14-balloon affair. Today, it runs for nine entertainment-packed days that include gas-balloon races, precision parachute teams, and an Old Time Air Show. A not-to-be-missed event is the "Mass Ascension," held on the first and last days, where 500-plus balloons take off at the same time. Other activities include a kite-flying contest, radio-controlled aircraft, dancing, ethnic food (Mexican), and an ice cream freeze-off. Held early Oct.

Albuquerque Internat'l Balloon Fiesta, 3300 Princeton NE, No S-24, Albuquerque, NM 87107, **505/883-0932.**

MIDWEST

AQUATENNIAL

Minneapolis, MN

In recent years, more than 2 million visitors have attended the various events scheduled for the 10-day Aquatennial. Despite the name, there are many events for landlubbers, including hot-air-balloon races, a tennis tourney, auto and bike races, a torchlight parade, band concerts, and fashion shows. On the aquatic side (there are 22 lakes in the area) are boat races at Lake Nokomis in which contestants build their boats entirely out of milk cartons, the Pepsi Water Ski Show of Stars at Lake of the Isles, fishing clinics and contests at Lake Calhoun, as well as the Pepsi Sailing Regatta. Held late July.

Minneapolis Aquatennial Assn, 702 Wayzata Blvd, Commodore Ct, Minneapolis, MN 55403, **612/377-4621;** *current schedule from the Connection,* **612/941-2501.**

FESTIVAL OF NATIONS

St. Paul, MN

One of the largest ethnic celebrations in the US features cuisine, music, folk dancing, folk art demonstrations, and exhibits of 7000 costumed volunteer participants from more than 50 ethnic groups. The International Institute of Minnesota has sponsored the Festival of Nations since 1932 as a showcase for the state's ethnic groups. All attractions and events, including 40 ethnic cafes and an international bazaar, are held under one roof at the St. Paul Civic Center throughout the three-day festival. Other festivals of note in the Twin Cities area are the Winter Carnival in Jan., and the Minneapolis Aquatennial (see) in late July. Held late April.

Festival of Nations, 1694 Como Ave, St. Paul, MN 55108, **612/647-0191.**

CHAMPIONSHIP RODEO

Sidney, IA

America's largest continuous outdoor rodeo puts on seven big performances every year in August, and the fun begins with a grand entry parade. Events within the enormous grandstands include bareback bronc riding, saddle bronc riding, steer wrestling, calf roping, bull riding, and barrel racing. Country music, a carnival and midway, and western-style food from barbecues to corn on the cob, add to the fun. Located about 50 mi SE of Omaha. Held early Aug.

Rodeo Ticket Office, Sidney, IA 51652, **712/374-2695.**

EXPERIMENTAL AIRCRAFT ASSN. INT'L. FLY-IN

Oshkosh, WI

The world's largest aviation event annually brings more than a thousand experimental aircraft to Wittman Field near Oshkosh, and for one week it becomes the busiest airport in the world. Yearly contests include the Oshkosh 500 air race, and awards for best custom builts, classics, rotorcrafts, antiques, ultra-lights, and warbirds. Approximately 800,000 participants and spectators attend the Fly-In convention, with foreign visitors from more than 70 different countries. Opened in 1983, the new Experimental Aircraft Association Aviation Center (off Hwy 41 at Wittman Field in Oshkosh), includes the world's largest privately owned collection of aircraft and aviation-related artifacts. The Fly-In is usually held late July-Aug.

Experimental Aircraft Assn, Wittman Airfield, Oshkosh, WI 54903, **414/426-4800.**

KING RICHARD'S FAIRE

Bristol, WI

Turn back the clock more than 400 years to an age of jousting, magic, and Old-English accents. This festival has them all and more than 275 artisans display wares of generally excellent quality—from leatherwork and wood carvings, to pewter and stoneware. Visitors can get their fortune told or test their skills at belly-dancing, fencing, and archery. A sampling of more than 40 available foods includes cornish hens, prime rib, roasted rabbit, and English fudge cakes. Guests can watch more than 35 demonstrations of craft-making and special attractions complete with a free-for-all mud fight and falconry demonstrations.

King Richard's Faire—Bristol, WI

Around 300 entertainers (500 during special events) include mimes, puppeteers, jugglers, dancers, troubadours, and minstrels. Each weekend revolves around a different theme ranging from dance and music, to magic and horse races. Located near IL/WI state line off I-94. Held on 7 consecutive weekends from early July.

King Richard's Faire, 12420 128th St, Kenosha, WI 53142, **312/689-2800,** or **414/396-4385.**

INT'L. FILM FESTIVAL

Chicago, IL

When American film festivals are considered, many people think first of New York or Los Angeles, but a growing number of critics feel that Chicago's pre-winter screenings are perhaps the most interesting and attainable. *Town and Country* suggests, "If you can see only one American film festival, make it Chicago's . . ." Called "A landmark on the American cultural scene" by the *Hollywood Reporter*, the 20-year-old film festival has showcased distinguished motion pictures from all over the world. The videos are featured in selected theatres and other institutions in the metropolitan area. Categories included are fiction, documentary, video arts, major releases, short subjects, student films, educational productions, animated subjects, and some television productions. Occasional talks are given by famous film-makers. Held mid-Nov.

Chicago Internat'l Film Festival, 415 N Dearborn St, Chicago, IL 60610, **312/644-3400.**

LINCOLNFEST

Springfield, IL

The state capital is imbued with the presence of Abraham Lincoln—at his former home, at his law offices, and at the Old State Capitol where he made his "house divided" speech. During this weekend extravaganza held around the 4th of July, you can see Honest Abe himself (a look-alike, of course), along with 40 other roving characters including a 14-foot tall Uncle Sam stiltman. Several city blocks are roped off for this free family street festival that features more than 100 events and entertainment on six stages. There's dancing in the streets, a large children's area and special events for senior citizens—a singalong, husband-calling contest, and microwave cookoff. You'll find street food galore at nearly three dozen concessions, a flea market, crafts, and antique autos. Special events include soccer challenges, frisbee throwing, a clown show, a yo-yo championship, and a fireworks display. There is, of course, the obligatory parade, as well as such competitions as a 5K foot race, tobacco-spitting and "most freckles" contests, bicycle races, dance and star look-alike contests, and a chili cookoff.

Convention & Visitors Bureau, 219 5th, Springfield, IL 62701, **217/789-2360.**

TULIP TIME FESTIVAL

Holland, MI

In 1927 a Holland high school teacher persuaded the city's population of largely Dutch heritage to plant 100,000 tulip bulbs. Since then, millions of tulips have been planted in the area, and Tulip Time has become one of the largest floral festivals in America. Other attractions include color-

ful parades, Klompen dancers, an authentic Dutch church service in two languages, and barbershop quartets. Each year, festival participants get down on their knees and actually scrub the street. This custom originates from the Netherlands where the good *Hauswaifs* washed the inside, the outside, and the surrounding area of their houses as well. Points of interest include a wooden-shoe factory, and "Little Netherlands," a small Dutch village complete with a 200-year-old windmill surrounded by 100,000 tulips. Held 4 days beginning on Wed, 2nd week of May.

Holland Tulip Time Festival, Inc, Holland, MI 49423, **616/396-4221.**

CIRCUS CITY FESTIVAL

Peru, IN

This small midwestern city has two claims to fame: It was the birthplace of Cole Porter, and the home or winter headquarters for 10 major circuses. Both Cole Porter and the circuses are gone, but for one week each summer the tradition of sawdust magic returns as a spectacular three-ring performance belies the fact that it's not a professional show. Performers are selected from more than 325 applicants in the Peru area, and each high school participant is awarded around $1000 in college scholarships for his/her dedication. NBC filmed an hour-long documentary about it called "Circus Town, USA." A festival highlight is the mammoth Circus Parade, always held at 10 am on the final Saturday of the celebration. Also of interest is the Circus City Festival Museum, which displays model circus wagons, original costumes and equipment, paintings, and other circus memorabilia. Held 3rd Wed in July.

Circus City Festival, Inc, 145 N Broadway, Peru, IN 46970, **317/472-3918.**

INT'L. AIRSHOW AND TRADE EXPOSITION

Dayton, OH

Barely more than a decade old, this attraction is claimed to have become the world's 5th largest event of its kind. Hosting about 175,000 visitors, each year's airshow includes at least one military flight team, six civilian performers, experimental and antique aircraft, WW II planes, parachute displays, hot-air-balloon rallies, and radio-controlled aircraft. Static displays of more than 100 aircraft are supported by manufacturers and other businesses and organizations at the trade exposition. Take I-75 N from Dayton to Exit 64 (Engle Road) and follow signs. Held mid-July.

Dayton Internat'l Airshow, 214 Terminal Bldg, Dayton Internat'l Airport, Vandalia, OH 45377. Or, Convention and Visitors Bureau, **800/221-8235** *(outside OH),* **800/221-8234** *(within OH).*

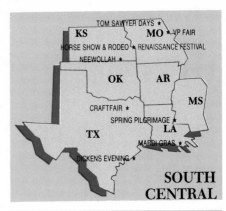

SOUTH CENTRAL

NEEWOLLAH

Independence, KS

Leave your raw eggs and soap at home because this halloween celebration was originated in 1919 as a sane, family-styled event to reduce vandalism. Today, Neewollah (halloween spelled backward) has become one of Kansas' largest annual festivities. A full week of activities includes the crowning of the Neewollah queen and coronation ball, a carnival, top performers such as The Osmond Brothers, Roy Clark, The Oak Ridge Boys, a Broadway musical, and a Grand Parade on the last day. In 1980 the festival became known worldwide when it added a segment called the International Music Festival. Famous performers come from as far afield as Australia, Bulgaria, Cuba, and Nigeria; the festival is judged and musicians are awarded prizes. Other attractions have included free street acts, a kiddies' parade, a hog-calling contest, and a fiddler contest. Performances located in various buildings, and in downtown Independence.

Chamber of Commerce, PO Box 386, 108 W Myrtle, Independence, KS 63701, **316/331-1890.**

AMERICAN CRAFT COUNCIL CRAFTFAIR

Dallas, TX

(See under San Francisco.)

DICKENS EVENING ON THE STRAND

Galveston, TX

During the first weekend in December, hundreds of carolers, bell ringers, jugglers, mimes, and bagpipers celebrate the start of the Christmas season in the restored Strand financial district of Galveston Island, about an hour's drive southeast of Houston. Named after the famous financial street in London frequented by a young Charles Dickens, Galveston's Strand was once the financial capital of the Southwest. Now it's a beautifully restored district of historic buildings featuring iron facades, gaslights, and more. This historical recreation of a Victorian Christmas is sponsored by the Galveston Historical Foundation. Persons in full Victorian costumes are admitted without charge.

Galveston Historical Foundation, Dickens Evening on the Strand, PO Drawer 539, Galveston, TX 77553, **409/765-7834,** *or* **713/488-5942.**

Tom Sawyer Days—Hannibal, MO

AMERICAN ROYAL LIVESTOCK, HORSE SHOW, AND RODEO

Kansas City, MO

From its beginning in 1899 as a Hereford Cattle show in a single tent, the Americal Royal has grown to become the largest combined livestock, horse show, and rodeo in the nation. The livestock show encompasses 11 breeds of cattle, seven varieties of swine, and eight breeds of sheep. Equestrian spectaculars include the six days of the American Royal Saddle Horse Show in which a number of world championship medals are presented, as well as shows devoted to quarter horses, Arabian/Morgans, and Hunter/Jumpers. The rodeo, which attracts about 500 cowboys competing for $75,000 in prize money, runs for a full week. Held late Oct—mid-Nov.

American Royal Assn Inc, 1701 American Royal Ct, Kansas City, MO 64102, **816/221-9800.**

RENAISSANCE FESTIVAL

Kansas City, MO

An authentic recreation of a 16th century village in the midst of a harvest celebration, the Renaissance Festival is presented by the Kansas City Art Institute. Here, peasants and townfolk, minstrels and merchants, artisans and jesters, mingle with royalty and guests in a hamlet where merriment reigns. Six theatres and three stages feature continuous entertainment and lighthearted drama, puppetry, music, juggling, and jesting. Also included are Renaissance sporting events, contests, exhibits, and food. Runs weekends only (but also Labor Day) for 6 weeks starting early Sept.

The Renaissance of Kansas City, 3706 Broadway, Kansas City, MO 64111, **816/561-8005.**

TOM SAWYER DAYS

Hannibal, MO

The days leading up to Independence Day are celebrated with a wide variety of activities related to Sam Clemens' writings in this small Mississippi River city, Mark Twain's famous hometown. Best-known events are the fence painting contest (more fun if you can get someone else to do your work) and the annual frog jump-off. But there are also concerts, raft races on the Mississippi, re-enactments of Civil War battles by local school children, crazy contests, and a variety of sporting events. A large fireworks display is touched off at the riverfront on the evening of July 4th. The delightful little town, an antiquer's mecca, is clustered with Mark Twain landmarks—the Mark Twain Boyhood Home & Museum, the Clemens Law office (where the author's father was JP), and the Mark Twain cave (where Tom Sawyer and Becky Thatcher were lost). For inexpensive family-style meals—all-you-can-eat platters of chicken and country ham—try Nick's Homestead.

Hannibal Tourism Commission, PO Box 624, 308 N Main, Hannibal, MO 63401, **314/221-2477.**

VP FAIR

St. Louis, MO

One of the most successful urban festivals in America has recently won extensive coverage by radio and television networks. Usually scheduled around the 4th of July, the fair brings to St. Louis top-name entertainers, daily air and water shows, major fireworks displays, exhibits by dozens of community and ethnic groups, hundreds of arts and crafts booths, and nearly every kind of food imaginable. Races are held for steamboats, balloons, bicycles, and marathon runners. Much of the action takes place in the Jefferson National Expansion Memorial below the famous Gateway Arch, but other events are held in Busch Stadium, along Wharf Street and the Mississippi Levee, Laclede's Landing, and various downtown streets. Festivities begin with the Veiled Prophet Parade, the fair's namesake from a fictional character in a poem by the Irish poet Thomas Moore. The first Veiled Prophet Parade was held in 1878. More than a century later the event has become so popular that attendance approaches 4 million.

VP Fair Foundation, 7701 Forsyth Blvd, St. Louis, MO 63105, **314/721-FAIR.**

MARDI GRAS

New Orleans, LA

Mardi Gras, which means "Fat Tuesday," is the last day before Lent and the culminating blow-out of New Orleans' Carnival season. But for two weeks preceding Mardi Gras, business is at a standstill and there are parades almost every day complete with elaborate floats, marching jazz bands, and doubloons and trinkets tossed to the crowds. On Mardi Gras day, more than a million people watch the great parade of Rex; the King of the Carnival is a well-known businessman, and the Queen is from a prominent family. Highlights include plenty of street dancing, two parades of magnificently decorated trucks, and the He Sheba costume competition for transvestites! The streets and public buildings are decorated in the official carnival colors—purple, gold, and blue. All of the parades and festivities are prepared by private citizens, usually members of sometimes small organizations called krewes. All balls and parties are private and can be attended by invitation only.

Tourist and Convention Commission, 334 Royal St, New Orleans, LA 70130, **504/566-5031.**

SPRING PILGRIMAGE

Natchez, MS

Visitors to this historic southern town are invited to tour a number of stately old mansions during this pilgrimage in March. Ladies in hoop-skirts welcome guests into magnificent homes furnished with antiques. Ticket prices vary depending on the number of homes visited (3-5). Two theatrical events are also part of the festivities: The *Confederate Pageant,* a drama by local talent featuring scenes of southern society in elaborate, antebellum costumes, and *Southern Exposure,* a satirical comedy making fun of the way southerners make money by opening their homes to northerners—a fitting topic after a day of tours! The former is held in the City Auditorium, the latter in the Natchez Little Theatre Playhouse.

The Natchez Spring Pilgrimage, PO Box 347, Natchez, MS 39120, **601/446-6631.**

NORTHEAST

AMERICAN CRAFT COUNCIL CRAFTFAIR

Baltimore, MD

(See under San Francisco.)

FESTIVAL OF AMERICAN FOLKLIFE

Capitol Mall, Washington, DC

The Smithsonian and the National Park Service help folk artists and artisans demonstrate their crafts in an annual outdoor living museum. Located in The Mall between the Washington Monument and the Capitol, this is the largest yearly cultural event in the nation's Capitol. Cultural displays include Anglo-American potteries, native American songs, salmon roasting, fiddling, and black expressions ranging from blues and gospel, to tap dancing and street drills. Concerts usually begin at 7 pm in the Sylvan Theatre (on the Washington Monument grounds). The National Heritage Program, usually held for five days, honors 16 recipients of National Heritage Fellowships, traditional artists, dancers, storytellers, and craftspeople. In all, more than 150 artists depict crafts from America and many foreign nations. Held late June—early July.

Festival of American Folklife, Smithsonian Institution, Washington, DC 20560, **202/357-1729.**

OLD DOVER DAYS

Dover, DE

Once a year, this festival provides tours of Victorian, Colonial, and even modern homes and gardens not usually open to the public. Many of the buildings and homes in the area were constructed during the 17th century; Delaware's State House—second oldest capitol still in continuous use—was built on the town Green in the late 1700's. Other activities include an opening parade, a band concert, and a dollhouse show. Past exhibits have featured old coins and paper currency, quilts, and Kent County memorabilia. Craftsmen display such skills as basketweaving and blacksmithing. (Children under 10 not admitted into private home tours.) Held early May.

Friends of Old Dover, PO Box 44, Dover, DE 19901, **301/736-4266.**

POCONO WINTER CARNIVAL

In and Around Stroudsburg, PA

People who enjoy outdoor winter sports can climb right into the thick of things, or watch from the sidelines as a number of resorts and ski areas around Stroudsburg celebrate the delights of winter. Events include a variety of ski races, some (such as the Michelob Light Big Two Challenge) open only to those 21 and over, others open to all skiers. The Newport Alive Ski Spree, usually held at Big Boulder Ski Area at Lake Harmony, schedules downhill races, obstacle runs, a sloppy slalom, and snow sculpting contest. The Dr. Pepper Recreational Race, a number of all-night ski feats, and a costume parade on skis add to the fun. A smaller number of events are scheduled for the skate and sled crowd. Sites include Big Boulder, Camelback, Masthope Mountain, Saw Creek, and Shawnee ski areas. Held late Feb-early March.

Pocono Mountains Vacation Bureau, Box K, 1004 Main St, Stroudsburg, PA 18360, **717/424-6050.**

CHERRY BLOSSOM FESTIVAL

Washington, DC

Festivities begin when 650 cherry trees, a gift from Japan in 1912, start blooming in early spring—ranging in color from deep-pink to white. The delicate trees have become a symbol of friendship and goodwill between the two nations. More than 500,000 people flock to DC for the Festival Parade and other highlights that include a high-school-band competition at the Kennedy Center Concert Hall, sporting events, arts and crafts, the Cherry Blossom Ball, and an opening picnic and reception. The Festival Queen is truly regal in her gold and pearl crown which was donated in 1957 by Mr. Yoshtaka Mikimoto—its estimated value is $500,000. Other activities include live music and entertainment in downtown parks, and displays of oriental art, fashion, crafts, dance, and music.

Downtown Jaycees, **202/296-8675,** *or Convention & Visitors Assn, 1575 I St NW, Washington, DC 20005,* **202/789-7000.**

Aquatennial—Minneapolis, MN

Circus City Festival, Peru, IN

MISS AMERICA PAGEANT

Atlantic City, NJ

This pageant has come a long way since its humble beginnings in 1921 as purely a Bathing Beauty Contest. Today, contestants are rated according to their poise, charm, personality, and talent, in addition to their physical beauty. The Miss America Pageant is a culmination of a year's competitions at the local, state, and national levels, and more than $2 million in scholarships are awarded annually. Representatives from each state gather in the Atlantic City Convention Hall for five days of competitions in the swim suit, evening gown, and talent categories. Tickets are available to the public for each night, but the final day—when the new Miss America is crowned—is often sold-out months in advance. The winner travels the US promoting the pageant's scholarships. -Held mid-Sept.

Miss America Pageant, Atlantic City, NJ 08401, **609/345-7571.**

LAKE CHAMPLAIN DISCOVERY FESTIVAL

Burlington, VT

Started officially in 1983, this is one of the youngest major festivals in the United States. However, it schedules more than 50 events including a hot-air-balloon extravaganza, a jazz concert series, an international fishing derby, a film festival, a float parade of boats, and the Samuel de Champlain sailboat race. Cultural events include a day of Scottish activities featuring a bagpipe competition, and a Shakespeare festival with madrigal singers and renaissance dancers. Hotels, stores, restaurants, and tourist attractions in the area offer reduced rates during June. Held June—early July.

Lake Champlain Regional Chamber of Commerce, PO Box 453, Burlington, VT 05402, **802/973-3489.**

LEAGUE OF NEW HAMPSHIRE CRAFTSMEN FAIR

Mt. Sunapee State Park, Newbury, NH

"Getting to know a region's crafts is a good way to experience the spirit and personality of a region," says New Hampshire league director, Richard Fitzgerald. "At the fair, you can watch a blacksmith or chairmaker employing centuries-old craft techniques while you are introduced to the latest in computer weaving and ceramic sculpture." For half a century, spectators and craftsmen have come together in brightly covered tents to examine traditional and contemporary crafts' techniques at the oldest such fair in the nation. Recent additions include the Living With Crafts exhibit, featuring fine objects dramatically displayed in home and office settings, and the Gourmet Shop, featuring cookware and delicacies, and the League Shop of Sunapee, with fashion displays, accessories, and toys. Held early Aug.

League of NH Craftsmen, 205 N Main St, Concord, NH 03301, **603/224-3375.**

AMERICAN CRAFT COUNCIL CRAFTFAIR

West Springfield, MA

(See under San Francisco.)

KENTUCKY FRIED CHICKEN BLUEGRASS MUSIC FESTIVAL

Louisville, KY

For three days in mid-September, the main stage and workshop at Louisville's Riverfront Plaza come alive with entirely free performances of the music born in central Kentucky. Besides featuring performances by the best bluegrass bands, the festival also brings a half dozen or so emerging groups to the state. Scheduled workshops allow bluegrass fans to learn more about the styles and techniques adopted by players of the banjo, fiddle, mandolin, and guiter. Workshops also available in vocals and clog dancing. Held mid-Sept.

KFC Bluegrass Music Festival, PO Box 32070, Louisville, KY 40232, **502/456-8704.**

NAT'L. STORYTELLING FESTIVAL

Jonesborough, TN

Folktales, fairy tales, mountain tales, and tall tales are only part of the calendar at this festival. Staged in a two-century-old town beneath brightly colored circus tents, there are more than 50 nationally known storytellers (occasionally from foreign nations) ranging from Jewish housewives to Ph.D.'s. In addition to hearing and seeing first-rate yarnspinners share traditional tales, mime-stories, and ballads, spectators can test their own skills at the "Swappin' Ground." On Saturday night everyone walks down to the Old Jonesborough Cemetery for ghost stories around a crackling fire. This was the first festival in America devoted to storytelling, and today it remains the largest of its kind. Sponsored by the National Association for the Preservation and Perpetuation of Storytelling (NAPPS), it is held 1st full weekend in Oct. Primitive and improved camping available. No motel accommodations in Jonesborough (shuttle buses to nearby towns). Located 6 mi E of Johnson City off Hwy 11-E.

NAPPS, PO Box 112, Jonesborough, TN 37659, **615/753-2171.**

MEMPHIS IN MAY INT'L. FESTIVAL

Memphis, TN

During selected days in May, Memphis comes alive with festivities all spiced with the flavor of a chosen foreign country. Recent countries feted include Israel (1983), Mexico (1984), and Australia (1985). Events include river races on the Mississippi, ethnic shows, the famous International Barbecue Cooking Contest, the yearly wine waiter's race, and children's programs. A wide variety of musical concerts include classical performances by the Memphis Symphony, as well as traditional American music—especially folk and jazz. Memphis' Beale Street, regarded by many as the birthplace of the Blues, has recently been restored and rededicated. The Beale Street Music Festival, held in late May, brings some of the top names in Blues music to the area. A recent innovation was the triathlon, a race incorporating bicycling, swimming, and running.

Memphis in May Internat'l Festival, Inc, 12 S Mid-America Mall, Ste 1224, Memphis, TN 38103, **901/525-4611.**

SPOLETO U.S.A.

Charleston, SC

This internationally acclaimed event combines the talents of world masters with gifted young artists, and brings the public 2½ weeks of the world's most comprehensive performing arts festival including opera, ballet, modern dance, symphonic, choral and chamber music, theatre, jazz, and the visual arts. It was originated as a counterpart to the Festival of Two Worlds held in Spoleto, Italy, by Pulitzer prize-winning composer Gian Carlo Menotti. Most events charge admission, but the Piccolo Spoleto ("Little Spoleto") complements those activities with mostly free performances by local and regional artists. Staged in various community centers, churches, hospital wards, and schools in historic Charleston, both the regular festival and Piccolo bring quality productions to underprivileged citizens and minorities. There are 125-140 performances during the festival, and they represent traditional, contemporary, and experimental forms of art. Free sidewalk attractions. Held end May—early June.

Spoleto USA, PO Box 157, Charleston, SC 29402, **803/722-2764.**

HELEN OKTOBERFEST

Helen, GA

The Alpine flavor of this resort town sprang from the dreams of three businessmen and an artist who thought that the Georgia highlands were a perfect backdrop for a Bavarian village. Today, German restaurants, chalets, and colorful window boxes provide a perfect backdrop for the yearly Helen Oktoberfest. Festivities include a kick-off parade, six weeks of the best in oompah-pah music, German food, Bavarian beer, delicious wurst, polkas, and balloon rides. In past years, entertainment has included the popular Stratton Mountain Boys with their Alphorns, the Edelweiss Singers, and the Alpine Village Cloggers. Held 6 consecutive weekends from early Sept—mid-Oct.

Chamber of Commerce, PO Box 192, Helen, GA 30545, **404/878-2181.**

Chapter 5

HISTORIC LANDMARKS

The known history of the US may not stretch as far back as some of the venerable countries of Europe, Asia, or Africa, but the fierceness and genuine spirit of America's past has made this country the world leader it is today. From Valley Forge, where Washington endured the ravages of a bitter winter that threatened to break the will of our young country's fight for independence, to the Alamo and San Jacinto, where Texas tenacity gave birth to a stunning military victory from the ashes of a stirringly heroic loss—the history of our country has come to symbolize the best hopes and dreams of mankind.

It is not only through the pages of books that we come to know and understand the giants of the American story. These historic heroes also belong to the diverse and sprawling land they came to love: Jefferson's Monticello, Lincoln's midwest, and Teddy Roosevelt's North Dakota Badlands. Foresight and planning have preserved many important historical sites in the US, making it possible for generations yet unborn to see places that have become known as "backdrops to history." Stand where Lincoln gave his moving Gettysburg Address . . . and feel the anguish of the leader of a torn country. Step into Mark Twain's boyhood home . . . and visualize a mischievous Tom Sawyer sneaking out of the upstairs bedroom. Visit a ghost town in Nevada . . . and try to stay immune from the gold fever that built these instant towns. From coast-to-coast and border-to-border, America is at once a living land, and the world's largest history book; ready to be read and explored, experienced and enjoyed.

NORTHWEST

FORT LARAMIE NAT'L HISTORIC SITE

Fort Laramie, WY

Fort Laramie, on the eastern Wyoming prairies, was a private fur-trading post from 1834-1849, and a military post from 1849-1890. It was a welcome refuge for travelers during the covered-wagon migrations to Oregon and California in the mid-1800s. Ft. Laramie was also a central point in the Army's bloody fight against the Plains Indians. Ranchers and homesteaders moved into the area in the 1870s, and the fort was abandoned in 1890. For nearly 50 years it fell into decay, until the historic site became part of the national park system in 1938. Several of the buildings, including the post trader's store, the bakery, and "Old Bedlam,"—an officers quarters believed to be the oldest surviving Army structure in Wyoming—have been restored. Many others are in ruins, some with only their foundations visible. The site is now of far greater interest for its historical significance than for its scenic value. Open daily except Christmas and New Years 8am—4:30pm (7am—7pm mid-June—Lab Day). Located about 3 mi SW of the town of Fort Laramie on US 26.

Supt, Fort Laramie Nat'l Historic Site, Fort Laramie, WY 82212, **307/837-2221.**

JOHN DAY FOSSIL BEDS NAT'L MONUMENT

John Day, OR

John Day Fossil Beds offer you the next best thing to a time machine: a chance to use your imagination as you visit this display of our evolutionary past. A tour of this park takes you steadily backward in time, as you explore the fossilized vestiges of life preserved within the colorful and ancient formations. A major part of the record of the Age of Mammals—the last 60 million years—derives from this area. It is truly an archive of pre-historic life, and only a fraction of its treasures have been removed for study. The three major sites in the region are Sheep Rock, Painted Hills, and Clarno. Each site features striking rock formations running the gamut of colors from red to green to gold, and numerous easily observable fossils. However, the park prohibits individual digging or removal of fossils or rocks. Park headquarters, in the city of John Day near the intersection of US 26 and US 395, contains a display of fossil replicas identical to those found in the park, as well as orientation literature, and other publications. No camping, lodging, or food facilities within the park.

John Day Fossil Beds Nat'l Monument, 420 W Main, John Day, OR 97845, **503/575-0721.**

FORT CLATSOP NAT'L MEMORIAL

Astoria, OR

"Great joy . . . we are in view of the ocean, which we have been so long anxious to see . . . the roaring made by the waves breaking on the rocky shores may be heard distinctly." So wrote famed explorers Meriwether Lewis and William Clark in their journal the winter of 1805-6. That season they established Fort Clatsop in northern Oregon— near the end of their trail-blazing journey from the Missouri River to the Pacific Ocean. During their three-month stay at the fort (named for the area's friendly Indian tribe), Lewis and Clark reworked their journals, and prepared significant maps of the areas they had visited. They left the fort in March 1806, and began their arduous, yet triumphant trek home. 150 years later, the fort was rebuilt by local citizens according to notes and plans by Clark. Other than the reconstructed fort itself, the main attraction of the monument is the Fort Clatsop Living History Program, which runs each summer. The program features demonstrations of frontier activities that were part of everyday life for the Lewis and Clark expeditioners. Colorfully-costumed park staffers step back into history to show visitors how candles, clothes, and other necessities were made in the early 1800s. Another fascinating demonstration is the building of an Indian-style canoe of the type used by the expedition. Park rangers, as costumed frontiersmen, add an authentic ambience to the fort, and are always ready to answer a visitor's question or share an amusing anecdote about life at Fort Clatsop. Open all year, every day, 8am—5pm (8am—8pm during summer). Located 4 mi S of Astoria (90 mi W of Portland).

Fort Clatsop Nat'l Memorial, Rte 3, Box 604-FC, Astoria, OR 97103, **503/861-2471.**

CUSTER BATTLEFIELD NAT'L MONUMENT

Little Bighorn Valley, MT

On June 25, 1876, Lt. Col. George Armstrong Custer, vastly underestimating the thousands of Sioux and Cheyenne warriors camped along the Little Bighorn River, led 260 soldiers to their massacre and a place in history as one of the most unforgettable disasters in American military history. Soon after the infamous Battle of the Little Bighorn, the battlefield became a popular tourist attraction, especially for those traveling the newly constructed Northern Pacific Railway. In 1893 the War Department began placing a series of retired soldiers in charge of protecting the area from souvenir hunters until much of the land, including the cemetery, was transferred to the National Park Service, in 1940. The Visitor Center in the northern extreme of the park has an informed staff to help guests plan tours, and a Custer museum display ranging from the regimental flag carried that fateful day to letters exchanged by Custer and his wife. Points of interest include: Custer Hill, where most of Custer's men were reburied at the base of a memorial shaft; the National Cemetery, where soldiers from many different wars are buried; and various battle sites. A one-hour guided bus tour over the battlefield and other points of interest (including the actual "Last Stand" area) is available for $1; children 50 cents. Located within the Crow Indian Reservation off US 212 about 15 mi S of Hardin. No picnic or camping facilities.

Custer Battlefield Nat'l Monument, PO Box 39, Crow Agency, MT 59034, **406/638-2622.**

Fort Clatsop National Memorial, Astoria, OR.

Covered Bridge, VT

SOUTHWEST

GENEALOGICAL LIBRARY
GHOST TOWNS
UT
CO
NV
SAN JOSE HISTORICAL MUSEUM
LOST CITY MUSEUM
PECOS NAT'L MONUMENT
OLD JEROME
CA
AZ
NM

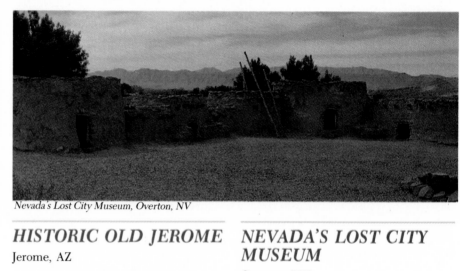

Nevada's Lost City Museum, Overton, NV

SAN JOSE HISTORICAL MUSEUM

San Jose, CA

This unique outdoor museum offers a view of San Jose much as it appeared near the end of the 19th century. Highlights include a 115-foot replica of an electric light tower that was to light the entire city in the 1900s, the ornate Victorian-era Umbarger House, a blacksmith shop at Dashaway Stables, the original Bank of Italy (forerunner to the Bank of America), comprehensive historical exhibits in the elegant Pacific Hotel, the Coyote Post Office, the Empire Firehouse, and various stores and offices. Visitors feel as if they've stepped into a page of California's history, as the sights and sound of a long-lost era return to life. From the south end of Kelley Park, visitors to the museum can ride the small-scale reproduction of the South Pacific Coast Railroad to other San Jose sights, such as the Japanese Friendship Garden. The museum is open 10am—4:30pm, Tue—Fri, and noon—4:30pm weekends. Admission: $1. Tours of the mentioned historic buildings are also included.

San Jose Historical Museum, 635 Phelan Ave, San Jose, CA 95112, **408/287-2290.**

HISTORIC OLD JEROME

Jerome, AZ

Jerome was once a roaring mining town with a population of 15,000 which produced a billion dollars worth of copper, silver, zinc, and gold between 1885 and 1953. Once the last mine was closed, a mass exodus of the settled workers ensued. Although the population is now just a few hundred, some of the old structures in the boom town have been restored. Highlights include the Jerome Mine Museum on Main Street (housed in an 1899 saloon), the 19th century Catholic Church, and the Douglas Museum in Jerome State Historical Park. The Gold King Mine, which visitors can enter ($1), is a mile north of town on Perkinsville Road. The most famous sight in Jerome is the "Traveling Jail," which has slid downhill some 200 ft from the spot on which it was built. The entire town was built on the steep slopes of Cleopatra Hill, and is gradually slipping down its face. Lodging in the town is extremely limited, but is available in nearby Cottonwood or Prescott.

Jerome State Historic Park, Jerome, AZ 85331, **602/634-5381.**

NEVADA'S LOST CITY MUSEUM

Overton, NV

Around AD 800, in the Moapa Valley of southeast Nevada, scores of Pueblo Indian villages stretched along the banks of a muddy river on a site that today is near a finger of man-made Lake Mead. The story of the Pueblo Grande de Nevada, or Lost City, is preserved at the Lost City Museum, 60 mi northeast of Las Vegas. On the museum grounds several pueblo-type houses of wattle and daub have been reconstructed on their original foundations. The Puebloans left the valley around AD 1150, never to return, but they left behind ruins extending for miles along the valley, ripe for excavation. Museum displays date back as far as 10,000 years, and include one of the Southwest's most extensive Pueblo collections, as well as artifacts left by Mormon settlers. Open daily 8:30am—4:30 pm.

Lost City Museum, Box 807, Overton, NV 89040, **702/397-8088.**

GHOST TOWNS

Virginia City and other locations, NV

The lure of gold and silver brought thousands of prospectors to the west in the mid-1800s, and fabulous finds such as the Comstock Lode turned places such as Virginia City (see Ethnic and Historic Villages) and Carson City into overnight boom towns. But when the tide of riches and miners went out, these "instant towns" were left high and dry. Virginia City, particularly, is full of the kind of rags-to-riches lore that made the gold rush famous. For a good overview, see the free movie, "Story of Virginia City," which runs continuously at the Visitor's Bureau on C Street, near the historic Courthouse. A few of Nevada's many other ghost towns are: Fort Churchill—34 mi NE of Carson City via US 50 and NV 2B. This was the site of Nevada's first military post, and its gaunt, weathered adobe buildings remain. Rhyolite—4 mi W of Beatty on NV 374, and a marked gravel road. Rhyolite is home to a famous house made of bottles during the 1907 boom, and restored by a movie company in 1920. Franktown—12 mi N of Carson City on US 395, and a marked road. This deserted locality was once a Mormon settlement and the second largest community in the state. Dozens of other Nevada ghost towns may be explored with help from tourist bureaus and Chambers of Commerce in the state.

Nevada Commission on Economic Dev, Carson City, NV 89710, **702/885-4322.**

Pecos National Monument, Pecos, NM

GENEALOGICAL LIBRARY OF THE MORMON CHURCH

Salt Lake City, UT

If you have a burning desire to pinpoint exactly when your great-great-grandfather O'Malley came to the US from County Cork, or if you wonder whatever happened to your great Aunt Cecily's branch of the family, this haven of roots research can be of considerable help. In a recent year, nearly one million people spent untold hours tracing their family histories in the enormous facilities of the Library's modern 28-story building in downtown Salt Lake City. Here, more than one billion names of people who have lived all over the world are available to amateur and professional researchers, who enthusiastically dig into 160,000 bound volumes and 1,250,000 rolls of microfilm (equal to 5,500,000 bound volumes). Records and facilities are open to the public without charge, and beginners at the Library can get acquainted with the massive stacks by taking a guided tour hosted by volunteers. The tour takes visitors to atlases, geographies, family histories, reference books, and census indexes, as well as to the catalog index of microfilm rolls and books. Open Mon, 7:30am—6pm, Tue—Fri, 7:30am—10pm, and Sat, 7:30am—5pm. Closed Sun and hols. Adjacent to Temple Square.

Genealogical Library of the Church of Jesus Christ of Latter-day Saints, 50 E North Temple, Salt Lake City, UT 84150, **801/531-2331.**

PECOS NAT'L MONUMENT

Pecos, NM

"The houses in this pueblo are in the manner of house-blocks. They have doors to the outside all around, and the houses are back-to-back. The houses are four and five stories, and every house has three or four apartments on each story, so that from top to bottom each house has 15 or 16 rooms." This is how Spaniard Gaspar Castano de Sosa, a 16th century visitor to northern New Mexico, described the pueblos of the Pecos Indians near the Pecos River. The village was settled about 1100, and the pueblos were constructed in the mid-15th century. Epidemics and tribal warfare in the 18th century nearly annihilated the people of the pueblo. In 1838, the remaining 17 inhabitants abandoned their Pecos homes to move westward to Jemez, leaving the pueblos deserted. Excavation and exploration of the site began 75 years later, and the Pecos Nat'l Monument was created in 1965. Since then, visitors and professional archeologists alike have shared the beauty and history of the Pecos Pueblo ruins. A ¾-mile self-guiding trail, starting at the Visitor Center, allows visitors to walk past the ruins; guided tours are also available. On weekends, Mem Day—Lab Day, various Hispanic and Indian craftspeople demonstrate traditional Southwest baking and artwork. Camping available in the Pecos Wilderness area north of the town of Pecos. Monument hours: 8am—6pm summer, off-season 8am—4:30pm. Located 25 mi SW of Santa Fe off I-25.

Supt, Pecos Nat'l Monument, PO Drawer 11, Pecos, NM 87552, **505/757-6414.**

MIDWEST

THEODORE ROOSEVELT NAT'L PARK

Near Watford City and Medora, ND

Although not as famous as the Badlands of South Dakota, North Dakota's badlands have some magnificent vistas—and fascinating history. During the 1880s, Theodore Roosevelt owned a number of major cattle ranches in this area, and it was his love of the land here that shaped his philosophy of practical conservation that helped preserve and expand our country's national park and monument system. The badlands straddle the final 200 miles of the Little Missouri River, and it was this river's moving water that cut fantastic shapes into the ancient high plains of this territory. The park's South Unit features the restored Maltese Cross Cabin, used by Roosevelt during his visits, as well as a number of scenic points, and a petrified forest. The North Unit is mostly of interest for its fine scenery and wildlife, including herds of lumbering buffalo, soaring hawks and eagles, and several prairie-dog towns. Between the two units is the site of Roosevelt's Elkhorn Ranch, a visit to which requires obtaining prior permission from the park superintendent's office. No buildings remain where the ranch once stood, and intrepid travelers must ford the Little Missouri River to reach the site. The nearby town of Medora appears much as it did when the Marquis DeMores founded it and named it for his wife in the 1880s. Of special interest is the Chateau DeMores, a 26-room frame structure built in 1884 for the Marquis and his wife and furnished in a grand European style. Guided tours available.

Supt, Theodore Roosevelt Nat'l Park, Medora, ND 58645, **701/623-4466.**

LINCOLN'S HOME

Springfield, IL

Springfield is so filled with the presence of Abraham Lincoln that you almost expect to see the stoic countenance and lanky build of our 16th president as you turn each corner. Lincoln lived and worked in Illinois' capital city for 25 years, leaving when he was elected president in 1860 of a swiftly dividing country. But the personal effects remaining in his former home, and the disarray of legal papers on his office desk seem to indicate that Big Abe left only yesterday. On a lot at the corner of 8th and Jackson Streets is the only home Lincoln ever owned. Bought from the minister who married him to Mary Todd in 1842, it was here that three of Lincoln's sons were born, and—after a two-month illness—one of them died. The furnishings are authentic period pieces, including many that belonged to the Lincoln family. The Visitor Center has other Lincoln exhibits, a bookstore, and a film on the great man's life. Open daily 8am—5pm; closed New Years Day and Christmas. Other Springfield Lincoln areas include his office in the building where he practiced law for ten years (6th & Adams Sts, 217/523-1010), his majestic tomb at the base of a 117-foot spire in Oak Ridge Cemetery (217/782-2717), and the Lincoln Depot where he gave his famous farewell address in 1861 before journeying to Washington and his place in history (10th & Monroe Sts, 217/785-3865).

Lincoln Home Nat'l Historic Site, 426 S 7th St, Springfield, IL 62703, **217/492-4241.**

Theodore Roosevelt National Park, Near Watford City and Medora, ND

Photo: National Park Service

LINCOLN BOYHOOD NAT'L MEMORIAL

Lincoln City, IN

The Lincoln family moved to this pleasant farm of rolling hills in the Indiana forests when Abraham was seven years old. When, in 1830, the family moved west, he was 21 years old, and ready to begin his historic public life. The memorial building on the grounds contains a small museum devoted to Lincoln memorabilia, and an auditorium where motion pictures and slide shows on his life are presented. Outside the building, graveled walks lead to the Thomas Lincoln Farm, the Lincoln Cabin Site Memorial, and the Lincoln Living Historical Farm, where the land is planted and farmed in the same way Lincoln and his family tended it more than 150 years ago. The path continues through lovely fields and woodlands. Open daily. Located S of Lincoln City on IN 162.

Supt, Lincoln Boyhood Nat'l Memorial, Lincoln City, IN 47552, **812/937-4757.**

George Rogers Clark Park, Vincennes, IN

Photo: Dennis Latta

GEORGE ROGERS CLARK NAT'L HISTORICAL PARK

Vincennes, IN

During the American Revolution, George Rogers Clark led a detachment of soldiers into Indiana to capture Fort Sackville at Vincennes to mark the beginning of the end of British dominance in the Old Northwest. The victory at Fort Sackville foiled British attempts to keep Americans out of the region north of the Ohio and west of the Appalachians, and set the stage for further American exploration westward. The George Rogers Clark Memorial on the site of old Fort Sackville, is a grand, Greek-style building encircled by 16 massive pillars. A bronze statue of Clark stands in the center of the rotunda, surrounded by large murals depicting important facets of Clark's campaign. The memorial was dedicated by Franklin Roosevelt in 1936. In summer, the "Trailblazer Train" operated by Vincennes University leaves from the old Territorial Capitol Building for 40-min guided tours of the Vincennes area (812/885-4339). Open daily. Free admission.

George Rogers Clark Nat'l Historical Park, 401 S 2nd Ave, Vincennes, IN 47591, **812/882-1776.**

SOUTH CENTRAL

MARK TWAIN BOYHOOD HOME

Hannibal, MO

Hannibal has been described as "the world's most famous small town" and as "everybody's hometown." Parts of the town will certainly seem familiar to visitors who have read works by Hannibal's most famous son, Samuel Clemens, better known by his pen name of Mark Twain (taken from the Mississippi riverboat call to indicate two fathoms—12 ft—of depth in the water ahead). The main attraction in town is Twain's boyhood home, a modest white clapboard house built by his father, Judge John Clemens, and inhabited by the Clemens family from 1844-1853. The home was presented to the city of Hannibal in 1911, and now includes a museum of Twain memorabilia. Hannibal is filled with other sites of importance in Mark Twain's early life. Grant's Drug Store, built in the 1830s, was once occupied by the Clemens family. The cave that was the inspiration for the cave where Tom and Becky were lost, and Tom and Huck found the robbers' ill-gotten gold is now appropriately called the Mark Twain Cave (314/221-1656), and is 1 mi S of town on MO 79. The Becky Thatcher Bookshop (314/221-0822) at 211 Hill St was, in the 1840s, the home of Laura Hawkins, real-life model for Becky Thatcher. National Tom Sawyer Days (see Fun at Festivals), held each year the week before the Fourth of July, is a good time to visit.

Tourism Commission, 308 N Main, PO Box 624, Hannibal, MO 63401, **314/221-2477.**

VICKSBURG NAT'L MILITARY PARK

Vicksburg, MS

General U.S. Grant's eventual victory during the protracted campaign around Vicksburg 1862-63 succeeded in bringing the Mississippi River into Union control and dividing the Confederacy to the east and west of its shores. The battle concluded with Grant's troops surrounding the city for six weeks, bombarding the Confederates and cutting off their lines of supply and communication. One of the most fascinating exhibits at this military park is the remains of the Union ironclad gunboat *Cairo*, which sank in the Yazoo River north of Vicksburg. The *Cairo* was steaming up the river early in the campaign to destroy Confederate batteries and clear enemy obstructions from the channel, when two explosions tore gaping holes in the boat's bottom. The *Cairo* became the first vessel in history to be sunk by an electrically detonated mine. The USS Cairo Museum displays artifacts from the boat, and is adjacent to Vicksburg National Cemetery. A visitor center, located at the park entrance on Clay Street (US 80) has maps of the battlefield engagements. Both the visitor center and the USS Cairo Museum are open daily except Christmas.

Supt, Vicksburg Nat'l Military Park, 3201 Clay St, Vicksburg, MS 39180, **601/636-0583.**

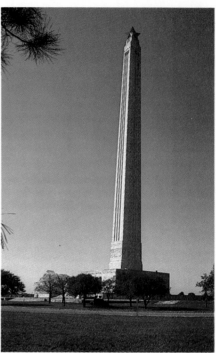

San Jacinto Battleground, La Porte, TX

SAN JACINTO BATTLEGROUND

La Porte, TX (Near Houston)

Where in the Lone Star state can you find a 35-foot high, 220-ton lone star? Appropriately, it's located at the site of one of the state's sweetest moments in history—it sits atop the San Jacinto Monument, towering 570 feet above the historic San Jacinto Battleground. It was here, on April 21, 1836, that General Sam Houston led 927 Texans against more than 1300 surprised Mexican troops, defeating them in 18 minutes. The next day, Mexican dictator Santa Anna was captured, and surrendered to Houston. With this battle, Texas won its independence from Mexico, and became a US state 10 years later. The Battleground Museum is located in the base of the Monument, which is the tallest masonry monument in the world (15 feet taller than the Washington Monument). The museum commemorates Texas' past from its days as a foreign possession to the early years of US statehood. Open daily 10am—6pm except Dec 24 and 25. Admission is free, but elevator rides to the top of the towering monument cost $1.50/adults, 50 cents/children. The battleship *USS Texas* is moored near the park, and can be visited for a small fee. The battleground is located 21 mi from downtown Houston off TX 225.

San Jacinto Battleground Museum, 3800 Park Rd 1836, La Porte, TX 77571, **713/479-2421.**

THE ALAMO

San Antonio, TX

This impressive two-story stone structure, originally a Spanish mission, will be known forever as "The Cradle of Texas Liberty." It was here, during Texas' struggle for independence from Mexico, that Davy Crockett, Jim Bowie, and 186 other heroic defenders held off Santa Anna and his 5000 troops during a 10-day Mexican siege. On March 6, 1836, columns of Mexican soldiers attacked the fortress from all sides. Twice repulsed by the defenders' musket and cannon fire, they concentrated their third and final attack on the weakened north wall. They finally broke through the Texans' lines and massacred all of the valiant freedom fighters, sparing only a few women and children. Santa Anna's army had sustained nearly 1600 casualties, or almost nine Mexicans for every Texan felled in the historic battle. "Remember the Alamo!" became the rallying cry of the Texans who defeated Santa Anna at San Jacinto (see) 46 days later, to win Texas its long-sought independence. The Long Barrack Museum at the site contains artifacts of Texas' history under six flags (France, Spain, Mexico, the Republic of Texas, the Confederate States, and the US), and shows film and slide shows about the state and the brave battle. The grounds are also home to an extensive research library and a souvenir and book shop. The site is open daily, 9am—5:30pm, except Dec 24, 25.

Convention & Visitors Bureau, PO Box 2277, San Antonio, TX 78298, 512/299-8123.

NORTHEAST

MINUTE MAN NAT'L HISTORICAL PARK

Concord, MA

The area surrounding this town and nearby Lexington can be truly called the birthplace of our country's independence. It was here that the first shot—the "shot heard 'round the world"—of the Revolutionary War was fired, as British redcoats clashed with members of the Lexington militia. The fire of freedom quickly spread to the southern and middle colonies, and a unified struggle emerged to march the colonies towards a united and independent future. Visitor centers along MA 2A (the "Battle Road" along which the redcoats marched to Concord and back to Boston) explain the events and significance of the minutemen and the Lexington/Concord area. Henry David Thoreau's famous Walden Pond, and the one-time home of Ralph Waldo Emerson are both south of the Battle Road in Concord. While the area surrounding MA 2A is rich in history, and ripe for sightseeing, it is also a heavily traveled state road. Park officials ask that you not cause traffic problems by slowing down to sightsee along this road; parking is available to explore the area by foot.

Supt, Minute Man Nat'l Historical Park, Box 160, Concord, MA 01742, 617/369-6993.

SALEM MARITIME NAT'L HISTORIC SITE

Salem, MA

In 1790 Salem was the 6th largest city in the US, and her port was one of the most bustling. On any day a dozen vessels—schooners, brigs, frigates—may have been seen entering or leaving the port. For many years, Derby Wharf, part of which was built in 1764, was the busiest section, and during the intervening years many additions were made as the wharf stretched half a mile out into Salem Harbor. Salem's importance as a port peaked around the War of 1812, and then steadily declined. Now Salem is a quiet community of charmingly preserved landmarks. Along Derby Street are a number of historic buildings, including Derby House, the oldest brick building in Salem (constructed in 1762); the Custom House, built in 1819; and the West India Goods Store built in the early 1800s. The area has been carefully maintained to appear much as it did more than 150 years ago. The National Historic site is centered on Derby St in Salem, about 20 mi NE of Boston. Special arrangements can be made for groups.

Supt, Salem Maritime Nat'l Historic Site, Custom House, Derby St, Salem, MA 01970, 617/744-4323.

The Alamo, San Antonio, TX

Covered Bridge, Woodstock, VT

VERMONT COVERED BRIDGES

Various Locations in VT

For many, the covered bridges scattered throughout Vermont are among the world's most scenic attractions. At last count, the state could boast of 114 such structures, a veritable cornucopia for the covered-bridge enthusiast. The superstructures of the bridges have a specific function as well as an undeniable rustic charm; the coverings help protect and preserve the wooden trusses that support the bridge. Covered bridges are scattered fairly evenly in valleys throughout the state, but particularly high concentrations can be found in the counties of Lamoille, Franklin, Orange, Rutland, Washington, Windham, and Windsor. For a superb brochure pinpointing the location of every bridge, write to the address below ("Vermont's Covered Bridges," by Neal G. Templeton).

Agency of Dev & Community Affairs, Montpelier, VT 05602, **802/828-3236.**

CASTINE HARBOR

Castine, ME

By 1667, when Baron de St. Castin arrived in the town that would eventually bear his name, Castine had already been settled for more than 50 years under such names as Majabigwaduce and Pentagoet. This Maine coastal town, boasting one of the deepest harbors on the eastern seaboard, was held successively by the English, the Dutch, the French, and the English again. It was not until after the War of 1812 that the US took possession of the town. The area around Castine Harbor is packed with historic buildings from the 18th and 19th centuries, some fully restored and open to visitors. Castine can also boast of two museums, a 9-hole golf course which is among the nation's oldest, and the Maine Maritime Academy, which offers a number of free attractions, such as *The State of Maine* training ship (open for tours from July—Apr), tours of the academy itself, and the Maritime Heritage Museum (207/326-4311).

Castine Historical Society, Box 238, Castine, ME 04421, **207/326-4639.**

FORT NECESSITY NAT'L BATTLEFIELD

Farmington, PA

In the summer of 1754, a newly-commissioned, 22-year-old Colonel led a group of English colonists against French soldiers in the opening battle for control of the North American continent at Fort Necessity. It was Colonel George Washington's first major military battle, and was the only time he would be forced to surrender to an enemy. In an example of historical irony to make any capitalist proud, the Father of our Country later came to own the land upon which he fought—and lost—his first battle. Other areas of interest on the battlefield are Jumonville Glen, site of an early skirmish in the war; Braddock's Grave, the last resting place of British Commander Edward Braddock, killed during the Battle of Mohongahela; and Mount Washington Tavern, a stagecoach inn that served travelers on the National Road in the early 19th century. Open daily, admission free. Located 11 mi E of Uniontown on US 40.

Fort Necessity Nat'l Battlefield, The Nat'l Pike, RD 2, Box 528, Farmington, PA 15437, **412/329-5512.**

GETTYSBURG NAT'L MILITARY PARK

Gettysburg, PA

In July, 1863, more men died on a series of formerly peaceful fields in Pennsylvania than had fallen in any other battle fought in North America before or since. On July 1, General George G. Meade's Union forces met General Robert E. Lee's surging Confederate troops at Gettysburg. For the next three days, the battle raged as more than 50,000 soldiers from both sides fell in defense of their separate ideals. When Lee's men were repulsed finally and decisively on July 3, they staggered back into Virginia, never again to reach as far north and never again to launch an offensive operation of such magnitude. Four months later the Gettysburg National Cemetery was dedicated to the memory of the men who battled there, and President Abraham Lincoln was invited to add "a few appropriate remarks." His 272-word speech lasted a mere two minutes, but history remembers the Gettysburg Address as a masterpiece of spoken eloquence, defining what America stands for and what the Union Army was valiantly fighting for. The battlefield where history was forged may be toured by car or on foot, and many memorials and historic battle sites dot the suggested tour route. Maps for self-guided tours are available at the Visitor Center, and licensed guides conduct two-hour tours ($12/car, $25/bus). The Visitor Center contains an extensive collection of Civil War artifacts as well as the enormous Electric Map, which gives a narrated skirmish-by-skirmish view of the historic 1863 battle (exhibits are free, but adult admission to the Electric Map is $1.50). At the Cyclorama Center, visitors stand in the middle of a 356' X 26' cylindrical painting of the climactic battle, as a sound and light program recreates highlights of the fighting (admission: $1). The Gettysburg National Cemetery, site of Lincoln's stirring speech, is adjacent to the battlefield. In the Cemetery is the Lincoln Speech Memorial—the only known monument to a speech—and the Soldiers' National Monument to veterans of our nation's wars.

Supt, Gettysburg Nat'l Military Park, Gettysburg, PA 17325, **717/334-1124.**

Fort Necessity National Battlefield, Farmington, PA

Valley Forge National Historical Park, Valley Forge, PA

DOVER HERITAGE TRAIL

Dover, DE

The town of Dover was planned by William Penn in 1683, a year after his arrival in America, and formally laid out in 1717. During the early 1700s, major construction efforts were made in the town. Succeeding years witnessed the construction of many fine homes and buildings, many of which can still be seen (and sometimes visited) by walking the well-planned Dover Heritage Trail. First stop should be the visitor center in the Margaret O'Neill Building on Federal Street fronting Capitol Square maps and other info about historic structures and events. Highlights include documents in the Hall of Records dating back to 1683; Christ Church, constructed between 1734 and 1747; Richard Bassett House, built in the early 1700s and once owned by a signer of the Declaration of Independence; and Ridgely House, built in 1728.

State Travel Office, 99 Kings Hwy, PO Box 1401, Dover, DE 19903, **800/441-8846** *(outside DE),* **800/282-8667** *(within DE).*

VALLEY FORGE NAT'L HISTORICAL PARK

Valley Forge, PA

If the hardiness and soul of the US was ever tested, it was during the harsh winter of 1777-78 when George Washington and his rag-tag army camped at Valley Forge during their fight for independence from England. The irregular, but dedicated soldiers endured the hardships of lack of food and equipment, and rallied around Washington's decisive leadership to eventually repel their distant oppressors. The home of Isaac Potts, which was Washington's headquarters during the challenging winter, has been beautifully preserved and is just one of the highlights in the national memorial at Valley Forge operated by the National Park Service. Another beautifully restored home is that of the Stephens family, overlooking the field used as the parade ground during the encampment, and used as headquarters by Rhode Island's General James Varnum. Reconstructions of huts built by soldiers, cannons placed in their original positions, and many other revolutionary exhibits can also be found. The Visitor Center located at the junction of PA 23 and PA 363 has various historic exhibits, a slide and film show, interpretive guides, and general info available. Free admission. Open daily 8:30am—5pm except Christmas. I-276 and I-76, US 202, and PA 23 and PA 363 allow easy access to the park.

Supt, Valley Forge Nat'l Park, Valley Forge, PA 19481, **215/783-7700.**

THE WHITE HOUSE

Washington, DC

The cornerstone of the White House was laid October 13, 1792, on a site selected by George Washington, and the first president to occupy it was John Adams in November 1800. Burned by the British in 1814, it was rebuilt and reoccupied by James Monroe in 1817. Over many years, alterations weakened the frame and extensive reconstruction was made between 1948 and 1950. In recent years, the appearance of the site has been changed dramatically by anti-terrorist devices installed during the Reagan Administration. Although the second and third floors—reserved for the Presidential family and guests—are closed to the public, many beautiful and historic rooms are included on the tour. Visitors can see the famous East Room, used for state balls and press conferences; the State Dining Room, with oak paneling installed by Teddy Roosevelt in 1902; and the 2700-volume presidential library. The White House is open to visitors 10am—noon, Tue—Sat. Visitors with physical handicaps may obtain wheel chairs at the NE Gate.

The White House, Washington, DC, **202/456-7041.**

FORT WASHINGTON

Washington, DC

Every Sunday afternoon at Fort Washington, soldiers in Union gray and Confederate blue uniforms meet, but not on a field of combat. These costumed troops present demonstrations of period military life weekly for visitors to this Washington, DC landmark. Built on the site of the first fortification created to defend Washington—Fort Warburton, which was destroyed on August 27, 1814—Fort Washington was completed in 1824, and has been altered little since. Its high masonry walls, gun positions, dry moat, and drawbridge are good examples of typical American coastal defense installations in the early 19th century. Fort Washington was abandoned in 1872, although the site was used sporadically in the years that followed for various defense purposes. In 1946, the area was included in the national park system, and opened to visitors. The park is open daily 7:30am—dark, although the fort may close slightly earlier. On the Maryland side of the Potomac, the site can be reached by crossing the South Capitol Street Bridge and driving south on I-295 and east on I-495. Turn right onto Indian Head Hwy (MD 210) and again right onto Fort Washington Rd.

Fort Washington, Nat'l Capital Parks-East, 1900 Anacostia Dr, SE, Washington, DC 20020, **301/292-2112.**

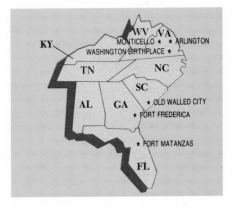

ARLINGTON NAT'L CEMETERY

Arlington, VA

Since its purchase by the federal government in 1883, Arlington National Cemetery has become a cherished national shrine commemorating the lives of many outstanding Americans who served in the armed forces. Among the interred are Presidents John F. Kennedy and William Taft, Robert Kennedy, Robert E. Peary, Oliver Wendell Holmes, Virgil Grissom, and, of course, the remains of unknown soldiers from American wars, including the conflict in Vietnam. Shrines and memorials include the Confederate Monument to the South's Civil War dead; the Maine Memorial, honoring those who lost their lives when the USS Maine was sunk, and the Tomb of the Unknowns itself. Permission to drive into the cemetery is only given to those with relatives or friends interred in the grounds. Sightseers must use pedestrian walks or take guided tours aboard official Tourmobile buses ($2; children $1; tickets at the Arlington Cemetery Ticket Booth). The cemetery is open 8am—7pm Apr—Sept, 8am—5pm Oct—Mar.

Supt, Arlington Nat'l Cemetery, Arlington, VA 22211, **703/557-0613.**

MONTICELLO

Charlottesville, VA

''All my wishes end where I hope my days will end . . . at Monticello.'' This was the wish of the author of the Declaration of Independence, the third president of the US, and the self-taught architect of the grand house Monticello: Thomas Jefferson. Jefferson began work on his labor of love in 1768 and did not consider it completed until he finished the final remodeling in 1809. He oversaw every aspect of the furnishing of his house, and nearly all of the furniture and ornamental objects at Monticello today were owned by Jefferson or his family. Jefferson equipped his home with a variety of gadgets—such items as the seven-day calendar clock in the entrance hall, the double glass doors in the parlor that both automatically open when either one is pushed, and the dumbwaiter and revolving serving door in the dining room, indicate his love of mechanical ingenuity. His days did indeed end at Monticello; he died there on July 4, 1826, and is buried in the family cemetery on the grounds. Guided tours of the house and its original decorations and furnishings are led daily Mar—Oct, 8am—5pm; Nov—Feb, 9am-4:30pm; closed Christmas. Located 3 mi SE of Charlottesville on VA 53.

Monticello, Box 316, Charlottesville, VA 22902, **804/ 295-8181.**

Monticello, Charlottesville, VA

GEORGE WASHINGTON BIRTHPLACE NAT'L MONUMENT

Westmoreland County, VA

George Washington not only *did* sleep here—he spent his very first night here. The first US president was born on his father's Popes Creek tobacco farm on February 22, 1732, and lived there until he was three years old and again for several years in his teens. Today, a Memorial House stands near the site of the original home, which burned down in 1779. Here, the National Park Service operates a colonial farm, recreating the sights, sounds, and smells of 18th-century plantation life. Furnishings in the house and kitchen, gardens of flowers and herbs, the crops in the fields, and the livestock are of types which help recall Washington's childhood days. Open daily 9am—5pm except Christmas and New Years. Free admission. Located on Popes Creek off the Potomac River 38 mi E of Fredericksburg, which can be reached via VA 3 and VA 204.

George Washington's Birthplace Nat'l Monument, Washington's Birthplace, VA 22575, **804/224-0196.**

OLD WALLED CITY

Charleston, SC

The aristocratic city of Charleston has some of the loveliest gardens and historic homes in the south, some dating all the way back to the 17th century. Perhaps the most glittering facet of this jewel of a city is the area known as the Old Walled City. This is a two-block by four-block quadrangle that was once enclosed in the manner of a European fortress-city. None of the walls remain, but many lovingly preserved and restored buildings stand in testimony to the area now known as a ''living museum.'' Although some buildings are private residences, and

closed to the public, a number of colorful and important sites are open to visitors. These include the first fire-proof building erected in the US, built in 1822; the City Hall, once a branch of the First Bank of the US, built in 1801; and the famous one-time slum of ''Catfish Row,'' the inspiration for Dubose Heyward's novel *Porgy,* and later, George Gershwin's *Porgy and Bess.* A horse- or mule-drawn carriage is a splendidly leisurely way to experience the blooming gardens and ornate buildings of the old Walled City and the rest of Charleston. A visitor information center at 85 Calhoun St is open daily from 8:30am—5pm.

Chamber of Commerce, PO Box 975, Charleston, SC 29402, **803/722-8338.**

FORT FREDERICA NAT'L MONUMENT

St. Simons Island, GA

When the mist from the Frederica River floats in over the crumbling walls that remain of Fort Frederica, you can almost picture how it stood in 1739, defending its town from Spanish forces. Established on St. Simons Island (see Island Escapes) in 1736, the fortified settlement of Frederica became General James Oglethorpe's military headquarters for operations against the Spanish in Florida during the Anglo-Spanish conflict of 1739-1748. At one point, the town contained a population of nearly 1500, and was the largest and probably most expensive British fortification in North America. In 1758, a fire destroyed most of Frederica's buildings, driving away all but a few soldiers. Five years later, Frederica was a virtual ghost town. In the 1950s the National Park Service excavated the site of the fort, and exposed the ruins of houses, streets, and the battlements of the fort itself. Self-guided tours may be taken of the ruins of both the town and the fort. A visitor center has numerous exhibits of fort artifacts and interpretive demonstrations of 18th century life. Open daily 9am—5pm (later during summer). Located 12 mi E of Brunswick on St Simons Island.

Supt, Fort Frederica Nat'l Monument, Rte 4, Box 286-C, St Simons Island, GA 31522, **912/638-3639.**

FORT MATANZAS NAT'L MONUMENT

St. Augustine, FL

The Spanish built this small stone fort in the early 1740s, before the level of the Matanzas River lowered, to control Matanzas Inlet—known as the ''back door'' to St. Augustine—from British attack. Although Rattlesnake Island, on which the tower was built, is more than 200 acres today, in the 1740s there was only two acres of dry land on which to build the fort. No battles were fought here, and the US eventually obtained the area through treaties, but never used the fort as a military station. Although extensive restoration of the fort has been made in modern times, most of the stonework is original. Accessible only by boat, the Park Service operates a free ferry capable of transporting 11 people at a time daily from 9am—4:30pm. For safety reasons, only a limited number of people can visit the small monument at any one time. The fort can be reached via FL A1A on Anastasia Island. Free admission. North of the Fort is St. Augustine itself, America's oldest city (see Ethnic & Historic Villages).

Supt, Fort Matanzas Nat'l Monument, 1 Castillo Dr, St Augustine, FL 32084, **904/471-0116.**

Chapter 6
THEME & AMUSEMENT PARKS

They used to be called amusement parks. Today, they're known as theme parks. By whatever name, these massive entertainment complexes continue to draw throngs of visitors seeking simple escape.

Certainly, they have become more sophisticated, more educational, and, in terms of sheer, unadulterated thrills, more hair-raising. They also have become diversified, with many parks devoted to such themes as fun in, on, and under the water, exhibitions of and performances by marine creatures (pet the whale, kiss the dolphin!), and the simulation of an African safari. Other themes range from chocolate and wild berries to circuses and monkeys, from the old South and pioneer West to the celebration of the Mississippi River.

Varied, too, are the activities available to park visitors. You can plunge into a swim-through aquarium, join the audience at a live TV show, explore a Hollywood back lot, or learn, "hands on," about computer science. There are water skiers to watch, as well as high-tech movies and Broadway-quality shows. And there are adventures, too, for the imagination, as visitors are transported to foreign lands and ancient eras. You can stroll past the Eiffel Tower or visit the Globe Theater of Shakespearean England, explore an old silver mine or hike through a tropical rain forest.

Modern technology has made the rides, now fashionably dubbed with such adjectives as "screaming" and "roaring," more thrilling and, hopefully (in view of occasional mishaps), more reliable.

Nonetheless, the attraction for millions remains that American tradition of simply escaping on a warm summer's day for an outing that comes complete with hot dogs, soft drinks, balloons, and souvenirs that are discarded long before the memories.

NORTHWEST

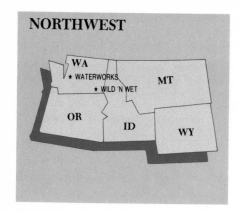

SOUTHWEST

UNIVERSAL STUDIOS

Universal City, CA

Tourists can watch daily performances of the parting of the Red Sea at this 420-acre monument to the USA's magic movieland. A 2½ hour tram tour takes visitors to see interior scenes, dressing rooms, and departments in make-up, wardrobe, music, and editing in the Front Lot. Versatile mock cities in the Back Lot replicate any locale in history during any season. The Prop Plaza has palm trees you can push over, a fake stagecoach ride where you bounce in place while the scenery rolls by, a jail house, and giant props you can climb on (scissors, table, telephone) from the movie, "The Incredible Shrinking Man" and from the TV series, "Land of the Giants." Tourists can watch repeat performances of a runaway train, a collapsing bridge, and a flash flood. The formal tour ends at the Entertainment Center, where it is followed by three hours of live shows including talking birds, trained animals, and a wild west fight staged by stuntmen. Located ½ blk N of Hollywood Frwy. Tours daily 8am-5pm during summer and hols (off-season schedules vary). Admission: $11; 3-11 $8.

Universal Studios, 100 Universal City Plaza, Universal City, CA 91608, **213/877-1311.**

MARINELAND

Rancho Palos Verdes, CA

Tourists can get into the swim of things—literally—by plunging into the 270,000-gallon Baja Reef tank—the world's only swim-through aquarium. It is one of four major cisterns and contains more than 1000 specimens of marine life. For visitors who don't wish to get wet, there are large observation ports. Also at the park is the seven-ton killer whale Orky, the world's largest animal in captivity (according to the *Guiness Book of World Records*). Marineland's Bubbles is the oldest and largest pilot whale in captivity. Visitors to this park on the Pacific can pet and even feed their favorite sea creatures. Open daily Apr-Sept and Easter and Christmas vacations. Admission: $9.50; 3-11 $6.85.

Marineland, 6610 Palos Verdes Dr S, Rancho Palos Verdes, CA 90274, **213/377-1571.**

LION COUNTRY SAFARI

Laguna Hills, CA

This is one of the first parks that started caging the visitors and letting the animals roam free. The tour is four miles—car windows must be closed, so air-conditioning is essential. Residents include bears, African buffalo, cheetahs, giraffes, and lions. You *can* get out of your car to visit the park area; highlights include a magic show, marionettes, petting village, kiddie rides, pony rides, and an arcade. Live animal shows feature baby animals, and well-trained birds performing skits. A narrated jungle cruise explores the Zambezi river, where you can spot birds and monkeys in the trees. (Another Lion Country Safari—different ownership—is located in W Palm Beach, FL, 305/793-1004.) Located at I-405 and Irvine Ctr Dr. Admission: $7.25; 3-11 $4.50 (one type of admission allows unlimited passage to the drive-through safari).

Lion Country Safari, 8800 Irvine Ctr Dr, Laguna Hills, CA 92653, **714/837-1200.**

WATERWORKS PARK

Issaquah, WA

This is one of the largest get-wet getaways in the northwest. It features 22 water rides with four 400-foot slides, a twisting inner tube run through tunnels, and a hill with eight speedy lanes. Two giant hot-pool baths keep guests warm between aqua-adventures, or during a water-break they can play volleyball or shuffleboard, or visit amusement arcades. The park has comparable rides for children, and a kiddie cove with fountains and water cannons. Facilities include a gift shop, food service, picnic area, and locker rooms. Take Exit 15 off I-90, next to Sammamish State Park. Admission: $7; 4-11 $5; under 4 and over 65 free.

Waterworks, 2005 NW Sammamish Rd, Issaquah, WA 98027, **206/453-5555.**

WILD 'N WET

Kennewick, WA

"Kamikaze," "Lover's Leap," and "Raider's Run," are just a few of the water chutes offered at this northwest oasis. The 9-acre park provides a full day of water activities with speed-slides, twisting slides, long slides (four more than 400 feet long), and drop-off slides that catapult their passengers into the landing pool—six feet below. Landlubbers have their choice between a basketball and volleyball court, a batting cage, or about 40 video games. If all this activity wears you out, relax in the hot-pool bath—large enough for 100 people, or enjoy a cool repast in the shaded picnic area. Other facilities include a 6000-foot swimming area, 1½ acres of astroturf for sun-seekers, a snack bar, and a gift shop. Open Apr-Oct 10am-9pm (off-season schedules vary). Located ½ mi E of Columbia Ctr on Canal Dr at Lincoln Way. Admission: $6.75; 4-5 and sr.cit. $2.

Wild 'N Wet, 6321 W Canal Dr, Kennewick, WA 99336, **509/735-8443.**

Six Flags Over Georgia, Atlanta, GA

KNOTTS BERRY FARM

Buena Park, CA

This park began as a roadside berry stand; 60 years later it has become the nation's third-most-visited theme park. It centers around the gold-rush era in the Old West, and guests who pan for gold almost always find a fleck or two. You can see a cancan performance, a cowboy stunt show, a fireworks display, an ice-skating spectacular, and a Spanish fiesta village . . . or ride a stagecoach, experience the parachute jump, boo the villain during a melodrama, and join the nighttime barn dances. There are several thrill rides including an upside-down corkscrew roller coaster that *Saturday Evening Post* called "a southern California landmark." The farm is still famous for canned berries, jams, and jellies, so don't forget to try some. Open Mem Day—Lab Day. Sun-Thur, 9am—midnight; Fri, Sat to 1am (off-season schedules vary). Located 2 mi S of Santa Ana Frwy on CA 39. Admission: $10.95; 3-11 $8.95.

Knotts Berry Farm, 8029 Beach Blvd, Buena Park, CA 90620, **714/827-1776.**

DISNEYLAND

Anaheim, CA

This is the father of theme parks as we know them today, containing some of the most sophisticated three dimensional animation in the world. Examples of this can be found in Bear Country featuring Audio-Animatronics musical bears, and in the Haunted Mansion and Pirates of the Caribbean attractions located in New Orleans Square. The magic of Fantasyland brings to life Pinocchio, Snow White, Dumbo and Peter Pan. Main St. USA houses nostalgia including a steam-powered railroad and an old-time cinema. Tomorrowland is famous for Space Mountain. You can explore the Swiss Family Robinson Tree House in Adventureland, or ride the Mark Twain riverboat in Frontierland. Each land has rides, restaurants, and entertainment relative to its particular theme. Plan to spend at least six hours. Located 26 mi S of Los Angeles on Harbor Blvd, off Santa Ana Frwy in Anaheim. Hours vary so call in advance. Admission: $14; 3-12 $9.

Disneyland, 1313 Harbor Blvd, Anaheim, CA 92803, **714/999-4000.**

MARINE WORLD AND AFRICA USA

Redwood City, CA

When Africa/USA was relocated in 1972 to Marine World on the San Francisco peninsula, it brought a unique combination of wildlife exhibits to the bay area. The 65-acre complex is surrounded by canals and waterways. A guided Jungle Raft Safari takes passengers close to ostriches, zebras, rhinoceri, tigers, and other exotic animals. Killer-whale and dolphin shows are performed daily. A number of exhibits in the Gentle Jungle, Seal Cove, Dolphin Exhibit Pool, and Ecology Theatre, give visitors a chance to touch, feed, and even ride some animals. Open year-round on weekends and school holidays; Wed-Sun spring and fall; daily 9:30am-dusk summer. Admission: $9.95; 60 and over $8.95; 5-12 $7.95.

Marine World/Africa USA, Marine World Pkwy, Redwood City, CA 94065, **415/DOL-PHIN.**

SIX FLAGS MAGIC MOUNTAIN

Valencia, CA

This family entertainment center features more than 100 attractions. Included are Magic Mountain—one of the world's largest dual-track wooden roller coasters, rafting trips down California's only man-made white water river, a new computer center, and the country's longest water-flume ride. The Great Rivers Ski Team performs on Mystic Lake and the US High Dive Team puts on shows Apr-Sept at the Aqua Theater. The Animal Farm includes a petting zoo for children. Open daily May 18-Sept 9, and weekends and school holidays the remainder of the year. Admission: $12.95; children under 48 inches $6.50. Located off the Magic Mountain Pkwy exit of I-5.

Six Flags Magic Mountain, PO Box 5500, Valencia, CA 91355, **805/255-4100.**

WILD ANIMAL PARK

Escondido, CA

This park's first priority is not to drape a lion over the hood of your car, but to insure the welfare of its wildlife sanctuary and research center. However, this non-profit, non-commercial off spring of the San Diego Zoo offers an exciting 5-mile safari through an 1800-acre preserve with more than 3500 animals from Asia and Africa. It's possible to see anything from a pride of lions to a herd of elephants. Narrated tours are given via non-polluting and silent monorails that don't interfere with natural habitats (for best view sit on right). The Kilimanjaro Trail is 1¼ miles and offers shaded viewing stations and picnic areas. Other attractions include an African village, animal and bird shows, petting zoo, simulated Australian rain forest, elephant and camel rides, and a gorilla colony. Famous entertainers perform on summer weekends. Located 30 mi NE via I-15, US 395, CA 163, then 5 mi E on CA 78 in San Pasqual Valley. Admission: $3.50; sr.cit. $2.50; 6-12 $1.

San Diego Wild Animal Park, Public Relations, Rte 1, Box 725E, Escondido, CA 92025, **619/747-8702.**

Six Flags Great Adventure, Jackson, NJ

MARRIOTT'S GREAT AMERICA

Santa Clara, CA

Newest of the thrill rides here is the Edge, a $2.5 million free-fall ride that lets daring visitors experience the ''rush'' of skydiving. Riders rapidly ascend 131-foot towers, experiencing G-forces of nearly 5.5, and then drop into a 2½-second, 65-foot fall. Other rides include three roller coasters (the Demon is said to be the scariest and most popular), two water flumes, the Sky Whirl triple-armed Ferris wheel, and many more. Open daily throughout the year from 10am. Located between Hwys 237 & 101 on Great America Pkwy. Admission: $11.95; 55 and over $7.75.

Marriott's Great America, PO Box 1776, Santa Clara, CA 95052, **408/988-1776.**

SEA WORLD

San Diego, CA

Here is the oldest of the three Sea Worlds owned by Harcourt Brace Jovanovich publishers. It was called by *Time* magazine the ''best planned, best stocked'' oceanarium in the United States. Penguin Encounter is a home for more than 400 birds of both the north and south polar regions. Other exhibits include dolphin petting pools, dolphin and killer-whale shows, a Fuji Japanese village, a newly enlarged California tide pool, ''Cap'n Kids' World,'' and much more. Guided tours, including several behind-the-scenes visits, are available for a small fee and take about 90 mins. Open daily 9am—dusk. Admission: $10.95; 3-11 & sr.cit. $7.95 (Passes good for a full year cost less than 2 regular tickets).

Sea World, 1720 S Shores Rd, San Diego, CA 92109, **619/222-6363.**

MIDWEST

KINGS ISLAND

Near Cincinnati, OH

For roller coaster fanatics, Kings Island is famous for the Beast, claimed to be the longest and fastest coaster in the world. The entire park has six themes: Hanna-Barbera land for youngsters, Rivertown of the 1800s, Oktoberfest, International Street, turn-of-the-century Coney Island amusement park, and the 100-acre Wild Animal Habitat. The enormous 1200-acre complex includes four unique roller coasters, a 2.5 million dollar Festhaus for music, shows, and food, and the Timberworld Amphitheatre for major musical attractions. Located in the Kings Island complex, but not in the theme park, are the College Football Hall of Fame, the Jack Nicklaus Sports Center (a huge resort inn and campground), and the enormous new Factory Outlet Mall. Open 9am daily, Mem Day—Lab Day, and selected weekends in spring and fall. Admission: $13.95; 60 and over $8.95, 3-6 $6.95.

Kings Island, Kings Island, OH 45034, **513/398-4000.**

SEA WORLD

Near Cleveland, OH

This popular Cleveland-area attraction is the only one of its kind in mid-America, the home of Shamu and Namu, the world's most famous killer whales. Features include a dolphin and beluga (white) whale petting pool, a tropical tide pool and aquarium, a world-class waterskiing extravaganza, an exotic children's playland with a life-sized pirate ship, and a magic theatre, with more than 20 attractions and exhibits in all. New for 1984 was Seaport Village, where a variety of crafts are demonstrated. Located 30-min SE of Cleveland on Rte 43, Sea World is open mid-May—mid-Sept from 9am. Admission: $10.95; 3-11 $9.95.

Sea World of Ohio, 1100 Sea World Dr, PO Box 237, Aurora, OH 44202, **216/562-8101.**

CEDAR POINT

Sandusky, OH

With 57 rides, including six roller coasters, here is one of the largest collections of thrill rides in the US. It is a 364-acre amusement/theme park located on the shores of Lake Erie with 225 guest dock spaces. In addition to rides, Cedar Point offers live musical shows, a full-service marina, a mile-long sandy beach, an aquarium, a marine-life show, a resort hotel, and an RV campground. Open mid-May—early Sept, and 2 weekends after Lab. Day. Located midway between Cleveland and Toledo, near Exit 7 on the OH Turnpike. Admission: $12.95; sr.cit. $8.95 (price includes unlimited rides).

Cedar Point, CN 5006, Sandusky, OH 44870, **419/626-0830.**

SIX FLAGS GREAT AMERICA

Gurnee, IL

This popular theme park located about 45 miles north of Chicago was sold in 1984 to the Six Flags Corp. New attraction for 1984 was the White Water Rampage, a 5-minute ride through man-made rapids. The park is noted for two excellent roller coasters, the American Eagle and the Demon, and a number of exciting water rides. The Pictorium Theatre boasts the world's largest indoor movie screen. Open daily 10am, May 20—Sept 3, and weekends only during spring and fall. Admission: $13.50; 55 and over $7.95.

Six Flags Great America, PO Box 1776, Gurnee, IL 60031, **312/249-1776.**

SOUTH CENTRAL

SIX FLAGS OVER TEXAS

Between Dallas and Ft. Worth, TX

A number of rides and attractions of regional interest add a bit of individuality to this Texas-sized addition to the Six Flags empire. The Oil Derrick in the Confederate Section is 300 feet high and is billed as the tallest land-based oil well in the world. Two large elevators carry as many as 30 visitors at a time to the observation deck. In the same section is Spelunker's Cave, in which "Bull Boats" carry passengers through tunnels populated by animated characters. The Run-a-Way Mine Train has five ore cars and was the first tubular steel rail roller coaster in the nation. Many other rides, shows, and attractions. Open daily mid-May—early Sept; weekends and hols during spring and fall. Admission: $13.95.

Six Flags Over Texas, PO Box 191, Arlington, TX 76004, **817/461-1200.**

AQUARENA SPRINGS

San Marcos, TX

What do a swimming pig, a magic act, and a mermaid have in common? They are featured in Aquarena Springs' submarine theatre! There's no stage curtain here; instead, the audience is submerged and the water stage features pageants, clowns, and a variety show set on the fabled sunken island of Atlantis. This all began as a hotel and golf course in 1928 and has expanded to include glass-bottom-boat tours, ferryboat rides, and Swiss gondolas which glide 120 feet above ground on their way to the sunken gardens. Visit Texana Village, an old west town with a saloon, general store, post office, and other buildings, all filled with artifacts from that era. This third largest attraction in Texas can be viewed from the Gyro Tower which raises tourists 250 feet straight up. Aquarena Springs is said to have the longest continuous record of Indian occupation in North America and artifacts dating back 13,000 years have recently been discovered there. The hotel has 25 historical rooms and an Olympic-sized swimming pool among other amenities. Located on I-35 between San Antonio & Austin in the Hill Country region. Plan at least 3 hrs for tours and sights. Admission: $8.95 (tickets sold for separate attractions).

Aquarena Springs, PO Box 2330, San Marcos, TX 78666, **512/392-2481.**

INT'L WILDLIFE PARK

Grand Prairie, TX

In a park which features more than 2500 exotic animals from around the world, visitors can see many of the sights in this 260-acre preserve from the privacy of their own cars. Free animal food is provided, and animals walk up to cars to feed. The safari includes one of the largest private collections of chimpanzees, elephants, and rhinos. Entertainment Village offers animal and boat rides, a train, a petting zoo, a baby-animal zoo, and a rare white tiger. Open daily Mar—Nov during daylight hours. Entertainment Village open weekends only spring and fall; daily in summer. Admission: $8.95 (discounts for groups of 15 or more).

Internat'l Wildlife Park, 601 Wildlife Pkwy, Grand Prairie, TX 75050, **214/263-2201.**

ASTROWORLD

Houston, TX

This park has 12 theme sections focusing on classic cultures and eras around the globe. Thunder River has the nation's first man-made river rapids which were designed in 1980; Western Junction is centered around the old west; Alpine Valley features an electric sleigh ride through the Alps; Fun Island is a Robinson Crusoe-type adventure; and Plaza de Fiesta celebrates a corner of Old Mexico. Trams from Astroworld parking lot carry visitors to Waterworld, an attraction with separate admission that includes the watery Wipe-Out speed slide, Run-a-Way River for tubing enthusiasts, Breaker Beach, an 815,000-gallon wave pool, and more. Open daily June-Aug and weekends spring and fall. Admission: $13.95 (other admission options available).

Astroworld, 9001 Kirby Dr, Houston, TX 77054, **713/799-1234.**

SESAME PLACE

Irving, TX

Bring the kids, yourself, and lots of energy to this futuristic play-park with enough activities to keep everyone busy for days. Sesame Place is geared toward children ages 3-13 but adults are invited to participate in almost everything. Jump into a pool of plastic hollow balls, climb the popular cargo net tunnels suspended up to 30 feet, and get lost in the water maze. There are more than 30 outdoor play activities, plus hands-on science exhibits and a computer center with some 70 educational games. Other highlights include a working replica of a TV studio, water slides, and "Bert" & "Ernie" Muppet shows. If the going gets too hectic visit the Adult Oasis with plenty of shade and TVs for viewing sports, news updates and stock-market information. Wear old duds (and/or bathing suit), slip-on shoes, and bring a change of clothes because you *will* get wet. Only health food, such as whole-wheat pizza and salads, is available. (Another Sesame Place is in Langhorne, PA, 215/757-1100). Located at Airport Frwy & Esters Rd. Admission: children $8.95; adults $5.95.

Sesame Place/Dallas, PO Box 3588, Irving, TX 75061, **214/445-0485.**

SIX FLAGS OVER MID-AMERICA

Near St. Louis, MO

Six historically themed areas represent Spain, France, Britain, the United States, and the states of Missouri and Illinois in this park with more than 100 rides and attractions. New in 1984 was the Rail Blazer roller coaster, in which passengers stand while racing along a track nearly ½ mile long. Also Thunder River white water raft trips, Screamin' Eagle wooden roller coaster, and a number of Broadway-style shows and water shows. Open daily May 18—Sept 3; additional weekends in spring and fall. Admission: $12.99; $17.99 for 2 consecutive days. Located along US 44 just W of St. Louis.

Six Flags Over Mid-America, PO Box 60, Eureka, MO 63025, **314/938-5300.**

OCEANS OF FUN

Kansas City, MO

Drinking and driving don't mix, but drinking and swimming do at this park featuring an adult pool with swim-up bar and underwater stools! There are some 30 water-related activities, so put on your bathing suit and experience the Typhoon—world's longest twin speed slide, a wave pool the size of a football field, or the Diamond Head—a triple water slide that loops around trees. If you would rather be *on* the water, you can rent rafts and paddleboats and use complimentary sailboats, canoes, and kayaks on the lake. The lake also has a water obstacle course complete with monkey bars, and a battery of water guns. Other attractions include water-ski shows, a playground, and sportswear shops. Locker rooms, restaurants, and picnic tables available, but food may not be brought in. Open 10am late May—late Aug. Located near Worlds of Fun (see); Exit 54 on I-435. Admission: $9.95 (1- & 2-day passports available).

Oceans of Fun, 4545 Worlds of Fun Ave, Kansas City, MO 64161, **816/454-4545.**

SILVER DOLLAR CITY

Table Rock Lake Area, MO

Journey back to the 1880s in this Ozark mining village. Frontier crafts are demonstrated throughout the city and the Spring and Fall Crafts Festivals highlight rare, historic skills, such as donkey-powered grain threshing, quilting, and barrelmaking (late Apr—late May/mid-Sept—mid-Oct). The rides also teach guests about ancient mining towns; boats take visitors through a flooded mine with animated characters and explosions; Rube Dugan's Diving Bell simulates an underwater trip—actually rocking the tourists' chairs; and guests can see Marvel Cave—returning to the surface via a cable railway. Other rides include Fire in the Hole, an enclosed roller coaster, and American Plunge Flume. The streets are lined with shows and characters, and a petting area has more than 150 animals. Bring your dancing shoes to the June Festival of Mountainfolks Music (mid-June). (Another Silver Dollar City is located in Pigeon Forge, TN, 615/453-4616.) Located 7 mi W of Branson on MO 76. Admission: $13.95; 5-10 $10.50.

Silver Dollar City, Marvel Cave Park, MO 65616, **417/338-2611.**

WORLDS OF FUN

Kansas City, MO

"Fury of the Nile," said to be the longest man-made white water river in the world, opened in 1984. It is a 4½-minute run through exploding geysers, waterfalls, twisting curves, and raging rapids. The park hosts five internationally themed regions: America, Scandanavia, the Orient, Africa, and Europe. Each area depicts its theme from food to entertainment and clothing; so depending on where you are, you can ride anything from the Cotton Blossom steamboat to a French taxi. More than 100 rides and attractions include four roller coasters, the Starbeam Music Machine—a video music history, the Shirt Tales cartoon characters, and Viking Voyager flume rides. The Incred-O-Dome is a round cinema; its visual and audio combination causes visitors to actually feel as though they are riding a roller coaster or an airplane. Oceans of Fun (see) is located next door; admission tickets are sold to include both parks ($18.95), however, they are separate and no shuttles are provided. Admission: $12.95 (1- & 2-day passports available). Open daily from 10am, late May—Aug. Some additional weekends. Located near exit 54 on I-435.

Worlds of Fun, 4545 Worlds of Fun Ave, Kansas City, MO 64161, **816/454-4545.**

NORTHEAST

SIX FLAGS GREAT ADVENTURE

Jackson, NJ

The nation's largest seasonal theme park is also the largest entertainment center in the northeast. Major rides at the park include the Freefall roller coaster, Parachuter's Perch, and the exciting Roaring Rapids. Also a part of the Great Adventure complex is the Safari, where guests drive in a zebra-striped jeep through a preserve populated by lions, tigers, bears, rhinos, elephants, giraffes, and monkeys. The Six Flags Corp. states that this is the largest safari outside of Africa. Open daily from 10am, Apr 29—Sept 18; selected weekends spring and fall. Admission: $15.25 (for theme park and safari); $14.05 (for theme park); $5.25 (for safari).

Great Adventure, PO Box 120, Jackson, NJ 08527, **201/928-2000.** *Recorded events hotline,* **201/928-3500.**

HERSHEYPARK

Hershey, PA

If you have a sweet tooth, you will love this 77-year-old theme park located in the chocolate capital of the world. Hometown of M.S. Hershey's famous factory, the park themes stem from the area's cultural heritage: Rhine Land (German); Tudor Square (English); and a Pennsylvania mining town (PA Dutch). It is one of the best parks to visit with children, offering many kiddie attractions including a playground, bumper cars, and other rides. ZooAmerica, located within the park, is a 10-acre walk-through area with about 200 animals and plant life indigenous to five regions of North America. Characters roaming streets are dressed as Hershey bars, peanut butter cups, Kisses, etc. Also nearby is Hershey Chocolate World; tours simulate the steps of chocolate production starting with the cocoa bean. Hershey Museum of American Life is adjacent to Hersheypark; attractions include American Indian collections, displays of Stiegel glass, and Hersheypark Arena (capacity 10,000) which hosts professional hockey, basketball, ice-skating, and variety shows. Located at US 322 & 422. Admission: $13.95; 5-8 $10.95.

Hersheypark, Hershey, PA 17033, **717/534-3005.**

RIVERSIDE PARK

Agawam, MA

This oldest and largest amusement park in New England features more than 100 rides and attractions, including a kiddieland, an International Plaza, shows and restaurants. Thrill-seekers head for the new Cyclone roller coaster which rises 112 feet above the ground, and, at one point, accelerates passengers from 0-60 mph in three seconds. A continuing beautification project is underway at this old park. Riverside is located on Rte 159 between Hartford and Springfield. Open daily March 31—mid-Oct from 11am. Admission: $9.95; 3-8 $6.95 (reduced tickets available to view shows and attractions only).

Riverside Park, PO Box 307, Agawam, MA 01001, **413/786-9300.**

CANOBIE LAKE PARK

Salem, NH

Although not among the largest, this park is one of the prettiest amusement centers in the US. Situated along the shores of scenic Canobie Lake, the park features three roller coasters, an antique carousel, a 24-gauge steam train, and an authentic paddlewheel riverboat for relaxing cruises around the lake. Patterned after a turn-of-the-century sawmill, the Log Flume ride carries passengers on a watery route through stately pines and up a high lift to a final slide. There are 38 rides in all for adults and children of all ages. Shows include a champion high dive. Open weekends only mid-Apr—May; daily from Mem Day—Lab Day. Admission: $4; sr.cit. & students $3; 6-12 $1.25.

Canobie Lake Park, Salem, NH 03079, **603/893-3506.**

SOUTHEAST

CYPRESS GARDENS

Winter Haven, FL

These gardens have been a major attraction in Florida for half a century, and their beauty is displayed along the Main Trail where tourists can stroll through 8,000 varieties of plants and flowers. Gardens of the World has 13 botanical theme areas including an All-American Rose Garden, an English courtyard, and a fern forest. Cypress Gardens is most famous for its water-ski revue where professionals ski in pyramid formations, jump from ramps, and perform on trick skis. Other highlights include the new Southern Crossroads, an antebellum town with theatres, magic shows, and rides, and the 6-acre Living Forest with ecology exhibits, a walk-through aviary, and a petting zoo. Open 8am-dusk. Fees vary.

Florida Cypress Gardens, PO Box 1, Cypress Gardens, FL 33880, **813/324-2111.**

WALT DISNEY WORLD

Lake Buena Vista, FL

Twice the size of Manhattan, this park has become the most popular attraction in the world. Magic Kingdom features more than 45 major attractions in Main St. USA, Fantasyland, Tomorrowland, Adventureland, Frontierland, and Liberty Square. However, this resort complex has much more to offer including Epcot Center with Future World and World Showcase—a fairly new addition geared toward adults. Future World has models of 21st century communities, robots, and hands-on exhibits. World Showcase features ten nations with replicas of architectural landmarks, shops, entertainment, and food. This area has a cultural exchange program bringing about 70 kids from around the world to work for a year and represent their countries. Walt Disney World has many vacation villas, resort hotels, more than 100 dining facilities, three 18-hole championship golf courses, beaches, horseback riding, and an 825-acre campground. Open every day of the year; Thur & Fri least crowded. Located 22 mi SW of Orlando at I-4 & 535. For accommodations inside park phone 305/824-8000. Admission: $12-$15 (multi-day passports available).

Walt Disney World Co, PO Box 40, Dept GL, Lake Buena Vista, FL 32830, **305/824-4321.**

Seaworld, San Diego, CA

ADVENTURE ISLAND

Tampa, FL

From the daredevil to the timid, and from grandpa to grandson, there's something here for everyone. Adventurers can climb the 34-foot mountain and take any one of five flumes 200-300 feet long. Or, they can try out the new 450-foot Barratuba slide which takes inner tubers down a twisting slide and through a tunnel. For thrill-seekers, the Gulf Scream speed slide drops five stories and reaches 40 mph. Paradise Lagoon is for guests who want to relax on white sandy beaches around a 9,000-square-foot pool fed by waterfalls. The Fountain of Youth is a children's area with a tire swing, a hand-over-hand rope ladder, and squirt guns. You can raft, body-surf, or frolic in a 17,000-square-foot pool with waves 3-5 feet. Other attractions include a cafe, volleyball facilities, and evening rock concerts. Open June—Aug, 10am-8pm (off-season schedules vary). Located 8 mi NE of downtown and 2 mi E of I-75. Admission: $9.25 (8 and under must have adult supervision).

Adventure Island, 4500 Bougainvillea, Tampa, FL 33617, **813/977-5833.**

WEEKI WACHEE

Brooksville, FL

This spring's measured depth is 137 feet but no one knows how much deeper it goes. It is known that this engineering showcase continues as one of Florida's most popular spectacles. It was used as a swimming hole until an ex-Navy frogman, who practiced underwater breathing techniques here, realized its potential in 1947. The first show was in a small auditorium built six feet below the surface. It was so successful that a new auditorium seating 500 was built 16 feet down. Tourists can watch underwater ballet, a musical production of "Mermaid Magic," comedy acts, acrobatics, and a magic show. Bird shows feature fowl that play poker, roller skate, ride a bike on the high wire, and perform other acrobatics. Explore nature on the wild-river cruise, and in the tropical gardens and rain forest. Buccaneer Bay, a water-themed park, is adjacent to Weeki Wachee (combination tickets available). Located 12 mi W on FL 50 at jct US 19. Open daily 9am-dusk. Admission: $7.05; 3-11 $4.80.

Weeki Wachee Springs, Inc, PO Box 97, Brooksville, FL 34298-0097, **904/596-2062.**

CIRCUS WORLD, INC.

Orlando, FL

If you've always wanted to run away to join the circus, this may be the next best thing! After a short demonstration, spectators are invited to test their skills on the trapeze and tightrope; children can try the low wire. This unique experience is one of many offered at the world's only circus-themed park, with a variety of shows to please everyone: a circus movie on a 6-story screen; an aqua circus; a circus parade; and a baby-animal circus. Other attractions include the Roaring Tiger roller coaster, a 16-story high ferris wheel, arcades, elephant rides, a circus menagerie, a magic show, and the chance to get your face painted like a clown's. Visit the circus-museum displays and the exotic animal zoo. The chipmunk cartoon characters perform song and dance concerts daily. Children enjoy the kiddie rides and play area. There isn't a lot of shade so bring hats and visit the shops and restaurants. Open daily 9am-6pm. Located on US 27 at I-4; 10-min from Disneyland. Admission: $11.50; 3-11 $10.50.

Circus World, Inc, PO Box 800, Orlando, FL 32802, **305/422-0643.**

MARINELAND OF FLORIDA

St. Augustine, FL

Thousands of marine specimens living much as they would in the open sea can be observed at the oldest marine exhibit of its kind (although recently improved) in the US. Trained porpoises perform astounding feats at the 1,500 seat Porpoise Stadium. The Margaret Herrick Shell Museum houses one of the finest collections in the southeast. At the Aquarius Theatre, visitors can experience the new multi-dimensional SpaceVision film, "Seadream." Two large Oceanariums house a wide variety of sea life, including sharks, Florida Manatees, and electric eels. Located on both sides of Hwy A1A between historic St. Augustine and Daytona Beach. Open daily 8am-6pm. Admission: $5; 6-11 $2.50.

Marineland of Florida, Rte 1, Box 122, St. Augustine, FL 32084, **904/471-1111.**

MIAMI SEAQUARIUM

Miami, FL

More than 10,000 species of marine life, including dolphins, sea lions, a killer whale, manatees, sharks, turtles, and tropical fish, as well as rare birds are on display on this 60-acre site leased from Dade County. This is the home of Flipper, star of 100 television shows. Seaquarium has been declared a wildlife sanctuary by the Tropical Audubon Society. On the popular Lost Island, rare birds, crocodiles and giant turtles live nearly in harmony. Attractions include tanks with viewing windows, jungle islands, tidepools, monorail, and a wide variety of shows including magic acts with animals. Open 9am-6pm (box offices closes at 5pm) every day of the year. Admission: $8; 6-12 $4. Located along the Rickenbacker Causeway near the entrance to Key Biscayne.

Miami Seaquarium, 4400 Rickenbacker Causeway, Miami, FL 33149, **305/361-5705.**

MONKEY JUNGLE

South of Miami, FL

One of the few protected habitats for endangered primates in the US can be found in this small but exotic park complete with hand-collected plants native to the Amazonian river basin. Here, nearly 500 monkeys roam free and uncaged in a 20-acre preserve. Visitors can walk through palm-draped caged pathways as squirrel monkeys chatter and swing acrobatically overhead. Guests are invited to stroll through a recreated rain forest also inhabited with monkeys. The forest requires 200 inches of rain each year so a network of irrigation lines traverse the jungle floor to supplement Florida's annual precipitation of 50 inches. Many rare species are successfully living and breeding in Monkey Jungle including the beautiful Golden Lion Marmoset which has red-gold fur and a thick mane, and the uakari, a primate with long red hair, a scarlet face, and a bald head. Asiatic apes and gorillas are also in residence. Open daily year-round from 9:30am-5pm. Admission: $5; 5-12 $2.50; sr.cit & military personnel $4.

Monkey Jungle, 14805 SW 216th St, Miami, FL 33170, **305/235-1611.**

Seaworld, San Diego, CA

BUSCH GARDENS, THE DARK CONTINENT

Tampa, FL

The most popular tourist attraction on Florida's West Coast provides authentic habitats in seven distinctly themed sections for more than 3000 animals. Inspired by yesteryear Africa, some of the more popular attractions include the Congo River Rapids, complete with 12-passenger rafts; Timbuktu, an ancient desert trading center featuring a dolphin theater; Marrakesh, a walled Moroccan-inspired village; and Bird Gardens, the original Busch Gardens with birds and lagoons. The Serengeti Plain houses a large collection of African big game; for $30, safari trucks take tourists onto the plain to shoot photographs without restricting fences, bars, or viewing windows. Open 9:30am–6pm (later in summer) throughout the year. Admission: $13.50.

Busch Gardens, The Dark Continent, PO Box 9158, Tampa, FL 33674, **813/977-6600.**

WILD WATERS AND SILVER SPRINGS

Silver Springs, FL

This park has found eight ways to combine slides and water to offer attractions for all ages. Climb a path to the branches of a 100-year-old oak tree to launch a watery descent. Or, visit the "Hurricane" with slides more than 400 feet long which take adventurers through a 120-foot lighted tunnel. There's a smaller flume for children and the Water Bonanza area for tots has wading pools, water forts, and squirt guns. Other attractions include mini-golf, volleyball, a frisbee court, and an Olympic-sized wave pool. Silver Springs is next door (combination tickets available) and offers glass-bottom-boat rides and a jungle cruise for viewing alligators, monkeys, and waterfowl. The water is so clear that several movies have been shot here including "Tarzan" and "Creature From the Black Lagoon." Open late Mar—mid-Sept; 10am-5pm; summer to 9pm. Located on FL 40. Admission: $6.50; 3-11 $5.50.

Wild Waters & Silver Springs, PO Box 370, Silver Springs, FL 32688, **904/236-2121.**

SIX FLAGS OVER GEORGIA

Atlanta, GA

The South's original family theme park has more than 100 rides, shows, and attractions thematically laid out over more than 330 acres. A member of Bally's highly successful Six Flags Corporation, the park features a dazzling and dizzying roller coaster, a white water rafting experience, and, new in 1984, "The Great Six Flags Air Racer" in which six-passenger biplanes "fly" 100 feet above the ground. Daily from 10am, May 28—Sept 3; weekends only during spring and fall. Admission: $13.50 for one day; $19.50 for 2 days.

Six Flags Over Georgia, PO Box 43187, Atlanta, GA 30378, **404/948-9290.**

STONE MOUNTAIN

Atlanta, GA

This park, the South's answer to Mt. Rushmore, encompasses the world's largest granite monolith (825 ft. tall). Generals Robert E. Lee and "Stonewall" Jackson, and Confederate President Jefferson Davis are carved onto the face of the rock. You can walk a trail or ride a cable car to the top to see the reflecting pool. The 3200-acre park also has 10 miles of nature trails. Other facilities include boat rentals, fishing, picnicking, tennis, 17 holes of golf, mini-golf, and a beach with waterslide. A restored antebellum plantation is complete with heirlooms, slave quarters, and cookhouse. Walk through the covered bridge to a section with reproduced industries from the Old South (free). Other highlights: train rides; riverboat rides on "The Scarlet O'Hara"; a Civil War museum; Confederate Hall, with light and sound show of Civil War in Georgia; and, an Antique Auto and Music Museum (cars from 1899). Daily concerts by a 732-bell carillon. Located 16 mi E on US 78. Admission: $4/car (fees for individual attractions).

Stone Mountain, PO Box 778, Atlanta, GA 30086, **404/469-9831.**

KING'S DOMINION

Doswell, VA

This 800-acre park has been called "the Disneyland of Virginia," and is packed with five themed lands. International Street duplicates European-style buildings and wide streets complete with a replica of the Eiffel Tower. A twin racing roller coaster called "Rebel Yell" is popular in turn-of-the-century Candyapple Grove. Old Virginia has a long flume ride, 19th century steam train, and antique cars. Cartoon characters roam the streets in Happy Land of Hanna Barbera and there are rides for children and adults. A monorail takes tourists through an African wildlife preserve in Wild Animal Safari. Other attractions include the acclaimed tallest man-made mountain which houses four fantasy rides, a free-floating white water raft ride in White Water Canyon, and the spooky Haunted River boat ride through a cave with animated spectres. Located 1 mi E of Ashland on VA 54, then 7 mi N on I-95. Open from 9:30am June—Lab Day (off-season schedules vary). Admission: $13.50.

King's Dominion, Box 166, Doswell, VA 23047, **804/876-5000.**

THE OLD COUNTRY, BUSCH GARDENS

Williamsburg VA

This 360-acre outdoor family entertainment park offers exciting rides, shows, shops, restaurants, and exhibits. It features eight authentically detailed 17th century European hamlets; Banbury Cross and Hastings (England), Aquitane and New France (France), Rhinefeld and Oktoberfest (Germany), Heatherdowns (Scotland), and San Marco (Italy). Other attractions include an arcade, an antique carousel, a Rhine River boat ride, animal acts, a magic show, and a reproduction of the Shakespearean Globe Theatre. Located 3 mi E of historic Williamsburg and 150 mi from Washington DC. Open daily mid-May—early Sept. from 10am (closing hours vary), and weekends only during spring and fall. Admission: $13.50 ($16.95 for 2-day passports).

The Old Country, Busch Gardens, PO Drawer F-C, Williamsburg, VA 23187, **804/253-3350.**

WATER COUNTRY USA

Williamsburg, VA

Water theme parks are known for having something for everyone and this 25-acre aquatic playground is no exception. Set in a rustic landscape are five major water experiences: the daring "Rampage" water chute which drops 40 feet at a 45° angle; "Surfer's Bay" swimming area the size of five Olympic pools capped with 3-foot waves and a four-tier sun deck; a "Runaway Rapids" white water experience on an inner tube; and the Polliwog Pond for the tadpoles in the family, complete with kiddie-size slides, fountains, and giant inner tubes. Facilities include a gift shop with beach wear, cafe, bathhouse and lockers. Located off I-64 in Williamsburg. Open 10am-8pm during summer (off-season schedules vary). Admission: $8.95.

Water Country USA, PO Box 3088, Williamsburg, VA 23187, **804/229-9300.**

MUD ISLAND

Memphis, TN

It has no body-jarring rides, yet its "theme" keeps visitors fascinated for hours. Located in the Mississippi River across from downtown Memphis, this entertainment and cultural center showcases the river from all aspects— historical, cultural, and scientific. A 5-block-long River Walk is a scale model of the lower Mississippi that faithfully reproduces every twist and turn with each step the visitor takes equalling about 1 mile. Flowing water rises and falls with the real river's changes; cities and towns are laid out in black slate; 75 markers pinpoint historic events. Other highlights: a recreated section of an 1870s packetboat; a full-sized replica of a Union gunboat in simulated battle; a Confederate shore battery; an extensive series of museums chronicling river history, including a 5-room music gallery; a river-themed children's playground; a 1928 towboat moored at the dock; and a 4,300-seat outdoor amphitheater with top-name entertainment. There are restaurants, food booths and shops, with access by monorail, steamboat or a walkway. Open 10am early-Apr—Dec (limited hours off-season). Admission: $5.75; Sr. Cit. $4.75; 4-11 $3.75.

Mud Island, 125 N Main St, Memphis, TN 38103, **901/528-3595.**

OPRYLAND

Nashville, TN

Opryland is a 120-acre musical entertainment theme park that emphasizes live musical productions, with facilities for as many as 15 fully staged shows in simultaneous performances. The high-quality shows, performed by young entertainers recruited by nation-wide auditions, are complemented by 20 rides and adventures, including the Grizzly River Rampage, a rafting trip on Opryland's own white water river. New in 1984 was the Screamin' Delta Demon which is like a bobsled on wheels. There are also restaurants, games, shops, and crafts demonstrations. The famous 1068-room Opryland Hotel covers 30 acres and claims more meeting, exhibit, and public space than any other hotel in the nation. Park guests can attend performances at the adjacent, legendary Grand Old Opry, watch stars perform each weeknight during a live variety show in the TNN Gaslight Studio, attend a Hee Haw TV show taping, and even record their own voices on stereo cassettes in mini recording booths. Open weekends spring and autumn; every day during summer. Admission: $13.25.

Opryland, 2802 Opryland Dr, Nashville, TN 37214, **615/889-6600.**

Chapter 7

NATIONAL PARKS & MONUMENTS

Glacier, National Park, MT

Photo: Danny On

Superlatives spring easily to mind when describing our National Parks. Within their boundaries are some of America's greatest natural resources and most scenic landscapes. In this land of contrasts, they embrace infinite geological variety, from Mt. Whitney, the tallest peak in the contiguous United States, to its lowest point of land shimmering in the furnace-heat of Death Valley. Within these National Parks you'll find the swampy, subtropical wilderness of the Southeast and the cool, sparklingly-clear lakes of the northland.

They protect America's deepest lake, oldest volcanoes, and the remnants of earlier civilizations, from pre-historic Indian dwellings and Spanish missions to relics of American pioneers. They contain painted desert, petrified forest, and towering stands of giant redwoods and sequoias. And, despite man's deprivations and because of his late-awakened interest in protecting our ecosystems, these parks are home to thriving populations of native wildlife.

There are the cool mountain streams of the high country, and the burning deserts of the arid southwest; there are columns and spires, towers and buttes, canyons and gorges, and a variety of other formation's wrought by time's passage and nature's hand.

For the active visitor they offer hiking, climbing, horseback riding, fishing, rafting and canoeing. Or you can explore a cave filled with onyx pillars and glistening formations . . . or photograph the rugged Pacific coastline or a tumbling waterfall . . . or admire the panoramic beauty of the Grand Canyon or the multi-hued, sweeping expanses of the Badlands. Stark and soft, accessible and remote, these parks are our natural inheritance and our bequest to future generations.

NORTHWEST

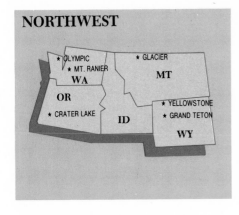

OLYMPIC

Nat'l Park, WA

From Alpine-like meadows to thick rain forests, and from towering mountains to the rugged Pacific coastline, Olympic National Park is a study in magnificently diverse habitats. The climate near sealevel is cool in summer and warm in winter, but torrential rains (especially between October and March) often last for days. US 101 is the principal through route for motorists, and numerous spurs give access to many of the park's most scenic areas. There are also a variety of hiking trails, some taking as much as a week or more to travel. Licenses are not required for fishing, but Washington State punchcards are needed for steelhead and salmon. A number of motels, cabins, and campsites are within the park.

Supt, Olympic Nat'l Park, 600 E Park Ave, Port Angeles, WA 98362, **206/452-4501, ext 230.**

CRATER LAKE

Nat'l Park, OR

Volcanic peaks, evergreen forests, and rolling mountains surround this huge, manificent lake high in the Cascades Range. Formed by an extinct volcano, this is the deepest lake in the US (2000 feet). Although the area is blanketed by snow for a large part of the year, heat from the summer sun is stored in the water and retards ice formation. Many of the roads in the park are closed by late fall due to snow, but OR 62, from the west and south, is open year-round and the park road to the lake is kept open whenever possible. There are many excellent backpacking trails (permit required), and guided boat and bus tours of the lake and surrounding areas. Accommodations available in Rim Village mid-June—Lab Day. Of special note is the rustic Crater Lake Lodge (see Inn Places), housed in a beautiful brick building. Camping at approved sites $7/night.

Supt, Crater Lake Nat'l Park, PO Box 7, Crater Lake, OR 97604, **503/594-2211.**

GRAND TETON

Nat'l Park, WY

Soaring more than a mile above the sagebrush flats of Jackson Hole, the Grand Tetons are relatively young geologically and, therefore, extremely rugged. Trips down the Snake River are popular with experienced canoeists, although a spill in the cold water is chilling and wet suits are a must. About 200 miles of trails are maintained for hikers. Because the Grand Tetons are so rugged, mountaineering is increasingly popular with experienced climbers (registration suggested). Park roads vary from modern paved routes to primitive trails, but major roads are cleared during winter. Numerous interpretive programs are offered by park rangers. Five campgrounds are operated by the National Park Service June—Sept.

Supt, Grand Teton Nat'l Park, PO Drawer 170, Moose, WY 83012, **307/733-2880.**

MT. RANIER

Nat'l Park, WA

More than 2,500 annual visitors make the climb to the 14,410-foot summit of magnificent Mount Ranier. However, less strenuous activities are also rewarding in this wonderfully scenic national park. The Wonderland Trail is a 90-mile challenge to hikers that circles the gleaming mountain, and takes about two weeks to cover. No license is needed to fish park waters, but ice fishing is prohibited. There are three modest campgrounds and a number of smaller ones, but only the camp at Sunshine Point is open year-round. Except for the roads from Nisqually Entrance to Paradise (WA 706), most roads are closed by snow late Nov—June or July. Of the three Visitor Information Centers, only the one at Longmire is open year-round. Park personnel warn visitors about the dangers of bears, glaciers, and avalanches.

Supt, Mt Ranier Nat'l Park, Ashford, WA 98304, **206/569-2211.**

GLACIER

Nat'l Park, MT

For hardy outdoor lovers who revel in the rugged terrain of the North Country, the lofty mountain ranges and ice-cold lakes in glacial valleys make this park a true elixir of the spirit. Recently, the park has been united with adjoining Waterton Lakes National Park in Alberta to become Waterton/Glacier International Peace Park. US Rangers conduct a variety of interpretive walks, hikes, and auto trips, during the brief summer months, usually mid-June—Aug. More than 750 miles of hiking trails extend throughout the park, and there are many campgrounds (permits required). Lakes are formed by glacial melts so the water is far too cold for swimming, but a heated pool is available. Officials do not attempt to clear most roads during winter.

Supt, Glacier Nat'l Park, W Glacier, MT 59936, **406/888-5441.**

YELLOWSTONE

Nat'l Park, WY

In 1872 the US Congress withdrew "from settlement, occupancy, or sale" 3472 square miles of land in northwest Wyoming to create the world's first national park. Not only is Yellowstone the oldest national park, it is also the largest (larger than Rhode Island and Delaware combined) and best-known park in the Continental US. The park's most popular attraction remains the Old Faithful geyser which still spews thousands of gallons of thundering water into the air with each eruption. At the Mammoth Hot Springs, mineral-laden waters flowing from deep within the earth have created tier upon tier of ragged and beautiful stone terraces. More than 700,000 gallons of water pour out each day, carrying an estimated *two tons* of limestone. More than 1000 miles of hiking trails (ranging from easy to challenging) traverse the sights and backcountry of the park. Visitors should be alert for bears, and rangers suggest hikers either talk continuously or wear bells to scare off the timid, but extremely dangerous, creatures. Campsites available first-come, first-served ($5-$6); sites usually full by noon during summer. Entrance fee: $2/vehicle (good for Yellowstone and Grand Teton National Parks (see)). Golden Eagle Passports ($10 annually).

Supt, Yellowstone Nat'l Park, WY 82190, **307/344-7381.**

Grand Teton, National Park, WY

Photo: National Park Service

Death Valley, National Monument, CA/NV

SOUTHWEST

★ REDWOOD
LASSEN VOLCANIC ★   NV   UT   ★ ROCKY MOUNTAIN
CANYONLANDS ★ ★ ARCHES
YOSEMITE ★ ★ BRYCE CANYON ★ CAPITOL REEF   CO
★ MUIR WOODS   ZION ★   ★ MESA VERDE
SEQUOIA & ★ ★ DEATH VALLEY   NM
KINGS CANYON   ★ GRAND CANYON
PETRIFIED FOREST ★   ★ SALINAS
CA   AZ   GILA CLIFF
JOSHUA TREE ★   ★ DWELLINGS
CARLSBAD CAVERNS ★

DEATH VALLEY

Nat'l Monument, CA/NV

Despite the harsh environment and furnace-like heat that bakes the valley six months of the year, more than 900 kinds of plants live within the park. Some have roots extending downward more than 60 feet in search of life-supporting water. In the late 1800s the famous 20-mule teams hauled out mined borax (used for cleansing and water softening) from Death Valley. Today, you can trace their path in 20-Mule-Team Canyon. Also of interest here is the lowest point in North America (282 feet below sea level). Because of the valley's size and the distance between major features, an automobile is essential. Fuel is available only at Furnace Creek, Scotty's Castle, and Stovepipe Wells. The park has nine campgrounds but only those at Furnace Creek, Mesquite Spring, and Wildrose are open year-round. Nearby, the Furnace Creek Inn & Ranch Resort offers choice accommodations either in the Spanish-style inn, or Old West ranch (see Inn Places). Carry at least 1 gallon of water per person per day when leaving civilized areas. For further info, write for, *Camping in Death Valley,* and *Getting Around in Death Valley Backcountry.*

Supt, Death Valley Nat'l Monument, Box 157, Death Valley, CA 92328, **619/786-2331.**

JOSHUA TREE

Nat'l Monument, CA

The arid ecosystems of the Colorado and Mohave deserts come together in this monument that encompasses some of the most interesting geologic displays found in California's deserts. The monument is named for the Joshua Tree, a picturesque plant that looks like a cross between a cactus and a pine. The desert area is made up of a series of mountains (up to 6000 feet) separated by flat valleys abundant with wild plants and animals. Visitor centers, ranger stations, and wayside exhibits are found along main roads leading into and through the monument, which is located about 140 miles east of Los Angeles. Nine campgrounds are available but visitors must bring their own water and firewood. Walks, hikes, and campfire talks are conducted by rangers mainly in spring and fall. Officials warn visitors about the dangers of poisonous rattlers, spiders, and abandoned mine shafts.

Supt, Joshua Tree Nat'l Monument, 74485 Nat'l Monument Dr, Twentynine Palms, CA 92277, **714/367-7511.**

MUIR WOODS

Nat'l Monument, CA

Located less than 20 miles north of San Francisco, Muir Woods is popular with city day-trippers who enjoy the six miles of marked trails through giant redwood forests. Trail-side exhibits, signs, and markers help explain flora and fauna. Abundant fog produced along the Pacific Coast keeps the climate in the V-shaped valley damp and cool; jackets are frequently needed even during the height of summer. The woods provide a home for Blacktail deer, squirrels, chipmunks, raccoons, skunks, harmless snakes, and a variety of birds. When Redwood Creek is swollen by winter rains, silver salmon and steelhead trout leave the ocean and fight their way upstream to spawning beds in Muir Woods.

Supt, Muir Woods Nat'l Monument, Mill Valley, CA 94941, **415/388-2595.**

YOSEMITE

Nat'l Park, CA

A number of the grandest sights in America are within Yosemite National Park: majestic rock mountains such as El Capitan, Half Dome, and the Sentinel Rock; famous waterfalls such as the Yosemite Falls and Bridalveil Fall; and spectacular scenic drives such as the one through Tioga Pass. Footpaths and paved walkways are scattered throughout the park—two of the most popular (both short) can be found at Bridalveil Fall and Lower Yosemite Fall. Camping and backpacking in the backcountry by permit only. Reservations required in Yosemite's auto campgrounds spring—early fall. Make reservations at the National Park Service Campground Reservation Center in Curry Village, or at any Ticketron office. Beware of bears; there have been more than 40 injuries from bears in recent years.

Supt, PO Box 577, Yosemite Nat'l Park, CA 95389, **209/372-4461, ext 264.**

SEQUOIA & KINGS CANYON

Nat'l Parks, CA

These two contiguous parks in central California are truly the lands of giants. The huge sequoia trees preserved and protected within are the largest living things in the world, the only survivors of the giant trees that once flourished over much of the world before the last great ice age. On the eastern boundary of Sequoia National Park is Mt. Whitney, highest peak in the US outside of Alaska. Both parks are accessible only from the west, along CA 180 from Fresno and CA 245 and CA 198 from Visalia. No roads cross the east-west width of the parks. Numerous campgrounds are open from June 1 until snow closes them in October. Lodges, cabins, and rooms can be reserved by writing, Sequoia and Kings Canyon Hospitality Service, Sequoia Nat'l Park, CA 93262.

Sequoia and Kings Canyon Nat'l Parks, Three Rivers, CA 93271, **209/565-3341.**

LASSEN VOLCANIC

Nat'l Park, CA

If you enjoy mountains and lakes, head for this park . . . it has 50 wilderness lakes and almost as many soaring peaks. Containing more than 160 square miles, the park is dominated by Lassen Peak, a 10,000-foot volcano last active around 1920. The park also contains vast coniferous forests, and a spectacular variety of wildlife including 50 mammals, 150 kinds of birds, and 12 different kinds of amphibians and reptiles. There are numerous self-guiding hiking trails and a scenic drive that half encircles Lassen Peak. Four campgrounds and five picnic areas are situated along Lassen Park Road. Non-powered boats may be used on all but a handful of the 50 lakes, but there are no boat-rental facilities in the park. Overnight accommodations available at Drakesbad Guest Ranch mid-June—mid-Sept.

Supt, Lassen Volcanic Nat'l Park, Mineral, CA 96063, **916/595-4444.**

Joshua Tree, National Monument, CA

REDWOOD

Nat'l Park, CA

Stretching along northern California's Pacific coastline from a point north of Eureka to just south of the Oregon border, Redwood National Park protects the giant trees from the area's highly active logging companies. These trees (the tallest plants on earth) form a natural canopy hundreds of feet above the forest floor, giving the park a cathedral-like presence. Although temperatures along the coast are always mild, sea breezes can bring massive and dangerous amounts of rain, especially during winter. All formal campsites within the park are operated by California. Reservations necessary in summer. Ticketron, PO Box 26430, San Francisco, CA 94126. For motorists, US 101 (see Scenic Drives) runs the length of the park, providing excellent views of the tall trees as well as the Pacific shoreline.

Redwood Nat'l Park, 1111 2nd St, Crescent City, CA 95531, **707/464-6101** *(24-hr info).*

BRYCE CANYON

Nat'l Park, UT

Mormon settler Ebeneezer Bryce lived here for five years, but little is remembered of him except his caution that it's ''a hell of a place to lose a cow!'' The beautiful columns and spires of the canyon were formed by geological faults and gradual erosion by rain, wind, and frost. The native Indian name for the area means ''rocks standing like men in a bowl-shaped canyon.'' Spectacular hiking trails run through the principal areas, and 35 miles of roads lead to many of the best scenic spots including Fairyland View, Sunset Point, Inspiration Point, Bryce Point, and Paria View (see Scenic Drives). Cabins available at Bryce Canyon Lodge May—Sept. Campsites open year-round but water not available after Oct. 1.

Supt, Bryce Canyon Nat'l Park, Bryce Canyon, UT 84717, **801/834-5322.**

CANYONLANDS

Nat'l Park, UT

A somewhat rough, dusty drive to a 6,000-foot-high Island in the Sky rewards visitors with one of the grandest views in the US: A vast expanse of canyons, spires, towers, buttes, and rivers. White Rim Trail, Shafer Trail and Elephant Hill in the Needles district are popular 4-wheel-drive areas (grades on Elephant Hill are as steep as 40 percent). For many, the ultimate experience at Canyonlands is a float trip on the roaring white water of either the Green River or the Colorado River and through Cataract Canyon. (Permits or professional guides required—applications available from park supt.) Commercially operated trips led by experienced, licensed guides are the safest and most popular. During summer, be sure to carry plenty of water whenever you leave established roads. (See Scenic Drives.)

Supt, Canyonlands Nat'l Park, 446 S Main St, Moab, UT 84532, **801/259-7164.**

ZION

Nat'l Park, UT

The most famous attraction in this park is Zion Canyon, formed by the Virgin River. A 13-mile round-trip drive takes visitors past the canyon and a number of well-known landmarks including the Sentinel, Court of the Patriarchs,

Bryce Canyon, National Park, UT

Mountain of the Sun, and the Great White Throne. A popular folklife festival held each September features pioneer crafts and vittles, storytelling, and children's games. South and Watchman campgrounds have unreserved sites year-round; more primitive sites elsewhere (camping permits from visitor center). Cabins operated by Zion Lodge; reservations are usually necessary in summer **(801/586-7686).**

Supt, Zion Nat'l Park, Springdale, UT 84767, **801/772-3256.**

CAPITOL REEF

Nat'l Park, UT

This park lies in the slickrock country of southern Utah, an area where water has cut monoliths, arches, and mazes of canyons out of a sandstone and shale desert. The park was named for one of its high ridges that resembles the dome of the US Capitol. Explored only within the last 100 years, much of the park is still a wilderness area. The park was home to the Fremont Indians 1000 years ago, and many tribal rock drawings remain. There are no services within the park, but two campsites are open year-round and there is backpacking by permit. Be sure to carry sufficient water in this desert environment and avoid camping in ditches subject to flash floods.

Supt, Capitol Reef Nat'l Park, Torrey, UT 84775, **801/425-3526.**

Carlsbad Caverns, National Park, NM

PETRIFIED FOREST

Nat'l Park, AZ

This park is a popular stop for westbound tourists, perhaps on their way to the Grand Canyon. It is notable for its petrified wood, prehistoric animal fossils, Indian ruins, rock formations, and desert landscapes—especially the famous expanse of colored sand in the extreme northern section known as the Painted Desert. Long Logs Trail, a marked footpath at the southern end of Petrified Forest, takes visitors past the largest collection of petrified wood in the park, and the Agate House ruins—a partially reconstructed building made of petrified wood. The Trail also offers views of fossil-rich badlands formations and desert wildlife. There are no developed campsites, but camping is allowed by permit in certain wilderness areas. Overnight accommodations in nearby towns.

Supt, Petrified Forest Nat'l Park, AZ 86028, **602/524-6228.**

ARCHES

Nat'l Park, UT

Located in southeastern Utah's red rock country, Arches National Park boasts the largest collection of natural bridges in the world. The smallest have just a three-foot opening (the minimal distance still considered to be a natural bridge). However, Landscape Arch is nearly 300 feet from base to base. The park can be entered only from the south, off US 163 near Moab. A visitor center near the entrance provides self-guiding auto-tour booklets, information on park attractions, and permits for backcountry travel. A popular activity in spring and summer is the guided Fiery Furnace walk, a two-hour tour through white rock formations that appear as if they had been burned to pinnacles of ash. The limited number of campsites near Skyline Arch are more popular in spring and fall, when the mercury is not as likely to rise above 100°F.

Supt, Arches Nat'l Park, 446 S Main St, Moab, UT 84532, **801/259-7164.**

GRAND CANYON

Nat'l Park, AZ

The most spectacular section of the world-famous chasm is contained within this national park. At one point the canyon is 18 miles wide and about one mile deep. The north rim averages about 1200 feet higher than the south and is usually closed except during summer because of heavy snows. Numerous facilities are located along both rims because crossing the canyon requires a drive in excess of 200 miles. However, strong hikers can cross via a 20-mile route on the Kaibab Trail. All campgrounds are first-come, first-served, although reservations are accepted at a few sites during summer. Mule trips of one or two days are available for persons over age 12 but weighing less than 200 pounds. Scenic flights with a close-up view above and below the rim, originate daily from Scottsdale, AZ (602/948-2400). Information about many other services can be found at visitor stations along both rims.

Supt, Grand Canyon Nat'l Park, PO Box 129, Grand Canyon, AZ 86023, **602/638-2411.**

Gila Cliff Dwellings, National Monument, NM

GILA CLIFF DWELLINGS

Nat'l Monument, NM

Of the numerous Indian ruins within this monument, the oldest are of a type constructed about AD 100-400. Others were created about a thousand years ago, but by the year 1400, the Mogollon Indians had abandoned the area entirely. Why they left or where they went is not known. A 44-mile drive heads north from Silver City on NM 15; the national monument is virtually surrounded by the Gila National Forest and Wilderness Area. Hiking, horseback riding, and camping are popular activities. Information about tours of the Indian homes, most built in natural caves, can be obtained at the visitor information center.

Gila Cliff Dwellings Nat'l Monument, Rte 11, Box 100, Silver City, NM 88061, **505/534-9461.**

Redwood, National Park, CA

SALINAS

Nat'l Monument, NM

On a ridge atop Chupadero Mesa in central New Mexico stand the ruins of an Indian pueblo and two massive 17th century Franciscan missions. The people of Gran Quivira (they called it Cueloze) lived in an area where two Indian cultures, the Mogollon and Anasazi, met and blended. The earliest Spanish explorers in the area entered the Salinas Valley near the end of the 16th century. A 30-minute walk through the Indian and Spanish ruins begins at the visitor information center, which displays many artifacts and distributes self-guiding tour folders. The nearby Shaffer Hotel Headquarters has a museum with an audio-visual presentation about the ruins. Located near NM 14 and NM 41, approach routes to the monument should be traveled only during good weather.

Supt, Salinas Nat'l Monument, PO Box 496, Mountainair, NM 87036, **505/847-2585.**

Petrified Forest, National Park, AZ

Photo: Dale Schicketanz

CARLSBAD CAVERNS

Nat'l Park, NM

Carlsbad Cavern is the largest of about 70 caves preserved beneath the harsh and rugged land of the nearly-47,000-acre national park. During summer evenings at sunset, hordes of bats can be seen flying out of the caverns—as many as 5000 a minute. The intricate patterns of water-dripped limestone are explainable in scientific terms, but remain awe-inspiring to even the most cynical observers. The centuries-long process has formed what seem to be colorful hanging "curtains" of rock along the cave's walls. Guided tours are offered year-round, but end at 2pm Sept-Apr. Above ground sites such as Walnut Canyon and the Capitan Reef Escarpment, can be approached by car. Nature trails are marked near the cavern entrance and Walnut Canyon. There are no overnight accommodations or campgrounds within the park, but numerous sites are nearby. Restaurant and gift shop adjacent to visitor center.

Supt, Carlsbad Caverns Nat'l Park, 3225 Nat'l Parks Hwy, Carlsbad, NM 88220, **505/785-2233.**

ROCKY MOUNTAIN

Nat'l Park, CO

The grandeur of high mountains and alpine valleys, crystal-clear lakes and sparkling mountain streams is nowhere more abundant in America than in this national park. Located in north central Colorado, fully one-third of the total area is above the tree line, and frozen tundra predominates in these areas. There are no permanent lodgings within the park, but plenty of rooms are available in nearby towns such as Estes Park. Five campgrounds scattered throughout the park are mostly filled to capacity early each summer day. More than 300 miles of magnificent hiking trails offer far more rewarding mountain experiences than the limited road system, although US 34 (Trail Ridge Road) is one of the great Alpine drives in the US (frequently closed during the winter). During the summer season, horses with guides can be hired in or around the park, but horses are permitted only on designated trails. Alpine and Moraine Park visitor centers are open summer months only.

Supt, Rocky Mt Nat'l Park, Estes Park, CO 80517, **303/586-2371.**

MESA VERDE

Nat'l Park, CO

Located near the Ute and Navajo Indian reservations, the majestic plateau of Mesa Verde is the site of extensive prehistoric Indian ruins. About 1300 years ago, American Indians built mesa-top villages and later great cities of stone in the cliffs of Mesa Verde. The Mesa Verde Indians abandoned their magnificent homes before Columbus discovered America. They were not found until more than a decade after the Civil War. The multi-room dwellings (sometimes called "America's oldest apartments") reach up to four stories, and were made of talus stones with Pinon pines as roof beams. These pre-Columbian cliff dwellings really are a "don't miss" attraction. There are free ranger-guided tours and a free 4-hour bus tour past striking scenery to Weatherhill Mesa. Plan at least a full day to explore. Bike rentals available. A lookout point, at 8,572 feet, offers spectacular views of four states. Camping is permitted only at the 500-site Morefield Village Campground near the park entrance. Modern, comfortable lodgings are available at the 100-room Far View Motor Lodge overlooking the Visitor Center. Reservations for rooms and tours are recommended (303/529-4421). Some ruins are open only in summer.

Mesa Verde Co, PO Box 277, Mancos, CO 81328, **303/529-4421.**

MIDWEST

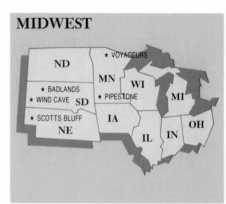

BADLANDS

Nat'l Park, SD

The Badlands are a wonderland of strange, colorful spires and pinnacles, massive buttes, and deep gorges. In 1976 new areas were added to the national park, including some lands on the Pine Ridge Indian Reservation. At the same time, nearly 65,000 acres were set aside as a wilderness area protected from roads or other kinds of development. Bison, Rocky Mountain bighorn sheep, prairie dogs, and other Great Plains wildlife roam the park. It is a wonderful area for backpacking, but stay alert for prairie rattlers. Backpackers are urged to contact a ranger before camping in the backcountry. Cabins, meals, and souvenirs available at Cedar Pass Lodge mid-May—mid-Oct.

Supt, Badlands Nat'l Park, SD 57750, **605/433-5361.**

Badlands, National Park, SD

Great Smoky Mountains, National Park, TN/NC

Wind Cave, National Park, SD

Wind Cave, National Park, SD

Wind Cave, National Park, SD

Glacier National Park, MT

Photo: Danny On

WIND CAVE

Nat'l Park, SD

Although the surface of this 28,000-acre park has become a sanctuary for bison, mule deer, prairie dogs, and birds, and also preserves the tall-stemmed grasses and delicate blossoms of the virgin prairie, most visitors are attracted by the 37-plus miles of twisting passageways in Wind Cave. Named for the stiff breeze that still blows out of the entrance, much of the cave remains uncharted; at least a thousand passageways have yet to be explored. Rangers lead cave tours several times daily Mem Day—Lab Day (off-season schedules vary). Mt. Rushmore National Memorial (see Manmade & Natural Wonders) is N via SD 87.

Supt, Wind Cave Nat'l Park, Hot Springs, SD 57747, **605/745-4600.**

SCOTTS BLUFF

Nat'l Monument, NE

A massive promontory rising 800 feet above the valley around it, Scotts Bluff once was part of the ancient High Plains that are now almost entirely eroded. The North Platte Valley, of which Scotts Bluff is the dominant natural feature, has been a human migration corridor for years. Well-worn traces of the famous Oregon Trail are still visible within the park. The summit can be reached by car, where parking is available. Grand vistas from a number of overlooks include views of famous landmarks such as Chimney Rock National Historic Site, Laramie Peak, and the Oregon Trail approach to Mitchell Pass.

Supt, Scotts Bluff Nat'l Monument, Box 427, Gering, NE 69341, **308/436-4340.**

PIPESTONE

Nat'l. Monument, MN

Long before the first white man reached the northern plains, Indians of many tribes were traveling up to 1000 miles to reach the sacred pipestone quarries of southwestern Minnesota. Indians battled for control of the land for many years until it was seized by the government in 1893 under the law of eminent domain. Many 19th-century settlers made it a point to visit this famous quarry where Indians found the raw materials for peace pipes. In addition to exhibits covering geology, history, archeology, and the pipestone crafts, there are some lovely scenic trails. A small stand of virgin prairie survives. The small park is adjacent to the north side of the city of Pipestone.

Supt, Pipestone Nat'l Monument, Pipestone, MN 56164, **507/825-5463.**

VOYAGEURS

Nat'l Park, MN

Practically adjacent to the Quetico and Boundary Waters Canoe Area, this park is a boater's paradise. In fact, watercraft must be used for travel within the park; automobiles are parked at the entrance. Boats, canoes, and other equipment can be rented from resorts just outside the park. The park is renowned for challenging walleye, muskie, and trout fishing (with many fish of trophy size), as well as for ice fishing. Fishing in Minnesota requires a state license; visitors crossing the Canadian border to fish must have an Ontario license. The park is home to the rare and rarely seen eastern timber wolf, and black bears are common to the entire region. Proper storage of food and disposal of refuse is a necessity to keep predators away from campsites. In season, trails through the woods are painted blue with an abundance of luscious, ripe blueberries (great for camp-baked pies!) and the area has a large harvest of cranberries. Nearby International Falls is a houseboater's Avalon, with a half dozen or so fleet owners offering rentals of these self-contained luxury craft. About 100 boat-in primitive campsites are scattered throughout the park, private and public campsites, as well as motels and rooms outside the park. Emergency weather info is given on 800 and 1230 on the AM dial.

Supt, Voyageurs Nat'l Park, PO Box 50, Internat'l Falls, MN 56649, **218/283-9821.**

Voyageurs, National Park, MN

HOT SPRINGS

Nat'l Park, AR

Situated in the small Zig Zag mountains southwest of Little Rock, Hot Springs is rich in history, and relatively close to civilization for a national park. In the early 1900s, huge, ornate buildings were constructed (in an area now coloquially known as Bathhouse Row) to cater to crowds of health-seekers anxious to soak in the "waters of the Washita." Although the tradition of mineral baths has declined, many people still enjoy the relaxing warm waters filtering up from the springs. With a favorable climate year-round, Hot Springs is a popular spot for horseback riders, boaters, anglers, and hikers. Scenic drives lead to views of woodlands and distant mountains, and to the nearby city of Hot Springs. There are more than 40 springs along the lower slopes of Hot Springs Mountain. At the source, the average water temperature is 143°F.

Supt, Hot Springs Nat'l Park, PO Box 1860, Hot Springs, AR 71901, **800/643-1570** *(outside AR), or* **800/272-2081** *(within AR).*

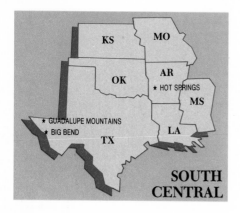

SOUTH CENTRAL

GUADALUPE MOUNTAINS

Nat'l Park, TX

Just south of Carlsbad Caverns National Park (see), the Guadalupe Mountains stand like an island in the desert, watching over the most extensive fossil-reef complex in the world; much of the park was covered by an enormous inland sea hundreds of millions of years ago. Some 80 miles of often *very* rugged trails are available to hardy hikers and backpackers, but note that this is rattlesnake country. Motorists can catch spectacular views of El Capitan and Guadalupe Peak, the highest point in Texas, from US 62-180. Free campgrounds near the Frijole Visitor Center and in the Dog Canyon area; hotel and motel accommodations at least 30 mi away.

Supt, Guadalupe Nat'l Park, 3225 Nat'l Parks Hwy, Carlsbad, NM 88220, **915/828-3385.**

BIG BEND

Nat'l Park, TX

The southern boundary of this park and its international boundary between the US and Mexico are formed by the Rio Grande River, and three major canyons cut by it. This rocky wilderness was once home to freely roaming dinosaurs, and now more than 1000 plants and trees (from cacti to pine) dot the magnificently stark landscape. The river borders the park for 107 miles, and trips down the Rio Grande can be made by obtaining a free permit at any ranger station; river-running equipment can be rented west of the park. Lodgings are provided by National Parks Concessions, Inc. (915/477-2291). Guided horseback tours can be arranged by calling 915/477-2374. All campgrounds, improved and primitive, available on first-come basis (small fee for improved sites). Park officials recommend carrying snakebite kits.

Supt, Big Bend Nat'l Park, TX 79834, **915/477-2251.**

NORTHEAST

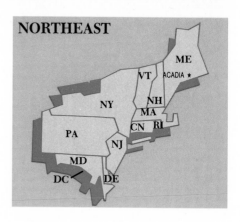

ACADIA

Nat'l Park, ME

(See Island Escapes.)

Acadia National Park, ME

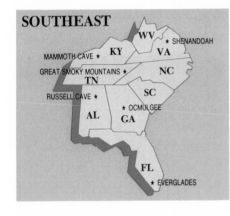

SOUTHEAST

GREAT SMOKY MOUNTAINS

Nat'l Park, TN/NC

Half in Tennessee and half in North Carolina, this park preserves the world's finest example of an unspoiled temperate deciduous forest. The more than 800 square miles of peaks and open valleys (locally referred to as "coves") are covered with more than 1400 types of flowering plants (best observed in full bloom early June—mid-July). The name "Smoky" refers to the smoke-like haze that blankets the mountains. Viewed from the observation tower at Clingmans Dome (closed winter), the mist and mountaintops become a dream-like sea of clouds and peaked islands. Some log cabins and barns have been restored to their pioneer-era condition, and are open to visitors. Rental horses available (except winter), but riding only permitted on designated horse trails. There are seven developed and three primitive camping areas (fees at developed areas); reservations may be required (615/436-9564). Exhibits and info available at any of three visitor centers in and around the park.

 Supt, Great Smoky Mts Nat'l Park, Gatlinburg, TN 37738, **615/436-5615.**

MAMMOTH CAVE

Nat'l Park, KY

Although there are a limited number of above-ground activites, the real appeal of this 52,000-acre park is the enormous limestone cave beneath the surface. More than 500 miles of twisting passageways have already been mapped—and more are being added every year. From the striking vision of up-reaching stalagmites and sturdily hanging stalactites to the smooth beauty of onyx pillars, the world's longest cave has some of the most original sights you'll ever see—above *or* below ground. Guided cave trips daily (except Christmas) throughout the year (times vary). The self-guiding Historic Tour can be started at any time. Cave temperature is a constant 54°F., so sweaters and jackets are needed. Walking is generally easy but there are many steps to negotiate. Riverboat cruises on the Green River through park wildlife areas can be enjoyed for $3 (502/758-2243). Above ground foot trails are known to include areas with poisonous snakes. Lodging at Mammoth Cave Hotel.

 Supt, Mammoth Cave Nat'l Park, Mammoth Cave, KY 42259, **502/758-2328.**

Great Smoky Mountains, National Park, TN/NC

OCMULGEE

Nat'l Monument, GA

Where the Ocmulgee River passes from the red clay land of the rolling piedmont to the sandy flat lands of the coastal plain, the rich native plant and animal life have led people to seek their livelihood here for more than 10,000 years. The area is noted for the relics of Indian mound builders who lived here for many generations. The visitor center houses a major archeological museum. Tours leave the museum for the Earthlodge, a restored ceremonial building with an original floor 1000 years old. The Temple Mound Drive leads to the three largest mounds as well as to the site of the British Colonial Trading Post. Opelofa Nature Trail leads past swamp and forest ecosystems along Walnut Creek. Located on the east edge of Macon, GA, the monument has no camping facilities.

Supt, Ocmulgee Nat'l Monument, 1207 Emery Hwy, Macon, GA 31201, 912/742-0447.

Everglades, National Park, FL

Everglades, National Park, FL

EVERGLADES

Nat'l Park, FL

The Everglades are the only subtropical wilderness in the US. The lifeblood of the area is a freshwater river 50 miles wide but only a few inches deep that flows slowly from Lake Okeechobee toward Florida Bay. The 1.4 million acres included in the national park is only part of this watery expanse. The park is home and protector to many rare or threatened species such as the American crocodile, the Florida panther, and the great white heron. Animals and birds are most visible and active during the dry winter season. The Main Visitor Center located about 11 miles southwest of Homestead, Florida, has information about hiking, boating, and open-air tram tours, led by rangers, of the Shark Valley area. Campgrounds are located at Long Pine Key and Flamingo. Reservations are accepted for winter months only, when a camping fee is charged. The park contains numerous marked canoe trails. The Gulf Coast Ranger Station offers boat tours Nov 1—May 1.

Supt, Everglades Nat'l Park, PO Box 279, Homestead, FL 33030, 305/247-6211.

SHENANDOAH

Nat'l Park, VA

Virginians and out-of-state visitors enjoy the magnificent Skyline Drive that follows the crest of the Blue Ridge Mountains for 105 glorious miles, offering glimpses and broad panoramas of the Piedmont to the east and the Shenandoah Valley to the west (see Scenic Drives). The national park runs along both sides of the drive, and is worth exploration on horseback or by foot, especially in fall when the nearly 100 varieties of trees burst into their annual chromatic splendor. Numerous campgrounds are scattered throughout the park. More than 500 miles of trails, some of them used heavily, are available to hikers. Park visitor centers can be found at Miles 4.6 and 51, but are open only during summer. Accommodations at Skyland Lodge (Mileposts 41-43), Big Meadows Lodge (Mile 51.2), and Lewis Mountain (Mile 57.5). Park headquarters is 4 mi E of Luray on US 211.

Supt, Shenandoah Nat'l Park, Luray, VA 22835, 703/999-2266.

RUSSELL CAVE

Nat'l Monument, AL

About 9,000 years ago, long before the first true civilizations arose in Egypt and the Near East, small groups of Indians began living in Russell Cave located in the hill country of northern Alabama. Successive bands of hunters with their families took shelter in this cave until about 1,000 AD. A record of at least 9,000 years of human life is held beneath the surface of Russell Cave. Exhibits of prehistoric cooking, weapons, and tools are in the visitor center and in the main cave entrance—the only access point that can be used without written permission. Demonstrations of ancient Indian life are presented periodically.

Supt, Russell Cave Nat'l Monument, Bridgeport, AL 35740, 205/495-2672.

Ocmulgee, National Monument, GA

Chapter 8

WINTER SPORTS OF ALL SORTS

Mt. Washington, White Mountains, NH

Photo: Bob Grant

Mark Twain once said, "Everybody talks about the weather, but nobody does anything about it," but there is something you can do about winter weather: enjoy it! This chapter gives you a whole season's worth of activities on or around snow. The emphasis, of course, is on skiing—downhill and cross-country—with descriptions of some of the finest slopes and trails in the country, the famous as well as the lesser-known. But this special section will also help you enjoy other wintertime outdoor activities.

Find out where in the city to go for giant, man-made toboggan slides. Discover where you can slide on an inner tube down a slope of ice and snow. Determine which are the hot spots for ice fishing. Pinpoint the meccas for ice skating. Included in this snow-season round-up are tempting trails for snowmobile enthusiasts and, for budding Olympians, a famous high-speed bobsled run that tests nerves as well as skills. This focus on winter fun spots will even tell you where to go to watch the exciting sport of dog-sled racing or the ancient Scottish game of curling.

Winter—once you decide to do something about it—can be custom-made for pleasure. These listings are designed to point you in the right direction—to stimulate you, the next time winter rolls around, to reach for your skis instead of your shovel.

NORTHWEST

WA
★ MT. RANIER NAT'L PARK
MT
★ BRIDGER BOWL
★ MT. BACHELOR
YELLOWSTONE NAT'L PARK
OR
★ WY
ID
★ SUN VALLEY
★ JACKSON HOLE

MT. RANIER NAT'L PARK

Ashford, WA

Even though the rugged face and craggy glaciers of Mt. Ranier (see Nat'l Parks & Monuments) are not available for skiing, a plentitude of winter diversions surround this majestic mountain. From the first snow of winter until May, Mt. Ranier's extensive cross-country and ski touring areas are open to the silent practitioners of these sports. Maps of the marked trails can be obtained at the Visitor Center, and lessons and equipment rentals are also available. Sliding down slick hills on inner tubes or saucers is a recently popularized winter thrill, and the park has enhanced the fun by removing timber and terrain dangers. Mt. Ranier has a supervised and maintained area with three runs designed for safe "adult or kiddie tubing." The area is next to the Paradise Inn, and operates from Dec—Apr. Perhaps the most unique and challenging cold-weather activities at the park are the snow- and ice-climbing seminars and expeditions organized by Ranier Mountaineering Inc. RMI offers a two-day climb on a Mt. Ranier glacier, or a five-day (and *extremely* strenuous) winter assault on the 14,410-ft. peak. Write: RMI, 201 St. Helens Ave, Tacoma, WA 98402 (Oct-May) or RMI, Paradise, WA 98398 (June-Sept).

Supt, Mt Ranier Nat'l Park, Ashford, WA 98304, **206/569-2211.**

MT. BACHELOR

Bend, OR

When is a winter sport not a winter sport? When it extends into summer! If downhill fever is bugging you, but the calendar says June, July, or even August, you can now enjoy your favorite winter activity in shirt-sleeve weather at Mt. Bachelor in central Oregon. A recently added chair lift transports skiers to the 9000-ft. summit of this volcanic peak, enabling them to take advantage of permanent snowfields covering a 3100-ft. vertical drop. The "Summer Season" begins May 1, and runs—weather and snow conditions permitting—until July or early August. Lessons are available, and non-skiers can also enjoy the ride and the view. Call to verify estimated closing date.

Mt Bachelor, Inc, PO Box 1031, Bend, OR 97709, **503/382-2442.**

YELLOWSTONE

Nat'l Park, WY

Winter comes early to Yellowstone. In September, the air turns cool, shadows lengthen, a thin skim of ice forms across puddles in the early morning hours; bull elk begin rounding up their harems, and an occasional herd of bison drifts across the lower geyser basin. It marks the beginning of a long season of winter fun in America's largest and oldest national park. The park is popular with those silent winter travelers, the snowshoers and cross-country skiers, yet is large enough to allow them to co-exist with their motorized brethren, the snowmobilers. Despite numerous restrictions—stay on the right side of marked trails only, maximum speed 45 mph, pre-registration—thousands of snowmobilers visit the trails during the mid-Dec—mid-Mar season. For ski tourers, the trails are seldom groomed and they may find themselves breaking trails as they explore the Yellowstone backcountry. There are no organized downhill facilities. Snowmobile fuel is available at Old Faithful, Canyon, and Mammoth Hot Springs stations. Warming stations are located at Mammoth Hot Springs, Old Faithful, Madison, Canyon, Tower Falls, Fishing Bridge, and West Thumb.

Yellowstone Nat'l Park, WY 82190, **307/344-7381.**

JACKSON HOLE

Teton Village, WY

The toughest and longest downhill runs in America are on Rendezvous Mountain, an ideal winter destination for experts anxious to get away from crowds slipping down the bunny slopes. Apres Vous, the second major downhill slope, is more appropriate to intermediates and even beginners. Nestled in the "hole," or high mountain valley region of Wyoming, and surrounded by the breath-taking peaks of the Grand Tetons, this area's sights and scenery are as famous and varied as its skiing. Grand Teton and Yellowstone National Parks are both less than an hour away. Accommodations are provided by Sojourner Inn, The Inn at Jackson Hole, and Alpenhof. Teton Village Property Management (800/443-6840) and Jackson Hole Realty (800/443-8613) offer condominium rentals—although more plentiful during the nonskiing season. Current snow conditions: 307/733-2291.

Jackson Hole Central Resrv, PO Box 510, Teton Village, WY 83025, **307/733-2292.**

SUN VALLEY

Sun Valley, ID

Ernest Hemingway, Ingrid Bergman, and Groucho Marx are among the luminaries who have enjoyed the fabulous downhill skiing on two mountains at this historic winter mecca developed by Averell Harriman for the Union Pacific Railroad in the 1930s. The four chair lifts on Dollar provide beginning and early-intermediate skiers with the excitement of Alpine thrills minus the major risks. But for experienced skiers looking for the best in downhill action, Sun Valley means "Baldy," actually four mountains in one served by 12 lifts and providing more than 750 acres of groomed runs and trails. For soaking away those ski aches, or just relaxing, try the two glass-enclosed pools. Week-long ski packages including seven nights lodging in Sun Valley Lodge, Inn, Apartments, or Wildflower Condominiums start at $364 per person, double occupancy.

Sun Valley Co, Sun Valley, ID 83353, **800/635-8261.**

BRIDGER BOWL

Bozeman, MT

Montana is known as the Big Sky Country, but at Bridger Bowl, they spell it "Big *Ski* Country." This ski haven in one of the nation's least populous states can rightfully be called one of winter's best kept secrets. Short lift lines and uncrowded slopes are the order of the day, but with Bridger Mountain's 37 meticulous trails and challenging 2000-ft vertical drop, this paradise won't remain undiscovered forever. Visit with your fingers crossed, and whisper the good news to only your best skiing friends. Runs are evenly divided between beginner, intermediate, and expert, while the longest run is a blistering 2½ miles. Of special interest is the New Year's Eve torchlit ski parade, and February's fabulous winter carnival. Bridger is only minutes from Montana State University, and the university town of Bozeman offers a wide variety of nightlife and other apres-ski activities. General info and lodging: 406/587-2111.

Bridger Bowl, 15795 Bridger Canyon Rd, Bozeman, MT 59715, **406/586-2787.**

Yellowstone National Park, WY

SOUTHWEST

LASSEN PARK

Lassen Volcanic Nat'l Park, CA

If you haven't skied down a volcano recently, here is the ideal place to start. The Lassen Park Ski Area is located inside the southwest entrance of Lassen Volcanic National Park, on Lassen Peak, which was an actively erupting volcano as recently as 1921. Where lava once flowed there are now six marked trails served by a new triple chair lift and two tows providing a lift capacity of 2800 skiers per hour. Most runs are carefully groomed, but some are left untouched after good powder snowfalls. The park operates daily from 9am—4pm seven days a week from Thanksgiving Day to Easter Sunday, snow permitting. Adult, all-day lift rates are $10/weekdays, $13/weekends and holidays. Complete Alpine ski rental packages start at $11 for adults, all day. Instruction available. Lists of accommodations obtainable from address below. Snow conditions: 916/595-4464.

Lassen Park Ski Area, 2150 N Main St #7, Red Bluff, CA 96080, **916/595-3376.**

BADGER PASS

Yosemite Nat'l Park, CA

Short lift lines are the rule at Badger Pass, the oldest established ski area in California. Four double chair lifts, a T-bar, and a cable tow serve nine different downhill runs. Lift tickets for adults are $14.50/all-day mid-week pass, or $15.50/weekends and holidays. Snow conditions: 209/372-1338. This National Park is also a growing mecca for cross-country enthusiasts. Especially popular is the 6000-foot Crane Flat, where varied terrain with wide meadows and gentle slopes makes for nearly ideal touring. For the dedicated Nordic skier, cross-country opportunities include multiday treks across the Sierra Nevada or to Tuolumne Meadows, and day trips to the Tuolumne Grove of giant sequoias, Gin Flat, and the Merced Canyon overlook. Other diversions offer a snow-cat tour to the top of the ridge (bring your camera) and showshoeing (rentals available). Evening activities in Yosemite Valley include ice skating, ski movies, special ski dinners, entertainment, Ranger-Naturalist programs, dancing, and a weekly ski buffet. Reservations required for all Nordic activities. For budget-conscious skiers, Midweek Winter Packages provide lodging and Alpine or Nordic skiing (but not both) for $30 per day. Located 23 mi from Yosemite Valley via CA 41 to Chinquapin junction turnoff; daily bus from valley at 9:15am—round trip $26.

Yosemite Park & Curry Co, Yosemite Nat'l Park, CA 95389, **209/252-4848.**

ALPINE MEADOWS

Tahoe Nat'l Forest, CA

Alpine Meadows operates under a license from the US Forest Service to run a ski area in the protected Tahoe National Forest. As you may expect, this arrangement makes for a beauteous marriage of sports and nature. The runs have been carefully and scenically planned to preserve the unadulterated state of the forest and mountain. Pine trees are abundant in the valley below 8637-foot Ward Peak, where most runs begin. Special 5-day adult lift tickets (about $100), interchangeable at Squaw Valley USA (minutes away), Northstar-at-Tahoe, Heavenly Valley, and Kirkwood. Single-day adult lift tickets for Alpine Meadows only are $22, $11 for children 12 and under. Total lifts include 10 double chairs, two pomas, and a T-bar. Of the 50 miles of runs, about 25% are for beginners, 40% for intermediate, and 35% for experts. The longest run is 2½ miles. Free ski shuttle service between the slopes and a number of area lodgings. Alpine Meadows reservations: 916/583-1045. Open Nov—May. Snow report: 916/583-6914.

Alpine Meadows Ski Corp, PO Box AM, Tahoe City, CA 95730, **916/583-4232.**

SQUAW VALLEY USA

Olympic Valley, CA

Nestled within five lofty peaks in the Sierras overlooking Lake Tahoe, the site of the 1960 Winter Olympics offers thousands of acres of skiable terrain, an annual snowpack of more than 400 inches, and an abundance of warm California sunshine. The main skiing mountains are Squaw Peak (8900 ft.), Emigrant Peak (8900 ft.), and KT22 (8200 ft.). The valley is serviced by 27 lifts, including an aerial tram and a brand-new, six-passenger gondola. For the apres-ski, snow-blind, or plaster-cast set, the gaming tables of Nevada are just minutes away. Accommodations in the area are on the expensive side, and 24-hour hedonists can spend a small fortune in an amazingly short span of time. For a brochure describing the complicated economic picture, call 916/583-5585. Located near I-80 about 200 mi E of San Francisco.

Squaw Valley USA Central Resrv, PO Box 2007, Olympic Valley, CA 95730, **800/825-7954 (resrv), 800/545-4350 (in CA).**

Breckenridge Ski Area, CO

Aspen, CO

SIERRA SWEEPSTAKES

Truckee, CA

See All-American Sled Dog Championships.

ALTA SKI AREA

Alta, UT

Located just 45 minutes from Salt Lake City's airport, Alta is noted for its dry, fluffy-powder, although packing machines keep many runs hard for those who don't like powder skiing. The four mountains towering above the Alta Lodge are Mount Baldy (11,068 feet), Sugarloaf (11,051 feet), Devils Castle (10,920 feet), and Point Supreme (10,595 feet). *Holiday* magazine called these scenic skiing peaks "the world's best." Of the eight chair lifts, five are in excess of 4000 feet long, and there are three rope tows. The longest run is a whopping 3½ miles. All day lift tickets are bargain priced at $12 for adults, even cheaper for a more limited number of runs. Apres-ski life at Alta is a series of enchanting spontaneous happenings—movies, talks, folk dancing, costume parties, bridge, chess, backgammon or simply stimulating conversations by a cozy fire. A true feeling of community exists at the seven lodges at Alta (Alta Lodge: 801/742-3500). A highly regarded instructional center, the Alf Engen Ski School, has 76 instructors.

Alta Ski Area, Alta, UT 84070, **801/742-3333.**

Breckenridge, CO

Photo: Courtesy of the Photo Shop, Breckenridge, Colorado.

SUNDANCE
Provo, UT

Robert Redford's compact but environmentally fascinating ski resort is a natural for lovers of the unspoiled outdoors as well as for downhillers on a budget. Even though they may not see Redford, adults can ski all day on 27 runs and make maximum use of two double chair lifts and one triple chair lift for less than the price of a night at the movies—$10; under 12 $7.50. On the slopes of 11,000-foot Mt. Timpanogos in Utah's Wasatch Mountains, the area is noted for its light, powdery snow. Plenty of novice and intermediate runs, as well as advanced terrain featuring some moguled and exceptionally challenging expert slopes. The longest run is 2½ miles. Ski in, ski out private cabins are available with plenty of advance reservation. Other accommodations available in Provo and Heber, both about 20 minutes from Sundance. The resort is also noted for its well-lighted trails frequented by night skiers—open weekday evenings only. The Sundance Tree Room—a restaurant with a full-size tree growing through the middle of it—features Redford photos and movie memorabilia, and is a must for film fans and skiers alike.

Sundance, PO Box 837, Provo, UT 84603, **801/225-4107.**

SNOWBIRD SKI RESORT
Snowbird, UT

Just a snowball's throw from the Sundance and Alta ski areas, Snowbird shares the light, powdery, and particularly abundant snow for which the region is noted. Here, the 3000-foot vertical Gad Valley and the 2900-foot drop of Peruvian Gulch present more than three square miles of varied downhill configurations. Lifts include a huge aerial tramway carrying 125 skiers in each cabin, six double chair lifts, and a specially designed beginners chair lift. Total lift capacity is 8810 per hour. For the skier who wants to try something different, the Wasatch Powderbird Guides offer helicopter flights to unserviced or otherwise inaccessible areas for premier virgin powder skiing. Snowbird also has extensive lodging facilities. Dormitory rooms are less than $25 per day (even less in late spring). Single rooms start at about $85, and a wide variety of packages are available. Reservations only: 800/453-3000. Located in Wasatch Nat'l Forest's Little Cottonwood Canyon—25 mi from downtown Salt Lake City.

Snowbird Ski Resort, Snowbird, UT 84092, **801/742-2222, 801/521-6040 (from Salt Lake City).**

VAIL
Vail, CO

One of the oldest, largest, most popular, and breathtaking downhill ski centers in the country is also a popular cross-country area. Cross-country trails include the town of Vail's trail, roughly paralleling I-70; the 11-mile Shrine Pass located atop Vail Pass; the beginner's Piney Lake above Red Sandstone Road, off North Frontage Road; Meadow Mountain, just south of Minturn exit off I-70; Tigiwon, off US 24 about two miles south of Minturn; Spraddle Creek on the northeast corner of the Vail exit on I-70; and the experts-only Game Creek, reached by taking chair lift #3 or 7 along Ptarmigan Range (permission from VA ski patrol required). Of course, for many, the true grandeur of Vail is the 10 square miles of mountain with the fantastic assortment of downhill slopes, some dropping a full 3000 vertical feet. The "in crowd" skiers still jet here to schuss and hobnob, but the atmosphere is more open and less cliquish than it once was. Vail is a rewarding experience for first-timers and old hands alike.

Vail Resort Assoc, 241 E Meadow Dr, Vail, CO 81657, **303/476-5677.**

COPPER MOUNTAIN RESORT

Copper Mountain, CO

The site of the 1984 US Alpine Championships has some of the most exciting ski terrain in America with 62 carefully sculpted trails and 17 lifts up 12,050-foot Copper Mountain and 12,250-foot Union Peak. Located in the Arapaho National Forest, there are also 35 kilometers of cross-country trails providing experience at a variety of levels—a quiet walk in the winter woods, a lope across open meadows, a fast run down the mountain on telemark skis, or the challenge of competition. Overall, the US Forest Service calls Copper Mountain, "the most nearly perfect ski mountain in the US." Extensive instructional programs for beginners to experts and children of all ages, even tots! Full-day tickets: $12/adults, $10/children. Equipment packages $11—$20 per day. Snowmaking capabilities ensure uninterrupted skiing Nov—Apr. The resort village, located 75 mi W of Denver, has more than 35 shops and restaurants, modern accommodations, and the new Copper Mountain Athletic Club, which features an indoor swimming pool, tennis and racquetball courts and spa.

Copper Mt Resort, PO Box 3001, Copper Mt, CO 80443, **303/968-2882.**

BRECKENRIDGE SKI AREA

Breckenridge, CO

Although most noted in recent decades for its silky smooth slopes best liked by the faint of heart, management at this ski area has recently added lifts to some of the perilous pitches once frequented only by the local cognoscenti. Now, a total of 79 trails on two mountains provide plenty of excitement and challenging terrain for skiers at all levels. The 12,020-foot Peak Nine has a vertical drop of 2390 feet. Lifts include 10 doubles, a quad, a triple, and two surface lifts. All-day lift tickets $20/adults, $9/children. Four-day Ski-the-Summit tickets, good at Breckenridge, Copper Mountain, Keystone, and Arapaho Basin are $80/adults, $40/children. Breckenridge also has 22 kilometers of maintained cross-country ski trails available for $4. Accommodations, rates and reservations: 800/221-1091. For 24-hour snow conditions: 303/453-6118. Free town shuttle.

Breckenridge Ski Area, PO Box 1058, Breckenridge, CO 80424, **303/453-2918.**

Vail, CO

ASPEN

Aspen, CO

In the late 1880s, Aspen was a boom town built on silver. Since the inevitable bust that followed, the mainstay of the town's success has been downhill skiing. The Victorian roots remain, from the 1889 Hotel Jerome in the center of town, to the Victorian buildings scattered throughout the village between the half-million dollar condos. An Aspen Skiing Company three-mountain lift ticket provides easy access to Aspen Mountain (3370-ft. vertical rise, 7 double chair lifts), Buttermilk Mountain (1972-ft. rise, 6 double chair lifts), and Snowmass (3596-ft. rise, 11 double chair lifts and 2 triple chair lifts). Per person package rates for 7 nights lodging and 6 day lifts start at around $200.

Aspen Skiing Co, Box 1248, Aspen, CO 81612, **303/925-1220.**

TAOS SKI VALLEY

Taos Ski Valley, NM

More than a few vacationing skiers have been known to pull into this secluded resort after driving the 18-mile access road from Taos, take one look at the moguled steep cliff known as "Al's Run," and make a U-turn for home—or to some easier slope. Fortunately, although half of the trails are for experts, there are plenty of inter-mediate trails. A total of 65 slopes are serviced by six double chair lifts and two surface units, bringing high-altitude skiing—ranging from 9207 feet at the base to 11,819 feet at the top—within everyone's reach. All-day universal lift tickets are $20/adults, $12/children 12 and under. A wide variety of accommodation packages include the popular seven-day "Learn to Ski Better Week" starting at less than $600 per person, double occupancy. "Martini Trees" (blue spruces with glass pitchers of ice-cold martinis waiting beneath the branches) are scattered throughout the slopes offering liquid courage to down-hillers. Around-the-clock snow conditions: 505/758-0088.

Taos Ski Valley, Inc, Taos Ski Valley, NM 87571, **505/776-2291.**

SIERRA BLANCA

Ruidoso, NM

Owned and operated by the Mascalero Apaches on tribal reservation land, the Sierra Blanca ski resort is in the heart of the Lincoln National Forest and is the most popular ski area in New Mexico. It's easy to understand why, with seven ski lifts capable of handling nearly 10,000 people per hour and 25 miles of ski trails ranging from beginner's level to expert. Adult lift tickets are $21/full day. Daily snow reports: 505/257-9001. (Be sure to call ahead; Sierra Blanca is located further south than most major US ski areas.) The nearby Inn of the Mountain Gods, 800/545-9011, (also owned, operated, and staffed by tribe members) offers a 2-day ski package for $131.50 per person, double occupancy, which includes two nights at the luxury resort, lift tickets on Sierra Blanca, ski rentals, transportation to and from the mountain, breakfast and more.

Sierra Blanca Ski Resort, Box 220, Ruidoso, NM 88345, **505/257-9001.**

MIDWEST

Photo: Mike Michaelson

NORTH SHORE MOUNTAINS

Northeast MN

A total of 203 kilometers of cross-country trails along the magnificently hilly and wooded Lake Superior shore, including extensive areas of Superior National Forest, makes this one of the premier ski touring centers in the midwest. Some trails utilize old logging or Indian paths, while others pass through pine and birch plantations. All levels of ability are represented, and most trails are free, but the State of Minnesota does require a cross-country ski license on some trail segments. Maps and info: US Forest Service, PO Box 338, Duluth, MN 55801. In addition, some of the best downhill skiing in mid-America can be found at Lutsen Mountain, which rises 1000 vertical feet above Lake Superior and offers five lifts and 20 slopes up to 1½ miles long (fee for lifts). Cross-country trails in the same area go gently downhill for miles. Although weather in the northern area allows for a long skiing season (usually into mid-Apr), the tempering effect of Superior helps skiers avoid the usually bitter upper midwestern temperatures. Resorts and inns along the trail include Lutsen Resort (800/346-1467, 800/232-0071 (in MN)), Bear Track Outfitting Co. in Grand Marais (218/387-1162), Chateau Leveaux in Tofte (218/663-7223), and Cascade Lodge in Lusten (218/387-1112). Lodge-to-lodge ski tours can be arranged, including forwarding of gear.

Lutsen-Tofte Tourism Assoc, Box 115, Lutsen, MN 55612, **218/663-7281.**

ALL-AMERICAN SLED-DOG CHAMPIONSHIPS

Ely, MN

Here's a winter sport that has—quite literally—gone to the dogs: dogsledding. For most, this is a spectator sport (perhaps with a little wagering on the side), but for the several thousand drivers who push their huskies across various tundras on the pro circuit, this can be an active diversion, a job, or even a way of life. The granddaddy of North American races is the grueling 1150-mile Alaskan marathon, yet, intriguing and very competitive races are held in the "lower 48." The largest of these races is the All-American Sled-Dog Championships at Ely, MN. The course in this January event runs over lakes, across portages and along wooded trails. Spirited cries of "mush!" ring out over the snow, as drivers urge their charges along

in four classes of competition: open, seven-dog, five-dog, and three-dog events. Also held at this race (and others), is the weight-pull competition, where trainers pit their strongest dogs against each other—pulling a weighted sled from a standing start. The purse here is $10,000, and while that can buy quite a bit of dog food, most contests have little or no monetary incentive for the winners. Motivation enough is the pure thrill of competition, and the pride of knowing your "team" has beat all comers. Another major US race is the annual Sierra Sweepstakes in Truckee, CA.

Ely Sled-Dog Committee, Box 247, Ely, MN 55731, **218/365-6123.**

MILLE LACS

Onamia, MN

Would you chop a hole in a frozen lake and sit in the wintery wind to try and catch a few fish? Many people—perhaps even many fair-weather anglers—would see that activity as the height of chilly folly, but for a surprisingly growing number of outdoor enthusiasts, ice fishing is a challenging, yet relaxing, winter activity. Many lakes that freeze solidly and remain that way throughout the winter (weather permitting, of course) allow ice fishing, but one of the country's premier spots for this sport is the famous "Thousand Lakes" area in the center of Minnesota. In fact, the original French name for the region, "Mille Lacs," is also the name of the 250-square-mile lake famed for its winter bouquet of giant crappie, bluegill, and Minnesota walleye. The skilled predators set up mini-metropolises of shelters, shacks and shanties to ward off the cold, and are separated from their wily aquatic prey by only three or more inches of ice. They sit on buckets, sleds, snowmobiles, folding chairs, boxes, or anything convenient as they battle for dinner or perhaps just the sport of it. Some

natives claim Mille Lacs was once an Indian burial ground, and is now haunted . . . while others claim it is the area that gave birth to the legend of timberman Paul Bunyan. Nearly all agree that when the big lake freezes over and the cities of patiently bundled anglers appear, Mille Lacs is the home to nonpareil ice fishing. State fishing license required. Maps and info available from address below.

Office of Tourism, 240 Brewer Bldg, 419 N Robert St, St Paul, MN 55161, **800/328-1461.**

CURLING

Stevens Point, WI

If you say "curling" to most people, the first thing they think of is hair. But, for a growing number of people from California to New England, curling means an ancient Scottish winter sport—a kind of shuffleboard on ice. There are more than 150 curling clubs scattered across 12 snowbelt states, and the US Curling Association claims nearly 15,000 members. Curling consists of sliding a "stone"—officially a 42 ½-lb. lozenge of granite with a protruding handle—towards a target of concentric circles 126 feet down the ice. Team members sweep the ice in front of the sliding stones with brooms to lessen resistance and control the speed and direction of the shot. Curling is popular wherever there is ice and a knowledge of the game—especially so in Wisconsin. Many towns in the state have curling clubs or teams. Info available through: WI Div of Tourism, Dept of Dev, 123 W Washington Ave, PO Box 7606, Madison, WI 53707, 608/266-2161. One such club is located in Stevens Point, WI, where locals invite visitors to observe this unfamiliar game, and perhaps try their hand at it.

Stevens Point Curling Club, Stevens Point, WI 54481, **715/344-1940.**

MT. VALHALLA RECREATION AREA

Chequamegon Nat'l Forest, WI

The 175 miles of snowmobile trails and 75 miles of cross-country skiing routes in this National Forest in northern Wisconsin are only the beginning of the cold-weather activities open for winter enthusiasts. In addition to these established trails, there are several hundred miles of un-plowed logging roads and numbered Forest Roads that snowmobilers and cross-country skiers are welcome to use. Trail maps are available from district ranger offices in Park Falls, Glidden, Medford, Hayward, and Washburn. Other ski areas in the vicinity of the forest are Mount Telemark, two miles east of Cable; Port Mountain, two miles southwest of Bayfield; and White Cap Mountain, three miles north of Upson. The area around Ironwood, Michigan, is also noted for cross-country skiing and the typical gentle slopes of the midwest.

Chequamegon Nat'l Forest, 157 N 5th Ave, Park Falls, WI 54552, **715-762-2461.**

WINTERGREEN

Spring Green, WI

With its 400-foot vertical drop, Wintergreen offers some of the most challenging downhill runs in the midwest. The longest trail, River Road, is 4100-feet long, and the steepest run, Liberation, has a 40% slope. In all, nine downhill runs are served by two double chair lifts and one J-bar. Snow-making facilities are available on almost all runs. Adult lift tickets are $12 on weekends and holidays, $9 on weekdays. Wintergreen's restaurant, Spring Green, was designed by famed architect, Frank Lloyd Wright, and nearby is Taliesin, formerly the site of Wright's home and studio. Taliesin is now a world-renowned architectural firm and school. Wintergreen also operates 28 kilometers of carefully groomed and packed cross-country trails. Located on County Trunk "C" just off WI 23.

Wintergreen Ski Area, Box 467, Spring Green, WI 53588, **608/588-2571.**

THE WORLD'S CHAMPIONSHIP SNOWMOBILE DERBY

Eagle River, WI

Squeeze the throttle and feel the wind in your face. Kick up a spray of snow as you fly over a frosted field or a frozen lake. For some, these sensations and many others make snowmobiling the ultimate winter sport. You can ride along major highways, travel deep into silent sanctuaries of pine and snow, or race in circles around a track. Alone or in groups, on marked trails or forging through virgin snow, snowmobiling—with its harmonious blend of man, machine, and nature—is a uniquely enjoyable experience. Wisconsin is a great place to try *and see* some of the best snowmobiling in the country. Each January, Eagle River is home to the World's Championship Snowmobile Derby. Nearly 800 competitors and 30,000 spectators descend on this motorized sledding mecca annually for the fast-paced racing on Eagle River's oval track. But when the races are over and the trophies are awarded, snowmobile fun in this town isn't over yet. Eagle River and the surrounding Vilas County have well over 100 miles of well-marked and maintained trails. Members of community groups split the chore of manicuring the trails with the two area-owned grooming machines, and they welcome enthusiasts from all over the country to try out their corner of Snowmobile Heaven.

Chamber of Commerce, Box 219, Eagle River, WI 54521, **715/479-8575.**

COOK COUNTY FOREST PRESERVES

Near Chicago, IL

With 66,000 acres of beautifully wooded land, the Forest Preserve District of Cook County nearly surrounds the city of Chicago, and offers an extensive array of winter activities for people who live in or near the city. Popular winter attractions include cross-country skiing, ice skating, sledding, and snowmobiling. There are five sites for tobogganing down artificial hills, with the tallest and longest being the very popular 6-chute Swallow Cliff run (also known as the Palos Hills). When the Forest Preserve lakes freeze solidly, virtual cities of huts and shelters appear as through-the-ice anglers try their luck. Ice fishing is allowed at most lakes, but licenses are required. The entire district, with a few exceptions for special use areas, is open to cross-country skiers.

Forest Preserve District of Cook County, 536 N Harlem, River Forest, IL 60305, **312/261-8400, 312/366-9420.**

Vail, CO

PINE MOUNTAIN

Iron Mountain, MI

The Ski Jump at Pine Mountain is famous throughout the world. Here, seven North American distance-jump records were established from 1939 to, most recently, 1980, when Austrian Olympic Team leader Armin Kogler made a flawless 399-foot jump. The graceful ski-jumpers fly the equivalent of an entire city block, and can reach air speeds of up to 70 miles per hour. There are 16 downhill slopes, of which West Wall, Hematite, and the Ski Jumping Complex are the most difficult. Of the four lifts, the 2800-ft. Spruce Double Chair is the longest. Two adults and their children under 17 can enjoy a special ski-week package including lift tickets, lodging at Pine Mountain Village Condos, and other amenities for $375. Adult single-day lift tickets $11/weekdays, $15/weekends and during the holiday season. Reservations: 800/321-6298.

Pine Mt Corp, Pine Mt Rd, Star Rte 2, Iron Mt, MI 49801, **906/774-2747.**

BOYNE MOUNTAIN

Boyne Falls, MI

"The Mountain," as only midwesterners could affectionately call it, offers some of the best downhill skiing in the Midwest. A total of 15 ski runs, up to 1½ miles in length, are carefully designed to get the most out of the 450-foot vertical drop at Boyne Mountain. Three four-place chair lifts, five two-place chair lifts, and two rope tows give a combined lift capacity of 15,000 skiers per hour. Even if you don't ski, the majesty of winter in this area can be experienced by hiking through the mountain's nearly 5000 wooded acres. For the cross-country enthusiast, the Boyne Nordic Center leaves nothing to chance. Five marked and groomed trails, together with a complete Nordic shop offering tours and lessons, combine to create an excellent experience for the "quiet sport" participant.

Boyne USA Resorts, Boyne Falls, MI 49713, **616-549-2441.**

Speed Skating, NYS

NORTHEAST

Vail, CO

Photo: Peter Runyon

MOUNT SNOW

Green Mountain Nat'l Forest, VT

No matter what type of skier you are, Mount Snow is the kind of mountain that can provide a challenge. With a 1700-foot vertical drop and a system of 52 trails and slopes spread over three mountain faces, and 1000 wooded acres, Mount Snow offers some of the best beginning and intermediate skiing in New England. And if the skiers in your party aren't all skiing the same terrain, you don't have to say goodbye each morning as you shuffle off to different ski areas; all three faces meet at the 3600-ft. summit, making lunch or other rendezvous easily arrangeable. A network of 14 lifts, including two skis-on gondolas, two triple chair lifts, and 10 doubles, makes getting to the top a snap. Summit Lodge offers meals and a warm place to reflect downhill options. Main Mountain area offers 38 trails, including the 100-yard-wide Snowdance slope. Sunbrook area, facing south, features two long, leisurely trails: Coldbrook and Moonwalk. The North Face is mostly for experts. Numerous lodging facilities in the area, some moderately priced. Lodging info: 802/464-8501. Snow conditions: 802/464-2151. Two-day lift passes are $40/adults, $24/juniors (slightly higher during holiday season). Located near VT 100, N of intersection with VT 9.

Mt Snow Lodging Bureau, 100 Mt Rd, Mount Snow, VT 05356, **802/464-8501.**

KILLINGTON SKI AREA

Killington, VT

Vermont's most famous ski region (after Stowe) offers ski mountains and more than 100 lodges, motels, and condominiums. A system of 90 trails and slopes connect Killington Peak (4241 ft.), Snowdon Mountain (3592 ft.), Rams Head Mountain (3610 ft.), Skye Peak (3800 ft.), Bear Mountain (3296 ft.), and Sunrise Mountain (2456 ft.). Outer Limits trail on Bear Mountain has pitches up to 62%, steepest in New England. The size and location of the peaks effectively change local weather patterns. This gives the slopes an enormous amount of base snow, while snow-making capabilities extend the season from mid-Oct—June (the snowmakers' unofficial motto is "we'll operate until you quit!"). Sixteen lifts are strategically located among the six mountains. Round-the-clock ski report: 802/422-3261. Lodging packages start as low as $177 for five days, per person double occupancy.

Killington Lodging Bureau, Killington Rd, Killington, VT 05751, **802/422-3711.**

STRATTON

Stratton Mountain, VT

Is it faster than a speeding bullet? Maybe not, but to bring a taste of Western skiing to the East, Stratton has created a "Super Trail." Almost a mile long and 300 feet wide, it is spiced with random islands of trees and promises spectacular downhill adventures for skiers of all abilities. This trail-of-trails is just one of many major improvements at this southern Vermont mountain that have made skiing more rewarding. Other additions include a million-dollar Sports Center with a variety of year-round fitness and sports facilities; $2.5 million rennovation of the Stratton Mountain Inn; and a hefty increase in manmade snow devices. These new features, added to the Vermont standbys of sunny trails and quaint surroundings, make Stratton an excellent choice for a full vacation or even a weekend getaway. In addition to great Alpine and Nordic skiing, there's throbbing nightlife, good shopping and antiquing nearby, and a full calendar of festivals, carnivals, and competitions. On the three faces of Stratton Mountain developed at this resort are 52 trails and slopes with more than 30 miles of groomed terrain. Eight double chair lifts, and one triple. Two-day lift tickets are $44/adults ($48 holidays) and $30/juniors ($32 holidays). Lift tickets are also honored at nearby Bromley. Current ski conditions: 802/297-2211.

Stratton Winter Vacations, Stratton Mt, VT 05155, **802/297-2200.**

Photo: NYS Commerce Dept.

STOWE

Stowe, VT

Vermont's premier ski resort features a full array of novice-to-expert trails on the state's highest peak, Mount Mansfield. On adjacent Spruce Peak, more than $2 million has been spent on beginner's trails in recent years to offset Stowe's "expert only" reputation. More than 20 feet of average annual snowfall is backed by extensive snowmaking machinery covering more than half of the area's skiing terrain. A total of 42 trails, ranging from novice to expert levels, have been developed—some quite long. For example, the novice Toll Road trail is a full 4½ miles in length. *Playboy* magazine rates Stowe's nightlife as the best among eastern winter resorts. Central Reservations: 802/253-7237. Although lodgings and lift tickets are not inexpensive, an extensive area transportation system makes free transit from mountain to village easy, even for those without automobiles. For expert skiers, Stowe's "Front Four" are unsurpassed New England ski trails.

Stowe Area Assoc, Box 1230, Stowe, VT 05672, **802/253-7321.**

Colorado

Photo: Peter Runyon

MT. WASHINGTON VALLEY

White Mountains, NH

Overcrowding and overfamiliarity have sent some skiers looking for an alternative to famous ski areas. Some disaffected thrill-seekers have discovered the Mt. Washington Valley area of New Hampshire. With more than $4 million state-of-the-art snowmaking machines, new lifts, and miles of new trails, the Attitash, Black, Cranmore, and Wildcats ski areas have proven themselves equal to the challenge of providing new fun to downhillers from all over the country. The more than 200 kilometers of cross-country trails surrounded by the White Mountain National Forest have also captured the interest of many tourers. Attitash features 20 downhill trails, four double chairs, limited daily ticket sales to avoid overcrowding, and exten-

sive snow-making capabilities. Black Mountain has 14 trails, many extra-wide, and four lifts. Three double chair lifts, a poma lift, and Skimobile tramway, as well as snow-making capabilities covering 60% of its terrain make Mt. Cranmore a popular site (and the original destination for White Mountain skiers). More than 2,000 feet of vertical rise and 31 trails mean Wildcat is the largest ski area in the valley. Snow conditions: 603/383-9356. Three-day passes allowing access to all four areas are $45/adults, $30/juniors. Reservations at inns and hotels: 603/356-3171. The surrounding towns of Conway, Center Conway, Jackson, and Bartlett are meccas for covered bridge enthusiasts or amateur New England historians.

Chamber of Commerce, Mt Washington Valley, NH 03860, **603/356-5701.**

MOUNT TECUMSEH

Waterville Valley, NH

The site of the 1984 Women's Alpine World Cup is noted for its cross-country as well as downhill skiing. The 15 trails serviced by eight lifts guarantee good skiing from Thanksgiving—mid-April, due to exceptional natural snowfalls and extensive snow-making capabilities. For the Nordic skier, the area has 60 kilometers of double tracked trails, groomed and patrolled daily, winding through the White Mountain National Forest, past peaceful streams, and along old logging trails. All-day lift tickets for adults are $16/during mid-week, and $20/weekends and holidays. Lodging info and reservations: 800/258-8988, New England and the East; 800/552-4767, NH; or 603/236-8371.

Waterville Co, Inc, Waterville Valley, NH 03223, **603/236-8311.**

CARRABASSETT VALLEY TOURING CENTER

Carrabassett Valley, ME

Ski tourers more accustomed to snow-rutted roads and golf courses will be surprised at the experience of gliding along carefully groomed, double-track trails maintained by this center near the Sugarloaf Mountain ski area. The 105-kilometer trail network here is well-marked and packed with state-of-the-art grooming equipment. Trails range from novice to expert, but all have one thing in common—the serene, wooded beauty of a Maine winter. For a detailed map, send 50 cents to the address below. Adult trail fees: $4.50/full day ($3/children and seniors). For lodging info, write the Sugarloaf Area Reservation Service, Kingsfield, ME 04947 (207/237-2861), but note that you will be competing for lodgings with hordes of downhillers in the area. Ice skating on an Olympic-sized outdoor rink, instruction, guided tours, and equipment rental. Located just S of ME 27.

Carrabassett Valley Touring Ctr, Carrabassett Valley, ME 04947, **207/237-2205.**

Mt. Van Hoevenberg Recreation Area, Lake Placid, NY

Photo: NYC Commerce Dept.

SUGARLOAF USA

Kingfield, ME

Highly regarded for its expert downhill slopes and miles of cross-country ski trails, Sugarloaf is the premier ski attraction in Maine. Rising above the boggy outback in the northern portion of the state, this mountain is big enough to handle all levels of skiers, yet friendly enough to make all visitors feel like honorary state-of-Mainers. Forty-four trails and slopes covering 36 miles (the longest is nearly three miles), are generally open mid-Nov—late Apr/early May. The 4237-foot Sugarloaf Mountain sports, in addition to great ski slopes and an average of 14 feet of annual snowfall, 433 condominiums, a lodge, a condo/hotel, and 29 private homes. Lifts include four passenger gondolas, seven double chair lifts, and four T-bars, one of them 3000 feet long. Lift rates $21/adults all day, $14/juniors. Day-long packages including lifts, lessons, and equipment, $44/adults, $37/children. Central resrv for lodgings: 207/237-2861.

Sugarloaf USA, Carrabassett Valley, Kingfield, ME 04947, **207/237-2000.**

THE BERKSHIRES

Berkshire Mountains, MA

Even though every February several hundred hardy cross-country skiers participate in the annual Ascent of Mount Greylock (the largest mountain in the Berkshires and Massachusetts), it is still undeveloped for skiing. But what the Berkshires lack in terms of the larger ski areas to the north, they more than make up for in charm and scaled down convenience. Taking Pittsfield as the central point, there are eight major downhill resorts, several small ones, and a dozen cross-country touring centers within a 35-mile radius. That adds up to 28 chair lifts, 17 ground lifts, and 20 rope tows, plus top to bottom snow-making capability covering 95% of the trails and slopes. A few of the resorts are: Brodie Mountain in New Ashford (413/443-4752); Bousquet Ski Area near Pittsfield (413/442-8316); and Otis Ridge Ski Area (413/269-4444). The Berkshires are also splendid cross-country territory. More than 100,000 acres of public land and state forests have hundreds of miles of primitive trails. More developed routes can be found at touring centers such as Cummington Farm, Bucksteep Manor, and Northfield. There are many rustic and historic inns in the area, and you may wish to stop at one or more (see Inn Places).

Berkshire Vacation Bureau, 20 Elm St, Pittsfield, MA 01201, **413/443-9186.**

MT. VAN HOEVENBERG RECREATION AREA

Lake Placid, NY

You don't have to be an Olympian to try out the bobsled run where medalists were clocked at speeds up to 90 mph during the 1980 Winter Olympics at Lake Placid. Visitors can ride the only bobsled run in the Western Hemisphere from the half-mile start, and zip through the famous "Little S" and "Zig Zag" curves accompanied by professional drivers and brakemen. Or, for more conventional winter thrills, ski where the best have skied: the more than 30 miles of track-set, well-groomed Olympic cross-country ski trails. Recreational loops vary in length from ½ mile to 4½

miles, and in difficulty from easiest to most difficult. Also open to public use (when not being used for competition) is the permanent Biathlon Stadium, and surrounding ski trails. First-class downhill skiing is available at nearby Whiteface Mountain (see).

Mt Van Hoevenberg Recreation Area, Lake Placid, NY 12946, **518/523-4436.**

WHITEFACE MOUNTAIN

Lake Placid, NY

People unfamiliar with upstate New York often find themselves unexpectedly awed by the grand setting of Lake Placid, located in the six-million-acre Adirondack State Park, and surrounded by 46 mountain peaks more than 4000 feet tall. Adirondack Park is larger than Yellowstone, Glacier, Yosemite, and Olympic National Parks *combined!*

Site of the 1932 and 1980 Winter Olympics, Lake Placid has hosted more world-class competitions than any other winter sports' center in the world. Whiteface Mountain, with the largest vertical descent east of the Rockies and one of the largest snow-making systems in the world, is the crown of this royal winter area. In fact, the 3216-foot descent from this 4867-foot mountain is greater than that found in many of the best-known ski resorts in the west. The mountain has seven lifts, 28 trails, two lodges, a ski school, rentals, nursery, and cocktail lounge. The area around beautiful Lake Placid is also noted for cross-country skiing, especially at the Mt. Van Hoevenberg Recreation Area (see) on NY 73 just 5 mi from the village. The Olympic bobsled run, which is available for public use, is also located at Mt. Hoevenberg.

Olympic Reg'l Dev Authority, Olympic Ctr, Lake Placid, NY 12946, **518/523-3107.**

Vermont

Chapter 9

MASTERFUL MUSEUMS

L.A. Museum Of Art, Los Angeles, CA

Museum haters — come back, all is forgiven. Far from being dull repositories of a dead past, today's museums are enthralling collections of history—painted, written, chiseled, or otherwise preserved. The quiet and regimented museums of the past have, in many cases, evolved into institutions that encourage touching and experiencing, and that are not hesitant to offer downright entertainment. Yes, mummies still stare silently out from behind 2000 years of history...while, from a more recent age, and sometimes under the same roof, the very rockets and rocks from the Apollo moon missions beg examination.

Museums spark those important questions: why? what? where? when? how? They tell the story, ancient and modern, of all recorded existence on this planet; they hold not only art and artifacts, but the very keys to our imaginations. They condense the "big picture" into small and real pieces that are easily digested and understood. They are—quite literally—living history books.

Today we have children's museums, art museums, historical museums, and industrial museums. There are museums celebrating achievements in sports and those honoring the discoveries of scientists. Some museums hang Picassos on their walls, while others hang vintage airplanes from their ceilings. Museums have become playgrounds of the mind, inviting visitors into a different age or place. These stationary time machines give us a glimpse, a taste, or a feast of historical perspective and vision...and they help unlock the doors to the future.

NORTHWEST

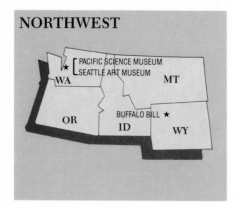

PACIFIC SCIENCE CENTER

Seattle, WA

Eager and perhaps apprehensive faces hover over a seismograph that constantly monitors volcanic activity at nearby Mount St. Helens, alert for new and potentially destructive tremors. However, the faces do not belong to geologists or seismologists, but to curious visitors to this "hands on" museum of science. Housed in six buildings originally designed for the 1962 Seattle World's Fair, and standing in the thin shadow of the famous Space Needle, this center is dedicated to helping the public understand and appreciate the fascinating world of modern science and technology. Students and adults alike are exposed to the capabilities and practical uses of all types of computers. The Pacific Northwest's only planetarium gives visitors glimpses of our vast solar system. Laser light beams perform in electrifying shows on a dome-shaped ceiling, while mystical music accompanies the action. Here, science is presented in an easily palatable form, without being condescending or boring. Of special note is the huge movie screen (three by six *stories)* of the IMAX Theatre, where specially made films on Hawaii and the Space Shuttle are shown. Open Mon-Fri, 10am-5pm; Sat & Sun, 10am-6pm.

Pacific Science Ctr, 200 2nd Ave N, Seattle, WA 98109, **206/625-9333.**

SEATTLE ART MUSEUM

Seattle, WA

Unless you are a devoted student of American art, you've probably never heard of Mark Tobey, Morris Graves, or Kenneth Callahan. However, the Seattle Art Museum displays works by these and other Northwest artists as prominently as other museums display their Picassos and Van Goghs; this is first and foremost a museum with a commitment to its community. In 1933 it opened as the first art museum in the Pacific Northwest. The original museum building — located in Seattle's Volunteer Park — was joined by the Seattle Center Pavilion Site in 1965. The two locations provide a total of 24,000 square feet of gallery and exhibition space. Among the museum's highlights are its internationally renowned Asian Art Collection, featuring paintings, ceramics, textiles, and jade pieces from Japan, China, and Southeast Asia. The museum also houses an extensive array of African sculpture, tribal masks, and other decorative artifacts in its Ethnic Art Collection. Other museum specialities include a collection of European paintings dating from the 14th century, and various Middle Eastern ceramics and sculpture. Open Tue-Sat, 10am-5pm; Thur, 10am-9pm; Sun 12pm-5pm. Both facilities closed Mon. Volunteer Park: 15th Ave E and E Prospect St: Seattle Center Pavilion: 2nd Ave N and Thomas St.

Seattle Art Museum, 1661 E Olive Way, Seattle, WA 98102, **206/447-4710.**

BUFFALO BILL HISTORICAL CENTER

Cody, WY

William F. "Buffalo Bill" Cody... accomplished buffalo hunter, Civil War soldier and scout, Pony Express rider, Wild West showman and western legend in his own lifetime. This museum, located in the town he founded and gave his name to in 1901, features a large collection of personal and historical memorabilia of this famed frontiersman. Among them are posters from his touring Wild West shows, guns and saddles used when he was Chief of Scouts for the US Army, and the congressional Medal of Honor awarded to him in 1872 for outstanding service to his country during the Indian Wars. The Historical Center also houses three other museums of western history: the Whitney Gallery of Western Art houses an original collection of western paintings and sculpture, including works by noted frontier artist Frederic Remington; the Winchester Arms Museum features more than 5000 different firearms in a collection started by rifle manufacturer Oliver Winchester; and the Plains Indian Museum preserves artifacts from records the histories of the Sioux, Cheyenne, Blackfeet and other Plains tribes. Closed Dec-Feb.

Buffalo Bill Historical Ctr, PO Box 1000, 720 Sheridan Ave, Cody, WY 82414, **307/587-4771.**

SOUTHWEST

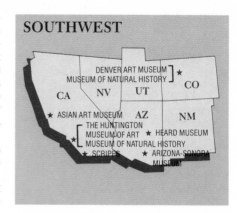

SCRIPPS AQUARIUM-MUSEUM

La Jolla, CA

As man's interest and dependence on the sea has evolved, so has his ability to research and explore the mysteries of the deep. The Scripps Institute of Oceanography on the shores of the Pacific at the University of California-San Diego is today the world's foremost center for the marine sciences. Its scientists have retrieved specimens, rocks and treasures from around the globe, many of which can be seen at this spectacular aquarium-museum. More than 300,000 yearly visitors marvel at more than 50 oceanographic exhibits. Twenty-two marine-life tanks make it simple to explore countless varieties of undersea life from the most distant realms. A man-made tide pool is just one of the many displays which make this fascinating science easily accessible to the layman. Open daily, no charge, 9am-5pm, including holidays.

Scripps Aquarium, 8602 La Jolla Shores Dr, La Jolla CA 92093, **619/452-6933.**

L.A. MUSEUM OF NATURAL HISTORY

Los Angeles, CA

One branch of this museum was made possible by the untimely demise of prehistoric animals who became trapped in a sticky asphalt bed—the famous Rancho La Brea Tar Pits. This building houses fossils and reconstructions of ice age animal skeletons including the Imperial Mammoth, California Saber-Tooth Cat, American Mastodon, and many extinct birds. The entire museum is the largest natural history collection in the western United States. Splendid galleries feature mammals of North America and Africa in their natural habitats, as well as birds, insects, and marine life. The Paleontology display includes dinosaurs and extensive exhibits of invertebrates. A gem and mineral display involves visitors with hands-on specimens, and features a guarded vault with dazzling exhibits of exotic precious stones such as the sapphire, emerald, ruby, and diamond. Displays of antique automobiles, US and California history, and South Pacific and pre-Columbian archaeology are also included. Admission: $1.50; 5-17, students & sr.cit. w/ID 75 cents (free 1st Tue of month).

Natural History Museum of Los Angeles County, 900 Exposition Blvd, Los Angeles, CA 90007, **213/744-3411, 213/744-3430.**

Pacific Science Center, Seattle, WA

L.A. MUSEUM OF ART

Los Angeles, CA

Imagine the nation's second biggest, second most populous city without a major art museum! Not until 1961 did leading citizens in Los Angeles decide to construct a major museum devoted solely to art, but when the decision was finally made, the plans went ahead with gusto. After an initial fund-raising drive that collected around $12 million, the museum was dedicated on May 30, 1965. Although the collection does not yet rival those in a number of more established municipal art museums, the British journal, *Apollo*, stated that "No other museum has come so far, so fast," and its holdings of Indian, Tibetan, Nepalese, and Southeast Asian art already are considered among the best in the world. Two Indian sculptures of particular note originated from the first-century A.D. Buddhist site of Sanchi—one of only two such displays in America. The Textiles and Costumes collections consists of 25,000 items including an English-silver-and silk gown from the 18th century, a 24-piece gown assemblage by Mariano Fortuny, and a man's red silk velvet doublet and red velvet breeches that comprise the only complete 16th century costume in any American museum. Among other important works are Bellow's *Cliff Dwellers*, Marsh's *Third Avenue El*, and Homer's *Cotton Pickers*. The still-young European collection has been bolstered considerably by a promised gift of collections from Armand Hammer.

*Los Angeles County Museum of Art, 5905 Wilshire Blvd, Los Angeles CA 90036, **213/857-6111**.*

ASIAN ART MUSEUM OF SAN FRANCISCO

San Francisco, CA

Quality and quantity have made this museum world-famous, and it's the only one in the United States entirely devoted to Asian art. Nearly 10,000 objects represent China, Japan, India, Southeast Asia, Nepal, Tibet, Korea, and Iran. Avery Brundage, an American businessman who was an Olympic contender and president of the International Olympic Committee for 20 years, donated nearly half of the museum's objects with artifacts of Chinese origin, including the celebrated Magnin Jade collection. Artifacts illustrate major periods and stylistic developments of the arts of Asia in many forms: sculptures, paintings, bronzes, ceramics, architectural elements, and decorative objects. The 11th-century life-size statues of the Khmer Royal Couple, carved in sandstone, depict the grandeur and pride of their era. Permanent displays on the first floor are dedicated entirely to Chinese arts. The two-floor museum can accommodate only a tenth of its treasures at any given time, so objects and displays are rotated periodically. Exhibits on the second floor are divided among various locations in the Orient. Free guided tours daily (415/387-5922). Open every day of the year 10am-5pm. Admission free 1st Wed of month.

*Asian Art Museum of San Francisco, Golden Gate Park, San Francisco, CA 94118, **415/558-2993**.*

The Heard Museum, Phoenix, AZ

Photo: Jerry Jacka

HUNTINGTON LIBRARY, ART GALLERY & BOTANICAL GARDENS

San Marino, CA

Where can you see the world's largest grouping of mature cacti, a Gutenberg Bible, and the famous Gainsborough painting, *Blue Boy*—all in one museum? The answer is The Huntington, often thought of as three museums in one with each section a major attraction in its own right... The 130-acre botanical gardens offers visitors a choice of a dozen different themes including The Rose Garden which traces this romantic flower's history for more than a thousand years, and The Japanese Garden groomed to exquisite perfection complete with colorful bridges, running streams, islands, and a five-room house—parts of which were imported from Japan. The art gallery emphasizes 18th- and early 19th-century works, including an impressive collection of French sculpture and art objects. Founded originally in 1919 as a research institution, scholars from around the world utilize its facilities every year. For this reason, public perusal is limited to Tue-Sun, 1-4pm. Admission free, but advance tickets required on Sun (213/449-3901).

*The Huntington Library, Art Gallery, & Botanical Gardens, San Marino, CA 91108, **818/792-6141**, **213/681-6601**.*

THE HEARD MUSEUM

Phoenix, AZ

Within the graceful Spanish colonial walls of this museum, a multitude of virtually unknown Native American treasures await. Said to be one of the world's best, this institute's major exhibit, with nearly 75,000 pieces, is the largest such display in North America. Along a timeline starting around 15,000 B.C., visitors encounter photomurals, maps, text, diagrams, and thousands of artifacts which bring the southwest's heritage to life. Oral histories, poems, and songs unfold cultural mysteries teaching visitors, for instance, why the Hopi believe that "corn is life," or why sacred mountains were thought to bring well-being and harmony to the Navajo. The famed kachina doll collection is 1000-strong—each representing different deified ancestral spirits believed among the Pueblo Indians to visit their communal dwellings from time to time. Other highlights include contemporary Navajo rugs, and three house-type reconstructions: the Navajo hogan; the Apache wickiup; and the Hopi corn-grinding room. Open Mon-Sat, 10am-4:45pm; Sun, 1pm-4:45pm. Closed hols. Admission: $2; sr.cit. $1.50; students & children 75 cents.

*The Heard Museum, 22 E Monte Vista Rd, Phoenix, AZ 85004, **602/252-8848**.*

ARIZONA-SONORA DESERT MUSEUM

Tucson, AZ

This living museum is often listed as one of the two best *zoos* in the US, a description that causes its supporters to declare, "But it's more than just a zoo!" And indeed it is. It is a garden of botanical wonders, a classroom of natural learning, a preserved relic of desert wildlife, and, yes, a rather good zoo as well. Although it only displays about 200 species of animals and 300 species of plants, all of these are native to the Sonora Desert area of Arizona, California, and Mexico. The ASDM was one of the first "zoos" in the US to use natural habitats and cage-less barriers to house animals, and a special underwater viewing room allows visitors a rare opportunity to see beavers, otters, and other creatures in their natural environment. Other highlights include a walk-in aviary where you can stroll past the realistic homes of desert birds, a garden of beautiful wild flowers and majestic cacti, and an orientation room full of facts and features about the world's great deserts. The recently finished Earth Sciences Center features a unique attraction: a man-made cave, artistically constructed to recreate southwestern desert caves. Visitors can wind their way through the realistic passages, possibly encountering a harmless bat or an inquisitive lizard. Nearly 500,000 people visit the museum each year; yet—perhaps because of its gentle and friendly atmosphere—this is one of the few institutions of its kind that does not feel the need to employ armed guards. Admission: $5; 13-17 $2.25; 6-12 75 cents. Open every day 8:30am-sundown.

*Arizona-Sonora Desert Museum, Rte 9, Box 900, Tucson, AZ 85743, **602/883-1380**.*

DENVER MUSEUM OF NATURAL HISTORY

Denver, CO

Picture yourself in Botswana. There's a herd of elephants in the background, while, closer at hand, zebras, warthogs, baboons, and other animals gather around a drying-up water hole. This is just one of 70 life-size dioramas that display animals from North and South America, Africa, Australia, and the South Pacific. Museum highlights include the only South American Mammal Hall in the US, reconstructed crystal caverns from Chihuahua, Mexico, an outstanding American Indian display, and a nonpareil exhibition of Colorado minerals. The Dinosaur Hall, always a delight for children, houses skeletons of a Diplodocus more than 75 feet long, a Stegosaurus, and a rare Plesiosaur. Denver's most popular tourist attraction is also the home for the Gates Planetarium and Phipps Auditorium. The Phipps Theater is currently featuring the IMAX motion picture projection system, said to revolutionize the movie-going experience with a screen 10 times the conventional size, and a superlative 6-track stereo system for on-site realism which, according to *Variety*, gives spectators "a stunning, breathtaking experience." Admission: $3; children $1. Closed Jan 1, Thanksgiving, and Dec 24, 25, & 31.

Denver Museum of Natural History, City Park, Denver, CO 80205, **303/370-6363.**

DENVER ART MUSEUM

Denver, CO

Founded in 1893 by local citizens with no funds, no art collection, and no permanent building, this museum has grown into the largest art institution between Kansas City and Los Angeles. Since its grand opening on October 3, 1971, it has become the major art resource for an eight-state region. The unique seven- story building is covered by 1 million gray tiles, custom-made by Corning Glass Works. Exhibits are arranged by floors starting at the Mezzanine (2nd Floor) with Art of the Northwest Coast, and moving upward to include exhibits from Africa and the South Pacific, Native American Art, American Art and Art of the New World, European Art, Asian Art, and Textiles and Costumes. Contemporary art and temporary exhibits are housed on the ground floor. Admission: $2.50. Closed Mon, Sun mornings, and major hols. Open Wed until 8pm.

Denver Art Museum, 100 W 14th Ave Pkwy, Denver, CO 80204, **303/575-2793.**

MIDWEST

WALKER ART CENTER

Minneapolis, MN

The accent at the Walker Art Center is on modern art in all of its amorphous and sometimes unpredictable forms— from a host of art objects to music, dance, film, theater, and education. The Center's permanent art collection includes O'Keeffe, Hopper, and Warhol, as well as European masters Moore, Miro, Arp, and Giacometti. Exhibits trace the development of 20th century art from cubism and abstract expressionism, to urban imagery and art dealing with personal subject matters such as anxiety and love. Hundreds of films, from Hollywood and foreign classics to avant-garde productions are screened each year. The museum sponsors or co-sponsors hundreds of music and dance concerts, experimental theater performances, and poetry readings each year—many staged throughout the Twin Cities area as well as at the center itself. Free admission (occasional fee for special exhibits). Ticket info: 612/375-7622. Closed Mon.

Walker Art Center, Vineland Place, Minneapolis, MN 55403, **612/375-7600.**

MILWAUKEE PUBLIC MUSEUM

Milwaukee, WI

One of the best kept secrets in the midwest is the Milwaukee Public Museum, the fifth largest natural history museum in the nation and the place where, in 1890, naturalist Carl Akeley invented the diorama. In keeping with this tradition, a new diorama completed late in 1983 features life-size models of dinosaurs in a Metasequoia swamp. Viewable from two different levels, it is the largest diorama in the world. Another popular exhibit is the new European Village, representing 33 ethnic cultures complete with homes and shops from various Old World countries and a working Swiss tower clock. Capturing the spirit of Old Milwaukee is the display which recreates the 1890s complete with flickering gaslights, cobbled streets, and old-time shops. Two other spectacular displays depict a bamboo forest in East Africa and a traditional Masai lion hunt near a savanna waterhole. The museum is also noted for its American Indian and pre-Columbian exhibits. Open daily except major hols from 9am-5pm. Admission: $2; children $1; maximum family rate $5.

Milwaukee Public Museum, 800 W Wells St, Milwaukee, WI 53233, **414/278-2700.**

CIRCUS WORLD MUSEUM

Baraboo, WI

Along the banks of the Baraboo River in central Wisconsin, is a city where the circus is always in town. Dedicated to collecting, preserving, and displaying circus history, the museum's many exhibits include circus railway cars, animal tents, authentic side show replicas, flamboyant posters, and other memorabilia from the past. However, the big attraction here, as at any circus, is under the Big Top where spectacular live performances and demonstrations are staged each day. Brightly decorated prancing ponies, elephant tricks and acrobatic feats are presented just the way they were 50 years ago. The nostalgic sound of old-style circus music filters through the air from the world's largest collection of circus musical instruments. Every morning, on the exact spot where the Ringling Brothers Circus was founded in 1884, you can see workers unload the circus train assisted by powerful Percheron horses. Children will especially enjoy the petting menagerie, the colorful street parade, and the 3000-piece miniature circus, incredibly realistic and accurate to the smallest detail. This mosaic of thrills, fantasy and adventure prompted Ernest Hemingway to write, "It is the only spectacle I know that, while you watch it, gives the quality of a truly happy dream." Open 7 days a week from mid-May-mid-Sept.

Circus World Museum, 426 Water St, Baraboo, WI 53913, **608/356-8341.**

THE TIME MUSEUM

Rockford, IL

How did people tell time 3000 years ago? When was the first wrist-watch made? How does an atomic clock work? The answers to these and other fascinating questions can be found at this extra-ordinary museum devoted to the science of horology—the study of timekeeping devices. First opened to the public in 1970, the collection features over 3000 items, ranging from ancient times to the present, and is regarded as the world's best collection of time-related pieces. The museum is divided into 16 separate areas which chronologically illustrate the historical development of time-telling instruments. Each period is represented by outstanding works of world-famous makers. The magnificent German astronomical and automaton clock designed by Christian Gebhard and his sons between 1865 and 1895, features a mechanized procession of the biblical apostles around the figure of Christ at noon each day (a la Glockenspiel). In addition to the countless varieties of mechanical clocks and watches, the museum also boasts a fabulous display of sundials, astrolabs, nocturnals, compendiums, incense clocks, water clocks, sand-glasses, calendars, chronometers and navigation devices. The museum is located in the Clock Tower Inn, a resort complex offering superior accommodations, three restaurants, two lounges, golf and tennis, indoor and outdoor pools, and a health club. It's a place where you can enjoy *spending* time, as well as *discovering* it. Open Tue-Fri, 10am-8pm, Sat & Sun, 10am-6pm.

The Time Museum, 7801 E State St, Rockford, IL 61125, **815/398-6000, ext 2941.**

Walker Art Center, Minneapolis, MN

FIELD MUSEUM OF NATURAL HISTORY

Chicago, IL

A pair of fighting elephants in the main entrance of this museum sets the stage for adventures in discovery, the stimulation of ideas, and not a few surprises. More than 10 acres of exhibit space are devoted to the display of 13 million articles in anthropology, botany, geology, and zoology. Popular attractions include a collection of mummies, an extensive exhibit devoted to Neanderthal Man, a Pawnee earth lodge, and a famous butterfly collection. The largest diorama in the museum depicts the flora and fauna around an African watering hole with 23 animals and mammals mounted in their natural habitats. You can even touch, try on, handle, listen to, compare, or examine under a magnifying glass the artifacts contained in a new gallery, The Place of Wonder. The world's largest faceted blue topaz rests in quiet splendor in an upstairs room. Open every day except Christmas and New Years. Admission: $2; 6-17 $1 (free on Fri).

Field Museum of Natural History, Roosevelt Rd at Lake Shore Dr, Chicago, IL 60603, 312/922-9410.

SHEDD AQUARIUM

Chicago, IL

Sift through sand for sea urchins, coral, and shell fragments. Touch live clams and oysters. Watch green moray eels lurk just inches from your nose, and harbor seals glide through the water. No, you're not at the ocean; you're at Shedd Aquarium on the shores of Lake Michigan. Darkened galleries set-off 200 exhibit tanks displaying some 5000 aquatic animals of 500 species — piranhas, sea horses, barracudas and nurse sharks, among others. A re-created coral reef is brimming with 300 rainbow-colored Caribbean fish. Divers daily enter the Coral Reef Exhibit and hand-feed fish while talking to spectators through built-in microphones in their masks. Divided into six galleries, the aquarium houses tropical, temperate, and cold saltwater, as well as tropical, temperate, and cold freshwater. Slide shows and lectures are given periodically on such topics as marine life on coral reefs around the world, and the art of shell collecting. Organized family programs include such activities as making prints of fish, squid and seashells, learning how to fish by spin-casting, and examining under a microscope water samples of Lake Michigan. A unique gift shop offers mother-of-pearl earrings, model kits for ship building, and a selection of related books. Open 9am — 5pm daily. Admission: $2; 6-17 $1; sr.cit. $.50.

Shedd Aquarium, 1200 S Lake Shore Dr, Chicago, IL 60605, 312/939-2438.

ART INSTITUTE OF CHICAGO

Chicago, IL

How can this museum fit 68 rooms into one gallery?! Because each room is a handmade miniature (built on a one-foot to one-inch scale), sequentially depicting the history of European and American interior design. The vastness of this storehouse is enough to overwhelm the most discerning visitor. It houses, for example, more French impressionist paintings than the Louvre in Paris, and is said to have the largest and most important combined museum and art school in the nation. Galleries include works by such luminaries as Monet, Renoir, Degas, and Van Gogh, while still others represent nearly every aspect of contemporary and historic art. Masterworks include El Greco's *Assumption of the Virgin,* Seurat's *Sunday Afternoon on the Island of La Grande Jatte,* and Grant Woods' *American Gothic.* Other highlights are the reconstructed Trading Room from the original Chicago Stock Exchange Building, and one of the largest historical assemblages of warfare and hunting equipment including gilded armor and ivory-stocked pistols. Half-hour gallery walks or slide lectures daily at 12:15pm. Special childrens' activities include games called, "I Spy" and "Scrutinizing Art," which are designed to teach youngsters about the museum. Tours covering museum highlights daily at 2pm. Lectures held Thur at 6pm. Contribution: $4.50; children, students and sr. cit. $2.25 (free on Thur).

The Art Institute of Chicago, Michigan Ave at Adams St, Chicago, IL 60603, 312/443-3500, -3600.

THE ORIENTAL INSTITUTE

Chicago, IL

Although this institute has been around for nearly 70 years, it is only recently that the general public has become interested in this collection of Egyptology. One problem has perhaps been the museum's name; chosen before the term *Near East* was coined, it belies the fact that five separate galleries display art and artifacts from Egypt, Mesopotamia, Anatolia, Iran, and Syria/Palestine. Many of the exhibits displayed in this small but elegant museum have been acquired through archaeological expeditions resulting in one of the world's major collections of antiquities—some as much as 9000 years old. King Tut, the youthful monarch who recently aroused the American public's interest, is also here, in the form of a 16-foot-high red quartzite statue that dominates the Egyptian gallery. Other notable relics include a Dead Sea Scroll fragment and jar, Persepolis artifacts, a reconstruction of a Jordanian graveyard, mummies (wrapped and unwrapped), and a 40-ton, rock Assyrian figure, dating back to 722 B.C., of a winged bull with a human head. The Suq, a small but unique gift shop, sells items made from molds of actual exhibits in the museum. Other souvenirs include sculpture and metalwork (some imported), as well as slides, games and books. Call for details about tours and special programs. Closed Mon and major hols. Free admission.

The Oriental Institute, 1155 E 58th St, Chicago, IL 60637, 312/753-2475, 312/753-2468.

MUSEUM OF SCIENCE & INDUSTRY

Chicago, IL

If you've never stepped aboard a captured German U-boat, toured a coal mine, walked through a 16-foot model of a human heart, or examined a spaceship that's orbited the moon, then you've never been here. America's oldest, largest, and most popular museum of science and technology attracts four million visitors annually from nearly 100 countries. It's a "please touch" kind of place where buttons to push, cranks to turn, and levers to lift will cause minds to stretch. Challenge a computer to a game of tic-tac-toe, watch baby chicks hatch inside incubators, or stroll down Yesterday's Main Street complete with brick pavement, gas lamps, and old-time ice cream parlor. The circus exhibit delights spectators with 22,000 animated miniatures bringing the history of the star-studded circus to life. More than 2000 exhibits in 75 major fields keep visitors coming back again and again. Open every day of the year. Free admission (fee for special exhibits).

The Museum of Science and Industry, 57th St & Lake Shore Dr, Chicago, IL 60637, 312/684-1414.

Field Museum Of Natural History, Chicago, IL

CINCINNATI ART MUSEUM

Cincinnati, OH

This museum is tailor-made! While some museums are unique because they are housed in one-time private estates, historical structures, or architectural marvels, the home to Cincinnati's collection is the first general art museum west of the Alleghenies specifically designed to be a museum. More than 100 galleries span 5000 years of almost every major civilization. Each collection tells the story of a culture. Art of the Ancient World displays many sculptures of deities reflecting a strong belief in afterlife; the Tribal Arts collection portrays a profound influence by geography and the environment; and the Costumes and Textiles section reflects the changing tastes and lifestyles in the history of our own country. This extensive treasure trove of delightful exhibits includes magnificent pieces of gold and silver from the Achaemenid period, an African collection of masks and ritual figures, and a singular display of musical instruments depicting the development of keyboard, stringed, and other orchestral instruments. The American Decorative Arts galleries also depict an economic cross-section of the American culture and way of life. Admission: $2; 12-18 $1; 3-11 25 cents. Closed Mon, Sun mornings, and major hols.

The Cincinnati Art Museum, Eden Park, Cincinnati, OH 45202, **513/721-5204.**

DETROIT INSTITUTE OF ARTS

Detroit, MI

Where would you expect to find the largest municipally-owned museum in the US? Or the largest collection of Native American art in North America. Or the third largest collection of Renaissance works outside of Europe? No, it isn't in New York, but rather in a town better known for machines than for masterpieces — Detroit. The Detroit Institute of Arts was founded in 1885, and now holds a permanent collection of more than 70,000 works. More than one million people visit this museum each year to view famous bodies of work, such as the Dutch and Flemish collections, with masterpieces by Rembrandt and Van Gogh, and the largest collection of German Expressionist works in the US. The Institute also holds some rather offbeat exhibitions, including a series of Charlie Chaplin films, a showing of rarely-seen Polish works, and a visual celebration of its home city's most enduring symbol—the automobile. The museum's public cafe open (11am-5pm) makes for an interesting stop, even if you're not hungry. The cafe's Renaissance charm is provided by actual decorations from three different Italian palaces. Open Tue-Sun, 9:30am-5:30pm; closed Mon and hols.

Detroit Institute of Arts, 5200 Woodward Ave, Detroit, MI 48202, **313/833-7900.**

CLEVELAND MUSEUM OF ART

Cleveland, OH

From 4000-year-old artifacts to works by living masters, this ambitious museum offers an unbeatable bargain — free admission to a world of aesthetic riches. Best known for its exhibits from the Orient, it houses one of the most complete collections outside the Far East. In addition, the museum has been praised by art critics for its Medieval works, prints, and drawings. Galleries are arranged chronologically with art pieces, sculpture, and paintings of the same era displayed together for a more complete cultural encounter. Regions represented include the Near and Far East, India, America, pre-Columbian Americas, Europe, Africa, and ancient Egypt, Greece, and Rome. Art classes, gallery talks, and events for adults and children are offered by an extensive education department. Closed Mon, Sun mornings, and some major hols.

The Cleveland Museum of Art, 11150 E Blvd, Cleveland, OH 44106, **216/421-7340.**

PRO FOOTBALL HALL OF FAME

Canton, OH

A seven-foot bronze statue of all-around athlete and gridiron star, Jim Thorpe, appropriately greets visitors to this complex of four modern buildings. As fans walk through the gently curving ramps, the history of America's favorite fall sport begins unfolding around them. Displays include countless mementos, photographs, displays, and high-tech presentations. Throughout the major exhibition areas, television monitors, taped voice recordings, question-and-answer panels, and selectable slide machines encourage each visitor to participate in the history of this uniquely American game. The annual Hall of Fame pre-season football game is played at Fawcett Stadium in Canton, and, since 1971, has featured rival teams from the AFC and NFC. Open every day of the year except Christmas. Admission: $3; 5-13 $1. Family admission: $8.

Pro Football Hall of Fame, 2121 Harrison Ave NW, Canton, OH 44708, **216/456-8207.**

THE CHILDREN'S MUSEUM

Indianapolis, IN

Here, delighted children and adults ride colorful hand-carved wooden animals on a turn-of-the-century carousel. But this isn't an amusement park — it's a museum. Despite its name, this museum is for children of any age, who can look at the marvels of science and history with an unjaded eye. Children will learn something new, and their parents will recall something they forgot. An actual Indianapolis 500 racing car waits for future speedsters to climb behind its storied wheel, while an Egyptian mummy preserved for 3000 years lies nearby inside a recreated tomb. Another exhibit uses video games as a fun way to teach about computers, energy, and economics. The key words here are 'touch" and "experience"—everyone is encouraged to get in on the action and let his or her imagination become the best of all possible teachers. Two of the most popular exhibits are a recreation of an 1890s firehouse (complete with fire pole, alarm, and horse-drawn fire engine), and a spectacular toy train set-up. Open Tue-Sat, 10am-5pm; Sun, noon-5pm. Closed Mon (open 10am-5pm Mem Day-Lab Day).

The Children's Museum, 3000 N Meridian St, Indianapolis, IN 46208, **317/924-5431.**

Museum Of Science & Industry, Chicago, IL

The Time Museum, Rockford, IL

AUBURN-CORD-DUESENBERG MUSEUM

Auburn, IN

The 1930s? From bread lines to champagne and caviar, and from unemployed masses to dazzling movie stars—it was a mad era. Typical of the times were the anachronistic Duesenberg automobiles. They easily topped 100 mph and sold for nearly $20,000—in the heart of the depression! Today, they're worth hundreds of thousands of dollars. This museum displays 140 such vehicles dating back to 1898, including the renowned Auburn boattail speedsters, the front-wheel-drive Cords, and many others. The building itself is listed in the National Register of Historic Places and its splendid Art Deco decor includes an elegant, sweeping stairway just inside the front door. Halls are lined with colorful mint-condition classics displayed on terrazzo tile floors beneath ornate chandeliers. Since 1955 Auburn has held the *Auburn-Cord-Duesenberg Festival*, assembling 200 antique automobiles and 150,000 spectators—said to be the "world's greatest classic car show" (Labor Day weekend). Highlights include an auction of 600 cars, the "Parade of Classics" down Auburn's treelined streets, and the museum itself. Displays are constantly changing because many cars are on loan and owners like to *use* them as well as show them off. Museum curators insist that these classics get driven quite a bit, but for the price, they hardly can be considered practical. Owners of these classic roadsters include such public figures as actors Dan Haggerty and Alan Alda, both of whom recently visited the museum to check out the market. Located at I-69 & IN 8, 20 mi N of Fort Wayne. Open 9am-9pm (off season schedules vary). Admission: $4; student/sr. cit. $2.50.

Auburn-Cord-Duesenberg Museum, Auburn, IN 46706, **219/925-1444.**

SOUTH CENTRAL

CARTER MUSEUM OF WESTERN ART

Fort Worth, TX

Amon Carter's hard work and zealous dedication was solely responsible for the establishment of this young, but reputable, art museum. Opened in 1961, it has not had the time to acquire the numerically diverse collections that are the hallmark of more established galleries, but the Amon Carter is rapidly gaining respect in its obvious specialty—the American West. Masterpieces include works by Remington, Homer, Wood, and O'Keeffe, all dedicated to portraying the pioneer spirit. The museum also features a distinguished collection of prints from famous paintings and drawings. Original masterpieces by the celebrated photographer of mother nature, Ansel Adams, includes majestic scenes of the Rio Grande, and the towering redwoods of northern California. Located within one block of the Kimbell Art Museum (see), the Fort Worth Art Museum, and the Fort Worth Museum of Science and History. Free admission. Closed Mon and some hols.

The Amon Carter Museum of Western Art, 3501 Camp Bowie Blvd, Fort Worth, TX 76113, **817/738-1933.**

KIMBELL ART MUSEUM

Fort Worth, TX

It has been said that behind every great man one finds a great woman. This adage, true or not, is exemplified by the Kimbells, who were solely responsible for the founding of this exquisite museum—Kay Kimbell with his millions, and Velma Kimbell with her instinct for quality. This combination was responsible for the nurturing of their world class collection including a Visee-Le-Brun self-portrait, Gainsborough's *Miss Lloyd,* and several Carots. Before Kay Kimbell died in 1964, he mandated that his numerous corporate holdings be used to found the Kimbell Art Foundation. Velma Kimbell respected those wishes and immediately donated her entire share of the property in exchange for a lifetime annuity. With such a beginning, the 1972 opening had to be a success, and it was—claimed by *Connoisseur* to be "quite simply the finest museum of its size in the United States." Housed in a unique award-winning architectural structure which takes advantage of the Texas sun through sky-lighted vaults, are selected works from the beginning of civilization to the present. Included are an abundance of works by El Greco, Van Gogh, Rembrandt, and Picasso. Also featured are Asian ceramics, sculpture, screens, scrolls, and pre-Columbian objects. The museum sponsors numerous lectures, concerts, dramatic and children's events, sketching workshops, and special tours. Free admission. Closed Mon, Sun mornings, and major hols.

Kimbell Art Museum, 3333 Camp Bowie Blvd, Box 9440, Fort Worth, TX 76107, **817/332-8451.**

MUSEUM OF NATURAL SCIENCE & BAKER PLANETARIUM

Houston, TX

From way back in time, to way out in space, this museum houses one of the largest natural history collections in the Southwest. You'll find dinosaur skeletons here, and also moon rocks. Attractions include a towering 70-foot-long Diplodocus skeleton, a collection of porcelain Boehm Birds, and Indian artifacts from South America to Alaska. The Wiess Hall of Petroleum Science and Technology

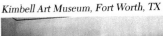

Kimbell Art Museum, Fort Worth, TX

houses one of the nation's foremost displays in this field with many touchable models and exhibits including electronic boards. A huge fiberglass mold of a great white shark hangs from the ceiling above a series of exhibits on coastal habitats; historical dioramas colorfully depict Texas history from 1543 — 1907; and a transparent anatomical mannequin realistically animates the human physiology in The Hall of Medical Science. Other exhibits cover energy, communications, gems and minerals, and space science. (Space enthusiasts should note that the mammoth Johnson Space Center is just southwest of Houston.) The Burke Baker Planetarium offers sky shows an average of 10 times per week. Open daily except Sun & Mon mornings, Thanksgiving, Christmas, and New Year's. Free admission to museum. Planetarium admission: $2; 5-11 $1.

The Houston Museum of Natural Science & Burke Baker Planetarium, 1 Hermann Circle Dr, Hermann Park, Houston, TX 77030, **713/526-4273.**

MUSEUM OF FINE ARTS

Houston, TX

This museum is Texas-sized, with its 11,000-work collection ranking as one of the most outstanding—and diverse — in the Southwest. Occupying three buildings, the sprawling museum includes the Bayou Bend mansion about five miles away, and the Alfred C. Glassell, Jr. School of Art across the street. Outstanding individual collections include the Straus Collection of Renaissance and Eighteenth Century works, the Beck Collection of Impressionist and Post-Impressionist paintings, the Kress Collection of the Italian and Spanish Renaissance, and the Target Collection of American Photography. The magnificent Bayou Bend mansion was the former home of Miss Ima Hogg (daughter of the late Governor James S. Hogg), and the 28-room estate houses one of the country's finest collections of American art and art objects. Exquisite furniture of the Chippendale period, rich Rococo Revival furnishings, and imported French panoramic wallpaper should please the most fastidious of art lovers. Guided tours of Bayou Bend offered Tue-Sat by reservation only (713/529-8773). The main museum is closed Mon, Sun mornings, and major hols. Free admission.

Museum of Fine Arts, Houston, 1001 Bissonnet St, PO Box 6826, Houston, TX 77265, **713/526-1361.**

ST. LOUIS ART MUSEUM

St. Louis, MO

This city, known as the "Gateway to the West," has gone through extensive changes in the last 20 years—with a thriving new convention center, as well as the renovation of old neighborhoods along the river under the shadow of the famous arch. However, not all is new! The St. Louis Art Museum was founded in 1880, and its collection has grown to emphasize Northern European works from the Renaissance to Rembrandt, as well as colonial to contemporary American, French Impressionist and Post-Impressionist, and German Expressionist works. Other notable collections include fine examples of 20th century European sculpture, American and European decorative arts, Chinese bronzes and porcelains, and primitive artifacts from central America dating from 2000 B.C. Tours of permanent exhibits free on Tue. Closed Mon, Tue mornings, and major hols.

St. Louis Art Museum, Forest Park, St. Louis, MO 63110, **314/721-0072 (recorded info), 314/721-0067.**

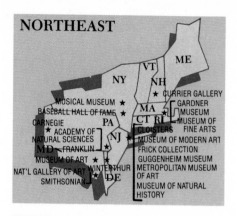

NORTHEAST

MUSICAL MUSEUM ★
BASEBALL HALL OF FAME ★
CARNEGIE ★
★ ACADEMY OF
NATURAL SCIENCES
FRANKLIN
MUSEUM OF ART ★
NAT'L GALLERY OF ART
SMITHSONIAN

ME
VT
NH
NY
★ CURRIER GALLERY
MA ★ GARDNER
★ MUSEUM
CT RI ★ MUSEUM OF
CLOISTERS ★ FINE ARTS
PA MUSEUM OF MODERN ART
NJ FRICK COLLECTION
GUGGENHEIM MUSEUM
METROPOLITAN MUSEUM
OF ART
WINTERTHUR MUSEUM OF NATURAL
DE HISTORY

GUGGENHEIM MUSEUM

New York, NY

This round, tiered monolith was dubbed a "marshmallow" and even a "clothes washer" when it was completed in 1959, and it *has* been said that Frank Lloyd Wright's architecture upstages the art on display in this museum! Exhibits are arranged along a quarter-mile-long ramp that spirals upward for six floors — leaving the building's domed, and sky-lighted core an Escher-type study in dizzy, white circles. Particularly noted for its constantly changing exhibits of avant-garde and experimental abstract works, the lively museum does maintain several permanent collections. Located along the winding way are masterpieces by Braque, Cezanne, Gauguin, Manet, Matisse, Picasso, Renoir, and Van Gogh. In the Pioneers of 20th-Century Art Exhibit, Chagall, Klee, and Mondrian are represented. Other credits include: one of the world's largest collections of paintings and graphics by Vasily Kandinsky; one of the most extensive collections of works by Paul Klee, and sculpture by Constantin Brancusi. Admission: $2.50; students w/ID and sr. cit. $1.50. Open Wed-Sun, 11am-5pm, Tue to 8pm; closed Dec 25.

Guggenheim Museum, 1071 5th Ave, New York, NY 10028, **212/860-1300.**

MUSEUM OF NATURAL HISTORY/ HAYDEN PLANETARIUM

New York, NY

This is, quite simply, the museum of museums. With a collection of more than 34 million artifacts and specimens, and nearly a million square feet of exhibition and public service space, the museum is the largest of its kind in the world. No institution has more birds, spiders, fossil mammals or whale skeletons. You probably would need a dozen lifetimes to examine the eight million anthropological artifacts, 16 million insect specimens, 230,000 amphibian and reptile specimens, 600,000 fish, 8.5 million invertabrae, 250,000 mammals and 120,000 specimens of rocks, minerals gems and meteorites. Fortunately, it won't take that much time to view the world's most complete collection of dinosaurs, including one of only two extant dinosaur mummies at the Hall of the Late Dinosaurs. In all, there are 38 exhibit halls open to the public. The Margaret Mead Hall of Pacific Peoples opened in 1984, and the Hall of South America will open in 1986. Gaze at one of the most famous gems in the world, the Star of India sapphire (563-carat, two inches in diameter) at the Morgan Memorial Hall of Gems, or drop in at the Arthur Ross Hall of Meteorites and touch the 31-metric-ton Ahnighito, the largest meteorite ever recovered. Smell fresh moss and see a giant 1300- year-old sequoia tree in the Hall of the North American Forests. There is always something happening at the museum. On weekends, you can learn about foreign cultures at the People Center and enjoy the music and dance of different cultures through performances by guest artists. The adjoining Hayden Planetarium opens up the heavens through a series of Sky Shows in a domed auditorium. The Planetarium also features important exhibits and traces the history of instruments used to study the celestial world.

American Museum of Natural History/Hayden Planetarium, Central Park W at 79th St, New York, NY 10024, **212/873-4425.**

Guggenheim Museum, New York, NY

METROPOLITAN MUSEUM OF ART

New York, NY

Occupying nearly 1½ million square feet, the Metropolitan is unrivaled in its encyclopedic range. Crediting many of its grand scale collections to 19th- and 20th-century millionaires (J.P. Morgan, J.D. Rockefeller, H.O. Havemeyer, and others), today there are more than three million works of art. One wing contains an entire temple; others house the largest American as well as Islamic collections in existence, and nonpareil holdings in European art outside its mother continent. The late Nelson Rockefeller donated his collection of primitive art to the museum, and other highlights include costumes from throughout the ages, musical instruments, mummies, and (in season) a Christmas tree ornamented with small, 18th-century Neopolitan sculptures. An important branch of the museum is The Cloisters (see) which exhibits art from the 12th-15th centuries. Closed Mon and some major hols. Contribution: $4; students $2; under 12 free w/adult.

The Metropolitan Museum of Art, 5th Ave at 82nd St, New York, NY 10028, **212/879-5500.**

THE CLOISTERS

New York, NY

Housed in a modern building incorporating sections of medieval monasteries and churches, this museum — a branch of New York's Metropolitan Museum of Art (see)— holds a fascinating collection of medieval art of various types. Located on a hill overlooking the Hudson River in northern Manhattan's Fort Tryon Park, this unique museum was made possible by a generous bequest by John D. Rockefeller, Jr., and opened to the public in 1938. Passageways and arched walkways open on colorful, Middle Age-style gardens (planted with herbs and flowers prevalent in those days). One almost expects to see a monk, hunched in prayer, shuffle by quietly on his way to the chapel or to his meager room. One of the oldest and most valuable pieces here is the Chalice of Antioch. Made of gilded silver and inscribed with bucolic religious figures, this artifact has been dated between AD 350 and 500, making it one of the oldest surviving chalices used for Christian Mass. Other important holdings include colorful tapestries, hand-written illustrated manuscripts, and intricate stained-glasswork. Open Tue-Sat, 10am-4:45pm; Sun 1pm-4:45pm. Closed Mon and Jan 1.

The Cloisters, Fort Tryon Park, New York, NY 10040, **212/923-3700.**

MUSEUM OF MODERN ART

New York, NY

You would certainly call Van Gogh's famous painting *The Starry Night* a work of art, but would you say that about Francis Ford Coppola's first movie, a horror film called *Dementia 13?* You would expect to see a collection of Picasso paintings and drawings in an art museum, but would you expect to see a helicopter hanging from the ceiling, or a sports car parked in a gallery space? You can see all of these things—and much more at the Museum of Modern Art. It is the merging of traditional and bizarre, of expected and eccentric, that have made the museum into

The Baltimore Museum Of Art, Baltimore, MD

Credit: The Magnolia Branch, Henri Matisse

the diverse marvel it is today. In 1939, when the museum moved into its present quarters in midtown Manhattan, President Franklin D. Roosevelt spoke to a nationwide radio audience, and called it "a living museum, not a collection of curios and interesting objects." And it keeps on living and expanding, recently opening a new West Wing that doubles the museum's gallery and exhibition space. In a collection of more than 100,000 paintings, sculptures, photographs, and prints (as well as more than 8000 films and 3,000,000 film stills), the visual statements of this century are represented in their full spectrum. Open daily, 11am-6pm; Thur, 11am-9pm. Closed Wed and Christmas.

The Museum of Modern Art, 11 W 53 St, New York, NY 10019, **212/708-9400.**

THE FRICK COLLECTION

New York, NY

Henry Clay Frick commissioned an architect to design him a mansion which could one day serve as a museum. Consequently, the Frick Collection displays a laudable assemblage of objets d'art and paintings in the ambience of an elegant, private estate. Some of the famous pieces include Renoir's *Mother and Children,* Rembrandt's *Self-Portrait* and The *Polish Rider,* and Gainsborough's *Mall in St. James Park.* The manor's exquisite furnishings and sumptuous, thick carpets are half the charm, providing a setting for the romantic works of Turner, Reynolds, and Lawrence. Other artifacts include Chinese porcelains, a Herat rug, 18th century French furniture with pieces crafted by Riesener and Lacroix, and Jean Barbet's bronze *Angel* housed in the tropical atmosphere of the Court room—rimmed with Ionic pillars under an arched atrium. Illustrated lectures given Thur and Sat afternoons (Oct-May). Introductory talks available Tue-Sat at 11am (Oct-May). An automated introduction is repeated many times daily June-Sept. Admission: $1 (Tue-Sat); $2 (Sun); students 10-16 and sr.cit ½ price (children under 10 *not* admitted).

The Frick Collection, 1 E 70th St, New York, NY 10021, **212/288-0700.**

THE MUSICAL MUSEUM

Deansboro, NY

Most museums keep their treasures behind glass or rope barriers — away from anything but the gaze of curious visitors. This museum is different—all but the most fragile pieces of its unique collection of antique music-making devices are available to be played or operated by the public. And what a collection it is! Here you'll find a machine built in 1912 that can play both a violin *and* a piano at the same time, and was voted one of the "eight greatest inventions of the decade" by the US Patent Office. One of the rarest pieces in the museum is the Welte-Mignon, an automatic piano made in Germany about 1910. Holes in the music roll control not only what note is played, but how long the original pianist held down the keys, and how hard the keys were struck. This helps the piano recreate a realistic performance, with the same expression and touch the pianist intended. The museum also has fine collections of antique music boxes, phonographs, and organs on display and available for demonstration. These include some of the first disc phonographs ever made, and precise miniature music boxes the size of a large pocket watch. The museum was founded—and is still run—by the Sanders family, and what started as their private collection of music boxes and nickelodeons is today dubbed a "Marvelous Musical Menagerie." Open daily, 10am-4pm, Apr-Dec (Closed winters).

The Musical Museum, NY 12B, Deansboro, NY 13328, **315/841-8774.**

NAT'L BASEBALL HALL OF FAME

Cooperstown, NY

This famous tribute to "America's favorite pastime" is located, appropriately, just a block from historic Doubleday Field—where baseball pioneers Graves and Doubleday first played the game more than a century ago on what then was a glorified cow pasture. Baseball's most celebrated memorial has been welcoming fans for nearly 50 years and combines photos, paintings, audio-visual techniques and exhibits of baseball memorabilia to depict the origins of the game. The Great Moments room houses 9-foot pictures that capture stirring moments from great games of the past. More than 200 baseball giants are immortalized in the Hall of Fame Gallery, and more than 1000 artifacts and memorabilia are cleverly arranged to show the history of baseball. Recreations of once great ballparks such as Ebbets Field and the Polo Grounds are contrasted with stadia of the modern generation. Just behind the museum is the National Baseball Library where Hall of Fame induction ceremonies are held every year. Films shown daily. Open every day except Christmas, Thanksgiving, and New Year's. Admission: $4; 7-15 $1.50.

Nat'l Baseball Hall of Fame, PO Box 590, Cooperstown, NY 13326, **607/547-9988.**

Nat'l Baseball Hall Of Fame, Cooperstown, NY

THE SMITHSONIAN INSTITUTION

Washington, DC

Known as "Uncle Sam's Attic," this museum—actually 14 separate museums — may not have one of *everything,* but. . .they're working on it. Created in 1846 according to the wishes of James Smithson, an Englishman who had never set foot in the US, this institution set forth to "increase and diffuse knowledge among men." Today, the Smithsonian is the world's largest museum complex, and its National Air and Space Museum is the most visited museum in the world. To many visitors, the original Smithsonian building—known as the "Castle" because it resembles one—symbolizes the noble and novel aims of the Institution. Built in 1855, the Castle now houses the Institution's offices and the transplanted grave of the benevolent Mr. Smithson. The holdings in the various museums are eclectic, historic, and fascinating — anything but staid. The National Museum of American history preserves the original Star-Spangled Banner that Francis Scott Key immortalized in our national anthem. The National Air and Space Museum proudly displays Lindbergh's Spirit of St. Louis and a touchable moon rock. The Hirshhorn Museum and Sculpture Garden exhibits large works by Rodin, Calder, and Matisse. The main draw at the National Zoological Park are the Chinese Giant Pandas. Other museums at the Smithsonian show the range of its holdings: from masterpieces by Monet to African textiles, from trailblazing photographs by Matthew Brady to Asian jades and bronzes. Both diverse and focused, the Smithsonian is a model for museums yet unbuilt, and an inspiration for generations yet unborn. Open daily, 10am-5:30pm. Closed Christmas.

Smithsonian Institution, 1000 Jefferson Dr SW, Washington, DC 20560, **202/357-2700.**

NAT'L GALLERY OF ART

Washington, DC

Although Leonardo de Vinci died nearly five centuries ago, his contributions in science, medicine, and art have helped shape the modern world. Appropriately, his only painting in the US is housed here, in a museum dedicated to the artistic heritage of America and Europe. The huge collection is divided between two buildings connected by an underground concourse. The West Building, adorned with majestic Ionic pillars and imported marble, stone, and travertine, was designed by the same architect who did the Jefferson Memorial. It is one of the largest marble structures in the world, and exhibits many masterpieces from the 13th-20th centuries. The smaller East Building opened in 1978 with a great many modern and avant-garde works, as well as changing exhibits of established masterworks. Twentieth century pieces include works by Picasso, Moore, Calder, Miro, and Pollock. A wide variety of free tours, lectures, films, and concerts are regularly available. A 50-minute Introductory Tour conducted Mon-Sat, 11am and 3pm; Sun from 1-5pm. Free admission. Closed Christmas, New Year's, and Sun mornings.

Nat'l Gallery of Art, 4th S & Constitution Ave, NW, Washington, DC 20565, **202/737-4215.**

THE BALTIMORE MUSEUM OF ART

Baltimore, MD

Inside this museum you'll find a "collection of collections," so called because it came into being in bits and pieces, as gifts from local art collectors and patrons. The museum's 120,000 pieces range from antiquity to the present, from 15th century Italian masterworks to a cigar store Indian. An entire wing is devoted to American painting, sculpture, furniture, and silver, as well as other decorative and architectural items. Many of these are shown amid antiques or collectibles in a series of period rooms. This is the home of the world's largest collection of works by Henri Matisse, considered France's foremost post-impressionist, and masterpieces by Picasso, Van Gogh, Cezanne, and Renoir, among others. One of the museum's most popular permanent exhibitions is called Arts of Africa, The Americas, and Oceania, which displays works from these regions in special glass cases that provide unobstructed views from several angles. A large outdoor sculpture garden combines trees, flowers, and fountains with works by Rodin, Calder, and other eminent sculptors. Open Tue-Fri, 10am-4pm; Sat and Sun, 11am-6pm. Closed Mon and hols.

The Baltimore Museum of Art, Art Museum Dr, Baltimore, MD 21218, **301/396-7101.**

ACADEMY OF NATURAL SCIENCES

Philadelphia, PA

Founded in 1812, this museum's roots stretch back to a time of bloodshed and dissention, but has grown to become an extensive repository of national treasures and research institute for scholars and scientists. Historic treasures abound including plant specimens gathered by Lewis and Clark during their famous explorations, mounted birds used as models for Audubon's paintings, and Thomas Jefferson's personal fossil collection. Realistic dioramas introduce visitors to the flora and fauna of North America, Asia, and Africa. Constantly changing exhibits on wildlife, ice age art, scientific myths, conservation, among other topics, keep visitors coming back for more. Popular exhibits include a 65-million-year-old restored dinosaur skeleton near the academy entrance, a large reconstruction of a watering hole on the Serengeti Plain, a fossil cave through which children can crawl, and rare Chinese pandas guarding their young in a mountain pass. Open daily 10am-4pm except Christmas, New Year's, and Thanksgiving. Admission: $2.75; 13-18, over 65 and military $2.50; 3-12 $2.25.

The Academy of Natural Sciences, 19th & Pkwy, Philadelphia, PA 19103, **215/299-1000.**

FRANKLIN INSTITUTE

Philadelphia, PA

This museum is so much fun, you might forget you're learning something! Four floors of visitor-activited exhibits, frequent live shows, lectures, and a planetarium and roof-top observatory make this science museum as popular with children as it is with adults. Entertaining, "hands-on" exhibits include computer terminals, a physics lab, a giant heart, numerous shipping and sailing demonstrations, a Boeing 707 that visitors can board, the world's largest pinball machine, even the tools needed to move a 500-pound block. During good weather, the roof is rolled back so that visitors can peer at sunspots, Venus, and other points of astronomical interest through the powerful telescope in the nation's largest public observatory. Also housed in the institute is the 93-ton Benjamin Franklin Memorial, a 20-foot-high massive, marble statue of Franklin reclining in a chair (a la Lincoln Memorial). The domed memorial room was designed after the Roman Pantheon—tastefully accented with marble and a sky-light. Open Mon-Sat, 10am-5pm; Sun noon to 5pm. Admission: $3.50; children $2.50.

The Franklin Institute, Benjamin Franklin Pkwy at 20th St, Philadelphia, PA 19103, **215/448-1200.**

CARNEGIE INSTITUTE

Pittsburgh, PA

Carnegie Institute realizes Andrew Carnegie's dream of housing two museums and a music hall under one roof. The Museum of Art includes paintings, sculpture, and decorative arts of all periods and schools with major holdings of French- and Post-Impressionist paintings from 1800 to 1945, contemporary American and European paintings and sculpture, and an outstanding collection of European and American furnishings and art objects. The Museum of Natural History features displays of 10,000 objects from all fields of natural history and anthropology. Popular new exhibit halls are the Hillman Hall of Minerals and Gems, Geology Hall, and Polar World. The Institute also houses a large music hall, a lecture hall, and the Museum of Art Theater for a full program of drama, music, poetry, films, and lectures. Closed Mon, Sun mornings, and major hols. Voluntary donations requested.

Carnegie Institute, 4400 Forbes Ave, Pittsburgh, PA 15213, **412/622-3131.**

WINTERTHUR MUSEUM & GARDENS

Winterthur, DE

The American antique collection here is so exquisite that the *New York Times* stated "no other collection comes even close in matching its range, its richness, and its quality." The house at Winterthur was first built in 1839 and its superlative collection began with the acquisition of a single antique chest of drawers in 1923. The original house was extensively remodeled to maintain period authenticity with detailed attention to anything from woodwork to fireplace walls, and has grown to a total of 196 rooms depicting 200 years of changing American styles. Decorative arts were acquired for minute finishing touches down to textiles, paintings, and even newspapers.

Rooms are often garnished with flowery treats from the spectacular—and equally impressive—landscaped gardens which surround the museum. There are 200 acres of rolling hills, lush meadows, ponds and streams carefully ornamented with thousands of trees, shrubs, wildflowers and bulbs. A year-round fantasia of color begins in spring with Chinese witch hazel and yellow-flowered cornel dogwoods, giving way to the yellow-blue conifers of the Pinetum in winter. Subtly curving paths provide self-guided walking tours year-round (open-air tram tours spring-autumn). Located off Rte 52 N of Wilmington. Open Tue-Sat, 10am-4pm. Closed Jan 1, Thanksgiving, and Dec 24 & 25. Admission (depending on season): $5-$7; students over 16/sr. cit. $3.75-$5.25.

Winterthur Museum and Gardens, Winterthur, DE 19735, **302/654-1548.**

Winterthur Museum & Gardens, Winterthur, DE

THE CURRIER GALLERY OF ART

Manchester, NH

Once described as a "little gallery on a grand scale," the Currier Gallery of Art is one of the most attractive museums in New England. Everything about this relatively small museum has been done beautifully. The building itself is a national landmark; the landscaped grounds are breathtaking. The collection itself was acquired by a policy that stressed quality over quantity, and each acquisition has been placed in a setting to maximize its enjoyment. Although the Gallery exhibits works from 13th century Europe to the present, including pieces by Monet and Picasso, its real strength lies in American art. Holdings include 19th and 20th century paintings, and a wide variety of American furnishings and art objects. Everything is placed in an uncommonly congenial atmosphere. Free admission. Closed Mon, Sun until 2:00pm, and major hols.

The Currier Gallery, 192 Orange St, Manchester, NH 03104, **603/669-6144.**

BOSTON MUSEUM OF FINE ARTS

Boston, MA

This museum doesn't depend upon special traveling exhibits to keep its corridors echoing with the clip-clop of street shoes and the humming murmurs of satisfied visitors. Founded in 1870, it has become universally respected for its permanent collections. Laurels include the most complete assemblage of Asian art under one roof in the world, the finest collection of 19th century American art in the world, as well as a rapidly growing number of contemporary works. The museum is also noted for its French Impressionist paintings, which include the largest number of works by Monet outside of France. Other curatorial departments include American and European Decorative Arts and Sculpture, Textiles, and the extensive Department of Printings, Drawings, and Photographs. Special exhibits held throughout year. Admission: $4; under 16 free. Closed Mon and major hols.

Boston Museum of Fine Arts, 465 Huntington Ave, Boston, MA 02115, **617/267-9300.**

ISABELLA STEWART GARDNER MUSEUM

Boston, MA

From the late 1800s until her death in 1924, Isabella Stewart Gardner was one of Boston's foremost connoisseurs of fine art. It is only fitting that her grand home now houses a lovingly assembled collection of paintings, sculpture, and manuscripts. The museum itself is a work of art—Mrs. Gardner visited the great capitals of Europe to gather the columns, arches, ironwork, and fountains which she incorporated into her stately home. The center Court was designed by Mrs. Gardner in the style of a Venetian courtyard of the 15th century, and is colorfully decorated throughout the year with blooming flowers grown in the museum's own greenhouse. On the second floor is the Tapestry Room, used weekly for classical concerts. The room derives its name from 10 large 16th century tapestries that dominate the decor, and help provide the room's fine acoustics. The museum's collection contains pieces by such well-known artists as Rembrandt, Matisse, Botticelli, Rubens, and Manet. Other exhibits of interest include one of the two surviving busts by the sculptor Cellini, a fragment of an original Tchaikovsky score, and a portrait of Mrs. Gardner by James McNeill Whistler. Open Tue 12pm-1pm; Wed-Sun, 12pm-5pm. Closed Mon and hols. $2 suggested donation.

Isabella Stewart Gardner Museum, 2 Palace Rd, Boston, MA 02115, **617/566-1401.**

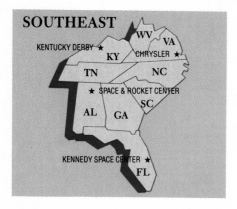

SOUTHEAST

KENTUCKY DERBY ★
WV
VA
KY
CHRYSLER ★
TN
NC
★ SPACE & ROCKET CENTER
SC
AL
GA
KENNEDY SPACE CENTER ★
FL

THE KENTUCKY DERBY MUSEUM

Louisville, KY

For more than 100 years, the Kentucky Derby has thrilled fans with its "most famous two minutes in sports," and this museum commemorates the men and the horses who have immortalized the annual "Run for the Roses." The museum replaces a small display of Derby memorabilia collected at Churchill Downs, and is topped by a replica of the Downs' famous Twin Spires. Inside, visitors will find exhibits on the breeding and training of champion horses, biographies of famous Derby jockeys, and many more facts and features about America's oldest continuously run horse race. Two special exhibits combine thoroughbreds and technology in a fascinating display. The first is a computerized race simulation, where visitors can "place bets" on the outcome to test their handicapping skills; the other is a stunning multimedia presentation featuring a 360-degree movie screen that surrounds visitors with the sights and sounds of an actual race. The Derby IQ Quiz gives trivia buffs a chance to test their racing knowledge, and the Derby Time Machine shows selected films of historic races and profiles to their famous participants. A must-visit for children and interested adults alike is the Museum's barn and paddock area, where visitors can observe stabled thoroughbreds. A gift shop and the Stallion Stakes Restaurant—perfect for an authentic Kentucky Mint Julep—round out this shrine to America's most famous race.

The Kentucky Derby Museum, Churchill Downs, 700 Central Ave, Louisville, KY 40208, **502/636-3541.**

THE SPACE & ROCKET CENTER

Huntsville, AL

Few of us will ever have the opportunity to pilot a spacecraft to the moon, fire a laser, or experience the force of triple gravity. However, you don't need to be an astronaut to experience these exciting adventures; simply visit this extraordinary facility. More than 100 relics of historic NASA flights occupy the main exhibit area. Included are the Mercury capsule *Sigma 7* and the heat-scorched *Apollo 16* vehicle which brought astronauts back from the moon in 1972. Participation is the operative word here. Walk through our galaxy in the "Space Dimension" exhibit, punch up a satellite picture of your home town, or try your skill at maneuvering a lunar module through an asteroid belt. The center's newest attraction is the "Spacedome," where you can experience in superrealistic detail the flight of the space shuttle. Outside, you can view more than 30 space vehicles, missiles and rockets which cover the four acres of Rocket Park. Nearby is the Marshall Space Flight Center, which can be enjoyed via a 2-hour bus tour. Unlike museums which celebrate artifacts and memorabilia from antiquity, the Space and Rocket Center asserts itself in the here and now, transporting its visitors to the outer limits of technology and imagination. Open: June-Aug 8am-6pm, Sept-May 9am-5pm, closed Christmas Day.

The Space & Rocket Center, Tranquility Base, Huntsville, AL 35807, **800/572-7234, 205/837-3400.**

KENNEDY SPACE CENTER

Kennedy Space Center, FL

Here's a museum that's a blast…and maybe even a *blast-off!* At NASA's Kennedy Space Center visitors can see historic reminders of America's quest to put men in orbit and on the moon, and possibly see one of the famous space shuttles launching into aviation's future. At the Visitor Center, mock-ups, models, and some actual spacecraft trace our extraterrestrial history, from satellite to spacewalk to shuttle. Films, flight demonstrations, and even real moon rocks are on display to pay tribute to the men who raced into the "last frontier," as well as to those on the ground who helped make it possible. The most famous items on display include the actual Apollo spacecraft that docked with the Russian Soyuz craft in the US-USSR cooperative flight of 1975, astronaut David Scott's Gemini space suit from a 1966 mission, and the command module simulator used to train moon-landing crews. Bus tours take visitors behind the scenes, past buildings where flight crews are trained and huge rockets are assembled. Visitors are often surprised to find that most of the land area of the Center is a protected wildlife refuge, where (among others) alligators, eagles, armadillos, and many species of endangered birds manage to coexist with blasting rockets and advanced technology. Tours also explore accessible areas of the refuge, giving sightseers a rare view of an American Bald Eagle's nest. Located 47 mi E of Orlando on FL 405. Call 800/432-2153 in FL only for updated launch info.

John F. Kennedy Space Center, Visitors Center, TWA-810, Kennedy Space Center, FL 32899, **305/452-2121.**

THE CHRYSLER MUSEUM

You won't find any automobiles here, but you will find why this museum was recently praised by the *Wall Street Journal* as "one of the top 20 museums in the country." An afternoon stroll through the more than 40 galleries reveals hundreds of works of art spanning most major civilizations and historic periods. The classic beauty of 18th and 19th century European art is well-represented by the works of French, Italian, Dutch, and German masters. A bust of Christ by Bernini has been hailed as "one of the greatest works of art in the country" by John Russell of the *New York Times.* Connoisseurs of French Impressionism and Post-Impressionism will revel in the canvases of flowering gardens, airy landscapes and sunny beaches by such renowned artists as Renoir, Degas, Monet, and Gaugin. The Institute's 10,000-piece glass collection delineates the 2000-year history of glassmaking, and includes one of the most important Tiffany collections in the world. 18th and 19th century American art is well-represented by such notables as Benjamin West, John Singleton Copley, Asher B. Durand and Thomas Cole. The impressionistic paintings of Mary Cassatt and Childe Hassam bridge the gap of early traditionalists and their modern counterparts. The contemporary galleries reflect the works of such recent artists as Andy Warhol, Jackson Pollock and Franz Kline. In addition to the best in fine art, the museum's collection includes artifacts from ancient civilizations, tribal masks from Africa, scrolls and costumes from the Orient, and furniture from France, England and Early America. Hours: Tue-Sat, 10am-4pm, Sun, 1pm-5pm. Closed Monday, New Year's Day, Independence Day, Thanksgiving Day, and Christmas Day.

The Chrysler Museum, Olney Rd and Mowbray Arch, Norfolk, VA 23510, **804/622-1211.**

Cincinnati Art Museum, Cincinnati, OH

Credit: Undergrowth with Two Figures, Vincent Van Gogh

Chapter 10

GOLF & TENNIS PLACES

Boca West, Boca Raton, FL

What do golf or tennis aficionados crave more than a hole-in-one or a perfect backhand? To find the ultimate course or court on which to play their favorite sport! This isn't always easy, because many fine tennis and golf facilities are within the hallowed sanctuaries of private country clubs or are operated by private associations, and thus are not available to the public. But non-members take heart! All of the entries here have met two requirements: excellence and/or uniqueness of playing conditions, and availability to the general public.

Intrepid linksmen can walk in the footsteps of the greatest golfers, past and present, on such challenging courses as wind-and-water-swept Pebble Beach, and venerable Pinehurst that echoes the achievements of golfing greats. Tennis enthusiasts can hone their skills with computerized and televised teaching aids at John Gardiner's Tennis Ranch or practice on any of 37 courts with an 11-member pro staff at Rod Laver's International Tennis Resort. The listings that follow include golf courses designed by some of the best golf architects such as Jack Nicklaus and Robert Trent Jones, and tennis clinics taught by such world-famous champions as John Newcombe and Arthur Ashe. We show you where to golf on oceanside links in the true Scottish tradition, or on green oases carved out of the shimmering desert; where to play tennis under pluperfect cloudlessly blue skies or in comfortable, climate-controlled domes.

In the US each year more than 17 million people golf for recreation while more than 25 million people play tennis (statistics courtesy A.C. Nielsen Co). If you're part of these huge numbers, or even if you've never tried these sports but want to, what follows are perfect spots to combine a relaxing vacation with some stimulating recreation. Note: Each entry is designated with a golf ( ) and/or tennis ( ) symbol to indicate its availability.

NORTHWEST

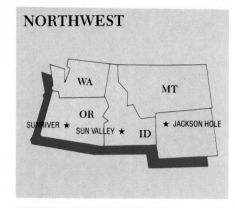

SUNRIVER

Sunriver, OR

Oregon, widely acknowledged as one of America's most beautiful states, is home to the uncommonly beautiful 3300-acre resort/residential community of Sunriver. Recipient of four diamonds from AAA and four stars from Mobil Travel Guide, Sunriver offers two fine 18-hole championship golf courses, one designed by Robert Trent Jones, Jr., the other featuring mid-fairway mounds and tougher roughs. Everything from rental clubs and golf carts to starting times and lessons from the PGA pro can be arranged at either of the two pro shops. Tennis is on 19 Plexi-Paved outdoor courts—plus three indoor courts at the Sunriver Racquet Club—which also has five racquetball courts (available to guests renting condominiums and resort homes). Tennis clinics and tournaments go on throughout the year. More than 360 spacious and luxurious condominiums nestled near the forest or golf links command incomparable views of the Cascade Mountains or the Deschutes River. Sunriver lodge houses dining and lounge facilities plus 77 deluxe kitchen suites and 134 deluxe bedroom units. A private airport brings guests and residents to this community 15 miles south of Bend, and recreation opportunities abound with two heated-swimming-pool complexes, stables, marina, nature center, arts and crafts center, gameroom and bike pavilion—and there's even a shopping mall.

Sunriver, Sunriver, OR 97702, **800/547-3922, 800/452-6874 (in OR).**

SUN VALLEY

Sun Valley, ID

Sun Valley in summer—why not? Enjoy the newly redesigned 18-hole golf course, remodeled by Robert Trent Jones, Jr., and recently named in the top 1% of well-designed courses by members of the American Society of Golf Course Architects. The mature, lush alpine course has long been a favorite of many guests, and has three teaching pros, practice fairways, pro shop and dining terrace. Next to the Sun Valley Inn and Lodge are 18 tennis courts, with a total of 85 courts in the area. Two-to five-day tennis clinics and private lessons feature Amten, the computerized ball machine and videotape system, plus pro shop and dining. Sun Valley is a complete family summer resort, with its separate, professionally staffed "Young Summer" programs for children and for teens. Ice skating in the sunshine, riding, dining, swimming in outdoor heated pools, mountain and river trips, fishing—that's Sun Valley in summer. (See Regal Resorts.)

Sun Valley, Sun Valley Rd, Sun Valley, ID 83353, **800/635-8261, 800/632-4104 (in ID).**

JACKSON HOLE RACQUET CLUB RESORT

Jackson, WY

In the sheer-granite-faced Wyoming mountains, hard by Yellowstone and Grand Teton national parks, (see Nat'l Parks & Monuments), is the tennis resort with probably the most magnificent setting of all. The Racquet Club Resort (AAA four-diamond rated) is the tennis center for the famed Jackson Hole recreation area. It features two outdoor and six indoor courts. For golf, the valley has an 18-hole, par-72 course designed by Robert Trent Jones. The resort itself, conveniently located at the foot of the Teton Mountain Range, provides guests with the convenience and luxury of vacationing in a tastefully decorated, fully equipped condominium, with a private balcony for experiencing the breathtaking alpine vistas. There's a three-hour peaceful scenic float trip—or take the daring white water run through the Snake River Canyon rapids. Guests also enjoy the Court Club, with eight racquetball courts, locker rooms, steam, sauna, whirlpools, indoor and outdoor swimming pools, jogging track and a complete Nautilus weight room. Outdoors is the place to be, with hiking, backpacking, riding, hunting and more—and of course, in winter, the fabulous skiing. There's even a personal-computer school and an aerobic-fitness program.

Jackson Hole Racquet Club Resort, Box 362A Star Route, Jackson, WY 83001, **307/733-3990.**

Innisbrook, Tarpon Springs, FL

SOUTHWEST

RANCHO BERNARDO INN

San Diego, CA

Now *this* is elegance … an utterly luxurious tennis and golf resort based on an early California theme. Memorable golf on the breathtakingly beautiful par-72 West Course, 6400 yards that demand accuracy with the championship character of the course evident with almost every hole. Links are garnished with four lakes, a stream, tricky doglegs, some 60 bunkers and strategically placed glittering silica-sand traps, and lush clumps of trees. For even more of a challenge there's the nearby 27-hole Oaks North Executive Course, with tough little par-3 nines that deliver their own kind of scaled-down action. Also on hand are five resident teaching pros, club storage, a shoe attendant and a top-of-the-line pro shop. The 12 tennis courts (four lighted) are terraced to enhance the beautiful landscaping, and the pro shop features only the best. Five USPTA pros at the Tennis College offer "intensive" or "strategy" curricula—both in depth. Accommodations at Rancho Bernardo are in seven red-tiled haciendas, together providing 236 deluxe rooms, executive suites and one- and two-bedroom suites, as well as the extraordinarily luxurious Palacio and Castillo suites. Two restaurants beckon with uncommon character and impeccable cuisine.

Rancho Bernardo Inn, 17550 Bernardo Oaks Dr, San Diego, CA 92128, **619/487-1611.**

TORREY PINES INN

La Jolla, CA

"A golfer's paradise," say the staff who run this lovely inn. No wonder. Adjacent to the Torrey Pines is the rolling turf of an 18-hole course. A breathtaking view of the blue Pacific Ocean stretches from virtually every hole. Home to the Andy Williams-San Diego Open Golf Tournament, it has been rated as one of the finest public courses in the world. Rooms and suites are tastefully furnished and designed for relaxing living, and the inn offers the inviting surroundings of the Seascape Dining Room and the Lantern Room Cocktail Lounge. The heated AAU-sized pool provides fun in the sun for the entire family. Nearby is the outstanding San Diego Zoo, Sea World theme park and the fascinating sights of old Mexico, as well as the elegant community of La Jolla. (See Romantic Rendezvous.)

Torrey Pines Inn, 11480 N Torrey Pines Rd, La Jolla, CA 92037, **619/453-4420.**

SILVERADO
Napa, CA

Here in the heart of the state's wine district lie the two finest 18-hole golf courses in Northern California, plus the largest and best-designed tennis complex. Both award-winning golf courses were designed by Robert Trent Jones and each bears its distinguished architect's signature: trees arching the fairways, traps and greens artfully positioned. The fine golf center includes a staff of top pros led by Bob Rosburg. Tennis players have an equally beautiful setting for their game with a random, open layout with wide, flowered walkways, patios, a mini-clubhouse, review decks and pro shop. There are 20 Plexi-Pave courts and a pro staff directed by Barry McKay. The 269 suites and studios at Silverado are uniquely private and personalized—none in a hotel setting, but in clusters with hidden courtyards, secluded swimming pools and quiet walkways. The beautiful 200-acre resort also features gracious restaurants serving the finest foods and wines, and the entire complex centers on a historic mansion built in the 1870s. Best of all, its setting is the exquisite Napa Valley, just a 45-minute drive from San Francisco.

Silverado, 1600 Atlas Peak Rd, Napa, CA 94558, **800/227-4700, 800/622-0838 (in CA).**

THE LODGE AT PEBBLE BEACH
Pebble Beach, CA

Imagine yourself standing in the ocean with perhaps a 9-iron trying to pitch from a rock-strewn shore, struggling, not merely to save par, but to complete the hole in the low teens! This scene actually occurred in the '60s during a Bing Crosby Pro-Am Tournament. The golfer . . . Arnold Palmer! That's the Pebble Beach life, and some say the utterly challenging, amazingly beautiful Pebble Beach course is the pinnacle of the golfing experience. Spectacularly set against the Pacific Ocean in the Del Monte National Forest, between Carmel and Monterey, (See Romantic Rendezvous), the Pebble Beach Golf Links has been consistently ranked in *Golf Digest's* top 10 courses. The Bing Crosby National Pro-Am tournament is held here annually, and golfers prepare for a long, challenging round at this outstanding course designed by Jack Neville and Douglas Grant. While guests at this elegant seaside resort, golfers can also test their game at the Robert Trent Jones-designed Spyglass Hill Golf Course, the historic Del Monte Golf Course (the oldest west of the Mississippi) or the par-3 Peter Hay Golf Course. Off the links, lodge guests enjoy the privileges of membership in the Beach & Tennis Club, with its 14 tennis courts, two paddle tennis courts, resident pro, teaching staff, heated year-round freshwater pool, sauna and wading pool. Nearby, explore the verdant forest from the Pebble Beach Equestrian Center's 34 miles of bridle paths, the five hiking and jogging trails and parcourse, and, by auto, the fabulous 17 Mile Drive (see Scenic Drives).

The Lodge at Pebble Beach, 17 Mile Drive, Pebble Beach, CA 93953, **408/624-3811.**

John Gardiner's Tennis Ranch, Scottsdale, AZ

SHADOW MOUNTAIN RESORT & RACQUET CLUB
Palm Desert, CA

Tennis magazine calls Shadow Mountain one of the top 50 tennis resorts in the US, and its 16 courts are the focal point of a full two- and four-day tennis clinic program headed by staff professional Leoncio Collas. Two paddle tennis courts and a well-stocked pro shop complement the tennis offerings. When it's time to relax there is Shadow Mountain's unique figure-eight-shaped pool, luxurious getaway accommodations of 200 studio units and condominiums, and many other pools and spas on the grounds. Within walking distance are El Paseo, the European-styled shopping boulevard of Palm Desert, plus fine restaurants and night life. Golfers will find 27 championship courses scattered throughout the valley. Located just 135 miles from Los Angeles in the shadow of the San Jacinto Mountains, the resort's own full dining and relaxation facilities maintain its four-decade image as a fully self-contained resort haven.

Shadow Mountain Resort & Racquet Club, 45750 San Luis Rey, Palm Desert, CA 92260, **714/346-6123.**

DESERT INN COUNTRY CLUB
Las Vegas, NV

Carved out of the desert more than three decades ago, the Desert Inn's legendary 7000-yard championship golf course is acclaimed—by seasoned pros and amateurs alike—as one of the finest and most exacting courses in the world. Home to numerous tournaments and enjoyed by entertainers, presidents and just good golfers, the 18 holes blanket nearly 200 acres of precious emerald greens and long, rolling fairways speckled with ponds, lakes and traps of white sand. The $3 million clubhouse includes a pro shop stocking apparel, equipment and accessories, rental clubs and motorized carts. For the tennis buff, there are five lighted tournament-class courts, perfect for beginner and pro alike. The resort is constructed in six golf- and tennis-themed areas, centered on a total of 818 individually designed guest rooms and suites. The newest Desert Inn feature is the 16,000-square-foot, world-class health spa, and there are more than 14,000 square feet of retail shops plus nine restaurants, snack bars and lounges. The showpiece Crystal Room presents Broadway-style musical productions. Don't miss the glamorous 50,000-square-foot casino . . . no Vegas resort is complete without one.

Desert Inn Country Club & Spa, 3145 Las Vegas Blvd S, Las Vegas, NV 89114, **800/634-6909.**

PALA MESA RESORT
Fallbrook, CA

This lovely little village north of San Diego is home to one of California's most challenging golf courses, winding through twisting oak and towering eucalyptus trees. The entire 6461-yard championship course has just two parallel holes, and a full staff of certified PGA pros for lessons. The lodge at Pala Mesa features more than 130 well-appointed rooms in the warm, friendly lodge, with gourmet dining, live entertainment, swimming, a Jacuzzi and tennis, too. Or, choose one of the 54 Fairway Condominiums, all spacious and newly decorated. For even more diversion, Sea World, San Diego Zoo, Wild Animal Park, Mission San Luis Rey and some of the finest vineyards in Southern California are all less than an hour's drive away. (See Theme & Amusement Parks.)

Pala Mesa Resort, 2001 S Hwy 395, Fallbrook, CA 92028, **619/728-5881.**

GARDINER'S TENNIS RANCH

Scottsdale, AZ

Tennis whites on court, and coats and ties and dresses in the evening—that's the international luxury resort atmosphere at John Gardiner's Tennis Ranch. The motto here is, "To play better is more fun." This elegant private resort has 24 championship courts including the world's most complete teaching court. Here you will find the Amten computerized ball machine and closed-circuit-television training room. Group and private instruction by a full pro staff is based on the Gardiner system, first developed more than 25 years ago. The gift and pro shops feature a full selection of apparel, gifts and equipment. A mainstay of the instructional program is the week-long Tennis Clinic, and the Ranch specializes in organizing tournaments for guests. During the Oct–mid-May season, special Junior Clinics and classes are offered for children visiting the Ranch with their parents. All guests enjoy luxurious Casita rooms or suites plus gourmet dining, swimming pools, whirlpools, saunas and massages.

Gardiner's Tennis Ranch, 5700 E McDonald Dr, Scottsdale, AZ 85253, **602/948-2100.**

TENNIS RANCH OF TAOS

Taos, NM

The only professional tennis facility in New Mexico, this 37-acre resort offers the possibility of tennis and skiing on the same vacation. Known for its unique pueblo-style architecture, the ranch has won design awards from the American Institute of Architects, and from *Sunset* and *House Beautiful* magazines. Six outdoor and two indoor courts are Laykold-surfaced, and instruction focuses on fundamentals for adults and families, beginners or advanced players. The main clubhouse area includes two racquetball courts, a bar and restaurant, heated swimming pool, sauna, hot tub and locker rooms. The studio and one- to three-bedroom condominiums, are fully furnished and equipped, including a Jacuzzi and sauna. The nearby town of Taos, a famous haven for artists, offers several fine dining spots, galleries, music performances and more. Nearby are fishing, hiking, and riding while the Taos pueblo and historic Santa Fe (see Romantic Rendezvous), are about an hour's drive away.

Tennis Ranch of Taos, PO Box 707, Taos, NM 87571, **800/624-4448, 505/776-2211 (in NM).**

RANCHO DE LOS CABALLEROS

Wickenburg, AZ

The contrasts of vigorous exercise on court and relaxing horseback rides are no more evident than at Rancho de los Caballeros. It's a place to play hard, but mostly the accent is on leisure and relaxation. The ranch has its own outdoor courts and the Oct–May season's often cool weather makes anytime court time. For golf, it's the exclusive los Caballeros Golf Club, where an 18-hole, par-72 course surrounds the ranch facilities. Natural desert rough contrasts with lush fairways seeded to be a deep green year-round. Rolling terrain, strategically placed bunkers, a three-acre lake and a backdrop of distant mountains make the course both beautiful and challenging. During the season, the weather is perfect for other outdoor activity: basking beside the unique pearl-shaped swimming pool, sharpening reflexes and hand-eye coordination on the trap and skeet range, joining the wranglers on a cattle roundup, or just strolling leisurely around the exquisite grounds.

Rancho de los Caballeros, Wickenburg, AZ 85358, **602/684-5484.**

MIDWEST

GRAND TRAVERSE RESORT VILLAGE

Grand Traverse Village, MI

Here in the beautiful northwestern Lower Peninsula of Michigan, a new course, named "The Bear," rages its 18 holes through cherry and apple orchards and towering hardwood forests, across clear streams and around four lakes. The Golden Bear himself, Jack Nicklaus, a master golf course architect, designed this rare stadium-style course, featuring large contoured mounding for major tournaments and 10 holes with water hazards. It's the showpiece of the year-round Grand Traverse Resort Village, an ideal vacation place for golfers and non-golfers alike. Situated on 850 acres, Grand Traverse has a 245-room hotel, more than 200 condominiums, four restaurants, four lounges and a health club with indoor tennis and racquetball courts, indoor and outdoor swimming pools, whirlpools, saunas, an exercise room and a masseur. Wintertime doesn't mean hibernation time at Grand Traverse. When the snows come, the resort turns into a cross-country skiing center. It boasts miles of scenic, well-groomed trails, including the longest lighted trail in the midwest, plus horse-drawn sleigh rides and ice skating, too.

Grand Traverse Resort Village, Box 404, Grand Traverse Village, MI 49610, **616/938-2100.**

BOYNE MOUNTAIN & BOYNE HIGHLANDS

Boyne Falls, MI

These sister resorts sprawling across 10,000 acres of northwestern lower Michigan, feature courses that challenge golfers while preserving the natural beauty of the land. Rolling hills, crisp forests, and clear mountain lakes surround the dark green links as they wind their way along the side of Boyne Mountain. For the past 10 years, *Golf Digest* magazine has ranked Boyne's Heather Highlands course as one of America's top 100 golf courses. And the Boyne complex offers three more championship-level 18-hole courses, as well as two 9-hole courses, driving ranges, putting greens, and fully-stocked pro shops. After an exhilarating morning of golf, you can relax in any of Boyne's heated pools, Jacuzzis, or saunas, or recreate that perfectly-placed drive or rim-circling putt with your partner over lunch at the Main Lodge or Highlands Inn. Tennis, horseback riding and sailing are also available, but the real stars here are top-notch golf and the serene beauty of Michigan. (See Winter Sports of All Sorts).

Boyne Mountain & Boyne Highlands, Boyne USA Resorts, Boyne Falls, MI 49113, **616/549-2441.**

EAGLE RIDGE INN & RESORT

Galena, IL

The warmth of an old New England inn, the amenities and conveniences of a modern full-service resort—plus one of the midwest's most scenic and challenging new golf courses, all add up to Eagle Ridge Inn & Resort, part of the huge Galena Territory development near the Mississippi River. Roger and Larry Packard met the demanding layout and construction standards for fine championship golf courses by blending the interesting, variegated terrain with well-placed tees, large greens and uniquely shaped sand traps. The inn itself offers an opportunity for succulently prepared meals, relaxing swims in the glass-enclosed 30' × 50' swimming pool and refreshing respite in the whirlpool or sauna. Children have a game room of their own to enjoy. Outdoors, besides golf, there is tennis, sailing, fishing, riding and just exploring. When the snows come, Eagle Ridge is just as much fun, with eight excellent cross-country ski trails, each carefully planned for a different level of expertise. Winter also brings sledding, toboggans, sleigh rides, ice skating, and even downhill skiing nearby. Guests can rent almost any equipment they need, winter and summer alike.

Eagle Ridge Inn & Resort, Box 777, Galena, IL 61036, **815/777- 2444.**

FRENCH LICK SPRINGS

French Lick, IN

This resort has been a symbol of elegance and luxury in the hills of southern Indiana almost since the turn of the century. Besides the beautiful 525-room hotel, the resort boasts two 18-hole golf courses. One course, "The Hill," was designed by the noted golf course architect Donald Ross. Typical of his style, the course is hilly with large, undulating greens, and there's no such thing as a level lie or a straight putt. The fairways are surrounded by oak and maple trees which are stunning in fall foliage. The other course, "The Valley," is longer but more of a pitch-and-putt course—built in the early 1900s for the rich elite looking for a relaxed, social game. For tennis, there are eight outdoor and 13 indoor courts. It's truly a vacation spot for the entire family with miniature golf, croquet, badminton, volleyball, bowling, health spa, horseshoes and two swimming pools (one bubble-enclosed) plus a wading pool. And, of course, there are the rich mineral springs —which first attracted French settlers here more than two centuries ago—that still provide their waters for refreshing and relaxing mineral baths. The only complaint that guests have is that there's too much to do!

French Lick Springs, French Lick, IN 47432, **812/935-9381.**

Boyne Mountain & Highlands, Boyne Falls, MI

AMERICANA LAKE GENEVA RESORT

Lake Geneva, WI

Only a 1-½-hour drive from the Chicago area in the lush Wisconsin countryside is this full-service, year-round golf and ski resort. There are two 18-hole golf courses, one of which was designed in the Scottish fashion—golfers need steady concentration and a fluid swing to contend with the narrow and briar-rough fairways. There are eight hard-surface outdoor and four indoor tennis courts. The indoor sports complex also includes six racquetball courts, Nautilus fitness center, men's and women's health spa and Fitness Monitoring program. Other outdoor activities include skeet and trap shooting, boating, riding, bicycling, miniature golf and strolling the 1400 rolling acres. Americana has its own private airport with a 4100-foot runway, and a 25-acre private lake. The low-rise eight-building complex of cedar, concrete and glass houses 340 rooms including 55 suites, every one with balcony overlooking the golf course and the Parcourse fitness track. Other amenities include indoor and outdoor pools, and four restaurants. Two miles west is the New England-like town of Lake Geneva, with fine shopping, dining and boat tours on the mansion-rimmed lake.

Americana Lake Geneva Resort, Hwy 50, Lake Geneva, WI 53147, **414/248-8811.**

SENTRYWORLD

Stevens Point, WI

There are not many championship courses where you will encounter a flower hazard; however, when you step to the tee at the Par-3, 150-yard 16th hole at SentryWorld, you'll be tempted to reach for your camera instead of your 7-iron. More than 90,000 flowers surround the green of this magnificent hole, where the multi-colored beds of snapdragons, petunias and marigolds are treated the same as water hazards. Robert Trent Jones, Jr. designed the course which is owned by Sentry Insurance, and it is one of the few national championship facilities available to the general public. SentryWorld was recently cited "the best new public golf course in America" by *Golf Digest*. It features the 6900-yard championship blue tee course, two intermediate lengths, and the red forward tees which play at a short 5200 yards. In addition to more than five acres of flower beds and plants, another distinguishing feature which sets SentryWorld apart from the crowd is its 35 acres of spring-fed lakes lined with large boulders. "Rarely are 18 holes so challenging and yet so elegant," remarks resident golf pro Bob Keith. Designer Jones has called his creation, "very possibly my Mona Lisa." The course is part of the Sentry complex which also contains six indoor tennis courts, five racquetball courts, restaurant, lounge, locker rooms, and pro shop. Six outdoor lighted tennis courts are also available to the general public.

SentryWorld, 601 N Michigan Ave, Stevens Point, WI 54481, **715/345-1600.**

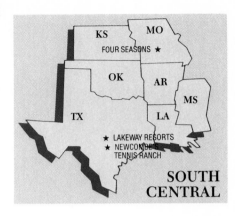

SOUTH CENTRAL

RESORTS OF LAKEWAY

Austin, TX

Take your choice between golf and tennis at this 5500-acre resort/residential community that is Lakeway. Choose golf and you get three magnificently groomed, championship 18-hole courses, one designed by Jack Nicklaus and all with picturesque views of the central Texas hill country. Pro shops at each course are completely equipped (including dining facilities), and a unique instructional facility features a 500-foot driving range, three separate practice holes and condominium accommodations. Choose tennis and you get the Tennis Center, with a full complement of lessons and clinics. In addition, The Hills of Lakeway Racquet Club offers striking courtside townhouses as well as 26 Laykold competition-quality courts, a lavishly equipped clubhouse with its own restaurant and lounge and a unique, racquet-shaped pool. *World Tennis* magazine has called The Hills of Lakeway one of the top 50 vacation spots in the world. Lakeway also boasts a private marina opening onto 65-mile-long Lake Travis, an Equestrian Center that includes a rodeo and riding arena, and a 3200-foot runway for private airplanes.

Resorts of Lakeway, 101 Lakeway Dr, Austin, TX 78734, **800/531-5001.**

LODGE OF THE FOUR SEASONS

Lake Ozark, MO

Located in the heart of the "show me state," this lodge shows *you* many different reasons why it calls itself "The Total Resort." The Robert Trent Jones Championship Golf Course challenges even the most seasoned competitor to keep head down and eyes on the ball and not on the spectacular panorama of luscious green woodlands and crystal blue water. In addition to the championship course, the lodge features a 9-hole Executive Course, putting green, driving range, pro shop and private instruction. The tennis facility features eight courts (two lighted), equipment rentals and lessons with the resident pro. However, if you want to get away from your game for a while, the nearby marina offers everything you'll need to take your holiday onto the water: boat rentals, skis and ski boats, sailing and skiing lessons, and cruises by day and by moonlight. The lodge offers a host of amenities, including four restaurants, three lounges, three night-

Americana Resort, Lake Geneva, WI

Sunriver, Sunriver, OR

clubs (dancing nightly), complete health spa, five outdoor pools and one indoor/outdoor pool. Other activities include trap and skeet shooting, bowling, bicycle riding, table tennis, ice skating and cross-country skiing (in season).

Lodge of the Four Seasons, Lake Rd HH, Lake Ozark, MO 65049, **314/365-3001, 800/392-3461.**

NEWCOMBE'S TENNIS RANCH

New Braunfels, TX

Serious about your tennis game? "Newk's" is the place for you. John Newcombe, one of the most extraordinary players in the history of tennis, has developed, along with famed coach Clarence Mabry and top-ranked Australian tournament player Graeme Mozeley, a team-coaching system that will enhance your potential and improve your game. Newk's, with 24 Laykold all-weather covered and lighted courts, has programs for adults at all levels and three excellent junior camps; from the Advanced Camp come the boys and girls on the prestigious Newk's International Touring Team. Newk's was originally a dude ranch so the air-conditioned cottages, courtside lodge rooms and two-bedroom apartments are designed for comfort and convenience. Nearby, you'll find fishing, water adventure, golf, and antiquing, while the beauty of old San Antonio is just a half hour's drive away. You'll enjoy some wholesome, downhome country-style cooking, especially the chef's Texas prime rib beef and barbecue. Since guests are at Newk's to learn and relax, there's no dressing up—tennis clothes may be worn to meals.

Newcombe's Tennis Ranch, Box 469, New Braunfels, TX 78130, **512/625-9105.**

NORTHEAST

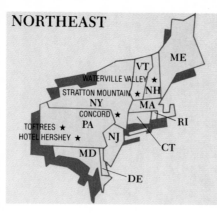

HOTEL HERSHEY & COUNTRY CLUB

Hershey, PA

Chocolate, chocolate, everywhere ... and three championship-level 18-hole golf courses plus two beautiful 9-hole courses ... and a full-service resort facility that could hold its own in any southern climate. That's the Hotel Hershey way of life. The west course was built in 1929 and is rated in the top 100 golf courses by *Golf Digest.* It annually hosts the LPGA Ladies Keystone Open, as well as a number of other tournaments throughout the golf season. The east course is known for being very long and difficult, measuring a full 7240 yards. Golf pros are on hand to assist novice-through-expert players and practice facilities include a driving range and putting greens. The hotel itself is an old, elegant edifice, which besides providing excellent tennis and dining and 270 tastefully appointed rooms and suites, offers a heated indoor pool, a sauna and outdoor activities including horseback riding. And, of course, you'll be in Hershey, Pennsylvania — "Chocolate Town, USA"—where you can tour the Hershey Museum of American Life, ZooAmerica and Hersheypark theme park (see Theme & Amusement Parks).

The Hotel Hershey & Country Club, 1000 E Derry Rd, Hershey, PA 17033, **717/533-2360, -2464.**

WATERVILLE VALLEY

Waterville Valley, NH

Families have been visiting Waterville Valley for more than 120 years. And today, there's still something for everyone here, where the emphasis is on family tennis and golf in the scenic setting of New Hampshire's magnificent White Mountains. Adults and children receive top-quality tennis instruction at daily clinics and through private instruction with Tom Gross, a USPTA professional who was formerly National Director of Tennis for Rod Laver Tennis Holidays. Golfers play the 9-hole, 2500-yard par-32 course. There's an Equestrian Center for trail rides and children's pony rides. Try swimming in Corcoran's Pond, which is fed by mountain streams, or in the various swimming pools at the 500-acre resort village's Snowy Owl Inn or Valley Inn & Tavern. Children aged 4-10 will love WINGS Day Camp—and so will their parents! The full-time recreation directory organizes day and evening events for families, with special programs for the kids. (See Winter Sports of All Sorts).

Waterville Valley, Waterville Valley, NH 03223, **603/236-8311, 603/236-8371 (resrv).**

TOFTREES RESORT

State College, PA

"You have to use every club in your bag when you play at Toftrees," says Jim Masserio, the resident pro. This par-72 course, designed by Edmund Ault, runs more than 7000 yards from the back tees. The rolling terrain and wooded hillsides of central Pennsylvania have been worked in so well that the course—judged the best resort course in the state—seems to be an extension of nature. Golfers can use the complete locker room—including a sauna. Visitors to the Toftrees Resort will find much more than golf to amuse them. Two restaurants with nightly entertainment and full recreational facilities (including a heated pool, tennis, platform tennis, a Parcourse Fitness trail, and hiking/biking trails) make Toftrees a fine spot for family vacations. Spacious lodge rooms, attractively furnished, are climate-controlled and include cable color television. Luxurious furnished rental condominiums are also available.

Toftrees Resort, One Country Club Ln, State College, PA 16803, **814/237-5311.**

Toftrees Resort, State College, PA

STRATTON MOUNTAIN
Stratton Mountain, VT

Late May through mid-September is the time for tennis and golf (with a little trout fishing on the side) in the beautiful Green Mountains setting of Stratton Mountain. Each summer, the Stratton Tennis Center features the Legends of Tennis Championship, with such longtime stars as John Newcombe, Rod Laver and Ken Rosewall. Throughout the season, the professional staff conducts weekend and five-day instructional programs. There are eight outdoor courts, with Har-Tru, red clay and hard surface, and four indoor courts as well as a complete pro shop. Golfers can take advantage of a magnificent 18-hole, par-72 championship golf course and the Stratton Golf School, a unique instructional program featuring a 22-acre "outdoor classroom" complete with videotape cameras for game analysis. Accommodations, obtainable through the Stratton/Bromley Lodging Bureau, offer a selection of more than 50 lodging facilities, with options ranging from bunkrooms to plush apartments with modern kitchens. Nearby are numerous fine restaurants, shops and night spots, as well as the New Life Health Spa and the Stratton Fly Fishing School at Stratton Lake and local, trout-stocked streams. (See Winter Sports of All Sorts.)

Stratton Mountain, Stratton Mountain, VT 05155, **802/ 297-2200.**

CONCORD RESORT HOTEL
Kiamesha Lake, NY

Ninety miles north of New York City, there's a center for great golf and tennis that's probably more famous for its enormous Singles Weekends than for anything else. But on the Concord grounds, golfers seek out an exceptional challenge on the celebrated 18-hole "Monster" course. A par-72 course, second-largest in the world at 7672 yards, the "Monster" was named one of America's top 20 by *Golf Digest* only three years after completion in 1963, and is still considered one of the top 50. The Concord also boasts the 18-hole International course and the 9-hole Challenger, plus the famous weekly Concord Golf School. As for tennis, how about 24 courts outdoors (free)—and 16 indoors. Also available are private, group and clinic instruction, occasional free clinics and exhibitions, and even racquet and shoe rental. The 1200-room Concord also features a full health club including daily exercise classes, and free team sports such as volleyball, handball, basketball and softball. Enjoy miles of trails and a full roster of winter sports with downhill skiing on Concord's very own mountain.

Concord Resort Hotel, Kiamesha Lake, NY 12751, **914/794-4000.**

SOUTHEAST

PINEHURST HOTEL & COUNTRY CLUB
Pinehurst, NC

Championship standards on the golf course, gracious service and timeless elegance in accommodations are what Pinehurst brings to the vacationer. Since 1898, golf at Pinehurst's six competitive courses has been evolving and prestigious amateur and professional tournaments have been hosted here throughout the years. All courses were landscaped with a hint of the Scottish tradition including rolling greens and rough fairways scattered throughout the links. Instruction is important, too, and Pinehurst is establishing a new golfing reputation and tradition with The Golf Advantage School, a series of week-long and daily clinics and individual and group lessons. Many lessons are scheduled in the Teaching Center, an indoor practice and teaching facility. Tennis lovers find 18 clay and six hard-surface courts (four lighted) nestled in a cool, refreshing pine grove. The Pinehurst Tennis Club, rated among the top 50 US tennis resorts, has an equally fine reputation for instruction. A new 18-hole course is scheduled to open soon. Near Pinehurst is the World Golf Hall of Fame, a museum and shrine dedicated to the sport of golf.

Pinehurst Hotel & Country Club, PO Box 4000, Pinehurst, NC 28374, **800/334-9560, 800/672-4644 (in NC).**

CALLAWAY GARDENS
Pine Mountain, GA

Put some variety into your golfing almost all year round… play the four very different courses of the lush, 2500-acre Callaway Gardens resort. Just over an hour's drive southwest of Atlanta, it's nestled deep in the foothills of the Appalachians. Callaway Gardens focuses its sports activities on its superbly maintained courses with 63 holes of golf—surrounded by the tall trees and beautiful lakes of the Gardens themselves. PGA and LPGA professionals offer the finest in instruction and two fully-stocked pro shops meet every golfer's needs. Tennis is almost as important at Callaway Gardens, with 19 lighted courts, a pro shop and high-quality professional instruction. The resort complex has a 345-room inn, 175 wooded cottages and luxurious villas for rent or sale. Guests can also enjoy fishing, riding, bicycling, skeet and trap shooting and from Oct-Mar, hunting for quail.

Callaway Gardens, Pine Mountain, GA 31822, **800/ 282-8181.**

WILD DUNES BEACH & RACQUET CLUB
Isle of Palms, SC

Golf magazine named this 18-hole beauty one of its Greatest 50 Courses in the World. Nestled alongside the Intracoastal Waterway and the Atlantic Ocean, the course incorporates the natural marshland, stately evergreens and impressive interior sand dunes into its player-perfect design. The Wild Dunes Tennis Center has a tennis pro on staff and features 17 Har-Tru courts (some lighted), and complete pro shops for both sports. Wild Dunes is the ideal family vacation spot—guests stay in luxuriously furnished private villas or cottages featuring full laundry, linens and kitchen facilities (dinnerware, dishwashers, ice-making refrigerator, and optional daily housekeeping). Ocean or pool swimming, a private marina with charter fishing boats, bicycling and picnicking, and fine dining at Edgar's round out this casual-living resort just 12 miles from historic Charleston. (See Historic Landmarks).

Wild Dunes Beach & Racquet Club, Isle of Palms, SC 29451, **803/886-6000.**

Wild Dunes Beach & Racquet Club, Isle of Palms, SC

SEA PINES PLANTATION

Hilton Head Island, SC

With five thousand acres of golf, tennis and the casual, luxurious resort lifestyle, Sea Pines truly offers something for everyone. Located in a golfer's and tennis player's paradise, on beautiful Hilton Head Island, golfers enjoy privileges at three championship courses: Ocean — with a spectacular Atlantic Ocean view on the 15th hole; Harbour Town Golf Links — consistently named a top-10 North American course with at least six of the toughest holes on the PGA tour; and Sea Marsh—an excellent scenic course for any golfer. A staff of Class A PGA teaching pros offers private and group lessons year-round and Bert Yancey conducts the Classical School of Golf. There are driving and putting ranges plus a pro shop at each course. Tennis is just as important—Sea Pines is America's largest tennis resort — with 80 courts in racquet clubs and villa neighborhoods throughout the complex, many fast-dry and night-lighted. And, there's a full clinic and lesson program featuring the "Tiny Tots" and the Doubles Clinic programs. Add nearly five miles of Atlantic beach, 25 swimming pools, two marinas, 41 miles of private roads and trails, a 605-acre forest preserve and nearly 1500 deluxe villas, hotel rooms and homes, and you'll never be without plenty of options and fun.

Sea Pines Plantation, Hilton Head Island, SC 29928, **800/292-GOLF, 803/671-2446 (in SC).**

SHIPYARD & PORT ROYAL RESORTS

Hilton Head Island, SC

Tennis Magazine said that here is "the most beautiful tennis complex not only on Hilton Head Island but maybe anywhere in the US." Their golf facilities are also top-notch with 63 holes on five courses; narrow, rolling fairways wind through scenic woodlands and are studded with quiet lagoons. For the tennis fan, there's the Shipyard Racquet Club, rated a Five-Star Tennis Resort by *World Tennis* magazine. Shipyard has 14 clay (eight lighted) courts and six Laykold. Guests may also play at Port Royal. For less strenuous pastimes, there's the 13-mile white-sand beach, and on the plantation four miles of beautiful trails plus swimming and a full health club. Nearby marinas charter an assortment of ocean-going craft for sailing or offshore fishing. Marriot's Hilton Head Resort is located within Shipyard Plantation and has top ratings from both Mobil Travel Guide and AAA. Situated on 800 acres overlooking the Atlantic coast, it offers scenic backdrops for both golf and tennis.

Shipyard & Port Royal Resorts, Hilton Head Island, SC 29925, **803/785-4256, ext 210.**

AMELIA ISLAND PLANTATION

Amelia Island, FL

Twenty-seven holes of golf…21 courts for tennis…take your choice. It's all in a 900-acre symphonic setting of massive sand dunes, golden sea oats, hideaway lagoons, and unspoiled tidal marshlands. Amelia Links is 27 challenging Pete Dye-designed holes. The resort's tennis facilities have earned its recognition as one of America's top 50 tennis resorts by *Tennis* magazine. There are 19 Har-Tru (some lighted), two Deco-Turf and one stadium court, plus All-American Tennis Academy tennis camps. In addition, the resort features a free-form pool, baby pool and restaurants for day and evening. The resort's accommodations include oceanfront rooms and one- to four-bedroom spacious, dramatically designed, furnished and fully-equipped villas. Supervised children's program and a program for teens, also available.

Amelia Island Plantation, Amelia Island, FL 32034, **800/874- 6878, 800/342-6841 (in FL).**

Diplomat Resort, Hollywood, FL

ROLLING HILLS GOLF RESORT

Fort Lauderdale, FL

Giant Spanish oaks and towering Australian pines combined with abundant water make the long course (6519 yards) at Rolling Hills as beautiful as it is challenging. The rolling terrain and contoured greens of the course add even more to its uniqueness. Designed by famed golf course architect William Mitchell, the 27-hole course is truly northern-style here in the perfect year- round climate of South Florida. Gracious accommodations in the 70-room lodge offer a casual atmosphere while the spacious sun deck, free-form pool and tennis courts, restaurant and lounge provide leisurely off-the-course activity. Rolling Hills' location is ideal, too — just a short drive to Fort Lauderdale's beaches, shops and restaurants, as well as three racetracks, the jai alai fronton, and the neon glitter of Miami.

Rolling Hills Golf Resort, 3501 W Rolling Hills Circle, Fort Lauderdale, FL 33328, **800/327-7735.**

DORAL HOTEL & COUNTRY CLUB

Miami, FL

The "Blue Monster" course gathers the greatest golfers in the world at Doral every year for the Doral-Eastern Open— one of the most important stops on the PGA Tour. Yet the Blue course is just one of five (four 18-hole championship courses and one 9-hole executive course) at Doral. In addition to golf, there are 19 tennis courts, both clay and all-weather (some lighted), and one of the world's largest pro shops. Doral's Director of Tennis is one of the tennis world's foremost celebrities, Arthur Ashe, while the resident pro is the former Davis Cup star from Colombia, Pancho Castillo. The lakes on the golf course are all well-stocked, which makes fishing the ideal late-day relaxer. The 650 rooms in this self-contained resort are located in eight separate lodges that fan out on both sides of the main building to front directly on the courses and courts. Restaurants and lounges are scattered over the 2400-acre grounds and there are fully-equipped health clubs for men and women.

Doral Hotel & Country Club, 4400 NW 87th Ave, Miami, FL 33166, **800/327-6334.**

INNISBROOK

Tarpon Springs, FL

With 63 great holes on three championship courses, the 1000-acre Innisbrook is the golf center of Florida. The Copperhead, up to 7031 yards, leads the group. The 6999-yard, par-72 Island calls for long and straight tee shots to avoid lakes and bunkers. Sandpiper, par-70, demands accuracy, its rolling fairways crisscrossed by water. Innisbrook is also home to tournaments and to the Innisbrook Golf Institute, headed by Jay Overton, a PGA tournament player. At Innisbrook's million-dollar Tennis and Racquetball Center, tennis is played on 11 clay and seven Laykold courts, with seven courts lighted for nighttime play. The Australian Tennis Institute, headed by Terry Addison, a former Australian Davis Cup player, specializes in teaching both beginner and advanced players. Innisbrook's spacious guest lodges offer a total of nearly 1000 individually owned condominiums rented to guests. Swimming pools, dining in the three clubhouses, and recreational facilities are within each lodge group. There's also a full health club, wildlife preserve and a complete roster of scheduled activities available for adults and children.

Innisbrook, PO Drawer 1088, Tarpon Springs, FL 34286, **800/282-9813, 800/237-0157 (in FL).**

THE DIPLOMAT

Hollywood, FL

Stretched along more than one-fifth mile of private Atlantic Ocean beach is The Diplomat, designed to fulfill everyone's dream of the perfect resort vacation. Two PGA 18-hole courses are dotted just right with lakes and sand traps. Each course has its own clubhouse, restaurant and pro shop. Rental carts and clubs are available. At the Diplomat Racquet Club, nine of the 19 wind-protected tennis courts are lighted for night play. Other amenities include five swimming pools, seven lounges, and nine restaurants presided over by an award-winning chef. A spa high atop the East Tower has separate men's and women's facilities, and supervised programs for children are offered. Luxurious hotel and VIP suite accommodations, horse and dog races and other nearby attractions at Fort Lauderdale and the Greater Miami area make this an exceptional sporting vacation.

The Diplomat, 3515 S Ocean Dr, Hollywood-By-The-Sea, FL 33022, **800/327-1212.**

GRENELEFE GOLF & TENNIS RESORT
Grenelefe, FL

For fine, uncrowded golf and full family vacation facilities, there's Grenelefe, on Florida's Gulf Coast just a 30-minute drive from Walt Disney World (see Theme & Amusement Parks). Grenelefe offers 54 holes on three championship golf courses. The West Course, designed by Robert Trent Jones, has been rated number one in the state for the past six years by *Florida Golfweek* magazine and one of the top 100 nationally by *Golf Digest*. The East Course and the new South Course are right behind West in popularity. David Leadbetter, Grenelefe's teaching pro, conducts the year-round Grenelefe Golf Studio—Florida's premier golf instruction center. Putting greens, driving ranges and a pro shop round out the facilities. The 13-court Tennis Complex is among *Tennis* magazine's top 50. Expert tennis clinics, clubs and camps are always available and include videotape analysis. For the entire family there's an adult and children's activity center with a full roster of events from which to choose. There are two restaurants, four swimming pools, and tranquil jogging/cycling trails that run through Grenelefe's 950 acres. Lake Marion offers 6400 acres of fishing for bass, speckled perch, bluegill and bream. Accommodations are in deluxe rooms and one- or two- bedroom Fairway Villas; children under 18 stay free when sharing with parents.

Grenelefe Golf and Tennis Resort, 3200 FL 546, Grenelefe, FL 33844, **800/237-9549, 800/282-7875 (in FL).**

SADDLEBROOK GOLF & TENNIS RESORT
Wesley Chapel (Tampa), FL

Designed and built by Arnold Palmer and Dean Refram, the 27 holes of golf at Saddlebrook have been rated among the top Florida courses by readers of *Florida Golfweek*. You'll experience water holes, sand hazards and fairways bordered by cypress and pine—so warm up on Saddlebrook's putting green and driving range. Or take a turn at tennis—11 Har-Tru (five lighted) and four Laykold courts are yours for the choosing. Awning-covered islands with water fountains and rest chairs are located between the courts. Take advantage of the resident golf and tennis pro staffs for a full schedule of instruction, and find all of the apparel, equipment and service you need at the pro shops, plus four restaurants and full health spas for men and women. Saddlebrook is a self-contained resort community, winner of four stars from Mobil Travel Guide and four diamonds from AAA. Accommodations range from deluxe hotel rooms in the centrally located Walking Village to rentals of more than 500 condominiums (daily housekeeping service). Cool off in the Superpool Complex complete with Olympic lanes, water sports, diving and a kiddie pool/play area, plus whirlpools, snack and swim shops, all surrounded by a beautiful ornamental garden.

Saddlebrook Golf & Tennis Resort, PO Box 7046, Wesley Chapel (Tampa), FL 33599, **800/237-7519, 800/282-4654 (in FL).**

BOCA WEST RESORT
Boca Raton, FL

Between Fort Lauderdale and Palm Beach is the elegant city of Boca Raton. Here is the sports-oriented Boca West, a carefully planned resort/residential community with 1436 acres of golf, tennis, canoes, bikes, lakes, cypress and green space that has hosted some of the great tournaments in recent golf and tennis history. *Tennis* magazine calls this one of its top 50 resorts, and it has 34 professional clay courts (many lighted) in a casual woodsy setting — plus expert instruction, advanced equipment and a full pro shop. The four golf courses (one at the stately Boca Raton Hotel and Golf Club, built in 1926 and now a sister resort to Boca West) are each noted for a unique challenge in design. These are supported by two driving ranges, a fully stocked pro shop and putting greens. *Golf Digest's* nationally known instructional school is held at Boca West. Accommodations are in spacious Hammocks (suites), villas and rooms, tucked away among tropical foliage with romantic verandas overlooking lush green fairways.

Boca West Resort Club, PO Box 225, Boca Raton, FL 33432, **800/327-0137, 800/432-0184 (in FL).**

SAWGRASS
Ponte Vedra Beach, FL

A self-contained resort community, Sawgrass is 4800 acres of a golfer's holiday and a tennis buff's dream. Most noted for golf, the resort features 54 championship holes, including a new 18-hole course designed by Pete Dye. You can also test your skills on the resort's championship Oceanside and Oak Bridge courses. For tennis there are 13 professional courts at the Racquet Club, which has hosted numerous tournaments and has been selected as a five-star resort (highest honor) by *World Tennis* magazine. The Beach Club features the adult-retreat Oasis Pool; the Olympic-sized pool is a family favorite. Dining is casually elegant, and there is live entertainment in the Topsider Lounge. Sawgrass even has a year-round activities staff to make sure everyone's visit is enjoyable.

Sawgrass, PO Box 600, Ponte Vedra Beach, FL 32082, **800/874- 7547, 904/285-2261, (in FL call collect).**

Laver's Tennis Resort, Delray Beach, FL

THE COLONY BEACH & TENNIS RESORT
Longboat Key, FL

The perfect tennis partner...every tennis player's dream. The Colony doesn't promise perfection, but they will try to match you with a partner of equal ability. Tennis on the 21 Plexi-Pave courts is free, and the staff of USPTA pros offers both group and Health-club facilities are complete with whirlpool, sauna, steam and massage. Swim in the large freshwater pool or in the Gulf of Mexico; stretch your muscles and enjoy games on the beach; sail, fish, bike, jog, play volleyball, or join in the daily aerobics program for fun and fitness. Golfing on a championship course is only minutes away. Longboat Key/Sarasota is a comfortable drive to other famous Florida attractions: Busch Gardens, EPCOT Center, Walt Disney World, Sea World, Cypress Gardens (see Theme & Amusement Parks) and elegant shopping at St. Armands Circle. The Colony's attention to detail is reflected in the accommodations. Beautifully wooded, clustered condominium apartments all contain fully equipped kitchenettes, living/dining area, sun balcony and a separate, private bath for each bedroom.

The Colony Beach & Tennis Resort, 1620 Gulf of Mexico Dr, Longboat Key, FL 33548, **800/237-9443, 800/282-1138 (in FL).**

LAVER'S INT'L TENNIS RESORT
Delray Beach, FL

Laver's is proud to be a tennis resort that offers more than racquet sports, but its tennis facilities draw guests from around the world. They enjoy 37 courts—27 Har-Tru (16 lighted) plus ten Tru-Flex (all lighted) and one Australian half- court. That translates to year-round tennis instruction by the 11-member professional staff, for adults and juniors at every level. The Laver's Tennis Host program matches players of comparable skills. Some of the top professional and amateur tournaments are played here, and many of the very best players come to show their stuff. Other recreation opportunities include three swimming pools, a whirlpool, racquetball, biking, jogging or hiking trails, a fully-equipped Nautilus health club plus award-winning restaurants. Nearby, choose between challenging golf courses, sun-drenched beaches, sailing, sport fishing, snorkeling and scuba diving — plus incomparable shopping and entertainment in close-at-hand Palm Beach and Boca Raton. The advantage in accommodations is luxurious, fully furnished one- or two-bedroom condominium suites with fully-equipped kitchens, and economical rates.

Laver's Int'l Tennis Resort, 2350 Jaeger Dr, Delray Beach, FL 33444, **800/327-1160, 800/432-2482 (in FL).**

Chapter 11

UNIQUE RESTAURANTS

The Cannery, Newport Beach, CA

You're in the Pacific Northwest, enjoying a trencherman's breakfast, the lumberjack proportions of which include oatmeal, eggs, bacon, ham, sausage, cornmeal mush, hash browns and pancakes. Through a picture window you watch the cascading spectacle of a waterfall that is higher than Niagara. This, we feel, is a unique dining experience. And that is what this section is all about — good food, plain or fancy, served in a unique ambience.

As you browse through these selections, you'll find a restaurant in Brooklyn where gas lighting still is used and where the meats are seared dark over anthracite coal to seal in the juices. There's an Irish pub in Seattle that really goes to bat for sports fans, and a purveyor of wurst in Milwaukee that offers 75 different kinds of sausages. Or maybe you'll be intrigued by the mid-eastern opulence of Moroccan restaurants in California and Colorado where eating with your fingers is *de rigeur* — or by an old tavern that once served the Delaware and Hudson Canal. In Kansas City you'll find what have been multiply-acclaimed as the "world's best ribs," in Texas an old stagecoach stop, in Chicago a lively Serbian club where you can enjoy Eastern European cuisine and join in lively traditional dances, and in Vermont an eatery where fresh maple syrup is dribbled deliciously over flaked ice. As you follow our lead, you'll meet Amish folk and fisherfolk — and you'll follow in the footsteps of presidents and movie stars.

These selections range from simple, downhome fare served in humble, but unique surroundings, to truly exotic food or haute cuisine presented in an ambience of decadent luxury. While we have not attempted to include information about prices, we believe the descriptions themselves will provide obvious clues as to cost. In any event, prices run the gamut from "budget conscious" to "credit-card tilt." Enjoy!

UNIQUE RESTAURANTS

NORTHWEST

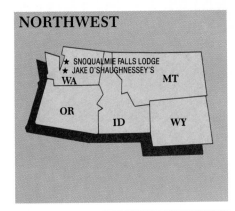

SOUTHWEST

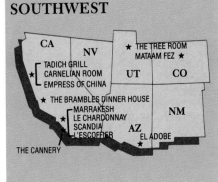

MARRAKESH
Studio City, CA

There's an air of authenticity here in a setting somewhat akin to an opulent Moroccan home. It's lavishly gilded with colorful tapestries made in ancient hand-sewn applique once used by nomads for tent decor. Moroccan ceramics, pottery, brasses, water colors and artifacts abound. Eight and nine-course dinners are favored, though a more diminutive five-course meal is offered. But there's no menu. Instead, a djellaba-clad waiter kneels beside your table, names the courses, translates and explains them. A ceremonial washing of the hands from a large silver bowl precedes the serving. This is necessary because you'll eat almost everything with your fingers and you'll be grateful for the tasty bread in more ways than one. The featured meal begins with Harira, a lentil vegetable soup seasoned with ginger and saffron. Then, in leisurely succession, you'll be served a colorful salad of marinated Moroccan vegetables, a B'Stilla (pastry-like layering of chopped chicken, scrambled eggs and almonds in a light flaky filo dough, baked and covered with powdered sugar and cinnamon), and charcoal broiled lamb kebobs sauced with a bowl of red liquid fire. The entree is chosen in a democratic fashion—by unanimous vote of the diners in your party. And it's a Solomon-like choice to be made from roast quail, chicken, rabbit or fish. A spoon comes next with couscous, a succulent mound of steamed cracked wheat smothered in colorful spiced meats and vegetables. Fruit, nuts and tea are yours to enjoy as the democratic tradition continues with entertainment provided in the form of both male and female bellydancers!

Marrakesh, 13003 Ventura Blvd, Studio City, CA 91604, **818/788-6354.**

JAKE O'SHAUGHNESSEY'S
Seattle, WA

You can't avoid catching up on the latest sports news here; it's a famous hangout for fans. The interior resembles a turn-of-the-century Irish pub, and the specialty is some of the best seafood in this seacoast city. Here you will find a fine fettle of fish every day of the week, including salmon slow-smoked over a fire of alder wood just as the Indians used to cook it. It's called cold smoking, which means the salmon stays firm and moist after absorbing the flavor of the wood smoke over a period of hours. It's heated just before serving. Atypical of the sporting world, where fire, flash and speed are highly prized, O'Shaughnessey's cooks its beef slowly. The Saloon Roast is encased in salt and cooked at low temperatures for half a day, the salt flavoring the meat and keeping the juices within. A 24-ounce Idaho baker called the Murphy, stuffed with corned beef, butter, onions, and sour cream complements any meal (in fact, it's big enough to be considered an entree). Sports fans especially appreciate Jake's bar, where more than a thousand different brands of booze stretch to the rafters.

Jake O'Shaughnessey's, 100 Mercer St, Seattle, WA 98109, **206/285-1897.**

SNOQUALMIE FALLS LODGE
Snoqualmie, WA

"This symbolizes the falls," the waitress says and, holding a bowl of honey high in the air, drizzles your individual portion into a smaller container. Through the dining room window you can see the real thing, a cataract of water cascading 270 feet into the gorge below. It's as spectacular as Niagara, and higher. Before or after your meal you can see and hear the roar up close on a walkway from which you can look up at one of the country's most picturesquely sited inns, a cedar-shingled structure dangling on the brink of a cliff. Although there are several luncheon offerings and dinner specialties, such as salmon from nearby Seattle's Puget Sound and fresh mountain trout from much closer waters, you must have the breakfast. It's the gut-busting kind that farmers, ranchers, cowboys, coal miners, and lumberjacks need in order to put in a hard day's work. Unlike these folk, however, you'll need about three hours to chow down on the oatmeal, eggs, bacon, ham, sausage, cornmeal mush, hash browns and pancakes. Breakfast ends with fresh fruit already set on the table.

Snoqualmie Falls Lodge, Snoqualmie Falls City Rd, Snoqualmie, WA 98065, **206/888-2451.**

L'ESCOFFIER
Beverly Hills, CA

The posh penthouse of the Beverly Hilton draws celebrity diners like a headliner's entourage. Muted tones of grey, rose and green form a backdrop for elegant silver, crystal, bouquets of fresh flowers and lilting music. Diners are offered one of the finest views of Los Angeles south of Mulholland Drive, and a stunning inlaid glass mosaic mural stretches the length of the room. Through it all, an unruffled staff serves trays laden with such comestibles as rich moist quiche Lorraine, double beef broth with seedless grapes and cheese straws, trout saute with cucumber pears, medallion de veau baked with asparagus, and a regal salad comprised of fried Camembert cheese with Boston lettuce and walnut dressing. Two prix fixe menus require considerable time to consume. Tempting dessert souffles dressed in chocolate, Grand Marnier and fresh raspberry, strawberry and other fresh fruits are justifiably world-renowned.

L'Escoffier, 9876 Wilshire Blvd, Beverly Hills, CA 90210, **213/274-7777.**

L'escoffier, Beverly Hills, CA

LE CHARDONNAY

Los Angeles, CA

A turn-of-the-century French bistro that would have found favor with the Lost Generation, even without the Left Bank, has recently begun operations in this busy un-French city. The ambience is deliberately evocative of La Belle Epoque and, more precisely, the Vagenende, a favorite haunt of co-owner Robert Bigonnet in his youth. In fact, the mirrored walls faithfully duplicate paintings of the windmills and fishing boats found similarly ensconced at the Parisian prototype. Lavish curved wood dividers and handsome posts decorated with brass coathooks give the bistro a cozy intimacy; a rainbow of French tiles and the amber lighting contribute to the effect. The flavor of oak and grapevine cuttings from a wood-burning rotisserie spice the air and the spitted chickens and meats cooked on the grill. Co-owner chef Claude Alrivy, who trained at Maxim's in Paris, offers a menu considerably different from most French fare served in the US. Consider, for example, the tasty sauerkraut, a concoction of cabbage, smoked salmon, eel, sturgeon and trout in chive butter. Or lamb curry, spiced chunks of meat with chopped tomato and raisins on a bed of rice accompanied by banana fritters with a piquant mango chutney. Desserts created by a Paris-trained pastry chef may inveigle you to linger after the main course. A tasty example is an outstanding chocolate cake, the richness of which is tastily muted by creme anglaise. California Chardonnays, uncharacteristic of French Bank bistros in the early 1900s, overpower the wine list.

Le Chardonnay, 8284 Melrose Ave, Los Angeles, CA 90046, **213/655-8880.**

SCANDIA

Los Angeles, CA

Simply put, this is one of the best restaurants on the globe. And the planet has honored it with enough award titles to fill four single-spaced typewritten pages. Viewed from any angle, the Sunset Strip setting is superb, and the menu ranges from merely ambrosial to sublime. The 40-year-old heritage developed by the late founder, Ken Hansen, constitutes a flavorful legacy to gastronomes the world over. The Danish room was meant for banquets, but almost from opening day it was needed for daily dining. Originally a cement patio with awning, the Belle Terasse is fully enclosed and decorated with white lattice work. The wine cellar downstairs features some of the best vinted products found outside a monastery. Here, kalvfilet Oskar was introduced to America, along with gravlax (cured salmon) and remains one of the most popular entrees. The favorite, however, sounds like a movie star's name—Biff Lindstrom; it's made with chopped sirloin, chopped beets, capers, and onions served with a fried egg on top. The L-shaped bar, topped with brightly polished brass, arguably is the best in the city. Tasty appetizers served at cocktail time include a zesty blue cheese dip or a chicken liver pate filled with pistachio nuts; nonpareil Swedish meatballs slowly simmer over a flickering flame. It's also the best place in town to gaze at the stars, Hollywood variety.

Scandia, 9040 Sunset Blvd, Los Angeles, CA 90069, **213/278-3555.**

THE CANNERY

Newport Beach, CA

Orange County is better known for its politics than its cuisine, yet here is a showcase for seafood in this ritzy port city near Los Angeles. It is a most unusual setting for a fine restaurant, housed as it is in an old factory with high ceilings and enormous windows that provide a frame for the picturesque bay. The ambience is created by a hodge podge of cams, thermostats, crates, wrenches, cogs, gears, gauges, winches, boilers, engines, tubes and tubs once used in the canning process. Fine food is available anytime, because fresh-caught fish are served almost from the instant they're heaved onto the dock. But for a real treat, try the Sunday brunch aboard owner Bill Hamilton's converted trawler, *The Isla Mujeres* (reservations required). Your serving crew will be headed by German-born manager Annerose Beech, a former waitress who is widely credited for making the whole thing work. Notable assistance is provided by abalone, lobster salad, shrimp scampi Mediterranean, rack of lamb and bife a Portuguesa.

The Cannery, 3010 Lafayette Ave, Newport Beach, CA 92663, **714/675-5777.**

TADICH GRILL

San Francisco, CA

If you're serious about seafood, or seriously interested in your date, this is a good place to enjoy both. The former is excellent both for lunch and dinner, and, although lunch is quite busy, you can usually find a nice cozy nook in the evening. Since Gold Rush days when 49ers were served from a tent, broiled and pan-fried fish have been served here to appreciative diners whose numbers grow each year. Newburg and cioppino dishes border on greatness. Seafood lovers especially savor the nutty flavor of pan-fried sand dabs and charcoal broiled rex sole. This ambidextrous establishment also specializes in great meat dishes, and you can enjoy a tradition first relished by famished miners with an order of truly excellent charcoal broiled eastern beef. The decor is not exactly splendiferous; it's supposed to resemble a men's lunchroom circa 1900 and it is quite successful in the effort. The menu is fresh daily, just like the food, and in season you will also find local Dungeness crab and oysters from the east coast or Seattle.

Tadich Grill, 240 California St, San Francisco, CA 94111, **415/391-2373.**

CARNELIAN ROOM

San Francisco, CA

This is one of the most exclusive and romantic dining rooms in the US. From the moment you enter the elevator that speeds upward 52 floors to the top of the city's tallest building, all of your senses vie for attention. Painstaking care has been taken to accommodate them—from the panoramic views and superb seasonal cuisine, to a collection of Louis XV and Louis XVI antiques and paintings imported from an 18th century French chateau. Three sommeliers are on hand to help you select from 36,000 bottles of wine stored in the glass-enclosed wine cellar in the sky. Several soups are presented, more or less au naturel: sea urchin soup is served in its bristly shell, papaya soup in a papaya shell, pumpkin soup in a pumpkin rind and broccoli soup in a cored apple. Palate beguiling entrees include McCorkle duckling with kumquats

and roasted almonds, and selected dishes from other restaurants around the country: sauteed grouper from Michelle's in Atlanta, escalope of veal Anthony from the 95th in Chicago (a silver award winner in the 1980 culinary Olympics held in Germany), and roast rack of lamb from Francois in Los Angeles. Carnelian? It's the name of the marble on the building.

Carnelian Room, 52nd Floor, Bank of America World Headquarters Bldg, San Francisco, CA 94104, **415/433-7505.**

EMPRESS OF CHINA

San Francisco, CA

They could serve raw hamburger on a cold bun here and you might not notice. Fortunately, however, the food matches the superb view of the city and the incredible decor. This Chinese roof garden restaurant tops the 6-story China Trade Center in the heart of Chinatown. Internationally acclaimed, its laurels have been pinned by architects and museum curators as often as by restaurant critics. The ambience is created by priceless art reflecting the Han Dynasty of 2200 years ago. All of China is represented by the extensive menu — lobster Cantonese, Manchurian beef, Shanghai kuo-tieh, Szechuan spice beef, Peking duck and Mongolian hundred blossom lamb are only a small sampling of geographic offerings. Most are cooked in a 70-foot Chinese wok-over-range said to be the biggest in the US. Exotic potables are erotically defined: Breath of the Empress is "a whisper of events to come"; two of the Empress' Whim "will make you an emperor," three "a conqueror," and Tiger Tail "will increase what you have, regenerate what you might have lost." Each of several dining rooms looks out on the breathtaking skyline, ranging from Telegraph Hill with glimpses of the Bay to Coit Tower and North Beach.

Empress of China, 838 Grant Ave, San Francisco, CA 94108, **415/434-1345.**

THE BRAMBLES DINNER HOUSE

Cambria, CA

Less than 10 miles from San Simeon and the ornate Camelot William Randolph Hearst called home, sits the tiny village of Cambria, a scenic collection of antique shops, a small plant that builds even smaller toy soldiers, and this English-style eatery focusing on roast beef and Yorkshire pudding. It's easy to miss on the gorgeous seacoast paralleled by California Highway 1, partially because of the superb ocean and mountain views on either side, and partially because the 100-year-old house in which the restaurant is located is so different from the kitschy plasticene environments of so many Golden State eateries. The house itself was once an antique gallery, and today the collection overflows into the waiting room where you will see tempus fugiting in all manner of clocks. Generous helpings of homemade oyster or pea soup start all dinners. You may be tempted to order a meat dish after sniffing the fine aroma of grilled steaks over an oak fire, or you can sample a host of tasty seafood entrees from nearby waters. Delicately seasoned abalone, scallops, oysters and prawns are features. The English trifle is a flavorful finish to any meal.

The Brambles Dinner House, Burton Dr, Cambria, CA 93428, **805/927-4716.**

MATAAM FEZ

Denver, CO

From the moment you sink into plush pillows beneath a tented ceiling you'll luxuriate in Moorish splendor, learn Moroccan customs and savor flavorful Mediterranean fare. A caftan-clad waiter bends to your low table and explains the colorful menu. An air of authenticity is lent by the traditional hand washing ceremony that precedes the meal, an important event as your meal will be eaten in true ethnic fashion—no utensils, except for the hearty soup (three salads come with it). True to its heritage, lambs are purchased and slaughtered in the moslem manner. This meat is served in a variety of ways—with honey and almonds, with eggplant, with apricot, with lemon and olives, and as a brochette. Other Moorish entrees feature rabbit, beef, vegetarian and fish dishes. Cornish game hen and couscous (a preparation with cracked wheat) are tasty mainstays. The B'Stilla, thin baked pastry, comes with every meal.

Mataam Fez, 4609 E Colfax Ave, Denver, CO 80220, **303/399-9282.**

THE TREE ROOM

Provo, UT

Unbeknownst to the world at large, this mountain retreat for almost 20 years has nourished famished skiers in an ambience dominated by a huge tree at its center. Owned and built by actor Robert Redford, he found his environmental sensibilities tested by the presence of an 100-year-old pine tree—rooted smack dab in the middle of his enterprise. True to his conscience, Redford and his partner erected the eatery *around* the obstacle. The structure itself resembles a log cabin and the interior is inspired by the old west. Although the resort is tucked into a canyon northeast of the city, the marvels of modern transportation have enabled chef Mont Farrer to prepare succulent seafood dishes with freshly caught specimens. Australian lobster tail, jumbo shrimp served with a tasty sauce created by the chef, deep sea halibut and skewered shrimp

rival entrees prepared at a dockside restaurant for freshness and flavor. A variety of sauces complement several entrees, notable among them the Sundance Brown Sauce that blankets a tasty melding of wild rice and beef. Reflecting another interest of the owner, plays and musicals are produced throughout the summer at an outdoor stage. (See Winter Sports Of All Sorts.)

Sundance Ski Resort, North Fork of Provo Canyon, UT 84603, **801/225-4107.**

EL ADOBE

Tucson, AZ

This is the home of the Immaculate Concoction, otherwise known as the popular Margarita—the one they build here is claimed to be perfect. Housed in a 130-year-old national landmark, it is proclaimed to be one of the best-preserved examples of frontier architecture in the southwest. Originally constructed as a home for a territorial entrepreneur named Charles O. Brown, the restaurant is located in an unspectacular downtown location in a region otherwise known for its extraordinary scenery. However, the comfort and ambience of the hacienda—especially the patio—makes up for the lackluster location. Scenery is provided by fig, pomegranate, orange, and palm trees that line the patio. A glass-enclosed porch also is popular for dining. Miniature pinatas—the largest collection in the southwest—are pinned to every available space, making it look as if they're celebrating Christmas all year long. Vigas hauled by ox team from nearby mountains are held by two-foot-thick adobe walls. The boards that support the roof originally were crates that contained glassware and mirrors shipped around the Horn to San Francisco, then freighted to Tucson by mule team. Although the fare is Mexican, it is prepared Sonoran-style (lightly seasoned), but blistering salsa is available for the courageous. The camarones con arroz, shrimp served on a bed of rice, are always a good bet because they are shipped fresh from Gyuaymas, a Mexican port 350 miles south of the border.

El Adobe, 40 W Broadway, Tucson, AZ 85701, **602/791-7458.**

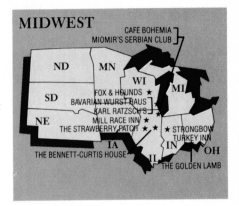

MIDWEST

FOX & HOUNDS

Hubertus, WI

Sometimes, when the moonbeams spill into the rustic interior through leaded window panes, this can be a most romantic spot. The setting is ideally located in a copse northwest of the rolling forested area carved by ice-age glaciers. This was once a frontier cabin and it still remains as one of six dining rooms. A collection of steins adorns the walls, and rough-hewn beams and open fireplaces complement the comfortable accommodations. The food is quintessentially German and shows the fine hand of its owners, the Ratzsch family (see Milwaukee). It's famous for a robust plate named choucroute garni a la Hetliger Huegel. It's a mouthful in more ways than one, combining as it does five different kinds of sausage in a blend of wine, bacon, smoked pork, apples and sauerkraut, and baked slowly in an earthen pot. The roast breast of goose, braised roulade of beef and hunter's casserole, tenderloin, chicken livers, mushrooms and scallions in a creamed wine sauce, also are popular entrees. And if you're still in the mood, a stroll in the moonlight to the Carmelite Monastery at nearby Holy Hill is a great way to end the evening.

Fox & Hounds, 1298 Friess Lake Rd, Hubertus, WI 53033, **414/251-4100.**

KARL RATZSCH'S

Milwaukee, WI

Germanophiles have been flocking to this Bavarian retreat since 1904, and usually with sufficient reason to return again and again. It's due not only to superb cuisine served in great helpings, but to an ambience that reflects the Old World and all of its charm. Dark paneling supports an enviable collection of priceless Meissenware, massive ornamental steins too beautiful to be called mugs, and lilting melodies issue forth from a string ensemble. Probably the best German fare in the nation is offered here, and the roast goose shank may well be the best in the world. Such superlatives are commonly attached to other dishes such as pork shanks with sauerkraut, sauerbraten and some more modern entrees: baked whole walleye, prime New York strip sirloin, scrod and shrimp. Fanciers of weiner schnitzel a la Holstein (boneless veal topped with anchovies, capers, and a fried egg) claim this entree is definitive here. They also serve something called a steinhager, a sort of gin-like liquor served, if you wish, with beer. Naturally, Rhine and Mosel wines are plentiful.

Karl Ratzsch's, 320 E Mason St, Milwaukee, WI 53202, **414/276-2720.**

The Tree Room, Provo, UT

Fox & Hounds, Hubertus, WI

CAFE BOHEMIA
Chicago, IL

If you're expecting to see artists in berets discussing literature and politics with a bearded poet droning in the background, you're in for a surprise. Huge helpings of truly unique dishes are the favored fare, and they come from far and wide, and include a host of wild game featuring venison, moose, buffalo and bear. At one time or another the restaurant has broiled, roasted, fried or steamed the flesh from enough exotic animals to fill a good sized zoo. While these offerings made the west side landmark famous, it remains true to its Austro-Hungarian heritage, flavorfully honoring dishes from that historic region in Europe. You might think you're in Prague sampling cuisine highlighted by pheasant, quail and duck. For the hearty carnivore, aged prime steaks weighing almost *four* pounds will fill the bill, and an array of seafoods, including a 2-½ pound lobster, should satisfy almost any other appetite. You can shed some of the calories with about a mile-long walk to the lake or cradle them in the comfort of a limousine (compliments of the house) on the ride back to your hotel.

Cafe Bohemia, 138 S Clinton St, Chicago, IL 60606, **312/782-1826.**

MILL RACE INN
Geneva, IL

Picturesquely situated in an old stone building at the edge of the Fox River, the board-walk covered river bank invites you to amble about and feed the ducks with bread provided by the restaurant. In its original incarnation, the inn was a blacksmith shop, abandoned in 1842 and resuscitated in 1933 as a tea room. The mill no longer exists, but the eatery was named for that part of the river that was diverted to turn the wheels of the mill; hence, mill race. The charm of the setting is enhanced by the open-air Gazebo bar and the Mill Grill. The commodious stone-walled dining rooms upstairs offer an extensive list of entrees highlighted by baked chicken and braised lamb shanks. The Mill Room specializes in steaks, prime rib carved by the chef, and a variety of tasty sandwiches served in a cozy atmosphere dominated by a fireplace. The arts are honored with renditions in song at the piano downstairs and the Mini-Chautauqua Series upstairs, and during warm weather with alfresco musical entertainment at the Gazebo.

Mill Race Inn, 4 E State St, Geneva, IL 60134, **312/232-2030.**

BAVARIAN WURST HAUS
Milwaukee, WI

The storybook, gingerbread exterior of this haus speaks of gemutlichkeit, with verses, phrases, scenes and flowers garnishing the facade. Inside, the walls, ceilings, sideboards and bar are adorned with antique plates, Bavarian scenes, German steins, pitchers, vases and mugs. The Teutonic decor includes steel swords and shields, banners and pennants, and garlands of ferns. Foot-stomping music complement a vast array of wunderbrats; the sausage kitchen manufactures 75 different kinds to eat in or take out. Standard German fare includes prodigious portions of pork shank, a quarter of roast goose, and Bavarian rouladen, in which the usual pickles and onions are replaced by pork sausage wrapped in sliced beef. Less Germanic fare includes broiled sea bass (also huge) covered with Hollandaise sauce and lightly topped with slivered almonds. The more traditional dishes are standouts: kasseler rippchen, a lean smoked chop; weisswurst, a light sausage; and the muenchner schlact platter which includes weiner schnitzel, weisswurst and kasseler rippchen—plus bread, soup, salad, potato dumpling and red cabbage. Save room for a helping of Bavarian cheesecake, apple strudel, or Black Forest cherry torte; dessert is included in the price of a meal.

Bavarian Wurst Haus, 8310 W Appleton Ave, Milwaukee, WI 53218, **414/464-0060.**

MIROMIR'S SERBIAN CLUB
Chicago, IL

Life is a cabaret, old chum, and in the Windy City it's run by gypsies whose mission in life is good times. And do they ever roll! On any given evening you will find Miomir Radovanovich spurring a napkin-waving audience on to greater heights as the festivities progress. The lively performances include Italian and Bulgarian songs, Russian folk dances and a Serbian violinist noted as much for his contortions as his string music. The menu is not comprised solely of traditional Yugoslavian fare; a wide variety of Eastern European cuisine is served. But the best entrees in this melange of good times undoubtedly is Serbian: kajmak, a fermented milk spread; corba, a beef and vegetable soup; ajvar, a pureed eggplant and purported contributor to long life; sarma, cabbage stuffed with veal, beef and rice and served in its broth; cevapcici, a sausage-shaped meat loaf…and then there's palacinke, a Serbian crepe, sauteed crisply, topped with confectioner's sugar and stuffed with raspberry jam. Now is the time to flash your napkin and work off some calories as the band plays on.

Miromir's Serbian Club, 2255 W Lawrence Ave, Chicago, IL 60625, **312/784-2111.**

Mill Race Inn, Geneva, IL

THE BENNETT-CURTIS HOUSE

Grant Park, IL

Remember the old 1940's Bing Crosby movie, "Holiday Inn"? The idea was a club created to put on special shows celebrating national holidays. Well, here's a restaurant located in a turn-of-the-century mansion, filled with antiques and collectibles, that does much the same thing—with its decor, and even with the presentation of the food. For example, in February, the eight-course dinner menu might include avocado stuffed with hot crab and garnished with heart-shaped beets (in honor of St. Valentine), beef hatchet—a spicy meatball mixture fashioned into the shape of an axe (honoring Washington's Birthday)—and an aspic mold of lime-flavored applesauce shaped as Abraham Lincoln. You get the idea. At Eastertime, an eight-foot rabbit (reminiscent of Harvey himself) greets you at the door, and inside there are colorfully-decorated Easter Egg trees, more than 1000 scattered eggs, a "strawberry patch," and Beatrix Potter music boxes on the tables. For Christmas, the mansion restaurant becomes a glittering fairyland, resembling a scene from Nutcracker Suite, with 15 Christmas trees, 800 handmade bows, 500 crystal snow flakes, collections of music boxes and miniature cottages from around the world, and 65 place settings of English Spode Christmas china. Halloween and Thanksgiving are similarly celebrated. Eight-course dinners and five-course lunches and brunches are prix fixe and prepared and served with tender loving care and a great deal of flair by owners Sam and Charlotte Van Hook. In summer, cool drinks and hors d'oeuvres are served in a carriage house flanked by ornamental flower beds, bubbling fountains and sweeping lawns.

The Bennett-Curtis House, 902 W Taylor St, Grant Park, IL 60940, **815/465-6025.**

STRONGBOW TURKEY INN

Valparaiso, IN

You could celebrate Thanksgiving here almost every day for a month and still not exhaust the flavorfully different ways they've learned to serve the nation's most festive fowl. It is smoked, roasted, fried, minced, sauteed, souped, pied, pated and salad-ed. It's especially lip-smackin' good in the form of pate, accompanied by homemade bread. Not that you need confine your dining enjoyment to turkey. Steak, chicken and shrimp dishes are delicious and some relatively new entrees are real stand-outs: coquille St. Jacques, shrimp Pescator, veal Oscar, wiener schnitzel, filet de boeuf Madeira, linzertorte and baked Alaska. The restaurant at one time was a ranch devoted to raising turkeys, but in 1940, highway builders sliced up the property. Owner Bess Davis cunningly conceived the eatery as a roadside temptation for passing motorists. The facility, named for an Indian chief, now is operated by Mrs. Davis' daughter and son-in-law, Caroline and Charles Adams, who preserve her recipes in their daily menu. Her cranberry sauce, made with whole ground oranges and other specialties, can be purchased to take home. A tasty array of desserts, many made with fruits from nearby orchards, includes pecan and apple pies and cream cheesecakes.

Strongbow Turkey Inn, 2405 US Hwy 30 E, Valparaiso, IN 46383, **219/462-3311.**

THE GOLDEN LAMB

Lebanon, OH

Americans have supped and slept here for almost 200 years, enjoying a virtual Shaker museum with food and furniture dedicated to the memory of the sect that settled the area. While the Shakers enjoyed a simple life, they spiced up their simple fare with herbs and other seasonings to create palate-satisfying dishes. Ten American presidents have graced the hostelry, sampling such dishes as flanked steak in a dressing that hints of basil, savory, sage and rosemary, and a rather famous braised lamb shank flavored with rosemary, thyme, bay leaves, mushrooms and onions. The Buckeye State's oldest inn features a tasty appetizer of sauerkraut balls consisting of deep-fried, finely ground pork and ham and kraut. One serving makes a meal for most people, so be prepared to share or loosen your belt for the entree. Butler County turkey, served with sage dressing, and pork loin with herb dressing also are popular main dishes. The Shaker lemon pie is the jewel in the inn's crown; it's a burnt brown color, flavored with nutmeg, and layered with molasses between filling and crust. Another lemony dessert is a stack pie, two wedges with a crust in the center and a curd dappled with lemon peel.

The Golden Lamb, 27 S Broadway, Lebanon, OH 45036, **513/932- 5065.**

THE STRAWBERRY PATCH

Princeton, IL

Situated in the middle of the hog-raising and corn-growing prairieland of western Illinois, this town is a long way (geographically *and* culturally) from France, and even from Chicago. Yet, tucked away in a cellar on Main Street is a charming Continental restaurant. Owner-chef John Pawula has big- city credentials. He is an alumnus of Chicago's famed Bakery, having trained under chef/author/food columnist, Louis Szathmary. Here, in a town where fried chicken and country-fried pork chops are king, you'll find elegant pates, creative soups such as crayfish bisque and cream of cauliflower, imaginative salads such as bibb lettuce with hazelnuts, and spinach with a classic mustard dressing, and such entrees as quail with pasta, crispy duckling served with a tart wild-cherry sauce, and veal Florentine. For dessert, there's a selection of homemade pastries (rich tortes, creamy layer cakes, and fruit tarts) that would be at home aboard the pastry cart of any big-city restaurant that flaunts its haute cuisine. As an alternative, there's a fine selection of imported cheeses. The ambience of the cool, basement restaurant (a sort of midwesternized country French) features wallpaper with a strawberry motif, cream-painted tin ceiling, white trelliswork, and framed, watercolor wildflower prints. The strawberry theme is repeated in the pattern of the bright green linen that centers snowy white tablecloths. The sizzling of pans emanating from a compact kitchen hidden behind the false-front of a country cottage (complete with red curtains), is testimony to John Pawula doing his culinary thing — the fruits of which are so admired that many patrons drive the 85-mile round-trip from Peoria simply to dine there.

The Strawberry Patch, 516 S Main St, Princeton, IL 61356, **815/872-8011.**

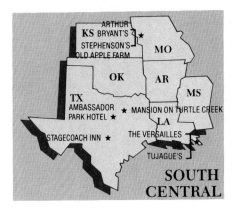

SOUTH CENTRAL

THE MANSION ON TURTLE CREEK

Dallas, TX

Sheppard W. King found a fortune in tall cotton, which enabled him and his wife to build on this property repeatedly—until they got it right, so to speak. The palatial setting now serving the landed gentry from Dallas and Fort Worth is the third structure on the site, as the Kings razed the first two. They spared little expense, importing some great European works of art. Other highlights include two tall pairs of early 19th Century Spanish Cathedral doors with hand-carved helmeted faces, and an awe-inspiring oak paneled library (part of the dining room) with stained glass windows. The inlaid dining room ceiling, which is composed of 2400 separate pieces of wood, took six carpenters eight weeks to install. The decor includes the coats of arms of the Barons of Runnymede (forbearers of Mrs. King), who were witnesses at the signing of the Magna Carta by King Edward III of England. The tasty fare offered here is reminiscent of New York's 21 — and with reason. The Manhattan management wrote the menu, which includes chicken with wild rice, Steak Diane, Scottish salmon, beluga caviar, and rack of lamb bouquetiere. The Kings, whose cotton got short in the 30s, would have been pleased.

Mansion at Turtle Creek, 2821 Turtle Creek Blvd, Dallas, TX 75219, **214/526-2121.**

The Mansion On Turtle Creek, Dallas, TX

Stagecoach Inn, Salado, TX

STAGECOACH INN
Salado, TX

The carriage trade between Dallas and San Antonio has been stopping here since the mid-1800's when fatigued stagecoach passengers were fed and hosteled before continuing their journey. The restful inn is built along the banks of Salado Creek near I-35. Care has been taken to preserve the inn's original cypress beams and oak floors, and the gigantic burr oak tree in the center of the complex is 500 years old. The inn has been a favorite watering hole for the likes of Sam Houston and General Robert E. Lee; intimate dining areas, once a small parlor and dining room, commemorate their patronage. A pioneer museum across the street is worth a gander and so are many of the nearby historic homes. The wayside respite has been operated by the same family for almost 40 years, and they've got the menu down pat. Tender and tasty turkey steak is drowned in mushroom sauce; a flavorful wine is used in basting the broiled flounder; the ham is baked in a glaze of glory (honey); and crispy hush puppies accompany every meal.

Stagecoach Inn, Box 81, Salado, TX 76571, **817/ 947-5040.**

AMBASSADOR PARK HOTEL
Dallas, TX

Dallas' oldest luxury hotel has been restored to its original European charm; comfort and service still speak of turn-of-the-century hospitality. Guests dine where presidents and their charges rested on the edge of frontier America. Cuisine is cajun and western; house speciality is tasty drusilla steak and mushroom sauce. The hotel has played host to celebrities such as Andy Barr and Sarah Bernhardt. Miss Bernhardt was so enamored with the cooking, she spirited away the chef. Intercepted at the border, she was told either to return him or leave Dallas forever. She handed him over. The hotel's colorful past includes its origins as a bordello and, during recent remodeling-owners discovered walled-in elevators and other interesting oddities. Now, amidst tastefully chosen appointments, a butler serves each floor of the hostelry. Across the street is Old City Park, the recreation of Dallas 100 years ago.

Ambassador Park Hotel, 1312 S Ervay, Dallas, TX 75215, **800/527- 3010, 800/442-4839 (in TX).**

STEPHENSON'S OLD APPLE FARM
Kansas City, MO

Modern restaurateurs spend a lot of time looking for novel themes, but the Stephenson brothers, Loyd and Leslie, were to their manor born. The restaurant sits on the edge of the family farm beside an apple orchard—across the road from a former drive-in where the brothers once hopped cars and learned the secret of smoking meats. Their somewhat arcane art accounts for a world-wide reputation for hickory-flavored hams, not to mention chicken, pork and beef, slow-smoked for seven hours before serving. The brothers' reputation as purveyors of great food spread with the addition of green rice—a casserole with cheese, parsley, onion, green pepper and spices, and fritters burdened with confectioner's sugar. Traditional side dishes include broccoli and cauliflower au gratin and scalloped zucchini squash. Former President Harry S Truman and wife Bess used to dine here, and daughter Margaret still does as well as Mrs. Lady Bird Johnson. You can mingle with celebrated visitors (or view their likenesses in a photo gallery) while you wait in the lobby, which is decorated with old farm tools. The wait—and usually there is one—is made more palatable by a keg of cold apple cider, yours to sample at will. Next door is a store where you can purchase corn chow chow (a spicy relish), pickles, apple butter, green rice, and other farm-fresh products. Lip-smacking potables are offered, too. The house speciality is a daiquiri made with fresh apples (or peaches, strawberries or bananas).

Stephenson's Old Apple Farm, Hwy 40 & Lee's Summit Rd, Kansas City, MO 64136, **816/373-5400.**

ARTHUR BRYANT'S
Kansas City, MO

Bryant's couldn't have fared better if it had built a better mousetrap after Calvin Trillin proclaimed the rib joint "the single best restaurant in the world." A monument to grease, Bryant's probably serves the best ribs in the world, and is euphemistically called a barbecue shack. It is unquestionably a great one. Chauvinistic *Chicago* magazine once sent a brace of investigative reporters to compare Bryant's ribs to those of the Windy City. The news-hounds enthusiastically declared the KC eatery winner by a rack of bones. They're crisp but tender, crunchy without being tough, sloppy but not too indecorous, and sauced with an indescribably red-orange concoction that is without doubt the tastiest conglomeration of spices that ever splattered a palate. While the secret sauce is the magic ingredient that makes the ribs unforgettable, barbecued beef—served in big mounds between slices of white bread—is the more popular offering. The french fries may also rank as the world's best. The sauce is jugged by the gallon and lugged 'round the world by aficionados.

Arthur Bryant's, 1727 Brooklyn, Kansas City, MO 64127, **816/231-1123.**

THE VERSAILLES
New Orleans, LA

Louis XIV would feel right at home here because the ambience is true to the memorable palace for which it's named. If you like cuisine francaise in a regal setting, you would like it too. It's not slavishly imitated to the last sunburst, which was Louis' trademark and the reason he was known as the Sun King, but does come awfully close. The restaurant is adorned with mirrors and red velvet, and fashionably illuminated by crystal chandeliers. The nuances of decor are attributable to Evelyn Preuss, but owner/chef Gunter Preuss is responsible for the subtleties of the flavorful fare. The royal menu is certifiably haute cuisine and reflects the personal attention of Preuss, who was trained in England, France, Switzerland, Sweden and Germany. The bouillabaisse Marsellaise is delectably creative and the savory escalope de veau financiere is a gastronomic work of art. The escargots Bourguignon en croute is a tasty appetizer of snails in a succulent sauce served in a hollowed-out round of French bread. Other distinctive dishes include the redfish dore, and cream of leek soup Chantilly. The chef will create your favorite meal by special request, and he boldly shares his famous recipe for bouillabaisse by printing it on a folder you can take with you.

The Versailles, 2100 St Charles Ave, New Orleans, LA 70130, **504/524-2535.**

TUJAGUE'S
New Orleans, LA

Long before such presidential dignitaries as DeGaulle, Roosevelt, Truman and Eisenhower sampled the Creole cuisine here, it was known to locals as the oldest stand-up bar in the city. Its fame as a watering hole dates back more than 130 years and, before that, it was an armory for Spanish artillery. By the time hostilities ceased, enterprising restaurateurs had none-too-subtly switched the ambience to reflect the French influence. They imported the cypress bar from Paris with its ornate antique mirror. Before it cleared customs in 1856 the 63-square-foot mirror had, for nearly 90 years, reflected the images of parched Frenchmen slaking their thirsts. The Tujague family commenced a tradition of culinary excellence in 1856 and the Latter family now maintains it with seven-course servings featuring both Creole and French dishes. The menu in New Orleans' second oldest restaurant changes daily with a choice of two entrees—ineluctably superb and always accompanied by shrimp remoulade, potage du jour, a tasty brisket of beef with horseradish sauce, salad, vegetable, and dessert with bracing chickory coffee. A balcony perched across from the French Market and famous 24-hour coffee house, the Cafe du Monde, provides a picturesque setting for a leisurely cocktail.

Tujague's, 823 Decatur St, New Orleans, LA 70116, **504/523-9069.**

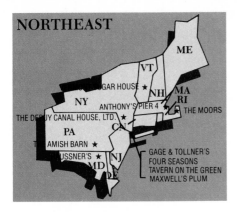

NORTHEAST

ME
VT
SUGAR HOUSE ★ NH MA RI
NY ANTHONY'S PIER 4 ★ ★ THE MOORS
THE DE UY CANAL HOUSE, LTD. ★ CA
PA
★ AMISH BARN ★ NJ
USSNER'S ★ MD DE
GAGE & TOLLNER'S
FOUR SEASONS
TAVERN ON THE GREEN
MAXWELL'S PLUM

ANTHONY'S PIER 4

Boston, MA

For the ichthyophagous among us—those who subsist on fish—this place ranks number one. Pollsters say it's also one of the top spots in the country to seal a deal, and a noted connoisseur of the grape gives the wine card a vintage label. The restaurant is located at the end of a converted pier that juts out into Boston Harbor, offering diners a spectacular view of traffic from Logan International Airport, seaport vessels in the harbor, and the Boston skyline. The ambience is created by early American marine decor featuring exquisitely etched scrimshaw, figureheads, casks, and other memorabilia of this nation's early sailing days. A brass bell is rung as ships of exceptional significance heave into diners' view, and the vessel's name, home port, destination and cargo description are announced. The lobster is superb, as well as the steaks which are open-hearth broiled. The baked scrod cannot be beat.

Anthony's Pier 4, 140 Northern Ave, Boston, MA 02210, **617/423-6363.**

THE MOORS

Provincetown, MA

In the whaling days of yore, Portuguese adventurers often sailed into the rocky waters of the New World, and a good many of them liked the cut of its jib. The cuisine they enjoyed on the Azores and Cape Verde Islands in the Atlantic, remained with them when they settled here on Cape Cod. There's no mistaking your whereabouts; thunderous ocean surf may be heard in the background and the interior is fittingly decorated with sailing memorabilia. Barrels prop up the bar and the tables, and nets, harpoons and other whaler's tools are scattered throughout the driftwood- paneled dining area. A Portuguese soup laden with vegetables and a brace of sausages makes a hearty beginning to any meal. Entrees that have stood the test of time are porco em pau, chunks of broiled pork tenderloin that have soaked up the juices of a spicy marinade, and pork chops that have been soaked in wine, vinegar, garlic and other spices. Camaro macao is zesty shrimp surrounded by bamboo shoots, water chestnuts, ginger, garlic, crushed red peppers and scallions. The seafood dishes also are prepared by conventional methods, but the unusual Portuguese offerings are a whale of a treat (see Romantic Rondezvous).

The Moors, Beach Rd & Bradford St, Provincetown, MA 02657, **617/487-0840.**

VERMONT SUGAR HOUSE

Royalton, VT

The piece de resistance here is flaked ice smothered with hot maple syrup. It's a fairyland for anyone with a sweet tooth, and a special room upstairs will provide all the details as to how the juice of the maple tree came to be. The menu alleges that an Indian squaw overboiled her man's moose entree in the sweet water of the maple tree, and he was very pleasantly surprised to find the syrupy residue more palatable than the meat. (The White Man's explanation in the museum upstairs is a little more technical.) In any event, Mrs. Annie Clifford has uniquely capitalized on the product and personally dispenses the syrup, which comes in a separate bowl, for you to spoon over the ice. It's accompanied by sour pickles and an occasional bite only whets your appetite for more—with apple cider, which, in the fall, is made on the premises. Pancakes, doughnuts, candy and maple pecan pie, all prepared by Mrs. Clifford, round out the menu.

Vermont Sugar House, Junction Rtes 14 & 107, Royalton, VT 05068, **802/763-8809.**

The Moors, Provincetown, MA

HAUSSNER'S

Baltimore, MD

You might say that this restaurant is kind of sketchy even though its menu contains more entrees than perhaps any other in the city. However, the sketches are part of a mammoth collection of art, original paintings by Rembrandt, Whistler, de Blass, Shreyer and others. From floor to ceiling you also will see bronzes, china, wood carvings, clocks and various works, all of which represent only a third of the priceless collection. One reason it is priceless is because it is not for sale. What *is* for sale includes more than 50 seafood dishes, some 40 meat entrees and as many sandwiches plus 30 vegetables. Crab, lobster and flounder are particularly good and several tasty German dishes are treated with care. Hasenpfeffer with spaetzles, wiener schnitzel a la Holstein (topped by a fried egg, anchovies, and capers), and sauerbraten with Tyrolean dumplings are toothsome and filling. The interior is spacious, made up of five row houses, so a museum-like stroll between courses is quite rewarding.

Haussner's, 3244 Eastern Ave, Baltimore, MD 21224, **301/327-8365.**

THE AMISH BARN

Near Bird-In-Hand, PA

Country cooking, a la carte or family style, is the specialty here in a structure built in the Amish fashion. You will see members of the Mennonite sect, which eschews modern trappings of electricity and automobiles, plowing the neat nearby fields with beasts of burden. Recipes have been developed by the Pennsylvania Dutch over a period of 250 years, and a traditional entree might include Speck Und Bona which is ham with green beans and boiled potato. ("Dutch" is an aberration of "Deutsch," meaning "German.") Don't despair, all menu offerings are translated from their German language and most, in fact, are in English. Another specialty is Chicken Bot Boi, chunks of rectangular pasta in broth, with boiled potato and a half breast of chicken. Meals begin with a bounteous salad bar, colorfully arranged with vegetables plucked from the garden you see from the dining room. Meals end superbly with such desserts as Shoofly pie and apple dumplings confected at the bakery on the premises. Heirloom-quality quilts, wall hangings and other cottage crafts from local artisans are on display at an upstairs gift shop.

The Amish Barn, Rte 340, between Intercourse and Bird-in-Hand, PA 17505, **717/768-8886.**

FOUR SEASONS

New York, NY

This is the home of tantalizing and delectable mysteries because (just as the name implies) the menu changes with the seasons and you must actually go there to learn the featured dishes. However, the uniformly superb fare puts the restaurant among the top five in the country, and not for food alone. Aesthetically, it is a triumph for famed architect, Mies van der Rohe. Fittingly for his philosophy—"less is more"—owners Paul Kovi and Tom Margittai have tastefully and artistically complemented the design with works of art that also change with the menu—except for the world's largest Picasso, one of the few constants. Although entrees are in a seasonal state of flux, the legendary menu offers just about any great meal you could name. The mahogany cake, the cheese tray and a superb wine list are about the only consumables that have earned permanent status.

Four Seasons, 99 E 52nd St, New York, NY 10022, **212/754-9494.**

THE DEPUY CANAL HOUSE, LTD.

High Falls, NY

Amateur chefs are not noted for their staying power, but John Novi, with eight months training in Italy, has been packing them in for almost two decades. At the ripe old age of 22 and with $4500 borrowed dollars he bought the two-story stone tavern in 1969. He opened the restaurant in order to get the money to restore the structure, originally built in 1797. It once served the Delaware and Hudson Canal, which ran through High Falls until 1899, and its history is depicted in one room which serves as a museum. A seven-course menu is served at a leisurely pace and fixed price. The inventive chef varies the meal with his muse. Whole fish are served with dough masks hiding their heads. The eclectic fare includes hominy vichyssoise, Szechuan sauteed breast of pheasant stuffed with sausage and pistachio nuts, sweetbreads and sauerkraut marinated in Russian vodka and blanketed in Greek filo dough. Tasty choucroute is served with two wursts and duck wrapped in miso. On the more sedate side are rack of lamb in orange glaze, apple crumb pie and ricotta cheesecake. Dinner will take at least three hours to complete so admire the falls cascading across the way — they're higher than Niagara, and between courses you're welcome to take a tour of the eye-popping kitchen with its collectibles, ancient copper pots and assorted what-nots.

The Depuy Canal House, Ltd, High Falls, NY 12440, **914/687-7777.**

TAVERN ON THE GREEN

New York, NY

You can still hitch your horse to a rail and partake of something stronger than sarsaparilla here in the middle of Manhattan. The building was originally a sheep fold constructed by Tammany's Boss Tweed, but was converted to a restaurant as a WPA project in the mid-30s. Maxwell's Plum creator, Warner LeRoy, with his flair for showmanship, re-converted it in the '70s and there's no denying his mark. Huge etched mirrors, copper and brass chandeliers, flowering trees, high-beamed ceilings and a 60-foot wooden bar inlaid with brass and copper, bear his signature. Its reputation for great food remains untarnished and succulent entrees include roast rack of lamb, dover sole meuniere, Muscovy duck breast, veal escalope, seafood pot au feu and grilled pigeon with shallots. The green of the title refers to the adjoining, famous (and notorious) Central Park and, if you like, they'll pack a picnic lunch for you to eat there.

Tavern on the Green, Central Park at W 67th St, New York, NY 10023, **212/873-3200.**

GAGE & TOLLNER'S

Brooklyn, NY

The meats and seafoods cooked here are darker than you'll find anywhere else—that's because they're cooked over anthracite coal, which creates a very hot fire that sears in the juices. But you needn't worry about darkness otherwise, brass lighting fixtures hang the length of the room and work with either gas or electricity. The gas remains because the proprietors distrust almost anything new-fangled, and has come in handy during recent blackouts. The eatery is more than a hundred years old (opened in 1879) and little has changed over the years. It is, in fact, the only restaurant in New York to receive landmark status for both its exterior *and* interior. The center-piece oak and marble bar on the first floor dates back to the opening and the tables are the same ones graced by the likes of Diamond Jim Brady and Lillian Russell. The cherry woodwork on the interior walls, and the burgundy velvet tapestry between the mirrors also are the genuine article. So's the menu. Oysters and clams are served in literally dozens of ways, and the soft-belly clam broil is renowned. For the carnivores, English mutton chops with sausage and kidney, and a variety of steaks, make for unique repasts in a pleasant old-time setting. However, some things do change: they no longer offer brollys to diners departing in a rainstorm.

Gage & Tollner's, 372 Fulton St, Brooklyn, NY 11201, **212/875- 5181.**

MAXWELL'S PLUM

New York, NY

This is a spectacle that gloriously assaults all the senses. Restaurateur Warner LeRoy created the scene much in the same manner as Cecil B. DeMille would assemble a motion picture. A formal dining room, bar and sidewalk cafe coexist in magnificent splendor, amid Tiffany stained glass ceiling and lamps, hand carved mirrors, rare ceramic animals and brass statues crafted circa 1900. It's the scene for swinging singles and showcases a menu that lures gourmets and gourmands from around the world. It is, in fact, the world's most copied restaurant, which led the original-minded owner to add new works in a 1982 renovation. Outstanding among them is a complex stained and painted glass collage of a damsel riding a huge jeweled Siberian tiger. The trademark—fresh flowers —graces every nook and cranny. Entrees are complemented by Devon cream from England, butter from West Germany, Dover sole flown fresh from Atlantic waters, homemade vinegar and mustard. Delectable continental and American fare is highlighted by such specialties as veal piccata, rack of lamb, charcoal broiled swordfish, steamed rock shrimp, duck salad and a super-rich chocolate fudge cake.

Maxwell's Plum, 1181 1st Ave, New York, NY 10021, **212/628-2100.**

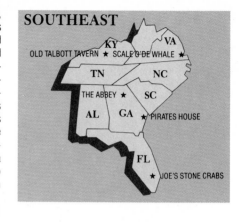

SOUTHEAST

OLD TALBOTT TAVERN

Bardstown, KY

The famous, such as Andrew Jackson and one-time vice president Aaron Burr, have dined here since the lodge opened in 1779. Country ham, smoked and salted, is the specialty of the house. It's a southern menu mainstay accompanied by eye-tearing red-eye gravy and soda bread made on the premises. A calorific pan-fried chicken sets the taste buds aglow. It's covered with seasoned flour and served with a cream gravy just made for dipping. A chicken and ham combo plate is available for those who can't choose between them. Another staple served at the old tavern is the famous Kentucky "hot brown" sandwich made with turkey and bacon under a blanket of cheese sauce. For more plebian tastes, steaks, shrimp, salads, and hamburgers are available. For dessert, choose between their belt-tightening peach cobbler and tasty chess pie—a honey-gold crust filled with beaten eggs, sugar, butter and flavored with vanilla. If you're stuffed, you might consider spending the night; on the other hand, there are only five rooms so it's better to make the decision well in advance.

Old Talbott Tavern, Court Square, Bardstown, KY 40004, **502/348-3494.**

Maxwell's Plum, New York, NY

Photo: Alan Schindler

PIRATES' HOUSE

Savannah, GA

The Jolly Roger flutters from two sides of the building, beckoning diners to hearty southern fare that includes fried chicken, Savannah red rice and candied yams. But Savannah is a seaport, and the galley here does more than justice to seafood gumbo, seafood bisque, and shrimp and crab au gratin casserole. Almost three dozen desserts are offered to top off the meal. Savannah's unique soft-southern accent flavors the voices of servers, and the setting's lore is as satisfying as the food. The restaurant is situated just a block from the picturesque Savannah River in Trustees' Garden, site of the first public experimental garden in the US, and part of a restoration project in a former slum. Inside is a maze of 23 dining rooms (actually nine connecting buildings) with a motif that signifies both literature and piracy. Robert Louis Stevenson lived across the street from the restaurant in the late 1800s and wrote part of *Treasure Island* in one of their dining rooms. Etchings from a rare edition of his classic tale adorn the walls, and an amazing electronically controlled tropical forest highlights the bar.

Pirates' House, 20 E Broad St, Savannah, GA 31401, **912/233-5757.**

THE ABBEY

Atlanta, GA

The non-sectarian continental cuisine is served here with medieval flair. The serving staff is garbed in old world monk's robes, befitting the beautiful surroundings — a former house of worship erected in 1915 for the congregation of the Methodist Episcopal Church. The craftmanship of a bygone era is preserved in massive stained glass windows, and enormous 50-foot arched and vaulted ceilings. Proprietors have gracefully complemented it with tapestries, statuary, monks' chairs and copperware that lend the setting a medieval ambience. The menu is prepared daily from scratch by some of the most experienced European chefs in the US. Their skill is flavorfully apparent in such dishes as roast goose, venison and pheasant. The list of entrees is quite extensive, but the monks are enlightening as to detail. Oenophiles will be pleased by the wine cart, and may choose to dine in the appropriately named Wine Cellar dominated by products from French vintners. For a more sedate gastronomic experience, the upstairs dining room is called the Sanctuary.

The Abbey, 163 Ponce de Leon Ave, Atlanta, GA 30308, **404/876-8831.**

Pirates' House, Savannah, GA

Pirates' House, Savannah, GA

JOE'S STONE CRABS

Miami Beach, FL

The uninitiated expect the flavor of stone crabs to resemble the better known cousin of the Chesapeake Bay, but they are in for a pleasant surprise. The succulent stone crabs, indigenous creatures to the nippy Atlantic, are a breed apart. They are served here in much the same fashion as they were in the 1930s when they first made the place a household name. (The waiters still dress in tuxedoes.) Stone crabs are served cool and, thankfully, their tough exterior is cracked in the kitchen. The meat is sweet, the texture rather like lobster, and comes with hot butter and mustard sauce. A popular but unlikely accompaniment to the claws are hash browns. Somehow they are a perfect match. The delicacy — stone crabs — is almost unique to Florida restaurants, although you occasionally find them in other parts of the country. One reason they are scarce and expensive is due to the conservation-minded legalities of harvesting. Fisherman can take only one claw from each crab and then they must return it to the deep; it'll grow another in a couple of seasons. Several fish from native waters make delicious entrees—yellowtail, red snapper and pompano among them. Tasty Key Lime Pie is a great finale. Open only during stone crab season from Oct—May. Unless you arrive almost at opening time, the wait can be as much as three hours.

Joe's Stone Crabs, 227 Biscayne St, Miami Beach, FL 33139, **305/673-0365.**

SCALE O'DE WHALE

Portsmouth, VA

This place really moves at night...and day, because it's built on pilings. The movement isn't great enough to cause alarm, but the sway is apparent. From the multi-level interior an almost constant array of activity spreads out on the water before you, including the scoop of the bridge you crossed reaching the Western Branch of the Elizabeth River. You can dock here for free and even leave your boat overnight if you give enough advance notice. The menu is broad and so many temptations make a choice of entree difficult, but broiled dishes are uniformly prudent selections (from more than 40 seafood listings), and the deluxe seafood platter provides an overview of several tasty delights. It showcases clam chowder, shrimp, oysters, crab cakes, flounder filet, and clams in the shell. Portions are prodigious or truly "jumbo" as many are called. The flounder dish, heaped with crabmeat, is another good choice and beef-eaters may select from various charbroiled meats. Home-based Piedmont Seyval Blanc, a medium-bodied white wine, is a refreshing accompaniment to most servings.

Scale O'De Whale, 3515 Shipwright St, Portsmouth, VA 23703, **804/483-2772.**

Chapter 12

HEALTH SPAS

Canyon Ranch, Tucson, AZ

At the modern American health spa the pungent smell of sulphur has been supplanted by the fragrant perfume of the lemon facial. Mineral water is a rarity, while the herbal body wrap has become derigeur. Today's guest goes in search of strict programming . . . and elegant pampering; of toned muscles, a trimmed waistline and an expanded mind.

Having evolved through the "fat farm" era, spas still help guests lose weight through low-calorie meals and exercise regimes, but they also stress the *maintenance* of good physical fitness and beauty. In fact, some require guests to work at getting in shape *before* arriving, and many provide exercise routines, diet plans, and menus to take home.

These fitness resorts often vary widely in philosophy and atmosphere, but all have organized programs for nutrition, exercise, and beauty treatments. Spa methodologies emphasize anything from physical exercise and healthy eating habits, to behavior modification techniques and holistic attitudes. Guests can visit a Spartan retreat with dormitory accommodations and a water diet menu for $450 a week, or pay more than $2,500 a week for a stay in one of the posh pampering palaces with canopied beds and private Jacuzzis. Daily meals can run as low as 500 calories and schedules can start as early as 6:30 am.

Complete salon facilities are usually available, and beauty treatments can be as simple as a massage, or as exotic as skin applications of seaweed or volcanic mud. Some offer personalized exercise programs, daily schedules, and diets according to individual goals and priorities. Other retreats are less structured and spa-goers sleep in late and leisurely take advantage of whirlpools, Grecian tubs, Swiss needle showers, Roman baths, and the inevitable beautiful scenery.

Nearly all spas are strategically located in scenic backdrops—from the Mohave Desert and the Santa Catalina mountains, to the thundering cataracts of Niagara Falls and the Long Island Atlantic coast. Ambience runs the gamut from Victorian mansion to exquisite Japanese rock gardens.

NORTHWEST

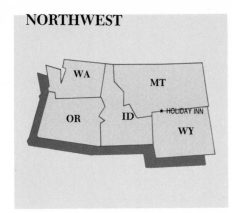

SOUTHWEST

THE PALMS AT PALM SPRINGS

Palm Springs, CA

Situated in a celebrity-studded resort, this retreat claims to offer low-priced luxury for spa-goers. The high elevation eliminates pollution, and the mountainous horizons help to reduce stress. Offering a complete fitness program in a vacation atmosphere, it has all the facilities and programs you'll need to get into shape: a modern gymnasium, spacious pool, sauna, and weight machines. A typical day begins with a hike before breakfast, and is filled with yoga, aquatic exercises, toning and strengthening techniques, and classes on body awareness. Evening lectures may cover anything from hypnosis to wardrobe management. You can unwind with a massage, enjoy a facial, receive a custom cosmetics treatment, or even treat yourself to a cellulite wrap, manicure or pedicure. Guests dine in the large Las Palmas dining room with a diet cuisine featuring fresh fruit, vegetables, homemade soups, and low cholesterol entrees. Meals are designed to help you lose up to a pound daily. Located in the incomparable climate of Palm Springs—home of challenging golf courses, fashionable shops, and exciting night life options.

Rates: $608 from Sun—Sun. The Palms, 572 N Indian Ave, Palm Springs, CA 92262, **619/325-1111.**

LA COSTA

Carlsbad, CA

This spa enjoys some of the best weather in the nation—the sun shines on this Pacific resort area more than anywhere else on the continent and the annual temperature fluctuates between 68 and 74°F. Located near San Diego, this 6700-acre spa is the largest in the United States and resembles an enormous country club. Special features include Roman baths, outdoor massages, Grecian tubs, private whirlpools, and classes on makeup techniques. The program includes a medical evaluation, skin analysis, and personalized meal planning with a dietician. Well-suited to couples, it offers unlimited golf and tennis privileges on La Costa's 27-hole course, and 25 all-weather surface tennis courts. A variety of classes include yoga, dance, stretch-and-flex, pool exercises, rigorous calisthenics and water volleyball. Spa facilities are complemented by such sybaritic treatments as four different facials, hair styling, manicures, pedicures, and herbal body wraps. Leisure activities include nightly movies and backgammon. Accommodations range from hotel rooms and suites, to golf and tennis cottages, chateaus, and villas. Located 90 mi S of Los Angeles; Rte 5 to La Costa Rd exit; left onto Costa del Mar Rd.

Rates: Single $275, double $405 (4-night minimum). La Costa, Costa del Mar Rd, Carlsbad, CA 92008, **619/438-9111.**

HOLIDAY INN OF THE WATERS

Thermopolis, WY

In 1896, the Shoshone and Arapaho Indians deeded 100 square miles of Wyoming to be preserved for the enjoyment of all Americans. Today, this area is Hot Springs State Park, home of picturesque chasms, mysterious tunnels and the world's largest mineral hot spring (35 feet in diameter) used for both therapeutic and recreational purposes. This spring is the ancestral roots of plush spa resorts as we know them today. The Holiday Inn of the Waters shares part of the 18,600,000 gallons of water surfaced every day by piping it directly into an ultra-modern bathhouse. Facilities include mineral steam baths, saunas, private soaking tubs and full-time massage therapists. There is also a fresh-water swimming pool and a year-round outdoor hot mineral pool. The area, part of the scenic Big Horn Basin, also boasts great sight-seeing, big-game hunting, skiing, snowmobiling and float trips.

Rates: Single $40, double $56. Holiday Inn of the Waters, Thermopolis, WY 82443, **307/864-3131.**

The Aurora House Spa, Aurora, OH

THE SPA AT SONOMA MISSION INN

Sonoma, CA

It may be true that there's no gain without pain when trying to keep fit, but this Spanish stucco spa is designed to pamper as you melt those extra pounds away. In an atmosphere of high skylights, soft pink lighting, restful earth-toned colors, and art deco decor, rooms feature plantation shutters, canopied beds and ceiling fans. Daily schedules begin with a mountain hike, warm-up exercises, or aerobics and calisthenics, perhaps followed by a swim in the heated pool or a workout on exercise equipment. Coddle yourself with hydrotherapy, herbal cleansing, and massages, along with body conditioning and weight-loss programs. Personalized nutritional regimes are determined according to hypertension, blood pressure, and the percentage of body fat; the low-calorie menus include such delectables as chicken with mustard sauce, and bouillabaisse with ruille, and a choice of juices or spring water. Situated in the heart of wine country, this spa even allows a little wine in its program. Hot-air-balloon rides glide guests over the surrounding vineyards. Basically for women, but there are scheduled men's weeks and couples' weekends. Located 1 mi W of CA 12.

Rates: Single $1800, double $1600 (5 days). Sonoma Mission Inn, PO Box 1, Boyes Hot Springs, CA 95416, **707/996-1041.**

BERMUDA INN

Lancaster, CA

This resort combines weight-loss activities with a fun-filled vacation in the high country of the Mohave Desert. Medically supervised programs include low-calorie meals planned by a staff dietician, and voluntary exercise classes conducted several times daily in the gym or one of the two pools. Other activities include jogging or bicycle riding (on a ½ mile lighted track encircling a lake), badminton, tetherball, swimming, volleyball, or general gym workouts. Nearby are facilities for golf, bowling, and tennis. Leisure activities include a putting green, arts and crafts, lectures and field trips. Massages are available for a nominal fee, and there is a boutique and beauty salon. Take CA 14 to Antelope Valley exit; turn right onto Ave L; left on Sierra Hwy. No gender or age restrictions, but not geared to children.

Rates: Single $115, double $76, triple $59 (per day). Bermuda Inn, 43019 Sierra Hwy, Lancaster, CA 93534, **213/625-3115 (resrv), 805/942-1493.**

THE OAKS

Ojai, CA

This co-ed spa, in a renovated country inn, offers a no-nonsense fitness vacation. Its pragmatic approach to health attracts mortals *and* celebrities such as Gore Vidal and Jeanne Crain—all striving for the common goal of body beautiful. Its fitness program begins in earnest with individual medical evaluations and a discussion of personal goals. Visitors choose from 14 classes including nature walks, aerobics, yoga, muscle-toning exercises in the pool, and classes on body awareness, self-image, and designing personal appearance. You'll eat low-calorie (500-750 per day) meals, swim in the pool, workout in the gym, and relax in the sauna. Beauty treatments are not a priority here, but they are available for an extra fee and are quite modern and thorough. Golf, tennis, and horseback riding can be arranged. Located in the center of town, and not far from the Los Padres National Forest.

Rates: Single $128 or $140, double $87-$103/person (per night). The Oaks, 122 E Ojai Ave, Ojai, CA 93023, **805/646-5573.**

THE ASHRAM

Calabasas, CA

This somewhat eccentric health retreat offers fitness fanatics a dream regime. Sometimes called "the toughest spa in the country," it still attracts the likes of Shirley MacLaine, Raquel Welch and Barbra Streisand. Its philosophy is that peace of mind and a new source of energy is attained through challenging the body's physical limits. A busy day begins with yoga and meditation at 6:30am. After breakfast, guests gather for a brisk two-hour hike, an hour of weight lifting and an hour of pool exercises. After lunch and a rest period, an hour of calisthenics is followed by a 1½-hour evening hike. The only beauty treatments offered are a daily massage and facial which help tired muscles make it through the week. Evening lectures cover subjects ranging from developing healthy habits to dream interpretation. Located about 30 mi NW of Los Angeles, but the exact location is kept somewhat secret; spa vans arrange to pick up guests at three local hotels.

Rates: Double $1300/week (no singles). The Ashram, 2025 McKain Rd, PO Box 8, Calabasas, CA 91302, **213/888-0232.**

THE GOLDEN DOOR

Escondido, CA

Considered by some health-seekers to be the "spa of spas," this Japanese-style oasis provides a luxurious, expensive experience in exercise, diet and relaxation. The program lasts a week and supplies shorts, T-shirts, jogging suits, terry robes, and rubber slippers. Guests are evaluated for general levels of physical fitness, and staff members help them plan their daily calorie intake. Activities include warm-up classes, spot exercises, aerobics or aquatic exercise, volleyball, dance, sauna, whirlpool, yoga, lectures, and pre-bed massages. Workouts are interspersed with juice breaks (for example, pear juice over ice), beauty treatments, and gourmet meals featuring fresh, mostly home-grown, produce. The Japanese influence is evident everywhere from the meticulously land-scaped rock gardens with raised wooden walkways, to

the fan-shaped whirlpool, shoji screens, and oriental antiques. Weeks alternate between women only, men only, and couples. Located 40 mi NE of San Diego.

Rates: $2675 (all singles, Sun—Sun). The Golden Door, PO Box 1567, Escondido, CA 92025, **619/744-5777.**

CANYON RANCH SPA

Tucson, AZ

Snuggled in the foothills of the Santa Catalina Mountains, this lush 28-acre resort offers programs for fitness beginners, for those who have slipped out of shape, and for the lean machines who sign up for every class. Guests are cossetted with savory (albeit nutritionally balanced) meals and chromatic sunsets, while being taught the importance of proper nutrition, exercise, stress reduction, and the control of alcohol and drug use. The staff includes nurses, fitness advisers, registered dieticians, psychologists, and biofeedback experts, and all programs are designed to be both fun and habit-forming. Physical activities include the perfunctory morning stroll, bicycle exercise, aqua trim, yoga, creative dance, stretch-and-flex, aerobics, and circuit weights. Eight charming adobe rooms fan around the spacious clubhouse, and the ultramodern 28,000-square-foot spa features airy carpeted gymnasiums, a fully equipped weight room, air-conditioned racquetball courts, Jacuzzis, steam and sauna—plus complete massage, herbal wrap, skin-care and beauty departments. Outdoors are six tennis courts, three swimming pools, and miles of scenic trails for bicycling, jogging, or guided mountain hiking. Co-ed facilities. Located just W of Tucson.

Rates: Single $1070—$1460, double $875—$1200 (7 nights). Canyon Ranch Spa, 8600 E Rockcliff Rd, Tucson, AZ 85715, **800/742-9000 (except AZ), 602/749-9000.**

Canyon Ranch, Tucson, AZ

MIDWEST

THE SPA AT OLYMPIA RESORT

Oconomowoc, WI

The myth that getting into shape requires a Spartan atmosphere of discipline and self-denial is dispelled at this posh resort and spa. Following the philosophy that one should be pampered after a good workout, the programs feature strenuous cardiovascular exercises along with massages, saunas and whirlpool relaxation. An appropriately named Rear Echelon Class focuses on the hips, stomach and derriere. Other classes include dancing, aquatic exercises and aerobic workouts. The tennis facilities are adequate though not as superbly manicured as the 18-hole golf course. This course winds around the resort and circles a ski hill which dominates the flat Wisconsin tableland. This hill and Olympia's indoor pool, racquetball, handball, and tennis courts guarantee year-round stimulation. Between the golf course and the resort's wooded lakefront property lies the newly prepared, expansive polo grounds. On summer Sunday afternoons, teams from throughout the midwest challenge the Olympia Polo Club as spectators line the field to cheer on the thundering equines. Adventurous options feature sailing, water skiing and horseback riding.

Rates: Single $1470, double $1160 (7 nights). The Spa at Olympia Resort, Oconomowoc, WI 53066, **800/558-9573.**

WOODEN DOOR

Lake Geneva, WI

A for-women-only, rustic retreat, this casual spa offers fitness classes to enhance both body *and* mind. Exercise classes are offered at three different levels to suit individual needs and include aerobics, modern dance, beginning ballet, yoga, hiking, and weight training. Seminars cover topics on self-awareness, behavior modification, nutrition, self-defense, and even plastic surgery. Guests share modern cabins accommodating 3-6 women, for a maximum number of 95 guests each week. Located on 54 acres of lakefront property, sailing, canoeing, and water skiing privileges are included in the price. Chicken and fish are common entrees, complemented by fresh fruit and vegetables for a daily diet around 900 calories. Beauty treatments available for a fee. (Another Wooden Door is located about 50 mi NW of O'Hare airport in Woodstock, IL.) Lake Geneva is about 90 mi N of Chicago. Open to women over age 18.

Rates: $289-$389 (5 days). Wooden Door, PO Box 830, Barrington, IL 60010, **312/382-2888.**

KERR HOUSE
Grand Rapids, OH

Step into Louise May Alcott's world of *Little Women* when you enter this exquisite hilltop Victorian mansion. Guests are thoroughly spoiled amid delicate china, wall-to-wall antiques, and a dedicated staff. Named for its original owners of 100 years ago, today this holistic retreat works with guests through behavior modification and physical fitness programs. Catering to guests which have ranged in age from 19 to 83, a heavy emphasis is placed on stress-management, and the exercise program revolves around yoga movement and other relaxation techniques. The five-day program (Sun-Fri) also includes a complete menu of body-pamperings from herbal and cellulite wraps, to a finger facial massage and a foot reflexology treatment. Breakfast is served in bed, and all meals emphasize natural cookery with such delectables as cold melon soup, spinach salad, and eggplant Parmesan. Kerr House caters primarily to women, but couples' and men's weeks are also held. Located 20 min from Toledo via Rte 65.

Rates: $1750 (5 days/Sun—Fri). Kerr House, 17605 Beaver St, Grand Rapids, OH 43522, **419/832-1733, 255-8364.**

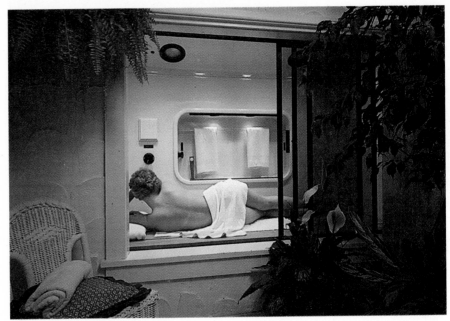

The Aurora House Spa, Aurora, OH

AURORA HOUSE & SPA
Aurora, OH

Situated in a century-old country manor, this spa pampers and reconditions its guests from head to toe. Aurora's special treatments and serene atmosphere amid antiques and exotic plants, attract a melange of patrons—housewives, businessmen, and even stalwarts from the Cleveland Browns football team. A number of spa packages range from a one-day "excursion" to a 6-day, 6-night "asylum." Services include a complete hair salon, facials, massages, a sauna, paraffin treatments (for softening skin), cellulite wraps, and a waxing room for hair removal. "The Habitat" is a small, space-capsule-type room in which guests experience steam, winds, and rain while lying naked on a wooden platform—an experience designed to invigorate and refresh skin and body. A beauty pampering treatment called "Repechage" ("second chance" in French slang), utilizes layers of aloe vera, seaweed and Dead Sea mud. The Repechage facial mask becomes very hard and guests can take the shell home as a souvenir. Cardiovascular exercises are offered along with yoga and dance. The 750-1000-calorie diets are high in natural and organic food. Open to men and women over age 18. Located near OH 82 & OH 36.

Rates: Single $1539, double $2700 (6 days). Aurora House, 35 E Garfield Rd, Aurora, OH 44202, **216/562-9171.**

KS MO
OK AR
MS
GREENHOUSE ★
LA
TX
PHOENIX ★

SOUTH CENTRAL

THE GREENHOUSE
Arlington, TX

For the woman who would like to be totally pampered and "made over," this is the place to go. The semi-tropical setting is accented with Oriental touches and bedrooms equipped with sunken bathtubs and embroidered linen. It is one of the most expensive spas in the country, where guests receive breakfast in bed—served with silver and china. Planned diets hover around 850 calories per day, with delicate spicing and creative preparation designed to help guests forget the absence of bulk. (Everyone dresses up for dinner, so take something suitable.) Luxurious facilities include a pool area decorated with lush potted greenery, exercise and massage rooms, whirlpool, sauna, and steam area. All beauty treatments are arranged with one technician to ensure individual attention from the toenails to the roots of the hair. This pampering is earned by a morning of hiking, stretch-and-flex, muscle toning, aerobics, and water exercises. Weekly programs include a Neiman-Marcus fashion show and lectures on self-improvement. Located in a W suburb of Dallas. Open to women over age 18.

Rates: $2450/week. The Greenhouse, PO Box 1144, Arlington, TX 76010, **817/640-4000.**

THE PHOENIX
Houston, TX

The Phoenix is an elegant spa on a 15-acre wooded estate dedicated to exercise, stress-management, and eating wholesome produce. Individual attention is a priority and each guest meets with the Director for an hour and ½ for one-on-one discussions. Programs emphasize cardiovascular fitness combined with muscular toning and stretching activities. Daily lectures and discussions on healthy living and current issues provide a stimulating environment for intellectual development as well as physical fitness. A full week of pampered rejuvenation revolves around a healthy diet, daily exercise, massage, and beauty treatments. A unique feature is the indoor track which can be computer programmed to monitor an individual's progress. Other facilities include an Olympic-sized pool, tennis courts, handball, racquetball, weight room, saunas, and whirlpool. Some activities take place in the adjacent Houstonian Fitness Center, a vast complex that includes the most modern in exercise and fitness facilities (memberships cost about $10,000). Complete medical evaluations are available. Located just W of Houston. Open to women only except for selected men's weeks.

Rates: $1850/week (Sun—Sat). The Phoenix, 111 N Post Oak Ln, Houston, TX 77024, **713/680-1601.**

Canyon Ranch, Tucson, AZ

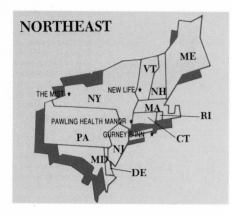

NORTHEAST

ME
VT
THE MIST ★
NEW LIFE ★
NY
NH
MA
RI
PAWLING HEALTH MANOR ★
GURNEY'S INN ★
CT
PA
NJ
MD
DE

NEW LIFE HEALTH SPA

Stratton Mountain, VT

Located at the base of Stratton Mountain (see Winter Sports) in Green Mountain National Forest, this alpine refuge promotes a healthy body and a sound mental attitude. This holistic philosophy is encouraged through diets of fruit, vegetables, and low-sodium chicken, fish, and vegetables. Every guest leaves with a professional diet plan and a list of wellness-minded recipes. Mornings start with a wake-up hike, and are filled with challenging classes in yoga, slimnastics, and dance aerobics. Afternoons are free for horseback riding, sailing, golf, and tennis at the nearby John Newcombe Tennis Center (see Golf & Tennis). A limit of 12-20 guests helps ensure informal groups and private attention. Beauty services are not a priority, but guests receive two massages per week, and are offered a variety of creative facials. Facilities comprise of a hot tub and sauna, two exercise rooms (one with gymnastic equipment), and an outdoor pool. Open to adults over age 16.

Rates: Single $900/week, double $800/week. New Life Health Spa, Liftline Lodge, Stratton Mountain, VT 05155, **802/297-2600.**

THE MIST

Niagara Falls, NY

What could be more perfect than to begin a day looking down on the majestic Niagara Falls? This spa is located only three blocks away and guests hike, jog and cross country ski (depending on season) to the Falls each morning via picturesque Goat Island which divides the American and Horseshoe Falls. The excursion is followed by stretch-n-strengthen routines, aquatic exercises, and dance aerobics. All visitors are medically evaluated, and take-home exercise programs are individually prepared. After a tasty lunch of perhaps crabmeat and vegetable pita, the pampering begins. Facials, body scrubs, massages, and foot reflexology treatments are all offered, with co-ed programs available for couples. Located in a private section of the Hilton Niagara Falls, the luxurious facilities include a swimming pool, Finnish sauna, whirlpool, and mirrored exercise room. Bicycles available at the hotel, and ice skating (in winter) at the nearby Niagara Falls Convention Center. Evening seminars on self-improvement. Co-ed facilities.

Rates: Single $887, double $740 (8 days). Niagara Hilton, c/o The Mist, Third & Mall, Niagara Falls, NY 14303, **716/285-3361, ext 162.**

GURNEY'S INN

Montauk, Long Island, NY

This elegant oceanside inn emphasizes beauty treatments and has one of the most extensive selections in the world. European-style saltwater treatments include the German thalassotherapy—a jet-circulated bathtub—and the French Vichy showers which alternate between fresh and saltwater. Located near vast stretches of white sandy beaches, restful coves and rustling woods, Gurney's has more than 40 rooms of gyms, massage rooms, beauty salons, saunas, and baths, and a spectacular 35x60-foot sea water swimming pool with a glass-wall view of the Atlantic. Options include the Fango Therapy, a soothing volcanic mud-and-paraffin body application, and a massage under the twinkling stars. A complete salon offers hair coloring and permanenting, along with other amenities. A medical evaluation and questionnaire helps the staff prescribe individual exercise programs and diets as low as 800 calories per day. Exceptional seaside edibles include oysters, clams, scallops, and fish, complimented with chicken and vegetarian entrees. Fitness programs include a private exercise class, and a range of options in weight lifting, pool exercise, stretch-n-strengthen routines, disco aerobics, calisthenics, yoga and swimming. Open to adults over age 18.

Rates: Single $1760—$2180, double $1820—$2240 (7 days). Gurney's Inn, Old Montauk Hwy, Montauk, NY 11954, **516/668-2345, -3203.**

PAWLING HEALTH MANOR

Hyde Park, NY

This restored Georgian estate is a year-round retreat emphasizing natural health principles. Only the agents of nature are employed to maintain and restore youthful vitality: sunshine, fresh air, exercise, natural foods, and rational fasting. The program is believed to reduce nervous tension, develop emotional equilibrium, and improve general physical well-being. The minimum stay is one week and weight loss is induced through controlled regimens of fasting (water diet), exercise and natural nutrition. Although exercise is not structured, guests may swim, hike, or use the spa's gym at their convenience. The manor also features solariums with showers for nude sunbathing, massages, and manicures. Immediately nearby are many historical sites: the Franklin D. Roosevelt Home and Library; the Vanderbilt, Ogden Mills, and Astor estates; Vassar and Bard Colleges; Woodstock Village, near where the famous 1969 music festival was held; and Rhinebeck Village, known for its displays of violets and anemones. A public golf course and riding stables are nearby. Open to adults over age 16.

Rates: $450/week. Pawling Health Manor, PO Box 401, Hyde Park, NY 12538, **914/889-4141.**

Gurney's Inn Resort & Spa, Montauk, Long Island, NY

New-Life Health Spa, Stratton Mountain, VT

SOUTHEAST

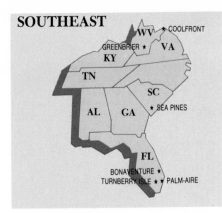

COOLFRONT RECREATION

Berkeley Springs, WV

Rustically located on 1200 lakeside acres in the shadow of West Virginia's mountains, TVs and telephones are scarce. An exceptional amount of recreational activities keep guests busy horseback riding, swimming, roller skating, boating, fishing, camping, and ice-skating and cross-country skiing during winter. Coolfront has five- or 12-day programs with aerobics, yoga, muscle toning, tennis, hot tub sessions, and swimnastics. Low-cal diets (750-1200 calories/day) and health lectures round out the regimen. Weekends are set aside for workshops on massage techniques, and periodic programs are offered for stress-management, and ''smokers anonymous.'' Guests stay in either the Woodland House Lodge or A-frame chalets, for a maximum capacity of 30 spa-goers. Located 2 hrs from DC.

Rates: Single $475, double $375/person (5 days). Coolfront Recreation, Berkeley Springs, WV 25411, **304/258-4500.**

THE GREENBRIER

White Sulphur Springs, WV

This antebellum paradise pampers the body *and* the palate, so weight watchers be wary! Situated amid 6,500 mountainous acres and 350-year-old oak trees, this white-pillared monument is dedicated to the same principles found in the first spas. A wide range of water-related treatments and facilities include hydrotubs, an indoor pool, bathhouses, the Skotch hose which strategically sprays tight muscles, and the famed White Sulphur Springs baths. Exercise programs are not formally scheduled, but staff will help guests with personal fitness plans. Recreational options include golf on three championship courses, croquet, horseback riding, skeet and trap shooting, platform and regular tennis, jogging along measured trails, cross-country skiing and ice-skating (in winter). One of the foremost resorts in the world (see Regal Resorts), Greenbrier is renowned for its perfectly manicured grounds and attention to detail. Every room is uniquely designed, with the emphasis on Southern charm; the ''Paradise Row'' guest houses are equipped with all the amenities of home. If first rate cuisine served beneath grandiose chandeliers aren't indoor diversion enough, try the billiard and pool tables, indoor tennis courts, table tennis, and exercise and game rooms. An extensive three-day medical evaluation available.

Rates: Double $202—$264/night. The Greenbrier, White Sulphur Springs, WV 24986, **304/536-1110, 800/624-6070.**

SEA PINES BEHAVIORAL INSTITUTE

Hilton Head Island, SC

Smoke too much, drink too much, eat too much? This fitness education center specializes in health maintenance programs designed to help change lifestyle patterns that are detrimental to overall health. Targets for intervention are inactivity, overeating, smoking, excessive reliance on alcohol, and stress reactions. All participants receive a complete medical evaluation that includes lab tests and physical examination. This institute is serious business and a variety of programs include a 26-day Weight Control Program and a five- or 12-day Executive Health Program. Exercise options include swimming, bicycling, golf, and use of a gymnasium. Clients reside in spacious villas adjacent to the Institute; couples may rent a villa at extra cost. Another retreat designed especially for controlling obesity is Green Mountain at Fox Run, located in Ludlow, VT, **902/228-8885.**

Rates: $3800 (26-day program), $1600-$2500 (Executive Health Program, 5-12 days). Sea Pines Resort, Hilton Head Island, SC 29928, **803/671-6181.**

Canyon Ranch, Tucson, AZ

PALM-AIRE

Pompano Beach, FL

As inspiration, weight-shedders might note that this spa helped Liz Taylor lose 20 pounds in three weeks. Whether beauty treatments are your main priority, or physical and mental fitness are your goal, this resort has superb facilities. Spa clothes are provided so all you need bring are your sneakers! Guests are started on exercise programs at home as soon as they pre-register. Upon arrival, a medical exam and a computer analysis determine weekly schedules, and then guests are off for sessions in aerobics, muscle toning and yoga. Classes are graded according to fitness and ability, but everyone is equally pampered. Guests receive six massages, herbal wraps, whirlpool baths, and facials in a week's time. Options include Roman baths, Swiss needle showers, saunas, steam rooms and a beauty salon. Toothsome menus might include flounder marinara or broiled lamb and still remain within calorie limits. Separate but nearly identical facilities for men and women include a solarium for nude sunbathing, a stress test area, Nautilus equipment and siesta rooms. It's a fun place for couples to visit because of the wide range of facilities, not the least of which are the Olympic-sized pool and patio, five golf courses and 37 tennis courts.

Rates: Single $2060, double $3170, triple $4408 (7 days). Palm-Aire, 2601 Palm Aire Dr N, Pompano Beach, FL 33060, **305/971-6000, 800/327-4960.**

BONAVENTURE INTER-CONTINENTAL HOTEL & SPA

Fort Lauderdale, FL

This lavish spa is designed for those who enjoy fitness and who adore being pampered. It's sparse but elegant. Computerized personal programs are designed according to a medical screening, as well as the individual goals and abilities of each guest. Workout options include aerobic walking, calisthenics, dance, and use of a skylighted weight-training room and exercise pool. Daily meals are based on a 900 calorie budget with an emphasis on variety, but diet snacks are provided to help visitors adjust to scanty meals. Extensive beauty treatments are available to both men and women; the separated facilities include steam rooms, saunas, whirlpools, several kinds of facials, a skin analysis session, and a full-service beauty salon. Located off Hwy 84 heading W.

Rates: Single $1435, double $1225/person (7 days). Bonaventure Inter-Continental Hotel & Spa, 250 Racquet Club Rd, Ft Lauderdale, FL 33326, **305/474-3300, 800/432-2673 (in FL), 800/327-0200 (outside FL).**

TURNBERRY ISLE

Miami, FL

If you own a fleet of luxury automobiles and you get bored shopping at Saks Fifth Avenue and Bloomingdales, then you've probably heard of this opulent spa. Generous accommodations include a mammoth sunken tub and a state-of-the-art stereo system; some rooms have a personal hot tub, a full-sized dining table, and a bar. Guests are invited to play the two 18-hole golf courses, 24 tennis courts and four racquetball courts. The spa is an extension of the resort, but it takes itself very seriously. The 4-day package allows guests a loofah massage, two herbal wraps and facials, and 12 fitness sessions. Spa guests get lots of attention in the morning classes because of sparse attendance due to late-risers. Facilities include indoor and outdoor pools, Nautilus equipment rooms, racquetball courts, sauna, indoor and outdoor massage areas, and hot and cold plunges. Creative cuisines are only 750 calories per day and surprising choices include a baked potato or barbecued chicken. All spa clothes are provided except shoes.

Rates: Single $1998—$2150, double $1325—$1450/person, triple $1175—$1200/person (6 nights). Turnberry Isle, PO Box 630578, Miami, FL 33163, **305/932-6200, 800/327-7028.**

Chapter 13

DUDE RANCHES & FARM VACATIONS

Skyline Guest Ranch, Telluride, CO

We owe the pleasures of today's dude ranches to the moneyed and curious Easterners and Britons who, generations ago, inveigled western ranchers to allow them the pleasure of their company—for a fee. Today, the same curiosity applies to farm life, and vacations down on the farm allow us to gratify our passion for the rural life without becoming a permanent part of it.

It's been said that a cowboy is no more than an appetite on a horse. Unquestionably, riding the range, baling hay, and branding calves will build quite a hunger, and westerners, in particular, know how to assuage such pangs. Bountiful repasts of steaks grilled over a fire of mesquite, barbecue-and-all-the-trimmin's cooked out of doors, wieners roasted over an oak fire, homemade bread, and pies and pastries rich with ranch-grown wild fruits and berries, have been part of a wrangler's daily fare since pioneer days. For many, hearty, home-cooked meals are a major part of the appeal of a vacation on a dude ranch or farm. Horses, the second ingredient of that cowboy definition, remain an integral part of farm and ranch life and, thus, horseback riding is immediately available or nearby to all of the facilities listed. And so are numerous other outdoor activities, because rural and western pleasures center on the outdoors. Thus, as a guest, you can ride, climb, hike, and swim…you can fish, hunt, take a pack trip, or help out with ranch and farm chores. You can take a hay ride, or do a hoedown…or, perhaps best of all, simply loaf and clear the cobwebs from your mind in a milieu of total, unpressured relaxation.

NORTHWEST

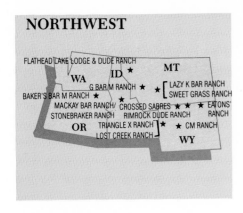

FLATHEAD LAKE LODGE & DUDE RANCH
WA
ID ★
MT
G BAR M RANCH ★
BAKER'S BAR M RANCH ★
[LAZY K BAR RANCH
SWEET GRASS RANCH
MACKAY BAR RANCH/ CROSSED SABRES ★ ★ ★ EATONS'
STONEBRAKER RANCH RIMROCK DUDE RANCH ★ RANCH
OR TRIANGLE X RANCH ★ ★ CM RANCH
LOST CREEK RANCH ┘
WY

BAKER'S BAR M RANCH

Adams, OR

There's room to spread out here. The 2500-acre ranch is nestled in the lush Blue Mountains of northeastern Oregon adjacent to the Umatilla National Forest 2161 feet above sea level. Guests get personalized transportation— that is, a saddle horse—for the entire stay. The cayuses graze on an undulating carpet of bunchgrass while guests drink in the pastoral delights of lush evergreens and wildflowers, drawing energy from deep draughts of bracing mountain air. Crystal pure drinking water comes from a spring and a pool is fed by warm waters gushing from a nearby cliff. Getting to the pool—via a cable-supported footbridge—is half the fun. Guest activities include fishing, square dancing in the rec barn, playing volleyball and basketball, or taking the opportunity to do absolutely nothing. Guests are welcome to help with an occasional chore, such as feeding the horses, which might help spend some of the calories acquired while enjoying homemade meals and camp-out cookin'. The ranch is located on the site of the historical Brigham Young Springs Resort; the hand-hewn log ranch house, built in 1864, was used during the Civil War as a stopover freight and stage station. $390-$400 weekly.

Baker's Bar M Ranch, Rte 1, Adams, OR 97810, **503/566-3381.**

MACKAY BAR RANCH/STONEBRAKER RANCH

Near Boise, ID

Two remote ranches 150 miles north of Boise offer as much or as little "civilization" as the heart desires. Both are in the far reaches of the River of No Return Wilderness, 2.2 million acres of rugged country, and both are accessible only by air or forest trail. Mackay Bar sits in a canyon between the South Fork and the main Salmon River, presenting all the amenities of a dude ranch even though it is in the middle of wilderness: a comfortable main lodge, modern guest rooms, pack llamas, and a menu that includes mouth-watering steaks, steelhead trout, and fresh salmon—complemented by ranch-grown produce. Mackay also offers a wide range of vacation packages and services, including guides and gear for fishing, hunting, white-water rafting, pack trips, and naturalist outings. Vacationers who really want to get away from it all go to

the Stonebraker Ranch, at 5500 feet in the Chamberlain Basin. Arriving by plane, guests then travel on horseback or by buckboard to the ranch, a group of hand-hewn cabins sequestered in a forest clearing. Glacial cirques and alpine meadows are close by; no electricity. You may want to use the more remote and Spartan Stonebraker as a take-off point for a hunting or pack trip—then settle back to enjoy the comfortable amenities of the Mackay Bar. $160 daily.

Mackay Bar Ranch/Stonebraker Ranch, 3190 Airport Way, Boise, ID 83705, **800/635-5336, 208/344-1881.**

G BAR M RANCH

Clyde Park, MT

This is a 3300-acre, private, game sanctuary—and a working cattle and horse ranch. As a result, in addition to encountering white-faced herefords and a string of ponies, guests frequently see mule deer, coyotes with their pups, bobcats, porcupines, skunks, gophers, woodchucks, pine squirrels and, occasionally, moose and bear. Several pairs of golden eagles live here. All this combines to delight shutterbugs, bird watchers, and nature lovers. For those of an historical bent, the lore of the west comes alive in the valley through which Jim Bridger led wagon trains on their trek to greener pastures. Stock-stealing Indians were thwarted here on Battle Ridge by soldiers from Ft. Ellis. Homesteading, moonshining and feuding are part of the ranch's colorful past. A ranch museum houses many artifacts of settlement days. Activities include horseback riding, mending fences, checking waterholes, tending to sick cattle and packing salt to the herd on summer range, trout fishing, horseshoeing, and eating copious quantities of thick, aged, home-cooked steaks from ranch stock and bakery products from the ranch kitchen. Ranch house rooms and comfortable cabins. $300-$325 weekly.

G Bar M Ranch, PO Drawer AE, Clyde Park, MT 59018, **406/686-4687.**

LAZY K BAR RANCH

Big Timber, MT

This working cattle-and-horse ranch was founded in 1880 and still is run by the same family. The ranch rambles over 20,000 acres in Big Sky Country; it produces its own pork, beef, milk, butter and cheese, as well as many vegetables. You'll find absolutely no organized activities of any kind, except for a Saturday night hoedown, and no television. Accommodations are cabins, with or without living rooms, ranging in size to accommodate families of up to eight persons. Bread and pastries are baked on the premises. For the angler, lunkers come in several varieties of trout—brown, brook, cutthroat and rainbow. The ranch has maintained a horse breeding program since 1900, so guests are assured a horse suited to ability and preference. Unlimited horseback riding is included in the fee. Nearby are Yellowstone National Park (See Nat'l Parks & Monuments), ghost towns, Indian reservations, and a colony of Hutterites—a peaceful, religious sect of farmers; horseback trips into the Crazy Mountains, which range from an elevation of 4000 feet at their base to well over 11,000 feet, are popular outings. $375-$475 weekly.

Lazy K Bar Ranch, Big Timber, MT 59011, **406/537-4404.**

SWEET GRASS RANCH

Big Timber, MT

This is a working cattle ranch and not a resort in any sense. Tucked away in a scenic valley in the foothills of the white-capped Crazy Mountains, the ranch offers the opportunity to take an active part in all phases of ranch life. Options range from the daily chores of milking cows and wrangling horses and the seasonal activities of fencing and haying, to mowing, branding horses and cattle, and packing salt to them in high summer pasture. Riding is a way of life here, through terrain that includes high alpine lakes, meadows blue with forget-me-nots, rugged foothills, and rolling low country. Fish are found aplenty in the creek, beaver ponds and lakes, and good hiking is outside your door. There are cookouts, moonlight rides, fish and steak fries, swimming, and rafting. Accommodations are comfortable rustic log cabins; no TV, but numerous sweeping vistas and an unstructured lifestyle. $350 weekly.

Sweet Grass Ranch, Melville Rte, Box 167, Big Timber, MT 59011, **406/537-4477.**

CM Ranch, Dubois, WY

FLATHEAD LAKE LODGE & DUDE RANCH

Bigfork, MT

Saddle sores are a way of life here for greenhorns, and the Saddle Sore Saloon is a good place to talk your way out of them. Horseback riding is part of almost every day's activities at this 40-year-old, 2000-acre ranch, but water sports aren't far behind. Flathead Lake, named for the tribe of Indians who inhabit their reservation on the south end of the lake, is the largest natural lake west of the Great Lakes. It's 30 miles long and 15 wide, comfortable for swimming and pure enough to drink. Fishing is for silver salmon and cutthroat trout or the Dolly Varden and Mackinaw species that reach 45 pounds. Nearby rivers and streams complement the water-based sports, which include waterskiing, sailing, white-water rafting, and canoe racing. The ranch also maintains a heated swimming pool. The rugged terrain, part of the Rocky Mountains of northwest Montana, just south of Glacier National Park, is ideal for hiking. Wildlife, such as bear, deer and the Bald Eagle, are abundant; the National Bison Range is only an hour from the ranch and daily trips are arranged to Glacier National Park, only 45 minutes away. $644-$686 weekly.

Flathead Lake Lodge & Dude Ranch, Box 248, Bigfork, MT 59911, **406/837-4391.**

CROSSED SABRES RANCH

Wapiti, WY

Originally established in 1898 as a stagecoach stop for visitors to nearby Yellowstone National Park (see Nat'l Parks & Monuments), this guest ranch is reputed to be the oldest such facility in Wyoming. Spacious, comfortable, heated cabins, complete with private baths, are picturesquely nestled in some of the most beautiful wilderness in the west. Horses, bred for the rugged terrain, will lead you over the same trails blazed by Jebediah Smith and other early frontiersmen in the heart of the Shoshone National Forest. Weekly activities include a guided tour of Yellowstone, white-water rafting on the Shoshone River, a visit to the Buffalo Bill Historical Center (see Masterful Museums), and Old Trail Town (see Ethnic & Historic Villages) in Cody, square dancing, and an overnight pack trip. The fishing in many of the jewel-like lakes and trout-filled streams is reported to be unbeatable. Children are welcome, and are given expert instruction in the ways of the west from experienced wranglers. Cookouts and ranch-style eatables contribute to the western atmosphere in this secluded mountain retreat, 7000 feet above the bountiful plains. $460 weekly.

Crossed Sabres Ranch, Wapiti, WY. 82450, **307/587-3750.**

Stonebraker Ranch, Near Boise, ID

TRIANGLE X RANCH

Moose, WY

This authentic working dude ranch has been owned by the Turner family for more than 50 years. Spectacular is a rather tame description for this enclave of outdoor pleasure, encompassed entirely by national park and forest lands. Located in the heart of awesome Jackson Hole country in the shadow of the magnificent Grand Tetons, the ranch offers superb scenery, abundant wildlife and a quiet, relaxed pace. Wrangling, haying, raising and breaking stock, shoeing horses, and all of the traditional activities of ranching are a way of life with which guests enjoy becoming acquainted. Hunters find elk, moose, and deer aplenty; cross-country skiers and snowmobilers criss-cross the vast lands in winter. Other diversions include horseback riding, river float trips, fishing, cookouts, square dancing, hiking, scenic tours, photographic expeditions, pack trips and swimming — there's also a special supervised children's ('Little Wrangler') program. $410-$575 weekly.

Triangle X Ranch, Moose Post Office, Jackson Hole, WY 83012, **307/733-2183.**

RIMROCK DUDE RANCH

Cody, WY

Behind the ranch is a towering range of steep canyons and peaks with trails leading to passes 10,000 feet high. This is the Absoraka range of the Rockies in the Shoshone National Forest and it provides a picturesque setting for most ranch activities. In a tradition true to the cowboy state, horseback riding is offered in many forms — on pack trips, overnight camping trips, or casual trail rides. Big rainbow and cutthroat trout are taken in the Northfork of the Shoshone River, while at Buffalo Bill Lake three and four pound lunkers are common. Indians once gathered at DeMaris Hot Springs, located near the ranch, for health rites in the warm sulphur pool. Now, ranch guests can swim there. Nearby also are the Buffalo Bill Museum and Whitney Gallery of Western Art (see Masterful Museums) and for a rootin', tootin' good time, the town of Cody really cuts loose on Independence Day. On the ranch, you'll find shuffleboard, table tennis, cards and a billiard table in the Remuda Room and a piano and large fireplace in the main ranch house. Accommodations consist of cabins with private baths; several have stone fireplaces. $60-$80 daily.

Rimrock Dude Ranch, Cody, WY 82414, **307/587-3970.**

EATONS' RANCH

Wolf, WY

The third and fourth generations of Eatons operate this 7000-acre spread in the shadow of Bighorn Mountains, which form a wall of granite and pine stretching 13,000 feet over the surrounding foothills. The Bozeman Trail once crossed this historic terrain, and Sitting Bull once used the area for his hunting grounds. Now, the ranch is used primarily for horseback riding, fly-fishing for trout along fast-running, boulder-strewn streams, and as a base for packing into the high country. Other activities include swimming in a large, heated pool, watching the wranglers' impromptu performances with the rope, dances in the recreational building, evening barbecues across the creek at the foot of a cliff, picnicking, and base-ball games between the dudes and the wranglers. For golfers, two courses are available in nearby Sheridan. Accommodations include several cabins, simply but comfortably furnished, with private baths. More than 120 colorful wildflowers have been identified on ranch property, and, in season, all pose prettily for the amateur photographer. $440-$465 weekly.

Eatons' Ranch, Wolf, WY 82844, **307/655-9285.**

Long X Trail Ranch, Grassy Butte, ND

LOST CREEK RANCH

Jackson Hole, WY

The view from the ranch across verdant Jackson Hole to the towering Teton Mountains is one of the most splendid sights on earth. Grand Teton soars 13,766 feet and 21 other peaks topping the 10,000-foot mark offer a visual feast that rates it one of the most majestic vistas in the world. The most widely known feature of Teton County is the range of mountains called *les Trois Tetons*, the three breasts, by early French trappers. Amid this scenic grandeur, ranch guests venture into the high country for hunting, fishing for scrappy species of cutthroat, Mackinaw, brown and rainbow trout, mountain climbing, river float trips, pack trips, skiing, painting, photography, hiking, boating, golf, snowmobiling, and ski touring. There are 10 million acres of national forests and parks around Jackson Hole dedicated to these activities. Elk, moose, deer, antelope, and bison roam free across an emerald landscape inset with sapphire lakes. Yellowstone National Park is 35 miles away. Accommodations are two-bedroom cabins, many with two baths, a living room, and private porch; the dining room opens onto a huge deck-porch. $599-$1004 weekly.

Lost Creek Ranch, PO Box 95, Moose, WY 83012, **307/733-3435.**

CM RANCH

Dubois, WY

Since 1927, guests have come here to watch working cowboys roping long-horned cattle, to ride the range, to fish, and to enjoy the great outdoors. Calves are branded in spring and the cattle are driven to high mountain range pasture for the summer. A year-round home for Les and Alice Shoemaker, the ranch is situated on the eastern slope of the main range of the Rocky Mountains at the mouth of Jakey's Fork Canyon. The canyon provides a fascinating opportunity for geological study because ice-age glaciers have exposed several layers and formations. A stream running through the canyon is fast, clear and full of brook, rainbow, and brown trout. The ranch is somewhat isolated; there's no road beyond the ranch, which is contiguous to the Fitzpatrick Wilderness Area of the Shoshone National Forest on the south and west. The nearest neighbors are more than 40 miles away across the Continental Divide, creating an almost endless expanse for riding. Each guest is furnished a horse for personal use. Guests stay in cabins of one, two or three rooms, each with private shower, bath, and porch. The 7000-foot altitude is ideal for a summer vacation—cool, yet below the range of the mountain storms that follow the Divide. Rates on request.

CM Ranch, Dubois, WY 82513, **307/455-2331.**

SOUTHWEST

Skyline Guest Ranch, Telluride, CO

WHITE STALLION RANCH

Tucson, AZ

Although only 17 miles from downtown Tucson, the ranch covers more than 4000 acres and guests can ride to their heart's content. The ranch operates a rookery of exotic birds, while activities include a cutting-horse exhibition and a pet longhorn that performs tricks. Several episodes of the TV oater, "High Chaparral," were filmed on the ranch. Quarter horses are raised here, and, as a result, guests are treated to two rodeos a week. Awaiting guests are adventurous, action-packed days in the sunshine, along with quiet and rest for those seeking tranquility in a relaxed informal atmosphere. Excellent meals are cooked in an Indian-style outdoor oven; comfortable guest rooms are wood panelled. Guests can hike the majestic Santa Catalina Mountains, swim in the heated pool, play tennis, horseshoes, or shuffleboard, or mosey over to the Happy Hour Saloon. $588-$609.

White Stallion Ranch, 9251 W Twin Peaks Rd, Rte 28, Box 567, Tucson, AZ 85743, **602/297-0252.**

THE ALISAL

Solvang, CA

Cathy Lee Crosby, Robert Vaughn, Doris Day, and Burt Lancaster relax here periodically, and Clark Gable liked it so well he selected the ranch library as the matrimonial site when he married Lady Sylvia. But star-gazing has no place on the schedule at this 10,000-acre working cattle ranch studded with ash and sycamore (*alisal* in Spanish). Tasteful, secluded bungalows with wood-burning fireplaces nestle amidst an almost infinite variety of entertainment: horseback riding, golf on a world-renowned championship course, tennis, boating, fishing for steelhead trout and swimming at a 90-acre lake, volleyball, badminton, and croquet. Herds of deer have the run of the place and guests see yellow billed magpies, acorn woodpeckers, raccoons, and bobcats on guided nature hikes. Haywagon rides in the moonlight. The restaurant serves western-style and gourmet dishes. Nearby are the: the scenic, historic Danish settlement, Solvang, (See Ethnic Villages), with its charming shops and Danish style architecture; Mission Santa Ines; and several vineyards and wineries. Charters available for whale-watching in season. $176 daily.

The Alisal, Box 26, Solvang, CA 93463, **805/688-6411.**

GREENHORN CREEK GUEST RANCH

Spring Garden, CA

They call it the Shangri-La of the Feather River country. It's high in the Sierras, about 70 miles from Reno, a land spiked with forests, softened with sheltered meadows, wildflowers, and awesome sunrises and sunsets. A mind-boggling calendar of events, mainly featuring the horse, greet guests in this fir-pine-and-aspen-laced retreat. Diversionary fare includes steak cookouts, hayrides, and bingo, poker and other card games in the saloon and dance hall. An after supper sing-along beside a bonfire is followed by square dancing; an "awards" banquet (for "happiest personality," etc.) is followed by a long-lasting, foot-stomping western country dance. A trout-stocked pond lies near the corral; the main buildings are comprised of a two-story frame structure with exterior verandas to resemble an old-fashioned frontier hotel, and several cabins. The latter feature high, open-beam ceilings, wood panelling, queen-size beds and verandas with porch swings. One evening is spent at a candlelight dinner, a little dressy. Meals are announced by a cook's banging on a big iron triangle, summoning guests to a chuck house furnished with tables fashioned from half rounds of pine. Nearby are the fairways of Feather River Inn—and 100 lakes and a thousand miles of streams, alive with rainbow trout and Kokanee salmon. Hikers, boaters, sailors, and water skiers will find all the means for their favorite activity close at hand. $395-$495.

Greenhorn Creek Guest Ranch, Box 11, Spring Garden, CA 95971, **916/283-0930.**

HIGHLAND RANCH

Philo, CA

In the heart of redwood country and surrounded by 250 acres of meadowland and forest swept by ocean breezes, this ranch offers miles of horseback riding trails through fragrant forests. The mounts are well-trained, the tables groan under hearty, well-cooked meals, and there is an apple orchard where you can pick fruit to take home. There's also tennis, buggy rides, swimming, canoeing, and paddleboating. Anglers will find excellent trout fishing plus populations of scrappy bluegill and crappie. You can take the famous redwoods trip on the Skunk Train, diesel rail cars that crisscross the Noyo River over several bridges and a tunnel through the mountains (see Romantic Rendezvous). It's seven hours round-trip. The ranch features a special program for children. Guest accommodations consist of 12 redwood cabins complete with private baths and fireplaces. $310-$330 weekly.

Highland Ranch, Box 150, Philo, CA 95466, **707/895-3294.**

CHOLAME CREEK RANCH

Cholame, CA

Five generations of the Van Horn family have operated this 800-acre spread for the last century. A great sense of history permeates the place; owners display the original deed signed by President Harrison and point out that the famed bandit Joaquin Murrietta was captured near here. The ranch is located in gentle rolling hills near Paso Robles, between San Francisco and Los Angeles, inland a little and uphill from the Pacific Ocean at an elevation of about 1500 feet. It's set along a quiet creek lined with cottonwood and willow trees. Doves, quail, cottontail rabbits, deer, and other wildlife abound. The area also is a natural habitat for several species of hawks and eagles. You can forage for wild herbs and vegetables with ranch hostess Gloria Van Horn, who spends 8 weeks each summer directing a camp program for children. Other activities include horseback riding, pony-cart rides, cookouts, hiking, fishing for catfish, fossil-and Indian-artifact hunting, touring nearby Indian encampments, bird hunting (in season), photographic expeditions, swimming in the pool, and helping with some ranch chores if you're an early riser. Or simply mellow out and enjoy the smog-free environment. From $60 per person daily.

Cholame Creek Ranch, Box 8, Cholame, CA 93431, **805/463-2320.**

Aspen Lodge, Estes Park, CO

Lazy H Ranch, Allenspark, CO

Colorado Trails Ranch, Durango, CO

Deer Valley Ranch, Nathop, CO

VISTA VERDE GUEST RANCH

Steamboat Springs, CO

Dudes and dudesses are welcome here year-round. In winter, there is breathtaking skiing, snowshoeing, cross-country skiing on about 20 miles of trails, and thrilling national competition at nearby Howelsen Hill jumping complex. This 1600-acre ranch lies in a secluded valley at an elevation of 7800 feet, surrounded by the Routt National Forest and the 12,000-foot peaks of the Zirkel Wilderness Area. Specialties are a quality riding and instructional program and raft trips on the Upper Colorado River. With 100 lakes and 900 miles of streams, there's enough fish to call it an angler's paradise. Other activities include rodeos, ballooning, hiking, hayrides, and gold panning. Golf and tennis facilities are nearby. Guests stay in hand-hewn log cabins with fireplaces and eat home-cooked meals prepared with ranch-grown provisions. Supervised activities for children. Rates: $70-$120 daily (includes all ranch activities).

Vista Verde Guest Ranch, Box 465, Steamboat Springs, CO 80477, **303/879-3858.**

LOST VALLEY RANCH

Sedalia, CO

For more than a hundred years this has been a working cattle and horse ranch, "lost", as it were, in a valley in Pike National Forest. It is about 60 miles from Denver or Colorado Springs. Guests stay in modern one-to-three bedroom cabin suites with fireplaces. Activities include horseback riding, with participants grouped according to ability, a weekly rodeo, and outstanding trout fishing in a three-mile-long private stream and three-acre lake. If they wish, guests may help with ranch chores and cattle round-ups. The ranch has a heated outdoor pool, a whirlpool, and Plexi-Pave tennis courts. There is a full-time children's program, and one for teens as well. Other diversions include pack trips and trap shooting. Summer festivities include square dancing, old fashioned melo-drama, cookouts, and staff musical performances. $475-$600 weekly.

Lost Valley Ranch, Box 70, Sedalia, CO 80135, **303/647-2311.**

LAZY H RANCH

Allenspark, CO

High in the Rockies near the fabulous resort town of Estes Park, this ranch is dedicated to good food, pleasing accommodations, well-trained horses, and robust family fun. There's a heated pool, a hot tub, and a recreation building. Pack trips into the mountains, fishing the rapid streams for trout, hiking, and shooting pool are part of the package. You can swap tales over a campfire at night. Rates include horseback riding and, if needed, instruction. There's even a special program for children 12 and under and a slate of activities for teens, too. The food is plentiful and home-cooked, outdoor meals feature chuck wagon breakfasts, trail picnics, and barbecues. Rides include a picnic lunch of sandwiches, fruit, and cookies packed cowboy-style in saddlebags. Accommodations are provided in the lodge and in cabins. Winter visitors will find cross-country skiing and tobogganing facilities. For unwinding, libations ranging from sarsaparilla to fancy Eastern drinks are served in the saloon. $360-$440 weekly.

Lazy H Ranch, Allenspark, CO 80510, **303/747-2532.**

LANE GUEST RANCH

Estes Park, CO

The European influence is felt here and seen in a sidewalk cafe on the ranch, enjoyed in the continental cuisine cooked from scratch. Not that the pleasures of the west, including native fare, are neglected one whit on this small but posh ranch located a thousand feet above Estes Park, bordering the million-acre Roosevelt National Forest. The ranch offers hiking and trout fishing in brisk streams, white-water rafting on the much brisker Colorado River, jeep rides to the top of the Continental Divide, wine-and-cheese horseback rides, visiting evening rodeos with ranch hands who give you the inside dope on what's happening. Golf is available nearby. The unspoiled wilderness area is home to many species of wildlife, including deer, elk and coyote; hummingbirds will land on your outstretched fingers. Frontiersman Kit Carson trapped beaver in this area and had a camp north of the ranch along the stream where guests hold cookouts. A special children's program includes horseback riding into the high country. $88—$103 daily.

Lane Guest Ranch, PO Box 1766, Estes Park, CO 80517, **303/747-2493.**

SKYLINE GUEST RANCH

Telluride, CO

The city, eight miles down the valley, is a nationally designated historic district with its roots deep in gold and silver mining days of a hundred years back. The ranch is surrounded by snowcapped 14,000 foot peaks of the San Juan Mountains, and the scenery is spectacular. In summer, the valley is awash in a sea of yellow dandelions, though the mountains are still covered with snow, inviting spring and summer skiing, glissading, and walking. As the season progresses, the alpine blanket of wildflowers becomes more brilliant and in fall the aspens are a shimmering gold. Lakes are abrim with feisty trout, deer may be seen in the woods, float trips on nearby rivers are arranged in season, and four-wheel-drive vehicles transport guests daily to special areas to begin their fishing, walking, picnicking, backpacking, horsepacking, or climbing adventures. Meanwhile, back at the ranch, a sauna is piping hot for day's end relaxation, swimming in the ranch lake is always on the schedule, sunset cookouts are usual, and the potbelly stove and fireplace in the spacious lodge are focal points for schmoozing. $420-$630 weekly.

Skyline Guest Ranch, Box 67, Telluride, CO 81435, **303/728-3757.**

LAKE MANCOS RANCH

Mancos, CO

Horseback riding is a way of life here. This ranch, at 8000 feet and nestled against the scenic San Juan National Forest, is stocked with more than 65 horses and it employs guides who can introduce you to a different trail each day in the great outdoors. Non-equestrians can enjoy a hike or a jeep ride, visit the ruins of the Indian dwellings at Mesa Verde National Park (see Nat'l Parks & Monuments), or relax in the Jacuzzi or heated swimming pool. Accommodations are comfortable. Surrounding the main buildings are cabins and the ranch house. Each cabin is fully carpeted and offers privacy and convenience (including your own refrigerator), plus daily maid service. Family cabins range from two to three bedrooms, all have a living room and two full baths. Accommodations for singles or couples are in spacious private guest rooms in the ranch house. $395 weekly.

Lake Mancos Ranch, 42688 County Rd, N Mancos, CO 81328, **303/533-7900.**

ASPEN LODGE

Estes Park, CO

Nestled between Long's Peak at 14,256 feet and Twin Sisters at 11,500 feet, this 82-acre facility was once called "truly Colorado" by a guest and the appellation has more or less become a trademark. The lodge is set behind a two-acre lake that is stocked with trout. Horseback riding stables are nearby, as are barbecue makin's tucked away in the columbines back in the woods. The lodge itself is symmetrical with a dining room on one end and a living room with a large flagstone fireplace at the other. Accommodations are provided in detached cottages, ranging from one to three rooms. During the summer season, the ranch offers hiking and backpacking, hot-air ballooning, sailing, stream fishing, jeep and river trips, 18-hole golf, tennis, and swimming. In winter, activities include ice skating, tobogganing, cross-country skiing on groomed trails, and ice fishing. A complete fitness center is being built; it'll include racquetball, Nautilus equipment, sauna, and Jacuzzis. On the drawing boards are a heated swimming pool and lighted tennis courts, and other activities on newly-acquired property. Write or call for rates.

Aspen Lodge, Hwy 7, Long's Peak Rte, Estes Park, CO 80517, **303/586-4241.**

THE HOME RANCH

Clark, CO

(See High Adventure.)

Aspen Lodge, Estes Park, CO

DEER VALLEY RANCH

Nathrop, CO

Billed as a "Christian Family Guest Ranch," this spread combines the best of outdoor activities in Colorado's high country with a sense of togetherness and camaraderie. While the emphasis is on families, singles and married couples are also welcome. The ranch's location — between Mt. Antero and Mt. Princeton—provides challenging hiking and climbing, and the ranch has four-wheel-drive vehicles for exploring the more traversable foothills. The ranch also has a stable of well-trained horses suited for expert and novice riders. Guest ranches are known for their hearty, home-style cooking, and Deer Valley is no exception. Recipes featured in the ranch's hearty Wrangler's Breakfast, outdoor Bar-B-Q Buffet, and chewy Cowboy Cookies are compiled in a cookbook that guests may take home. The family atmosphere of the ranch induces many guests to return. In fact, the owners offer a free one-week vacation after a family has visited the ranch for 10 years and report that many families have collected on that offer. Note: Alcoholic beverages are not allowed at the ranch. Located 6 mi W of Buena Vista on CO 162.

Deer Valley Ranch, Nathrop, CO 81236, **303/395-2353.**

Deer Valley Ranch, Nathrop, CO

SINGING RIVER RANCH

Questa, NM

Accessible 12 months a year, this secluded mountain retreat is located in the Carson National Forest, 8000 feet above sea level on the banks of Cabresto Creek, a portion of which burbles through the property. Facilities include a variety of guest accommodations: a lodge, cabins, and trailer park. It is centrally located near many of New Mexico's recreational, cultural, scenic, and historic centers. For example, the noted artist's colony of Taos is only 30 minutes away, the Santa Fe Opera a few miles farther south, and colorful Indian villages offering fry bread and hand-made jewelry abound. Summertime pursuits include stream and lake fishing, hiking, jeep sightseeing tours, and horseback riding using mounts from nearby stables. An indoor solar-heated pool, game room, and lounge round out the facilities. Nearby are ghost towns, museums, Indian pueblos, and spots for dancing, plus some restaurants featuring quality continental cuisine. Rates on request.

Singing River Ranch, Box 245, Questa, NM 87556, **505/586-0270.**

COLORADO TRAILS RANCH

Durango, CO

Here you'll find an opera house, but no opera, a cowgirl cook who's really a fine chef, and 500 rugged acres adjacent to the San Juan National Forest. Tens of miles of trails for horseback riding include many designed for cantering horses. Topography varies, depending on the chosen route, but guests are never far from spectacular views as they ride the ridges and open meadows through tall stands of timber and across sparkling streams. Breakfast rides feature sausage and Indian bread made from scratch and fried over an oak brush fire. Homemade buttermilk pancakes come with. Cowboys routinely entertain with rope tricks, songfests usually follow dinner, and daytime is filled with tennis, swimming in a heated pool, fishing for numerous varieties of trout in streams, rivers and lakes, testing skills with bow and arrow on an archery range, shooting skeet and trap, or shooting rifles on a range. Vallecito Lake, 12 miles from the ranch, is used for waterskiing and power boating. There are hiking and nature trails, and photo opportunities abound. Once-a-week hayrides are standard. For quiet relaxation, a parlor is decorated with antiques, inlaid card tables, and turn-of-the-century furnishings. The opera house is used for community singing, staff talent shows, and square dances. $545-$755 weekly.

Colorado Trails Ranch, Box 848, Durango, CO 81301, **303/247- 5055.**

BEAR MOUNTAIN GUEST RANCH

Silver City, NM

On the northern edge of Silver City, this small, ornithologist's retreat is a homey and inexpensive place where you can get back to nature, particularly if you are fond of bird watching. Silver City schoolboy Billy the Kid once roamed the area. The ranch house itself is a rambling pueblo-style structure built in the 1930s; rooms are commodious, with

Double JJ Ranch, Rothbury, MI

south-facing sun porches, a relic of its days as a sanitorium. The main hacienda is accompanied by two guest cottages with kitchens. Nearby are the Gila Cliff dwellings —North America's first primitive dwelling area (see Nat'l Parks & Monuments). Also at hand are hot springs, lakes, streams, and an immense national forest, as well as desert mammals and reptiles. Guests generally see at least 30 species of Southwestern birds and from Apr-Oct at least five of these will be varieties of hummingbirds. Prices are exceptionally low, the atmosphere is friendly, and the food is home-cooked. $38-$40 daily.

Bear Mountain Guest Ranch, Box 1163, Silver City, NM 88062, **505/538-2538.**

LOS PINOS

Cowles, NM

This small and unique summer guest ranch in the heart of the Sangre de Cristo range of the Rocky Mountains is 45 miles from the picturesque capital, Santa Fe. It's located near the headwaters of the Pecos River, at an elevation of 8500 feet—surrounded on every side by lofty peaks topping 13,000 feet, with summer temperatures averaging 76 degrees at noon and 40 degrees at night. Food is taken very seriously. Hearty appetites are sated with plenty of fresh milk, cream, fresh fruits, vegetables, meat and poultry purchased locally; breads and pastries are baked on the premises. Sparkling streams and hidden lakes make the Upper Pecos area a tempting spot for trout fishermen —the river runs right through the ranch. Horseback riding is the chief form of recreation; mounts are Rocky Mountain ponies, sure-footed and gentle, but spirited enough to interest the experienced rider. Pack trips can be arranged; trails wind through dense pine and spruce carpeted by wildflowers. Elk, deer, wild turkey, and grouse inhabit the forest. $325 weekly.

Los Pinos, Box 8, Rte 3, Terraro, NM 87573, **505/757-6213 (summer), 201/538-0700 (winter).**

MIDWEST

DOUBLE JJ RANCH

Rothbury, MI

This is a party place—it advertises itself as a special resort for "big kids," featuring live entertainment nightly and two 'good time" dances weekly. Owners issue a standing offer to refund the money to guests who can honestly say they didn't enjoy themselves and so far there have been no takers. Fun aside, it's also the largest working horse ranch in the state, on 1000 private acres. One standard fee paid at the beginning of the stay takes care of everything. Included are three all-you-can-eat meals a day and, to burn off those calories, plenty of horseback riding (on 900 acres of ranch trails and thousands more acres in the Manistee National Forest). All sports equipment, other than for fishing, is provided. Among activities are: canoeing, mini-golf, rifle-range shooting, tennis, swimming indoors or outdoors (in one of two stream-fed lakes), archery at a range, baseball, and volleyball. $419 weekly.

Double JJ Ranch, Rothbury, MI 49452, **616/894-4444.**

SYCAMORE SPRING FARM

Churubusco, IN

Located seven miles north of Churubusco, this working farm, with cattle and crops, serves as a country inn. Guests come for peace and quiet and good food in a pleasant setting. The Colonial-style guest house is modeled after a 17th Century Williamsburg, VA farmhouse. The woodwork is beautiful cherry and the floors are dotted with exposed handmade nails. The 10-room house contains five bedrooms, two of which are reserved for guests. There are never more than two guest groups at the farm, which makes it a very low-key place to get away from it all. Since there are no organized activities, guests can amble around the Amish countryside, browse auctions, and shop for bargains at local flea markets. Guests who wish to swim or fish can get a free pass to the nearby state park. And if so inclined, guests can slip on their grubbies and help with chores around the farm.

Sycamore Spring Farm, Churubusco, IN 46723, **219/ 693-3603.**

LONG X TRAIL RANCH

Grassy Butte, ND

Located in the picturesque Badlands country along the Missouri River, this ranch is a rustic slice of the days of the cowboys. The owners call it a living legacy of the Old West, and cowboys still roll their own cigarettes with makin's carried in their jeans. Though it does boast of a few modern amenities (indoor plumbing and showers), those hoping for an easy-living resort should look elsewhere. Accommodations include single, double, and dormitory facilities, and spaces for campers. The varied activities revolve around the wide open spaces of the Badlands: trail rides, pack trips, stagecoach rides, canoeing, nature walks, horseshoe pitching, campfire cookouts, and barbecues. Chuckwagon feasts include homemade rolls and butter, rhubarb, strawberry and cherry pies. The ranch sponsors an annual 'suicide ride," which is not really a

killing undertaking but a wild, rough, country horse race combing rodeo skills and race track competition, which thrills guests and a thousand spectators every September. Rates on request.

Long X Trail Ranch, Grassy Butte, ND 58634, **701/ 842-2128.**

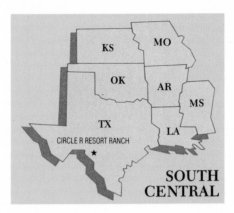

SOUTH CENTRAL

CIRCLE R RESORT RANCH

Medina, TX

They call this a working ranch, but out-and-out play is a big part of it. Guests can test their marksmanship at trap and skeet shooting as well as at a rifle range, improve or develop skills at archery, and try their luck at a fishing hole. Other leisure-time pursuits include tennis, swimming, golf, square dancing, and boating on the river. They breed horses here and the 550-acre spread is honeycombed with riding trails. Guests are treated to a rodeo in a lighted arena where genuine cowboys and real dudes strut their stuff. At night, you can either sing along with guitar-strumming cowboys, or get in some dancing to western tunes. No need for anyone to travel far to explore a western ghost town—there's one right on the ranch, as well as a private airstrip. $60 daily.

Circle R Resort Ranch, Box 1376, Medina, TX 78055, **512/589-2469.**

NORTHEAST

CONSTITUTION OAK FARM

Kent, CT

An hour-and-a-half north of New York City, this is a bed-and-breakfast retreat for weary urbanites, sprawling along some 200 acres in a peaceful, picturesque setting resembling a New England postcard. Part of the relaxed allure of this guest farm is that there's virtually nothing to do, unless you want to help milk the herd of Holsteins that roam the wooded farm or stroll the rolling meadows, luxuriate in the clear, clean air, and admire the neatly tilled fields. Guests appreciate the charming antiques that decorate the Colonial-style farmhouse, collected by three generations of family ownership, read a great deal of the time, and snack throughout the day. Most meals are taken at nearby restaurants, of which there are many, some quite excellent. It's easy to get to know your fellow guests—the farm accommodates only nine at a time, insuring an intimate, restful environment. $35-$40 daily.

Constitution Oak Farm, Beardsley Rd, Kent, CT 06757, **203/354-6496.**

THE INN AT EAST HILL FARM

Troy, NH

Picturesquely sited at the foot of Mount Monadnock is a quaint inn with guest rooms and cozy cottages that caters to the family. Staff are selected for their interest in children and most activities are planned with them in mind. Special events are scheduled for teens. Youngsters are encouraged to pet rabbits and lambs, hunt for eggs and ride ponies; a wading pool is set aside for their use. But adults aren't neglected: there are two outdoor swimming pools, one indoor pool, a sauna, lake beach, tennis, horseback riding, and mountain climbing. A pond adjoins the inn and it's ideal for rowing. At Silver Lake, a few miles away, guests can swim, waterski, and fish for hornpout (catfish) and trout. Nearby are golf courses, auctions, and the Cathedral in the Pines, an outdoor non-denominational chapel. Children are encouraged to help feed the pigs and calves, and like-minded adults are allowed to help. $245 weekly.

The Inn at East Hill Farm, Troy, NH 03465, **603/ 242-6495.**

The Home Ranch, Clark, CO

Photo: © Ken Jones

ROCKING HORSE RANCH

Highland, NY

Barely a couple of zip codes from New York City, this luxury resort near the Hudson River sports a string of horses that work year-round to provide enjoyment to vacationing riders. Ranch hands brag that their horses have been ridden every day except two for nearly 20 years, and that includes some heavy blizzards. There's about 500 acres all told, but 10 of those are a lake that gets exceptionally heavy use; skiing, snowmobiling, and ice skating in the winter, and water skiing, fishing, and paddling in the summer. Guests can try their skill at archery and rifle ranges, limber up city muscles on scores of hiking trails or on two outdoor tennis courts, or test the 18-hole golf course nearby. Activities more familiar to urbanites are also numerous, including an indoor pool, badminton, table tennis, and softball. Live entertainment is offered nightly, and succulent fare includes roast prime ribs of beef, London broil, and filet of sole purchased at a local market. $70-$95 daily.

Rocking Horse Ranch, Highland, NY 12528, **914/691-2927, 212/925-3385 (in NY).**

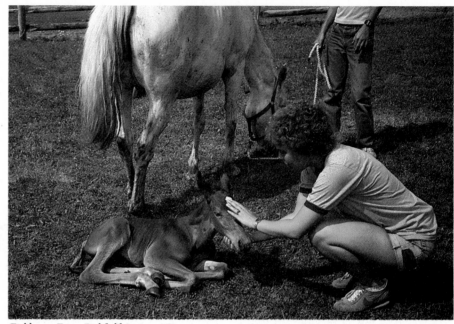

Fieldstone Farm, Richfield Springs, NY

ROUNDUP RANCH RESORT

Downsville, NY

For almost four decades one family has owned and/or operated the 2000-acre guest ranch, overseeing a range of activities that include an indoor ice-skating rink with a glass-enclosed heated lounge, surrey rides, and Saturday night rodeos. Weekend horse-drawn sleigh rides also are part of the wintertime slate of events, and riding is a year-round possibility by virtue of a huge indoor arena. Hundreds of miles of scenic riding trails cross the ranch, which provides for a host of outdoor activities with tennis courts, nine-hole golf course, shuffleboard, archery, and badminton. Skiing lessons and ski equipment rental are available in winter. Nightly entertainment is offered in the El Gaucho Room and cocktails are served in three other areas. Special weekends that include horsemanship clinics and hoedowns or similar events are staged throughout the year. $45 daily.

Roundup Ranch Resort, Downsville, NY 13755, **607/363-7300.**

Double JJ Ranch, Rothbury, MI

FIELDSTONE FARM

Richfield Springs, NY

A raft of activities—including paddling them (rafts)—are in store for guests here, not the least of which is pitching hay. Big fields of the horse food are grown here on 200 acres about 190 miles north of Manhattan. Horseback riding is one of the main attractions, but numerous water sports, centering on farm ponds, also are available. Anglers are sure to find a lunker in the bass-stocked waters—if they're smart; the bass are wily. There's a pool for swimming. Hiking, hayrides, cookouts, and games such as tennis, baseball, table tennis, basketball, and volleyball round out the slate of events. Accommodations are provided in housekeeping apartments in seven cottages. For baseball fans, a trip to the Hall of Fame (see Masterful Museums) at nearby Cooperstown provides a fascinating and definitive overview of "America's Favorite Pastime." Auctions, museums, and antique shops also are in the vicinity. Children are occupied by a playground, and by hunting for frogs and salamanders. $165-$295 weekly.

Fieldstone Farm, Rose's Hill Rd, Richfield Sprgs, NY 13439, **315/858-0295, 607/547-8740 (in NY).**

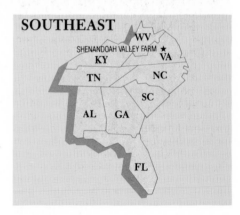

SOUTHEAST

SHENANDOAH VALLEY FARM

McGaheysville, VA

This is a great jumping off spot for touring some of the most spectacular scenery in the US, and for absorbing Americana at several historic landmarks. The farm is situated in an area just off scenic Skyline Drive (See Scenic Drives) and within an hour's drive of Thomas Jefferson's home, Monticello, at Charlottesville (see Historic Landmarks), and Woodrow Wilson's birthplace at Staunton. The caverns of Luray are within hailing distance and so is Natural Bridge. The cottages are tastefully appointed with Early American furnishings and fireplaces. The farm itself raises Black Angus cattle on some 200 acres of forested land dappled with pastures, a spring, and a stream; fishing and swimming facilities are available and there's a mountain ideal for hiking and picnicking. Tennis buffs will enjoy the lighted all-weather courts. Horseback riding trails and golf are nearby as are auctions and antique shops. $35 daily.

Shenandoah Valley Farm, Rte 1, Box 76, McGaheysville, VA 22840, **703/289-5402.**

Chapter 14
ISLAND ESCAPES

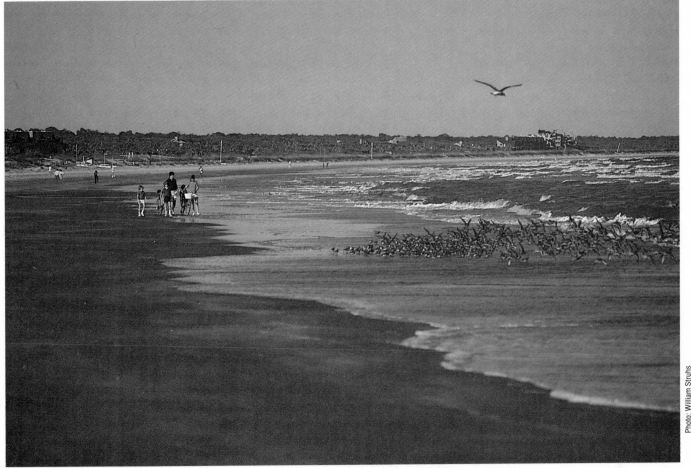

Kiawah Island, Near Charleston, SC

Photo: William Struhs

There is something remote and mysterious about vacationing on an island, even one that is severed from the mainland by only a sliver of water or connected by a short causeway. Perhaps the appeal is in the psychology of isolation, of cutting one's traces and putting water between oneself and the grinding realities of daily routine.

Our listings for island escapes range from Hemingway's old stomping grounds in Key West, to Mackinac Island, home of the stately Grand Hotel in northern Michigan; from popular Nantucket and Martha's Vineyard off the east coast to the San Juans, 172 of them sprinkled in the cool waters of Washington's Puget Sound. Although this book generally confines itself to the Continental United States, no listing would be complete without America's western jewels, the Hawaiian Islands—thus, we have included a brief overview of each.

Our idyllic isles, in freshwater as well as salt, offer a surprisingly rich mix of diversions—from steeping yourself in Colonial history or nautical lore, to watching herds of wild horses swim a channel; from fishing and crabbing to picking wild berries and observing migrating birds; from hang gliding and skin diving to whale-watching and beachcombing. You can be first to see the sun rise, on Mount Desert Island, or last to see it set, at Key West.

NORTHWEST

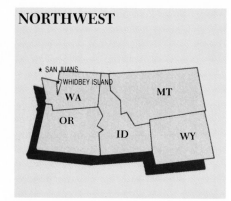

SOUTHWEST

CHANNEL ISLANDS NAT'L PARK

West of Santa Barbara, CA

If you're looking for queen-size beds and cocktail lounges, these five islands off the coast of southern California may not be for you. They attract hard-core nature lovers and offer a treasure trove of natural variety. Anacapa Island is popular with skin divers because of its wide assortment of marine life. Take the self-guided nature trail and watch the antics of the sea lions and harbor seals around the rocky shores. During January and March you might even sight migrating whales. Santa Barbara Island is a terrace surrounded with steep cliffs rising some 500 feet; a plateau offers great views of the mammals on the shores directly below, where the huge elephant seal is a sometimes visitor. Self-guided and ranger tours explore the many caves, coves, and blowholes. Santa Barbara and Anacapa have small visitor centers with wildlife and nature exhibits, and both allow camping (by permit). San Miguel Island is covered with "fossil forests" which give it an eerie look. It also has more species of seals and sea lions than any other place in the world because of its large and attractive "hauling out" area where the mammals can pull themselves onto the rocks. The other two islands, Santa Rosa and Santa Cruz, are privately owned; information about public access obtainable from park supt. Island Packer Cruises available year-round from Ventura (805/642-3370, -1393). Visitors center in Ventura offers information, exhibits, and audiovisual programs about the islands.

Park Supt, 1901 Spinnaker Dr, Ventura, CA 93001, **805/644-8262.**

SAN JUANS

North of Port Angeles, WA

If you like variety in your travel adventures, the San Juans are for you. There are 172 of them sprinkled in Northern Puget Sound, many connected by a ferry system. You can either take your car and use the 500 miles of paved and gravel roads, or rent a bike and explore. You'll find coves, occasional whales, tiny villages, thick forests, fjord-like vistas, soaring eagles, and both modest motels and plush resorts. Enjoy hiking, boating, golfing, camping and swimming. Orcas Island (largest in chain) has four freshwater lakes and a boat launch. Mt. Constitution is also on Orcas and provides visitors with a view from 2400 ft. from a lookout and tower. The Whale Museum houses exhibits about the lives of whales and porpoises. Ferryboats daily from Anacortes; for schedules phone 800/542-0810.

San Juans Chamber of Commerce, Box 98, Friday Harbor, WA 98250, **206/378-4600.**

CATALINA ISLAND

Off the Coast of Southern California

The only inhabitable island along the entire California Coast, this popular day-trip and vacation spot was once famous for the Catalina Casino, a 14-story circular building erected by the late William Wrigley, which served as host to the big bands of Tommy Dorsey and Glenn Miller. Some 20 miles long and eight miles wide, the island is about 20 miles west of Long Beach (near Los Angeles). Catalina's tourist-oriented town, Avalon, has about 2000 permanent residents and scores of hotels, as well as a busy marina at Avalon Bay. Sportfishing is excellent—for swordfish, tuna, sea bass, and a variety of other species. Catalina Cruises provides daily service to the island from Long Beach and San Pedro (213/775-6111). Island attractions include: El Rancho Escondido, the Wrigley Arabian Horse Ranch, Eagle's Nest Lodge, and the Catalina Casino.

Chamber of Commerce, Avalon, Catalina Island, CA 90704, **213/510-1520.**

WHIDBEY ISLAND

West of Everett, WA in Oak Harbor

Driftwood-littered beaches leading to sharp cliffs abound in this rustic islet separated from the mainland by the treacherous waters of Deception Pass. Whidbey Island is set apart by much more than a body of water. This sleepy farming country houses some of the oldest settlements in Washington, and blockhouses still stand that protected settlers' homes from Indians during the White River Massacre. The 49-mile-long island is never wider than 10 miles and contains a scattering of roadside stands, farmers markets, and lonely roads leading to secluded beaches. Whidbey is a logical route for travelers heading north from Seattle. After the ferry crossing from Keystone to Port Townsend on the southern tip, tourists can take highways 525 and 20 north, or explore the numerous villages where you are never more than three miles from salt water. South Whidbey State Park and historic Fort Casey State Park offer camping, picnicking, swimming and fishing. Deception Pass State Park shares its 5,000 acres with Fidalgo Island to the north; more than 250 campsites, picnic facilities, freshwater swimming and miles of beach are accented by beautiful views and an abundance of hiking trails through fragrant forests.

Chamber of Commerce, PO Box 152, Coupeville, WA 98239, **206/678-5434.**

Isle Royale Nat'l Park, Near the Canadian Border

MIDWEST

Isle Royale Nat'l Park, Near the Canadian Border

ISLE ROYALE NAT'L PARK

In Lake Superior Near the Canadian Border

Most of the land on this 40-mile-long island is pure wilderness, ideal for hearty backpackers, campers, and canoeists (who should avoid the open waters of Lake Superior). More than 170 miles of hiking trails offer spectacular views of Lake Superior and the Canadian mainland, and the only means of overland travel on the island. There are no roads and wheeled vehicles of any sort are prohibited throughout Isle Royale. Camping is permitted but open fires in most campsites are not, so a self-contained fuel stove is a necessity. (Free camping permits from the park headquarters.) The chilly waters of Lake Superior discourage most swimmers, but the waters surrounding the island offer a northern paradise to boaters. For the less adventuresome, a variety of comfortable accommodations can be found at Rock Harbor Lodge near the northeastern tip of the island. Inhabiting the island are notable moose herds and wolf packs, who crossed from the mainland over the ice during winter. Scheduled transportation by boat is available from Houghton and Copper Harbor, Michigan, and from Grand Portage, Minnesota. The park is open Apr 16-Oct 31 with full service offered mid-June—Aug 31.

Nat'l Park Service, Isle Royale Nat'l Park, Houghton, MI 49931. Winter Address: Nat'l Park Service, Mammoth Cave, KY 42259. Lodge info, **906/337-4993 (in winter: 502/773-2191).**

Grand Hotel, Mackinac Island

APOSTLE ISLANDS NAT'L LAKESHORE

North of Wisconsin in Lake Superior

The wooded, rocky shores of these historic islands beckon the adventurer. There are no modern accommodations but guests are invited to make their own "dream sites" where camping is available (some primitive). Stockton Island, one of the most visited, offers campsites and interpretive programs from mid-June–late Aug. Wilderness area features boating and fishing. Five historic lighthouses are sprinkled throughout the islands. The Raspberry Island Lighthouse Adventure offers a 1½ hour cruise to the island, and a guided tour of the lighthouse and grounds. Tourists bring sack lunches to enjoy on the beach ($8.50; 6-12 $4.30). Madeline Island is part of the group (not under federal jurisdiction); here you can find housekeeping cottages, restaurants, and cross-country skiing. This 14-mile-long island houses the Madeline Island Historical Museum. Located on the site of an American Fur Co. Post, four pioneer log structures were combined to house artifacts from the log company, lighthouse era, and native Americans (beads, clothes, canoe, etc.). Cruise info: Apostle Island Cruise Service, 715/779-3925, or Madeline Island Ferry Line, 715/747-2051.

Apostle Islands Nat'l Lakeshore, Rte 1, Box 4, Bayfield, WI 54814, **715/779-3397.**

MACKINAC ISLAND

In the Straits Joining Lake Michigan and Lake Huron

The name Mackinac is almost synonymous with the Grand Hotel, the island's famous summer resort which has provided the location for several well-known motion pictures, including 1979's "Somewhere in Time" starring Christopher Reeve and Jane Seymour. The 275-room hotel features fine food, live music and entertainment, and a wide variety of sporting activities. Formal attire is required in the evenings. Although automobiles are not allowed on the island, carriage tours and visits to nearby historical places such as Fort Mackinac and the Astor Fur Trading Company can be arranged through the hotel management. The 2,000-acre Mackinac Island State Park begins where the hotel grounds stop. The island has a Lilac Festival in June and the famous sailboat races from Chicago in July. The hotel is open mid-May—Oct.

The Grand Hotel, Mackinac Island, MI 49757, **906/847-3331 (in winter: 517/487-1800).**

BASS ISLAND

In Lake Huron North of Sandusky

This year-round resort claims the nation's best smallmouth bass fishing during spring; June-August are good for walleye, and ice-fishing for walleye and perch is popular. This island can be reached by ferry or airplane and offers boating, swimming, bicycling, picnic grounds, yacht facilities, golf and waterskiing. A tour train near the ferry offers 50-min. island tours from mid-May—mid-Sept ($3; children $1.50). Another way to see the sights is from Perry's peace monument; the observation deck provides views of nearby islands and Canada. Other highlights include Perry's Cave, Crystal Cave, and the Heineman Winery. Cave tours from Mem Day-Lab Day (Perry's Cave: $1.50; 6-12 $.75. Crystal Cave: $2; 6-12 $1.00). The Crystal Cave tour includes the winery, vineyards, and tasting. On South Bass Island, camping, cabins and nature programs are offered. Ferries available (call for time and seasons) from Port Clinton (285-3491) and Catawba Point (285-2421), or fly in from Port Clinton (285-3371) on the "world's shortest airline."

Bass Island, Put-In-Bay, OH 43456, **419/285-2112.**

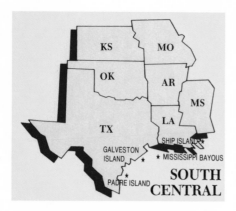

SOUTH CENTRAL

MISSISSIPPI BAYOUS: AVERY AND JEFFERSON ISLANDS

Near New Iberia, LA

An eight-mile deep mountain of salt near the Gulf of Mexico has formed one of the most unusual and striking islands in the United States. Rising out of the marshlands surrounding it, Avery Island is covered by a thin skin of rich topsoil which allows a wide variety of plants to flourish. The 250-acre Jungle Gardens (entrance fee) includes plants selected for their beauty and imported from throughout the world. Hidden walkways meander through the lavishly landscaped grounds which also have roads for sightseers traveling by car. Another part of the garden is maintained as a bird sanctuary. Nearly 20,000 heron families are hatched and raised each year in Bird City. On nearby Jefferson Island is Live Oak Gardens, opened to the public for the first time since 1980 when a mining disaster forced the attraction to close. In addition to the gardens, the island features a conservatory and restored 1870 mansion. Accommodations are available in Lafayette.

Visitors Commission, PO Box 52066, Lafayette, LA 70505, **318/232-3737.**

Galveston Island, Southeast of Houston

Galveston Island, Southeast of Houston

PADRE ISLAND

Near Corpus Christi, TX

Stretching more than 110 miles along the Texas gulf coast from Corpus Christi southward to Brownsville, Padre Island represents one of the longest, largely undeveloped coastal beaches in the Continental United States. Only the north and south ends of the island are developed. Accommodations can be found at both sites. Much of the long, central portion of the island is open only to 4-wheel drive vehicles able to navigate the shifting sands along the beaches. For those who like hardy adventure in a wilderness setting with an absolute minimum of convenience, it affords an uncommon experience. Vehicle traffic is permitted along much of the beach. Boating, hiking, shelling, fishing, and camping are popular activities along the protected shore. Beachcombing here is a serendipitous pleasure, with the Gulf tides depositing objects from as far afield as the Azores and South America.

Padre Island Nat'l Seashore, 9405 S Padre Island Dr, Corpus Christi, TX 78418, **512/937-2621.**

SHIP ISLAND

South of Biloxi, MS

Ride a Pan American boat (often followed by porpoises) on a four-hour cruise to this barrier island 12 miles south of Biloxi in the Gulf Island National Seashore (round-trip $10; 3-10 $5). The island has seven miles of sun-bleached beach flanked by dunes and pounded by gentle surf from the Gulf of Mexico. Enjoy surf swimming, surf fishing, snorkeling, camping, boating and picnicking. The island is steeped in history, serving as headquarters for French exploration in late 1700's, and also as a base for the British fleet when it attempted to take New Orleans in 1815. Fort Massachusetts was constructed just before the Civil War and offers tours Mem Day—Lab Day. Guides are also on hand for "beach walks"—the maritime version of nature hikes. In addition, you can learn the art of casting nets. Enjoy free primitive camping on the eastern section of the island, and free guided tours by boat in Davis Bayou. No motor vehicles or glass allowed; pets must be leashed.

Ship Island, 3500 Park Rd, Ocean Springs, MS 39564, **601/875-9057.**

GALVESTON ISLAND

50 Miles Southeast of Houston

The pirate Jean Lafitte established the first European colony on the southwest's most famous island in 1817. Totally rebuilt after a disastrous hurricane in 1900, Galveston offers many of the most popular attractions in Texas, including the 10-mile seawall along the Gulf of Mexico, the Strand National Historic Landmark District, the East End Historical District (with dozens of fine old mansions included in the National Register of Historic Places), Sea-Arama Marineworld, Seawolf Park, and 32 miles of clean, sandy beaches. A visit to Anico Tower, the island's lone skyscraper at One Moody Plaza, provides the opportunity for a free trip to the 20th floor observation room between 2-4pm for a bird's-eye view of the island and a glimpse at an extensive visual history of Galveston. Overnight camping permitted on some beaches. Important annual events include a Shrimp Festival with cook-offs, dancing and blessing of the fleet, (mid-April) and the yuletide Dicken's Weekend on The Strand (See Fun at Festivals).

Visitors Bureau, 315 Tremont St, Galveston Island, TX 77550, **409/763-4311.**

NORTHEAST

MOUNT DESERT ISLAND

Directly Coastward from Bangor, ME

Escape to this storybook, green forested island surrounded by Maine's trademarks—a rocky coastline and blue waters. Bar Harbor, the largest town, is dotted with resorts, summer homes, campsites, and roadside lobster shacks. Acadia National Park occupies nearly half of Mt. Desert Island and surrounding smaller areas. The park offers 100 miles of hiking trails, as well as guided nature walks and boat cruises with park naturalists, and a 56-mile auto tape-tour available at visitor center (207/288-3338). Acadia surrounds Cadillac Mountain (1,530 ft.), the highest point on the US Atlantic coast. Tourists arrive here before dawn and huddle beneath blankets to await the first US Continental sunrise. Other attractions include museums, narrated bus tours, and year-round ferry service connecting Southwest Harbor, Isleford, Great Cranberry Island, Sutton Island, and Northeast Harbor (207/244-3575).

Chamber of Commerce, Cottage St, PO Box 158, Bar Harbor, ME 04609, **207/288-5103.**

CASCO BAY ISLANDS

Off the Southern Coast of Maine

There are about 365 islands in this bay, or "one for every day of the year," as the locals say. They were carved by ice-age glaciers and their rocky cliffs and pine trees break the horizon in nearly every direction. Not only do the sizes of the islands vary, but so do the legends that accompany them—from tales of ghosts, Captain Kidd and buried treasure, to Indian myths. The Bailey Island bridge, located in northern Casco Bay, is one of few made with uncemented granite blocks laid honeycomb-style to let the tide flow through. The Giant Staircase on Bailey is a scenic rock formation of natural steps dropping 200 ft. to the ocean. Great Chebeague Island has an extensive resort with a golf course, hotel and cottages. Although many islets, such as Cliff, Jewell, Peak's and Orr, have little-to-no overnight accommodations, they still offer rich one-day cultural experiences. The islands can be explored via Casco Bay Lines (Portland) which offers daylight, sunset, and moonlight cruises of Portland Harbor and Casco Bay.

Casco Bay Lines, PO Box 4656, Portland, ME 04112, **207/774-7871.**

MARTHA'S VINEYARD

Off the Coast of New Bedford, MA

One of the most popular resort areas along the North Atlantic seacost is found around the triangle formed by the southern shore of Cape Cod and the islands of Nantucket and Martha's Vineyard. The varied landscape of Martha's Vineyard includes clean beaches, rolling farmland, trout streams, seacliffs, sand dunes—and a hefty dose of commercialism here and there. Ferry service is available from Hyannis, but reservations are recommended (and a must during the summer months). Cars and motorbikes can be rented on the island. There are about a half dozen small towns on the island, but Edgartown is the oldest and most interesting for its architecture in the colonial style. Of the many possibilities for accommodations, the Charlotte Inn in Edgartown (see Inn Places) is probably the most highly rated.

Vineyard Haven Chamber of Commerce, PO Box 1698, Martha's Vineyard, MA 02568, **617/693-0085.**

NANTUCKET ISLAND

30 Miles South of Hyannis, MA

The Gulf Stream warms the waters of the Atlantic to around 70°F. near this island that was once the whaling capital of the world. Be sure to make reservations for the long ferry trip from Hyannis Port well in advance (800/225-3122, in MA 800/352-7104). Ferry service is also available from Martha's Vineyard. Once you have arrived on this historic island, the sense of the past will be almost overwhelming. The oldest home on Nantucket was built in 1686, and carefully preserved buildings from the 18th and 19th centuries are almost everywhere. Many beaches line the north side of the island and boats can be rented at various locations in the busy and well protected Nantucket Harbor.

Chamber of Commerce, Pacific Club Bldg, Lower Main St, Nantucket Island, MA 02554, **617/228-1700.**

THOUSAND ISLANDS SEASHORE

Northwest Border of New York in the St. Lawrence Seaway

This abundance of rocky islands is famous for its beautiful scenery, numerous parks, and private clubs and large residences built by millionaires in the early 1900's. The most famous is 6-story $2.5 million Boldt Castle on Heart Island. Successful hotel magnate, George C. Boldt, built it as a present for his wife (cruises available from several islands). There are 1800 isles spanning 52 miles throughout the lower part of the St. Lawrence Seaway near the northeastern corner of Lake Ontario. Just over half are in Canada and they range from a mound of rocks with perhaps a single tree, to islands several miles long. The numerous parks offer swimming, boating, fishing, water sports, playgrounds, and camping. Tourists get encompassing views of 200 islands via the 5-span international bridge which connects New York and Ontario mainlands. Alexandria Bay, the beautiful island resort center, offers the usual park facilities, plus golf, tennis, and a water-themed amusement park. Clayton Island has three state parks and the Thousand Island Shipyard Museum, with exhibits of antique boats and nautical hardware.

Thousand Islands Bridge Authority, Collins Landing, Box 428, Alexandria Bay, NY 13607, **315/482-2501.**

FIRE ISLAND NAT'L SEASHORE

Off the South Shore of Long Island, NY

This 32-mile-long barrier island, seldom more than a half mile wide, offers an incredible study in contrasts nearly within sight of New York City's skyscrapers. There are nearly a dozen and a half vacation communities, and a 7-mile stretch of the island designated by Congress as a national wilderness—the only such area in New York

Mount Desert Island, off the coast of Bangor, ME

State. Those willing to hike into the interior can enjoy the island much as it must have appeared to the first Europeans to see it four centuries ago. Overnight camping is permitted with advance registration. Popular beaches include those at Sailors Haven Visitor Center and Smith Point West Visitor Center. Ferries operate May-Nov from Sayville (516/589-8980), Patchogue (516/475-1665), and the park headquarters near Patchogue on the mainland. Parkway access can be found at the north and south ends of the island.

Fire Island Nat'l Seashore, 120 Laurel St, Patchogue, NY 11772, **516/289-4810.**

ISLAND BEACH STATE PARK

40 Miles North of Atlantic City off the Coast of NJ

Enjoy the Atlantic surf with fishing rod and bathing suit on this barrier island. It's divided into three zones: northern third is a botanical preserve; central third is a recreational area with bathing beach, bathhouse, concessions, areas for surfing and scuba diving; southern third contains wildlife sanctuary and fishing area. Nature tours are conducted through the botanical and wildlife section. Fires are welcome because the tide leaves too much driftwood for park authorities to monitor. The beach's maritime plant and animal environment has remained virtually unchanged for thousands of years, and nearly all species of bird common to eastern North America uses the park as a rest area during migrations. The Aeolium nature center depicts the park's vegetation and wildlife. At a "touch table" youngsters can handle starfish, horseshoe crabs, whelk egg cases and eel grass. A self-guided natural history trail features examples of maritime vegetation and a marsh. Enjoy a picnic among sand dunes, pick tart beach plums in late summer. The park is accessible by car.

Island Beach State Park, Box 37, Seaside Park, NJ 08752, **201/793-0506.**

SMITH ISLAND

Southern Chesapeake Bay, MD

This island utopia is accessible only by boat and offers a quiet retreat from fast-paced life. It is comprised of three fishing villages and has a variety of seafood restaurants. This Methodist colony has descended directly from its 17th century ancestors; islanders still make their living from fish and shellfish. Visitors often comment on the friendliness of the watermen, finding that they enjoy sharing their culture with guests. Sommers Cove Marina offers one-hour cruises to the island and bus tours of the villages. Time is given to stroll the quiet streets and talk to the islanders (4½ hrs.-301/425-2771). Another option is to spend the night at one of three guesthouses. They usually serve an evening meal in the Smith Island tradition—family style with lots of fixings—and a full breakfast. Or, spend an entire week at the four-bedroom "Somerset" cottage (John & Addelle Schmick - 301/673-2368). Experience island lifestyle by arriving via the mail boat—perhaps sharing your seat with a shopper returning from Salisbury, or sandwiched between crates of soft-shelled crabs. Virginians can reach the island via the "Teresa Ann" departing from Reedville (801/453-3430).

Chamber of Commerce, Box 292, Crisfield, MD 21817, **301/968-2500.**

BLOCK ISLAND

Near Point Judith, RI

The charms of the 19th century eastern seacoast have been carefully preserved on this 11-mile island, but planning is a must. Accommodations, although they range from medium-sized hotels and inns to guest homes and summer cottages, can be limited, especially during summer weekends. Reservations should be made well in advance. The island, 12 miles out to sea, is accessible by boat or plane. Ferries operating from Point Judith (401/783-4613) and New London (203/442-7891) carry cars by advance registration only. A little planning can bring you all of the century-old charms of this quiet resort island, as well as a total escape from golf courses, fast-food restaurants, and traffic lights. Yours to enjoy are surf casting, deep-sea fishing trips, spectacular seascapes seen from clay cliffs, a state park with surf bathing, and, in spring and fall, the natural extravaganza of massive bird migrations.

Chamber of Commerce, Block Island, RI 02807, **401/466-2436.**

ASSATEAGUE ISLAND NAT'L SEASHORE

Off the East Coast of MD

A complete island adventure awaits tourists on this 37-mile barrier reef shared by two states. Each state operates a visitor center and activities include boat cruises, beach sports (bathhouses and lifeguards in summer), surf fishing and clamming demonstrations, slide shows and campfire gatherings. The landscape varies from sand dunes and forests, to the marshes where ponies roam wild on the Maryland side. Explore the nature and auto trails for various animals and countless birds. Hike-in and canoe-in campsites are available for hardy adventurers, as well as family and improved campsites. Other attractions include Chincoteague National Wildlife Refuge, and Assateague State Park. Easily accessible from the N via MD 611, and from the S by bridge through Chincoteague Island (see). Visitor center open year-round except major hols and weekends Jan-Feb.

Visitor Center, Rte 2, PO Box 294, Berlin, MD 21811, **301/641-1441.**

Assateague Island

SOUTHEAST

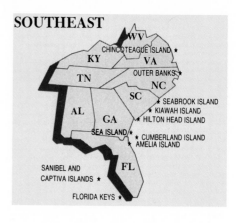

CHINCOTEAGUE ISLAND

Just South of the MD Border in the Atlantic Ocean

Once upon a time, a Spanish galleon carrying horses shipwrecked off the coast of Virginia, or so the legend goes. The horses swam to Chincoteague Island and today they are only somewhat bigger (but more graceful) than Shetland ponies—their growth stunted from eating marsh grass for several generations. The bulk of these horses are left to roam wild on nearby Assateague Island (see), where the habitat is more conducive. However, in order to prevent over-grazing, every last Wednesday in July the horses are rounded up, cattle-herding style, to swim the inlet back to Chincoteague. The following day the foals are sold at auction, and on the third day the remainder swim back to Assateague. Crowds of more than 25,000 descend upon Memorial Park to watch the spectacle and horses usually sell for $300-$1,000. This seven-mile islet is also known for its oysters, said to be some of the best in the East. Other attractions include the Oyster Museum of Chincoteague, the Refuge Waterfowl Museum, and the Chincoteague Miniature Pony Farm, said to have the smallest ponies in the world. The island is accessible by car taking US 13 to VA 175.

Chamber of Commerce, Beach Rd, PO Box 258, Chincoteague, MD 23336, **804/336-6161.**

Sea Islands, off the Georgia Coast

OUTER BANKS

Off the Northern Coast of NC in the Pamlico Sound

Historical intrigue, mystery, and legends galore await tourists on this 175-mile chain of narrow islands that spans Cape Lookout and Cape Hatteras national seashores, and stretchs north to Back Bay, VA. Legends say that Hatteras Island was settled by shipwrecked sailors from Devon, England, and that the village of Ocracoke, settled in the 17th century, was headquarters for the pirate Blackbeard. Today, Ocracoke houses the Cape Hatteras visitor center and offers free ferries to Hatteras Island. The Wright brothers did their first flying experiments on the dunes of Kill Devil Hills, located a little north of Cape Hatteras. Visit the museum and see the field where the first flight took place. Just to the south is Nags Head (see High Adventure), a year-round beachcombing town with a flight school that offers lessons in windsurfing, sailing, ultralight aircraft flying, and hang gliding on soft dunes swept by Atlantic winds. The national seashores are noted for their long expanses of sandy beaches and wild flowers. Available recreation includes boating, sailing, sportfishing, swimming, picnicking, camping, and waterfowl hunting (in season).

Chamber of Commerce, PO Box 90, Kitty Hawk, NC 27949, **919/261-3801, -2626.**

SEABROOK ISLAND

Near Charleston, SC

Practically touching Kiawah Island (see), Seabrook's entire 2,100 acres was purchased in 1972 by the Seabrook Island Company, which now develops it. Visitors can rent private villas and beach houses, and enjoy the accommodations at the Oceanside Club. Activities include organized boating and sailing programs, horseback riding, ocean and creek fishing, shrimping and crabbing in the tidal marshes, as well as golf on two championship courses and tennis on clay composition tennis courts. If vacation planning with a minimum of fuss is attractive to you, Seabrook reservationists can supply all the information you need on accommodations, golf and tennis packages, and swimming and fishing facilities.

Seabrook Island, PO Box 32099, Charleston, SC 29417, **803/768-1000.**

HILTON HEAD ISLAND

Off the South Carolina Coast

The largest sea island between New Jersey and Florida, Hilton Head has become one of the premier resort areas in the United States, as well as a permanent home for more than 10,000 people including many celebrities. Famous for saltwater as well as freshwater fishing, more than a dozen major golf courses, hundreds of tennis courts, miles of unusually wide, sloping beaches, and scores of other attractions. Thousands of rental condominiums, villas, and homes are available in addition to rooms at resorts and inns. The entire southern tip of the island is owned by Sea Pines Plantation, a 5000-acre resort complex which, among many other activities, is host for the Heritage Golf Classic and the Family Circle Magazine Cup tennis tournament. Bicycling—particularly on the hard-packed beaches—is a popular pastime, as is crabbing. Seafood restaurants abound (don't miss She Crab Soup) and beach cookouts are popular events at the resorts.

Chamber of Commerce, PO Box 5647, Hilton Head Island, SC 29938, **803/785-3673.**

KIAWAH ISLAND

Near Charleston, SC

Like neighboring Seabrook Island (see), Kiawah is being developed by a single owner, the Kiawah Island Company. Before the Civil War, the island was the home of rich plantations and the original plantation home, the Vanderhorst Mansion, still stands, although thick forests reclaimed almost all the farmland after the war. Redevelopment in the 1970s brought the famous Gary Player Golf Course, two complete tennis centers, elegant shopping facilities and restaurants, four separate lodges comprising the Kiawah Island Inn, and a wide variety of rental villas and cottages. All the usual southern Atlantic beach activities can be enjoyed on this island easily accessible by car.

Kiawah Island Resort, PO Box 12910, Charleston, SC 29412, **803/768-2121.**

CUMBERLAND ISLAND

Off the Georgia Coast

One of the largest and least-developed islands along the eastern Intra-Coastal Waterway, Cumberland's 17-mile Atlantic beach is usually deserted except for birds and marine life. The Cumberland Island National Seashore was established in 1972, and currently about 85 percent of the total area of the island is protected. Camping for up to one week is permitted. Dense oak forests in the interior support wild horses, wild turkeys, deer, and other forms of wildlife. Activities include clam digging, fishing, swimming, beachcombing, birdwatching, and sightseeing, for which a major attraction is the unusual ruins of the Carnegie mansion, Dungeness. Gracious accommodations are offered at the Grayfield Inn, a turn-of-the-century mansion. Cumberland Island is accessible only by boat and small airplane. The R.W. Ferguson ferry visits the island five times a week, departing from Fernandina Beach, FL.

The Greyfield Inn, 4 North 2nd St, Chandlery Bldg, Drawer B, Fernandina Beach, FL 32032, **904/261-6408.**

Sea Islands, off the Georgia Coast

SEA ISLANDS (SEA, ST. SIMONS, AND JEKYLL)

About 30 Miles North of Okefenokee Refuge, Off the Georgia Coast

Of the more than a dozen islands hugging the Georgia shoreline south of Savannah, sometimes called "The Golden Isles," only St. Simons was never privately owned. Once used by Edward Teach, the infamous Blackbeard, as a labyrinth in the sea to hide himself and his stolen treasures, a number of these islands are of interest to vacationers and occasional treasure hunters. St. Simons, the largest of the three islands covered here, has a number of major golf courses, first-class resort hotels, night clubs, and specialty shops. Neighboring Sea Island boasts of The Cloister, one of the highest rated resorts in America. Jekyll Island became a state park after World War II. Accommodations there are available in restored cottages once used by vacationing millionaires.

Chamber of Commerce, Neptune Park, St. Simons Island, GA 31522, **912/638-9014.** *Tourist Bureau, 1 Beachview Dr, Jekyll Island, GA 31520,* **800/841-6586,** *in GA* **800/342-1042.** *Also see Cumberland Island.*

AMELIA ISLAND

Just North of Jacksonville, FL

Situated in the Atlantic Ocean near the northeastern border of Florida, Amelia Island is noted for summers somewhat cooler than can be found on the Florida mainland, making it an ideal year-round vacation spot. Highlight of the island is the famous Amelia Island Plantation resort, permanent home of Chris Evert Lloyd and John Lloyd. The resort is noted for championship golf courses, tennis courts, and magnificent beaches. The town of Fernandina Beach, 10 miles north of Amelia Island Plantation, has been listed in the National Register of Historic Places for its varied Victorian-style architecture. The community is also one of the most prolific shrimping villages in the southeastern US.

Fernandina Beach-Amelia Island Chamber of Commerce, PO Box 472, Fernandina Beach, FL 32034, **904/261-3248.** *Or Amelia Island Plantation, Amelia Island, FL 32034,* **800/874-6878 (in FL 800/342-6841).**

The Florida Keys, FL

THE FLORIDA KEYS

Off the Southern Tip of Florida

The 113-mile-long Overseas Highway connects this famous chain of 29 islands which separates the Atlantic Ocean from the Gulf of Mexico. Key Largo, largest and northernmost island in the chain, is home to Pennekamp Coral Reef State Park, first underwater park in the United

States and a mecca for divers and glass-bottom-boat trippers. Other highlights along the chain include Theater of the Sea in Islamorada, Sea World's Shark Institute in Layton, the State Park at Bahia Honda, the National Key Deer and Great White Heron Refuge on Big Pine Key, and Orchid Gardens on Summerland Key. Southernmost isle is Key West, where Hemingway and Audubon created some of their masterpieces and whose homes now are museums. Popular Key West attractions are tours of America's southernmost city via the motorized Conch Train, and nightly gatherings to watch the sunset, a carnival-like ritual that attracts musicians, singers, clowns, stunt artists, and other itinerants who perform for tourists. Florida Keys Chambers of Commerce are located near mile markers: 106, 82, 68, 49, 31, and on Key West.

Florida Upper Keys Chamber of Commerce, PO Box 274-C, Key Largo, Florida 33037, **305/451-1414.**

SANIBEL AND CAPTIVA ISLANDS

Near Fort Myers, FL

These two narrow islands, situated in the Gulf of Mexico about 15 miles from Fort Myers, have a long and colorful history. They have been visited by Caloosa Indians, Spanish Conquistadores (including Ponce de Leon), slave traders, 18th and 19th century pirates, and, more recently, scores of tourists enchanted by their tropical charms. Home to nearly 7000 residents, the well-developed islands have many hotels, resorts, and housekeeping cottages available on a rental basis, yet nearly half of the total land area is protected for wildlife refugees. The islands contain some of the world's best shelling beaches, and provide sanctuary for more than 200 species of birds. The J.N. "Ding" Darling National Wildlife Refuge has walking trails and an observation tower. The two barrier islands are connected by a short bridge and to the Florida mainland by the Sanibel Causeway at Punta Rassa. Make winter reservations well in advance.

Sanibel-Captiva Chamber of Commerce, PO Box 166, Sanibel Island, FL 33957, **813/472-3232.**

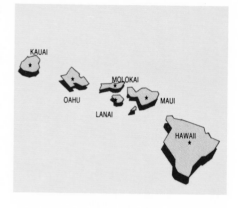

HAWAII

Southernmost of the Hawaiian Islands

Hawaii's largest isle, with an area greater than all of the remaining islands combined, is often described as a land of beautiful contrasts. Within its relatively large 4000 square miles can be found jet-black beaches formed by volcanic sand, lush forests with more than 20,000 varieties of tropical flowers, valleys resembling the deserts of Arizona and New Mexico, and volcanic peaks more than 13,000 feet above the nearby Pacific Ocean. Among the many attractions are two of the state's great waterfalls, Rainbow Falls and Akaka Falls, and the towering Hawaii Volcanoes National Park, where visitors can sleep and even play golf on one of the world's most active volcanoes. At Kealakekua Bay, Captain James Cook met his death when the natives discovered he was not their god Lono. A hill outside the harbor of Kawaihae is one of the few known areas where human sacrifices were performed. The island also is the site of the largest individually owned ranch in the US, the quarter-million-acre Parker Ranch. Dozens of large and small resorts and hotels can be found in the cities of Kawaihae, Kailua-Kona, Keauhou, Naalehu, Punalu'u, and Hilo.

MOLOKAI

Hawaiian Islands

Stretched between the larger islands of Maui and Oahu, Molokai is long on history and exotic scenery but relatively short on vacation-conscious visitors. Only a handful of major hotels dot the island, but the new Kaluakoi resort on the west end of the island, which has currently completed construction of more than 250 Polynesia-styled units, is attracting considerable interest. The lush Halawa Valley on the eastern end is now almost virgin jungle, the result of hundreds of families fleeing the area never to return before an advancing tidal wave in 1946. The starkly beautiful and often inaccessible north coast is formed by towering cliffs plunging nearly vertically into the Pacific. A 19th century Belgian priest began a leper colony along the north coast peninsula of Kalaupapa, and a government operated treatment center remains there to this day. There are only a few roads on the island, but miles of foot paths and 4-wheel drive trails beckon rugged explorers anxious to get away from it all. Attractions not to be missed include Kalaupapa Overlook, Palaau park, Halawa Valley and the hike to Moaula Falls, and the Molokai Ranch Wildlife Park.

Hilton Head Island, off the South Carolina Coast

Waimea Canyon, Kauai, Hawaiian Island

LANAI
Hawaiian Islands

With only 47 miles of total coastline and a mere 18 miles across at its widest point, tiny Lanai is the site of the world's largest pineapple plantation, the nearly-15,000-acre Castle and Cooke farm, parent company of Dole Pineapple. With just over 2,000 residents, Lanai has few famous landmarks that distinguish the other islands in the chain, but for some, it does have its charms. Near Lanai City is a no-charge 9-hole golf course. For sportsmen there is hunting and fishing. It's open season year-round for fishing anywhere and—in some portions of the island—for bow and arrow hunting. Sheep, antelope, quail, deer, turkey, partridge, pheasant, and wild goats will tempt the skillful hunter. A bumpy ride or a long hike will bring the visitor to one of the best preserved Hawaiian ruins in the islands, the ancient village of Kaunolu. The island's only hotel is Lanai Lodge, where rental cars can be acquired. The cool, mountainous, off-the-beaten track atmosphere of Lanai may appeal to those who really want to get away from it all.

OAHU
Hawaiian Islands

Mile for mile, Oahu is the most famous and popular of all the Hawaiian Islands. Some of the hottest action west of Hollywood can be found in downtown Honolulu and along the miracle mile of Waikiki Beach. Hotels, restaurants, and nightclubs in Oahu's population centers nearly burst with kinetic energy and beaches and clubs along the coast are the sites for many championship surfing meets and golf tournaments. Of cultural and historic interest are the extensive Polynesian Cultural Center at Laie, exhibits at Pearl Harbor, the East-West Center adjacent to the University of Hawaii campus, the Honolulu Academy of Arts Museum, Lolani Palace (once the only throne room under American flag), and Byodo-In Temple. Scenic wonders include the famous Diamond Head at the southern end of Waikiki Beach, Waimea Falls Park, and Nuuanu Pali, Oahu's scenic masterpiece, where Kamehameha the Great in 1795 forced thousands of Oahuan warriors to leap to their deaths. There are more hotels and resorts on Oahu than on any of the other islands, the vast majority centered around Waikiki.

Hawaii

MAUI
Hawaiian Islands

Sometimes called "the Valley Isle," Hawaii's second largest island almost touches the northern point of the big island of Hawaii. The island is dominated by the 10,000-foot dormant volcano Haleakala, "the House of the Sun," where visitors to Haleakala National Park can stare down into the largest volcanic crater in the world. The wild, wet lowlands of Maui are often covered with magnificent rain forests. For many years during the 19th century, the area around Lahaina (first capital of the kingdom of Hawaii) provided harbors for a thriving whaling industry. The fascinating Whaler's Village Museum is located about eight miles north of Lahaina, which was also the site of the oldest school west of the Rocky Mountains. Major resort areas include Kapalua, Kaanapali, and Wailea, where golf, tennis, swimming and other tropical activities can be enjoyed in settings of breathtaking beauty.

KAUAI
Hawaiian Islands

Many experienced travelers regard little Kauai as the most scenic of all the majestic Hawaiian Islands. With little more than 30,000 residents, the island's coastline is unspoiled and picturesque, and yet hotels and luxury resorts are abundant along the shore. The wild and often untamed interior boasts of the world's wettest spot, Mt. Waialeale, where rainbows are born and the hunting is plentiful, as well as what is regarded by many as the world's most beautiful sight—Waimea Canyon. The view from Rte. 55 along the entire western rim is magnificent, appearing much like the Grand Canyon cut into a lush, tropical setting. Other points of interest include Menehune ditch, an ancient aqueduct built before the Hawaiians came, Kokee Park adjacent to Waimea Canyon, Kalalau Lookout, Hanalei Valley, and Paradise Pacifica, a unique exhibit of island scenery, wildlife, and ethnic heritage viewed during a narrated train ride. Like novelist Jack London who wrote of the island's beauty, few visitors will forget this tiny jewel in the Pacific.

Akaka Falls, Hawaiian Island

HAWAII VISITORS BUREAU
Visitor Information Offices

2270 Kalakaua Ave.
Honolulu, HI 96815

441 Lexington Ave.
New York, NY 10017

180 N. Michigan Ave.
Chicago, IL 60601

209 Post St.
San Francisco, CA 94108

3440 Wilshire Blvd.
Los Angeles, CA 90010

Chapter 15

SCENIC DRIVES

Shunpiking! The word was coined for the practice, preferred by many motorists, of using quiet, scenic sideroads to avoid the noisy, monotonous throb of America's turnpikes. By no means the shortest distance between two points, these byways twist and turn, climb and narrow, as they bisect golden fields, pastoral meadows, and backwater villages. What they lack in directness, they more than compensate for with character and charm.

From simply being "alternate routes," many of these backroads have become celebrated in their own right as "scenic drives"—where getting there is *most* of the fun. In other cases, roads have been built primarily to showcase local scenery, scaling mountains and forging through wilderness.

One of America's most famous scenic drives is US 1, which hugs California's untamed coastline—overlooking the sea from craggy bluffs. Others, too, provide a view from aloft. In South Dakota, ascend Iron Mountain in a series of hairpin turns and hardrock tunnels; in Minnesota, climb 600' on Skyline Drive to a national hawk watch area; in Colorado, conquer what is said to be the world's highest road—rising nearly three miles above sea level.

Roads with more of a domesticated and historical bent include: a tour of 34 covered bridges in Indiana; the Natchez Trace which follows a trail blazed by Indians and early pioneers; and one of the longest suspension bridges in the world connecting the two peninsulas of Michigan. Drive past the antebellum homes of the south, the weathered red barns and white-steepled churches of New England, and through unspoiled country backroads and rolling hills in the midwest.

Wherever you go, drive slowly to enjoy the scenery, stopping frequently to explore artist colonies and quaint villages, ancient lighthouses, or clear mountain lakes—to buy fresh vegetables at a roadside stand, to visit a cider mill, or to watch a storm rolling in off the ocean.

NORTHWEST

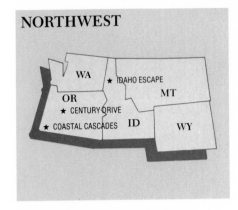

storm-watching in winter (when the mercury will occasionally rise above 60°F), draws spectators to witness huge waves crashing against austere cliffs. Historic Oldtown, numerous gift and antique shops, and a Cheddar Cheese Factory are located in coastal Bandon, also home of an autumnal Cranberry Festival (late Sept), and it is a favorite destination for rock hounds who often find agate, jasper, and other semi-precious stones along the beach. Eastbound incentives via Rtes 42 and 138 can be found at the Wildlife Safari in Winston—a drive-through wildlife preserve where cheetahs, tigers, elephants, and other exotic animals are free to roam, and skiing (in season) at Diamond Lake.

Dept of Transportation, 101 Transportation Blvd, Salem, OR 97310, **503/378-6309, 800/547-7842.**

IDAHO ESCAPE

Lake Coeur d'Alene Area, ID

Idaho, famed for its potato crop, also offers a rich natural bounty of spectacular scenery. In fact, the northern panhandle is becoming a favorite destination because of its serene beauty — mountainous terrain, lava beds, sand dunes, ice caves, lush evergreen forests, and more than 2000 lakes. Following I-90 east from Coeur d'Alene (see Romantic Rendezvous), you'll enter the primitive woodlands of Coeur d'Alene National Forest, dominated by moderately steep to rugged mountains. In autumn, the changing colors are particularly striking because of the contrast between the golden tamaracks and the dark, green firs and pines. At Old Mission State Park just south of I-90, you can view Idaho's oldest standing building—a beautifully preserved church built by a Jesuit Missionary in the 1850s. Rte 3 runs south from I-90 and winds its way through fertile farmlands, wooded foothills, and near the Coeur d'Alene River which is especially good for trout fishing in summer and fall. Further south at St. Maries is the world's highest navigable river, the St. Joe. Canoeists run the 12-mile stretch terminating near the ghost town of St. Joe—once the site of a flourishing mine. Just west of St. Maries, stretching for 6000 acres, are the rolling hills of Heyburn State Park, bordering the shores of Chatcolet Lake. The park is a year-round recreation center—camping, hiking, picnicking, swimming, and boating in summer; cross-country skiing, snowmobiling, and ice-fishing in winter. Two miles inside the park on Rte 5 is a splendid view of the St. Joe river as it meanders between the Chatcolet and Round Lakes.

Travel Council, Statehouse, Boise, ID 83720, **800/635-7826, 208/334-2470 (in ID).**

CENTURY DRIVE

Cascades Lakes Area, OR

This relatively short (100 mile) tour begins at Bend, OR (see Romantic Rendezvous)—a heavily-forested town on the banks of the Deschutes River. Located in the shadow of the Oregon Cascade Mountains, Bend is virtually a year-round recreation center for fishing, hiking, boating, camping, and snow skiing. The tour follows OR 46, west from US 97, crossing pathways used by early explorers, trappers, and hunters, amid high meadows and sparkling lakes that reflect beautiful snowcapped peaks. In Deschutes National Forest, thousands of acres of green pines captivate with their distinct variance in size, density, and color, due to differences in age, soil, moisture, and elevation. Further along is a magnificent view of Three Sisters and Broken Top peaks as you ascend the rise at Bachelor Butte Wayside. This is the gateway to the Cascades Lakes Country where dormant volcanic peaks dominate the skyline. South is Dutchman Flat, a barren pumice desert surrounded by a lush green forest. Rising from the flatlands, motorists are greeted by a display of summer wildflowers in a glade leading to Todd Lake, one of the many beautiful and scenic high alpine lakes in the region. Rare Roosevelt elk, tenacious coyotes, and valuable (and protected) mink can be seen along the route, and there are numerous fishing spots — particularly good for trout, steelhead, and salmon.

Supt, Forestry Service, 211 NE Revere St, Bend, OR 97701, **503/388-2715.**

COASTAL CASCADES

Brookings—Bandon, OR (US 101)

Skirting the Pacific coastline from Santa Barbara, CA to Olympia, WA, legendary US 101 offers more than a thousand miles of natural and man-made wonders. Focusing on 113 miles of this remarkable road in Oregon, US 101 shadows the rugged coastline and takes motorists past green inland valleys and clear mountain lakes. Near the state's southern border sits Brookings, known as "Home of the Winter Flowers" because of its annual Azalea Festival, and boasting beautiful beaches, charming art galleries, and seafood- brimming restaurants. The spectacular drive north to Bandon from Brookings, takes you past miles of broad beaches and shifting sand dunes which hide glistening lakes. Kite-flying, crabbing, beachcombing, and fishing are the most popular shore activities;

Monterey Peninsula, CA

Sparks Lake, OR

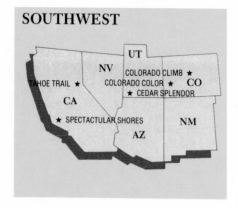

SOUTHWEST

Durango/Silverton Narrow Gauge R.R.

SPECTACULAR SHORES

Big Sur—Monterey, CA (CA 1)

Hugging the rugged coastline along sheer, forbidding cliffs which plunge downward to sheltered coves and secluded beaches, CA 1 is perhaps the most famous, and most scenic road in America. Drive through sun-dappled clearings in the 400,000-acre Los Padres National Forest, past the crashing surf of Big Sur, or search for precious stones on the rocky beach at Jade Cove. As the horizon continues to rise and fall journeying northward from Big Sur, you'll pass the Point Sur Lighthouse and the impressive Bixby Creek Bridge, rising 285 feet above the gaping canyon below. Further north is Point Lobos, known for its jagged rocks and Monterey cypress. Located on a curving beach at the foot of rolling hills, sits the artists' and writers' retreat, Carmel—named for the Spanish Friars who first settled there. This quaint village abounds with colorful flower gardens, diverse art galleries, and magnificent homes bordered by cypress-lined avenues. The Seventeen Mile Drive to Pacific Grove takes you past the rocky, flower-edged shoreline; picnicking and seal-watching are popular at Cypress Point Lookout and at Seal and Bird Rocks. From Pacific Grove Gate, take Ocean View Boulevard along Monterey Bay where red-roofed, white stucco houses look out onto sugar loaf beaches and an emerald harbor. In winter, thousands of monarch butterflies migrate to Pacific Grove, which is often referred to as "Butterfly Town USA."

Convention & Visitors Bureau, PO Box 6977, San Francisco, CA 94101, 415/974-6900.

Boardman State Park, OR

TAHOE TRAIL

Around Lake Tahoe, CA/NV

Where in this country is there a lake so clean that a white dinner plate is visible 200 feet below the surface? Lake Tahoe's water is 99.7% pure, and its 72 miles of shoreline are some of the most dramatic in America. Bisected by the California/Nevada state line, the mountain lake is 6225 feet above sea level, and more than 1600 feet deep. The lake is rimmed with paved roads, and to best enjoy the view, leave South Lake Tahoe following NV 89 west into National Forest lands. The Pope-Baldwin Recreation Area features miles of alpine beach as well as the Historic Estates Tour through mansions built more than 100 years ago. NV 89 climbs north past a lateral moraine formed by ice-age glaciers. Take in excellent views of the lake from the Eagle Point State Campgrounds. Bliss State Park is next on your lakeside trek, followed by the sparkling beaches of Meeks Bay. Travel east on NV 28 near the state line, where many of the older hotel/casinos are located, as well as the Ponderosa Ranch where the famous television western *Bonanza* was filmed, which offers horseback riding, gift shops, and an amusement park. From Incline Village, the road heads south along the east shore of the lake through forests of pine and fir, eventually intersecting with NV 50. A right turn will bring you to Cave Rock Zephyr Cove and to the Heavenly Valley Tram which offers a splendid vantage point, 2000 feet above the sparkling lake.

Convention & Visitors Bureau, PO Box 6977, San Francisco, CA 94101, 415/974-6900.

COLORADO CLIMB

Mount Evans, CO

Rising above the foothills of the Rocky Mountains to an altitude nearly three miles above sea level, Mount Evans boasts what is believed to be the world's highest highway. Following I-70 west from nearby Denver to the small village of Bergen Park, you've already ascended 7500 feet. Past Bergen Park, CO 103 twists and turns through pine and aspen forests, occasionally revealing glimpses of distant snowcapped peaks — including neighboring Pike's Peak to the south. As you continue your ascent, the air will become thinner and cooler, plant life will diminish, and you'll feel the urge to stop at many of the turnouts to muse over spectacular views. Echo Lake, your last chance for food and drink before the summit, is an ideal spot for a picnic, but it is not unusual to find snow here in June, even when the mile-high city of Denver is basking in 90°F. Follow CO 5 from Echo Lake for the final 4000-foot climb to the top, hugging the mountain for no less than 14 miles. Summit Lake lies about 1000 feet from the crest—where the water is bone-chilling at any time of the year. The final stretch is the steepest and the vegetation is scarce—unable to grow in this arctic-like wasteland. The road becomes a series of switchbacks, finally reducing itself to nothing more than a beaten dirt trail for the final few hundred yards. Take time to enjoy the spectacular panorama and revel in your accomplishment before beginning the ride down. The road is open mid-June—Oct. Check local weather conditions beforehand.

Div of Parks & Outdoor Rec, 1313 Sherman St, Denver, CO 80203, 303/839-3437; 303/639-1111 (road conditions); 303/398-3964 (Nat'l Weather Service).

CEDAR SPLENDOR

Cedar City Area, UT

"Look—The morn, in russet mantle-clad, walks o'er the dew of yon high eastern hill."—*Hamlet*, I,i. Such spectacular early-morning vistas are a common sight in southern Utah, a veritable palace of regal redrocks, massive granite monoliths, and cavernous canyonlands. Beginning in Cedar City, home of the Utah Shakespearean Festival (Jul-Aug) and the heart of Utah's Color Country, the towering columns, Sphinx-like statuary, and gingerbread bluffs have provided the backdrop for countless Hollywood classics — from "Drums Along the Mohawk" to "The Electric Horseman." Take I-15 south to Kolob Canyon in the northwest corner of Zion National Park (see

Nat'l Parks & Monuments). Crimson canyons and wind-worn cliffs vie for attention, and many diversions include camping, fishing, swimming, and rock hunting. Head back north on I-15, then east on Hwy 14 to Strawberry Point, where the 8000-foot-high rock formations in the chasm change colors with variations in light throughout the day and with each season—and are said to resemble thrones, cathedrals, and temples. Eight miles north of nearby Navajo Lake on Hwy 143 are the primeval forests and wind-eroded facades of Cedar Breaks National Monument—a magnificent, multi-hued natural amphitheatre rising over 10,000 feet, surrounded by lava beds and bristlecone pines—the oldest known living trees on earth. Return to Cedar City and perhaps catch a Shakespearean performance under the stars.

Travel Council, Council Hall, Capitol Hill, Salt Lake City, UT 84114, **801/533-5681.**

San Juan Mountains, CO

Photo: Denver & Colorado Convention & Visitors Bureau

COLORADO COLOR

San Juan Mountains Area, CO

US 550 is also known as the "Million Dollar Highway," partly because of the low-grade ore which intermittently flecks its surface, but more so because of the views afforded its travelers—green valleys, abysmal canyons, and glistening lakes bordered by towering snowcapped peaks. The region is best known as the southern terminus of the historic Silverton railroad, which, loaded with tourists and railroad buffs, still labors through the spectacular San Juan Mountains. The road parallels the narrow-gauge tracks and alternately rises and falls as it twists and turns across the rugged terrain—following one of the old toll road routes where ore had to be removed by pack mules. Continuing north, you'll pass through historic mining sites, and at Silverton, there's a still-thriving mining center complete with reconstructions of businesses and homesteads, and a three-story jail now home to the Historical Society Museum. The western route from Durango along US 160 (known as the Navajo Trail) takes you through verdant forests of ponderosa pine, juniper, and gambel oak. The La Plata Mountains rise majestically to the north, and the waving hayfields of the Mancos Valley stretch to the south. The imposing rugged escarpment looming to the southwest is the Mesa Verde ("green table"), site of the primitive Indian dwellings at Mesa Verde National Park (see Nat'l Parks & Monuments), where a 20-mile scenic drive takes you from the base of the Mesa to the magnificent ruins at Chapin Mesa.

Visitors Bureau, 225 W Colfax Ave, Denver, CO 80202, **303/892-1112.**

MIDWEST

MN
SUPERIOR'S SKYWAY ★
ND   MICHIGAN'S MAJESTY ★
SD   WISCONSIN WATERFRONTS
★ IRON MOUNTAIN ROAD   WI   MI
RIVERSIDE ROADWAY
NE   IA   IN   OH
SPOON RIVER VALLEY ★   COVERED
IL   BRIDGES

SUPERIOR'S SKYWAY

Duluth, MN (Skyline Parkway)

This 27-mile drive rises 600' above Duluth and not only offers spectacular views of bay, harbor, and river, but is a national hawk watch area. Natural wonders abound on this twisting trailway past birch-filled ravines, tumbling brooks, placid ponds, and blue-gray cliffs. Views of Mediterranean-like white-painted houses, ocean-bound ships on Lake Superior, and snaking ore trains are common. Minnesota Point, the seven-mile peninsula which reaches across the lake toward the Wisconsin shore, is Duluth's playground for outdoor recreation. Artists, photographers, and naturalists are drawn to its gently rolling dunes and sandy flats, while swimmers and sunbathers flock to its many fine beaches. From your vantage point on the parkway, you can look down at a progressive city which boasts many examples of spectacular contemporary architecture, a new convention and entertainment complex, a 25-acre zoo, and a host of historic museums.

Travel Info Ctr, 240 Bremer Bldg, 419 N Robert St, St Paul, MN 55101, **612/296-5029, 800/328-1461, 800/652-9747 (in MN).**

Covered Bridge, Parke County, IN

Photo: Mike Michaelson

SPOON RIVER VALLEY

Galesburg/Havana Area, IL

There's a rich bounty awaiting motorists who take the Spoon River Scenic Drive. Rewards come not only in the pastoral splendor of the rolling farmland of western Illinois, but also in meeting friendly, down-to-earth farm folk, and in reaping the rich harvest of the land and its people. You'll meet hog raisers and, perhaps, take home a hickory-smoked ham or a slab of fresh bacon; you'll visit with farmers and retirees who, by way of a hobby, refinish antique pieces of golden oak furniture and you'll perhaps acquire a handsome rocker or ornate dresser to grace your home; and you'll meet farmers' wives who, during the long winter months, produce lovingly-wrought quilts and beautiful applique and, in fall, gather and dry sprigs of orange-scarlet bittersweet and other wild flowers. The scenic inspiration for Edgar Lee Master's verse classic, *Spoon River Anthology,* is the locale for this 65-mile diversion through rustic villages and over unspoiled country backroads and rolling hills. Picnic areas are abundant in parks along the carefully marked route which parallels the historic river. Upon commencing your drive at London Mills, a series of clamshell-shaped signs direct you through Ellisville, Mt. Pisgah, and Babylon Bend, ending at Lewistown in the south. The drive is like a trip back to the mid-19th century—past old mills, churches, and a hotel and blacksmith shop which have been restored and are now museums. Autumn is enchanting here, ablaze with color and festivities. The Spoon River Valley Fall Festival in October features residents costumed in period dress, demonstrations of early crafts, and flea markets. In every town along the route there are art and antique shows, and an endless variety of scrumptious homemade cooking—butterflied pork chops, whole-hog sausage sandwiches, and pies galore.

Chamber of Commerce, 154 E Simmons St, PO Box 631, Galesburg, IL 61401, **309/343-1194.**

IRON MOUNTAIN ROAD

Black Hills, SD

It is *impossible* to exceed 30mph on this winding mountain road, and many people drive much slower to take in the breathtaking views. Connecting Custer State Park and Mount Rushmore National Memorial (see Man-Made & Natural Wonders) in the enchanting Black Hills, US 16A was regarded as an engineer's nightmare when it was first designed in the 1930s. Slowly climbing its way through tall ponderosa pines, it arrives at the top of Iron Mountain in a series of hairpin turns, dizzying switchbacks, and hardrock tunnels. The tunnels were designed so that their openings would perfectly frame Mount Rushmore, some 17 miles distant. Another view of this world-famous monolith and the surrounding territory is afforded from Norbeck Lookout at the mountain's summit. Other equally scenic roads in the Black Hills include the Needles Hwy (US 87), Rimrock West Hwy 44, Boulder Canyon Dr, Palmer Gultch Rd, and Spearfish Canyon Dr.

Div of Tourism, PO Box 1000, Pierre, SD 57501, **800/843-1930, 800/952-2217 (in SD).**

RIVERSIDE ROADWAY

The Great River Road, IA/IL

This scenic drive stretches for 75 miles along the Mississippi River, from Dubuque, IA to Rock Island, IL. It is part of the Great River Road, which hugs the banks of the "Big Muddy" for some 3000 miles from Minnesota to the Gulf of Mexico, and offers travelers the best route to explore the scenic and historic resources of the Mississippi River Valley. A picturesque starting point is Dubuque, IA, where you can board the Fenelon Place Incline Railway — a cable car which takes you up steep bluffs, 300 feet high, for an unobstructed view across the river of the wooded, hilly terrain of Illinois and Wisconsin. Nearby Crystal Lake Cave features rare and beautiful underground geological formations adjacent to an ultra-clear lake. At Galena, visit the home of former president, Ulysses S. Grant, and other historic buildings such as an elegant 1859 Victorian mansion, and a Civil War "Steamboat Gothic" estate. Board an old paddlewheeler at the Rhododentron Showboat Museum in Clinton, IA, which displays artifacts and specimens of Indian lore. The former home of the Sauk and Fox Indian nations is on the grounds of Black Hawk State Park at Rock Island, IL and Arsenal Island (on the river between Rock Island and Davenport, IA) contains a replica of the blockhouse at Fort Armstrong built to protect Canadian fur traders. The Great River Road has received more than $300 million since 1973 for road improvements, scenic and historic preservation, recreation trails, and tour info centers.

Great River Rd, 205 Victoria Crossing, 867 Grand Ave, St Paul, MN 55105, **612/224-9903.**

MICHIGAN'S MAJESTY

Mackinaw City—Paradise, MI

While Michigan may be one of the most industrialized states in the nation, it is also one of the most beautiful boasting more than 36,000 miles of rivers and streams, and 11,000 inland lakes. Mackinaw City is located at the northern tip of the Lower Peninsula and you can see the sun rise over one Great Lake (Huron), and set over another (Michigan). The Mackinac Bridge, one of the longest suspension bridges in the world, stretches for five miles to unite the Upper and Lower Peninsulas of Michigan. Crossing the Strait of Michigan via the "Mighty Mac," you'll come upon the historic port of St. Ignace where Father Marquette, the Jesuit Missionary and explorer, settled more than 300 years ago; a 52-acre memorial depicts his life and adventures. US 2W will lead you along the southern shores of the Upper Peninsula, past Lake Michigan's deep blue waters and into the thick woodlands of the Hiawatha National Forest — scenic inspiration for Longfellow's famous poem. Pointe Aux Chenes (Point of Oaks) is a popular spot with swimmers and picnickers. Rte 117 north takes you to Rte 28 east and Soo Junction where visitors can explore Tahquamenon State Falls Park via a train and boat tour — no other means of transportation can penetrate this dense wilderness. The town of Newberry, via Rte 123 north, is a popular winter destination for tobogganers and cross-country skiers, and the well-stocked Tahquamenon River near Paradise is a favorite tributary with fishermen.

Travel Bureau, Box 30226, Lansing MI 48909, **517/373-1195, 800/248-5700, 800/292-2520 (in MI).**

Spoon River, IL

Parke County, IN

Spoon River, IL

Parke County, IN

Photos: Mike Michaelson

WISCONSIN WATERFRONTS

Door County Peninsula, WI

Famous for its fall foliage, quaint villages, fish boils, and miles of shoreline, Door County is often referred to as "the Cape Cod of the midwest." WI 57 and 42 crisscross the peninsula all the way to its tip, and motorists often spend days exploring rolling woodlands, limestone bluffs, quaint fishing villages, and fragrant orchards. A good starting point is Algoma (east of Green Bay) on WI 42, where visitors can sample apple and cherry wine at the Von Stiehl Winery. North on WI 42 is Sturgeon Bay; a narrated boat tour takes visitors past many Great Lake ships in the process of being built, remodeled, or just at anchor. One mile north of Valmy via WI 57 and east on Clark Lake Road, is Whitefish Dunes State Park and Cave Point County Park. The constant pounding of thunderous waves from Lake Michigan creates natural caves which may be explored during a refreshing stroll along the beach. North on WI 57 is Baileys Harbor — the oldest village in Door County, and one of the best harbors on the east shore. In late May, 4000 acres of apple and cherry blossoms add a splash of pastel color to this always picturesque town. North to Hwy Q will take you to the Ridges Sanctuary, noted for its wild plants, including the lady-slipper — a wild orchid unique to the area. Follow Hwy Q to the water's edge and walk across a narrow strip of land to tour the Cana Island Lighthouse, built in 1851. Return to WI 57 and continue north to Sister Bay — a collection of eclectic waterside villages where you can pick your own cherries, stroll through galleries and boutiques, or sample Swedish cuisine. Don't miss that Door County tradition, the fish boil (held regularly at several locations), where whitefish steaks, potatoes, and other vegetables are boiled in a huge kettle over an open hardwood fire.

Chamber of Commerce, Green Bay Rd, PO Box 215, Sturgeon Bay, WI 54235, 414/743-4456.

Mackinac Bridge, MI

Photo: Travel Bureau, Lansing, MI

COVERED BRIDGES

Parke County, IN

Hoosiers will quickly tell you that New England doesn't have a monopoly on covered bridges. In fact, there are no fewer than 34 in a single Indiana county — Parke County, 55 miles west of Indianapolis and bounded to the west by the slow-moving Wabash River. These rust-colored enclosures, many built more than a century ago to protect bridges from the ravages of weather and time, span still-running creeks and trickling brooks; their weathered timbers, rustically set amid stands of hardwoods and swathes of emerald pastureland, inspire visitors to reach for pen, brush, or camera. In fact, these bridges, and the tours and festivals that celebrate them, have become an important part of the economy of this rural county where rolling hills are blanketed by dense, hardwood forests, where beef and hog farms are nestled in tiny valleys, and where narrow lanes wind, tunnel-like, through fields of tall corn that crowd in from either side. The bridges attract tourists — 500,000 during the 10-day Covered Bridge Festival during early October — and these visitors have spawned a thriving local industry in arts and crafts. You'll find tiny shops and studios, many creatively fashioned from rickety old barns and abandoned stone buildings, where you can shop for beautiful quilts, hand-made furniture, pottery, antiques, a whole range of arts and crafts, and such country foodstuffs as corncob jelly, thick blackberry preserves, hickory-smoked, sugar-cured hams, and whole-hog sausage. A map, suggesting four separate tours, each with a varying number of covered bridges along the route, will guide you around the county. Most tours start at centrally-located Rockville, the county seat, with its handsome courthouse built of red sandstone. Nearby is Billie Creek, a recreated, turn-of-the-century village and farmstead where costumed guides demonstrate old-time crafts. Other county highlights include: Bridgeton, with a double-span bridge built in 1868 and a

dam and grist mill (buy a sock of freshly-ground cornmeal to take home) that is one of the most photographed spots in the county; Marshall, a small farming community where you'll find an old-fashioned soda fountain at Spencer's Corner Barn; and Rosedale, where the Civic Center is packed with crafts people, many of them demonstrating their skills. Festivals include: Maple Fair (Feb — Mar), Quilt Show (Aug), and Sorghum-Cider Fair (Sept). As you tour this picturesque county, don't miss the popular local breakfast of biscuits smothered with creamy, sausage-rich gravy.

Tourist Info Ctr, Box 165, Rockville, IN 47872, 317/569-5226.

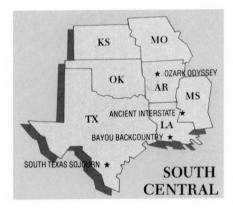

ANCIENT INTERSTATE

Natchez Trace, MS/AL/TN

What began as a wilderness road blazed by Indians and early pioneers hundreds of years ago is today a near-complete 450-mile scenic parkway cutting its way from Natchez, MS to Nashville, TN. The drive, which roughly follows the route of the original Natchez Trace, takes the traveler past primitive Indian dwellings, historical landmarks, nature trails, and recreation areas. In many places, it is possible to walk typical sections of the old trace to get a first-hand look at an old frontier road. Recent excavations have revealed that the trace was populated by humans as long as 8000 years ago. Roadside markers indicate points of interest along the way, such as Emerald Mound in Natchez, the third largest remaining Indian mound in the US. It was built by ancestors of Creek, Choctaw, and Natchez Indians to support their temples and ceremonial buildings. Chickasaw Village in Tupelo (between US 78 and MS 6) is the approximate site of an ancient Indian village. Here, audio-visual presentations and nature trails demonstrate facets of the Chickasaw way of life. Parkway headquarters and Visitor Center are located 5 miles north of Tupelo; facilities include a museum room depicting the history of the area, and information on self-guiding trails, wayside exhibits, and crafts demonstrations along the route.

Supt, Natchez Trace Pkwy, RR 1, NT-143, Tupelo, MS 38801, 601/842-1572.

Cypress Lake, Lafayette, LA

BAYOU BACKCOUNTRY

Lafayette, LA—New Orleans, LA

While US 90 may not be the fastest route from Lafayette to New Orleans, it does offer many interesting diversions. Driving south from Lafayette, you'll pass through the rustic town of St. Martinville — site of the Longfellow-Evangeline Commemorative Area, and the Acadian House Museum—and New Iberia, with the white-pillared splendor of Shadows-on-the-Teche, the antebellum plantation of wealthy planter, David Weeks. The landscape is painted with blossoming azaleas, camellias, and massive oaks draped with Spanish moss. Also in New Iberia is the Konriko Rice Mill, the oldest operating rice mill in America. Continuing south along US 90, you'll arrive at the colorful seaport of Morgan City on the banks of the winding Atchafalaya River. Swamp Gardens is the attraction here, the location of the first Tarzan movie (1917) and accessible via numerous tour boats. The wafting, salt-filled breezes of Houma-Terrebonne (the Good Earth), signal your arrival at the Gulf of Mexico, where the deep-sea fishing is just as superb as the eating at any of the local restaurants. Specialties include oysters, shrimp, crabs, crawfish, and even alligator — all prepared Cajun-style (zesty and spicy).

Office of Tourism, PO Box 44291, Capitol Station, Baton Rouge, LA 70804, **504/383-1825.**

OZARK ODYSSEY

Near Ozark Mountains, AR

The Arkansas River cuts a wide valley between rising bluffs in the shadow of the Ozark Mountains. Highway 7 runs north of the river and, for breathtaking beauty, it makes little difference what time of year you make the drive: In spring, profuse blossoms on the redbud and dogwood trees contrast with the yellow-green of new buds; in summer, hundreds of shades of green line the valleys that are studded with wildflowers; in fall, the hardwoods come ablaze in a myriad of colors; shirt-sleeve days are not uncommon in December and January. From Russelville, follow Hwy 7 north to Dover in the foothills of the Ozarks, and browse through antique shops and flea markets. Continuing north, you'll pass great forest lands bordered by the majestic mountains, seen to best advantage from numerous lookout points. Nature lovers, backpackers, and photographers may enjoy a sidetrip to Fort Douglas—site of Arkansas' largest natural bridge—and Haw Creek Falls, an area of rugged terrain and churning waters on the Big Piney River. Some of the rural, gravel-lined roads may be less than perfect, but the ruggedly beautiful landscape makes the detour worthwhile.

Dept of Parks & Tourism, 1 Capitol Mall, Little Rock, AR 72201, **501/371-1511, 501/371-7777.**

SOUTH TEXAS SOJOURN

San Antonio Area, TX

San Antonio is home to the "Cradle of Texas Liberty"—the Alamo (see Historic Landmarks)—and it is also the launching spot for a scenic and storied drive through southern Texas. Leaving San Antonio, follow I-35 north to TX 46 north, which will lead you to Natural Bridge Caverns, an underground tangle of rock formations and caves which reach a depth of 250 feet, and stretch for more than a mile beneath Texas ranch country. Return to I-35 and continuing north you'll next pass through New Braunfels, a community settled in 1845 by German immigrants. Highlights include a preserved and restored immigrant village, and a "Wurstfest" celebration each November. Head north on River Road from New Braunfels as it parallels the Guadulupe River (great catfish!) to Rte 32 at Sattler. A northwest tack on Rte 32 and three miles west on Rte 1623 at the Blanco River, brings you to the site of 120-million-year-old footprints of a massive Brontosaurus—one of the largest of all dinosaurs. From Blanco, travel north on US 281 to Johnson City, and the working ranch that was known as the Texas White House during Lyndon B. Johnson's administration. Also at the LBJ National Historical Park are the former president's birthplace and grave. The last leg of this drive runs west on US 290 to Fredericksburg, also settled by German immigrants shortly after New Braunfels. Many Old World customs are still in evidence.

Visitor Info Ctr, 317 Alamo Plaza, San Antonio, TX 78205, **512/299-8155, 800/531-5700, 800/292-1010 (in TX).**

Skyline Drive, VA

NORTHEAST

HIGHWAY OF HISTORY

Mohawk Trail, MA

Following a path originally blazed by the Pocumtuch Indians in 1663, this east-west highway (Rte 2) stretches for 63 miles from the Massachusetts-New York line, to Miller Falls on the Connecticut River. From the Mohawk Trail Concert Series at Charlemont in summer, to superb downhill and cross-country skiing in winter, the trail is an avenue to more than 100 attractions—all cloaked in the seasonal beauty of the Berkshire Hills and the Connecticut Valley. Browse in any one of a host of antique shops, art galleries, country stores, flea markets, street fairs, and craft shows, or take in a play at a summer theatre in Williamstown or Greenfield. Natural wonders abound along this route including the view from Mount Greylock at 3491 feet-highest point in Massachusetts, the Bridge of Flowers in Greenfield—a deserted trolley bridge which was transformed into a garden of shrubs and flowers by a woman's club in 1929—and a natural bridge in North Adams with 30-foot marble walls attesting to thousands of years of natural erosion since the ice age. Info booths located along the highway at Williamstown, North Adams, Charlemont, and Greenfield, provide up-to-date reports on local activities.

Chamber of Commerce, 69 Main St, N Adams, MA 01247, **413/663-3735.**

VERMONT VISTAS

Woodstock Area, VT

This 155-mile tour of the Ottauquechee Valley, postcard-pretty at any time of the year, is particularly recommended for viewing fall foliage. Take US 4 east from Woodstock to White River Junction—the spot to sample local maple syrup and other goodies confected from Vermont's famous sweetner, as well as to shop for fine woolen products at local boutiques. Take US 5 north to East Thetford, and after a home-style lunch at a country inn or a leisurely picnic under a sheltering maple tree, continue on VT 113 past the rustic cottages of tiny Post Mills and Chelsea to VT 110, and then head north to Barre. The Rock of Ages (exit 6, I-89) is the site of the world's largest granite quarry; a train ride through the excavation is available in summer, and everyone gets a free granite specimen. US 302 leads you north to the state capital, Montpelier, where the Wood Art Gallery exhibits more than 250 paintings of Thomas Watterman Wood, in addition to representative works of American artists from the 1920s and 1930s. The Vermont State House is an impressive example of Doric and Corinthian architecture, crowned with a 14-carat gold-leaf dome. Take US 2 west to Middlesex, and then VT 100 south to Stockbridge. The landscape is dotted with white-steepled churches, weathered red barns, and green meadows, against a backdrop of snowcapped mountains. VT 107 east will take you to VT 12 south, the final leg of your journey back to Woodstock. Fall foliage conditions: 802/828-3239.

Travel Div, 134 State St, Montpelier, VT 05602, **802/828-3236.**

YANKEE COUNTRY

Hartford Area, CT

This picturesque inland city, plentiful in scenic parks, historic museums, and colonial mansions, is the point of departure for a 90-mile excursion over the rolling hills and flower-dotted meadows of the Connecticut Berkshires. You'll be wooed by roadside offerings along the way — fruit-and-vegetable stands, cider mills, picnic areas, and old-fashioned country inns—as you navigate rural byways flanked by miles of stone walls dating back to the Colonial period. Follow I-91 north to exit 45 at Warehouse Point, home of the Connecticut Electric Railway Trolley Museum with more than 40 vintage trolleys (1892-1947) on display. Take Rtes 140 & 75 west to Rte 20, and follow Rte 20 west to Riverton where a collection of Lambert Hitchcock's famous 19th century furniture is displayed at the Hitchcock Museum. West River Road heads south through the 200-year-old sheltered pines of People's State Forest and into lovely Pleasant Valley where a 680-acre wildlife sanctuary is located with more than 180 species of birds. Follow Rte 181 south to Rte 44, and take Rte 44 east to Avon, home of the Farmington Valley Arts Center. This historic stone building, which served as an explosives warehouse in the Revolutionary War, today houses an art gallery and artists' studios. Return to Rte 44 east, and then follow Rte 10 south to Rte 4 east, which will lead you back to Hartford and complete your loop. On the way back, visit the Noah Webster House and Museum in West Hartford, birthplace of America's first lexicographer.

Div of Economic Dev, 210 Washington St, Hartford, CT 06106, **800/243-1685, 800/842-7492 (in CT), 203/566-3977, -3385.**

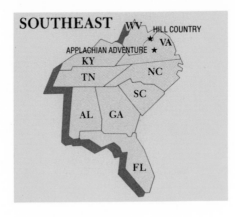

SOUTHEAST

APPALACHIAN ADVENTURE

Skyline Drive, VA

Winding its way for 105 miles along the peaks of the Blue Ridge Mountains through Shenandoah National Forest, Skyline Drive is a nature lover's road. VA 130 east from I-81 will take you across Natural Bridge, a stunning limestone formation rising 215 feet above Cedar Creek, and regarded as one of the great wonders of the world. The speed limit is 35mph along the entire drive, which allows you to appreciate the myriad of wild forest flowers, twisting vines growing over massive overhanging boulders, and trout-brimming streams. Autumn aficiandos are in for a special treat with more than 100 species of tree displaying their fall colors. Enjoy a roadside picnic at any of 75 scenic overlooks; chipmunks, squirrels, white-tail deer, and an occasional bear and bobcat make the park a veritable wildlife sanctuary. More than 400 miles of paths along the Appalachian Trail parallel the drive through the park, and a good starting point for a hike is Skyland at 3860 feet —the highest point on the drive. The trail leads to Little

Stony Man Cliffs — an outstanding vantage point for embracing a panorama of blue mountains, forbidding cliffs, and distant flower-dotted meadows.

Supt, Shenandoah Nat'l Park, Luray, VA 22835, **703/999-2266.**

HILL COUNTRY

Harpers Ferry, WV

With an average elevation of 1500 feet, West Virginia justly deserves its title as the Mountain State. The rolling ridges of the Appalachian Mountains, which traverse the state's eastern third, provide many opportunities for motorists to view the region's spectacular scenery. Driving west on Rte 340 from Harpers Ferry, occupied in turn by both sides during the Civil War, the road winds past battlefields, ruins, and buildings which date back to that historic conflict. Today, the heavily wooded countryside dotted with placid lakes is tranquil and peaceful — a remarkable contrast to the bloodshed and violence which ravaged nearby Antietam where 23,000 casualties were sustained in the famous Civil War battle on September 17, 1862. South on Rte 220, spelunkers will delight in seeing the longest ribbon stalactite in the world at Smoke Hole Caverns (closed mid-Nov — Mar). Continuing south on Rte 28 is the southern branch of the Potomac River which is bordered by quaint farms and rolling meadows. This pastoral setting is in sharp contrast to the breathtaking escarpment of the Seneca Rocks—a massive formation of Tuscarora sandstone rising 960 feet, yet only 15 feet wide at the top! Rock climbers may test their skill by ascending the face. However, the magnificent view from the summit is not denied those without the skills or inclination to climb — a tame pathway also leads to the top. Spruce Knob (4863 feet) is further south on Rte 28 and offers a panorama of nine mountain ranges from its observation tower, but beware: The misshapen spruce trees are evidence of the severity of the winds at this exposed peak.

Trav Dept Program, Charleston, WV 25305, **800/624-9110.**

Blackwater Falls, WV

Chapter 16
FISHING & HUNTING SPOTS

Fishing

Photo: ©SD Dept. of Game, Fish & Parks

Quail Hunting

Photo: David E. Morris

To many hunters and fishermen, the quality of the outdoor experience—man in harmony, as well as in conflict, with nature—and the technical excellence of equipment and technique are as important as the quarry itself. Thus it was that Hemingway's Nick Adams, a young man desperate to heal the wounds of war, sought the remoteness of a northern Michigan forest of sweet ferns and tall jack pines and the challenge of a fast-running trout stream.

Absorbing the first shock of the icy-cold water, he felt the fast current suck at his legs; strung on a thong around his neck was a bottle containing 50 medium brown grasshoppers, caught when the grass was still wet with morning dew; bulging his breast pocket were his fly book and the onion sandwich wrapped in oiled paper ready for lunch; downstream, a mink scampered across a logjam and disappeared into a swamp. Nick was ready—with flyrod, heavy, double-tapered line, leader, and bait, all carefully assembled—to do soul-purging battle with hungry trout. He fished alone because he believed that other fishermen "spoiled" the experience.

It is this experience, when savored alone or enjoyed in good company, that is the essence of the following suggestions. They will take you to those same Michigan northwoods favored by Nick Adams, this time when they are deep in midwinter snow, in search of plentiful snowshoe rabbits. And to Hemingway's own favorite fishing grounds off Key West, where you might hook into a trophy-sized marlin and join a muscle-tearing battle of several hours. In crisscrossing the country with rod and gun, we have attempted to select spots that offer not only a fine experience, but also a good expectation of bagging the quarry.

Many factors affect a person's success: hunting or fishing pressure from other sportsmen, both daily and seasonal weather patterns, always-changing habitats, cyclical population fluctuations, his own ability, and plain old luck. But the areas listed below have, year after year, consistently offered some of the best hunting and fishing in the country.

NORTHWEST

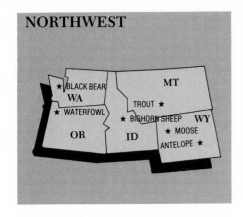

MONTANA RIVERS
(TROUT)
Southwestern MT

No area is blessed with so many world-class trout streams as is southwestern Montana. The Missouri, Yellowstone, Beaverhead, Big Hole, Bitterroot, Gallatin, and Jefferson are all outstanding, but many experts consider the Madison to be the finest trout stream in the world. Rainbow, brown, brook, and cutthroat trout thrive in these pure, icy waters, and fishing is usually best after the spring run-off of snow. Most anglers wade into the fast-moving streams and use fly-fishing tackle; the appropriate type of fly depends on local conditions, and a visit to a nearby tackle shop usually yields wise advice. This region's main appeal is the close proximity of these great rivers. They are located just two or three hours apart, enabling fishermen to hit them all during a week's vacation with little trouble. Regulations vary from stream to stream, so contact the Fish and Game Dept for complete info. Fishing best mid-June–mid-July, and steady through fall.

Montana Rivers, Dept of Fish, Wildlife & Parks, 1420 E 6th Ave, Helena, MT 59620, **406/444-2535.**

TETON NAT'L FOREST
(MOOSE)
Northwestern WY

The Teton Forest north of Jackson is one of the few spots in the continental United States where good moose hunting may be enjoyed. However, it's not easy. When most people think of moose, they envision serene, passive animals munching away on aquatic vegetation. However, during the hunting season, when bulls are in rut, these animals are far from passive; they become very aggressive and sometimes dangerous. Hunters, therefore, must be knowledgeable and experienced. Moose tend to reside in the high country during the early season, and good spots to find them in the mountains are small, open willow marshes that are tucked into the huge pine forests. Then, as the weather turns cold and snow begins to fall, the moose move down to the valleys. There, they are often found by small streams or ponds close to spruce, willow, and cottonwood trees. Guides are required for nonresident hunters, and you must apply for a permit between Jan 1 and Mar 15 of the year you want to hunt. Hunters travel on horseback. Seasons vary depending on zone, but generally range mid-Sept–Dec.

Game & Fish Dept, License Section, Cheyenne, WY 82002, **307/777-7631.**

WYOMING PLAINS
(ANTELOPE)
Central/Eastern WY

Wyoming is an excellent hunting state for many species of game, but for antelope, it is definitely *the* best. Millions of acres of public hunting lands are available, with a choice of public hunting areas. With 325,000 animals, there are more antelope here than in any other state, and more than 100,000 licenses are issued each year—more than the total of all other states combined. Thunder Basin National Grassland (northeast of Casper) contains 600,000 acres and is especially productive. Hunting in Wyoming is done on the vast, open prairies. Hunters drive around in trucks or four-wheel-drive vehicles until they spot a herd; then the trick is to stalk close enough to get a good shot. Stalking skills and long-range marksmanship are vital, since out in the vast, open prairies, there is no place for a hunter to conceal himself. Seasons range mid-Aug–mid-Dec.

Game & Fish Dept, Licensing Section, Cheyenne, WY 82002, **307/777-7631.**

OLYMPIC PENINSULA
(BLACK BEAR)
West of Seattle, WA

The thick rainforests blanketing the western part of this state are the stomping grounds for thousands of black bear. With the highest kill total in the country, about 3000 bears are taken each year; and when they are too populous, special spring and summer seasons are opened. The hunting challenge is magnified in this jungle-like environment because visibility is always poor—especially in the fog and mist so common to this climate. Guides with trained bear hounds are almost a necessity. If the dogs can tree the bear, and if the hunter can keep up with his hounds, he will have a relatively easy shot. Relying on the tenor of their hunting dogs' barks, hunters can tell when a bear is trapped, and then move in for the kill.

Olympic Peninsula, Washington Dept of Game, 600 N Capitol Way, Olympia, WA 98504, **206/753-5707.**

SAUVIE ISLAND
(WATERFOWL)
North of Portland, OR

This island, which is located at the confluence of the Willamette River, Columbia River, and Willamette Slough, encompasses 56 square miles of rich farmland. Heavily cultivated in fields of buckwheat, millet and corn, and blessed with the mild winters common to this region, Sauvie is an ideal winter haven for ducks and geese. All shooting is done by decoying and some hunting parties set out as many as 500 at one time. Anywhere from 250,000 to 500,000 ducks, and from 25,000 to 80,000 geese predominantly Canada and snow geese, winter here. Wigeon and pintails are the main duck species—arriving on Sauvie after leaving Alaska—and they are often joined by mallards migrating from Canada. There are about 35 private clubs, and the Sauvie Island Wildlife Area covers some 12,000 acres. To attract waterfowl, the Fish and Wildlife Commission plants, and then leaves unharvested, about 1000 acres of grain fields. Shooting is consistently good Oct–Dec.

Sauvie Island, Fish & Wildlife Dept, Info & Education Section, Box 3503, Portland, OR 97208, **503/229-5403.**

RIVER OF NO RETURN WILDERNESS
(BIGHORN SHEEP)
Central Idaho Rockies

Many hunters consider a bighorn sheep trophy the "holy grail" of hunting—the ultimate, elusive trophy of a lifetime. And for good reason...you really have to earn that set of horns. This is a hunt only for serious, patient, and skilled hunters. Only a limited number of permits are issued every year (about 125) and it may take years to draw one permit. When you do, it's imperative to be in top physical condition in order to tackle this formidable wilderness area. There are no roads, so travel is done by foot, horseback, or boat, and hunters must cover many miles in the 10,000-foot-high mountains, and be able to make very difficult, 400-yard shots. Realistically, you'll probably get one shot at a ram—and that's it—for your *lifetime*! However, most hunters who capture this elusive prize, consider the long wait and the physical ordeal to be worth it. Season open in Sept.

River of No Return Wilderness, Dept of Fish & Game, 600 S Walnut, PO Box 25, Boise, ID 83707, **208/334-3700.**

Photo: Wyoming Game & Fish Dept., Credit: LuRay Parker

Antelope

SOUTHWEST

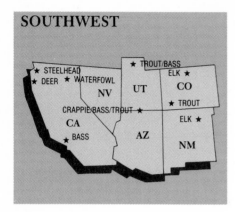

CALIFORNIA RAINFORESTS
(DEER)

Northwestern CA

These rain-drenched forests receive more than 100 inches of precipitation annually and, as a result, the region contains some of the thickest, most impenetrable vegetation found in North America. But, for hunters who are willing to endure an arduous foray into this forbidding terrain, the rewards can be spectacular. This is the habitat of the largest black-tailed deer in the United States. In fact, five California counties—Siskiyou, Trinity, Shasta, Humboldt, and Mendocino—have produced more record-book blacktails than the states of Oregon and Washington combined. Two major tactics are used: 1) driving, when several hunters move in a parallel line and drive the deer to a waiting shooter; or 2) setting up a stand along a known deer trail, hoping a deer will pass underneath. Much of the blacktail hunting here is done on national forests. The main firearms season extends Aug–Nov, depending upon zone.

Dept of Fish & Game, 1416 9th St, Sacramento, CA 95814, **916/445-3531.**

LAKE CASITAS (BASS)

North of Los Angeles, CA

Familiar as the site of the rowing competition during the 1984 Summer Olympics, Lake Casitas is also one of the prime bass fishing lakes in the country...and arguably one of the most scenic. It borders the Los Padres National Forest, and is nestled at the base of the magnificent Santa Ynez Mountains known as the home of the California condor, a huge, vulture-like bird with a wing spread of up to nine feet. The lake's main appeal, though, is in the fact that a fisherman has a chance to catch the next world-record largemouth bass. (The record of 22 pounds 4 ounces has stood for more than 50 years). In 1980, a fisherman pulled a 21 pound 3¼ ounce bass from Lake Casitas — the second-largest bass ever taken. Good places to fish are the many coves along the mainland and Main Island, the lake's biggest island. Wren's Nest and Dead Horse Canyon are two excellent inlets worth trying. Mid-Feb–mid-Apr is the best time to fish. This is a magical time on the lake, when the chaparral vegetation is lush and green after the winter rains.

Casitas Municipal Water Dist, 11311 Santa Ana Rd, Ventura, CA 93001, **805/649-2233.**

KLAMATH RIVER
(STEELHEAD)

Far Northwestern CA

The northern tip of California remains virtually unchanged since the days of the Gold Rush. It's still a land of immense pine forests and sharply rising, jagged mountains. The Klamath River, which runs for about 200 miles from Iron Gate Reservoir at the Oregon/California border to the Pacific Ocean, slices through this beautiful wilderness, and provides some of the finest steelhead fishing on the West Coast. Fishermen use tough, wooden drift boats to negotiate the fast-moving current. Five-pound steelhead swimming upstream to spawn are normally caught —although some 10-pound fish are landed every season, and most anglers catch at least a dozen fish a day, and are allowed to keep three. The river's last few miles are spectacular as it cuts through majestic redwood forests. The best period to fish is Oct–mid-Apr.

Shasta-Cascade Wonderland Assn, 1250 Parkview Ave, Redding, CA 96001, **916/243-2643.**

TULE LAKE NAT'L WILDLIFE REFUGE
(WATERFOWL)

Northern CA

The Oregon-California border is the site of some of the finest waterfowling in the West. In season, when the first pallid light of dawn begins to brighten the eastern sky, thousands of geese and ducks leave Tule Lake and fly west to feed in the grainfields surrounding nearby Klamath Lake. Hunters who station themselves in a blind on 1000-foot-high Sheepy Ridge—between the two lakes—can intercept the birds as they fly overhead. Most of the ridge is open to the public; some of it is controlled by private hunting clubs. Season open Oct–Nov.

Refuge Mgr, Tule Lake Nat'l Wildlife Refuge, Tulelake, CA 96134, **916/667-2231.**

FLAMING GORGE RESERVOIR (TROUT/BASS)

Northern Tip of UT

This man-made lake, formed in 1962 by a giant dam blocking the Green River, is well-named. In early morning and twilight, the steep canyon walls are indeed aglow in resplendent shades of red and orange. The reservoir is huge: 91 miles long and covering more than 65 miles of surface. It extends from pine-covered mountains in the southern part of the area to plains and desert in the north. Beneath the dam, the Green River offers exceptionally good rainbow trout fishing. The lake itself boasts some of the finest trout fishing in the West. In fact, the world-record brown trout, weighing 33 pounds 10 ounces, was caught in Flaming Gorge in 1977. The biggest browns are found in Hideout Canyon, Sheep Creek, and Lucerne Valley at the southern end of the lake. Besides the big browns, lake trout, rainbow trout, and smallmouth bass are also found. Fishing is done in the reservoir itself throughout the year; spring and fall are the most productive seasons.

Div of Wildlife Resources, 1596 W North Temple, Salt Lake City, UT 84116, **801/533-9333.**

Photo: John F. Reginato

Steelhead Fishing

LAKE POWELL
(CRAPPIE/BASS/TROUT)
AZ/UT Border

About 20 years ago, Glen Canyon Dam was built on the Colorado River, creating a huge reservoir: Lake Powell. In intervening years, this 180-mile-long lake has developed into the best fishing lake in the Southwest. It offers visitors superb fishing for many species, Grand Canyon-like beauty, and privacy (there are more than 2000 acres of shoreline). Striped bass, largemouth bass, bluegills, walleyes, and northern pike are all found in the lake, but Powell is best known for its superb crappie fishing and it's not unusual to catch 100 crappies in a single day. Because this lake is so huge, many people rent houseboats and spend several days exploring the many coves and harbors. There are five marinas with complete facilities (guides available): Wahweap, Rainbow Bridge, Bullfrog, Halls Crossing, and Hite.

Del Webb Rec Properties, Box 29040, Phoenix, AZ 85038, **800/528-6154.**

VERMEJO RANCH (ELK)
Northeastern NM

For years, this once-private 450,000-acre ranch has been considered one of the elite elk-hunting spots in North America. A few years ago, the Pennzoil Company turned over about a quarter of this property to the US Forest Service. This is now public land and there are about 2500 elk on the newly opened property—dotted with hundreds of lakes and streams, forests of aspen and conifers, and many alpine meadows that the elk use to feed. Since the herd is carefully controlled, many of the bulls reach record-book sizes. However, obtaining the prize requires rigorous work because hunting is done at high altitudes and in heavy timber. The season usually runs Oct–Dec. The best hunting is in early Oct, when bulls are in rut.

Dept of Game & Fish, Villagra Bldg, Santa Fe, NM 87503, **505/827-2923.**

SAN JUAN BASIN (ELK)
Near Durango, CO

This region offers hunters a fine opportunity to enjoy a classic American big-game hunt. Encompassing part of the west slope of the Rockies, the San Juans have changed little since the days of Kit Carson and Jim Bridger. This is some of the steepest, roughest country in the West. Elk love it. Unless you live in this vicinity, it's best to hire a guide who will supply vehicles, horses, tents, pack boxes, camping gear, and food. Particularly good areas to hunt are the Sand Creek, Turkey Creek, and Buckles Lake territories. Guides take clients, via horseback, to hunting areas at or near timberline amid dense spruce and fir, in forested areas dotted with some big, open meadows. This is not a trip for a novice or for the timorous, since hunters may expect to spend several days on the trail. Only experienced, well conditioned sportsmen are likely to succeed. The best times to hunt are very early and late in the day, when elk come out of the meadows to feed. The 10-day elk season is normally held late Oct.

Div of Wildlife, 6060 Broadway, Denver, CO 80216, **303/297-1192.**

SUMMIT COUNTY (TROUT)
West of Denver, CO

This region is probably best known for its skiing; it contains such well-known ski resorts as Breckenridge, Copper Mountain, and Keystone (see Winter Sports Of All Sorts). But many of the pure, icy mountain streams and lakes in this area also provide some of the finest trout fishing in the West. Experienced fly fishermen will especially enjoy casting for the brown, brook, and rainbow trout found in these waters. In Dillon Reservoir — the largest lake in the region—anglers sometimes catch 20-pound brown trout, while 10-pounders are common. Giberson and Heaton bays are especially productive in Dillon Reservoir and the Blue River is one of the best trout streams for catching lunker brown trout. Ten Mile Creek, Snake River, Arkansas River, Meadow Creek, Miner's Creek, French Creek, Indiana Creek, and Pennsylvania Creek also offer fine fishing. Other good lakes include Wheeler and Cataract. In addition, many small beaver ponds near Copper Mountain Resort hold plenty of small fish that are fairly easy to catch, and are ideal hotspots to take youngsters. Best fishing in July, Aug, and early Sept. Guides available but not necessary for experienced anglers.

Summer the Summit, Box 267, Dillon, CO 80435, **303/468-6607.**

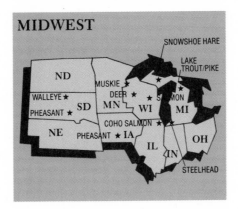

LAKE OAHE (WALLEYE)
Central SD

In the late 1950s and early 1960s, the US Army Corps of Engineers put up a series of dams on the Missouri River as it flowed through the central part of South Dakota. This created several lakes: Oahe, Sharpe, Francis Case, and Lewis and Clark. All provide fine fishing for walleyes and other species, but Oahe—the biggest—probably offers more facilities and opportunities for nonresidents. Oahe is 230 miles long, and starts just north of Pierre and runs all the way to Bismarck, ND. Fishing improves year-by-year, and the outlook is promising. Less than 700,000 people live in South Dakota, and since Oahe alone covers about 375,000 acres of water, there are plenty of spots to fish. In spring and fall, the tributaries of the lake offer the best walleye fishing. In summer, the southern, deeper end of the lake is the place to go. Oahe also contains plenty of northern pike, rainbow trout, white bass, and chinook salmon.

Game, Fish & Park Dept, 445 E Capitol, Pierre, SD 57501, **605/773-3485.**

Pheasant Hunting

SOUTH DAKOTA PRAIRIES (PHEASANT)
South-Central SD

During the 1940s, South Dakota offered what may have been the best pheasant hunting ever experienced by mankind. Then the birds' numbers dropped dangerously low in the 1960s due to drought and intensive farming. But in the last few years, the pheasants have been making a strong comeback, and now this region provides some of the best pheasant hunting in the country (second only to Iowa). Since Lake Oahe — a massive reservoir on the Missouri River — was built in the early 1960s, farmers have had an irrigation source that enabled them to grow corn, wheat, and milo. As grainfields flourished, so did the birds. Much of this land is open to the public and many landowners gladly give permission to hunt on their property after the first week or two of the season, generally held mid-Oct–early Dec.

Game, Fish & Parks Dept, 445 E Capitol, Pierre, SD 57501, **605/773-3485.**

IOWA (PHEASANT)
East-Central/Southwestern

This state is a mecca for pheasant hunters. More ringnecks (about 4 million) live in Iowa than in any other state, and the countless cornfields provide perfect habitat for the birds. Early in the season, hunters should try to get permission from private landowners to hunt on their property. Late in the season, hunters will enjoy good hunting by choosing one of the state's 250 public hunting areas. Especially fine spots are Riverton Wildlife Unit, Rathbun Wildlife Area, Elk Grove Wildlife Area, Otter Creek Marsh, Ricke Lake, Walters Creek, and Meadow Lake. Hunting is often a group affair, as hunters line up in a straight line and walk through the cornfield stubble, hoping to flush the birds ahead of them. Such events are always festive, party-like occasions. Season generally runs early Nov–early Jan.

Conservation Comm, Wallace State Office Bldg, Des Moines, IA, 50319, **515/281-5145.**

BOULDER JUNCTION (MUSKIE)

Northern WI

Boulder Junction is called the Muskie Capital of the World, and for good reason. There are 195 lakes within a nine-mile radius of town, and more muskellunge, that hard-fighting giant of North American gamefish, are landed in these waters than anywhere else in the world. Catching these fish, though, is always extremely difficult. The muskie is the biggest, meanest, smartest and, perhaps, the most elusive freshwater gamefish in North America. Even anglers who spend several days on the water are lucky to catch one and that, of course, is the wonderful, seductive attraction of this fish. Landing a tenacious muskie, which can attain a length of eight feet, is one of fishing's greatest accomplishments. There are many guides in the area, or you can simply rent a boat at one of the scores of marinas in town and try your own luck.

Chamber of Commerce, Box 286, Boulder Junction, WI 54512, **715/385-2400.**

WISCONSIN (DEER)

Northern Region

The northern section of Wisconsin, with its blend of farmland and dense forests, contains some of the largest white-tailed deer in the country. If you're going after true, trophy-class whitetails, this is the place to go…and has been for a long time. In fact, the No. 1 Boone and Crockett record-book whitetail (typical antlers) was taken in 1914 in Burnett County on the Mississippi River. Wisconsin grows mammoth deer because it provides an ideal habitat —lush fields for feeding and dense woods for bedding. Forests of oak, hickory, and walnut offer good cover and also yield natural food in the form of a huge crop of nuts. Additional food is obtained from cultivated fields that annually produce fine crops of corn, wheat, and soybeans. As a result, the deer here grow to massive proportions, and some weigh more than 300 pounds. Most sportsmen set up stands along deer trails. Much hunting is done on private land, and because of an overpopulation of deer that eat and damage crops, farmers generally grant permission quite readily. Many state and national forests are also open to hunters.

Dept of Natural Resources, Box 7921, Madison, WI 55707, **608/266-2621.**

WASHINGTON ISLAND

(SALMON)

Tip of Door County Peninsula, WI

King (chinook) salmon have made a strong comeback in the Great Lakes, and perhaps the best fishing for this species is done in Lake Michigan near Washington Island, WI. During the peak season, a fisherman can expect to catch several 20-pound-plus chinooks in one day. The best fishing occurs from early July to late August, when tens of thousands of the great fish gather in the deep channels between the many islands in the area. Trolling is the primary technique. Depending on water temperature (they prefer 50°F) the salmon are caught in depths ranging from as little as 25 feet to as much as 200 feet. The best fishing is done either in very early morning or at

Hunting

dusk. In spring, these waters also provide superlative fishing for brown trout. During slow fishing periods, the wonderful scenery can help compensate for the lack of action as the boat parallels many heavily-forested, unpopulated islands. Deer sometimes are seen along the shoreline, while an occasional eagle soars overhead. Ferries leave for the 45-minute trip to Washington Island about every hour from Gills Rock at the tip of the peninsula (see Scenic Drives).

Mike Lane Charters, 410 Northview Rd, Green Bay, WI 54301, **414/465-8848.**

CHICAGO SHORELINE

(COHO SALMON)

Southern Tip of Lake Michigan

In the 1960s, Lake Michigan was hurting. Gamefishing was virtually dead and commercial fishing had entered a serious decline. Lamprey eels, entering the lake from the ocean via the St. Lawrence Seaway, were insidiously attacking and destroying the lake's populations of lake trout and whitefish. And at the same time, the lake was inundated by huge schools of alewives—tiny fish of no commercial value that washed ashore in the millions, befouling beaches. Then came a noble experiment, the implantation of Pacific salmon. It worked. The salmon thrived in the lake and grew fat on alewives. Meanwhile, the incursion by lamprey was controlled by selective chemical kill-off. As a result, the beaches were clean again, and an exciting new brand of sportfishing was born in Lake Michigan. Even a few hundred yards off the Chicago skyline, anglers can now enjoy outstanding fishing for coho and chinook salmon. Cohos are the most common of the two species, and they usually weigh between eight and 10 pounds. Occasionally, a fisherman will land a much-larger—and rarer—chinook, which can tip the scales at 25 pounds. Fishermen who own boats can use one of the public launching ramps run by the Chicago Parks District. Or, many charter boats are available for half- or full-day trips at Burnham Harbor, next to Meigs Field.

Chicago Sportfishing Assn, 25 E Washington St, Ste 823, Chicago, IL 60602, **312/922-1100.**

UPPER PENINSULA

(SNOWSHOE HARE)

Northern MI

By early January, many hunting seasons are closed. But in northern Michigan, when heavy, midwinter snow blankets the quiet forests of the Upper Peninsula, this is the peak time to hunt snowshoe rabbits. Michigan's northern cedar and balsam swamps hold huge populations of these tasty game animals. Much of this region is state and national forest land, so anyone can hunt on it. Best hunting spots are Ottawa National Forest (with 886,000 acres) and Hiawatha National Forest (839,000 acres). The UP is a five-hour drive from Detroit, and well worth it. There is little pressure because hunters usually have the vast forests to themselves. The season runs early Oct–Mar.

Dept of Natural Resources, PO Box 30028, Lansing, MI 48909, **517/373-1263.**

ISLE ROYALE NAT'L PARK (LAKE TROUT/PIKE)

Northern MI

This Lake Superior island is one of the truly unique ecosystems in the country, holding viable populations of both wolves and moose. With some of the country's best fishing for northern pike and lake trout, anglers can fish from canoes on several lakes: Wood, Richie, Siskiwit, Todd Harbor, and Duncan Bay (Wood and Richie are probably the best). Most fishermen fly in from Houghton, and stay on the island for a week, trying a new lake every day. In these untouched, seldom-fished lakes, 20-pound pike and 25-pound lake trout are plentiful. And since fewer than 200 fishermen seek these fish every season, they are anxious to hit anything thrown to them. A special highlight of an Isle Royale fishing trip is to hear, as you sit around a campfire in the evening, the eerie howling of timber wolves. The best months to fish are May, June, and Sept. (See Island Escapes.)

Northland Outfitters, Hwy M-77, Germfask, MI 49836, **906/586-9801.**

MICHIGAN CITY

(STEELHEAD)

Lake Michigan Shoreline, IN

At first glance, the last place one would expect to find world-class steelhead fishing is in Lake Michigan near the heavily industrialized cities of Gary, East Chicago, and Michigan City. Yet the very southern tip of this Great Lake is the home of the Skamania strain of steelhead, which was imported from Washington State in the early 1970s. These fish vary in weight from 12 to 20 pounds, and are considered the largest, toughest-fighting strain of steelhead. Indiana was the first state in the Midwest to import this strain, and although other Midwestern states (notably Michigan and Wisconsin) are following suit, most of the best fishing is still just off Indiana's 50 miles of shoreline. Most fishermen rent charterboats and troll for the fish, and the current record is 24 pounds 13 ounces, set in 1983. Once you hook one, anticipate a ferocious fight, and expect to lose about as many fish as you land. Mid-June–mid-Aug is the prime season.

Convention & Visitors Bureau, 1503 S Meer Rd, Michigan City, IN 46360, **219/872-5055.**

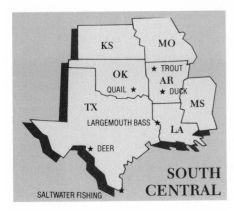

SOUTH CENTRAL

WHITE RIVER (TROUT)

Northern AR

This is perhaps the finest trout fishing stream in the South. Every spring, as the dogwoods bloom, painting the banks with pastel color, trout anglers gather along 100 miles of fishable water in search of trophy brown trout. In fact, the second-largest brown trout ever caught (33 pounds 8 ounces) was taken here in 1977. Located below Bull Shoals Reservoir, the White's water flow is controlled by the dam. During the low-water (nongeneration) periods, fishermen are particularly successful if they find deep pools where trout have congregated. The section of the river from Bull Shoals Dam to Cotter normally provides the largest fish—browns in the 25-pound class. More are caught on live crawfish or peeled crawfish tails fished on the bottom. Many fishermen prefer to float down the river on a small boat, enjoying the scenery of the picturesque Ozarks. Various docks and ramps are found at Bull Shoals Dam, Cotter, Buffalo City, Norfork, and Calico Rock.

Game & Fish Comm, 2 Natural Resources Dr, Little Rock, AR 72205, **501-223-6300.**

BAYOU METO WILDLIFE MANAGEMENT AREA (DUCK)

Southeast of Little Rock, AR

This area of pinoak bottomlands and willow sloughs offers the best "flooded timber" duck hunting in the country. Although several species of duck are present, mallards are predominant. Every October, about a third of the WMA is purposely flooded by the opening of sluice gates and levees, allowing hunters to enter the flooded timber by small boats. The great appeal of this region is that decoys aren't needed; hunters, wearing camouflage clothing, simply wade in and take a stand, using duck calls to attract their quarry. Arkansas offers a long season, from fall through spring, although shooting is allowed only in the morning. Because this area is so huge and hard to navigate, a guide is recommended (general map and guide available).

Game & Fish Comm, 2 Natural Resources Dr, Little Rock, AR 72205, **501-223-6351.**

TOLEDO BEND RESERVOIR (LARGEMOUTH BASS)

LA/TX Border

This lake is the largest man-made body of water in the South, and the fifth-largest in surface in the US—covering 185,000 acres. It was formed by the dam on the Sabine River, and creates part of the boundary between Texas and Louisiana. Toledo Bend's miles of standing timber provide a perfect habitat for huge, largemouth bass. Five-pounders are commonplace, and 10-pound fish are sometimes taken. In fact, many national bass fishing tournaments are held here each year. The weather is always warm, and since the lake is enormous, anglers can usually find a solitary spot to fish. Many launching sites and marinas.

Sabine River Authority of Texas, Toledo Bend Div, Rte 1, Box 270, Burkeville, TX 75932, **409/565-2273.**

SOUTH PADRE ISLAND (SALTWATER FISHING)

Southern Tip of TX

This is one of the greatest saltwater fishing spots in North America, due mainly to the variety of fishing available. Surf casting, fishing from piers and jetties, or deep-sea fishing are all effective techniques. Offshore charterboats take anglers out into the Gulf of Mexico to catch kingfish, dolphin, bonito, sailfish, marlin, barracuda, blackfin tuna, red snapper, scampi, and grouper. Surf fishermen take redfish, speckled trout, sand trout, sheepshead, croaker, skipjack, drum, and flounder. In the Laguna Madre channel between the island and the mainland, fishermen catch tarpon, mackerel, ling, jackfish, pompano, blue runner, and jewfish. The fishing seasons vary widely, depending on the migrating patterns of various species, but excellent fishing for at least some species is available every month of the year.

Tourist Bureau, PO Box 2095, South Padre Island, TX 78597, **512/943-6433.**

OKLAHOMA PLAINS (QUAIL)

Southeastern OK

The finest quail hunting in the country can be found in the Sooner State where, in most years, more bobwhite quail are shot than in any other state. In a single season, hunters sometimes bag more than three million birds. The best hunting for these small, plump game birds is done in the southeast and, although much of this region is private, landowners generally are very cooperative and in many cases encourage people to hunt on their land. In addition, there are many state-run lands open to the public, such as certain sections of the Ouachita National Forest. The season generally runs late Nov–mid-Feb.

Dept of Wildlife Conservation, Box 53465, Oklahoma City, OK 73152, **405/521-3851.**

DEL RIO (DEER)

Southern TX

There are more than one million deer in Texas, which makes bagging an average-sized animal relatively easy. But for hunters who want a true trophy whitetail, a private ranch in far southern Texas is the place to go. Here, ranchers hire professional biologists to keep the deer herd balanced so that conditions are optimum for bucks to grow to large sizes. This land of rolling plains, thornbrush, and scrub oak is cut by deep canyons. Deer often hide in these chasms, especially in thickets along dry washes. Hunters employ an unusual tactic: they stop and throw rocks into these gullies to startle the deer and drive them out into the open. In this region, 10- and 12-point bucks are commonly taken. Dolan Creek Hunting, Inc offers guided hunts on five huge private ranches. Though costs are expensive (between $1000 and $1500), hunters enjoy a 90% success ratio. The season runs mid-Nov–early Jan.

Dolan Creek Hunting, Inc, Box 420069, Del Rio, TX 78842, **512/775-3129.**

FISHING & HUNTING SPOTS

NORTHEAST

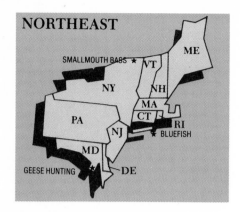

SMALLMOUTH BASS ★

ME

VT

NY

NH

MA

CT

PA

RI

★ BLUEFISH

NJ

MD

GEESE HUNTING ★

DE

season. The numerous corn, wheat, and soybean fields on the Shore provide ample food for the birds. In addition, the thousands of ponds and tidal rivers along the Chesapeake Bay ecosystem supply ideal nesting grounds. Most shooting is done in standing blinds or pit blinds placed in favorite feeding fields. The birds rise up after resting during the night, and fly out to feed in the grainfields. A good decoy spread will usually lure the birds in close. Since much of the hunting is done on private farmlands, it's a good idea to book a trip in advance with a guide who has access to these lands. Hunting is especially good Nov and Dec.

Office of Tourist Dev, 45 Calvert St, Annapolis, MD 21401, **301/269-3517.**

EASTERN SHORE
(GOOSE HUNTING)
East of Chesapeake Bay, MD

Maryland's Eastern Shore is arguably the finest Canada goose hunting area in the world. Everywhere one looks, for hours at a time, great V-shaped flocks of geese glide across the sky. Sometimes thousands can be seen at one time. Most hunters make their three-bird limit in a couple of hours. The reason the "Shore" is a goose hunter's paradise is because this region is the chief wintering spot for most of the Canada geese that live along the East Coast; more than 500,000 birds reside here during the hunting

THOUSAND ISLAND AREA *(SMALLMOUTH BASS)*
St. Lawrence River, NY

The stretch of the St. Lawrence River from its originating point at Henderson Bay in Lake Ontario downstream to Alexandria Bay (a span of 50 miles or so) is arguably the finest smallmouth bass fishing region in the United States. The area is aptly named, for there really are more than a thousand islands of all shapes and sizes everywhere you look (see Island Escapes). It's such a huge region that good fishing spots abound. Fishermen will catch smallmouths over shoals, rock piles, gravel bars,

ridges, ledges, and other structures, and anglers usually have little trouble reaching their six-fish limit. The smallmouths here are huge for the species: five-pound fish are frequently landed. Although there are innumerable islands to fish, particularly good areas are Wolfe Island, Bayfield Island, Hinckley Flats, Feather Bed Shoals, Carleton Island, Linda Island, Hill Island, and Wellesley Island.

Chamber of Commerce, 403 Riverside Dr, Clayton, NY 13624, **315/686-3771.**

MONTAUK *(BLUEFISH)*
Eastern Tip of Long Island, NY

The turbulent waters off Montauk Point, where Long Island Sound meets the Atlantic Ocean, unquestionably offer the finest bluefish fishing in the country. Because of its location, Montauk is a crossroads for many species of migrating fish. In late summer and early fall, huge schools of blues begin their migration southward and pass right by Montauk Point. Most fishing is done on large charter boats or party-boats, and anglers troll "umbrella rigs" that have about 10 colored worms on 10 separate hooks. It's not unusual for one boat to take 25 15-pound bluefish in a single outing. The Cartwright Grounds, about six miles south of the Point, are especially productive. Striped bass and bluefin tuna are also plentiful during the fall.

Montauk Marine Basin, c/o Carl Darenberg, W Lake Dr, Box 610, Montauk, NY 11954, **516/668-5900.**

Geese

Photo: Robert C. Fields

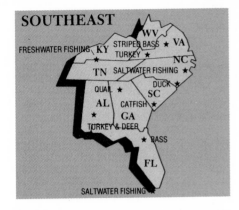

SOUTHEAST

FLORIDA (BASS)

Central and Northern Regions

Year in and year out, this state offers the best bass fishing in the United States. Its warm climate and nutrient-rich waters allow largemouth bass to grow larger here than anywhere else. It's practically impossible to pin down specific waters because the bass fishing is good almost *anywhere*. Small ponds and canals hold fish just as big as in larger lakes, but many of these smaller waters are on private land. However, several good-sized lakes do offer consistently fine fishing: Lake Tohopekaliga, Cypress Lake, Lake Hatchineha, the Harris chain of lakes, Lake Eustis, Lake Dorr, and Lake Yale — all near Orlando; Orange and Lochloosa lakes south of Gainesville; the lower reaches of St. Johns River from Sanford up to Astor; Lake Okeechobee near Winter Haven; Rodman Reservoir near Orange Springs; Crescent Lake near Crescent City; and Hurricane Lake in the panhandle. Basically, you are within an hour's drive of a top-flight bass water from nearly any major Florida city. In the hot, steamy Florida summers, the fish are sluggish — best fishing is in fall and spring.

Game & Fresh Water Fish Comm, 620 S Meridian St, Tallahassee, FL 32301, **904/488-1960.**

KEY WEST

(SALTWATER FISHING)

Tip of Florida Keys

Its always-balmy temperatures and the surrounding clear, turquoise waters make Key West one of the more pleasant spots to visit in the United States (see Island Escapes and Man-Made & Natural Wonders). This region also offers anglers exciting saltwater fishing in an incredible variety. Anglers interested in strapping themselves in a fighting chair to do battle with large gamefish, find the Gulf Stream waters a haven for marlin, sailfish, wahoo, tuna, and dolphin. The nearby coral reefs contain grouper, barracuda, mackerel, kingfish, and snapper, while, as a bonus, the many wrecks (some dating back to pirate days) claimed by the reefs around Key West, now are home to amberjack, cobia, and giant grouper. The flats (very shallow waters) around Key West also attract tarpon, and is one of the best areas for catching permit fish in the Western Hemisphere. Some of the most productive fishing is enjoyed Nov–Apr, an ideal time to visit this sub-tropical city, America's most southerly, when much of the country is suffering blizzards and subzero temperatures.

Chamber of Commerce, 402 Wall St, Key West, FL 33040, **305/294-2587.**

KENTUCKY AND BARKLEY LAKES

(FISHING)

KY/TN Border

These long, narrow "sister" lakes were created when the Tennessee Valley Authority dammed the Tennessee River (to form Kentucky Lake) and the Cumberland River (to form Barkley Lake). Today, the two lakes hold huge numbers of crappies, bass, catfish, sauger, and bluegills. If you want to be sure that you catch a lot of fish (but probably not a trophy) this is the place to go. This area is especially suited to family recreation. It's easy for youngsters to catch fish; there is a wide variety of campsites, motels, and trailer parks, as well as many other recreational opportunities. In most cases, fishing is best in spring and fall when the fish are found closer to shore. The spring crappie run is especially noteworthy; there is a 60-fish limit, and many anglers catch that many in a single day. In October and early November, the limestone outcroppings and underwater gravel bars at the mouths of bays are fine places to find Kentucky (spotted) bass. Dock pilings, stumps, and fallen trees are likely to shelter fish. Fishermen from shore should try those areas. During the hot, muggy summer, anglers will have the most luck on a boat in the middle of the lake, fishing in deeper water and holes.

Public Service Dept, Land Between The Lakes, Tennessee Valley Authority, Golden Pond, KY 42231, **502/924-5602.**

WESTERVELT LODGE

(TURKEY AND DEER)

West-Central AL

This private plantation, which is situated along the Tombigbee River flood plain, contains 11,000 acres of pine ridges and hardwood bottomlands—prime turkey habitat. During the spring turkey season, hunters staying at the lodge accompany a guide who takes them to their own 1000-acre private hunting area (usually a small clearing deep within the woods). Then they try to "call" male gobblers within shooting range. Westervelt also offers a three-day turkey school that is considered the most comprehensive in the country. During a typical two-day session, guests stay in modern rooms within the lodge, with three meals served each day. Westervelt also offers deer hunting in the fall. Some of the biggest racks in the state have been taken here, and hunters have an excellent chance of getting their buck. The turkey season runs mid-Mar–late Apr; the deer season mid-Nov–Jan. Turkey and deer hunts cost about $350 per person, per day.

Westervelt Hunting Lodge, PO Box 2362, Tuscaloosa, AL 35403, **205/556-3909.**

JEFFERSON & WASHINGTON NAT'L FORESTS (TURKEY)

Western VA

This beautiful wilderness, located in the picturesque Blue Ridge Mountains in far western Virginia, is the epicenter of more than two million acres of prime turkey hunting. It's all public land, but because of the vastness of this area, turkey hunters have these woods pretty much to themselves. Shooting hours run from 30 minutes before dawn to 11am. Hunters, wearing camouflage clothing, call to the birds, trying to get them close enough for a shot. Cover in this extremely hilly terrain is mostly oak and hickory, with a lot of low brush. Upon request, the offices of the state forests will provide excellent maps. Spring season mid-Nov–mid-May; fall season mid-Nov–mid-Dec.

Jefferson Nat'l Forest, PO Box 241, Roanoke, VA 24002, **703/982-6274.** *Washington Nat'l Forest, Federal Bldg, Harrisonburg, VA 22801,* **703/433-2491.**

SMITH MOUNTAIN LAKE (STRIPED BASS)

West-Central VA

Nestled in the foothills of the Blue Ridge Mountains, this 20,000-acre lake contains what probably are the most productive striped-bass waters in the East. Each year, anglers catch at least 500 striped bass weighing 15 pounds or more. Many others, in all probability, are never reported. The best fishing is enjoyed Mar—June, usually at twilight, when the sun sets over the Blue Ridge foothills, and the stripers come close to the surface to feed on baitfish. This is truly exciting fishing: schools of stripers will literally create white water as they rip through the huge schools of baitfish on the surface. Within a compact area of an acre, it is possible to encounter a school of 1000 stripers — and catch one on every cast. There are also walleyes, muskies, and smallmouths in the lake.

Saunders Marina, Rte 1, Huddleton, VA 24104, **703/297-7532.**

Saltwater Fishing

Photo: Fla. Keys Tourist Dev. Council

Photo: David E. Morris

Deerhunting

SANTEE COOPER LAKES *(CATFISH)*

Southeastern SC

The twin lakes of Marion and Moultrie are rightly nick-named, "Catfish Capital of the World." The second-largest blue catfish (67 pounds 7 ounces) and the world-record channel catfish (58 pounds) were taken from these waters, which encompass more than 171,000 acres. There is also excellent fishing for striped bass, largemouth bass, and panfish. The catfish tend to stay toward the bottom, and they favor dark water. During a bright midday sun, they will often take refuge at depths of around 50 feet. The biggest fish are taken in the main lake, where knowledge-able fishermen look for submerged old ditched riverbeds or holes that dip 35 to 50 feet under the surface. At dusk, fish move up to feed on the flats, which are only 20 feet deep, and respond well to live minnow baits. Prime fish-ing mid-Apr–mid-Oct.

Wildlife & Marine Resources Dept, PO Box 167, Columbia, SC 29202, **803/758-0059.**

BURNT PINE PLANTATION *(QUAIL)*

North-Central GA

Though fine quail hunting can be experienced throughout many regions of the country, this private game ranch is something special. It covers nearly 20 square miles of woodlands, interspersed with one-acre plots of rye and wheat grass. The plantation's open fields and fencerows are managed exclusively for bobwhite quail and mourning doves. At times, these fields are controlled-burned to make room for new cover for the birds. Hunters can either bring in their own bird dogs, or hire a guide and his dogs from the plantation. Quail may be hunted Oct-Feb, doves in Sept. Hunters stay either in separate cabins or in rooms at the main lodge, and three meals a day are included in the package. Deer can also be hunted at Burnt Pine—they are plentiful, but only average in size.

Burnt Pine Plantation, 291 Pat Mell Rd, Marietta, GA 30060, **404/953-0326.**

Photo: David E. Morris

OUTER BANKS
(SALTWATER FISHING)

Far Eastern NC

The long, narrow Outer Banks offer fishermen a unique opportunity. Nowhere else on the East Coast does the Gulf Stream—the warm ocean current that attracts hundreds of species of fish—come so close to a land mass. As a result, fishing is available for many interesting species of fish. The area is probably best known for its surf fishing; anglers can wade right out into the surf and haul in 20-pound bluefish and stripers (in late fall) and big, 40-pound channel bass (in spring). In Pamlico Sound, to the west, which separates the Outer Banks from the mainland, fishermen can catch weakfish, flounder, and cobia. On the ocean side, just off shore, boat fishermen can land king mackerel, false albacore, and tarpon. In the Gulf Stream itself lurk hard-fighting, huge gamefish—white marlin, blue marlin, dolphin, and tuna. There are many wrecks along this stretch of coastline, and boat fishermen above these wrecks can catch amberjack, barracuda, sailfish, and kingfish. Surf fishing is best in spring and fall. Ocean fishing is good every season except winter.

Fishing Unlimited, RR1 Box 600, Nags Head, NC 27959, **919/441-5028.**

LAKE MATTAMUSKEET NAT'L WILDLIFE REFUGE *(DUCK)*

Eastern NC

This 50,000-acre refuge near Swanquarter, is the winter-ing home of more than 20 species of duck, including pintails, wigeon, mallards, black ducks, teal, wood ducks, shovelers, canvasbacks, redheads, scaup, and ringnecks. The mild winter temperatures and ocean climate (the ref-uge borders Pamlico Sound) keep temperatures above freezing most of the winter. Hunters set up blinds around many of the thousands of tiny ponds, lakes, and flooded cropfields that draw the ducks. Hunting is centered around the lake itself, which is 18 miles long and five miles wide. About 40,000 acres of it are very shallow, no more than two feet deep. Sometimes 3000 ducks can be found in one large pond. Hunting is done mid-fall–Jan.

Refuge Mgr, Lake Mattamuskeet Nat'l Wildlife Refuge, New Holland, NC 27885, **919/926-4021.**

Chapter 17

HIGH ADVENTURE

Skydiving

Photo: U.S. Parachute Assn., Credit: Paul Proctor

There's adventure in the air—in many cases, quite literally! Perhaps it's because we need the fillip of calculated risk as relief from humdrum jobs. Maybe the pioneer spirit that drove our forefathers westward is resurfacing. Whatever their motivation, millions of Americans are seeking thrills from skydiving, white-water' river running, spelunking, and other pulse-quickening pursuits.

There often is a serenity about those who return from a high-adventure vacation—whether it's a day outing or a 28 day expedition. It comes from knowing that they have challenged Mother Nature in rushing rapids or on snow-capped peaks—and won. Who could ever forget the blood-pumping experience of jumping into freefall from a plane at 12,000 feet or careening around a racetrack at 125 mph on one of the fastest sets of wheels on earth? Yes, danger is involved, and one should be apprised of it when contemplating one of these trips. However, most of these experiences are appropriate for average citizens, as long as they are in reasonably good health and are equipped with the determination to push themselves that extra step, to test their mettle against some of the most awesome recreational challenges.

Usually, the rewards of high adventure are well worth the risk and effort. The wilderness experiences chosen for inclusion in this book often have multiple attractions. A heart-pounding run down the wild Colorado River provides glimpses of our Indian and pioneer history amid the rugged and blazing Rocky Mountain canyons. Those who take an Outward Bound winter dogsledding expedition return home with extra self-confidence and the strong character built from working with others and from taking off into the wilderness solo. And after wafting through the air in a hot-air balloon, champagne glass in hand, you'll never again look at a sunset as just the end of another day.

So whether you choose to scale the Adirondack's Mt. Marcy, to soar from the towering dunes of North Carolina strapped to a hang glider, or to explore the murkily mysterious netherworld of Cumberland Caverns on all fours, let your spirit soar!

NOTE: An international scale classifies rivers from I-VI in order of difficulty. We have included their ratings, where applicable, and the numbers generally translate to be: I = Beginner, II = Advanced Beginner, III = Intermediate, IV = Advanced, V = Expert, and VI = Unnavigable. However, ratings do vary according to season, region, and local interpretation.

NORTHWEST

[Map showing: MOUNTAINEERING, WA, WILDERNESS EXPERIENCES, MT, RAFTING, OR, RAFTING, KAYAKING/RAFTING, RAFTING, ID, COVERED WAGON TRIPS, WY]

COVERED WAGON TRIPS

Tetons, WY

For families who want to trace the path of our western pioneers amid the beautiful Tetons, Wagons West offers covered wagon treks through an historic region of Teton National Forest, Jackson Hole, and the Wind River Range. These covered-wagon odysseys are two days (one night), four days (three nights), or six days (five nights) and appeal to vacationers of all ages. Tours simulate the frontier atmosphere by sticking to unused roads where it's unlikely that other campers will be encountered; however, certain amenities are provided that Jim Bridger and other 19th-century fur trappers never heard of—such as rubber tires and foam-padded seats on the replica wagons that are pulled by teams of gentle horses or mules. Wagon-train members can take a turn at escorting the caravan on horseback and take guided horseback treks into the majestic Wyoming Tetons and Rockies foothills. Choice of sleeping accommodations lets travelers set their own level of comfort: they can sleep under the stars, in a deluxe teepee, or in their own wagons. Camaraderie is strong as latter-day pioneers gather to appreciate the sight of a soaring eagle, to spoon up open-air meals from the chuckwagon, and to enjoy the evening wagon circle, campfire, and singalong. Cost: $175 (2 days); $420 (6 days).

Wagons West, LD Frome, Outfitter, Afton, WY 83110, **307/886-5240.**

RAFTING

Middle Fork of the Salmon River, ID

One of the most famous white-water rivers in the US drops nearly half a mile over the most navigable stretch, with nearly 100 rapids punctuated with stretches of calm water. Fed by mountain springs and melting snow, the crystal clear water passes through the most extensive wilderness areas south of Alaska. Camping areas for the exclusive use of this outfitter range from forested spots to sandy beaches; many feature hot springs, hiking trails, and abandoned cabins. Fishing for salmon and other species is legendary. Dubbed "America's Switzerland," this wilderness is heavily populated by mountain sheep, deer, elk, bear, and enough western species to delight the most discriminating birdwatcher. High Adventure River Tours offers an extensive six-day trip along the Middle Fork ($795). Reserve well in advance.

High Adventure River Tours Inc, Box 581, Jerome, ID 83338, **208/543-4521.**

RAFTING

Lochsa River, ID

The Indian name Lochsa means "rough water," and that is an understatement. Just north of the better-known Salmon River, the Lochsa offers white-water thrills at their most challenging. Although the river is relatively short, not even extending beyond the Idaho panhandle, it offers mile-after-mile of explosive thrills. Even experienced river runners should not attempt this stretch of churning water on their own. Those who can wrench their attention from the white-water task at hand may catch sight of trophy-sized bull elk as well as bear, deer, moose, and goat. Available craft include oar rafts (rowed by guides), paddle rafts, and inflatable kayaks. The outfitter supplies transportation from city of departure, all meals, waterproof bags and camera boxes to protect personal gear, and wetsuits to protect runners from the Lochsa's icy clear water. Offered are one-, two-, and three-day trips ($55-$275/person) late May-Aug 10, for persons older than 14.

River Odysseys West, Rte 12, Box 854A, Spokane, WA 99203, **509/534-2024.**

WILDERNESS EXPERIENCES

Clearwater River, ID

If the big, national wilderness outfitters seem a little too impersonal for you, Leo Crane's operation may provide just the right, intimate introduction to Idaho's expansive wilderness. Visitors to the remote Clearwater River area, known as the "Elk Capital of the World," are treated to once-in-a-lifetime views of grazing elk herds as well as cougars, bears, and meandering deer. Birdwatchers should keep an eye on the pristine sky for a glimpse of majestically soaring eagles, and anglers will delight in bountiful catches of rainbow trout and Kokanee salmon in

Kayaking

the rivers, streams, and mountain lakes. Five-day pack-trips tailored to anglers or photographers, traverse spectacular mountains ($450/person, $800/10 days). Riding experience is not necessary. A number of other fishing packages are available. Remote island cabins, accessible only by boat, can be rented for $300 for the first week, $150 the next. Boats can also be rented. Fishing licenses available upon arrival ($14.50 for 7 days).

Clearwater Outfitters, 4088 Canyon Creek Rd, Orofino, ID 83544, **208/476-5971.**

MOUNTAINEERING

Northwest WA

Based on the edge of the North Cascades, this tour operator offers some of the most exciting and demanding mountaineering experiences in the Northwest. Trips include Alpine backpacking, bicycling, and mountaineering packages that take adventurers through some of the most beautiful wilderness in the continental US. Most are strenuous, meant only for those in good shape who can run two miles easily (smokers discouraged). One of the most popular trips is the Stehekin Sojourn, a five-day summer backpack trip that covers 50 miles over snow-capped peaks, through awesome cedar forests, to the Alpine village of Stehekin, ending with a boat ride down scenic Lake Chelan. Also offered are a Pacific Crest llama trek, and a Pasayten Wilderness Journey that draws photographers from coast to coast. Seminars (5-25 days) are offered on mountaineering, snow and ice climbing, rock climbing, and trekking and climbing in the Caucasus. For advanced skiers, Liberty Bell's heli-skiing tours (fly-in by helicopter) are not to be missed, featuring runs of 2500-4000 vertical feet and the only glacier skiing in the US. Summer vacationers can also take one of the outfitter's river rafting, kayaking, or boardsailing trips, ranging from rapid-running on the Methow River to tranquil paddling around the San Juan Islands (see Island Escapes).

Liberty Bell Alpine Tours, Star Rte, Mazama, WA 98833, **509/996-2250.**

KAYAKING/RAFTING

Illinois River, OR

"Untouched" is the word for the Illinois River and its Kalmiopsis Wilderness Area environs, and those who seek solitude in remote and rugged southern Oregon won't find a better spot for white-water adventure. One of the few true wilderness rivers on the West Coast accessible by raft, the Illinois is relatively short, but the thrills during its brief springtime running season are anything but. Runners on the Illinois will encounter few examples of the human species: a private boater or two may appear, but only three outfitters are authorized to run trips for the public on this river. Sundance Expeditions Inc is one of them, and this outfitter encourages white-water enthusiasts to work with its staff to custom-tailor trips designed to make the most of your visit to this pristine wilderness of virgin forest. Three-and four-day "Spring Thriller" trips available mid-Apr–mid-May ($335–$395). Also offered are comprehensive basic, intermediate, and advanced kayak programs, which run Apr–mid-Sept and teach kayaking on the Rogue, Smith, and Umpqua Rivers (3-9 days, $190–$855 per person).

Sundance Expeditions Inc, 14894 Galice Rd, Merlin, OR 97532, **503/479-8508.**

Mountain Climbing

RAFTING

Rogue River, OR

Among the first of seven rivers designated "wild and scenic" by Congress in 1968, the Rogue is rich in history as well as white-water thrills. Zane Grey once fished here and his cabin still stands at Winkle Bar. Much as they did more than a century ago, people still pan for gold along stretches of this stream, which extends all the way to the Pacific. The river is also noted for steelhead and rainbow trout. For the river runner looking for a challenge, the Rogue is hard to beat. It tosses rafters through churning rapids and then drifts them gently downstream; it plummets them over a 12-foot vertical ledge, and rockets them toward huge, menacing boulders. Patrons of this outfitter rest for the next day's rapid running in rustic lodges or at even more rustic campsites in the shadow of the towering canyon walls (average canyon depth, 3000 feet). A variety of guided tours, including summer rafting trips, fall steelhead-fishing parties, and winter fishing trips, are offered.

River Adventure Float Trips, PO Box 841, Grants Pass, OR 97526, **503/476-6493.**

SOUTHWEST

[Map of the Southwest region showing: UT, CO, CA, NV, AZ, NM with activities marked: RAFTING, LLAMA PACKING, SOARING, WILDERNESS EXPERIENCES, HORSEBACK, SPORTYAKING, MOUNTAINEERING, SKYDIVING, SPELUNKING, WILDERNESS HIKING]

RAFTING

Klamath, CA

This is the wild-water river that can convert the armchair adventurer into an avid river-runner. Northern California's Klamath River has the spectacular canyons, shoreline features, and pulse-quickening rapids that have made it a favorite among West Coast white-water enthusiasts, but it also features short rapids and initially easy paddling—perfect to transform a beginner into an experienced runner. And its warm water is a bonus for tyros and pros alike. Abundant wildlife along the shore includes bear, deer, osprey, otter, and blue heron, and there is even a rare bald-eagle nesting area. Paralleling the tough-to-easy versatility of the popular Klamath River itself, these trips offer the option of riverside camping, rustic cabins, or deluxe lodging, complete with pool overlooking the river. Three-day guided tours of the Klamath in one-man inflatable kayaks offer beginners the security of expert guides and the adventure of truly "paddling one's own canoe" (about $300/person).

Orange Torpedo Trips, PO Box 111, Grants Pass, OR 97526, **503/479-5061.**

SPELUNKING

California Caverns/Moaning Cavern, CA

Two prime examples of California mountain caverns, California Caverns and Moaning Cavern, offer spelunkers a variety of subterranean thrills and a unique view of history. Spelunkers can follow in the footsteps of John Muir, Bret Harte, and Mark Twain on the "wild cave" tour of California Caverns, which involves climbing rocks, scaling a 60-foot ladder, squeezing through small, unlighted passageways, and crossing 200-foot-deep lakes on rafts—an extremely strenuous tour. For a $49 fee, cavers are supplied with coveralls, gloves, and miner's hat with light. The five-hour tour begins at 9:00am daily June-Oct and weekends in Nov. Participants must be in good health, not pregnant or overweight, and at least 12 years old. Less strenuous "Trail of Lights" tour is available ($4). Located 10 miles east of San Andreas, near Mountain Ranch, CA in the heart of Calaveras County. Moaning Cavern, first explored by gold miners in 1851, lies in the heart of California's historic Mother Lode area and can be explored by serious spelunkers on the $25 Adventure Tour. Featured are an optional 200-foot rope descent through the cavern's main chamber and strenuous exploration of the lower passages and rooms — crawling through tight spaces, climbing a 70-foot vertical ladder, and examining human bone fragments still embedded in the limestone from ancient accidental falls into the cavern. The three-hour tour is available only by reservation to people in good health, age 12 and older. Located 9 mi N of Columbia State Park (see Ethnic & Historic Villages) on Parrotts Ferry Rd in Vallecito.

California Caverns & Moaning Cavern, PO Box 78, Vallecito, CA 95251, **209/736-2708.**

SKYDIVING

Perris, CA

If you're the kind of adventurer with your head in the clouds, here's the spot to head for a complete skydiving experience. Since the first sport parachutists began competing at the Cleveland Air Races more than half a century ago, the ranks of weekend enthusiasts have burgeoned. Today, there are approximately 500 parachuting clubs scattered throughout the US, with participants from all walks of life. Perris Valley caters to would-be parachutists and experts, and those at all levels of experience in between. Novices start with a thorough ground course that allows students to train and jump on the same day (time and weather permitting). Advanced instruction teaches experienced jumpers how to parachute to a target and how to perform acrobatic maneuvers in freefall. For those without "feet of clay" the very first jump can be made in accelerated freefall, from as high as 13,000 feet. For jumpers interested in preserving their feats for posterity, Perris Valley provides a color videotape of first jumps made on weekends; a staff photographer is also on hand. Class times change from season to season; call or write for reservations and fees. Located close to southern California's major entertainment centers and 1½ hours east of LA Int'l Airport.

Perris Valley Paracenter, 2091 Goetz Rd, Perris, CA 92370, **714/657-8727.**

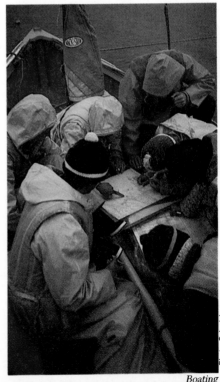

Hang gliding

WILDERNESS EXPERIENCES

San Francisco, CA

From raft trips down dozens of famous rivers, to backpack or horseback trips in nearly every major wilderness area; from mountain trail maintenance expeditions, to bike treks: nothing else in America can compare with the scope of wilderness experiences offered by this world-famous and ecology-minded organization. Sierra Club trips appeal to people of all interests and at all levels of outdoors skill; there is virtually a trip for everyone who wants to revel in the beauties of our natural landscape and learn about conservation and natural history. Forays into varied wilderness areas include backpacking trips that require 65 miles of hiking per week (around 80 different trips are offered), Alpine and backcountry base-camp trips that offer mountain climbing and fishing, burro trips that cover rugged territory 8000-11,000 feet above sea level (no children under seven), water trips that range from tranquil canoe paddling to rough white-water rafting, and more. There are also less demanding bicycle, junior backpacking, and family trips, plus service trips, during which one can return something to the wilderness that provides so much pleasure. Destinations range from a canoe and backpack trip to the unique Pine Barrens of southern New Jersey, to a burro trip to the lakes and peaks south of Mt Whitney in Sequoia Park for a week of canyon and peak climbing. (The Sierra Club also offers trips to sites in Alaska, Hawaii, and abroad.) Short paragraphs describing available expeditions fill a 100-page book. Fees range from less than $100 per person to thousands of dollars. The best way to find out what it's all about is to become a Sierra Club member (dues start at $29).

Sierra Club, PO Box 7959, San Francisco, CA 94120, **415/981-8634.**

RAFTING

Tuolumne River/Kings River, CA

The rivers of the Sierras are so diverse in natural wonders that it's no easy task to single out one for the best river running. We can, however, point to two that offer some of the wildest rides available in California. The Tuolumne River, situated between Modesto and Yosemite National Park, is often touted as the "Mercedes-Benz of Sierra rivers," and this superlative is well deserved. White water that ranges from Class II to Class V rages ever downward, dropping an average of 40-45 feet per mile, and rushing past the wildflower-studded hills forested with oaks and evergreens that have contributed to this river's 1979 recommendation for National Wild & Scenic River status. While the Kings River, southeast of Fresno in Kings Canyon, may come in second to the Tuolumne in difficulty of rapids (the Kings rapids range from Class III-IV), it makes up for it in size and speed. This largest of Sierra rivers becomes huge during spring runoff, with fierce currents and waves reaching 10 feet. Among outfitters serving these rivers, Zephyr offers one- and two-day trips on the Kings for $65 to $160 per person May-Aug; (experienced runners of 15-55 years only during May 15-June 15 spring runoff); and two- and three-day trips down the Tuolumne Apr-Oct for $225-$315 per person.

Zephyr River Expeditions, PO Box 3607, Sonora CA 95370, **209/532-6249.**

WILDERNESS HIKING

Superstition Wilderness, AZ

(See under Washington, DC.)

HORSEBACK MOUNTAINEERING

San Juan Mountains, CO

(See under Washington, DC.)

WILDERNESS EXPERIENCES

Denver, CO

Courses given by the Colorado Outward Bound School can prepare you for a lifetime of adventuring. As the oldest and largest of the five US Outward Bound schools, the Colorado school has served more than 35,000 people since its formation in 1961 and continues to expand its programs, designed to build character and confidence during hazardous wilderness situations. Courses are conducted mainly in the Rockies and the Southwest, in deserts, on mountains, and on white-water rivers; programs are offered for youngsters (14-15 years), college students, adults, and corporate and youth groups. Courses run from four days to three months and take place in all seasons: white-water rafting and river wilderness courses in summer, ski mountaineering in winter, canyonlands backpacking and climbing in spring and fall, and more. The 18-day ski mountaineering course (minimum age 16) is the most physically demanding and takes participants from 10,000-foot-high Leadville Mountain Center in the Rockies through the rugged territory of the Continental Divide. Students learn to build a snow cave, take off for a two- or three-day solo communion with nature, and end the trip with a six- to 10-mile marathon. Reserve well in advance.

Colorado Outward Bound School, 945 Pennsylvania, Denver, CO 80203-3198, **303/837-0880.**

RAFTING

Colorado River, CO

Satan's Gut, Last Chance, Funnel Falls — these aptly named rapids reflect the wild and dangerous character of America's favorite wild river. In fact, the Colorado is so rough in spots that veteran river runners may be surprised to learn that even beginners can navigate some stretches. While many outfitters serve this mighty river, Colorado Adventures Inc. offers one of the best selections of Colorado River runs. White-water enthusiasts can choose from one- to five-day trips of varying difficulty, May-Sept. One of the most popular trips — a one-day jaunt that serves as an ideal introduction to white water — takes runners through typical Rockies backcountry and whips them through narrow rock canyons, into a winding canyon floor, and back into the narrows over moderate rapids. The scenery is so gorgeous that many beginners end the day vowing to become lifetime river runners. Anyone over age five can take this run (perfect for families), because guided oarboats are offered as well as self-paddled boats. Also for ages five and over, another trip begins near the river's headwaters and crashes through redrock canyons rife with golden eagle and redtailed hawk. For big white water, try trips through Westwater and Cataract canyons, both of which feature glimpses of ancient Indian history. One-day trips run from $44 per person, five-day trips from $510.

Colorado Adventures Inc, PO Box 773088, Steamboat Springs, CO 80477, **303/879-2039, 800/332-3200 (in CO), 800/332-2439.**

Llama Packing

LLAMA PACKING

Clark, CO

Home Ranch, near Steamboat Springs, is not for "dudes." True, each of the hand-built cabins for 20 on this 650-acre ranch is equipped with a hot tub, and there are so many amenities that patrons of this former cattle ranch can plan a very comfortable vacation. But Home Ranch is unique in that it also provides a friendly South American llama for anyone who wants to take a wilderness packtrip into the surrounding Rockies. Llama packtrips, which must be booked separately, are four nights, five days long and begin on Mon during summer months. Once the llamas are packed, a guide and cook lead up to six persons to a base camp in the Mount Zirkle wilderness area, northeast of the ranch, where the elevation is 9000-10,000 feet. The view of surrounding peaks, snow-capped year-round, is spectacular, as is the verdant base camp territory, thick with rainbow-hued wildflowers all summer long. The cook and guide provide everything needed, leaving packtrippers free to take advantage of the fabled mountain-lake fishing and vigorous hiking. For those who want to sample some of everything the rugged West has to offer, there's also horseback riding, trout fishing, hiking, and winter cross-country skiing over 18 miles of groomed trails.

Home Ranch, PO Box 822T, Clark, CO 80428, **303/ 879-1780.**

SOARING

Boulder, CO

The pleasures of soaring span the generation gap. Children can learn to solo at age 14, and of the 16,000 enthusiasts associated with the Soaring Society of America, a good many are grandparents. Whatever their age, flyers will find that the Boulder, Colorado area has excellent soaring conditions throughout the year. The Cloud Base, Inc., located at the municipal airport two miles from downtown Boulder, offers full soaring services, including instruction, introductory flights, quality sailplanes, towing services, and cross-country flights. Newcomers to soaring can expect to spend about $1500 learning to fly

gliders; power pilots with a private license can get a private glider rating with at least 10 solo flights, which will run about $600. In this most spectacular of settings, one can soar over the easy terrain of the huge sandstone slabs called the Flatirons, or in the shadow of the Rockies situated to the west. One of the best "waves" (winds that rise upward after buffeting the mountains) found anywhere in the world is generated by the Arapahoe Peaks of the Front Range during Sept-Apr, and some of the best "thermal lifts" (rising warm air) occur Mar-Sept.

The Cloud Base, Inc, Airport Rd, Boulder, CO 80301, **303/530-2208.**

RAFTING

Green River, UT

As notable for its Indian and frontier history as for its intermittent stretches of white water, the Green River is most easily run under the leadership of a licensed guide. (An extensive list of outfitters and guides is obtainable at the address below.) Without one, it is necessary to obtain a permit (given by lottery). Applications must be received by March 1. In addition to the many rapids along this stretch of the Green River, there are interesting geological formations in the canyons-literally something to see around every bend. Look for old mine shafts and the remains of a ferry that operated until 1952 at Sand Wash. Archaeology buffs will find many signs of the Fremont Indians who lived in the area AD 900-1275, including some of the most elaborate petroglyphs (rock carvings) in Utah. Mule deer and other big game can be found here, in addition to chukar partridge, ducks, geese, coyotes, bobcats, and a variety of fish. The flavor of the Old West pervades the river area; the cowboy in all adventurers will love to explore McPherson Ranch, said to have been a stopover for cohorts of outlaw Butch Cassidy.

US Dept of the Interior, Bureau of Land Mgmt, Moab Dist, Price River Resource Area, PO Drawer AB, Price UT 84501, **801/637-4584.**

Mountaineering

RAFTING

Colorado River, UT

For an introductory taste of white-water adventure, Tag-A-Long Tours guides vacationers on a one-day trip down the mighty Colorado (see also Colorado River ,CO). Vacationers visiting the Canyonlands National Park area can boast back home that they've rafted one of the nation's great white-water rivers — without risking life and limb. This is an adventure for beginners who have only about eight hours to spare, and the "moderate" rating of the rapids along this stretch of the Colorado makes it perfect for families with little river-running experience. This veteran outfitter (the only one authorized by the National Park Service for both land and river trips in Canyonlands National Park), picks rafters up at Moab campgrounds or motels, provides them with life vests and watertight cases for personal gear, and launches rafts upstream from Moab into calm water. Soon the pace picks up, as experienced boatmen guide the craft through some of the best white-water wilderness in the West. Intermittent stretches of calm water allow for picture-taking, exploring, and swimming stops, where adventurers can take in ancient Anasazi Indian ruins and natural wonders that range from mesas to sheer cliff walls. Cost: $29.50; under 17 $21.75 (includes picnic lunch).

Tag-A-Long Tours, 452 N Main St, Moab, UT 84532, **801/259-8946.**

SPORTYAKING

Green, San Juan & Dolores Rivers, UT/CO

If the word "sportyak" conjures visions of an athletic beast of burden, anyone who sees this newly popular river craft for the first time will be convinced it is a strange breed indeed. While sportyaks have been used for river expeditions since 1963, they are only now coming into wide use by recreational river-runners, who find their unsinkability, sturdiness, and rigidity perfect for white water. The small (seven- to eight-foot-long) skiff is to this day the smallest craft ever to navigate the Grand Canyon. Fastwater Expeditions offers trips down the Green, San Juan, and Dolores Rivers in southeastern Utah and southwestern Colorado (near Lake Powell and the "Four Corners" junction of UT, CO, AZ, and NM) exclusively in sportyaks for those who like their river running fast and furious. Trips on these Colorado River tributaries cover 100 miles of the Green through Desolation and Gray Canyons or 85 miles of the San Juan in Utah. Dolores River runs are "specials only," scheduled when the river is not being diverted for irrigation and conditions are just right (for qualified Fastwater Expeditions veterans only). Seven-day San Juan River trips are $625 per person (May and June); nine-day Green River trips are $750 per person (June-early Sept); 10- and 12-day tours on the Green run from $825 to $985 per person.

Fastwater Expeditions, PO Box 365, Boulder City, NV 89005, **702/293-1406.**

MIDWEST

SPELUNKING

Wyandotte Cave, IN

Wyandotte has one of the largest underground mountains of any known cave in the US. You can see it on the tourist-oriented two-hour tours through lighted passageways that leave every hour on the hour during business hours. But serious spelunkers will want to make reservations for the five- or eight-hour guided tours that lead through non-commercial areas of the cave. These tours offer spelunkers a real challenge with several long crawls and some climbing. Spelunkers will get a much more detailed view of a paradigm of Indiana's limestone cave formations on the extended tours, including rare, twisted helictites and other unusual formations. Carbide lights are prohibited, but lanterns are provided. For prices and other information, call or write the address below. Located south of Hwy 64 on Rte 62 not far from the Ohio River.

Wyandotte Cave, Leavenworth, IN 47137, **812/738-2782.**

SKYDIVING

Sandwich, IL

The danger inherent in plummeting from a plane at 3000 feet is at once the appeal and the deterrent to aspiring skydivers. Well, Skydive Sandwich!, boasting state-of-the-art training facilities and a staff that includes world record holders and national champions, claims to take the risk out of parachuting and leave only the excitement.

Ultralights

Offering both first-jump and advanced instruction, Skydive Sandwich! allows students to jump the first day, equipped with static lines and radio instruction during descent. Beginners take a three hour videotape class (followed by a 10-page exam) which includes close-up pictures of students dangling from airplane struts at 3000 feet, and rare footage of parachute malfunctions which were actually staged by seasoned veterans in order to teach students how to handle emergencies. Four more static line jumps qualify learners for freefall (complete with "first freefall" certificate), which can be immortalized on videotape for $45 to $210. Also available is a freefall program, featuring jumps from 11,000 feet with parachutes opening at 5000 feet and a gliding descent about six minutes long. Just 60 miles west of Chicago, the school holds first-jump courses every Sat, Sun, and hol at 9:00am as well as weekday instruction by appointment. Make reservations for weekends or weekdays in advance. Fees depend upon learning level.

Skydive Sandwich! Parachute Ctr, Inc, Rte 34, Skyline Center, Sandwich, IL 60548, **815/786-8200.**

BALLOONING

Bolingbrook, IL

Imagine yourself wafting over the prairie, champagne glass in hand, basking in the golden warmth of sunset or sunrise. If your definition of adventure includes such romantic details, Illinois Balloons, Inc has the trip you seek. The company, the oldest of its kind in Illinois, features the services of chief pilot Russ Hardy, recipient of the highest distinction for pilot achievement (level VII) and takes passengers up in the air at sunrise and two hours before sunset every day of the year (weather permitting) for 60- to 90-minute rides. For those who yearn for the controls, there's balloon-pilot training. Illinois Balloons attempts to schedule your flight (booked two weeks in advance) for the departure site (Clow Airport or Barrington Hills) closest to you and will call booked passengers a couple of hours ahead of departure to confirm that weather conditions (clear skies, three miles minimum visibility, light winds) are optimum. Per passenger costs are $100 on weekdays, $120 on weekends, and a prepaid $35 deposit will not be refunded to no-shows. Excluded are those under age 15 and over 75 and anyone weighing in excess of 240 pounds; also, no physically handicapped passengers, or women more than three months pregnant.

Illinois Balloons, Inc, PO Box 1458, Bolingbrook, IL 60439, **312/739-0400.**

ULTRALIGHTS

Aurora, IL

If you are awed by the enormity of today's jumbo jets, here's a type of aircraft that may amaze you with its *miniscule* dimensions. These midgets of powered-flight are called ultralights, and some one-seater models can be as light as 250 lbs with wingspans as short as 30 feet. At Wheatland Airport, 40 miles southwest of Chicago, the Ultralight Air Company operates three intersecting 2000-ft grass runways for these small, humming craft. This seemingly primitive airbase has become a midwestern mecca for ultralight enthusiasts. During the peak flying season (May-Oct), the airport buzzes with activity as aviators of all ages, from all walks of life, take to the sky in tiny, brightly-colored aircraft. Although pilot's licenses are not mandatory for some sizes and models of ultralights, UAC requires all prospective pilots to complete a hands-on training program—for beginners or experienced flyers. The pinnacle of the sport is designing and/or building your own ultralight craft (following safety specifications), and the expert staff at UAC will examine and test-fly your handiwork. For the uninitiated or curious, a two-passenger model is available at the airport for demonstration rides, and aficianados say that once you've been bitten by the bug...you'll be back for more!

Ultralight Air Company, 1214 S 5th St, Aurora, IL 60505, **312/851-5597.**

BALLOONING

Muscatine, IA

Up, up in the air with a bottle of champagne and a soaring heart—what could be more exciting? Nothing, according to American Balloon Services Inc., founded and operated by Tom Oerman, full-time balloonist and world duration record setter. Humans first took to the sky on Nov 21, 1783, when two men ascended in a hot air balloon in Paris. For the better part of two centuries, ballooning was pretty much reserved for the rich, the obsessed, and the weird. But times have changed. By the late 1970s, a surge of interest in the sport had greatly increased the number of licensed balloon pilots. Today, there are nearly 3000 FAA-certified hot air balloons operating in the country. For those who want to try their hand at ballooning, American Balloon Services offers a pilot-training program and an ongoing schedule of passenger flights. Conditions permitting, some flights even end with an exciting "wet" landing on the Mississippi or other rivers.

American Balloon Services Inc, 113 Park Ave, Muscatine, IA 52761, **319/264-1878.**

Scuba Diving

RAFTING

Wolf River, WI

The Wolf is probably the most famous white-water stream in the Midwest and, unique among most rivers in the area, there is always enough water for small rafts. The beautiful Wolf was at the top of the original list of 64 rivers chosen for "wild and scenic" status but has never been included in the system; fortunately, this wild habitat that is home to blue heron, eagles, ospreys, deer, beaver, and mink will be protected by the state's ongoing purchase of all Wolf River frontage. The exceptionally clean water (some say it is even safe to drink) between Hollister and Markton is most popular but can be overcrowded during spring and summer weekends. Drops are about 12 feet per mile and current approaches eight mph. Rapids in this boulder-strewn river, with international ratings of II-III, are runnable from the time the ice melts to about late Oct, and most rafting runs are 10 miles long, take four to six hours, and are suitable for anyone over 12. A number of commercial outfitters supply rafts and gear for about $12/day per person. Wolf River Lodge outfits rafters for runs in the Langlade County segment of the river. To the south, the river is steeper and more difficult, but here runners can use only the Menominee Indian Reservation outfitters because they own the land and therefore have a monopoly on the raft trips. Anyone can raft the Wolf in relative safety, but experts advise that only those with considerable experience in canoeing and kayaking should opt for those types of craft. Wolf River Lodge offers canoe and kayak schools five days a week, plus a 10-hour weekend course, that will prepare canoeists and kayakers for the Wolf.

Wolf River Lodge, Inc, White Lake, WI 54491, **715/882-2182.**

SPELUNKING

Wind Cave Nat'l Park, SD

Here's a cave, operated by the National Park Service, where you can walk and observe or crawl and explore—via special four-hour spelunking tours ($5 per person). Tours include an orientation and safety discussion before entering the cave, and actual time underground is about three hours. Spelunking tours are usually conducted mid-June–mid-Aug only. Those who choose this tour over the guided tours will spend most of their subterranean time on hands and knees, some of it on the stomach, and should plan to have a change of clothes (no shower facilities available). The pre-spelunking discussion introduces the group to the fascinating geological features of this 60-million-year-old cave. Rare views are afforded of cave formations such as "boxwork" and "popcorn," and of unusual formations that resemble animated figures. Although pioneering spelunkers are making headway into the far recesses of Wind Cave, there are still more than 1000 passages that have never been explored. Reservations are suggested but cannot be made more than a month in advance. Restricted to people in good physical condition over age 13 (14 to 17-year-olds must have parents sign a release). (See Nat'l Parks & Monuments.)

Wind Cave Nat'l Park, Hot Springs, SD 54447, **605/745-4600.**

DOGSLEDDING/ MOUNTAINEERING

Long Lake, MN

Anyone who has heard the "Call of the Wild" and yearns to answer it should contact Voyageur Outward Bound, one of five Outward Bound Schools in the US (see also Colorado Outward Bound School). While various seasonal courses are offered as far north as Canada and as far south as the Rio Grande in Texas, the unique focus of this school is wintertime adventure. In keeping with the worldwide Outward Bound philosophy, this school has designed a wealth of challenging experiences for those who want to brave the elements, build character, and learn to work as part of a team. Adventurous dog-sled and ski expeditions take students of the wilderness into the great north woods for a trip reminiscent of those undertaken by 18th-century fur trappers. By the end of an eight- to 21-day trek along the Minnesota/Canada border, groups of 8-10 could hold their own with the likes of Sergeant Preston of the Yukon, building lasting skills in working with dogs and sleds, snowshoeing through virgin powder, cross-country skiing over frozen tundra, and safely crossing icy rivers and streams. The dogsled expedition is also available to youth with educational and motivational problems (28 days), and to the physically or developmentally disabled (8 days). Fees for the dogsled expedition (those over 15 only) run from $575 to $1500 per person. Reserve well in advance. Other winter courses take students canoeing, backpacking, and desert hiking to the Rio Grande River in Texas and to the Minnesota/Canada border area.

Voyageur Outward Bound School, Box 250, Long Lake, MN 55356, **612/473-5476, 800/328-2943.**

RAFTING

Superior Boundary Waters, MN

(See under Washington, DC.)

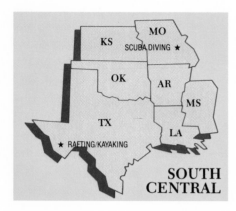

SOUTH
CENTRAL

RAFTING/KAYAKING

Canyons of the Big Bend, TX

This historic river forms the border between two cultures —the US and Mexico—and the resultant area diversity can be seen at its best on one of Outback Expeditions' canoe, kayak, or raft trips. The more remote sections of the Rio Grande are protected by US National Parks and Wild & Scenic River status, and natural wonders along the way include canyons with walls rising as high as 1800 feet, cane thickets, desert, bluffs, and rock outcroppings. Waterfowl and small game can be seen, and fishing is good. Rafting, canoeing, and kayaking trips take adventurers to Colorado Canyon (one or two days), Santa Elena Canyon (two or three days), Mariscal Canyon (three or four days), Boquillas Canyon (three or four days), or Pecos River (canoes) (four to seven days); longer trips (300 miles) can be arranged upon request. Spring and autumn bring the most favorable river-running conditions, with rapids of advanced beginner to intermediate rating (Class II-III). During high-water periods, rafts or kayaks will be used; low water conditions are appropriate for canoes. Anyone who foregoes a boatman to paddle his/her own craft gets a 10-percent discount.

Outback Expeditions, PO Box 44, Terlingua, TX 79852, **915/371-2490.**

SCUBA DIVING

Bridgeton, MO

Where once miners toiled by the light of a flickering lamp, scuba divers can now explore this flooded lead mine, hovering weightlessly in sparkling gin-clear water. West End Diving Center brings all the best together for scuba divers in this 'billion gallon lake'—a flooded lead mine last worked in the '60s. Divers can enjoy their sport year-round in an ideal setting with 100' visibility and a constant temperature of 58°F. A total of 10 dive trails take divers through mammoth archways, past beautiful calcium falls, and around 200-foot solid-rock pillars—all of which provide excellent opportunities for photography. A shack at a depth of 80 feet where miners once reported to work each day, a mile trail with wooden stairs, and sundry mining equipment scattered about, all make for a macabre setting. The Center provides classes for beginners and advanced divers, and equipment is available for rent—including instamatic cameras to capture the cathedral-like majesty of the caverns. For landlubbers, mine tours are given of above-water passageways, and there are antique shops, a playground with old mining implements, and a restaurant. Divers must be certified and age 15 or older. Reservations required.

West End Diving-Bonne Terremine, 11215 Natural Bridge Rd, Bridgeton, MO 63044, **314/731-5003.**

NORTHEAST

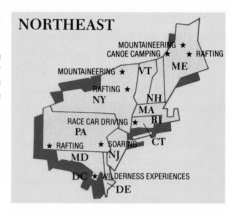

MOUNTAINEERING

Baxter State Park, ME

Mountain climbers and other outdoor adventurers flock to Baxter Peak, highest mountain in Maine, for good reason. A major feature of this 200,000-acre wilderness park, the peak was known as Katahdin before the parkland was donated to the state of Maine by former Governor Percival P. Baxter in the 1930s. The climbing can be strenuous (no children under six allowed above the timberline), but the rewards are many: orchids, ferns, and alpine plants abound; fossils can be foraged; and the 46 mountain peaks and ridges (18 above 3000 feet, with Baxter Peak at 5267 feet) shelter an abundance of wildlife. Camping facilities include lean-to sites, tent sites, bunkhouse, and cabins, allowing mountaineers to decide how Spartan they want to go. The park is well protected, and visitors should become familiar with rules and regulations—no feeding the bears! No camping, climbing, or mountain hiking allowed during the winter without special permit from park supervisor.

Baxter State Park, 64 Balsam Dr, Millinocket, ME 04462, **207/723-5140.**

RAFTING

Kennebec, Penobscot & Dead Rivers, ME

One trip to the wild portion of the Hudson River or to Maine's Kennebec, Penobscot, or Dead rivers will convince skeptics that the Northeast is more than an overpopulated industrial wasteland. Northern Outdoors offers a variety of white-water raft trips to give river runners a taste of the wild and historic Northeast in just a day or two. Mini-vacation packages are two days long; overnight wilderness camping trips to the Kennebec for families or singles are two days long and cover 23 miles. The whitewater expeditions, however, are for the most adventuresome canoeists. One-day trips take rafters to the Kennebec headwaters; to the northern New York Hudson River Gorge high in the Adirondacks; to Dead River, which is available only a few days a year, offers very high water, and is very popular; and to the West Branch of the Penobscot, which offers alternating stretches of calm water and rushing rapids. Most trips are available to those over age 14. One-day river trips cost $60-$80 per person, overnight Kennebec trips run $140, and mini-vacations are $140-$180.

Northern Outdoors, PO Box 100, Rte 201, The Forks, ME 04985, **207/663-4466.**

Dogsledding

Photo: Will Goddard

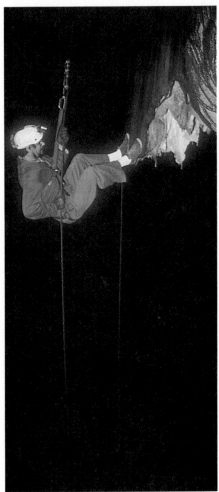

Spelunking

CANOE CAMPING

Millinocket, ME

Canoeists can explore the last extensive undeveloped region in the Northeast by arranging an unguided canoe-camping trip. The outfitter will help you plan your trip and will provide complete outfitting (or any individual items you need), but no guides—you're on your own. Target rivers include the Allagash, Upper West Branch of the Penobscot, St. John, and East Branch of the Penobscot— and there's a suitable destination for everyone, from novices to experienced white-water runners. For those who prefer lake canoeing, there are trips to Telos, Chamberlain, Eagle, Churchill, and Chesuncook lakes. The "Cadillac" of these trips is the 100-mile, seven-day trip on the Allagash River, beginning at Telos Lake and ending at Allagash Village. Best for those with a lot of flat-water canoeing experience, this trip combines peaceful lake canoeing with moderate rapid running through surrounding spruce-fir forest; sharp ears can listen at nighttime for the haunting cry of the loon. Trips to the Upper West Branch of the Penobscot are ideal for novices, while East Branch and St. John River trips are only for those with white-water canoeing experience. Reserve well in advance by mail; the outfitter has no summer phone service.

Allagash Wilderness Outfitters, Box 620, Star Rte 76, Greenville, ME 04441, **207/695-2821** *(radio contact, May 1-Nov 30); 36 Minuteman Dr, Millinocket, ME 04462,* **207/723-6622** *(Dec 1-Apr 30).*

RAFTING

Ohiopyle State Park, PA

This churning river is famous for its quiet flatwaters, dizzying whirlpools, and massive boulders — all in a dramatic, narrow gorge that was cut out of the Laurel Highlands by years of the river's raging force. A seven-mile stretch of foaming action through Ohiopyle State Park is the most famous—and most treacherous—part of this exciting river; rapids are extensive and formidable, and all but expert river runners should make use of one of the four outfitters serving the Yough (pronounced "yock"). River highlights include: steep, rocky cliffs on the Ferncliff Peninsula side of the river; dense, lush woodlands; dramatic Ohiopyle Falls; and drops of as much as 40 feet within a 300-yard span, including a 16-foot vertical plunge at the falls. Yough runners also witness one of the most successful river reclamation projects ever undertaken in the US. Industrial development and recreational use put a heavy strain on the Yough's natural wonders. By the 1930s, much of the original forest had been cut and the river and streams polluted. Thanks to reclamation efforts of the 1950s and 60s, appearances of whitetail deer, opossum, beaver, otter, mink, muskrat, hawks and owls, wild turkey and other wildlife have become more frequent.

Ohiopyle State Park, Box 105, Ohiopyle, PA 15470, **412/329-4707, -4704.**

SOARING

Erwinna, PA

With or without a motor this is *the* spot for soaring in the Northeast — and also the place to go to experience daredevil stunts first hand. Located at Van Sant Airport in beautiful Bucks County, Posey Aviation, Inc., offers a variety of soaring experiences seven days a week within an easy drive from Philadelphia and Trenton. Sailplane lessons, which cost $25-$30, include instructor, tow, and sailplane rental. Students can qualify for the FAA flight test for glider pilots after seven hours of solo time; licensed power pilots need only 10 solo flights to get a glider

Soaring

rating. A bird's-eye view of the scenic Delaware River can be had in privately owned or rented sailplanes, or the uninitiated can just go along for the ride with one of Posey's pilots. Power planes are also available for rent, including classic Piper Cubs, biplanes, and open-cockpit craft. Again, the option of just going along for the ride is open, including a barnstormer ride and an aerobatic biplane flight that includes a looproll, hammerhead, and snap roll. Sailplane rides run from $29 for the standard ride to $59 for the famous mile-high ride; power plane rides are 10 or 20 minutes long and run from about $10-$49 for the aerobatic flight.

Posey Aviation, Inc, Van Sant Airport, Erwinna, PA 18920, **215/847-2770.**

RACE CAR DRIVING

Canaan, CT

The dreams of would-be race car drivers come true at the Skip Barber Race Series, held four weekends at Lime Rock Park (as well as 13 other weekends at eight different circuits). Speed buffs don't need to own a racecar or break the bank account to participate in this series of races, nor do they need a nuts-and-bolts knowledge of auto mechanics. Skip Barber supplies the cars, mechanics, and racing gear — racers provide the skill (obtained through instruction) and the guts. It all starts with the Skip Barber Racing School's Three Day Competition Course, which costs $975 and teaches prospective racers everything they'll need to know—sometimes more than even the seasoned pros know! Again, Barber provides all that participants need. The course can be waived for those who have racing experience or credentials from another school, but most racers opt for this unbeatable learning experience before entering the racing series, getting lots of experience driving at speeds exceeding 100 mph. Each of the four race series weekends at Lime Rock Park costs $795 and covers two races, two warm-up sessions, and an extended practice session. Racers can choose to drive in one or all of the series weekends.

Skip Barber Racing School, Rte 7, Canaan, CT 06018, **203/435-0771.**

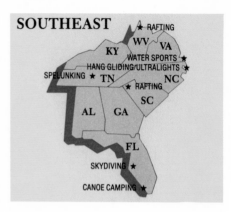

SOUTHEAST

Ballooning

MOUNTAINEERING

Mt. Marcy, NY

Although the Adirondack Mountains of northern New York are less than half the height of major peaks in the Rockies, the statistics can be a bit misleading, since the bases of Adirondack Mountains are much closer to sea level than the larger mountains to the west. There are four well-marked trails leading to the summit of the 5344-foot Mt. Marcy, tallest peak in New York state, but the ascent is long and arduous, although not technical. Shortest route at seven miles is the Van Hoevenberg Trail, which begins at the parking lot of the Adirondack Loj, nine highway miles from Lake Placid Village (see Winter Sports Of All Sorts). Toughest trails are Hopkins Trail, which is 10½ miles long and usually requires more than a day to complete, and The Range Trail, which is extremely steep in spots and is considered the most difficult as well as the most scenic. Panoramic vistas of the surrounding peaks and the many crystal-blue lakes, streams, and ponds can be appreciated on the way up and from the top of Mt. Marcy, which is more than a mile high and was appropriately named Tahawus, "Cloud Splitter of the Indians," before it was renamed Marcy after a New York governor. Those who reach the summit will be standing on a portion of the divide for the St. Lawrence and Hudson River systems.

NY State Dept of Environmental Conservation, Albany, NY 12245, **518/891-1370.**

RAFTING

Hudson River, NY

(See under Kennebec, Penobscot & Dead Rivers, ME.)

WILDERNESS EXPERIENCES

Washington, DC

A wide variety of often extensive wilderness experiences in the western, southeastern, and northern US are offered by this national organization. Hiking trips, horseback treks, and canoe tours, some lasting several weeks, are organized in virtually all of the major wilderness areas of the US. Per-person-prices range from $330 for a six-day hike in the Superstition Wilderness of Arizona to $915 for an 11-day combination raft and horse tour of the Quetico-Superior or Florida Everglades areas. Most specialized equipment is provided by the outfitter. The aim of the Trail Riders program is to allow AFA members opportunities to enjoy and learn about the natural resources of our wilderness. Since its inception in 1933, the program has expanded to offer more trips to an ever-widening selection of sites. A horseback trip to Colorado's San Juan Mountains lasts six days with two camp stops at 11,000 + feet. Highest trail elevation is 13,000, and from there riders can bask in the glories of the wildflower-strewn high country. Side rides and main trails will take equestrians past waterfalls, wild meadows, and snow-capped peaks, and the trip ends via an historic old cattle drive trail. Also offered are strenuous canoeing adventures with such trips as its Everglades Wilderness Exploration, a seven-day foray into the mysteries of this tropical preserve—a must for those who enjoy observing rare plants and marine life—with glimpses of the vestiges of shell mounds built by Seminole Indians. Schedules, prices, and trip descriptions available—send a stamped, self-addressed #10 envelope.

AFA Trail Riders, 1319-18th St, NW, Washington, DC 20036, **202/467-5810.**

WATER SPORTS

Virginia Beach, VA

It's no wonder that Virginia Beach has long been a mecca for water-sport aficianados—it has virtually something for everyone, going far beyond casual body-surfing and air-mattress-floating. Along 28 miles of ocean beach fronting this bustling resort town are all types of sailing experiences, including catamaraning and wind surfing, plus jet skiing, scuba diving, and snorkeling. Features of the Chesapeake Bay area make this an intriguing spot, whether one views Chesapeake Light Tower, examines Chesapeake Bay wrecks (dating from 1900-present), or tries spear-fishing. Costs may range from about $20 an hour to rent a boardsail to $300 a day for a charter fishing trip for six. How much one spends will depend on whether lessons in the chosen sport(s) are needed; also be prepared in many cases to put down a hefty deposit for rented equipment. Generally, the season for water sports is Apr-Oct, although there are exceptions and peak times: beginners should stick to May 15-Sept 15 for boardsailing, while experts can pursue this sport Apr 1-Dec 1; best season for jet skiing usually is May 1-Oct 1.

Virginia Travel Council, 202 N 9th St, Ste 500, Richmond, VA 23219, **804/266-0444.**

RAFTING

Chattooga River, SC/GA

The river where the motion picture *Deliverance* was filmed is the most thrilling (and at certain places the most suicidal) white-water river in the Southeast. It is also one of the few remaining free-flowing streams in the region, protected in 1974 by Congress under the Wild and Scenic Rivers act. The final section of the Chattooga, from US 76 to Tugaloo Lake, is extremely dangerous, with extensive rapids, undertows, and falls. Best time for challenging this river is spring, when the water is fairly high. Section IV is not for the uninitiated—or for those who like to "warm up" to a river; on this run, rafters are plunged right into the action via precipitous Seven Foot Falls. The Chattooga, which falls an average of 490 feet per mile, is surrounded by picturesque South Carolina scenery and features extensive wildlife and trout populations that draw hordes of hunters and anglers to the area every year. Canoe, kayak, and rafting equipment available. Two-day river runs at around $100 per person.

Wildwater Ltd, Long Creek, SC 29658, **803/647-9587.**

Rafting

RAFTING

The Cheat & New Rivers, WV

The Cheat River of northern West Virginia and the New River in the southern portion of the state offer white-water enthusiasts two unique views of this lovely state. Although popular stretches of these two Appalachian Mountain rivers are relatively short (half-day or day trips are about the maximum), the white-water action is intense, especially during spring. Standing waves as high as 12 feet or more are not uncommon in either stream, and all but expert runners should contact a licensed guide. Spring rains add challenge to the already-rough white water of the New River, and it's at that time of year that the torrential rapids resemble those of the Rockies, giving the river the nickname "Grand Canyon of the East." Flowing northward through a 1000-foot-deep gorge toward the foothills of central West Virginia, the New River drops about 240 feet in 14 miles for river-running excitement unparalleled in the East. An 11-mile run through Cheat River Canyon, to the north, features 20 furious rapids and is also most exciting during spring, when water levels are highest. At that time, six-place rafts usually replace the four-place models, and if the water rises above the cut-off for the canyon, rafters can run the "Narrows," a longer run that takes less time than the canyon run because the rapids are even swifter.

Office of Economic & Community Dev, Travel Dept, State Capitol, Charleston, WV 25305, **304/348-0190.**

SPELUNKING

Cumberland Caverns, TN

One of the largest caves in the US is Cumberland Caverns, located in about the center of Tennessee. Beware: Legend has it that Aaron Higgenbotham, who accidentally discovered this cave in 1810 and got lost when his torch burned out, was so terrified by his surroundings that when rescuers found him several days later, his hair had turned white! Although this registered National Landmark is generally operated as a tourist-only attraction with the usual well-lighted, well-managed trails, there are exceptions. Organizations can arrange special 14-hour tours that start in the evening in the commercial areas and proceed to undeveloped sections for two hours of exploring that requires spelunking skills—crawling, climbing, and slithering for more than a mile underground. The tour includes an overnight stay underground. Experienced spelunkers may also be able to participate in the annual Christmas Party, deep within the cave's noncommercial areas. Finally, dedicated speleologists whose motives are scientific, may be able to convince management to allow them to explore and map some of the cavern's nether reaches. Features to catch on the spelunking tours include 15-foot-high Monument Pillar, a stalagmite lauded as the "most beautiful speleothem"; eight waterfalls, including one more than 80 feet high; and a treasure trove of gypsum flowers, domepits, and cave wildlife such as bats and blind fish. The hawk-eyed (or over-imaginative) might even catch a glimpse of the ghosts of earlier, lost explorers.

Roy Davis, Mgr, Cumberland Caverns, McMinnville, TN 37110, **615/668-4396.**

HANG GLIDING/ ULTRALIGHTS

Nags Head, NC

Hang gliding is about as close to flying like a bird as human beings can get. And Kitty Hawk Kites has the optimum setting for this air sport. Nags Head, on the Outer Banks, is within view of where the Wright Brothers launched the modern world into flight. And Jockey's Ridge—the tallest sand dune in the East (the equivalent of 13 stories) is used for flights and instruction. Special mountain clinics are offered in addition to the many instructional courses, but sand provides easier landings than the rougher mountain terrain. Beginner's instruction usually culminates in flights of 75-200 feet at 5-10 feet above the beach; advanced gliders can learn to make 90o turns, spot landings, and glide at much higher altitudes. Certified instructors are on hand to teach you to fly an ultralight—a one-man aircraft powered by a 30 hp engine, which can take its pilot into the blue for two hours on only three gallons of gas. Whether the flying machine is an ultralight or the giant kite contraption used for hang gliding, these air sports are not for the faint of heart. Kitty Hawk Kites has served some 35,000 people with an excellent safety record, but patrons will be required to sign a waiver explaining the risks involved. A three-hour beginning course costs $44; a full pro package is $350.

Kitty Hawk Kites, PO Box 340, Nags Head, NC 27959, **919/441-4124.**

SKYDIVING

Zephyrhills, FL

This Florida spot welcomes thousands of skydivers from all over the world every year, and it's known as one of the best parachute centers in the country, especially for advanced jumpers. Four world RW (relative work) parachuting championships have been held here, where skydivers hook up in formations of two or more. Zephyrhills does offer instruction to beginners at about $100 on weekends, and students will jump the first day after about half a day of instruction. However, the majority of jumpers who head for this site are serious enough to own their own gear. Weather is good year-round, and for those who want a lot of action the best time to go is Oct-Apr. From May to September, the temperature rises, and most Zephyrhills activity takes place on weekends. Jumps are made from a DC-3 that holds 40 jumpers; a Cessna 1906 is used for smaller loads. A feature that draws many enthusiasts to this center is the unique relative work instruction program, which is acclaimed for teaching complicated aerial formations. Jumps (you supply the gear) cost $1 or so per thousand feet; most jumpers opt for about 12,000 feet.

Zephyrhills Parachute Ctr, PO Box 1101, Zephyrhills, FL 34283, **813/788-5591.**

CANOE CAMPING

Everglades, FL

(See under Washington, DC.)

Chapter 18

ETHNIC & HISTORIC VILLAGES

Two journeys, often intertwined, await the traveler in search of the roots—and the soul—of historic and ethnic America. One journey is back in time to the days of America's earliest settlers, the Pilgrims who suffered and survived the deprivations of that first harsh winter as they struggled for a foothold in the New World, and to the era of the courageous pioneers who pushed our frontiers ever westward. The second odyssey in this flight of fantasy transports you across oceans, as you visit, within the heartland of America, transplanted, microcosmic slices of Europe the way it was 100 years ago and more.

Journeying back in time you'll find the recreation of a bustling canal town, a New England country village of the 1830s where you can dine early-American style, and a whaling and trading port complete with tall ships, old salts, and sea shanties. You'll visit the boisterous cow towns of the old West where the Colt was the only law and where lonely Boot Hill awaited the vanquished, the rebuilt boom towns where gold fever once raged, and lone outposts where lonely men fought off attacks by hostile Indians. You'll discover vivid reminders of the War of Independence and of conflicts in which America's native Indian people were the oppressed, and the historic site where the resilient Cherokee tribe re-established its identity and dignity after the infamous forced march along "The Trail of Tears." And as you journey figuratively across geographic and political boundries, you'll visit Swiss and Swedes, Norwegians and Germans, Danes and Finns. You'll hear spoken the native languages of these countries, along with the dialect of Elizabethean English. You'll gain insights into the beliefs and mores of early religious settlers—the Quakers and Shakers, the Harmonists, Mennonites, and Amish. And you'll taste Swiss hunter's sausage, hearty Swedish pea soup, and the delectable shoofly pie of the Amish. Yes, America is a melting pot of peoples. But it also is a land in which separate cultures, customs, and religious persuasions have found the space and the freedom to flourish.

Old Salem, Winston-Salem, NC

NORTHWEST

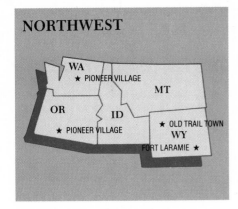

PIONEER VILLAGE

Cashmere, WA

This community restoration honors those pioneers who, in the years following the Civil War, endured hardships, loneliness, and danger to move the frontier across the Rocky Mountains and open the Far West. Authentic, primarily log-walled, structures gathered throughout Chelan County have been reassembled as a late 19th-century Northwest outpost, a saints-and-sinners world of juxtaposed Christian missions and boisterous saloons. There are primitive doctor's and dentist's facilities, barber and millinery shops, and the post office where new settlers anxiously awaited news from loved ones back home. Included are a western-style community smithy, a gold assayer's office, a general store, a one-room schoolhouse, a print shop, and early family cabins that show masterful broad-axe and dovetailing log construction techniques. A splendid museum contains a comprehensive collection of historical artifacts that journey from 9,000 years ago on up to the arrival of white pioneer settlers; it details the rich culture of the Indian tribes who lived along this river basin. Summer, daily 10am-4:30pm.

Pioneer Village, Chelan Hist Soc, PO Box 22, Cashmere, WA 98815, **509/782-3230.**

PIONEER VILLAGE

Jacksonville, OR

Pioneer spirit is alive and well in this friendly, beautifully-restored vintage Gold Rush community that managed to survive mid-19th-century devastations of mud-slides, smallpox, and fire. But unlike so many other familiar boom-town sagas with tragic endings, hardy Jacksonvillers persisted in rebuilding their town with a stunning treasury of brick masterpieces. Included are more than 80 meticulously refurbished landmark structures and more than a few artisans and shopkeepers intent on maintaining the look and feel of a bygone era. Among the highlights: The Old Jailhouse—now an instructive hands-on children's museum, populated by resident "pioneers," featuring pioneer tools and crafts; the restored United States Hotel; the old county courthouse—now the Jacksonville Museum—containing some of the best historic exhibits in the Northwest; and 20 antiquated Gold Rush period structures which resemble a western movie set. Jacksonville is also home of the renowned Britt Music Festival and not far from the Oregon Shakespearean Festival in Ashland, from Crater Lake National Park, and from rafting on Oregon's magnificent, challenging Rogue River.

Pioneer Village, Southern Oregon Hist Soc, PO Box 480, Jacksonville, OR 97530, **503/899-1847.**

OLD TRAIL TOWN

Cody, WY

The color and drama of the Old West lives on at this historic location, where Buffalo Bill and his associates surveyed the first town site of "Cody City" in 1895. Old Trail Town consists of 25 buildings, dating 1879-1900, plus 100 horse-drawn vehicles, and an extensive collection of memorabilia of the Wyoming frontier. Visit the "hole in the wall" cabin, a popular rendezvous for Butch Cassidy and the Sundance Kid; inspect bullet holes that perforate the doors of the Rivers Saloon, a favorite watering hole for cowboys, gold miners, and other colorful characters; and view the cabin where the Indian scout, Curly, the only survivor of General Custer's command at the Little Big Horn, lived until his death in 1923. Other historic structures include a livery barn, post office, school, and blacksmith shops. The Trail Town Cemetery is the final resting place for such notables as John "Jeremiah" Johnson and buffalo hunter Jim White. Be sure to visit the adjacent Buffalo Bill Historical Center (see Masterful Museums).

Old Trail Town, PO Box 2777, Cody, WY 82414, **307/587-2297.**

FORT LARAMIE

Fort Laramie, WY

(See Historic Landmarks.)

SOUTHWEST

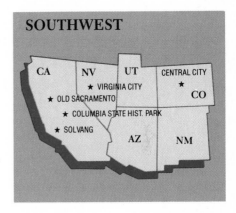

SOLVANG

Solvang, CA

Windmills gently creak in the breeze as the sun shines down on golden thatched roofs. The aroma of freshly baked pastry wafts over cobblestone sidewalks. You could very easily believe you were on a street in Copenhagen. Instead, you have discovered the Danish capital of America—Solvang (Sun Valley), tucked away in the heart of the beautiful Santa Ynez Valley. Founded more than 70 years ago by Danish clergymen, and settled by immigrants of Danish extraction, this quaint village abounds in Scandinavian flavor, and draws more than two million visitors annually. The native language can still be heard in homes, churches, and on the streets. If you time a visit during Danish Days (third week Sept), you can treat yourself to an *aebleskiver* breakfast (fried dough rolled into a small ball, with juice and coffee) served on the streets, while taking in the sights and sounds of roving singers and folk dancers, dressed in Old World Danish costumes. Competition is fierce among the bakeries, who will woo you with a wide assortment of breads, pastries, cookies, and cakes. Authentic Danish recipes are the featured fare at the local restaurants where the smorgasbords offer dozens of delectables including marinated herring, wilted cucumbers, and red cabbage and meatballs. For a taste of Denmark without ever leaving the USA, you need to know only one Danish word—Solvang.

Visitors Bureau, PO Box 465, Solvang, CA 93463, **805/688-3317.**

Old Trail Town, Cody, WY

COLUMBIA STATE HISTORIC PARK

Columbia, CA

"Gold! Gold!" When James Marshall exclaimed those words in January, 1848 he set in motion one of the most extraordinary movements in American history—The Gold Rush. Boomtowns sprang up overnight in the hills of the Sierra Nevada drawing hopeful prospectors from across the land in quest of the Mother Lode. Far from being a ghost town, Columbia is alive with the sounds, sights, and activity of yesteryear. Private tenants occupy most of the 21 restored buildings (further restoration is underway), which include a harness shop, restaurant, antique shops, barbershop, and an old-fashioned candy store. Year-round activities feature crafts demonstrations, tours of old mines, stagecoach rides, plays at the Fallon Theatre, and films and exhibits about the town's history. Of course, no visit would be complete without trying your luck at panning for gold. Visitors have been known to return home with a souvenir shiny nugget or two. Surrounding Tuolomne County is rich in recreation and points of interest. Highlights include nearby Yosemite National Park (see Nat'l Parks & Monuments), Railtown 1897 Historical Park, and countless scenic rivers and lakes where fishing, camping, boating, and even hot-air ballooning are found in abundance.

Columbia State Historic Park, PO Box 151, Columbia CA 95310, **209/532-4301.**

OLD SACRAMENTO/ SUTTER'S FORT

Sacramento, CA

Imagine the exhaustion and relief of an 1860 Pony Express ironman, who, as the last of a relay team of 80 riders, finally completed the perilous 1,966-mile cross-country mail run here at its western terminus in less than 10 days. Old Sacramento was also a strategic mid-19th-century headquarters for Wells Fargo & Co. and the earliest Western Union facility, a central staging area for the gold prospecting 49-ers, and the starting point for the western branch of the transcontinental railway, whose final spike was hammered in 1869 at Promontory Point, Utah, some 700 miles away. Such epical events of the Old West are much in evidence in California's historic capital. A 4-square-block restoration along the Sacramento River contains the 100,000-square-foot California State Railroad Museum, and the 1870 Central Pacific Railroad Passenger Depot, a train buff's paradise with more than 30 examples of puffer-belly-era rolling stock. (Steam train rides along a six-mile route on summer weekends.) Other displays and buildings, include the original Wells Fargo and Western Union offices in the B.F. Hastings Museum/ Building, well-stocked period shops such as the Huntington-Hopkins Hardware Store, the Old Eagle Theater and, from the settlement's lusty era of barge traffic, a Jack London-style waterfront along the river. Nearby is historic Sutter's Fort, the earliest non-Indian settlement in California's Great Central Valley, founded in 1839 by Swiss immigrant pioneer, John Augustus Sutter. With help from friendly Indians, his small party built a crude fort of sun-cured adobe to protect the soon-to-boom community, later named Sacramento. Today, Sutter Fort State Historic Park is a restored and recreated frontier outpost with blacksmiths, cooks and candlemakers,

carpenters and coopers, all in period dress, talking period language, and living an 1840 pioneer's life down to authentic menus. Both the Fort and other Old Sacramento historic attractions are open daily, except Thanksgiving, Christmas and New Year's Day. Guided tours and self-touring material available.

Old Sacramento/Sutter's Fort, California Dept of Parks & Rec, PO Box 2390, Sacramento, CA 95811, **916/445-4209.**

CENTRAL CITY

Central City, CO

Remember the fabled poem "Face On The Barroom Floor"? You can see it interpreted in the elegant Teller House hotel, one of many popular attractions in this restored classic Gold Rush community. In its 19th-century heyday, Central City missed being elected capital of Colorado by a scant *three* votes. This so-called "richest square mile on earth" boasted a population substantially larger than Denver, just 40 miles to the East. And in a sincere, albeit garish, gesture to honor a visit by President Grant, community fathers once paved a portion of main street in solid silver (gold bricks being overruled as too mundane!) No precious metals gild the streets today, but the town and surrounding Gilpin County yield an historical wealth of vintage honky-tonk saloons, widely varied period museums and exhibits, mine tours, ghost-mine camps, good restaurants and shops, and authentically refurbished Victorian lodgings. During summer, the splendid, heavy-stone 1878 Opera House offers major musical and theatrical productions that have showcased such performers as Lillian Gish, Helen Hayes, and Julie Harris. Central City also hosts the annual summer Ragtime and Traditional Jazz Festival and an adult soapbox derby called the Gravity Grand Prix. Nearby are miles of challenging back country Aspen trails for hiking and horseback riding, plus six campground facilities—all at

an altitude of 8000 feet where the clear Colorado air is rarified and exhilarating.

Central City, Central City Business Assn, PO Box 456, Central City, CO 80427, **303/582-5251.**

VIRGINIA CITY

Virginia City, NV

To this day the Comstock Lode, discovered in 1859, stands as the world's all-time record for gold and silver— an incredible $400 million in ore taken from this steep-sloping arid Nevada landscape. Such was the awesome value of these mineral deposits, that they have been said to be largely responsible for financing the Union Army's triumph in the Civil War, and for subsidizing a substantial portion of the development of San Francisco. Although this tiny community, self-styled "the liveliest ghost town in the West," is a frail shadow of its former self, it remains a remarkable repository of old boardwalks, 22 saloons, and many elegant, extravagantly furnished Victorian mansions constructed by suddenly wealthy miners. In 1875, a wind-whipped conflagration virtually flattened the town, but it quickly re-emerged as one finds it today. Many of the mansions are open for public inspection (hours and seasons vary). Underground still lies an incredible network of some *750 miles* of mining tunnels that produced this wealth; these, too, are popular tourist attractions. As a result of strict Historic District guidelines, local accommodations are limited—but Carson City is only 14 miles distant, Reno but 23, and the resort playgrounds of both north and south Lake Tahoe are only 40 miles away. Meanwhile, Virginia City offers hiking, swimming, tennis, and dirt biking, an abundance of arts, crafts, and antiques, plus a singular curiosity in October—National Championship Camel Races.

Chamber of Commerce, Virginia City, NV 89440, **702/ 847-0311.**

MIDWEST

AMANA COLONIES

Amana, IA

Since the seven Amana colonies were founded in 1854 as centralized, planned, and patterned villages, farming has been the principal activity. The rich northeastern Iowa River Valley soil has provided abundant yields of corn, soy beans, alfalfa, oats, and beef cattle. The original 800 Amana settlers, of German, Swiss, and Alsatian ancestry, came to escape persecution and pursue a visionary faith called the Community of the True Inspirationalists. Part of their adopted lifestyle embraced the concept of communal enterprises, a blend of brotherhood and economics with each individual contributing what he or she did best. The result was an extraordinary variety of finely-crafted 19th-century pioneer furniture, clocks, embroidery, calico dresses, hand-loomed woolen items, whole-grained cereals, Westphalia-style smoked meats, wines of German character, and the exceptional Old World baked offerings from a number of community kitchens. These early Amana traditions (more recently joined by state-of-the-art industry in major household appliances) continue to be the Amana trademark of excellence. Awaiting today's visitor is a first-hand sampling of all of these goods at their source, combined with a host of historic buildings, numerous museums, including the significant Museum of Amana History open Apr-Nov, and tempting regional restaurants.

Amana Colonies, The Amana Society, Amana, IA 52203, **319/622-3051.**

VESTERHEIM

Decorah, IA

Vesterheim (western home) is a word used by Norwegian immigrants to refer to their frontier homes in the New World. Since 1877, the Norwegian-American Museum has operated Vesterheim, an outdoor historic village with authentically preserved pioneer buildings. Through house furnishings, costumes, tools, toys, and other artifacts, the Museum tells the story of Norwegian immigration to America. Commonplace duties and chores in the immigrant pioneer's life are demonstrated at the restored Stone Mill and at the authentic blacksmith shop, both dating from the 1850s. The little town of Decorah, named for an Indian Chief, is in the extreme northeast corner of Iowa and is also noted for picturesque trout and canoe streams. Nearby are massive limestone formations along the Upper Iowa River and explorable caves of rock and ice. Open daily 9am-5pm. Admission $3; 7-15 $1.25 (off-season schedule and prices vary).

The Norwegian-American Museum, 520 W Water St, Decorah, IA 52101, **319/382-9681.**

HISTORIC BISHOP HILL

Bishop Hill, IL

Hardy, industrious Swedes, driven from their homeland by religious persecution, created this charming community in the prairie heartland. Hardy? They *walked* the 160 miles from Chicago, arriving in the fall of 1846, and spent that first bleak winter in makeshift dugouts, subsisting on meager rations. By spring, nearly 100 had perished. Industrious? Within a few years they had created a communal society, built a solid village of hand-made bricks, and were producing sturdy wagons, fine carriages, linens, furniture, and other products that established Bishop Hill as a major trade center. Today, the village enjoys National Landmark status and offers quiet, tree-lined streets, well-preserved historic buildings, craft studios, antique and gift shops, Swedish-flavored eateries, and a number of colorful festivals. More than a dozen original buildings remain, including the Steeple Building where visitors can browse through a museum and view a 30-minute film chronicling the settlement of the colony and its restoration. The Colony Church, with black walnut pews—separate sections for men and women — has wood and wrought-iron chandeliers, copies of brass chandeliers colonists remembered in Swedish cathedrals. It houses more than 100 paintings of Olof Krans, a self-taught artist whose austere canvases capture the harsh life of the prairies and whose stern-faced portraits depict many of Bishop Hill's immigrant founders. The Red Oak, a small eatery that once was the general store, is cheerfully decorated with Scandinavian pottery and china. It serves hearty, open-faced sandwiches on Swedish rye, and Scandinavian-style early dinners on Sundays. Swedish-style sandwiches, homemade soup, and a daily luncheon entree are served in the Victorian dining room of P. L. Johnson. Conversion of the old colony administration building soon will provide an attractive bed-and-breakfast inn, The Three Seasons. Special events include: *Jorbruksdagarna,* an agricultural festival with harvesting demonstrations, crafts, and games (Sept); *Julmarknad,* a Christmas market featuring decorations, gifts, and Swedish foods and baked goods (Nov); and Lucia Nights, the traditional Swedish festival of lights (Dec).

Bishop Hill State Historical Site, Bishop Hill, IL 61419, **309/927-3345.**

Amana Colonies, Amana, IA

LITTLE NORWAY

Blue Mounds, WI

The tiny village of Mount Horeb reflects its Norwegian heritage with annual outdoor performances of The Song of Norway (Sats late June-July), an annual *Kafe Stu* (July), featuring traditional Norwegian foods served by authentically costumed villagers, and in shops selling imported arts and crafts, foodstuffs, crystal, porcelain, and linens. Nearby is Little Norway, an outdoor museum (also known as *Nissedahle,* "Valley of the Elves") that includes a small but outstanding collection of Norse antiques at the homestead of an early Norwegian settler to this tiny valley nestled among wooded hills. The buildings of the homestead site include a log cabin, barns, and sheds, all dating from 1856. Inside the buildings, costumed guides show off the arts and crafts of these Norwegian pioneers. Also on the grounds is the Norway Building, built in Norway as a pavillion for the Chicago Columbian Exposition of 1893. The building is a replica of a *Stavekirke,* a 12th century Norwegian church. Nearby are the strikingly beautiful crystaline formations of Cave of the Mounds (with 18 underground rooms). On evenings of "Song of Norway" performances (held on Cave grounds), a family-style restaurant serves Norwegian specialties.

Little Norway, Blue Mounds, WI 53517, **608/437-8211.**

Historic Bishop Hill, Bishop Hill, IL

Caesar's Creek Pioneer Village, Wayneville, OH

LITTLE SWITZERLAND

New Glarus, WI

Going to New Glarus is like taking a trip to Switzerland... without leaving the US. This small community nestled in the rolling hills of southern Wisconsin has all the sights and sounds of Switzerland, spiced with festivals, singing, dancing, and folklore. Chalet-style buildings sport colorful flower boxes, shops sell lace, embroidery, cheese, and *landjaeger* sausages favored by Swiss hunters, and yodelers perform in local inns and restaurants where fondue and wiener schnitzel are featured menu items. Founded in 1845 by 108 emigrants from the Canton of Glarus, the village has successfully retained its original Swiss flavor and many customs survive. The main preservator in the town is the Swiss Historical Village, the site of a replica pioneer village. Exhibits include log cabins, a log church, a one-room schoolhouse, and other structures furnished in the manner of 19th century Swiss settlers. Other attractions include the Chalet of the Golden Fleece (a museum displaying more than 3000 Swiss items, from dolls to kitchenware), the historic Swiss paintings in Puempel's Tavern at the village entrance, the annual Little Switzerland Festival and Heidi Drama (late June), the Alpine Festival and Wilhelm Tell Drama, held outdoors with mounted performers and performances in English and the original German (early Sept), and the New Glarus Marathon Run (mid-Oct).

NEWTAP, Box 713B, New Glarus, WI 53574, **608/527-2095.**

OLD WORLD WISCONSIN

Eagle, WI

Visitors to Old World Wisconsin smell fermenting sauerkraut, see flax blooming in the sun, watch new potatoes being dug, taste freshly-churned sweet butter, and hear the shrill whistle of the huge steam engine at threshing time. These are the slices of living history that visitors take home with them from this complex of eight reconstructed ethnic farmsteads and an 1870s crossroads village located on 576 rolling acres of wooded farmland. Farms, log cabins, and churches built by Finns, Germans, Danes, Norwegians, and Yankees have been painstakingly restored by the Wisconsin State Historical Society on the

lovely and expansive preserve. Here, with all of their senses, visitors become attuned to the diverse customs and lifestyles of the settlers who, in the 1800s, came to Wisconsin from every corner of Europe. Men in authentic costumes more than a century old put up hay, tend to livestock, and plant fields and gardens the same way the immigrant pioneers did; village women make soup and candles, card wool, and weave and dye fabric. The enormous complex, which includes a restaurant featuring ethnic dishes, is open May-Oct. Located about 35 mi SW of Milwaukee, just S of Eagle on WI 67 in the Kettle Moraine State Forest.

Old World Wisconsin, Rte 2, Box 18, Eagle, WI 53119, **414/594- 2116.**

HENRY FORD MUSEUM & GREENFIELD VILLAGE

Dearborn, MI

Here are historic homes and workplaces filled with the drama and personalities of those who, within these walls, changed the course of history. This 240-acre outdoor museum is dedicated to demonstrating the effects of the Industrial Revolution on everyday life: the cast-iron stove that replaced the fireplace; mass-produced furniture; and the incandescent lighting devices that supplanted the kerosene lamp. Craftsmen can be seen using traditional techniques to blow glass, make pottery, and forge tools. Highlight of the village is Edison's actual Menlo Park laboratory, just one of nearly 100 structures in the living museum. Next door is the Henry Ford Museum which houses the country's finest collections of cars, airplanes, steam engines, and power machinery. Further tracing the changes that technology has wrought on everyday tools and implements, visitors can inspect crude wooden plows displayed next to modern tractor plows, and compare the canoes and Conestoga wagons of yesteryear to the sleek cars and aircraft of today. Both museum and village open

year-round 9am-5pm. Admission: $8; 6-12 $4. Located on Oakwood Ave near Michigan Ave.

Henry Ford Museum & Greenfield Village, PO Box 1970, Dearborn, MI 48121, **313/271-1620.**

NEW HARMONY

New Harmony, IN

In 1814 the Harmony Society formed of Lutheran Separatists from Wurttemberg, Germany, purchased 30,000 acres of land in southern Indiana on the banks of the Wabash. Their leader, the charismatic Father George Rapp, preached total celibacy and the second coming of Christ in their lifetimes. From 1814 to 1824, the Harmonists perfected a cosmopolitan and efficient community. More than 20 products were marketed as far away as New Orleans and Pittsburgh, and the per capita income and cultural amenities rivalled larger Eastern centers. In 1825, a Scottish intellectual, Robert Owen, having had success with progressive labor practices in his own factories turned his attention to the creation of a utopia. Believing firmly that environment forms man's character, he bought New Harmony and invited a host of scientists, writers, and educators to participate in his dream. Owen was destined to sell his venture in 1828 at a loss of 80% of his personal estate, but not before various innovative firsts such as free kindergarten and education for women. Today, the New Harmony experience includes 12 exhibition buildings, some standing side-by-side with contemporary buildings, and various other exhibits such as a recreated labyrinthian network of hedges intended, while strolled through, to symbolize the choices taken during a lifetime. Present-day structures such as the Roofless Church and the internationally acclaimed Anatheum which serves as the visitors center, continue the radical tradition that this quiet town has seen. Open daily 9am-5pm except Christmas and New Years. Admission: $5; 6-18 $3 (4 hours). (Shorter tours at reduced rates.) Located on the Wabash River at Rtes 66 & 68, 7 mi S of I-64.

Historic New Harmony, Inc, Visitor Reception, New Harmony, IN 47631, **812/682-4474.**

Henry Ford Museum & Greenfield Village, Dearborn, MI

Photo: Joan Liffring

Amana Colonies, Amana, IA

SOUTH CENTRAL

SCHOENBRUNN VILLAGE

New Philadelphia, OH

The American Revolution was just around the corner when, in 1772, David Zeisberber established a Moravian missionary village in Schoenbrunn, Ohio's first white settlement. This German Protestant sect, which believed in pacifism and neutrality, converted Indians by persuading them that peace and order reap greater rewards than hostility. Ten years later, 72 of the Christian Indians were brutally massacred, having been accused of assisting the British Indians against the American militia. During the confusion of the war, the 60 log and clapboard houses of Schoenbrunn were abandoned, and some buildings were partially destroyed. The Ohio State Historical Society acquired the site in 1923 and the first cabin was restored in 1927—the meeting house and schoolhouse were rebuilt the following year. Today, the village consists of 19 structures, several of which have been halted in varying stages of completion to show construction techniques, plus a cemetery, and 2½ acres of planted fields. Interpretive guides answer questions and demonstrate typical crafts such as cooking, sewing, candle-making, field work, chinking, and mat-weaving. Located on US 250 1 mi southeast of New Philadelphia.

Schoenbrunn Village, PO Box 129, New Philadelphia, OH 44663, **216/339-3636.**

CAESAR'S CREEK PIONEER VILLAGE

Waynesville, OH

When the US Corps of Engineers was asked to construct a flood-control dam on Caesar's Creek near Waynesville, they discovered a series of log homes hand-crafted by Quaker settlers in the early 1800s. A group of local residents banded together to begin the slow task of relocating and restoring the structures. A 2½ story house (with full basement) from 1807 is the only one on its original site; the other buildings have joined it around a picturesque village green to demonstrate what many 19th century pioneer settlements looked like. The Quaker village contains five homes, a general store, a schoolhouse, a Quaker meeting house, a log smokehouse, a barn, a number of accessory buildings, and various farming exhibits. Work on the restoration is still in progress, but visitors are welcome on weekends. Caesar Creek Lake, formed by the dam, is now a popular vacation spot. The pioneer village is located just off Oregonia Rd near Waynesville.

Caesar's Creek Pioneer Village, PO Box 329, Waynesville, OH 45068, **513/897-1120.**

SWISS/AMISH VILLAGE

Sugarcreek, OH

Authentic Swiss costumes, *Steinstossen* (stone-tossing), *Schwingfest* (Swiss wrestling), and free polka-band entertainment are just a few of the annual late-Sept festival attractions that celebrate the heritage of this historic "little Switzerland of Ohio." Many of Sugarcreek's Swiss Village residents are direct descendants of Old Country immigrants whose influence is manifest in the community's architecture, customs, and some 17 varieties of superb, locally produced Swiss cheese. The prosperous surrounding rolling farm country is also home to America's largest concentration of Amish, who date back to hardy pioneer Moravian missionaries of the late 18th century, and can be easily spotted today journeying in immaculate horse-drawn buggies, or at work in community livestock barns and blacksmith shops. Of special historical interest is the Alpine Historical Museum (daily Apr-Oct) highlighting early village, farm, and Amish traditions. Elsewhere in the Tuscarawas County area are a number of other local museums and quaint restored or reconstructed log villages and sites such as Ohio's first permanent white settlement, Schoenbrunn (see), located a few miles south of Canton and Football's Hall of Fame (see Masterful Museums). The region abounds in craft and specialty shops, Amish homestyle restaurants, and comfortable accommodations.

Swiss/Amish Village, Convention & Visitors Bureau, PO Box 232, New Philadelphia, OH 44663, **216/343-4476.**

THE RANCHING HERITAGE CENTER

Lubbock, TX

Have you ever wondered what life was really like in the old west? Well, strap on your chaps and get ready to step back into history at this fascinating restoration of 20 ranching structures. Cowboy and greenhorn alike will be able to reminisce at the one-room schoolhouse, the blacksmith shop, the milk and meat house, the bunkhouse, and the ranch headquarters. The eastern hills and man-made ridges isolate the buildings from nearby modern surroundings. The Center draws more than 100,000 visitors each year from the US and abroad. Exhibits are held continually, featuring saddle wagons, branding irons, Western art and bronzes. In addition, reenactments of "how it was done" are provided to demonstrate soap-making, baking, shoeing horses, furniture making, sheep shearing, milk churning, spinning, weaving, and needle arts.

Ranching Heritage Center, PO Box 4040, Lubbock, TX 79409, **806/742-2498.**

Amana Colonies, Amana, IA

187

TSA-LA-GI, Tahlequah, OK

TSA-LA-GI

Tahlequah, OK

For America's noble, early-19th-century Cherokee Indians, the infamous year-long forced-march—the "Trail of Tears"—in 1838 was a holocaust of heartbreak, blizzards, disease, and hunger. More than 4000 died in this cruelly-administered federal effort to relocate the Cherokee Nation from their native southeast US domains to the wilderness of northeastern Oklahoma. Nonetheless, the resilient Cherokee spirit persevered. In the "Golden Years" before the massive disruption of the Civil War, they established Tahlequah as their nation's capital, built a public-school system, established seminaries which taught such subjects as Latin, algebra, vocal music, grammar, and geography, and sent top scholars off to America's highest institutes of learning in the East. As Oklahoma's most historic town, Tahlequah still serves as the tribal center with some 43,000 Cherokees living in the immediate area. Their proud heritage—from a rich archaeological pre-history to more modern accomplishments, including the career of Will Rogers, that "most familiar Cherokee of them all"—is impressively displayed. Highlights include: the Cherokee Heritage Center; the Cherokee National Museum; performances of a dramatic pageant, "Trail of Tears," at an outdoor amphitheater; and the recreated 17th-century working village of Tsa-La-Gi, which eloquently demonstrates the resourceful, ancient, and ultimately triumphant dignity of the Cherokee culture. Located about 3 mi S of Tahlequah, open year-round, (outdoor drama early May–Labor Day).

Tsa-La-Gi, PO Box 515, Tahlequah, OK 74465, **918/456-0511.**

INDIAN CITY, USA

Anadarko, OK

An authentic restoration of Indian dwellings and the recreation of a way of life, Indian City is on the site of the massacre of the Tonkawa Indians by a band of Shawnees and other mercenaries during the Civil War. Planned and constructed under the supervision of the University of Oklahoma's Dept of Anthropology, the attention to detail will fascinate anyone interested in traditional Indian life.

The dwellings are set in seven separate mock villages, and represent seven different tribes. The authentic Indian homes range from simple "wickiups" (small thatched huts) to familiar conical tepees to elaborate multi-story pueblos. Numerous artifacts, such as tools, utensils, weapons, musical instruments, and toys help illustrate the American Indian's ancient way of life. Tours conducted by Indian guides start every 45 minutes from 9:30am, and take about 30 minutes to complete. Dancers perform for most tours; a Plains Indian Ceremonial is conducted many Saturday nights. A museum and a KOA campground are also on the premises (campground reservations: 405/247-9043). Located 2½ mi SE of Anadarko.

Indian City, USA, PO Box 695, Anadarko, OK 73005, **405/247-5661.**

OLD COWTOWN MUSEUM

Wichita, KS

You may think that you're walking onto the set of a frontier movie, but this isn't Hollywood—the buildings are real. You are on location in historic Wichita. The 36 restored structures which cover 17 acres depict the pioneer period from 1865-1880. As you stroll through this quaint village back into history, you can't help but marvel at the painstaking detail rendered in the authentic decor, furnishings, and artifacts. Your journey will take you through simple rustic homes, a blacksmith's forge, harness and saddle shop, corner drugstore, saloon, and the old jail. There is something here for everyone. Costumed characters populate the streets during weekends in summer, and the Sedgwick County Fair is the big attraction in October. A Victorian Christmas is recreated on six consecutive evenings after Thanksgiving, complete with music, food, games, and entertainment. There are not many museums where you can see, hear and smell what life was like during a particular period of history, but at Cowtown, it happens every day. Open daily, Mar-Dec, Mon-Fri, Jan-Feb, 10am-5pm, admission charged, special tours by reservation.

Old Cowtown Museum, 1871 Sim Park Dr, Wichita, KS 67203, **316/264-0671.**

DODGE CITY

Dodge City, KS

The Earp and Masterson brothers, Doc Holliday, Wild Bill Hickok, Buffalo Bill, Big Bill Tilghman, Shoot-Em-Up Ike, One-Eyed Jake, Toothless Nell ... a seemingly endless legacy of this most infamous of all six-shooter communities sits at the top of the 1000-mile Santa Fe trail. Five distinctly American terms originated in this rootin' tootin' town: "Stinker" (as originally applied here to buffalo hunters); "Joint" (as in saloon); "Stiff" (as in rigid corpse); "Red Light District" (originating from visiting railroad workers who left their lanterns in front of the many brothels); and "Cooler" (the first official jail—actually a well into whose chilly depths drunks were lowered until sober). Another of Dodge's grim realities was the original Boot Hill—a high, lonely bluff where gunfight losers were unceremoniously wrapped in blankets and buried with their boots on. Unquestionably, no 19th-century western town enjoyed greater notoriety than the "Wickedest Little City in America." And quite possibly no present-day western community extracts greater commercial profit from its wild, utterly reckless beginnings. Kansas' number one tourist attraction is the combination of Boot Hill Cemetery and an activity-loaded replica of 1875 Front Street, both in the heart of today's downtown community. Here, and in other parts of the city, one can find stagecoach rides, High Noon boardwalk gunfight showdowns, Miss Kitty's Long Branch Saloon complete with period-style variety shows and barbecue suppers, and a multitude of historic buildings and sites, small museums, shops and assorted period-related amusements.

Chamber of Commerce, Box 939, Dodge City, KS 67801, **316/227-3119.**

Mystic Seaport, Mystic, CT

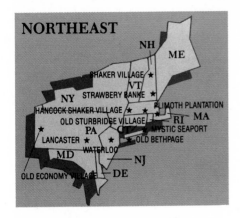

NORTHEAST

WATERLOO VILLAGE

Stanhope, NJ

Armaments for Washington's Continental Army were forged in these steep Sussex County hills not far from the Delaware Water Gap. And not long after, Waterloo became a key lock-and-plane terminal along the old Morris Canal, northern New Jersey's first bulk-freight transportation system. Today, this restored historic village recalls its days as a bustling early 19th-century inland port. Surviving is a still-operational 1790 blacksmith shop, a gristmill and sawmill, and a general store stocked with reproduced period crafts made by the Village's skilled artisans. The church, in continuous use for 120 years, holds Sunday services, and more than 15 other early buildings include inns, taverns, an Ironmaster's mansion, an apothecary, herb-drying rooms, broom and cabinet shops, a weaving barn, and pottery shed. Seasonal events include antique and arts festivals and, mid-June–early Sept, a renowned summer music festival with a wide-ranging program that includes jazz and ragtime, country and bluegrass, as well as chamber music, ballet, opera, and symphonies. Open Tue-Sun, Apr 13-Jan 2. Basic Village hours: 10am-6pm to Oct 3; closes at 5pm, Oct 5-Jan 2. Admission: $4; seniors $3; 6-12 $2 (higher prices for some special attractions).

Waterloo Foundation For The Arts, Inc, Waterloo Village, Stanhope, NJ 07874, **201/347-4700.**

OLD BETHPAGE

Bethpage, NY

This skillfully assembled working model of a typical early 19th-century farm village recalls the time when Long Island was "vegetable garden" to New York City. Throughout the year are seasonal fairs, holiday celebrations, militia drills, temperance meetings, period dances, music, and parades. Visitors can enjoy wagon rides and a schedule of special events that include candle-making, quilting, canning, and a clambake. The setting includes authentically furnished houses, a schoolhouse, tavern, barns, farm animals, era shops, operating blacksmith and carpentry shops—a village peopled with costumed resident "interpreters" who represent life as it was here some 150 years ago. Actually, Old Bethpage never historically existed as a single community. Restoration has painstakingly brought together bonafide historic structures from various parts of Long Island to establish this impressive vintage composite. Approximately 37 miles east of New York City, the Village is only a few minutes' drive from any of Nassau County's major parkway exits with brown-and-white signs marking the route. Open Tue-Sun all year except Christmas, Thanksgiving and Easter. Admission: $3, children & sr.cit. $1.50. Group rates and foreign-language audio tour materials available. Free parking and ample lodging in the immediate vicinity.

Old Bethpage Village Restoration, Round Swamp Rd, Bethpage, NY 11804, **516/420-5288.**

OLD ECONOMY VILLAGE

Ambridge, PA

In 1804, a group known as Harmonists came to America from Germany, seeking religious and societal freedom. In 1824, they established the pastoral village of Economy along the Ohio River in Western Pennsylvania. Although the Pietist society at Economy, the longest-lived of three Harmonist towns in the US, was dissolved in 1905, Old Economy Village still thrives today as a preserved example of an immigrant communal settlement. The core of the village remains, including: the large Feast Hall, used for meetings and communal meals; the Great House, the rather garish home of George Rapp, the Harmonist leader and prophet; and the cabinetmaker's, the tailor's, the cobbler's and other various shops. Costumed guides roam the 6.7 acres of the village, answering questions and taking on the roles of actual Harmonist followers, as documented by society records and writings. These volunteers also give periodic demonstrations of weaving, spinning, baking, quilting, candlemaking, and many more traditional pioneer tasks. Open 9am-5pm, weekdays, 12-5pm, Sun; closed Mon.

The Harmonie Assn, Inc, 14th & Church Sts, Ambridge, PA 15003, **412/266-4500.**

LANCASTER COUNTY

Lancaster, PA

When hearty local cooks tell you, "Kumm esse!" ('Come eat!'), they aren't kidding. Delicious shoofly pie, snitz and knepp, funnel cakes, and other specialties available at a broad selection of family-style and smorgasbord restaurants, are reasons enough to visit this historic center of Pennsylvania Dutch culture. The region was settled in the late 17th and early 18th centuries by hard-working, fundamentalist Christian Amish and Mennonite pioneers, the descendants of whom are known as "the plain people." The term "Dutch" is misleading. It is a colonial adaptation of "Deutsche," the area's predominant ancestry being German. And aside from distinctive ethnic foods in this rural southcentral Pennsylvania retreat, what one finds today is an unmechanized, brotherly way of life, time-removed customs, one-room schoolhouses, unadorned dress, and farming and transportation methods carrying on pretty much as they have for centuries. Lancaster County abounds in picturesque farmer's markets, historic homes open for public tours, covered bridges, hex signs, folk art and crafts, and lodgings that range from conventional hotels/motels and quaint country inns to accommodations on working farms where visitors are invited to help with the chores. An excellent way to enjoy "the Lancaster experience" is via one of several Amish farm tours with a guide to explain the unique character of this ancient, deeply religious way of life. And one friendly request to bear in mind: Because of the literal Biblical restriction forbidding "graven images," visitors are asked not to snap people-pictures without permission.

Visitors Bureau Dept 2000, 1799 Hempstead Rd, Lancaster, PA 17601, **717/299-8901.**

Old Sturbridge Village, Sturbridge, MA

Photo: Clay Nolen

Old Bethpage, Bethpage, NY

SHAKER VILLAGE

Canterbury, NH

When Englishwoman founder Mother Ann Lee and her tiny handful of "Shaking Quakers" first reached New England shores in 1774, the Declaration of Independence was yet to be written and the American Revolution was about to erupt. The Shakers, too, were seeking freedom, both for their religion and for their advanced utopian beliefs. By 1792, this industrious little Shaker colony, which held all goods in common, had become established in New Hampshire, 30 miles north of Concord. In its peak years, half a century later, Canterbury Shakers numbered some 400 and had earned international renown for their classically simple, yet functionally inventive building, furniture, and handicraft designs. Today, 22 of the early colony's historic still-standing buildings and 600 acres of its field, woodlot, and waterway systems have been preserved as a living museum of Shaker culture. Resident Shaker Sisters guide visitors through five historically furnished buildings relating Shaker customs and culture. Daily attendance is restricted to a few hundred to maintain the site's striking tranquility. Special events scheduled May–late Oct include craft demonstrations, heritage workshops, a series of Shaker-related art exhibits, children's programs, and meals. Friday evening candlelit tour/dinners in the Creamery Restaurant features authentic Shaker menus. A gift shop sells a wide array of traditionally simple mementos, as well as meticulously reproduced Shaker furniture. Open 10am-5pm, Tue-Sun (including hols), May-Oct 20. Admission: $4; children $1.50.

Shaker Village Inc, Canterbury, NH 03224, **603/783-9977.**

STRAWBERY BANKE

Portsmouth, NH

"Do you want to wake up some morning and find nothing here but beer joints, honky-tonks, and bowling alleys?" This angry question was posed by plain-spoken Portsmouth Yankee town librarian, Dorothy Vaughan, at a local Rotary Club meeting back in 1957. It had the effect of a call-to-arms in this little-known, historic New England seaport whose origins date back to 1623. What the town populace has accomplished since is the creation of a 10-acre waterfront outdoor museum and cultural resource, incorporating some 37 restored architectural treasures dating from 1695. Some houses have been simply preserved and adapted for modern use as offices and shops; others are on display as educational exhibits covering archaeology, traditional trades, and the evolution of architectural styles and construction techniques spanning four centuries of New England history. Designed to entertain as well as educate, Strawbery Banke's year-round activities include hands-on workshops and historical games for kids, vintage songs and stories, and elaborate period decoration projects in furnished houses. There are horticultural symposiums on historic gardens, clinics on restoring old houses, seminar-workshops on boat-building, instruction on watercoloring and other historic art forms, crafts fairs, charming seasonal events such as the annual Christmas candlelight stroll, and original children's theater productions. Admission $5.50; sr.cit. $4.50; students $4; 6-16 $3; families $5 (special group rates). Open Apr 15-Nov 15 (some facilities open year-round).

Strawbery Banke, PO Box 300, Portsmouth, NH 03801, **603/436-8010.**

Old Sturbridge Village, Sturbridge, MA

HANCOCK SHAKER VILLAGE

Pittsfield, MA

Located in the hills of western Massachusetts, this restored 18th century village depicts the farm life and crafts of the Shakers, America's oldest surviving religious communal sect. The "City of Peace" as it was called, dates back to 1790 and was the third of 19 Shaker communities established in the northeastern and midwestern US. This national landmark provided a home for Shakers until the last members left in 1960. With 20 restored buildings and 1000 acres of rolling farm and woodland, the "City of Peace" is now a popular tourist attraction. The most interesting building is the magnificent Round Stone Barn, erected in 1826. The efficient shape of the structure allowed farm workers to water and feed cattle in a simple circular operation around the perimeter, leaving a massive center space for hay and grain storage. In other exhibits, crafts people meticulously reproduce Shaker wooden and tin goods, furniture, and confections. Visitors are also able to participate in special cooking, dancing, and farming demonstrations. Open daily 9:30am-5pm, Mem Day-Oct. Special group tours and demonstrations may be arranged at other times. Located at the jct of US 20 and MA 41, 5 mi W of Pittsfield.

Hancock Shaker Village, PO Box 898, Pittsfield, MA 01202, **413/443-0188.**

PLIMOTH PLANTATION

Plymouth, MA

Pilgrims who survived the first terrible seasons in this most historic of all Colonial American settlements, endured what to the end of their days they would always remember as "The Starving Time." Facing the tiny colony was the dark wilderness of an unknown continent. Behind lay the bleak horizon of the open sea. Their slender supply of food was shared by stragglers from outposts along the coast and with the Indians who later helped save them. Meanwhile, their spring planting was a disaster. Corn, parched by drought, lay withered in the fields. Before their first year was over, half of them had died. Based on extensive research, today's recreated Plantation conjures the stark original 17th-century colony, complete with 1627-vintage timber houses, furnishings, farm animals, and even a full-scale replica of the Mayflower. But the most intriguing resurrection is the people themselves — a museum staff intensively trained to "impersonate" such known Pilgrims as John Smith and William Bradford, as well as seamen who crossed the Atlantic in subsequent years to establish the first surviving English colony in the New World. Not only do they dress in period clothing and perform typical daily routines of the era, they also speak in the dialect of the time — the Elizabethan language of Shakespeare. Open daily from 9am-5pm Apr-Nov. Admission: $5.50; 5-13 $3. Located 3 mi S of downtown Plymouth on Warren Ave (Rte 3A), or exit 4, Plimoth Plantation Hwy, from Rte 3.

Plimoth Plantation, PO Box 1620, Plymouth, MA 02360, **617/746-1622.**

MYSTIC SEAPORT

Mystic, CT

The middle 19th century. It was a time of Herman Melville's "Moby Dick," of rugged individuality, romance, and adventure—yet also an isolated time when sailors spent years cramped aboard ship, a lonely time that saw grizzled mariners crafting whalebone and ivory scrimshaw or carving fine woods into delicate keepsakes for loved ones left behind. And it was a perilous time when sea-farers raised Sabbath hymns to their Protector. These sailing days represent one of America's proudest and most unique heritages, an era enshrined at this 37-acre preserve of maritime history. That bygone ship-building, whaling, and trading-port lifestyle is captured amidst the large sailing vessels moored here, the scores of small craft prototypes and museum exhibits, and the impressive complex of more than 60 mid-19th-century buildings, lofts, sheds, chapels, and taverns of bustling waterfront

New England. From a distance, the Seaport, with its masts, spars, weathered shacks, and shingles, resembles an ancient sea captain's lithograph. But this is indeed history at anchor where everything floats or works, and where a staff of several hundred interpreter-guides are on hand, many over 70 years of age with sea water in their veins and an intimate understanding of nautical traditions. Invariably, their spry Yankee wit adds to the visitors' fun. There are many kinds of adult handicraft courses, scores of "live" demonstrations, strollers singing sea chanties, an elaborate planetarium that offers celestial navigation instruction, open fireplace cooking, and seafood festivals. Open year-round except Christmas: May-Oct, 9am-5pm; Nov-Apr, to 4pm. Admission: $8.50; 5-15 $4.25.

Mystic Seaport Museum, Inc, Mystic, CT 06355, **203/572-0711.**

OLD STURBRIDGE VILLAGE

Sturbridge, MA

Dinner in a country village! If this sounds intriguing, during a visit to Sturbridge you can become immersed in an early-American dining experience employing open-fireplace cooking techniques, historically-authentic preparations and kitchenware — even down to helping to chop firewood and clean up. It's one of many historic adventures offered in this 1830-era, New England village, a functioning community authentic to the smallest detail. Visitors are transported to the early 19th century amid 200 acres of period structures including churches, water-powered grist and wool-carding mills, a district school, tinsmith and broom shops, wool-dyeing and woodcrafting facilities, a sawmill, pottery shops, a shoemaker, law office, tavern, a bank, general store, and a working farm, complete with teams of oxen and horse-drawn ploughs. Sturbridge is a constant hive of day-long seminars on early craftsmanship ranging from cabinet-making and coopering to spinning, tinsmithing, broom-making, and basketry. There are also special days where participants don period dress and literally take on the arduous working routines of an early American farm family. Week-long preparations for Thanksgiving include musket turkey shooting and hearth-baking. All "receipts" are taken from period cooking texts, turkeys are roasted on vintage tin-reflector ovens, and the full traditional dinner is served in the Village Tavern (reservations mandatory), and includes oyster bisque, steaming harvest vegetables, herb stuffing, old-fashioned cranberry sauce, cornbreads, Marlborough puddings, mince and pumpkin pies, fresh fruits, and home-pressed ciders. Open all year except Christmas and New Year's and Mondays, Nov 26-Mar. Hours: 9am-5pm, Apr-Oct 27; 10am-4pm, Oct. 28-Mar 31. Admission: $7.50 (adults), $3.50 (children 6-15), under 6, free. Group rates available.

Old Sturbridge Village, Sturbridge, MA 01566, **617/347-3362.**

OLD SALEM

Winston-Salem, NC

Founded in 1766 by members of the Moravian Church (an early Protestant group), this lovely and painstakingly restored congregation town, peopled by costumed guides, includes hand-hewn buildings, many from the 18th century, such as a tobacco shop, a bakery, a boys' school, a firehouse, a tavern, a shoemaker's shop, and a number of private residences. The Home Moravian Church Sanctuary, still in use, was built in 1800. Also on the grounds is the Museum of Early Southern Decorative Arts, presenting art objects from the old South in 15 period rooms and four galleries. Other historic points of interest in Winston-Salem include Bethabara Park, site of the first Moravian settlement in NC, and several re-created Salem gardens, sprinkled throughout the grounds of Old Salem and Bethabara Park. Old Salem open every day of the year except Christmas from 9:30am-4:30pm (1:30pm-4:30pm on Sun). Combination tickets for entrance to the museum and all restored buildings is $8 for adults, $4 for children 6-14. Museum-only tickets also available. Located near Old Salem Rd, S of its intersection with US 40.

Old Salem, Inc, Drawer F, Salem Sta, Winston-Salem, NC 27108, **919/723-3688.**

HISTORIC BATH

Bath, NC

Founded in 1705, and the oldest community in North Carolina, Bath is a vibrant crossroads of mid-Atlantic Colonial history. Numbered among its earliest inhabitants were men of great refinement and wealth, as well as notorious pirate Edward Teach, better known as Blackbeard. Farms and tobacco plantations prospered in this fertile bottomland, and local merchants, operating small stores within their houses, enjoyed lively trade with Indians and with the great overseas cargo schooners. As North Carolina's seat of government and a major stop along the great Colonial north-south post road, this village attracted a worldly flow of settlers, strolling players, tinkers, peddlers, farm-produce wagons, ministers, and colonial dignitaries, keeping inns and taverns astir with news and excitement. Most of present-day Bath exists within its original quarter-square-mile where an historically-designated district of preserved and restored vintage structures includes the state's oldest surviving church and residence. Swindel's, housed in a 19th-century brick building, still operates as a general store; an outdoor drama, "Blackbeard: Knight of the Black Flag," is a weekend attraction, mid-June-mid-Aug. Beach-loving, sailing, surfing, and other watersport enthusiasts are attracted by the warm waters of the famous Hatteras Inner and Outer Banks region (see Island Escapes). A Visitor's Center offers brochures and an introductory film. The historic Bath Guest House Inn provides sumptuous Southern-style breakfasts and bicycles for guests. Open year-round, Mon-Sat, 9am-5pm; Sun, 1pm-5pm. Admission: $1; kids 50 cents.

Historic Bath, PO Box 148, Bath, NC 27803, **919/923-3971.**

HISTORIC CAMDEN

Camden, SC

Fever for independence was by no means universal in upper South Carolina, but little support for the British came from this oldest inland settlement of 1750 Irish

Shakertown, Harrodsburg, KY

Williamsburg, VA

Quakers. Consequently, General Corwallis took over the town, making it the final stronghold before the ultimate British defeat at Yorktown. When the Red Coats abruptly departed Camden in 1781, left behind was a unique collection of swords, muskets, coins, cannon balls, and cooking utensils, plus six small surrounding forts and substantial remains of the old community. Today, an historic district recreates this period, complete with perfectly detailed dioramas, restored log cabins filled with antique museum pieces, and the magnificent Judge Kershaw mansion taken over as Cornwallis' headquarters. The visitor encounters a charming unpretentious historical exposure here, including something the British never had— southern hospitality. Much of the area offers winding, self-guided hiking trails, lined with historic markers, fort sites, and deep-woods picnic areas. Operating year-round, except Mon, (unless a hol.) Winter: (Sept 1-May 31), Tue-Fri, 10am-4pm; Sat, 10am-5pm; Sun, 1pm-5pm. Summer: (June 1-Aug 31), Tue-Fri, 10am-5pm; Sat & Sun same as winter. Admission: $1.50; kids $1.

*Historic Camden, Box 710, Camden, SC 29020, **803/432-9841.***

SHAKERTOWN

Harrodsburg, KY

Each time we use a flat broom, a wooden clothes pin, a circular saw, or a washing machine, we can thank the inventive Shakers. This religious sect, once known derisively as "Shaking Quakers"—after jerking bodily motions that were a ritual of their worship — believed in far-sighted notions of racial and sex equality, staunch pacifism, scientific agriculture and experimental farming, and total celibacy with wives living in separate quarters from their husbands. Sad, but small wonder that their numbers are no longer with us. The last Shaker in this 5000-acre Kentucky farm settlement died in 1924. But this historic village preserves 27 original 19th-century buildings that still hold a sense of peace and the godly way of life that once governed the entire community. A self-guided tour enables visitors to see 40 rooms of Shaker furnishings in the Centre Family House and watch broommakers, joiners, coopers, spinners, weavers, and

quilters carrying on their trades. You can also sleep in authentic Shaker lodgings. More than 70 guest rooms are furnished with traditional hand-woven rugs, curtains, and classically simple Shaker furniture reproductions (see Inn Places). Shaker breakfasts, lunches, and dinners are offered in a restored dining room. Open 9am-5pm from mid-Mar-Nov, although a curtailed schedule is in operation during winter. Admission: $4.50; 12-18 $2.00; 6-11 $1.00. Prices for hour-long riverboat rides on the Kentucky River are the same.

*Shakertown at Pleasant Hill, Rte 4, Harrodsburg, KY 40330, **606/734-5411.***

COLONIAL WILLIAMSBURG

Williamsburg, VA

From 1699 to 1780, Williamsburg served as the capital of the Virginia Colony. Here, Washington, Jefferson, Patrick Henry, George Mason, and other patriots helped shape the foundations of our government. In 1926 John D. Rockefeller and others began the task of restoring a large part of the original town to its 18th-century condition. Today, more than 170 acres have been preserved, including 88 buildings, and 90 acres of gardens and greens. In addition, 50 other major buildings have been rebuilt according to exhaustive research, making this by far the largest and most comprehensive 18th century restoration project in the US. Using tools and methods that were common in the 18th century, craftsmen in more than 20 shops create goods that range from ragpaper books to elegant wooden cabinets, all before the public's curious gaze. Also represented are examples of the recreational side of colonial life, including the reconstructed Raleigh Tavern where George Washington was known to lift a few tankards of ale. Exhibits include more than 225 period rooms, 20 craft shops with live demonstrations, the Abby Aldrich Rockefeller Folk Art Center, and the 650-acre Carter's Grove Plantation nearby. Admission plans vary from the year-long Patriot's Pass for unlimited admission ($21 for adults, $10.50 for children 6-12) to the 10-admissions

ticket offering a slightly limited choice of 10 separate exhibits at the visitors choice ($10 for adults, $5 for children).

*The Colonial Williamsburg Foundation, PO Box C, Williamsburg, VA 23187, **800/446-8956, 800/582-8976** (in VA).*

ALEXANDRIA

Alexandria, VA

Robert E. Lee's father, the Revolutionary War hero "Light Horse Harry," made his home here. It was also George Washington's hometown with a still-existing country-style church that contains the private Washington pew. Today, this ancient seaport, founded by Scottish landowner, John Alexander, in 1749, conveys its heritage via a collection of more than 2000 restored and preserved 18th and 19th century buildings. Old Town Alexandria, a living architectural textbook, presents fine examples of elegant Georgian, Federal, Greek Revival, and Victorian styles. Supported by a variety of interpretive exhibits, are: Lyceums, taverns, an Athenaeum, and an 18th-century town hall/market square complex complete with whipping posts; a Presbyterian meeting house with the Tomb of the Unknown Revolutionary Soldier; the George Washington National Masonic Memorial containing a clock that stopped at precisely the time of Washington's death; and old Fort Ward—now an outstanding Civil War museum with an adjoining 40-acre park, outdoor amphitheater, and picnic area. These are just a few highlights of a self-guided walking tour beginning at the 1724 Ramsay House official visitor's center (221 King St) where free brochures and an orientation film are available. Free admission to most tour sites, but check for varying hours. Annual events include historical observances, concert series, a popular Scottish Games and Gathering of the Clans Festival, and a second-to-none Washington's Birthday bash.

*Tourist Council, 221 King St, Alexandria, VA 22314, **703/549-0205;** 24-hour taped message on special events, **703/549-SCOT.***

Shakertown, Harrodsburg, KY

Chapter 19

ROMANTIC RENDEZVOUS

Poconos, PA

Do your fantasies conjure *the* idyllic romantic rendezvous for you and your special someone? Is it perhaps a rustic lodge in the Smoky Mountains? A misty seaport village off the tip of Cape Cod? Or a secluded inn on craggy cliffs above the Pacific?

Chosen especially for traveling twosomes, the following destinations promise an atmosphere of intimacy and seclusion. Couples can discover the secrets of a New England village; explore arts and crafts galleries in the Ozarks; taste the flavor of fisherfolk heritage; stroll down shaded, narrow streets; and feel unsullied, virgin-beach sand between their toes. Brown County, Indiana offers the charm of homespun art colonies, miles of horseback trails, and vivid fall colors. Other towns enchant their visitors with festivals featuring country crafts, street dancing, and regional cooking, such as free boiled shrimp.

Our listings span the United States in an effort to introduce hideaways—some traditional, many that are off the beaten track—which create an ambience of mystique and romance. You might want to stroll through a Swiss village that has never seen a traffic light, or discover specialty shops and boutiques selling hand-blown glass, handknit sweaters, and fine antiques. Whatever you're looking for—horse and buggy rides, moonlight dancing on a boat, heart-shaped bathtubs, a private penthouse, or cobblestone streets lined with moss-draped oaks—we've tried to include them all, and more.

And wherever you go, these romantic rendezvous promise a scenic backdrop and roots buried deep in history. Investigate, for example, the covered bridges of the Berkshires, admire stately antebellum mansions along the Gulf of Mexico, or taste-test wine at a local, scenic vineyard.

There's nothing quite like the discovery of a picturesque village that can become your own "special place"—whether it's nestled in the mountains, along a logging river, or overlooking a sparkling harbor. Each haven has its special charm and personality, and perhaps there's one waiting just for you.

Many of our listings include suggested inns, resorts, and/or restaurants; you should always make reservations to ensure accommodations—especially for weekend rendezvous.

NORTHWEST

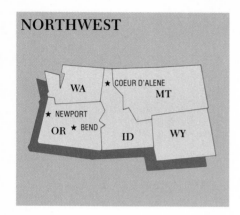

summits of some, such as Pilot Butte, Paulina Peak, and Lava Butte, offer easy access to spectacular views of the Cascade Range. In winter, many of these peaks, as well as others in the Cascades, provide superb downhill skiing slopes. In summer, a wide assortment of geological oddities, including underground lava tubes, the world's largest forest of lava-cast trees, and Newberry Crater (remains of a massive volcano that collapsed into itself) can be explored. Spectacular scenic drives also surround the area, providing views of the Deschutes River, McKenzie Pass, and the 97-foot-high Tumalo Falls. Pine Mountain Observatory, largest in the Northwest, welcomes visitors seven days a week. Just to the northeast, the town of Sisters has been restored to its original frontier character.

Chamber of Commerce, 164 NW Hawthorne Ave, Bend, OR 97701, **503/382-3221.**

SOUTHWEST

NEWPORT

Pacific Coast, OR

Few scenic wonders can woo couples better than the stunning Pacific seacoast of the Northwest. Oregon's shoreline is considered by many to be the most picturesque coast in the world, and the compact, neat-as-a-pin village of Newport is smack in the middle of it. Along US 101 are magnificent views of craggy cliffs, deep inlets, sandy beaches, shifting dunes, lighthouses, and promontories (see Scenic Drives). Newport has many buildings dating from the Victorian era, and has enjoyed popularity as a resort for well over a century. For a truly romantic getaway, stay at The Inn at Otter Crest just 10 miles north (see Inn Places). Overlooking the craggy Pacific coast from atop a cliff, this cedar-sided lodge offers a long list of resort amenities. Much of the character —and romance—of Newport derives from Yaquina Bay, where the Yaquina River meets the Pacific. Here, in addition to the town and the fishing port, is Yaquina Bay state park and the famous Old Yaquina Bay Lighthouse, built in 1871 and since restored and used as a maritime museum. Nearby attractions include: the Underseas Garden (267 Bay Blvd), regarded by many as the loveliest display of indoor marine life in the Northwest; the enormous Mislaw National Forest, comprised of a number of lovely beaches operated as state parks; and the Oregon Dunes National Recreation Area. The city sponsors a seafood and wine festival (late Feb) and a sailing regatta (late Apr). Highly regarded among a number of fine resort/motels are the Embarcadero (503/265-8521), and Salishan Lodge (503/ 764-3600) (see Regal Resorts).

Chamber of Commerce, 555 Coast Hwy, Newport, OR 97365, **503/265-8801.**

BEND

Central OR

Lovers who enjoy the great outdoors at its finest will love this four-seasons resort area on the sheltered eastern side of Oregon's Cascade Mountains. The area juxtaposes tall, coniferous evergreens with a backdrop of sloping volcanic tableland capped with a series of dormant volcanoes. The town of Bend is located along the banks of the Deschutes River, noted for its fine canoeing, superb fishing (14- to 20-inch rainbows are common), and spectacular scenery. The immediate area around Bend was once the site of extensive volcanic activity. Massive cones left by extinct volcanoes dot the landscape. Roads leading to the

COEUR D'ALENE

Northern ID

Here is America's grand wilderness, where the human spirit soars like the tree-covered mountains guarding the crystal-clear lakes and unspoiled streams below them. Here, famous Lake Coeur d'Alene and the picturesque city at its northern shore can be just the beginning of an adventure as large as the western sky. In summer, you and your special someone can disport around either of two enormous, deep lakes, Coeur d'Alene and Pend Orielle. Together, they offer hundreds of miles of shoreline and varied recreational opportunities including water skiing, wind surfing, ferryboat tours, and seaplane rides. Or explore the more intimate Hayden Lake, or any one of dozens of rivers and bubbling brooks meandering through the hills just beyond the town. Drier but equally enchanting experiences await on hiking and bicycle paths through valleys speckled with wildflowers and on horseback trails winding through wooded, mountain slopes. Other activities include: pack trips; hayrides; mining tours; helicopter rides; and water slides. In winter, major ski areas, both Alpine and Nordic, as well as hundreds of miles of snowmobile trails are nearby, offering plenty of ways to fill up the hours before apres-ski time.

Chamber of Commerce, PO Box 850, Coeur d'Alene, ID 83814, **208/664-3194.**

SAUSALITO

North San Francisco Bay, CA

Half the fun of Sausalito is getting there from the south, via San Francisco and the Golden Gate Bridge (see Man-Made & Natural Wonders). Located at the North terminus of the famous bridge, the town is noted for its artist residents and for the enormous harbor and marinas that make it San Francisco's yachting center. The huge Sausalito Art Festival is held on Labor Day weekend, but formal as well as decidedly informal galleries are year-round attractions. The eclectic Village Fair (777 Bridgeway), housed in a three-story building once used by Chinese as a gambling and opium den, now offers a variety of imports and unusual arts and crafts sold in small specialty shops. At 2100 Bridgeway is the San Francisco Bay and Delta Hydraulic Model, a 2-acre building containing a model that reproduces tidal action, plus a variety of related exhibits. Sausalito is an excellent home base for tours of the wine country to the North, especially in the Napa Valley. Several inns, notably Casa Madrona and Sausalito, offer comfortable accommodations in well-preserved old rooms furnished with antiques. Among the many highly regarded restaurants are Ondine and Casa Madrona.

Chamber of Commerce, PO Box 566, Sausalito, CA 94965, **415/332-0505.**

Steamboat Springs, CO

Carmel, CA

NEWPORT HARBOR AREA

South of Los Angeles, CA

Sun, surf, and sand. The trademarks of southern California's Gold Coast are much in evidence here. Sometimes called the American Riviera, this seaside area is known for its many specialty shops and atmospheric restaurants. Couples can amble down shaded streets lined with elegant waterfront villas, and/or lounge on six miles of sand overlooking a sparkling harbor painted with streamlined yachts and rainbow-striped spinnakers. A favorite destination is Balboa peninsula, a six-mile-long finger of land offering resort accommodations, seaside recreation, and boat excursions to nearby Catalina Island (see Island Escapes). Balboa Island is one of the largest in the area and can be reached by car via Marine Ave. Sailboat tours point out the beachfront homes of many celebrities, while motorized craft and sailboats can be rented at several locations for a more private exploration of the harbor and the open Pacific. South Coast Plaza Village, in Costa Mesa, provides unique shopping with 70 shops and restaurants clustered around a Village Green, and cobblestone streets bordered with old-fashioned lamp posts imported from London. A well-kept secret is the elaborate Magic Island entertainment complex, an adults-only extravaganza featuring everything from Las Vegas-style stage acts to intimate, late-night dancing. Although the $4 million establishment is a private club, many area hotels can arrange temporary memberships. The harbor hosts a Charter Boat Parade late Aug, a Christmas Boat Parade late Dec.

Chamber of Commerce, 1470 Jamboree Rd, Newport Beach, CA 92660, **714/644-8211.**

PALM SPRINGS

East of Los Angeles, CA

A world-class resort area particularly noted for its golf, tennis, and outdoor trails, Palm Springs may appeal to couples interested in finding luxurious surroundings on a moderate to king-sized budget. Since its discovery by Hollywood celebrities in the 1920s, the town has evolved from a sleepy village on the edge of the desert to a sprawling city with more than 200 hotels, motels, and resorts dedicated to vacation luxury. No less than 40 golf courses, most of tournament quality, lie within a 20-mile radius. Of the more than 300 tennis courts in the area, many are lighted for night play. Palm Springs has more swimming pools per capita than any other city on earth, and social sunbathing is one of the most popular activities. For the more energetic, there are miles of hiking, bicycle, and bridle paths winding through the desert canyons. The Palm Springs Aerial Tramway offers an escape from the desert heat in spectacularly rapid fashion. In the 15-minute climb to the top of 8516-foot Mt. San Jacinto, from the blazing desert floor through pine forests to a ski area at the summit, the temperature drops 40°F—the equivalent in climate of a trip from Mexico to Alaska. A restaurant at the top has a panoramic view of the shimmering desert. At night, area discos, theatres, and night clubs pulsate with top entertainment and a sprinkling of Hollywood celebrities. For many, a romantic evening includes a leisurely stroll under the star-filled desert sky.

Convention & Visitors Bureau, Municipal Airport Terminal, Palm Springs, CA 92262, **619/327-8411.**

CARMEL

Near Monterey Peninsula, CA

Verdant pine forests, virgin beaches, rugged seascapes, and clear, blue water...It's hard to imagine a more serendipitous setting than Carmel and the Monterey Peninsula just north of it. Carmel is rapidly developing a reputation as the honeymoon capital of the west, and a number of world-famous attractions are in or near the quiet village. Commercialism is low-key here; instead of neon signs, the village relies on meandering streets, flaky-fresh pastries in bakery shop windows, markets selling imported cheeses, and haute cuisine, to attract your attention. Point Lobos Reserve is an outdoor museum of rare, natural beauty, where whales can be seen migrating in spring and fall, and a variety of cormorants, pelicans, sea lions, sea otters, and waterfowl can be spotted year-round. Nearby are Pebble Beach golf resort (see Golf & Tennis Places) and the famous 17-Mile Drive (see Scenic Drives)—unforgettable for its picturesque splendor. Also of note is the 1771 Carmel Mission (open to visitors daily) and the Tor House (Fri/Sat by appointment), a remarkable structure built entirely of granite found along the coast. Carmel's beaches are beautiful, but the cold ocean water and dangerous tides are not conducive to swimming. Instead, explore the beautiful countryside on the Monterey Peninsula. Remember to take sweaters for the foggy, summer days and cool evenings.

Carmel Business Assn, PO Box 4444, Carmel, CA 93921, **408/624-2522.**

Santa Barbara, CA

SANTA BARBARA

North of Los Angeles, CA

Many have called it "America's French Riviera." Baron Philippe de Rothschild journeys from France to spend his winters here, so perhaps he agrees. The natural beauty of this year-round, residential and resort area begins at the palm-lined Pacific beaches, continues northward and upward through the foothills, and on into the cool coastal mountains. Historic Yacht Harbor, home for well over a thousand fishing and pleasure boats, features a paved walkway over the main breakwater that makes possible a half-mile walking tour into the harbor. Directly opposite the main breakwater is Stearns Wharf, a three-block-long extension of State Street with shops, eateries, and great fishing spots. Nearer the mountains is the famous Mission Santa Barbara, founded in 1786 and still in use two centuries later. In the foothills, on Mission Canyon Rd, is the 60-acre Botanic Gardens which preserves, in addition to native trees, wildflowers, shrubs, and cacti, an historic dam built in 1806 by Indians under the direction of mission padres. The city's Hispanic past has left reminders everywhere, including the red tile roofs that top many downtown buildings and the well-known Royal Presidio, the ruins of a Spanish fortress presently being refurbished. The city has a number of small but excellent museums and plays host to seasonal arts and crafts shows as well as to music and dance performances. The beauty of 30 miles of white sand beaches around Santa Barbara is only slightly marred by the presence of offshore oil rigs.

*Conference & Visitors Bureau, PO Box 299, Santa Barbara, CA 93102, **805/965-3021.***

SCOTTSDALE

Central AZ

Life in Scottsdale, as well as in neighboring Phoenix, revolves around the certainty of one thing—sunshine. With reportedly more sun-filled days than any other place in the US, and an average yearly temperature of 72°F, this red-hot resort mecca perennially attracts couples. A striking diversity in natural landscape and thus, in recreation, allows visitors to choose between a leisurely game of golf or tennis and a relaxing day at poolside, or try hang-gliding, hot-air ballooning, jeep treks into the desert, rock climbing, or even tubing down the nearby Salt River. Open-air trolley cars provide easy access from the many resorts, to shopping areas known for good browsing and a wide range of commodities, including western gear, Indian crafts, and designer clothes. Cultural festivals are held frequently, and the area has more than 90 fine arts galleries. The "Green Belt," a 7½ mile landscaped area spanning Scottsdale, offers expansive parks, bicycle paths, hiking trails, and swimming pools. For those in search of the romance of the Old West, the attractions include Rawhide, an 1880s frontier town, and several horseback riding ranches, some offering cowboy cookouts under the stars. For lovers of natural beauty, the area around Scottsdale is unsurpassed, and includes the Grand Canyon (see Man-Made & Natural Wonders), Monument Valley, the Petrified Forest (see Nat'l Parks & Monuments), and Meteor Crater. Tours of two futuristic centers of architecture, Paolo Soleri's studio and Frank Lloyd Wright's Taliesin West, are available.

*Chamber of Commerce, 7333 Scottsdale Mall, PO Box 129, Scottsdale, AZ 85252, **602/945-8481.***

Steamboat Springs, CO

SANTA FE

In the Sangre de Cristo Mountains, NM

First-time visitors seeking a romantic getaway in this city will find that Santa Fe is filled with a wealth of surprises, and resplendent with historic and ethnic charm. For such a well-known city, the population is tiny, barely passing the 50,000 mark. Nestled on a desert plateau 7000 feet high, Santa Fe's altitude is nearly a half mile higher than Denver's, the famous "Mile High" city, and the rarified air gives the town a mild, four-seasons climate unusual for the Southwest. This picturesque capital has acclaimed opera performed outdoors atop a crest (June 30-Aug 25), while festivals fill the summer calendar, culminating in the Fiesta (mid-Sept), a nearly 270-year-old folk festival that offers historical pageantry, arts and crafts, and street dancing. Santa Fe is the oldest continually used seat of government in the country. Established in 1610 by Spaniards, it soon became the capital of the "Kingdom of New Mexico." Spanish, Mexican, and Indian heritage influence much of the city's architecture, and the narrow, winding streets in the downtown district testify to Santa Fe's age. Historical highlights include: San Miguel Mission, the oldest mission church in the US; a number of historic Catholic cathedrals; and the oldest house in America, built more than 800 years ago by Indians. Nearby are a number of Indian pueblos, the oldest *cities* in the US. Renowned as one of the leading art centers in the country, the city has more than 100 galleries. The Santa Fe ski basin, reached by a breathtaking, 20-mile drive through the Sangre de Cristo Mountains, is famous throughout the Southwest.

*Convention & Visitors Bureau, PO Box 909, Santa Fe, NM 87501, **800/528-5369.***

STEAMBOAT SPRINGS

In Rocky Mountains, CO

Lovers who enjoy the rugged outdoors will appreciate this four-seasons ski resort area high in the mountains. In winter, invading hordes of skiers test the downhill slopes and such cross-country trails as the 10,000-foot Rabbit Ears Pass. Scenic escapes include a number of drives, designed for photographers, into the mountains just out of town (some of which are accessible only in summer). These include the famous Rabbit Ears Pass about 20 mi southeast of the city, Buffalo Pass, which crosses the Continental Divide and leads to a number of remote lakes, and Fish Creek Falls, named for a mountain-fed waterfall nearly 300 feet high. Steamboat Springs is so-named because of the 100 or so mineral springs active in the area, and the Steamboat Health and Recreation Association operates a year-round pool fed by spring water in excess of 100°F, in addition to saunas and tennis courts. The adjacent 141,000-acre Routt National Forest is popular for hiking, fishing, camping, and picnicking. During off-season (winter here often extends Nov-May), accommodations are less expensive.

*Resort Chamber Assn, Box 773377, Steamboat Springs, CO 80477, **303/879-0880.***

Scottsdale, AZ

MIDWEST

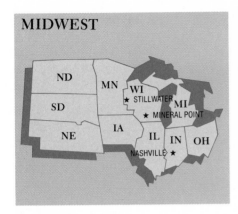

MINERAL POINT

Southwest WI

The romance of England's rugged west country lives on in this charming town, founded in 1827 when Chicago was still a mud flat. A true renaissance town, it has attracted artists and artisans and others with a sense of history who have lovingly restored its old, stone buildings. The Chesterfield Inn dates back to 1834 when it was one of the territory's first stagecoach inns. When settlers from Cornwall, England, renowned for their mining skills, came to this booming lead-mining town in the 1830s, they brought expertise in stonecutting and masonry and built sturdy cottages. The Chesterfield Inn, built of native limestone, is a fine example of this craftsmanship, and offers three comfortable guest rooms and a dining room featuring Cornish specialties. An outdoor-dining patio is set against a steep stone bluff containing the remains of two cave-like dwellings. During the lead rush, miners chiseled these so-called "badger holes" as temporary homes. Stop at this hostelry for afternoon tea—Cornish tea biscuits and saffron bread served with butter and preserves. Or enjoy a hearty miner's stew—thick with meat, potatoes, and vegetables and served with homemade bread. Delectable English desserts include bread pudding with caramel sauce and *figgyhobbin*, pie crust wrapped around a filling of raisins, brown sugar, and cinnamon. Ubiquitous around Mineral Point is the Cornish pasty—a hot, crusty turnover brimming with meat and vegetables, a portable meal that miners once carried to work in their pockets. Pasties are served at many local cafes. The Walker House, undergoing complete restoration, is a beautiful stone building (circa 1836) which will offer guest rooms and traditional Cornish fare. Shake Rag Alley is an arts/crafts colony housed in reconstructed rock and log buildings. "Shake Rag" comes from the custom of women shaking a rag from their doorways, signaling miners home to lunch. Pendarvis is a restoration of miners' houses, authentically furnished, that includes a rowhouse with a traditional *kiddlywink*, a cozy Cornish pub. The scenic drive into Mineral Point via WI 23 takes you past rustic farmhouses, quiet streams, and lush green meadows in the heart of Wisconsin's dairyland.
Tourist Info Ctr, PO Box 75, Mineral Point, WI 53565, **608/987-3201, -2361.**

Nashville, Brown County, IN

NASHVILLE

Brown County, IN

The steeply rolling hills, lush valleys, thick forests, and homespun art colonies of Brown County will surprise many people who picture Indiana as a land of flat corn fields. But here it is, a touch of the Ozarks planted just north of the Ohio River, a popular weekend getaway for couples from St. Louis, Chicago, and other midwestern metropolises. This rustic county exudes homespun charm, with bluegrass music festivals, edibles that include hickory-smoked ham, hot fried biscuits, persimmon pudding, and hickory-nut pie, an old-time drugstore with a marble soda fountain, and towns with the improbably colorful names of Gnaw Bone and Bean Blossom. Sometimes referred to as "Log Cabin Country," Brown County has more than 50 historic log cabins and many are still in use (tours available). Nashville is home for hundreds of artists and artisans who specialize in country crafts, a score or so of antique shops, and half a dozen museums. Art galleries ranging from Nashville's large Brown County Art Gallery and Brown County Art Guild, to tiny studios, dot the town and much of the county, featuring oil paintings, jewelry, wood carvings, handmade textiles, flower art, and cornsilk dolls. The 15,000-acre Brown County State Park, largest in Indiana, offers lovely views from roadside lookout points, and miles of hiking and horseback riding trails. The fall foliage here is a polychromatic extravanganza, and miles of bicycle paths and picnic spots provide up-close enjoyment. Accommodations are available in the state park's Abe Martin's Lodge, as well as at a number of quaint inns in Nashville.
Chamber of Commerce, PO Box 164, Nashville, IN 47448, **812/988-2785.**

STILLWATER

On the St. Croix River, MN

The charm of a Victorian-era rivertown and the beauty of a National & Scenic Waterway combine to give this town a particularly romantic quality. Back when lumberjacks rode the logs downriver—deftly maneuvering them with log poles, and neighboring St. Paul was still a village called Pig's Eye, Stillwater was a hustling river town. The clearing of forests by the rugged men of this frontier town soon won the entire St. Croix Valley its reputation as "King Pine." These glory days are not yet lost upon the people of Stillwater; the lumber industry is still active and its history is celebrated annually in its St. Croix River Festival and Lumberjack Days. Today, the lower portion of the St. Croix is still a lazy-moving, wide stream full of wildlife, delightful scenery, and inviting backwaters and sloughs. Couples can appreciate the picturesque environs by staying at the Lowell Inn—its colonial motif along the banks of the river is in keeping with the historic significance of the town. Three dining rooms furnished with a Dresden china collection (for display only), acid-etched stained glass windows, and Williamsburg ladder-back chairs, make dining an elegant event. For both white-water and quiet-water enthusiasts, the St. Croix is a popular canoeing and rafting stream, flowing through the unspoiled and often heavily forested banks of the protected valley. Autumn illuminates the valley in brilliant colors.
Chamber of Commerce, PO Box 586, Stillwater, MN 55082, **612/439-7700.**

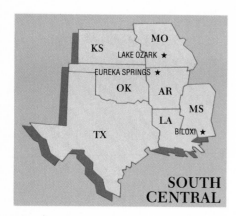

SOUTH CENTRAL

BILOXI
Gulf of Mexico, MS

Take a lovely peninsula in the Gulf of Mexico surrounded by 26 miles of sandy beaches; pepper liberally with French, Indian, Cajun, English, and Spanish heritage; add dashes of antebellum elegance and maritime adventure; and bake the mixture year-round under a warm southern sun and — voila! — call it Biloxi. Graceful homes with sweeping lawns and bay windows front the blue Gulf or oak-shaded lanes, and an average temperature of 67°F is conducive to a full calendar of festivals, parades, and fishing rodeos. The Annual Shrimp Festival and Blessing of the Fleet (1st weekend in June) is a 300-year-old religious ceremony asking God for successful fishing in the coming season. Music, dancing, free boiled shrimp, and a parade of gaily decorated boats are among the colorful festivities. Community life revolves around the Gulf of Mexico, and a 138-year-old lighthouse stands as an historical, maritime tribute; the 65-foot-high monument is still in use and offers visitors a stunning coastal view. Spend an idyllic day along the shore, picnicking and fishing off piers in Gulf Marina State Park. Flounder, drum fish, shrimp, and crab are commonly caught, and 24-hour security makes midnight fishing viable. Tours of the Mississippi Coast will take you past 65 historical and geographical sights, including some of the South's most stately antebellum homes. Hotels and resorts offer dancing to live music and a wide variety of outdoor activities. Area restaurants prepare excellent ethnic and seafood dishes. One, the French Connection, is located on grounds that were originally part of Beauvoir, the estate of Confederate leader Jefferson Davis (tours daily). About 12 miles south of Biloxi is Ship Island (see Island Escapes), accessible by tour boat.

Chamber of Commerce, 1036 Fred Haise Blvd, Biloxi, MS 39530, **601/374-2717.**

EUREKA SPRINGS
Northwest AR

Clinging to the gentle Ozark Mountains like a transplanted Swiss village, this lovingly restored Gay Nineties resort town almost seems to whisper, "for lovers only." The quiet beauty of this magical place has seemed to defy description for more than 100 years, even though little has changed. Eureka Springs has yet to see its first traffic light. For more than a century, the village has been shaped by the rolling mountains surrounding it. No two of the town's 230 streets cross at right angles. St. Elizabeth's is the only church on the continent where the street level entrance is through the top of the bell tower. The Ozark Mountains have long been a center for arts, crafts, and folk music, and more than 600 artists and craftspeople live and work in Eureka Springs. Much of their handiwork is sold in quaint stores and workshops around town. The first week in November is usually the time for the famous Ozark Folk Festival, widely imitated but never surpassed by other area villages. Late October and early November is also the time when the hardwood forests covering the hills begin to turn color and the rust-to-crimson foliage paints the horizon in every direction. But at any time of year, the town's beautifully restored Victorian homes and businesses make Eureka Springs one of America's most romantic destinations.

Chamber of Commerce, Box 551, Eureka Springs, AR 72632, **501/253-8737.**

LAKE OZARK
Lake of the Ozarks, MO

With 1372 miles of irregular shoreline, Lake Ozark is replete with enough scenic nooks and crannies to delight its faithful, year-round vacationers. Enjoy the Ozark Highlands aboard a *Tom Sawyer* paddlewheeler, or arrange your own prime-rib-dinner cruise, or an evening dance while serenely floating across the lake (Casino Pier: 365-2020). For the adventuresome, helicopter and seaplane rides are available, and boats can be rented at a variety of marinas including those near Bagnell Dam. Just south of Lake Ozark, near the town of Osage Beach, is the sprawling Lake of the Ozarks State Park. Occupying about 90 miles of shoreline, the park features several large public beaches and boat ramps, miles of hiking and horseback trails, and tent and trailer campsites. Lodge of the Four Seasons and Marriott's Tan-Tar-A Resort (see Regal Resorts) both have topnotch accommodations, although more modestly-priced rooms are available if you prefer. Even if you don't stay at the Four Seasons, visit its Toledo Room for a superb continental meal and a lovely view of the lake.

Lake of the Ozarks Assn, PO Box 98, Lake Ozark, MO 65049, **314/365-3371.**

NORTHEAST

OCEAN CITY
Atlantic Coast, MD

Whether it is joining the crowds on Ocean City's boardwalk, chartering an ocean-going yacht for fabulous offshore fishing, or getting away from it all on a secluded island, this popular resort city can appeal to almost everyone seeking an exciting (or restive) romantic getaway. Maryland's only ocean resort features a 3-mile-long boardwalk, complete with the usual nautical atmosphere, amusements, and summertime crowds. Surf casting and pier fishing can result in excellent catches, but the finest sport fishing (Ocean City is considered the white-marlin capital of the world) is found in deep ocean canyons about 50 miles offshore. For a truly romantic rendezvous, escape to nearby Assateague Island (see Island Escapes). Primitive campsites that can be reached only by canoe or relatively long hikes, offer private and peaceful getaways. If this sounds a bit too quiet and primitive, many of the resort motels in Ocean City offer live music and late-night dancing throughout most of the year, and there is harness racing June-Labor Day at Ocean Downs Raceway (5 mi W of town).

Chamber of Commerce, Rte 1, PO Box 310A, Ocean City, MD 21842, **301/289-8559.**

Eureka Springs, AR

MT. POCONO

Pocono Mountains, PA

These rustic mountains of northeastern Pennsylvania are noted for their rugged beauty and as a honeymoon mecca for Easterners. Nearly a dozen resorts cater especially to newlyweds and to the otherwise romantically inclined. On Mt. Pocono alone, there are four: Strickland's Mountain Inn and Cottages; Mount Airy Lodge; Pocono Garden Lodge; and Paradise Stream Honeymoon Resort. Satisfying a demand for exaggerated luxury, and for seclusion, these resorts typically provide such amenities as individual chalets, Jacuzzis, heart-shaped sunken bathtubs, private indoor swimming pools, penthouse villas, and roman suites. Pine and hardwood forests cover much of the steeply rolling countryside, making outdoor jaunts a delight. The numerous lakes and streams hidden throughout the hills are excellent for fishing, canoeing, swimming, sailing — and wooing. Attractions within a few miles of Mt. Pocono include a scenic drive to Pocono Knob, the Amish exhibits at Pennsylvania Dutch Farm (see Ethnic & Historic Villages), Memorytown, USA (a complete old-time village with Hex Shop and more), and two state parks. Southeast of Mt. Pocono is Stroudsburg, near the site of the scenic and historic Delaware Water Gap. There are a variety of festivals throughout the year.

Vacation Bureau, Box PR, 1004 Main St, Stroudsburg, PA 18360, **717/421-5791.**

SARATOGA SPRINGS

Central NY

Lovers who enjoy quiet Victorian elegance, relaxing mineral water baths, fine music and dance, and the whirlwind social and recreational activities surrounding thoroughbred racing at its dressiest will enjoy this historic, European-style resort. In the 1880s, fashionably attired men and their parasol-twirling ladies promenaded along the shaded paths in Congress Park, where naturally carbonated mineral springs produced water that for many years was all the rage as a health tonic. Much of this dressy and elegant spirit still pervades the area, and many of the springs are still active. The Performing Arts Center at Saratoga Spa is home in July to the New York City Ballet and in August to the Philadelphia Orchestra. A variety of other cultural events are staged June-Labor Day. Saratoga Spa is a 2000-acre state park just south of town. Located within are a number of internationally famous mineral baths, the Spa Summer Theatre, a spectacular swimming pool, a golf course, and the renowned Gideon Putnam Hotel, *the* place to stay (or at least see and be seen) in Saratoga Springs. The hotel is famous for its sumptuous honeymoon packages. Saratoga Race Course is the nation's oldest active thoroughbred racetrack. The action takes place only during a 24-day period in Aug, but Saratoga Harness Raceway has a considerably longer season.

Chamber of Commerce, 494 Broadway, Saratoga Springs, NY 12866, **518/584-3255.**

Poconos, PA

CAPE MAY

Southern Tip of NJ

A visit to the nation's oldest seashore resort is like a romantic journey into the past, to the era when the austere homes of whaling crews were gradually being supplanted by the mansions of Victorian high society. Cape May is both a 25-mile-long peninsula, poking into the Atlantic, and a town located at its extreme tip. The town of Cape May boasts no fewer than 600 authentically restored Victorian-style homes and business establishments, the largest collection of such structures in the US. Tree-lined streets and the gorgeous homes fronting them begin just a short block from the seaside promenade. Best times to see these spectacular residences, inside as well as out, are during the three yearly open house festivals (July, Oct, and Dec). During the crowded summer tourist season, walking is about the fastest form of locomotion in town, but old-time trolleys and rented bicycles are also popular. Like any full-fledged ocean resort, Cape May has a number of marinas, clean beaches, a fishing wharf, a variety of nautical clubs, fine antique and souvenir shops, and a number of excellent restaurants, ranging from elegant dining rooms in Victorian buildings to informal sidewalk cafes. For particularly romantic accommodations, try one of the many restored guest houses or historic old hotels (see Inn Places).

Chamber of Commerce, PO Box 109, Cape May, NJ 08204, **609/884-5508.**

NIAGARA FALLS

Northwestern NY

For more than a century, the thundering falls of the Niagara River have beckoned honeymooners from around the world. Undoubtedly, it is the splendor of the Falls themselves that attract the love-struck, and one of the most thrilling ways to view the magnificent cataracts is by boat — enveloped in the mist near the base of both the American and Horseshoe Falls (many tours available). Or, couples can dine while enjoying Niagara Falls from the Top of the Falls Restaurant — every table has an unforgettable panorama. In downtown Niagara, the glass-enclosed Wintergarden is a year-round tropical park with ponds, a waterfall, and more than 7000 trees, shrubs, and flowers. Flanked on either side by Rainbow Mall and near the newly renovated Main St. specialty shops, Wintergarden is the hub of tourist activity. In winter, the falls freeze into rippling, crystal prisms, and the Festival of Lights transforms the town into a sparkling wonderland (between Thanksgiving and New Year's). Other popular attractions in the city are the Niagara Wax Museum, the Aquarium of Niagara Falls, the Schoellkopf Geological Museum, with numerous exhibits and A/V programs presenting a 500-million-year history of the Falls, and Old Fort Niagara. About seven miles north is historic Lewiston, where vintage shops and restaurants built in the 1820s have been carefully restored. Within walking distance of downtown Lewiston is Artpark, featuring a wide variety of cultural activities. (See Man-Made & Natural Wonders.)

Convention & Visitors Bureau, 4th St, Niagara Falls, NY 14303, **716/285-2400.**

Litchfield, Berkshire Hills, CT

NEWPORT

Narragansett Bay, RI

The salty air of the Atlantic and the carefully preserved mansions and summer cottages of America's elite families from the Gilded Age, go hand-in-hand on this island-like peninsula. Once the nation's most opulent resort area, many mansions are now open for public inspection. The Breakers, a palatial summer residence for Cornelius Vanderbilt, is the most stunning of the grandiose estates in Newport. The most relaxing and romantic way to see the grand old buildings in Newport is to travel on the old-style trolley that snakes by or near most of the popular sites (passes sold at Chamber of Commerce). Hammersmith Farm, established in 1640, is still in operation and may be toured Apr-Oct. The 28-room cottage built on the premises in 1887 was once the summer residence of the family of Jacqueline Kennedy Onassis. The building served as the Summer White House from 1961 to 1963. Newport Harbor is home base for the America's Cup races and for a variety of interesting seafood restaurants. Visitors to Newport should also consider excursions to the nearby island resorts of Block Island and Martha's Vineyard (see Island Escapes). In Newport, a wide variety of private guest homes and inns provide rooms in historic settings (401/846-5444).

Chamber of Commerce, Ten America's Cup Ave, Newport, RI 02840, **401/847-1600.**

SALEM

North of Boston, MA

The romantic charms of maritime New England are exemplified at Salem, where rolling, tree-lined streets wind past stately 17th and 18th century homes and tiny graveyards. The town's many paths following the shore are often used by bikers, joggers, and pedestrians who take pleasure in enchanting views of postcard-pretty Salem bay dotted with bobbing yachts and brightly-colored buoys. The skyline of Salem as seen from Derby Wharf has remained essentially unchanged for 300 years. The wharf is part of Salem Maritime National Historic Site (see Historic Landmarks) which also protects the historic Customs House, where Nathaniel Hawthorne once worked. Derby street is home to the *House of Seven Gables,* the setting for Hawthorne's famous novel. Also along Derby Street is Pickering Wharf—a six-acre complex, in the style of a New England fishing village, of shops, seafood restaurants, and amusements. Although the infamous Salem Witch Hunts remain the town's greatest claim to fame, it is remarkable that this bit of regional hysteria occurred only during seven months in 1692. The Witch Dungeon (featuring reenactments of a witch trial), Witch House (restored home of a witchcraft judge where the accused were "questioned"), and Witch Museum are popular tourist attractions. The nine acres of Salem Common are surrounded by well-maintained historic homes and provides yet another tranquil setting for scenic strolling.

Chamber of Commerce, Old Town Hall, Salem, MA 01970, **617/744-0004.**

AMHERST

North of Springfield, MA

About her home town, Emily Dickinson wrote, "Here seems to be a bit of Eden...Fairer it is and brighter than all the world beside." This quaint college town has an alluring way of combining the cosmopolitan qualities of a campus with the rural atmosphere known to this area. Tree-lined streets, red-brick towers, and Victorian homes provide a New England ambience, and the usual college-town amenities abound: concerts; theatre; film; lectures; art exhibits; and intercollegiate sports events. A free bus service transports students and visitors around campus, to the many specialty shops downtown, and to the center and heart of Amherst—a green, shaded village common. Steeped in history, literary and otherwise, are many reconstructions of historic villages within an hour or two's drive (see Ethnic & Historic Villages). The immediately surrounding area is rural, and the country roads that twist through undulating farmland are best explored via rental mounts available at many local stables. Tours are available through the historic home of Miss Dickinson as well as the homes of other celebrated locals such as Robert Frost, Noah Webster, and William Cullen Bryant. Nature lovers enjoy the beauty of the enormous Quabbin Reservoir, which supplies metropolitan Boston with water, located just east of Amherst. Hiking trails, boat rentals, picnic areas, and canoeing are all favorite pastimes for visiting couples. Every spring the town rallies to drain the precious sap from its maple trees; visitors are welcomed into maple camps to see how syrup and sugar are made and to taste the delicacy of sugar on snow (early Mar-early Apr).

Tourism Dev Council, 11 Spring St, Amherst, MA 01002, **413/253-9666.**

PROVINCETOWN

Cape Cod, MA

Nowhere in America is the provincial charm of quiet fishing villages and the site of momentous historical events so happily married as on Cape Cod. And Provincetown, at the very tip of the cape, is the distilled essence of America. Here is where the Mayflower first landed in 1620. Here, too, is where the brother of Norseman Leif Erickson came ashore to repair the keel of his boat some 600 years earlier. And, here, is a misty, mystic spot for lovers, old and new. To the credit of the administrators of the National Seashore around Provincetown, the beaches at the tip of Cape Cod today look much the same as they did to the early Viking and Pilgrim explorers. Except for the changing shapes of the wind-and-surf-swept dunes piling up around the 30 or so miles of open beaches, nary a motel, home, or gas station has been allowed to alter the age-old splendor of the coastline. The singular exception to the ban on improvements is an eight-mile stretch of paved bicycle trails and a few old fishing shanties that are being allowed to return to the sandy earth according to their own, natural rhythms. There are also three low-impact, self-guiding nature trails, two at Pilgrim Heights and another in the Province Lands. Along the narrow streets of Provincetown, which retains the flavor of 19th century Portuguese fishermen who settled there, is much to see—museums, historic sites, arts and crafts galleries, and fine restaurants, including those specializing in Portuguese cuisine (see Unique Restaurants). The most romantic way to see the sights is via horse and buggy, starting just outside Town Hall on Commercial St. The cape is best seen during spring and fall, before and after the summer tourist season. Whale-watching tours leave MacMillan Wharf mid-Apr–fall.

Chamber of Commerce, PO Box 1017, Provincetown, MA 02657, **617/487-3424.**

Saratoga Springs, NY

Portland, Casco Bay, ME

WILLIAMSTOWN

Northwestern MA

One of the loveliest towns in New England, rich in history and quiet tradition, is nestled in the rolling, pastoral landscape of the Massachusetts Berkshires. Community life revolves around George Williams College, which has a provincial charm all its own, and is well worth a walking tour. The Williams Inn is adjacent to campus bordered by a wide, tree-lined thoroughfare through historic Williamstown. Couples can stay at the inn and be within walking distance of most cultural attractions and the unique shops downtown. For gift ideas, The Studio displays exquisite wares of wool, rare woods, hand-blown glass, and pottery, and The Cowbell specializes in handknit sweaters, items of brass, and knickknacks from the orient. One of the biggest attractions is the small but superb Clark Art Institute featuring a major collection of Renoir, as well as some American art and artifacts. But the romantic setting of Williamstown is half of its enchantment, and couples shouldn't pass up the chance to explore the gorgeous New England hills and country valleys. East of town off Rte 2 is 3500-foot Mt. Greylock, highest point in the state with views ranging as far as the Hudson Valley and the Green Mountains of Vermont. Here, hikers can join up with a section of the Appalachian Trail and with other footpaths which cross the summit. Just east of Williamstown, Rte 2 follows the famous Mohawk Trail (see Scenic Drives), a fascinating excursion ultimately leading to New York's Finger Lakes. Between Williamstown and Pittsfield is a major historic recreation, Hancock Shaker Village (see Ethnic & Historic Villages). From Pittsfield, it is a short drive to major classical and jazz concerts at Tanglewood in Lenox. Autumn is the time when the rolling hills and farmlands of the Berkshires are perhaps the most magical and romantic.

Chamber of Commerce, 69-½ Main St, North Adams, MA 01247, **413/663-3735.**

LITCHFIELD

Berkshire Hills, CT

The Berkshires are, for many thousands of annual visitors, the quintessential New England experience—a place to unwind among glorious scenery, covered bridges, art and music festivals, and Norman Rockwell-like images of rustic life in the hinterlands of the Northeast. Cutting across Massachusetts and a corner of Vermont as well as Connecticut, the Berkshire Hills (they'll look like mountains when you see them) are popular playgrounds for harried residents of New York, Boston, and other cities along the Eastern Seaboard. The romantic appeal of Litchfield, in the northwest corner of the state, is its classic New England charm. Here is where you can bicycle down country lanes lined with hedgerows, past quiet New England farms and fields dotted with wildflowers, tour historic villages and gracious country estates, and stop at country inns for hearty food and drink. Litchfield itself is an outstanding example of a New England town from the 1700s. Among the historic homes are Oliver Wolcott's house, where a statue of George III was melted into bullets by the ladies of the town for the Sons of Liberty, and the birthsite of Harriet Beecher Stowe, author of *Uncle Tom's Cabin*. Perfect for romantic strolls is the White Memorial Foundation, a 4000-acre park with more than 30 miles of hiking and horseback trails, located just west of town on Rte 202. Just east of Litchfield is the Haight Vineyard, featuring tours and tastings daily May-Dec. Within day-tripping distance is Tanglewood in Massachusetts, site of famous music festivals and the summer home of the Boston Symphony.

Travel Council, PO Box 1776, Marbledale, CT 06777, **203/868-2214.**

PORTLAND

Casco Bay, ME

If variety is the spice of both life and love, then the little seacoast town of Portland is a feast for the adventuresome spirit of every romantic. The pounding surf, the rugged mountains of Maine, clear inland lakes, a potpourri of significant historical attractions, and even the foreign charms of Canada are accessible from this picturesque maritime community. Myriad summer resort islands dot the blue horizon in Casco Bay, and couples can explore them during daylight, sunset, and romantic moonlight cruises (see Island Escapes). The Old Port Exchange is a restored area of 19th century Portland; cobblestone streets are lined with shops featuring such specialities as wood-working, toys, and fabric weaving, plus quaint,

old-time restaurants. America's first lighthouse, commissioned by George Washington, still stands here. Today, visitors are welcomed into numerous historic homes, including that of Henry Wadsworth Longfellow, and can climb to the top of historic Portland Observatory for a 100-mile panorama of land and sea. Whether for sightseeing in summer or skiing in winter, the east coast's finest mountains are just a short drive inland. Nearer the sea is an assortment of fine eateries (locals claim that there are more restaurants per capita in Portland than anywhere else in the US) where fresh lobster is king. At Portland's historic harbor, visitors can rent sail boats or motor boats or book passage on tour boats or on a ferry to Canada, or simply watch the trawlers come in and unload the day's catch.

Greater Portland Chamber of Commerce, 1428 Free St, Portland, ME 04101, **207/772-2811.**

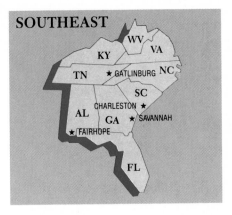

SAVANNAH

Southeastern GA

A surprisingly cosmopolitan city in the heart of the Deep South, eclectic Savannah can always fit the way you feel. Its roster of restaurants and clubs run the gamut: ballroom dancing and ice cream parlors; bluegrass music with beer, or harpists with dinner; ethnic foods and hotdog stands. The shirt-sleeve climate makes sightseeing a joy, and more than 5000 majestic, moss-draped oaks keep Savannah shady and green year-round and known as "The Walking City." Streets are punctuated with lush squares and grand mansions, and a riverfront plaza utilizes restored cotton warehouses for more than 75 boutiques, as well as taverns, restaurants, studios, and museums. A brick concourse is ideal for strolling, picnicking, and shipwatching. The enormous 2½-square-mile National Historic District bordering I-80, has an impressive list of "must see places" for architecture and history buffs. (Historic inns and hotels are located within the district.) Horse and buggy rides are popular ways to enjoy the Victorian charms of the city, and are especially romantic under moonlight. Or take a riverboat cruise of the harbor and port. The labyrinth of waterways leading to the Atlantic are also the sites of a number of historic forts, Fort Washington being the largest and most interesting. The tidal marshlands, fed by brackish saltwater and three major rivers, are also excellent places for exploring, beachcombing, and fishing. *Victory Drive* is a world-famous, three-mile stretch of stately mansions, preserved as a memorial to servicemen of World War I.

Convention & Visitors Bureau, 301 W Broad St, Savannah, GA 31499, **912/233-6651.**

Charleston, SC

CHARLESTON
Southeastern SC

A long and rich history has given Charleston the name, "Mother City of the South." Historic shrines, landscaped gardens, winding streets, and detailed iron lace gateways exude the high manners of noble aristocracies from ages gone by. Much of the history of the area is contained in the restored buildings and exhibits of Old Charlestown (see Historic Landmarks), and the best way to explore this district is on foot. Tours begin at White Point Gardens (Murray Blvd and E Battery), the tip of a peninsula offering a view of the harbor and Fort Sumter Nat'l Monument, where the Civil War began. Many of the buildings date from the 18th century and include the infamous Provost Dungeon, Cabbage Row (the inspiration of "Catfish Row" from Gershwin's *Porgy and Bess*), Old Slave Mart (now a museum), Dock St. Theatre, and a number of historic homes, churches, and commercial buildings. To get into the romantic spirit of the by-gone era preserved in Charlestown, try tours of the old district in horse-drawn carriages or aboard old-time trolleys. Perhaps even more romantic than the charming, historic buildings, are the fine examples of southern gardens near the city. Magnolia Plantation and Gardens is a three-century-old garden and waterfowl refuge along Rte 61. Slightly farther north is Middleton Place Gardens, the oldest formal gardens in America.

*Visitor Info Ctr, Box 975, 85 Calhoun St, Charleston, SC 29402, **803/722-8338.***

GATLINBURG
Great Smoky Mountains, TN

Few words can adequately express the somber sensuality of the Smokies. Few places equal their romantically remote, yet easily accessible, setting. Visitors to the lofty peaks and high trails are gradually introduced to a hush that can be downright unnerving at first. Adding to the magic is an almost ever-present ethereal haze, more like an incantation than a misty cloud. But there is a ruggedness here as well, both to the land and to the hearty people who live and work in the hills. There are 16 peaks in the Smokies higher than 6000 feet, all among the highest points east of the Rockies. Gatlinburg is nestled next to one of the highest, the 6593-foot Mount LeConte, within the borders of the enormous Great Smoky Mountains National Park (see Nat'l Parks & Monuments). In terms of permanent residents, Gatlinburg is tiny. But its population of 3000 manages to support accommodations for some 25,000 daily visitors. Virtually all of the major motel chains are represented, but for hardy couples not afraid of a five-hour hike up the side of a mountain, none can compare with LeConte Lodge near the summit of Mount LeConte. Operated by the National Park Service, the seven snug cabins and three lodges are as rustic and isolated as any spot in the eastern US (615/436-4473). For those uninterested in a strenuous hike, three skylifts operate within or near Gatlinburg. Also in town are a number of stores featuring mountain handicrafts, and several fine restaurants including the highly regarded Burning Bush and Open Hearth.

*Chamber of Commerce, PO Box 527, Gatlinburg, TN 37738, **615/436-4178.***

FAIRHOPE & POINT CLEAR
Eastern Shore of Mobile Bay, AL

Romance and southern hospitality seem to go hand in hand. Smile at passersby along the beaches lining the calm and warm waters of Mobile Bay, and just about everyone smiles back. They, too, know the quiet delights that abound in the little resort towns stretching along the bay from Spanish Fort to the north to Point Clear to the south. Beautifully maintained parks and public beaches dot the shoreline, and high bluffs near Spanish Fort offer panoramic views of the bay and the city of Mobile just across it. The municipal pier, marina, and yacht club at Fairhope attract thousands of saltwater enthusiasts every year. Also in Fairhope is the Square-Rigger restaurant (205/928-1291), highly regarded for its stuffed flounder, softshell crabs, and Colonial atmosphere. Just to the south, in Point Clear, is probably the most famous of all the historic resort hotels in the south, Marriott's Grand Hotel (see Regal Resorts). The 650-acre grounds, resplendent with moss-covered oaks, shimmering lagoons, and spectacular formal gardens, are tailor-made for romantic strolls and quiet outdoor *tete-a-tetes*. Although most of the joys of the eastern shore are quiet ones, middle-of-the-night joviality reigns during the unpredictable summer "Jubilee." This is when the fish go wild! Bottom-dwelling denizens break their normal routine and either float on the surface of the water or actually crawl up on shore. Flounder, eel, and shrimp comprise a few, and crabs have been known to scuttle right out of the water and up trees. The exact reason is not known but it's believed to be a periodic deficiency of oxygen in the water which drives them up for air. Whatever the reason, it's said that on a good night you can fill your freezer!

*Eastern Shore Chamber of Commerce, PO Box 507, Fairhope, AL 36533, **205/928-9324.***

Charleston, SC

Chapter 20

CITY WEEKENDS

Photo: Mike Michaelson

New Orleans, LA

For those who work in a big city, the tendency on weekends is to escape from it. Yet, many American cities are storehouses of cultural and recreational wealth, unbeatable for pure entertainment. Why not commute in reverse? Check in at a hotel for a weekend — bargain packages often are available as hoteliers strive to fill rooms jammed during the week with business guests and conventioneers. Then take time to explore and enjoy.

Awaiting in Chicago, are distinct ethnic neighborhoods, including the Swedish and Lithuanian enclaves described here. In Boston, you can relive some of the most crucial days in American history. In Baltimore, you can wander a revitalized waterfront, shopping, dining, and snacking within a gleaming new indoor marketplace, visiting fascinating museums and historical sights, and viewing the old Colonial port from aboard a tour boat.

If you live in a small town or a rural area, by all means visit a city for a weekend. Within large cities you can concentrate on exploring special areas—street markets, waterfronts, restored historic neighborhoods, expansive parks, and clutches of museums and galleries. In smaller cities, you can sample a cross-section of attractions—in Fort Wayne, for example, there's an old fort, a delightful compact zoo, a botanical gardens with three different climate zones, and a gleaming museum of antique cars. Memphis and Nashville have historic sections that revolve around music.

More and more cities are undertaking massive urban renewal projects to wipe out urban blight and create attractive new areas, usually around an historically authentic theme. The results add up to some great weekend excursions.

Although we have included only a small sampling of suggestions for city escapes, the intent is to indicate the *range* of fascinating diversions that cities have to offer and, perhaps, inspire you to head for town—instead of out of it.

NORTHWEST

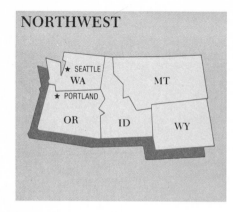

SUBTERRANEAN CITY

Seattle, WA

Two events in Seattle's history—the 1889 fire, and the 1962 World's Fair—left remnants that are fascinating spots to visit in this growing metropolis. After the devastating fire in 1889, city planners decided to raise the street levels, and simply rebuild *over* the remainder of the old city. This left many homes, shops, and sidewalks below the new street level. This preserved bit of history lay undisturbed for decades until Bill Speidel started exploring the forgotten subterranean city in the 1960s. Speidel began taking curious friends down to see the underground marvels, and word soon spread. Now he offers walking tours of the historic catacombs, past once-elegant hotel lobbies, dusty storefront windows, and cobweb-draped doorways. The tour is also filled with tall tales and short stories about Seattle's bawdy past. Visitors learn about the lady barbers who fronted for an opium den, the birth of the modern "massage parlor," and the old town's sewer system, which caused toilets to erupt twice a day at high tides. Nearby and above ground is Seattle Center, the site of the futuristic 1962 World's Fair. This 74-acre landscaped complex is the hub of Seattle culture. The dominating feature is the famous Space Needle, a 605-foot spire that has come to be known as the city's "trademark." From its observation deck visitors can see all of the city, and most of the surrounding lakes and mountains. The Center is also home to the Seattle Opera and Symphony, the Fun Forest Amusement Park, the Pacific Science Center, and a pavilion of the Seattle Art

Museum (see Masterful Museums). A 90-second monorail ride whisks you the 11 blocks from the Center to downtown (or vice versa).

Bill Speidel's Underground Tours, 610 1st Ave, Seattle, WA 98104, **206/682-1511.** *Seattle Ctr, 305 Harrison St, Seattle, WA 98109,* **206/625-4234.**

URBAN OREGON

Portland, OR

Despite the fact that Portland suffered through Indian wars and the money-scarce years following the Civil War, it still blossomed into the largest city in Oregon—largely due to its location near the confluence of the Willamette and Columbia Rivers. A major deepwater seaport, Portland is a rapidly growing city with more than two dozen office buildings constructed during the last decade—the most well-known modern landmark is the Portland Building, its blue-tiled facade has won architectural awards and the notorious title, "municipal bon bon box." Only momentarily daunted by a dousing of volcanic ash in 1980 (compliments of nearby Mount St. Helens), downtown Portland offers shoppers everything from major department stores and malls, to antique and specialty shops. The Old Town district features a wide variety of shops and boutiques housed in some of Portland's most historic buildings, and the Yamhill Marketplace is a 5-level atrium-style mall with more than 30 shops featuring bakeries, a farmers market, and an art gallery. Relax on the grassy environs of an amphitheater and watch a summer play, splash around in a city fountain (it's legal!), or take a day-trip to nearby Willamette Valley and tour a vineyard. In a city known as a leader in rose culture, visitors are invited to stroll through the International Rose Test Gardens, and/or celebrate with thousands of others during the annual Rose Festival in June (see Fun at Festivals), for a week to 10 days of floral and boat parades, sports car races, and outdoor concerts. Although the town is a growing metropolis, its picturesque environs often charm visitors into staying an extra day or two. Graced on the east side by the snowcapped Cascade Mountains, and to the west by the forested hills of the Coast Range, buildings are limited to 40 stories in order to preserve the view. Portland boasts 160 parks, including the northwest Forest Park with 4700 forested acres crisscrossed with hiking and running trails, and said to be the largest wilderness area located inside an American city. Jake's Famous Crawfish (226-1419) is a popular destination for fresh seafood and entrees flown in from as far away as New

Zealand, and Westin Benson is one of the best-known luxury hotels in the area, offering a variety of amenities and vacation packages (228-9611). Bed and breakfast lodgings are available in a variety that ranges from suburban homes to houseboats.

Convention & Visitors Assn, Inc, 26 SW Salmon, Portland, OR 97204, **503/222-2223.**

SOUTHWEST

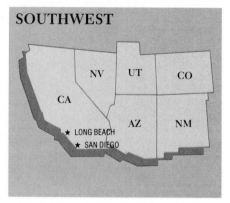

PACIFIC PARKLAND

San Diego, CA

This city, with its pluperfect climate (71°F. average annual temperature, low humidity, and meager annual rainfall) and with magnificent vistas ranging from ocean to desert to rugged mountains, offers diversions enough to fill dozens of weekend getaways. It is imbued with history, dating back to the original native Indians and to 16th century Spanish conquistadores, and it has a dominant Mexican flavor because of its proximity to the border (Tijuana is just 17 miles south of downtown). Its incomparable zoo is world renowned, and Sea World (see Theme & Amusement Parks) is a perennially popular marine amusement park. Plus there are beaches, boat rides, and a charming Old Town, restored site of San Diego's original settlement. But San Diego also is a city of beautiful, expansive parks, perfect for weekends out of doors (*the* place to be in San Diego). In fact, Balboa Park, the cultural heart of the city, could keep you pleasantly diverted all summer long. Within its 1400 acres are fountains, ponds, miles of walkways alongside gardens, lawns, and lush vegetation, and the famous zoo with an aerial tramway and more than 3200 animals (800 species) roaming large, open areas confined by natural barriers. Also in the park are concerts by the world's largest outdoor organ (with 5000 pipes)—and one of America's greatest concentrations of museums, art galleries, and theaters. Here is where theater-lovers go for Shakespeare festivals at the Old Globe Theatre, and for musical and dance events at the Starlight Bowl. Space buffs head for NASA exhibits at the San Diego Aero-Space Museum, displays and memorabilia honoring the heroes and heroines of flight at the International Aerospace Hall of Fame, and to the world's largest theater planetarium at the Reuben H. Fleet Space Theater and Science Center. For art lovers, the park offers Old Masters at the Tinken Art Gallery, and a wide range of European, early-American, Oriental, and contemporary art at The San Diego Museum of Art. The park also houses an excellent Natural History Museum and, for sports fans, the San Diego Hall of Champions. For a spectacular overview of San Diego, drive the road fringed with palms and

Portland, OR

Photo Greater Portland Convention & Visitors Association

cypresses to Point Loma, site of the Cabrillo National Monument. As America's most visited national monument it receives more tourists than the Statue of Liberty. It also is a great spot for whale-watching during the migration season.

Convention & Visitors Bureau, 1200 Third Ave, Ste 824, San Diego, CA 92101, 619/232-3101.

RENAISSANCE CITY

Long Beach, CA

A fishing village, water sports, a retired ocean liner, gondola rides down canals, pedicabs for hire, wine-tasting, unusual restaurants, a thriving artists colony, a score or more of antique shops, fine hotels, comfortable bed-and-breakfast inns, and a good measure of sunshine — all within one city. These are the ingredients for a relaxing weekend getaway in Long Beach, which is becoming known as the "The Renaissance City." An unusual place to stay is the Hotel Queen Mary, the regal liner whose passenger list once included such names as Gable, Astaire, Churchill, and Vanderbilt. She's still afloat and docked at Long Beach Harbor, offering comfortable restored cabins, restaurants, shops, and a lounge with entertainment. Even if you don't stay aboard, you can relive the luxurious heyday of transatlantic crossings with a tour of the *Queen*. Alongside rests another retired legend, Howard Hughes' famed flying boat, the *Spruce Goose*, the largest airplane ever built (see Man-Made & Natural Wonders). European-style lodgings are available at Bettenhausen's Seal Beach Inn (see Inn Places), located

within 300 yards of the beach. Shoreline Village is a waterfront shopping/dining area, themed as a fishing village, that threads through the harbor. It is quintessentially Californian, with wooden decks, alfresco dining areas, stand-up bars, and glass-enclosed dining rooms full of gleaming brass and hanging plants. As you stroll its planked boardwalks, stopping to admire a lighthouse or trim yachts at anchor straining against creaking ropes, you can buy a fresh cookie or an ice cream to munch on, or stop at the Rainbow Pier Fish Market for a bowl of chowder or fresh fish or shellfish. The village has two major restaurants, five cafes, 30 shops, boutiques, and galleries, and a gleaming authentic 1906 carousel. Water sports enthusiasts will want to head for Alamitos Bay (birthplace of windsurfing), where lessons and rentals are available for windsurfing and sailing (Sabot class). Unusual dining spots include Kalemegdan, for Yugoslav cuisine served at a small, family-run restaurant; hearty breakfasts (or huge luncheon burgers) in the morning sunshine on the patio at Hamburger Henry; and The Filling Station (it formerly was a gas station), featuring tempting sandwiches, a wide selection of omelets, creative salad combinations that are large enough for two, and lots of locally-produced relishes, preserves, and other canned goods to take home. At Naples, a picturesque community threaded with canals, you can take a romantic ride in a gondola and enjoy a wine tasting at Morry's of Napes, the oldest gourmet wine and liquor shop in Los Angeles county. A major event, the Long Beach Grand Prix (late Mar), brings international racing drivers to compete around the streets of town in Indy-style cars.

Convention & Visitors Bureau, 180 E Ocean Blvd, Ste 150, Plaza Level, Long Beach, CA 90802, 213/436-3645.

San Diego, CA

Long Beach, CA

Photo: Mike Michaelson

MIDWEST

TIME CAPSULE TOWN

Fort Wayne, IN

The two kitchen helpers, wearing long dresses, cotton bonnets, and severe, floral aprons, were chopping vegetables for a beef stew and fashioning cornbread loaves for the oven. The blue-coated soldier, gossiping with the women, wore a tall leather shako with a plume. Having been shooed by the busy women, he turned to the camera-toting visitors and introduced himself as Sgt. Ezekiel Harris. Nodding at their "St. Louis" T-shirts, he asked, "What news of the Missouri Territory," explaining that he was to receive bounty land there as payment for fighting in the War of 1812. This vignette, enacted at Old Fort Wayne, is typical of what today's visitor will find upon entering this authentically reconstructed fort and stepping into an 1816 time capsule. Daily chores are performed by accurately costumed military and civilian personnel who engage in spirited conversations with visitors about social or political issues of the time. Quilting, spinning, weaving, sewing, and candlemaking are carried on inside the timbered fort; outside are vegetable gardens, a blacksmith shop, and an Indian encampment. Dramatizing a typical day at the Fort, soldiers drill, fire and clean muskets, split wood, and make lead musket balls. Each year a series of colorful weekend events revolve around folkcrafts, music, cooking, and military encampments. History is evident elsewhere in modern Fort Wayne: the Lincoln Library and Museum contains an impressive collection of books, documents, and other Lincoln memorabilia; there are separate museums devoted to art, history, and firefighting; and the Auburn-Cord-Duesenberg Museum at nearby Auburn has a collection of more than 100 classic automobiles (see Masterful Museums). Other diversions for weekenders include an excellent compact zoo where electric cars take visitors on a safari through an African veldt, and a botanical conservatory comprised of three buildings—the Tropical House, the Arid House, and the Showcase, devoted to major seasonal displays. Fort Wayne offers excellent community theater and, for outdoor lovers, canoe trips down three rivers that played an important role in the town's history. A major annual event is the Johnny Appleseed Festival (mid-Sept)—the grave of Johnny Appleseed (John Chapman) who died in 1845, is at Fort Wayne. The Marriott offers excellent accommodations and amenities and a sumptuous Sunday brunch.

Chamber of Commerce, 825 Ewing St, Fort Wayne, IN 46802, **219/424-1435.**

Fort Wayne, IN

Photo: Mike Michaelson

LIVELY ARTS
Cleveland, OH

Once a beleaguered, bankrupt city, denigrated as "the mistake on the lake," Cleveland has undergone a remarkable renaissance. It has become a cultured, black-tie town that is an important center in arts and entertainment—and an excellent weekend destination for theater-going and gallery-hopping. It has an orchestra and art museum of world class, opera and ballet companies of growing stature, and Playhouse Square Center, a dazzling, $27 million restoration of three grand movie palaces. The old Ohio, Palace, and State theaters are being returned to their original 1920s elegance, replete with hand-painted murals, plush velvet seats, Carrara marble walls, and crystal chandeliers copied from the Palace of Versailles. The Center will showcase cabaret-style theater and Broadway productions, and will be home to the Cleveland Ballet and Opera and the Great Lakes Shakespeare Festival. Other weekend diversions in Cleveland, particularly appropriate for families, include: the Cleveland Aquarium, with a live crocodile, sea horses, octopi, and seals; Cleveland Metroparks Zoo, with 1300 animals and a six-acre African plains area; The Cleveland Museum of Art, with its Egyptian mummy cases and a medieval armour court (complete with a mounted knight in armour); the Cleveland Museum of Natural History, full of dinosaurs, birds, and stuffed animals; the Cleveland Health Education Museum, with blinking, talking, walk-through exhibits of the human body; and the Crawford Auto-Aviation Museum with meticulously restored cars and planes. The city offers skyline views of sparkling Lake Erie, an 18,500-acre string of woodland parks, called the "Emerald Necklace," and fascinating shops and unusual eateries along a waterfront restoration known as the Flats. Don't miss a Saturday morning visit to the colorful West Side Market with 130 indoor and outdoor stalls offering a variety of produce and scrumptuous ethnic dishes, ranging from Hungarian strudel to Ukranian pirogies.

Convention & Visitors Bureau, 1301 E 6th St, Cleveland, OH 44114, **216/621-4110.**

ETHNIC INFLUENCES
Chicago, IL

Take a weekend — or several — to explore Chicago's ethnic neighborhoods. The options are many, for while Sandburg's "city of the big shoulders" is a melting pot, it also is a city in which ethnic groups cling to their cultures. There's a thriving Chinatown and well-defined Polish, Irish, and Italian neighborhoods in addition to the two microcosmic ethnic areas highlighted here—one on the city's south side, the other near its northern edge. Many of Chicago's 150,000 Lithuanians live in Marquette Park, an area they settled in the late 1800s, finding jobs at the nearby Pullman Works and stockyards. Lithuanian Plaza Court resembles a small European town, dotted with tiny cafes, delicatessens, and specialty import shops. Here you can buy Lithuanian books, records, dolls, dishes, and other old- country goods, and taste such dishes as sauerkraut soup, potato pancakes, roast pork, stuffed cabbage, and meat-filled blintzes or dumplings. A street fair (late June) brings entertainment stages, a dance tent, costumed folk dancers, Lithuanian arts and crafts, and booths vending beer and food. Chicago's Swedish community is centered along four blocks of N. Clark Street (between Foster & Balmoral). Here are a trio of Swedish restaurants where you can sample such fare as potato sausage with yellow turnips, pancakes with traditional ligonberry sauce, and hearty open-faced sandwiches. For take-home Scandinavian food, two delis, with sacks of yellow peas and shelves lined with an assortment of canned fish and packages of potato-dumpling mix, offer such cheeses as Jarlsberg, Havarti, brie, and samsoe, plus pickled herring, lutefisk, and schmaltz. Import shops stock china, crystal, stainless steel ware, and Scandinavian arts and crafts. Accomplishments of Swedish-Americans are attractively presented at a small museum. Annual events include a summer festival (mid-June) and the traditional St. Lucia Festival and crowning of the Queen of Light (Dec 13).

Convention & Tourism Bureau, McCormick Place-on-the-Lake, Chicago, IL 60616, **312/225-5000.**

Cleveland, OH

Photo: ©Mark C. Schwartz

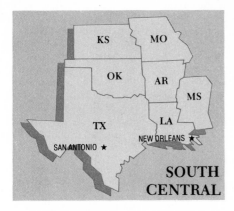

KS
MO
OK
AR
MS
TX
LA
NEW ORLEANS ★
SAN ANTONIO ★

SOUTH CENTRAL

CULTURAL CROSSROADS

San Antonio, TX

Imagine a place where the sun shines 300 days a year (and where they claim that summer goes to spend winter), where graceful streets give way to gently-sloping hills, a place rich and diverse in ethnic tradition. That place is San Antonio, a city that represents a variety of the 26 different cultures which originally settled in Texas. It's a great town to explore on foot, especially as you wander along the lovely Paseo del Rio (River Walk), tracing the course of the San Antonio River which snakes through town. This riverside walkway, lush with foliage, is bordered by shops, boutiques, galleries, and eateries. For dinner, pick an outdoor terrace along the river and enjoy a Texas-style steak or authentic Mexican cuisine. Or enjoy the view from the river, aboard a spry water taxi, sight-seeing barge, or a do-it-yourself pedal boat. The historical district of La Villita, the city's original settlement with 18th century adobe buildings and bordered by palms and bougainvillea, is today an arts community with a wide variety of galleries and shops. As visitors stroll leisurely through this old quarter, they can watch local artisans create blown glass, pottery, candles, woodwork, and other crafts—or custom-order a pair of rugged boots and watch them being made. Nearby is the Alamo (see Historic Landmarks), where you can relive the 1836 battle when Davy Crockett, Jim Bowie, and 186 other Texans lost their lives in gallant defense of the old Spanish mission. This heroic stand is recreated with 10 color projectors, five screens, and polyphonic sound at a theater-museum. Across the street is the Long Barrack Museum and a church, all that survive from the beseiged mission. Market Square distills the Mexican flavor of the city. This colorful marketplace, with drifting Mariachi music and gas-lighted streets, has shops and arcades crammed with wood crafts, handmade serapes, jewelry, and other imports from south of the border. On the south side of town is the King William district where German craftsmen and merchants settled and built elaborate homes in the 1840s. Annual celebrations include La Fiesta, a 10-day party, reminiscent of New Orleans' Mardi Gras, commemorating the Battle of San Jacinto (Apr); and the Texas Folklife Festival (Aug).

Convention & Visitors Bureau, PO Box 2277, San Antonio, TX 78298, **512/299-8123, 800/531-5700** *(outside TX),* **800/292-1010** *(in TX).*

DOWN BY THE LEVEE

New Orleans, LA

The fabled French Quarter, with its raucous Bourbon Street, sedate Royal Street and historic Preservation Hall, is a magnet to visitors. But there is plenty of diversion, too, for weekenders who roam the area around Decatur Street, which borders the Quarter and parallels the Mississippi. There's the river itself, with its timeless barge traffic, tourist paddleboats, and quiet spots along the levee for rest and contemplation. And, alongside, the bustling French Market, offering a cornucopia of fresh fruit and vegetables ... luscious ripe tomatoes, decorative wreaths of garlic, and mesh sacks of pecans. Its neighbor is a flea market where, amid stalls vending discounted jeans, a few genuine antiques, and mounds of assorted junk, reproductions of bordello tokens are a popular curiosity. Adjacent to the flea market is the old U.S. Mint, now housing a museum where fascinating exhibits trace the history of jazz, presenting the story with sepia photographs, snatches of music, visitor-activated narratives, and a collection of the instruments of the famous. The building also houses an outstanding Mardi Gras Exhibit, full of colorful costumes and floats, while on the grounds is one of the original streetcars of the Desire route. Across from the French Market is Central Grocery and several other Italian groceries, festooned with cheeses and smoked sausages and hams. Prepared here, amid barrels of olives and pungent, tempting aromas, are huge muffuletta sandwiches—a circular, loaf-sized bun filled with layers of an olive-oil based salad, meat, sausage, and cheese. Other "don't miss" culinary experiences in this area include: Creole cooking at Tujague's, a moody restaurant and bar established in 1856 (see Unique Restaurants); a late-night (or early morning) visit to Cafe Du Monde for strong, bracing *cafe au lait,* laced with chicory and served with hot *beignets*—square donuts sprinkled with powdered sugar; and, in season (Feb-June), a sidewalk crawfish boil at Coop's Place, a small, open-fronted bistro with a Cajun kitchen and an oyster bar. The old Jackson Brewery, built in 1891, has been renovated to provide a new riverside spot for shopping, outdoor dining, and people watching.

Tourists & Convention Commission, Inc, 334 Royal St, New Orleans, LA 70130, **504/566-5011.**

NORTHEAST

ME
VT
NH
NY
MA ★ BOSTON
CT RI
PA
NJ
BALTIMORE ★
MD
DE

CULTURE ON THE CHARLES

Boston, MA

Spend a weekend. Live a lifetime. Experience a century or two. Boston, situated on the Charles River, is a fascinating blend of the old and the new, and no visit would be complete without taking the Freedom Trail, a 1½-mile pedestrian tour of historic old town including: the Old Bookstore where meetings were held by such writers as Emerson, Hawthorne, and Longfellow; the site of the notorious Boston Massacre; Paul Revere's house; and the Bunker Hill Monument. Juxtaposed against its colorful past, modern Boston is the hub of a sprawling metropolis and considered the commercial, financial, and cultural center for a six-state region. Greater Boston, often referred to as the higher education capital of the US, draws thousands of teachers, students, and visitors from all over the world to its dozens of institutions, prep schools, and the eminent Harvard University and Massachusetts Institute of Technology. A mecca of cultural amenities, the Shubert, Colonial, and Wilbur Theaters feature trial runs of Broadway shows, and a host of smaller theaters—many connected with the universities—are active during the school year. Whether you prefer chamber music or punk rock, Boston's nightlife has a niche for everyone: The elegant Plaza Bar in the Copley Plaza Hotel draws a sophisticated crowd to its top-name performances; Pooh's Pub features excellent

Norfolk, VA

Photo: Mike Michaelson

jazz groups in a more informal environment; and Jack's offers popular music by mostly local musicians for a come-as-you-are crowd. Autumn is perhaps the best time to visit Boston—escaping the humidity of summer and chill of winter—and a perfect time for a stroll through Beacon Hill. The beautiful gas-lit and tree-lined streets of this venerable neighborhood were the top real estate for Boston's prominent families during the 19th century. One of the best panoramic views of the city and its environs is afforded from the John Hancock Observatory—60 floors up, and multimedia shows of Boston, both historical and contemporary, are given regularly. The Ritz-Carlton, conveniently located on the Public Garden and within walking distance of the Newbury Street shops, is a proper and elegant Bostonian experience (536-5700); dining facilities run the gamut from the exquisite Continental menu at The Voyageurs (354-1718), to Elsie's, serving monstrous sandwiches to the college crowd (354-8781).

Convention & Tourists Bureau, Prudential Plaza, Box 590, Boston, MA 02199, **617/536-4100.**

BAYSIDE BOUNTY

Baltimore, MD

Here is another city that has taken massive strides to remove urban blight. The result is a sparkling new waterfront with dozens of attractions ideal for weekending. Centerpiece of the city's 45 miles of waterfront is Harborplace, twin glass-enclosed pavilions with more than 140 shops, boutiques, and restaurants that bustles with activity day and night. Supplanting decaying wharves and docks and grim warehouses, this lively marketplace in the Inner Harbor is the spot to go to dine on fine seafood (don't miss the crab cakes at Phillips and the polish sausage at Ostrowski's!), shop at food markets, scout for unusual gifts and collectibles sold from kiosks, stalls, and pushcarts, and enjoy people-watching in a festive atmosphere. Rising up from the waterfront, the pentagonal World Trade Center has an observation deck that provides an overview of the city — a good starting point for a weekend in and around Inner Harbor. On Pier 3, the National Aquarium has 6000 specimens exhibited on several levels, with sharks and puffins, a steamy tropical rain forest, a coral reef, a "touch me" shellfish display, and a reproduction of Iceland's Sea Cliffs. It provides great family entertainment, as does the Maryland Science Center and Planetarium at the southwest corner of Inner Harbor. Here, you can challenge computers, dabble with scientific experiments, walk through a model of a human cell, and relax for an orbit of outer space. Baltimore has been an important seaport since Colonial times, and a visit to Inner Harbor would be incomplete without going aboard ship. Options include a number of harbor cruises, a visit to Pier 1 and the anchorage of the U.S. Frigate *Constellation*, built in 1797 and the oldest naval ship afloat, as well as a National Historic Landmark, and a trip to Pier 4 to tour the World War II submarine, *USS Torsk*. Boats depart the Inner Harbor for narrated cruises to Fort McHenry National Monument and Historic Shrine (also accessible by auto). Tours of this doughty fort with its 20-foot-thick walls and a view from the ramparts that inspired Francis Scott Key to pen the National Anthem, include a visit to the powder magazine and officers' and enlisted men's quarters, and military drills conducted by "soldiers" in the manner of 1814 when the fort thwarted an attack by the British fleet.

Office of Promotion & Tourism, 110 W Baltimore St, Baltimore, MD 21201, **301/752-8632.**

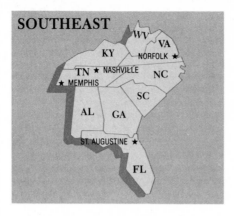

SOUTHEAST

COLOR IT COUNTRY!

Nashville, TN

Song writers, recording stars, aspiring musicians, avid fans of popular music, and curious tourists — they are drawn to Nashville like flies to a country hog. Nashville, often dubbed "Music City, USA" is the heart and soul of the popular-music industry, producing more than 50% of all American record singles. If you're planning a tour of Music Row, the section of town where music publishing companies and recording studios, many in charming old houses, are juxtaposed with office high-rises, a good starting point is The Country Music Hall of Fame and Museum. Here, the story of popular music unfolds via 16 permanent exhibits (plus several changing exhibits, two theaters showing rare film and TV clips, and the Hall of Fame itself). Among a rare collection of instruments, costumes, photographs, and other memorabilia, you'll find an old Cajun triangle, fashioned from a hay rake, the gaudy costumes of the singing cowboys (and girls), Elvis Presley's gold Cadillac complete with gold-plated TV, Willie Nelson's sneakers, Minnie Pearl's trademark floral hat and stringbean banjo, and the sequined, tassled outfits of country stars past and present. A short walk from

Memphis, TN

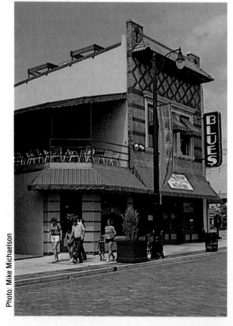

Photo: Mike Michaelson

the museum is RCA's historic Studio B, where hit songs were recorded by such stars as Hank Snow, Eddy Arnold, Jim Reeves, Chet Atkins, Dolly Parton, and Elvis Presley. Tours of this cradle of recorded popular music include a multi-media presentation and a simulated mix-down session of a recent country hit at which visitors are invited to play studio instruments — sometimes producing some remarkably acceptable music. Country-music fans won't want to miss the opportunity to step on stage at the Ryman Auditorium, where every Saturday for 31 years — from 1943 to 1974—the music of the Grand Ole Opry rang out across America. At this old brick tabernacle with rows of wooden pews you can explore backstage corridors and see the dressing rooms, stage sets, microphones, and props that were used by the great country performers. Of course, the show itself lives on at Opryland, U.S.A. (see Theme & Amusement Parks) where you can see a live performance of the Grand Ole Opry, visit the set of a Hee Haw taping, or join the audience of a radio or TV show. The Opryland Hotel offers first-rate accommodations and good food and entertainment in a setting of lush, indoor gardens, pools, and fountains.

Chamber of Commerce, 161 Fourth Ave N, Nashville, TN 37219, **615/259-3900.**

OLDEST TOWN

St. Augustine, FL

The golden sun beats down on red-roofed haciendas. On narrow streets, vendors push their rickety carts or catch a quick siesta in shaded doorways. The history of this town stretches back more than two centuries before the American Revolution. No, this isn't a sleepy village near Madrid, or anywhere else in Spain. It's St. Augustine, the US's oldest town, seasoned with more than a bit of old world flavor. The town was founded in 1565, and it is believed also to be the site where Ponce de Leon landed 50 years before that, in search of the fountain of youth. During the town's long and winding history, it has been ruled by Spain, Britain, the Confederate States, and the US. In fact, St. Augustine flew the Spanish flag for nearly a hundred years longer than it has been a US city! In recent years, massive restoration and renovation projects have preserved important historic sites in the town, earning it the sobriquet, "a Hispanic version of Williamsburg, VA" (see Ethnic & Historic Villages). The major landmark of St. Augustine is the massive Castillo de San Marcos, a fortress erected in the late 1600s to protect the town from English invaders and Indian raiding parties. At the time of its construction, it cost Spain the equivalent of $30 million. The restored village district—known as San Agustin Antiquo—is located along five enchanting blocks of St. George St, and features historic buildings reconstructed and redecorated to reflect different periods and styles from the town's past. These range from a mid-18th century neighborhood store to an upperclass Spanish residence to an early 19th century US territorial outpost. Other points of interest include the supposed site of Ponce de Leon's Fountain of Youth, and an alligator farm featuring a zoo of Florida wildlife, and the offbeat entertainment of alligator wrestling. The entire area is compact and lends itself easily to leisurely walking tours. There are also quaint horse-drawn carriages and sightseeing train tours. Be sure to check out one of the many Victorian-style bed and breakfast inns (see Inn Places).

Chamber of Commerce, 75 King St, Lightner Bldg, St Augustine, FL 32084, **904/829-5681.**

Historic District, Portsmouth (short ferry ride from Norfolk, VA)

REBIRTH OF THE BLUES

Memphis, TN

Beale Street, the "birthplace of the blues," has been rescued from neglect and is itself reborn as a lively complex teeming with shops, eateries, nightclubs, and theaters. In its heyday, Beale Street, with bars and pawnshops, dance halls and gambling dens, all interspersed with cotton brokerage houses, was close to the steamboat landing and a major center of commerce and entertainment for southern blacks. In 1909, W.C. Handy's band was hired to drum up crowds for a mayoral candidate. The song he wrote, later known as "Memphis Blues," launched a new sound that set off a chain reaction around the music world. Today, in Handy Park, beneath a statue of the blues great, trumpet in hand, aspiring musicians beat out the plaintive blues notes. "The sound" — along with jazz, country, rock, and soul music—also may be heard elsewhere along the renovated strip, in clubs such as the New Daisy (a former movie house, circa 1940), Club Handy, and W.C.'s Cafe. The Old Daisy, operated by the Center for Southern Folklore also presents performances by original blues artists and rising young talent. The Center also offers a 25-minute multimedia show which traces the history and music of the street. From the music of Handy to B.B. King, the show presents the tales and music of the storekeepers and shoppers, bankers, political leaders, and musicians whose lives and dreams are part of the Beale Street experience. With Beale Street's remarkable renaissance, clubs are again attracting top-name performers, the likes of Lou Rawls and Charlie Rich. Don't miss a visit to the dry-goods store of A. Schwab that has been operating on Beale St. continuously for 100 years and whose motto is, "If you can't find it at Schwab's, you're better off without it." At this huge emporium with green-painted walls and an old wooden staircase, you'll find an eclectic jumble of goods ranging from shoes and overalls to fascinating voodoo supplies—candles in various colors designed to fix everything that ails you, from financial woes to romantic aspirations. Nearby, the Orpheum Theatre, built in 1926 for vaudeville and movies, and where Houdini and Burns and Allen once performed, has been meticulously restored as a performing arts center.

Convention & Visitors Bureau, 203 Beale St, Ste 305, Memphis, TN 38103, **901/526-1919.**

WINNING WATERFRONT

Norfolk, VA

It once was a notorious navy town, with the inevitable neon strip of rowdy bars and burlesque houses. The navy is still there. In fact, popular tours of the world's largest naval base often include an open house aboard ship—perhaps a recommissioned hulking battleship of World War II vintage. But the town itself has changed. Massive redevelopment has transformed Norfolk into an attractive, modern city, an ideal destination for a fulfilling weekend getaway. Activities center around the revitalized waterfront. Check into the luxurious, 10-story Omni International Hotel (weekend packages available), and enjoy gourmet dining, lively lounges, and relaxed people-watching at the airy Riverwalk Cafe. Adjacent is The Waterside, a "festival marketplace" offering an eclectic mix of more than 120 shops and eateries in a nautical setting that includes full-size wooden figureheads suspended from the ceiling. This bustling marketplace, a melange of sound, color, and the wafting aroma of food, has flower stands, pushcarts, market stalls brimming with fresh produce and cheeses, and, mixing with the crowd, street performers—musicians, jugglers, mimes, and the like. It houses several fine restaurants (try Phillips for superb seafood), plus two dozen specialty food booths serving local and ethnic delicacies ranging from raw oysters to souvlaki, and 30-plus kiosks vending handmade stoneware, woodcarvings, and other arts and crafts. Alongside is Town Point Park, which offers concerts and festivals summerlong, many of them saluting Norfolk's various ethnic communities. Other attractions around Norfolk include: The Douglas MacArthur Memorial, the general's final resting place with 11 galleries of exhibits and a collection that ranges from his famous corncob pipe to historic military documents; The Chrysler Museum, containing many old masters and one of the world's major glass collections (see Masterful Museums); The Moses Myers House, a Georgian beauty built in 1792 by a local merchant and containing more than 70% of the original furnishings; harbor boat tours, dinner cruises, and a ferry boat to sister city, Portsmouth, where an historic district awaits exploration; tours of Norfolk aboard a shiny blue trolley; and a cluster of antique shops set on quiet streets amid restored homes.

Convention & Visitors Bureau, Monticello Arcade, Norfolk, VA 23510, **804/441-5266.**

New Orleans, LA

Chapter 21

VACATIONS AFLOAT

Buffalo National River, AR

Vacations on the water can be romantically free and spontaneous. Once the windjammer has set sail for the open seas, or the canoe is shoved off-shore, boat vacationers are free to roam coastal and inland waters at will—stopping, perhaps, to steam lobsters over a driftwood fire, exploring remote coves in the Ozarks, hopping from island to island in the San Juans, or dropping anchor in a different New England port each night.

For those desiring a primitive adventure, try canoeing down the Lewis & Clark Trails in Montana, or drift by giant redwood trees in California—pausing for a taste-test or two at the many wineries along the way. In Vermont canoeists can paddle by day and stay at a series of rustic colonial inns by night—or simply choose a sandbar or beach on which to pitch a tent. In New York, a packet boat relives the era of canal travel.

For those who prefer comfort afloat, houseboats are the choice. Many are equipped with all the amenities of home—air conditioning and heating, carpeting, gas grills, refrigerators, and cutlery. With these vessels you can explore the jungle-flanked waterways of the St. Johns River in Florida, drift across placid Lake Mead in Nevada where you can enjoy the contrast between the desert and fjord-like coves, or beach your boat along the banks of the Mississippi at La Crosse, Wisconsin for a daytime excursion or a night-time layover.

We also have included a few mini-cruise ships which represent the most luxurious in water travel. Relive the era of paddlewheelers aboard the *Mississippi Queen*, complete with jazz bands and moonlight dances, or take a week-long cruise on the northern Mississippi River via the *Viking Explorer*, with side trips to a steamboat museum and an old lumber town.

But perhaps the most unique floating crafts are the clippers. Passengers are encouraged to help crew the windjammers by taking a turn at the helm, plotting a course, hoisting and/or lowering sails, and coiling the halyards. If you would rather *watch* the 5000 square feet of sail billowing in the wind, that's O.K. too, but most people readily volunteer to cast the anchor when stopping for a spontaneous picnic or party.

Whatever kind of of vacation afloat you choose, they all afford plenty of time for relaxing, to sit back and savor the scenery—from mountain landscapes and limestone cliffs, to antebellum houses, live oaks dripping with Spanish moss, and the splendid color of fall foliage.

Note: Listed prices reflect high season fees; off-season cost (usually Sept—Apr) can run as much as 40%-50% cheaper.

NORTHWEST

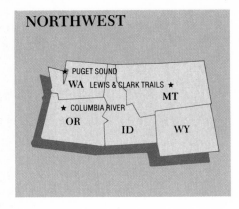

PUGET SOUND

(CRUISE)

Seattle, WA

Get together some friends and set your own itinerary on a plan-it-yourself cruise off the coast of Washington. These off-season tours (Sept-mid-May) allow guests to determine the course of their journey and stop at the different San Juan Islands in the Puget Sound (see Island Escapes). The 65-foot *Stephanie Ann*, a plush vessel with five double staterooms and a crew of four, serves seafood bought from passing fishermen — or the galley will prepare your own catch. Passengers have the use of two 14-foot skiffs to fish for salmon, set crab pots, make explorations to such places as Butchart Gardens and Princess Louisa Inlet, or stop over at Victoria, British Columbia's beautiful garden city, for a round of golf. *You* set the itinerary. The ship accommodates only 10 aboard for a night, but you can get together a group of as many as 35 and stay overnight at hotels during your voyage. Simply let the cruise line know where you want to go and they'll arrange everything. $1450 per day, plus $30/day/passenger, and fuel.

Bendixen Cruises, 818 W Argand St, Seattle, WA 98119. **206/285-5999.**

COLUMBIA RIVER

(CRUISE)

Portland, OR

Striking contrasts in great natural beauty are the order of the day—every day—during this seven-day cruise from Portland, OR to Lewiston, ID, and back. Few places in America offer more rugged country or more beautiful scenery than the Columbia River valley, which originates near Portland. Sea winds warm the western part of the state and promote lush vegetation, but just on the other side of the Cascade Range are snow-clad peaks, giant waterfalls, and semi-arid regions. During the 900-mile journey, which includes a short voyage on the Willamette River to the Columbia, up to Astoria and on to Lewiston, there are several stops: Visit the town of Fort Clatsop (see Historic Landmarks) where the Lewis and Clark expedition wintered; explore the new Maritime Museum on the waterfront; or take a ride aboard a jet-powered watercraft on Snake River in Hell's Canyon. $1100-$1700/week.

Exploration Cruise Lines, 1500 Metropolitan Park Bldg, Olive Way at Boren St, Seattle, WA 98101, **800/426-0600.**

LEWIS & CLARK TRAILS

(CANOE)

Fort Benton, MT

The violent conquest of the Indian Territory, vital to the pioneers' need to reach the Northwest, is evident throughout the colorful, 150-mile journey on the Upper Missouri river from Fort Benton to James Kipp State Park. The Missouri River Outfitters rent canoes for do-it-yourselfers, and also have equipment and a guide available. Their 35-foot boat, *West Wind*, accommodates 18-24 passengers on 1- to 5-day trips ($55); guests sleep on shore and the outfitter provides tents and food including a campfire breakfast to begin each day. The Mullan Trail originates at Fort Benton, an outpost that saw the passage of fur traders from 1830 for half a century through the gold rush days and ultimate settlement of the northwest. The woodchoppers for the steamboats were often killed by Indians when they went ashore for fuel, and their graves line the banks of the river. Also still standing are the remnants of log cabins, and rifle pits surrounded with barricades, which were dug by soldiers during the steamboat era to protect their freight from marauding Indians. The three most traveled sections of the river are from Fort Benton to Coal Banks Landing, 42 miles; from Coal Banks Landing to the Judith Landing, 48 miles; and from Judith Landing to Kipp Park, 61 miles. The first section is most heavily traveled, but wildlife abound because there are numerous islands and protective vegetation. The area from Coal Banks Landing is more isolated and scenically distinguished by a region known as White Cliffs—unusual rock configurations formed during the glacier age. The wildest part of the river is from Judith Landing, where the river travels through a rugged, narrow canyon which contains the Cow Island steamboat landing and the Nez Perce crossing. $10/day.

Missouri River Outfitters, Inc, Box 1212, Fort Benton, MT 59442, **406/622-3295.**

SOUTHWEST

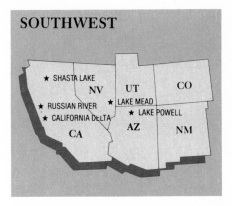

SHASTA LAKE

(HOUSEBOAT)

Redding, CA

Houseboating has come into its own in California, probably the only other place in the country comparable to Florida in that respect, and this lake offers the same kinds of opportunities for fun on the water. Numerous islands dot the lake and explorers will find several equipped with campgrounds, many of which are accessible only by water. Bays and inlets spike the perimeter in profusion, creating peaceful moorings and good bases for tours afoot. There are several marinas and resorts; plus good fishing throughout the mountain lake's 30,000 acres of surface water (370 miles of shoreline). Free tours are offered at Shasta Dam and there's a two-hour tour of nearby Lake Shasta Caverns that includes a boat ride. The town of Redding, which provides access to the lake from the south, is 250 miles north of San Francisco. $1000-$1500/week.

Bridge Bay Resort & Marina, 10300 Bridge Bay Road, Redding, CA 96003, **916/275-3021.**

Maine Windjammers, Around Rockport, ME

Photo: Carolyn Bates

VACATIONS AFLOAT

CALIFORNIA DELTA
(HOUSEBOAT)
Bethel Island, CA

This is the Everglades of the West, the region formed by two of the Golden State's famous rivers—the Sacramento and the San Joaquin—as they wend toward the Pacific Ocean. An ideal destination for houseboaters, this region is noted for remote, secluded coves, thriving flora and fauna, and excellent fishing for hefty scrappers such as sturgeon, striped bass, steelhead trout, and catfish. Days filled with sunbathing or waterskiing may be capped in the evening by a sampling of the exciting nightlife offered at dozens of small towns and villages throughout the region. Best time of the year is fall, but the climate is pleasant throughout the year. Charter boat fishing is available and you can picnic and camp at numerous sites. Instruction for navigating the waterways with the easily-handled houseboat is available at most rental agencies. $750-$1100/week.

*Island Holidays, PO Box 373, 3955 Willow Rd, Bethel Island, CA 94511, **415/684-2884.***

LAKE MEAD
(HOUSEBOAT)
Near Las Vegas, NV

This giant reservoir, framed by the Grand Canyon at one end and Hoover Dam at the other, is within a dice-throw from Las Vegas. Its 550 miles of shoreline and fjord-like coves are best seen by houseboat, and many rentals are quite luxurious featuring air conditioning, carpeting, and the equipment to make a strawberry dacquiri. Awesome desert scenery—sometimes resembling a painted movie set—beckon shutterbugs, while swimmers and skiers are drawn to the blue-green hues of the water. Several beaches dot the shore; some are sandy and smooth, others rocky and rough. Desert bighorn roam the arid terrain, but are wary of intruders; underwater canyons and caves await adventurous scuba divers and, near the lower gateway to the Grand Canyon, the waters are cold and the fish are fighters. Catfish, largemouth bass, rainbow trout, and stripers all seem tastier in this setting. At Lake Mead you'll find a floating restaurant and cocktail lounge worth a visit; marinas also located at Echo Bay and Temple Bar. $1000-$1500 weekly.

*Play Mate Resort Marinas, 730 S Cypress, La Habra, CA 90631, **213/691-2235, 714/871-1476.***

RUSSIAN RIVER
(CANOE)
Healdsburg, CA

The scenic grandeur of Northern California is as different from its southern part as day is to night. Nowhere is it more evident than while canoeing down the Russian River, which originates in the Coast Range near Ukiah. The river flows southward, then bends to the west and passes giant redwood trees and huge vineyards, resorts and camps galore. For the novice paddler, Cloverdale is the best put-in point as the river is fairly gentle from that point on; above Cloverdale the water level varies and should be carefully scouted in advance. The Simi Winery is in

Healdsburg, and various others are within a few paddle-lengths of the shore. You can put in at numerous sites, whether for a stroll amid often verdant banks or picnicking at a short stretch of rock-strewn sandy beach, exploring a vineyard or watching birds and other wildlife. Near the mouth of the river, where it meets the Pacific Ocean, is Fort Ross State Historic Park—site of a Russian trading post and fort built in 1812. $28/1 day; $40/2 days; $55/5 days.

*Trowbridge Recreation, 20 Hillsbrook Ave, Healdsburg, CA 95448, **707/433-7247.***

LAKE POWELL
(HOUSEBOAT)
Page, AZ

The panoramic beauty of this body of water, forged from the Colorado River, stretches 186 miles from Page to Canyonlands National Park in Utah (see Nat'l Parks & Monuments). Its shoreline is almost the same length as the entire eastern seacoast of the US and is choked with largemouth bass, crappie, striped bass, walleye, rainbow trout, and northern pike. The houseboat is the preferred mode of travel because it is easy to handle and completely self-contained. Rentals are available at four large marinas in various sites along the lake. Boat camping is also popular—boaters simply haul their small craft ashore and sleep in a tent or under the stars. A leisurely cruise should include a visit to Rainbow Bridge Canyon (see Man-Made & Natural Wonders), which features the largest stone arch on earth. Bird watchers will find a spectacular array of species from eagles and owls, to great and blue heron; wildlife includes bobcats, bighorn sheep, mountain lions, and porcupines. Day trips from the Waheap Lodge also are available. $675-$1350 weekly.

*Del Webb Rec Properties, PO Box 29040, Phoenix, AZ 85038, **800/528-6154, 602/278-8888** (in AZ).*

MIDWEST

INTERNATIONAL FALLS
(HOUSEBOAT)
Minnesota/Canada Border

If you enjoy the wilderness, yet also cherish your personal comfort, the perfect compromise could be a houseboat vacation on Rainy Lake. This huge, 400-square-mile expanse of water with close to 3500 miles of shoreline and more than 3000 islands, is nestled between Minnesota and Ontario. A typical day could, perhaps, begin with an outdoor breakfast of pancakes made with freshly-picked blueberries; a shore lunch with fillets of freshly caught fish and a visit from a black bear; and at night, docking alongside a white, sandy beach under a myriad of stars and watching the glow of the northern lights illuminating the dark horizon. Fishing is great and the lake is home to trophy-size muskie—a 42-pounder pulled from here was the largest caught in Minnesota in 1982. Literally a houseboating mecca, Rainy Lake supports four houseboat operators, with yet others located on adjoining lakes to the east. The lake itself is so large that it takes two full days' cruising by houseboat to journey from International Falls to Kettle Falls at its easterly tip—with another large arm reaching north into Canada. Guides are suggested during your first day. $500 to $1200/week.

*Greater Int'l Falls Area, PO Box 169, Int'l Falls, MN 56649, **218/283-9400.***

Minnesota Voyageurs Houseboat, MN

BOUNDARY WATERS
(CANOE)

Ely, Grand Marais, Tower, MN

Early voyageurs explored the wilderness in birchbark canoes, and this scenic glory is accessible virtually only by canoe. It is one of the most primitive areas in the US and is off-limits to motorized crafts. Although almost 200,000 people travel through it every year, you needn't fear crowding because the area is vast—running for 150 miles along the Canadian border and joining Canada's Quetico Provincial Park, combining for more than 300 square miles of wilderness. It is alive with wildlife—soaring bald eagles, lumbering black bears (which can be a nuisance—and dangerous), browsing moose and deer, and howling timber wolves. Permits are limited, and while there is no fee, paid reservations will ensure your choice of entry point. Professionals will outfit your expedition for about $800/week (four person). Roughing it can be unsettling for the novice—seemingly nearby shorelines can be miles away, sometimes the wind can be more than a bit discouraging, and even if you know how to read the map provided, be prepared to find yourself off course a few times. But the spectacular natural vistas forged by extraordinary volcanic eruptions, the chance to drink pure water from the lake in which you're paddling and the opportunity to pick berries, portage your canoe the way early explorers did, and sample the succulent and plentiful pike and bass cooked over a fire in the great outdoors, makes it all worthwhile. $15-$40/day (depending on outfitter).

Chamber of Commerce, Ely, MN 55731, **218/365-6123;** *Chamber of Commerce, Grand Marais, MN 55604,* **218/387-2524;** *Chamber of Commerce, Tower, MN 55790,* **218/753-4070.**

Photo: Mike Michaelson

International Falls, MN

NORTHERN MISSISSIPPI
(CRUISE)

St. Paul, MN

For sheer luxury on the water, a cruise on the Mississippi aboard the *Viking Explorer* is hard to beat. The yacht—actually a mini-cruise ship with room for 42 passengers—calls St. Paul home port, with berths at La Crosse, WI, New Orleans, Memphis, St. Louis, the Quad Cities, and other ports. Tours last three, five, six, seven, or eight nights on travels between St. Paul and these cities, and include meals with homemade breads and pastries. The ship docks several times, and a bus tags along allowing passengers to make interesting side trips. Stay in an old lumber town, take a gander at a steamboat museum, stroll through apple orchards, and visit a winery. And all that is just on the shortest cruise offered, three nights from St. Paul to LaCrosse. Along the way, you'll see sandy beaches, white and blue herons, travel through several locks and miles of lily pads and around islands in the stream. If you opt for the 1700-mile junket on Ol' Man River to or from New Orleans, you'll not only become intimately acquainted with one of America's great rivers, but you'll see mansions of the old south, Civil War battlefields, and fascinating changes in the landscape, which includes Spanish moss and mistletoe misting the trees. $294-$784/one way.

Padelford Packet Boat Co, Inc, St Paul, MN 55107, **800/328-1472, 612/227-1100.**

UPPER MISSISSIPPI
(HOUSEBOAT)

La Crosse, WI

You can drink in the natural beauty of the Dairy State almost any time of the year from a houseboat on the Upper Mississippi River. Some of the most picturesque stretches of the mighty river course through Wisconsin, past restored homes of immigrant families who settled the land, near some fine hiking trails, and through waters choked with fighting fish. The center of most houseboating activity here is in La Crosse, which itself is a fine attraction. The *La Crosse Queen,* a steam-driven paddlewheeler, berths here; it features weekend cruises in May and two-a-day trips through the summer. For an easy-going exploration of these waters try putt-putting north from La Crosse past Onalaska and into Lake Pepin. Along the way you'll skirt Trampealeau Island, Winona, MN, and Alma, WI. You can beach your boat almost anywhere for shore-side excursions or a night-time layover. Several houseboat rental firms headquarter at La Crosse, and all offer an hour or two of instruction for piloting the docile craft. Most boats have complete galley, stereos, and barbeque facilities. Summer rates for the smaller houseboats range from about $495/3-days; $695/week.

Convention & Visitors Bureau, Box 1895, La Crosse, WI 54601, **608/782-2366.**

AU SABLE RIVER
(CANOE)

Grayling, MI

The most favored canoeing river in Michigan, and possibly the US, owes its popularity to the trout that populate the upper reaches. The 180-mile stream flows through the beautiful Huron National Forest, and once was a major floating thoroughfare for the logging industry. Despite the number of people who paddle it, heavy traffic is unusual except just below the Grayling put-in. There are more than enough campsites along the forested banks and you can catch a lunker almost anywhere. Rental cottages are available, but most are for a minimum one-week stay and open only during the summer. To avoid the crowd, you could put in some 25 miles downstream at Wakeley Bridge and paddle hard for three days to reach the Mio Dam, or make it a five-day float with more leisurely strokes. The annual Au Sable Canoe Marathon draws 20,000 people to watch some 30—40 sturdy souls compete in a 210-mile race, portaging five dams and canoeing through an entire night (date varies). Competition is open to anyone over 18 years old, and applicants are divided into amateur and professional status. The most scenic time of year is May—Sept. Be sure to check fishing regulations as three different areas of the stream come under special fly-casting rules. Outfitters supply equipment and transportation for 1- to 7-day trips from $19-$150/canoe.

Chamber of Commerce, 100 W Michigan, Oscoda, MI 48750, **517/739-7322.**

SOUTH CENTRAL

LAKE OUACHITA
(RV RAFTS)

Mountain Pine, AR

Amphibious vacations afloat are possible here by utilizing a craft popularly known as the Camp-A-Float—a barge-type cruiser containing more than adequate room to carry an RV. Its principal use is for making forays onto the 200-plus uninhabited islands in the lake which is 16 miles west of Hot Springs National Park—the water is flat and ideal for cruising. Many campers bring their own RV and strap it to a rented barge, but you can rent one with an RV already tied down. Float to a particular island and spend the entire vacation there as if it were your personal resort (it's unlikely you'll encounter many visitors). If you bring your own RV the cost for 1- to 7-day trips is $75-$475. If you rent a barge-cum-RV, the tab is $115-$700.

Supt, Star Rte 1, Box 1160, Mountain Pine, AR 71956, **501/767-9366.**

MISSISSIPPI
(STEAMBOAT)

New Orleans, LA

The mystique captured by Mark Twain will never die so long as there's a paddlewheeler afloat on the Mississippi, and the *Mississippi Queen* and *Delta Queen* cruise in the fashion of the golden era of steamships with all the comforts and amenities of modern life. The boats throb with throaty brass rhythms and twangy tunes from jazz bands, and echo mellow strains perfect for romantic starlit dancing. The peppery cuisine of the cajuns and French-influenced New Orleans fare titillate the palate and soothe the senses amidst opulent furnishings. The *Mississippi Queen* commissioned in 1976, is the largest and most luxurious paddlewheeler ever built and sister *Delta Queen* is so carefully preserved it's hard to believe she's past 50 and logged in the National Register of Historic Places. The two rove up and down the Mississippi and Ohio Rivers,

offering glimpses of antebellum plantations straight from the pages of *Gone With the Wind*, and mute scapes scarred by battle or decorated with neat whitewashed fences. Stops are occasionally made to tour a station once used by the Underground Railroad, and to visit historic villages such as Nauvoo, IL where Joseph Smith, founder of Mormonism, established a thriving religious colony and later was assassinated, and New Harmony, IN (see Ethnic & Historic Villages) where Lutheran Separatists built a relatively cosmopolitan and economically efficient community. Once a year the two paddlewheelers battle it out in a 10-day race from New Orleans to St. Louis. $115-$425/person/night.

The Delta Queen Steamboat Co, 511 Main St, Cincinnati, OH 45202, **800/543-1949.**

DE SOTO NAT'L FOREST
(CANOE)

Brookland, MS

Floating down the Black Creek is so remote and peaceful, that the plop of surface-feeding fish is about the only sound you hear. The longest trip possible is 33 miles from the landing at Big Creek to Fairley Bridge, and the lazily-drifting current pulls downstream at only about 1mph, affording the paddler ample opportunity to snag one of the plentiful bass, bream (pronounced 'brim'), or catfish, or contemplate the heavily forested banks, colorfully accented with flowering shrubs. Numerous broad sandbars dot the surface and are ideal for picnicking or overnight camping. Bird watchers may not find any new species to list, but there are native fowl aplenty and lush scenery begging for immortality in a color photograph. This is basically a gentle stream, but rapid increases in water level require boaters to keep a sharp lookout for submerged logs and snags. Several put-in sites, including boat ramps, are in the area, and a rough map provided by the Forest Service shows the spots. $16/day/canoe.

Black Creek Canoe Rental, PO Box 213, Brookland, MS 39425, **601/582-8817.**

LAKE OF THE OZARKS
(HOUSEBOAT)

Osage Beach, MO

The state's largest lake, about midway between St. Louis and Kansas City, is a major playground of the midwest. The man-made lake was formed when the Osage River's Bagnell Dam was completed in 1931, so commerce has had a long time to develop. There are more businesses catering to houseboaters and other water adventurers here than on any lake of comparable size in the country — swimming, fishing, and water-skiing are the main attractions. Lake of the Ozarks stretches snake-like through the heart of the Ozark Mountains, the 60,000-acre body of water containing some 1300 miles of shoreline. The region is rugged, heavily wooded, and famed for great bubbling springs and caves formed by underground streams. Lake of the Ozarks State Park is at the southeastern end of the lake. For a breathtaking experience, catch the two-hour Fort Of The Osage Water Show at Osage Beach, featuring water skiing, jumping, and hang gliding. $235/day (plus tax & fuel).

Link's Landing, US 54, Osage Beach, MO 65065, **314/348-2741.**

BUFFALO NAT'L RIVER
(CANOE)

Northern AR

Some of the country's most spectacular scenery is best viewed from a canoe, paddling down 120 miles of this mountain stream bordered by limestone cliffs and forested banks. The upper reaches of the river are the most scenic, and although there's some white water, clear and quiet streams predominate, and good campsites dot the river banks. If you're new to this water sport, begin at Steel Creek, southwest of Harrison. A few miles downstream at Hemmed-in-Hollow, there's a great trail for hikers accessible from the river with scenic overlooks from towering cliffs, a natural bridge, and a 200-foot-high waterfall. One-, two- and three-day floats on the lower, slower part of the river begin at Maumee, Woolum, and AR 14. Small craft with motors, called "john boats," are also available for rent. $15-$20/day/canoe (plus shuttle fees).

Buffalo Nat'l River, PO Box 1173, Harrison, AR 72601, **501/741-5443.**

Buffalo National River, AR

Mississippi Queen, On The Mississippi

Delta Queen, On The Mississippi

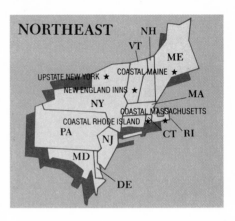

NORTHEAST

COASTAL MAINE
(WINDJAMMERS)
Around Rockport, ME

Pack your duffel bag and board one of 13 schooners registered with the Maine Windjammer Association. Debarking from cities on the central coast of Maine, the vessels head north to Mt. Desert Island (see Island Escapes), sailing the Atlantic for six days. Combining nostalgia, history, and fun, passengers are encouraged to help hoist and furl the sails, coil the halyards, and take the helm—much the same as it was done in the 19th century. The hard work produces hearty appetities and typical meals include pot roast, home-baked oatmeal bread, and oven-hot pies. Once a week the schooners stop at a secluded beach for a lobster bake over a driftwood fire. Because of changing weather conditions, there are no set itineraries, but the clippers always stop to visit fishing villages, historic towns, and deserted islands. Dress is casual—denims, T-shirts, and bare feet—but be sure to take along sweaters and rain gear. Some of the windjammers have limited use of hot water, and small, but comfortable, quarters have portholes for fresh-air snoozes. Keep a sharp eye out for seals, porpoises, whales, and picturesque lighthouses. Cruises available June — Sept. $325-$425/6 days.

*Maine Windjammer Assn, Box 317P, Rockport, ME 04856, **207/236-4867.***

NEW ENGLAND INNS
(CANOE)
North Thetford, VT

The hearty Puritans and the rugged Indians of the New World saw their land from a birchbark canoe—making camp along the river as they traveled the countryside. A unique inn-to-inn canoeing tour allows you to repeat their experience, but under decidedly more comfortable circumstances. By day you paddle a canoe; at night you relax at various charming country inns along the route (with bed and board reserved by tour operator). The Connecticut River is New England's longest (it bisects the state that bears it name). Guided tours on the Connecticut, which include stopovers at rustic colonial inns, are offered every summer by Vermont school teacher Art Sharkey. Paddlers are treated to river views of picturesque villages, quaint New England towns, and historic sites along the route. You are met at Hanover, New Hampshire, and driven to Haverhill. Up-close looks at old farmhouses and inns begin in Haverhill, where group tour participants spend the first night at an inn built in 1810, and furnished with numerous antiques. The second night is spent at Sharkey's own Stone House Inn in North Thetford, an 1835 farmhouse perched on the riverbank. The second day on the river takes you to Hanover, NH, home of Dartmouth College. The tour concludes with dinner at Moose Mountain Lodge. $200/person.

Art Sharkey, Stone House Inn, N Thetford, VT 05054, **802/333-9124.**

COASTAL MASSACHUSETTS
(CLIPPER)
Vineyard Haven, MA

The wind and tide determine the night's anchorage among the seaports of southern New England, and the clipper, *Shenandoah*, docks in a different port every night. She is the only non-auxiliary, square-rigged vessel operating under the American flag, and all of the sails require hands aloft to set them, take them in, and stow them. All this must be done while the vessel is underway. This work is known as Norwegian Steam and passengers pitch in, especially when lifting anchor and making sail. Sailing in the wake of the whalers, clippers, and privateers of old, the *Shenandoah* passes picturesque shores highlighted by stark silhouettes of granite wharves, venerable lighthouses, gray-shingled white-trimmed cottages with neat picket fences and wild roses, weathered wooden boat houses, and sand dunes with rippling beach grass. Yankee fare prepared on board over a coal-fueled fire features chowders, roasts, homemade breads, and pies. Anchorages, depending upon the whim of wind and tide, may include Nantucket (see Island Escapes), Edgartown, Cuttyhunk, Newport (see Romantic Rendezvous), Bristol, Mystic (see Ethnic & Historic Villages), New London, and Greenport. Quarters are small, but not cramped—bunks will accommodate 6' 6"—and in the main saloon a brass ship clock keeps time amid ship comforts and implements of an era that passed this way a century ago. $450/person/week.

Capt R.S. Douglas, Coastwise Packet Co, Inc, Vineyard Haven, MA 02568, **617/693-1699.**

UPSTATE NEW YORK
(CANAL CRUISE)
Albany, NY

Among canal buffs, the inland water routes of upstate New York rank high, but there is only one packet boat cruising these historic waters — the *Emita II*, called a packet because it carries passengers on a regular schedule. There are trips from Buffalo to Syracuse, Syracuse to Albany, and the longer Albany-Whitehall cruise. The 120-mile three-day cruise from Albany to Whitehall and back travels past the Watervliet Arsenal, which has manufactured munitions for American use in every war fought since 1810. Nearby is the Cluett and Peabody shirt factory, the somber setting for Theodore Dreiser's *American Tragedy*. The packet passes the Saratoga National Historic Park, where the British Army was defeated on Oct 7, 1777, by a band of patriots led by Benedict Arnold. On the second day out, the boat docks briefly at Whitehall, known as

Maine Windjammers, Around Rockport, ME

the birthplace of the US Navy because Arnold built some ships there in 1776. Breakfast, lunch, and dinner are served aboard ship or at a picnic spot alongside the canal. The fare is plain, but tasty; cold cuts for lunch, and steaks grilled on an open fire for dinner. A chartered bus takes passengers to the Queensbury Hotel in Glens Falls for two nights; there's time to take in the Victorian architecture of the town and the hotel bar is a good spot for a nightcap. $260-$800/round trip.

Mid-Lakes Navigation Co, Box 61A, Skaneateles, NY 13152, **315/685-8500.**

COASTAL RHODE ISLAND
(SCHOONER)
Newport, RI

The *Bill of Rights* is an authentic replica of an 1856 gaff-rigged top sail schooner and, for many, an important part of a vacation voyage aboard her is the chance to take a turn at the helm, plot a course, or hoist a sail. With her 6300 square feet of sail, she stops in such famous old New England harbors as Mystic (see Ethnic & Historic Villages), Stonington, Port Judith, and Block Island (see Island Escapes). Specific ports of call depend upon prevailing wind and tide, and other anchorages usually are part of the itinerary, including the Elizabeth Islands, Pandanarun, Edgartown on Martha's Vineyard, or Nantucket (see Island Escapes). Windjammers sometimes find themselves halting in mid-voyage for a spontaneous picnic or party, and the various ports of call offer several hours of sightseeing, shopping, and solitary beaches. On board, hearty home-cooked meals are served in the main salon and occasionally there are candlelight dinners complemented by wine and served on fine pewter. A buffet-style meal under the stars or a shore picnic on a deserted beach present equally pleasant alternatives. There are 16 private staterooms, from single- to four-berth arrangements, with bunks six and a half feet long, and the rooms have easy access to the head and shower. Linens are provided, but no maid service; the crew of six attends to everything else. Cruises available for 2, 3, 4, and 7 days from $200-$475.

Capt J.M. Davis, Jr, 110 Wilcox Ave, Pawtucket, RI 02860, **401/724-7612.**

ST. JOHNS RIVER
(HOUSEBOAT)

Deland, FL

Exploring the St. Johns River in sub-tropical central Florida is somewhat akin to a jungle safari. This area has 150 miles of navigable waterways and helpful entrepreneurs have opened up a vast territory for exploration by greenhorn riverboat pilots. The means is provided by rental houseboats, and the operation for the novice is made relatively simple by a captain's manual, river chart, and a half-hour course in handling the bulky craft, which range from 36 to 47 feet long. The shallow-draft pontoon houseboats offer all the conveniences of home, and the St. Johns—renowned as the "Bass Capital of the World"—offers a variety of fish, wildlife, and breathtaking scenery. Just north of the home port is Astor where the Blackwater Inn serves up mouth-watering hush puppies, and Hall's provides great fried fish sandwiches. Just south of the marina is the Hontoon Dead River, populated by sunning turtles, prowling racoons, and blue herons stalking for fish. Near the river is Hontoon Island State Park, marked by big shell mounds left by the Timucuan Indians who lived there 3000 years ago, and a tall observation tower. On down the St. Johns is Blue Springs Park where you'll find a path leading past a swimming hole across a boardwalk through a copse and ending at a "boil"—a spring from which gushes millions of gallons of water each day. Blue Springs is home to one of the rarest of water creatures, the 1000-pound snub-nosed manatee, or sea cow, which can startle you with the breathing noise it makes when breaking the surface—but don't be alarmed, they're vegetarian. $700-$1500/7 days.

Sunshine Line, Holly Bluff Marina, Box 3558, Deland, FL 32720, **904/736-9422.**

FLORIDA'S INTRACOASTAL WATERWAY

Sebastian, FL

You can explore more than 400 miles of the Atlantic intracoastal Waterway in a floating summer cottage, aka houseboat. Using Sebastian, just south of the Kennedy Space Center, as a base, you can cruise north as far as Jacksonville, and as far south as Boca Raton—about 100 miles. There's a lot to do at the starting point including swimming, 'catting around in a Hobie, surfing, fishing, and clamming. Southward, through the St. Lucie Locks, is Lake Okeechobee where lunkers abound, but don't miss

the Gilbert's Bar House of Refuge in Stuart, the only remaining life saving station for shipwrecked sailors, which is now an historic site restored to the 1800s. There's good anchorage south of Stuart at Peck's Lake, a small inlet just off the Atlantic Ocean. Southward still, at Jupiter, is Burt Reynolds' Dinner Theater, which specializes in seafood; outdoor diners can enjoy the view of Jupiter inlet and lighthouse. $795/week.

Sebastian Houseboat Rentals, Indian River Dr, Sebastian, FL 32958, **305/589-7575.**

CENTER HILL LAKE/ DALE HOLLOW LAKE
(HOUSEBOAT)

Lancaster, Celina, TN

About an hour's drive from Nashville's Grand Ol' Opry, you'll find Center Hill Lake—some 18,000 acres of water with 415 miles of shoreline. Bass, crappie, walleye, and stripers populate these waters in great numbers, and trout fishing is nearby. The Cove Hollow Marina offers float trips via rental canoes with pickups arranged as needed. This is a good base for deer hunting in the fall, but the houseboats are the big attraction; they can be rented by the weekend or the week (three-day minimum in summer). This is a year-round resort, so you'll find a number of people on perpetual vacation — living in houseboats docked in slips at the Yacht Club. If you prefer to float by day and keep landlegs at night, rustic cabins with all of the comforts of home are available ($500-$1200/week). Most of the marinas are on the multi-branched Dale Hollow Lake, a 63-mile-long lake that edges into Kentucky, are near Celina. $500-$700/week.

Cove Hollow Resort, Rte 1, Lancaster, TN 38569, **615/548-4315.** Horse Creek Marina, Rte 3, Box 290, Celina, TN 38551, **615/243-2125.**

LAKE CUMBERLAND
(HOUSEBOAT)

Albany, KY

Within a day's drive of most of mid-America you can rent sumptuously furnished houseboats and loose the ties of civilization on this 101-mile-long lake with 1225 miles of shoreline. An ideal destination for houseboaters, Lake Cumberland is easy to navigate due to its depth and protection from the weather by the surrounding scenic mountains. Privacy is afforded by the numerous coves that line the shore, and the lake's rural setting, 150 miles from the nearest major metropolis, keeps the environment pollution-free. Seventy Six Falls is a pleasant spot to spend an evening roasting hot dogs and marshmallows and listening to the gentle roar of the cataract (located on Indian Creek). The high walls of the mountains surrounding the lake keep the water smooth and white-cap free—excellent for water skiing, and, in season, anglers will find plentiful bass, crappie, and bluegill. As for swimming, simply anchor your boat and dive in. There are lots of islands to explore and nearby are excellent dining, horseback riding, hiking trails, tennis, and golf, plus swimming pools, a country store, and gift shop. Boats come with all the necessities, from linens to cutlery, plus a gas grill for cooking the catch of the day. A mecca for houseboat rentals, Conley Bottom Resort (606/348-6351) also is widely recommended. $810-$1260/week.

Grider Hill Boat Dock, Hwy 734, Albany, KY 42602, **606/387-5501.**

SHENANDOAH RIVER
(CANOE)

Luray, VA

A float trip through the Shenandoah Valley, particularly in the fall when the leaves are changing, is a lot like a motor trip along the famed Skyline Drive (see Scenic Drives). The river flows northward through banks lined with apple orchards, robust oaks, hickory trees, and poplars. Depending upon your endurance and desire, trips can last 1—5 days. Outfitters supply canoes, paddles, and life jackets, and will arrange for a pick-up when you reach your destination. Chances are excellent you'll see deer, and maybe some elk, in between netting your catches of bass, carp, perch, pickerel, pike, or trout. Eateries at hamlets along the river offer fresh fish sandwiches, as well as country ham and red-eye gravy. The suggested put-in point is near the colorful Caverns of Luray, worth a looksee before dipping your paddle into the river. The Shenandoah empties into the Potomac River near Harper's Ferry. The area is famed for John Brown's raid on the federal arsenal there. However, the scenery offers what is arguably one of the most picturesque vistas in the country—Thomas Jefferson said the view was worth a voyage across the Atlantic. $29.50/day.

Shenandoah River Outfitters, RFD 3, Luray, VA 22835, **703/743-4159.**

LAKE SIDNEY LANIER
(HOUSEBOAT)

Lake Lanier Islands, GA

This lake is in the foothills of the Blue Ridge Mountains, and offers 47,000 acres of water with 700 miles of shoreline and almost infinite exploration possibilities. The Chattahoochee and Chestatee rivers feed the lake, constructed as part of a hydroelectric power dam, and numerous coves, bays, and islands rim the shore and dot the lake. Houseboaters will find numerous species of birds, including doves, marsh hens, ruffed grouse, and ducks. Bass and catfish are plentiful and aficionados claim they never taste better than when cooked over a driftwood fire on shore. Picnic sites are plentiful, as well as beaches and resort activities. $725-$1000/7 days.

Lake Lanier Islands, Box 605, Buford, GA 30518, **404/945-6701.**

Lake Cumberland, KY

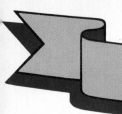

INDEX

INDEX